SOUTHERN EDITORIALS ON SECESSION

PREPARED AND PUBLISHED UNDER THE DIRECTION OF
THE AMERICAN HISTORICAL ASSOCIATION FROM THE IN-
COME OF THE ALBERT J. BEVERIDGE MEMORIAL FUND.

FOR THEIR ZEAL AND BENEFICENCE IN CREATING THIS
FUND THE ASSOCIATION IS INDEBTED TO MANY CITIZENS
OF INDIANA WHO DESIRED TO HONOR IN THIS WAY THE
MEMORY OF A STATESMAN AND A HISTORIAN.

The American Historical Association

SOUTHERN EDITORIALS
ON SECESSION

Edited by

DWIGHT LOWELL DUMOND, Ph.D.

ASSISTANT PROFESSOR OF HISTORY
UNIVERSITY OF MICHIGAN

GLOUCESTER, MASS.
PETER SMITH
1964

PRINTED IN U. S. A.

INTRODUCTION

The purpose of this volume of newspaper editorials is to show the variety, conflict, and concurrence of opinion in the southern States during and shortly before the crisis of secession. The files of seventy-two papers, published in all parts of the South, were examined. From them were chosen in the first instance nearly 2,000 editorials to be considered. The final selection was with a view to variety, clearness, and cogency of argument. Some preference was given to such as were extensively clipped and commented upon in other journals.

Among the editors of the papers here most used were numerous men prominent in the journalistic profession and in political affairs. Robert Barnwell Rhett of the Charleston *Mercury* and George D. Prentice of the Louisville *Journal* have been mentioned by historians as the chief journalistic spokesmen of the two major opposing popular elements in the South. This is hardly warranted, for those who stood with Rhett as disunionists *per se* and those who like Prentice were unconditional unionists were far fewer than those whose attitude was open to very considerable change by the repercussion of events. Rhett supported Breckinridge in the presidential campaign, and Prentice supported Bell; but in no other respect was either consistently representative of any large group of citizens; and in the newspaper world they stood alone. Rhett's refusal to countenance a reunion of the Democratic party after the rupture at Charleston and Prentice's denunciation of the Washington Peace Conference were typical of their individualism.

In New Orleans were two leading independent papers of established reputation and wide influence among the conservative merchant and planter classes of the lower South. The *Picayune,* owned by George Wilkins Kendall and Francis Asbury Lumsden, had occupied an enviable position since the days of the Mexican War. Neither of these men was active in 1860, and Lumsden was lost in a storm on the Great Lakes during the heat of the campaign. Most of the editorials were written by Alva Morris Holbrook, with occasional contributions from Kendall. The *Bee,* published as a bilingual sheet, was equally conservative and even more influential than the *Picayune* because of its large circulation among the Creole population. Both papers indicated an intention to support the nominee of a united Democracy, but supported Bell after the final schism at Baltimore. Following the election of Lincoln, they urged secession and the formation of a southern confederacy as soon as it was clear that the North was not disposed to listen to measures of conciliaton.

Of the remaining Constitutional Union journals, the Nashville *Patriot* and Nashville *Republican Banner* were outstanding. The majority of the editorials of these two papers were written by Ira P. Jones and R. K. Walker, respectively. They were insistent in asserting that William L. Yancey was the leader of a disunion conspiracy and that the disruption of the Charleston Convention was engineered to further the plans of the disunionists *per se*. Both papers denied the constitutional right of secession, but urged resistance by revolution following Lincoln's call for troops.

The Richmond *Examiner,* edited by William Old, was undoubtedly the most fully representative of the southern-rights papers which supported Breckinridge for the presidency. The brilliance of its editorial columns was but slightly less than that of the Charleston *Mercury*. It was hardly less conservative than the New Orleans *Bee* or *Picayune,* as steadfast in its support of the southern-rights platform as the leading Breckinridge organs of the lower South, and more voluminous in editorial comment than any other paper with the possible exception of the Nashville *Patriot*. Other conservative papers of the Breckinridge Democracy were the Nashville *Union and American,* edited by Leon Trousdale and John C. Burch; the Raleigh *Standard,* the Louisville *Courier,* and the *Kentucky Statesman*. More closely allied to the Charleston *Mercury* were the New Orleans *Delta* and the Jackson *Mississippian,* organs of John Slidell and Jefferson Davis.

The three leading Douglas papers of the lower South were the Augusta *Constitutionalist,* the Mobile *Register,* and the New Orleans *True Delta*. The *Constitutionalist* was owned by James Gardner and edited by Henry Cleveland. Gardner was prominent in Georgia politics, frequently mentioned for the governorship, and a close personal friend of Hershel V. Johnson. The *Register* was owned and edited by John Forsyth, leading opponent of William L. Yancey in Alabama politics and, together with Seibels of the Montgomery *Confederation* and Figuires of the *Southern Advocate,* an organizer of the Douglas Democracy in that State after the Charleston Convention. The *True Delta,* edited by John Maginnis, was the official organ of Miles Taylor, Chairman of the Douglas national campaign committee, and of Pierre

Soulé, who organized the Douglas party in Louisiana, wrote the resolutions adopted by that party's convention at Donaldsonville, and headed the contesting delegation to the Baltimore Convention.

Many of these editors were delegates to the national party conventions, all were prominent in State politics, and some were nationally known. Few men were more intimately acquainted with the intricacies of party politics or more thoroughly sensitive to the trend of opinion in their several localities with regard to matters of national concern.

*   *   *

A rapid survey of conditions, events, and reactions will give a setting for the documents which follow. A general disquietude at the South followed John Brown's raid into Virginia. The incident was of little consequence in itself; but the widespread sympathy expressed for Brown made those connected with the institution of slavery more keenly apprehensive of the future. Their concern arose rather from the fear of what anti-slavery agitation might effect thereafter through political action than from what it had accomplished already by violent methods. The possibility of a Republican victory in the coming presidential election stimulated the discussion of measures for the defense of southern institutions. The former Whig newspapers revived the perennial demand for commercial independence. The extreme southern-rights press disapproved of further wrangling, and advocated immediate separation if federal legislation and patronage should pass to the control of the anti-slavery party. The more liberal Democratic journals were content with enumerating an imposing array of southern grievances and calling attention to the danger of open warfare unless steps were taken to eliminate slavery agitation from the public forum.

Early in 1860 the legislatures of South Carolina and Mississippi proposed a southern conference at Atlanta and sent commissioners to urge the participation of Virginia. Concurrent state action in defense of southern rights was desired. A demand for assurances, if supported by a united South, might arrest anti-slavery agitation at the North. In any event, it was thought, coöperative action would eliminate factional feuds at home and insure harmony if more drastic measures should prove desirable. The Charleston *Mercury,* Jackson *Mississippian,* Richmond *Examiner,* and Richmond *Enquirer* labored faithfully to promote the project. The Nashville *Patriot,* Richmond *Whig,* Vicksburg *Whig,* and other journals opposing the project charged South Carolina with attempting to precipitate disunion by getting the South committed in advance to secession unless the North should concede the demands to be made. So strong was the general aversion to any and all tendencies toward disunion that even those papers which earnestly advocated retaliatory state legislation and military preparation for eventual hostilities opposed the project. In vain did its proponents insist that divided counsels would foster disunion. The conference did not meet, political parties were sectionalized, and separate state action became the trump card of the immediate secessionists at the turn of the year.

Meanwhile, the state convention of the Alabama Democracy framed a series of demands in behalf of southern rights, thereafter known as the Alabama Platform (Appendix II). Shortly afterward the legislature of Alabama provided for a state convention in the event of a Republican victory in November. The Alabama platform was not of novel content. Jefferson and Madison had made it a truism that the powers of the federal government were derivative and limited. Calhoun's doctrine of concurrent majority had popularized the theory that there must be a self-protecting power in the hands of the minority. The right of slaveholders to enter the Territories with their property had been asserted clearly in the debates over the Wilmot Proviso. The doctrine of the duty of Congress to correct the action or supplement the inaction of a hostile territorial legislature had now become stereotyped in refutation of popular sovereignty; and the right of secession was in the minds of a multitude a matter of course. Other state delegations had been instructed to withdraw from national conventions unless their principles were embodied in the party's platform. But for the first time social creeds and political theories were threatening to disrupt the Democratic party. In that event a Republican victory in the presidential election, and a dissolution of the Union in defense of southern institutions from prospective dangers, appeared to be inevitable. William L. Yancey was the leading spirit in establishing this advanced position, which the New Orleans *True Delta,* Mobile *Register,* and Montgomery *Confederation* condemned as the first step in a preconceived disunion program. The independent press inclined to the same opinion, the New Orleans *Bee* predicting that Douglas would be the nominee at Charleston, "unless Southern ultraists are bent upon discomfiture and ultimate disunion."

Jefferson Davis and Judah P. Benjamin were pressing to a conclusion in the Senate a protracted discussion of the right of slaveholders in the territories to protection by congressional legislation, with Douglas and his doctrine of popular sovereignty on the defensive. The debate in Congress was reflected in the newspapers; and, though few slaves were in the Territories and fewer were likely to go thither, that phase of the question of the rights of slavery under the Constitution became the main theme of the presidential canvass. The situation, though anomalous, is not incomprehensible. An aggressive political party at the North, seeking control of the federal government, was professing that the exclusion of slavery from the Territories was the limit of its designs against the institution. But the champions of southern rights believed the attack upon slavery in the Territories was but a first step in a program of ultimate emancipation, and chose to fight at the outer defenses. The Charleston *Mercury* was almost alone in believing that slavery would have expanded under the protecting mantle of congressional legislation. Most southern-rights journals were satisfied to claim congressional protection as a constitutional right without discussing the necessity of its practical application. The former Whig papers frequently denounced the demand for congressional protection as an abstraction, but they seldom denied its validity. The Douglas Democrats contended that the territorial legislature could lawfully exclude slavery, either by non-action or by unfriendly legislation. They claimed as an historical basis for this doctrine the theory of non-intervention, and charged the southern-rights men with assuming an advanced position.

This question of the rights of slavery in the Territories, revivified and clarified for the first time by this preliminary discussion, carried over into the presidential canvass, and lines were tightly drawn on a sectional basis. The Republicans demanded congressional exclusion and received only 3 per cent of the popular vote in the upper South. The Douglas Democrats supported the doctrine of popular sovereignty, recognized as hostile to the institution of slavery. They polled only 7 per cent of the popular vote in the lower South, constituting but 3 per cent of Douglas's total vote; and only 8 per cent of the popular vote in the upper South, representing 5 per cent of his total vote. The Constitutional Unionists denounced the doctrine of popular sovereignty and asserted the duty of protection by the federal government, although denying its immediate necessity. In the election they received only 2 per cent of the vote in the free States, representing 13 per cent of the total votes cast for Bell. Moreover, Bell received 66,058 votes in Kentucky, but only 12,194 in Ohio, 5,306 in Indiana, and 4,913 in Illinois. Douglas received 187,232 votes in Ohio, 115,509 in Indiana, and

160,125 in Illinois, but only 25,651 in Kentucky and 36,516 in the entire lower South.

The question of whether Congress could abdicate its power to protect persons and property in the territories threatened the disruption of the Charleston Convention from the moment of its temporary organization, April 23. The northern delegates dared not risk their political fortunes on the chance of a popular endorsement of southern rights. The southern delegates were not willing to accept popular sovereignty. The Cincinnati Convention, 1856, had postponed the crisis by referring the question to judicial determination. The decision had now come in the Dred Scott case, but Douglas denied that it fulfilled the conditions of the party compact because it did not arise out of an attack on slavery by a territorial legislature. The nomination of Douglas on the Cincinnati Platform, therefore, would give it a popular sovereignty interpretation. The nomination of a southern-rights man would operate equally to the advantage of that section. There was no escape from the dilemma.

Two delegations from New York were present at Charleston, each claiming to have been regularly appointed. The Fernando Wood delegation was solidly anti-Douglas. The Dean Richmond delegation contained forty Douglas men and thirty opposed to his nomination. The Dean Richmond delegation was seated and, operating under the unit rule, cast thirty-five votes against the southern-rights men on every important issue. By virtue of these thirty-five votes, the Douglas forces were able to establish a voting rule which released Douglas minorities in uninstructed delegations and submerged southern-rights minorities in delegations instructed to vote as a unit. The southern-rights men secured a majority report from the platform committee, but were defeated by a vote of 165 to 138 on the floor of the convention. The delegations from five States and in part from four others then withdrew and partially effected a new political organization. The Douglas forces were unable to muster the 202 votes required for a nomination, but refused to compromise. Other southern delegations were restrained from deserting the rump convention by assurances from the New York delegation that the platform would be reconsidered. That delegation drafted a new platform which was acceptable to the remaining delegates from the upper South. Howard of Tennessee introduced it as a resolution, and it was pending when the Convention adjourned to reassemble at Baltimore, June 18.

The question of disunion was brought to the fore when the opposition press denounced the proposed Atlanta Conference and the Alabama Platform as disunion projects. Douglas repeated the charges during the Senate debates and included in the ranks of the disunionists all those who opposed his nomination at Charleston. Too much had been said by the extreme southern-rights men about secession in event of a Republican victory to leave any doubt on that subject. Naturally those who advocated that action were also most insistent upon the adoption of a southern-rights platform by the national Democracy. When delegates from nine States deserted the Charleston Convention, therefore, the Douglas Democrats sought to discredit them by the charge that they were breaking up the party to insure the election of Lincoln and thus further their secession program. Irregular conventions were held in Louisiana, Alabama, Georgia, and Arkansas, and Douglas delegations were sent to the adjourned convention at Baltimore.

During the month of May the entire press of the South was engaged in discussing the important questions involved. Did the bolters break up the convention for the purpose of insuring the election of the Republican candidate? Should their constituents send them back to Baltimore to reunite the party on the basis of the Tennessee Resolution? Was that resolution a sufficient guarantee of southern rights? Should the project of the so-called Constitutional Democratic party be sustained and delegates sent to perfect its organization at Richmond? Did the former delegates have a right to seats at Baltimore unless reaccredited by state conventions of newly elected delegates?

The controversy was bitter, with the South Carolina newspapers alone opposing concession or compromise, and insisting upon permanent separation. The New Orleans *True Delta,* which had long advocated the nomination of Douglas at Charleston, very shrewdly complimented Rhett, Yancey, and Mouton as "frank, manly and plain spoken on this Union question. . . . They went to Charleston to make a sectional issue they had long contemplated and had conspired to mature; they made their move, got beaten, but not disgraced, and they hoisted the banner of revolution. We honor them for their frank and open proceeding, while condemning and repudiating it." The Mobile *Register,* Montgomery *Confederation,* and *Southern Advocate,* whose editors were the leading Yancey opponents within the Alabama Democracy, and the Augusta *Constitutionalist,* which endeavored to make a distinction between non-intervention and popular sovereignty while supporting the former and had advocated the nomination of a southern man on the Cincinnati Platform, all joined in

claiming that the bolters had surrendered their rights to further participation in the adjourned convention. They supported the *True Delta*
in a demand for newly elected state conventions; participated in convening them, without too much concern about regularity and strict
party lines; and secured the appointment of contesting delegations to
Baltimore pledged to support the nomination of Douglas on the
Cincinnati Platform.

The Richmond *Examiner* had endorsed R. M. T. Hunter for the
nomination at Charleston, but had indicated a willingness to support
Douglas if he should receive the nomination. It did not approve of
forcing the issue of a southern-rights platform in the national convention. The Richmond *Enquirer,* Louisville *Courier,* and Nashville
Union and American had advocated, respectively, the nomination of
Henry A. Wise, James Gutherie, and Andrew Johnson. All united in
urging the bolters from the Charleston Convention to resume their
seats at Baltimore. They agreed that the Tennessee Resolution would
be a satisfactory basis for compromise, but insisted that any further
attempt to force the nomination of Douglas would result in the complete disruption of the party.

The New Orleans *Bee,* believing that the campaign probably would
be conducted on sectional lines, had been ready to support the nominee
of the Charleston Convention. It preferred Douglas on the Cincinnati
Platform in view of the fact that no free State was likely to vote for
congressional protection. Following the rupture at Charleston it said:
"Abolitionism in one quarter, fierce and intractable, and Disunionism
in another, wily and resolute, have combined to destroy its [the Democratic party's] prestige, weaken its resources, demoralize its courage,
and sap its energy." Nevertheless, it advised the opposition to follow
the previous plan and, awaiting the nomination of the adjourned
convention, support its nominee. It did not endorse the policy of a
separate opposition ticket until the final schism in the Democracy
occurred at Baltimore. "Because Whigs and Democrats once opposed
each other, when parties were national, is there any reason they should
now keep up the warfare when they are confronted with a party whose
triumph would imperil the Union?" asked the New Orleans *Crescent,*
requesting the Constitutional Union Convention to endorse the
prospective nominee of the Democratic party, on the ground that he
alone could defeat the Republican candidate. Both papers eventually
supported Bell.

The New Orleans *Picayune* and the Augusta *Chronicle and Sentinel* denied that the bolting delegations could reënter the Baltimore Convention "without abandoning their lofty positions," denounced the Tennessee Resolution as unsatisfactory to the South, and agreed that the rupture at Charleston made necessary the nomination of a presidential candidate by the Constitutional Union party at Baltimore. A far different reason for that action was advanced by the Nashville *Patriot*, which sought to submerge the slavery agitation and unite conservative elements in both sections within the ranks of a truly national party. This position was assumed also by the Louisville *Journal*, which demanded protection for the slaveholders in the Territories, but did not intend to endorse a dissolution of the Union on the basis of its denial. It deprecated the election of any other candidate than Bell on the ground that if a Republican were elected the country would be "threatened with anarchy, treason, civil war, and disunion," while the success of a Democrat would be followed by "the most embittered factional quarrel that one [*sic*] country has ever known, not so sanguinary but equally as vindictive as that of the rival houses of York and Lancaster."

Meanwhile, the regular party organizations in the lower southern States adopted somewhat diverse courses, though they concurred in endorsing the action of the bolting delegations at Charleston. These delegations were partially reorganized and for the most part accredited both to Richmond and to Baltimore. The South Carolina delegation was accredited to Richmond only, and the Florida delegation was given permission to apply for admission at Baltimore at its own discretion. Their plans for the preservation of the party on the basis of the Tennessee Resolution, however, were foiled by the Douglas forces, who made adherence to their chief the test for admission at Baltimore. That action completed the work of cleavage begun at Charleston. Having purged the convention of southern-rights men, they converted an actual strength of 141 votes into an unanimous nomination by resolution.

On the last day of the regular session, June 23, 231 delegates who had been regularly elected to the convention and had not applied for admission, had been refused admission, or had withdrawn, assembled at the Maryland Institute for consultation. They decided to complete the organization of the Democratic Constitutional party begun at Charleston, adopt a platform, and nominate candidates for the presidency and vice-presidency. No one was allowed to participate in the proceedings unless possessing credentials as a regularly elected delegate.

Each delegate was permitted to cast only the vote to which he was entitled, and no State was allowed a vote in excess of that to which it was entitled by actual representation. The southern-rights platform embodied in the second majority report at Charleston was adopted unanimously, and John C. Breckinridge and Joseph Lane were nominated as the party's candidates.

Disunion became the all-absorbing topic in the campaign at the South after the final separation at Baltimore. A majority of those who believed that the election of Lincoln would constitute sufficient reason for secession supported Breckinridge. In an effort to combat sectionalism both North and South, the survivors of the old Whig and American parties had organized the new Constitutional Union party. Its strength was in the upper South, and it was not a Union party in the sense that its members were willing to forego resistance in any and all contingencies. They agreed that the South ought to resist a Republican administration conducted along the lines of the Chicago platform. They accused the Breckinridge Democrats of destroying the unity of their party for the purpose of furthering secession. They denied the necessity of forcing to a conclusion the sectional issue of the rights of slavery in the Territories. They urged that resistance be delayed until some overt act had been committed. Many of them denied the constitutional right of secession and inclined to revolution *en masse* as the proper mode of ultimate resistance, but they were not inclined to deny the right of ultimate resistance in one form or another.

Both parties were interested in defeating Lincoln, the Breckinridge Democrats because they expected in sequel to his election an insidious attack upon slavery as an institution in the States; the Constitutional Unionists because they knew his election would be followed by a determined effort to consummate a dissolution of the Union. As the campaign neared its close, both parties advocated fusion in a last desperate effort to defeat Lincoln by throwing the election into the House of Representatives. They could not submerge party differences sufficiently to effect union at home, but they did concentrate upon New York as the State most favorable to success. At the South this fusion movement had an important result in softening the bitterness engendered during the heat of the campaign, an important preliminary step in the realignment of parties upon new issues following the election of Lincoln.

The New Orleans *Crescent* expressed the general attitude at the South toward Lincoln's election: "we read the result in the face of every citizen upon the street. There is an universal feeling that an insult has been deliberately tendered our people, which is responded to, not by noisy threats or passionate objurations, but a settled determination that the South shall never be oppressed under Lincoln's administration." The press immediately applied itself to the task of clarifying new issues. Should the South acquiesce in the election and do nothing until forced into resistance by overt acts of aggression? Should all action be postponed, at least until Congress might have time to adopt definitive constitutional amendments satisfactory to the South? Should resort be had to direct interstate negotiation, a united South submitting a statement of grievances with demands for redress to the northern States? Should a southern convention be held and the South retire from the Union as a unit? Should the South rely upon separate state secession and coöperate afterward in forming a southern confederacy?

The immediate secessionists largely favored separate state action. A few advocated concert of action along previously determined lines. All others, until January, 1861, passed under the general designation of coöperationists. After the turn of the year those who remained opposed to secession were denounced as submissionists by the secessionists and lauded as Unionists by the northern press. Coöperationists favored a convention of delegates from the slave States to discuss grievances and determine upon a program for concerted action. The fear of southern disintegration along new lines of sectionalism, and the belief that united action was the surest approach to foreign recognition and the surest escape from attempted coercion, were impelling motives. Others were sanguine of northern concessions and expected to preserve the Union by securing definitive constitutional amendments. Some favored secession in event of failure; others would wait for overt acts of aggression. Some no doubt hoped by delay to frustrate the entire movement.

During the month of November the editorial columns of the newspapers were devoted to a discussion of southern grievances, prospective evils either in the Union or out of it, the possibility of securing definitive amendments to the Constitution, and the proper action demanded by the result of the election. "The day of compromise passed away with the seizure of California by the North, and the expulsion of the South from the Territories. The day of concession passed away with the election of Lincoln." Thus spoke the New Orleans *Delta,* with the concurrence of the Charleston *Mercury,* Columbia *South Carolinian,*

Jackson *Mississippian,* Montgomery *Advertiser,* Wilmington *Journal,* and other former Breckinridge papers. The Richmond *Enquirer* was disposed to recommend delay of action until the northern people gave some further indication of their general attitude, saying as late as November 20 that the question before the South was, "What will the Northern States do, or leave undone?" Within two weeks it joined in denouncing as submissionists all who were not actively supporting secession. The Louisville *Courier,* Nashville *Union and American,* and *Kentucky Statesman* were willing to make one more effort at conciliation in Congress or through the medium of a southern convention.

The trend of opinion in the lower South is clearly indicated in the editorial columns of the New Orleans *Crescent.* Speaking of the election, November 9, it said: "The Northern people, in electing Mr. Lincoln, have perpetrated a deliberate, cold-blooded insult and outrage upon the people of the slave-holding States. . . . Last Tuesday there was no disunion party in New Orleans. Today we would not care about trying the issue at the ballot-box." Next day it said: "that the country is threatened with fearful perils, there is not room for the shadow of doubt. That a dissolution of the Union is imminent, admits scarcely room for question. That we are on the eve of revolution and war, is equally clear." Four days later it declared that all prospect of concession from the North was "remote and shadowy," and raised the banner of immediate secession. Another Constitutional Unionist paper of New Orleans, the *Bee,* declared after the election that there was "no possible excuse for hasty and precipitate action on the part of the South." A week later it believed it to be the "palpable and undeniable duty of the South to seek redress within the Union, if possible." Three days before Congress convened, it approved immediate secession on the ground that "Whatever may have been the former belief or hope of conservative men, the issues of Northern injustice and Southern rights have gathered such rapid and overwhelming power as to extinguish all expectations of tinkering the difficulty by compromise." Equally rapid was the conversion of three Douglas papers, the Mobile *Register,* Montgomery *Confederation,* and Augusta *Constitutionalist.*

Most of the papers in the upper South, without distinction of previous party affiliation, agreed in sentiment with the Nashville *Patriot* when it said: "We desire to exhaust all peaceful and temperate remedies for a redress of our injuries, before resorting to those of violence and war . . . but let the Republican party understand that being for the Union is not to be for the principles on which their party is based." The restraining power of Congress and the Supreme Court, the conservatism of Lincoln, and a friendly reaction in the North following the election were urged as evidence that the South had nothing to fear for at least two years.

In order to promote harmony and concurrent action without a general conference and its attendant delay, the immediate secessionists resorted to the device of interstate commissioners. They became the diplomatic corps of the secession movement. Before the program was well under way they had arranged for a conference of delegates from any and all States to follow promptly upon their secession; and thus they robbed the coöperationists of their principal ground of argument. On the other hand, the precipitate action of the lower South, without first consulting those States which would suffer most in event of war, created a resentment not easily effaced. "Of all coercion that we ever heard of, this is the most arrogant, the most despotic, the most unnatural, ungrateful and monstrous," said the Nashville *Patriot.* That action gave countenance to the already prevailing idea that the lower South did not want to preserve the Union on any basis. Nor was the statement that separation was neither a remedy for past grievances nor a guarantee of future security easily answered. In large measure the press of the lower South resorted to the expedient of ignoring unpleasant issues, and trusted to time, Republican intransigence, and a natural affinity of interests to overcome opposition in the upper South.

Meanwhile opponents of secession sought in Congress to procure an intersectional compromise. Early in December special committees for the consideration of the state of the country were secured in both houses of Congress, and innumerable measures of conciliation were proposed. Neither house was able to arrive at any practical solution of the problem. Failing to secure favorable action on proposed constitutional amendments, the advocates of conciliation turned their attention to securing a national convention. Their efforts in that direction likewise failed, the Republican majorities steadfastly refusing to countenance the southern demands for additional guarantees and indicating an intention to resort to arms in the maintenance of national authority.

Without entering into a detailed account of congressional proceedings, the peculiar composition of the Committee of Thirty-three, the refusal of Republican congressmen to enter into the spirit of conciliation or agree to a national convention, and the speeches of Senators Hale,

Wade, and Seward must be indicated as important elements in the shaping of majority sentiment in the South. Those who had urged delay on the ground that the immediate secessionists had incorrectly judged the strength of the anti-slavery sentiment at the North, and those who hoped that definitive constitutional amendments of such nature as to allay the apprehensions of the southern people would be forthcoming, were completely discomfited. The inflexible opposition of Republican congressmen to the several proposals designed to prevent civil war broke down differences of opinion and united the two great parties in the lower South. South Carolina seceded December 20, and secession majorities were elected in all the gulf States before January 8. By that time the only paper of importance in that section still opposed to secession was the New Orleans *True Delta,* and it was wavering in response to the shifting of Buchanan's attitude on coercion.

The Louisville *Courier* dispelled all doubts of its position, December 27, when it said: "Death itself is no more inevitable than that they [the border slave States] will have to stay with their enemies of the North; or go with their friends of the South; or, making enemies of both the North and the South, set up for themselves." The Augusta *Chronicle and Sentinel,* Gallatin *Examiner,* and New Orleans *Bee,* all former Constitutional Unionist journals, surrendered to secession about the same time and for the same reason. The Nashville *Union and American* announced its new platform after Seward's speech in the Senate: "Aged men will turn from the perusal of his speech mourning that they should have lived to see the genius of our Constitution destroyed by the fierce fires of Fanaticism. . . . The day of submission is past and the day of our exodus has arrived. We will risk the danger of the wilderness." "Why will not men see and acknowledge the truth?" said the Wilmington *Herald,* February 7, admitting that there was no longer hope of compromise and urging the immediate secession of North Carolina. Three days later the Nashville *Republican Banner,* one of the few prominent journals which had not raised the banner of resistance, gave advance notice of its ultimate position: "We would not have the people of the Free States misunderstand our position. . . . They must not suppose because the disunionists made an attempt—abortive though it was—to stigmatize the majority as 'submissionists,' that that majority have any purpose of submitting to the Republican electioneering dogma that the people of the Southern states are to be excluded by legislation from the privilege of settling in the Territories with their slaves."

The last phase of the secession movement began with the removal of Anderson to Fort Sumter in Charleston harbor and Slemmer to Fort Pickens at Pensacola. Popular excitement reached such proportions in the lower South that state authorities resorted to the extreme means of seizing federal forts and arsenals in order to prevent collisions between federal troops and irresponsible mobs. The advanced position already taken by these seven States left no doubt that a southern confederacy would be formed early in February. The rapid sequence of events completely transformed the problem presented to the upper South for solution. There was no longer a question as to whether the election of Lincoln justified a dissolution of the Union. It was dissolved already. Constitutional guarantees which in the first instance would have been satisfactory to the upper South if approved by Congress would no longer suffice, because conciliation was now virtually hopeless. The Republicans had indicated a willingness to witness the development of a situation from which final separation or civil war were the only escapes. The right of coercion thus replaced the right of secession as the most important issue, and to the advantage of the separationists. Moreover, in event of final separation, the upper South must go with the southern Confederacy or remain as a hopeless minority in the Union without protection for their peculiar institution or markets for their slave surplus. Some favored joining the Confederacy in event of final separation. Others favored resistance in event of attempted coercion. A few advocated armed neutrality to prevent hostilities.

The disruption of Buchanan's cabinet, followed by the sending of reinforcements to the southern forts, was interpreted both at the North and at the South as indicating a determination to enforce federal authority in the seceding States. Northern state legislatures passed resolutions endorsing that program, and the Republicans in Congress sought to force the issue to a conclusion under a Democratic administration. Every state legislature in the upper South had endorsed the Crittenden amendments or similar proposals, and had indicated a determination to resist coercion. Civil war was dangerously near when Virginia, January 19, proposed the Washington Peace Conference and sent emissaries to the South and to Washington to prevent hostilities. That action arrested a rapid trend of popular sentiment in favor of immediate secession, defeated the proposed state conventions in Tennessee and North Carolina, and elected conservative delegates to the Virginia convention. "We mean to push the experiment of adjustment and settlement of this controversy to the last honorable and reasonable limit, and when we have done that unsuccessfully, we will set up for ourselves in a lawful way, and accept the consequences whatever they may be," said the Nashville *Patriot*.

The Washington Conference Convention met February 4. Its sessions were secret, and no intelligent discussion in the press of its probable success was possible. Moreover, Lincoln was journeying leisurely to Washington during the month of February, and his first public utterances since the election diverted attention from everything else. It may be said safely that his speeches at Springfield and Indianapolis converted more people to secession than did his inaugural address a month later, the Wilmington *Herald* tersely remarking: "Lincoln is on his way to Washington, with the Chicago platform for his gospel, and coercion for his motto." The Nashville *Patriot* also went a step further in the direction of resistance when it said: "Mr. Lincoln, we hope, will learn by the 4th of March that the Chicago platform was made for a Presidential Campaign; that it was totally repudiated by about fourteen States of the Union, and that if the government is administered strictly according to its provisions, the government must go to pieces." From that position it was but a short step to the denunciation of his inaugural as evidence that "he appeared to regard his own personal consistency . . . as of more importance than the preservation of the Union." Little opportunity was ever presented to the press for a discussion of the report of the Washington Conference Convention. News of its failure reached the people at the same time as the inaugural. From that time until Lincoln's call for troops nothing occurred to bring definitive action in the remaining slave States; but that event may be regarded as less of a cause and more in the nature of an occasion than surface indications show.

The Louisville *Journal,* regarding destruction of the Union as the certain extinction of American freedom, had opposed the Washington Conference Convention on the ground that it was a secession snare. Defiant rather than representative of public opinion in either section, it called upon Kentuckians, April 23, to stand by their State and "let her soil be the asylum for the moderate men of both the North and the South, where they may sojourn in peace and avoid the strife and horror of civil war."

For facilitation and cordial assistance I am indebted to Miss Edna J. Grauman of the Louisville Public Library; Mrs. Mary M. Pohlmann, custodian of the city archives of New Orleans; Miss Harriett Smither,

State Librarian of Texas; Mrs. Mary B. Owen, State Librarian, Montgomery; Joseph P. Breedlove, Librarian of Duke University; H. R. Mc Ilwaine, State Librarian, Richmond; Ernest W. Winkler, Librarian of the University of Texas; Miss Stella M. Drumm, Librarian of the Missouri Historial Society, St. Louis; Robert J. Usher, Librarian of the Howard Memorial Library, New Orleans; Miss C. S. Freret, Louisiana State Museum Library, New Orleans; Mrs. John Trotwood Moore, State Librarian, Nashville; Miss Ella Mae Thornton, State Librarian, Atlanta; and Donald Coney, Assistant Librarian, University of North Carolina. Dr. Dunbar Rowland, Director of the Department of Archives and History, Jackson, Mississippi, increased an already deep sense of gratitude by giving unrestrained access to the department's valuable collection. J. B. Bassick of New Orleans eliminated difficulties in the way of making photostats from newspaper files in the City Archives and the Cabildo. Miss India W. Thomas, Assistant House Regent of the Confederate Museum, Richmond, performed a similar service. E. R. Dabney, in charge of the newspaper files at the University of Texas, Peter A. Brannon and Miss Margaret Hails, of the Department of Archives and History, Montgomery, and Liston Lewis of the Carnegie Library, Nashville, extended many courtesies, in addition to giving freely of their time and advice.

CONTENTS

CONTENTS

CONTENTS

PAGE

SOUTHERN EDITORIALS ON SECESSION

SOUTHERN EDITORIALS ON SECESSION

I. THE CONTEST OF 1860

(*The Kentucky Statesman*, Lexington, January 6, 1860)

The Constitution of the United States, the laws of Congress giving practical force to its guarantees and the decisions of the Supreme Court, expounding and construing the laws, have secured to slave property in the States and Territories all the protection that is claimed or needed. That Congress has no power to interfere with slavery in the States is admitted. The fugitive slave law providing for the rendition of slaves escaped into other States, perfects the remedial protection to the institution as it exists in the States. In the Territories slave property is equally well guarded against invasion. It is now decided that neither the Federal nor Territorial government has the power to interpose between the slave holder and his property, either to wrest it from him or impair his rights.—More than this, it is decided to be the duty of both these governments to secure every species of property, including slaves, all needful protection. And here arises the only political issue under the Constitution which now divides parties. It is contended that the Supreme Court have not decided it to be the duty of Congress to enact protective laws for slave property, and that the opinion of the judges upon that point was *obiter dicta,* and not binding as a judicial decision. We hold a different position, claiming as we do, both the right and duty of the government to protect the citizen in the enjoyment of all his rights of property. We believe the court so decided, and with that decision, the South as a section, is content. But this issue loses its practical importance and becomes an abstraction in view of the universal admission that there is no necessity for any such legislation at this time, and that slave holders in the Territories do not now ask the enactment of any laws for the further protection of their rights. And when it is

3

further conceded, that in all probability the necessity of such legislation will never arise, and that probably the time may never come, at least not for years, when an aggrieved slave holder will go to the doors of Congress demanding the exercise of this power, this question must disappear from the arena of party politics and lose its place in political platforms.

But there are issues, and important issues outside of the Constitution, which soon must be tried, and these questions will subordinate to their consideration all others not of immediate and practical importance. The repeal of the fugitive slave law—legislation guaranteed by the Constitution—the reversal of the Dred Scott decision through the reorganization of the Supreme Court, the abolition of slavery in Territories and the exclusion of any more slave States regardless of the people, the abolition of slavery in the District of Columbia and in the forts, arsenals and dockyards of the United States, whether located in free or slave States, the prohibition of the inter-State slave trade and finally constant unceasing war upon the institution in the States are now the avowed purposes of the republican party, and in their solution is involved the existence of the confederacy. If the republican party, now a most formidable organization, shall succeed in attaining control of the government, its history leaves no doubt that it will undertake to carry out these purposes, and if so the whole power of the federal executive will not be able to coerce the subjection of receding States. We do not now discuss the propriety of such a course in the southern States, nor undertake to say what ought to be the result of the election of a black republican President. But we do undertake to say that in such an event we do not believe that the disaster can be prevented. The question should be treated as a practical issue and discussed with a fair estimation of what will, and not of what should ensue upon its either solution. The contest of 1860 will inevitably be a struggle between the democratic nominee of the Charleston Convention and the candidate of the black republican party, and upon the result we believe hangs the destiny of this Union. Men can not and have no right to ignore the dangers which encompass the Union, nor close their eyes to future events so closely foreshadowed in the signs of the times. It now becomes the duty of patriots, of all who love the Union and seek its continuance so to shape their course and employ their influence as to avert a result fraught with such calamity.

The clear and unequivocal presentation of this alarming issue is the prominent feature of Mr. Breckinridge's Frankfort speech, which has been published in our paper. He responds to the interrogatories of those who had requested him to define his position on the slavery question, and gives his opinion so clearly and unequivocally that none now can misunderstand it. But he then throws all such questions behind him, and moved by that alarm which the condition of public affairs and the state of feeling indexed at Washington must bring to every patriot, presents the dangers which threaten the republic, points out the calamity ahead and the only means by which it can be avoided. It is no time now to discuss abstract questions, no time now to anticipate contingencies, to wrangle about the position of men and parties when they occur. The question now to be tried comes home to the fireside of every citizen, involves the Union itself. Means must be taken to overthrow and destroy the republican party, to defeat its aspirations to power and crush it out as a political organization in the country. Its success will overthrow the government and that issue must be tried in 1860. We invite attention to this speech as embodying facts and arguments worthy the consideration of every man, no matter to which party he is attached. It is characterized by no spirit of alarm; but is calm, moderate and sincere. Let it speak for itself.

2. THE LAW WHICH CONTROLS AND THE INCENTIVE WHICH PROMPTS THE POLITICAL ACTION OF THE NORTHERN STATES OF THE UNION

(Richmond Semi-weekly Examiner, January 6, 1860)

Those who anticipated any beneficial results from the Union meetings in the free States, have little reason to rejoice at the evidences of popular sentiment and feeling recently given in the most conservative city of the North, and in the interior of the most wealthy, populous, and powerful State in the Confederacy. Not a fortnight has passed since every paper in the South teemed with the details of a grand Union meeting held in the city of New York. People were told that the dormant but potent conservatism of the Empire State was aroused, and in spite of the repeated failures of the spasmodic and intermittent efforts of that enfeebled element in Northern society, the timid and credulous Union idolaters of the South begun to receive this and similar demonstrations in the seaboard cities of that section as omens of a popular reaction which was to end our political "thirty years' war," and to furnish a cure for all the ills to which the body politic is subject. But the ruling genius of free society was not alarmed by these magnificent delusions, nor did it sleep over them. The high priest of Black Republicanism was wandering back from his European tour, and the unexpected and unwelcome appearance of RICHARD THE LION-HEARTED amid the sports at Ashby de la Zouche did not appal the minions of his indolent and hollow-hearted brother, or encourage the English loyalists more, than the sudden arrival of SEWARD disconcerted the Conservative reactionists, and animated the Black Republican cohorts. The thunders of an hundred cannon, the vociferous greeting of an immense multitude, welcomed him to the commercial emporium of the Union; the authorities of the city voted him its freedom. At Albany, at Syracuse, at Auburn, he was received with every demonstration of public rejoicing, and with all the assurances of popular confidence and support. From the villages and rural districts of the interior came forth the sounds of a people's welcome, as if to a great public benefactor and a trusted representative of popular will and sentiment. And why was this seen, amid a people not apt to pay for what it has not received, nor particularly demonstrative of grateful or sudden impulses of any kind? Why was this ovation rendered to the living politician by those who had suffered the greatest genius their section had produced for half a century to sink almost unnoticed and unhonored to his grave, and have apparently forgotten him in less than a decade? Why does VAN BUREN vegetate at Lindenwold, and why do PIERCE and FILLMORE still live unnoticed, "all weak and withered of their force," and indebted for casual mention and kindly memory to Southern friends alone? Why are DICKINSON, SEYMOUR, O'CONNOR, CUSHING, &c.,[1] seen only at fitful periods of temporary excitement and then forgotten in their hopeless and profitless struggles for influence and position? Why is DOUGLAS fast sinking in public esteem, even in the Northwest, and forced to cast his eye Southward "with the lingering last look of despairing?" These men had position, genius, ability, energy and great skill in public affairs, and all, save one, are in the vigor of life. Why should they fall, in despite of supports which generally sustain men greatly their inferiors? The answer is simple: They were at war with the popular sentiment, which is the law of the society in which they lived. Why does SEWARD head the political movements and lead the people, their agents and representatives in the Northern section of the Union? His abilities are fair, but not great, his name is connected with no leading measure, with no marked event in the political history of

---

[1] Daniel Stevens Dickinson of New York, Thomas H. Seymour of Connecticut, Charles O'Connor of New York, and Caleb Cushing of Massachusetts.

the country; his personal influence, even with his associates, does not seem to be commanding; his competitors do not fear him in debate, nor in any intellectual contest. Even in the Senate and in his own State, he was never known to have a large personal following. But, although thus destitute of position, of the qualities and the apparent elements of power, which are considered requisite to make and mark a popular leader, he is the undisputed head of a great popular party, in communities where the genius of unlimited popular sway riots in licentious triumph. The solution of this problem is not difficult. He, alone, of all the men of action and intellect in his section, saw early the law which controls the mind of the Northern masses, and the incentive which impels the Northern heart to recognize, to obey and to execute that law. He seized the idea promptly, he grasped it firmly, and he retains and uses its power with unscrupulous energy and with unremitting industry. When he proclaimed that the people of the North had a "higher law than the Constitution," he knew what he said, and more, that the people for whom he spoke felt and acted on his idea, though they might not understand or interpret his words. The law which commands obedience to the mandates of the physical force of an unrestrained numerical majority is the operative law, not only with the masses in the free States of the North, but in all communities where no divisions or orders of society are established or recognized, and where the conservative influence of domestic slavery does not supply the deficiency of restraining checks. In the Northern States the popular power has no check but the popular reason and will. A law such as this acting upon a society singularly energetic and adventurous, greedy after wealth and lusting for power, has no limit but the measure of its own power, and that measure is the extent of the physical force of the numerical majority of the people. That force is stimulated to action by one unvarying and universal incentive: the desire for the acquisition and use of power and property. The temper to acquire, the spirit to appropriate, thus unrestrained, operates under a universal law of human nature with a continuous and unremitting energy, against which plighted faith and constitutional checks will ever prove feeble and worthless defenses. There is but one defense of practical value and real efficiency: it is the ability and will of the minority to resist the action of the ruling majority whether seen in the operation of established government, or in the less usual form of unlicensed violence. The majority makes, and construes, and executes the law.—The minority, while living under government, but obeys and submits to the law thus made and construed. No defense provided for it by mere government is in its control or at its service. The majority does not even recognize the existence of the minority where the idea of the supreme authority of the numerical majority prevails, as it does in the Northern States of this Union. And SEWARD and his followers sweep away even the restraints of good faith and plighted honor from their creed. The whole history of Black Republican legislation demonstrates this. Upon their idea, as the majority of 1859 is not the majority of 1860, the majority of this year will not acknowledge the right of the majority of the last, to bind it by its enactments, still less will it admit the law adopted by the ancestry in one century as of binding authority upon the posterity in another. They at once assert the right of the majority in a society to form laws for the government of that society in reference to its then present condition, and they will not be bound by restraints which forbid the majority, that is themselves, to assume power which is within their reach, and which nothing but a law passed some seventy years before (in their view) prevents their using. To a people possessed with such an idea, and studiously taught to believe that this Union and its government is but the government and Union of one people, the rights of the States, and the construction of the Constitution, are of course no barriers. They deny the right of resistance or secession to the States, and they will alter or put their own construction on the Constitution. The prompt annulling by some,[2] and the universal evasion of the Fugitive Slave Law by all Northern States, and the refusal of the majority in that section to recognize the decision of the Supreme Court in the Dred Scott case as law, are but two of numerous instances in our history, to prove the inefficiency of legal, judicial or constitutional defenses against the encroachments of majorities who hold physical power. The Black Republicans did not reject the validity of the compromises of 1850, on the special idea which operates with those who adhere to constitutional compromises and attach to legislative compromises only the moral weight of plighted faith and honor. No, they put constitutional and legislative compromises on the same footing. If they do not denounce both "as leagues with hell and covenants with death," they hold them equally as unjust restraints upon popular will and power. They hold the fundamental and ordinary statute law as but the expressed will of the temporary ruling majority, and binding only

[2] For an abstract of the so-called personal liberty laws, see the *National Intelligencer*, December 11, 1860; or [James D. McCabe], *Fanaticism, and its Results: or Facts versus Fancies* (Baltimore, 1860), pp. 23–28.

until another majority shall repeal them. SEWARD uttered no sentiment construed as heretical by Northern politicians, when his higher law doctrine is thus explained. Let any one converse with Northern politicians, or read their speeches, and then reflect if this is not the prevailing sentiment there.

When the memorable Rochester speech was made, SEWARD was still in unison and not in advance of Northern sentiment.—The announcement of an irrepressible conflict between free and slave society, startled no one North of the Potomac, nor do we see why it should have surprised one South of it.—He might desire, indeed, that the enthusiasts and political jobbers in the North might apply this conflict to free and slave labor, but he knew that was not true. Between rival kinds of labor in the same community, subject to the same municipal regulations, there may be contests and antipathies—but the two kinds must be really rivals, in actual contact, using the same markets, and vending and buying the same articles. Between two kinds of labor, producing different articles, bartering or selling the products of their industry to each other, there is no antipathy, but a natural, mutual and rational dependence, and there is peace and not conflict. And there is still more unity of interest and inducements to peace, when they have no collision about local laws, are separated by broad geographical lines, and have distinctive peculiarities due to climate, habits and race. Neither SEWARD nor the Black Republicans believe, or act on any such absurdity, as the popular interpretation of this speech attributes to him. What was true, and what the history of anti-slavery agitations proves to have been true in the beginning and to be equally true now, is the reality of a stern contest waged by the buying, manufacturing, trading, speculating populous section, to obtain uncontrolled power over the producing and sparsely populated Southern section of the Confederacy. This contest was the moving cause which made the aggressive section of the Union adopt the idea of the rightful supremacy of the physical force of the popular majority, as the ruling principle in free communities. And where such a principle and such a nation control a majority in any society, there is an "irrepressible conflict" between the two opposing sections. And it must result in the abandonment of their principle, and the purifying [of] their motives, or in the ascendency of that section in the common government, or in the severance of the union of the two. One of the three results from such a conflict is inevitable.

In uttering this idea SEWARD was but popularising a familiar idea, and giving a less offensive expression to what might have startled the timid or unmasked some pretender who still found it convenient to wear a veil of conservatism in the ranks of the Black Republicans. He showed that he saw the results of the long sectional contest, and had marshalled the elements of political and social power in his section, and was prepared to push them on to farther and more substantial conquests. The man, it seems to us, must have been strangely deluded or wilfully blind, who has not seen for years that this contest about slavery was not confined to that institution, but embraced the whole principle, policy and objects of government. In every political contest in which this institution has been brought prominently forward, the primary object of its assailants has stood broadly and glaringly out. In the very adoption of the Constitution, they gained political power by bringing it forward, and deprived the slaveholder of two-fifths of his rightful power in the House of Representatives and of nearly as much in the Electoral College. In every contest about territory they have brought it prominently forward, and either by compromise or by unconditional plunder, deprived the Southern people both of the land and the political power which attached to it. In their contests about the Tariff they seldom mentioned the institution, for there the loss of their own commercial and agricultural strength was to be compensated by getting the votes of Southern delegates.—When Northern wealth was dependent upon protective duties, the section was conservative on slavery and Union-loving on principle; when it was able or forced to do without such protection, they became fanatical and disunionists, all on principle—the principle which operates on all men in all ages, and teaches them to appropriate the power and property of others.—They stand now committed to the doctrine of no more slave territory; they are favorable to Protective Tariffs and the whole system of class legislation, which must enrich their section, enlarge its political power, and throw the whole support of government, and of tribute to domestic manufactures on the producing States of the South. By legislative action, and by popular assemblies, they are placing the construction of the constitution by the numerical majority of the people, and even by their State Legislatures, above the decision of the Supreme Court; thus stripping the exposed minority of the South of the last defenses left under the constitutional Union of these States. Such acts are far more instructive and infinitely more dangerous and authoritative than any speech of any man. They show beyond doubt, that SEWARD is but the representative of his section. It needed not the reception given him in New York, to show that the political conflict between the sections had known no abatement, that the Northern majority had neither ruth nor relenting; that the fell spirit of aggression was neither sated by past triumphs, nor gorged by its abundant plunder. We trust that the people of the South will close their ears to the delusive promises of the merchant princes in Fifth Avenue, and hearken to no more tattle about popular reactions which, like sorrow, "endure for a night," but unlike it, are not precursors of "joy that cometh in the morning." Let them look at this matter as it is, as a conflict that must be settled, as a danger that is upon them, as an issue which delays and subterfuges cannot avert, as a trouble inseparable from the political and social condition of the Confederacy. Let them look neither to the Federal Government nor to popular movements in the free States for comfort or succor in time of need. But to their own power and authority. They should insist that every public man, either in office or a candidate for one, should stand at once upon defined and common ground with the people of the South. Let them assume a position at once, which will ensure them equality in, or security and independence out of the Union. If they are to stay in the Union, they should know on what terms; but let them be prepared to achieve independence, and maintain their honor and equality in whatever political position they may have to assume.

3. A Bad Sign

(*The New Orleans Bee,* January 18, 1860)

The Democratic State Convention of Alabama, which assembled a few days ago at Montgomery, has initiated a course of action which, if imitated by other Southern commonwealths, will most probably result in a disastrous political rupture, and may possibly precipitate a dissolution of the Union. The full account of the proceedings has not come to hand, but we learn by telegraph that the Convention adopted by a large majority a series of resolutions insisting upon the principle that it is the duty of Congress to protect slavery in the Territories, and requiring the Alabama delegation to Charleston to insist upon the endorsement of the platform by the National Democratic Convention before nominating a candidate for the Presidency, and in case the Convention fail to do so, they are instructed to withdraw and take no further part in the proceedings. In other words, the Democracy of Alabama have resolved that the National Democratic Convention shall affirm their particular and ultra Southern view of the slavery question, and it is only upon that express condition that they will consent to remain in the Convention, and participate in the selection of a Presidential candidate.[1]

It must be acknowledged that Alabama has assumed a bold—we may say, a dangerous position. She undertakes in advance to dictate a platform to a convention of delegates representing the entire Democratic party. Instead of leaving the subject to the body specially invested with authority to frame a programme of principles which will command the approbation of the party in every quarter of the Union, she virtually places before the Convention the alternative of accepting her particular views, or of witnessing her secession from that assemblage. The course pursued by Alabama denotes a foregone conclusion, and indicates clearly enough, as far as she is concerned, a rooted distrust of the Democracy of the free States, and a settled determination to enforce upon them her extreme doctrines, or failing therein, to strike the first blow towards the denationalization of the only party which can be relied upon as antagonistical to Black Republicanism. The wisdom and expediency of this decision may well be questioned.

Heretofore, Alabama, while invincibly Democratic, and strongly Southern rights, had never sanctioned any policy tending even remotely to the dissolution of the Union. Her resolves at the late Convention prove how profoundly agitated the public mind of the State must have been by recent developments of abolition insanity, and how completely shaken must be the confidence hitherto felt by her leading men in the integrity and soundness of the Southern Democracy. At a single leap Alabama has almost placed herself side by side with South Carolina. It is doubtful whether the latter State will so far recognize the Charleston Convention as to elect delegates to that body; but should she do so, we may feel altogether certain that they will be instructed to pursue a line of action at least as trenchant and decisive as that traced by Alabama. The example set by the latter will probably be followed by Georgia and Mississippi, and may meet the sanction of all the cotton-growing States. Now it is palpable that if any considerable number of Southern States go before the Charleston Convention with the unflinching resolve to compel the formal recognition and endorsement of the theory of federal protection of slavery and a Congressional slave code for the Territories —tenets which the Democracy of the North will never sanction—there is a complete end to all prospect of harmony. A national Democratic nomination will be rendered impracticable. The refusal of the majority

1 The resolutions, written by William L. Yancey, were thereafter known as the *Alabama Platform*. See Appendix I.

of the Convention to adopt the Alabama platform will be the signal for the withdrawal of most of the Southern delegations. The remaining members of the Convention may nominate candidates, but they will be to all intents and purposes sectional nominations. The South, in its turn, will select its champions, and then we shall have precisely that condition of things which the Charleston *Mercury* long since counseled and advocated—viz.: a sectional Democracy confined to the South, while everywhere else parties will be considered as more or less tainted with Abolitionism.

We need scarcely say that so lamentable a result would prove absolutely ruinous, not simply to the fortunes of the Democracy, for that would be of comparatively little consequence, but to the hopes of those national, conservative citizens, who cling to the Union and its preservation as the means of consolidating our liberties, our prosperity and our strength. If the Democratic party break to pieces, we can discover no bulwark to the encroachments of fanaticism, and therefore no safety to the South. The Union cannot possibly survive sectionalism in every part of the republic.

4. SOUTHERN POLICY

(*Vicksburg Daily Whig*, January 18, 1860)

Whilst this journal would by no means advocate the commercial independence of the South, as a distinctive measure, intended as an initiatory step for dissolving the Union; still, we are free to declare that, in our opinion, the South ought, without further delay, to commence a system of measures for her own protection. The Southern Conventions,[1] as they are called, which have from time to time assembled, were not only abortive, but positively injurious. Those assemblages, indeed, were conceived in a spirit of Disunion, and were hot beds for the speedy propagation of *fire-eating* sentiments. Such being their character, this journal, of course, had no sympathies with them, nor did we ever expect any substantial good to spring from their deliberations. However, it is manifest to even a casual observer of ordinary intelligence, that the policy in trade and commerce uniformly pursued by the South is not only blind and simple, but absolutely suicidal to our pecuniary prosperity.

By mere supineness, the people of the South have permitted the

[1] See William Watson Davis, "Ante-Bellum Southern Commercial Conventions," in The Alabama Historical Society, *Transactions*, V, 153–202; and Herbert Wender, "Southern Commercial Conventions, 1837–1859," in Johns Hopkins University, *Studies in Historical and Political Science*, XLVIII, No. 4.

Yankees to monopolize the carrying trade, with its immense profits. We have yielded to them the manufacturing business, in all its departments, without an effort, until recently, to become manufacturers ourselves. We have acquiesced in the claims of the North to do all the importing, and most of the exporting business, for the whole Union. Thus, the North has been aggrandised, in a most astonishing degree, at the expense of the South. It is no wonder that their villages have grown into magnificent cities. It is not strange that they have "merchant princes," dwelling in gorgeous palaces and reveling in luxuries transcending the luxurious appliances of the East! How could it be otherwise? New York city, like a mighty queen of commerce, sits proudly upon her island throne, sparkling in jewels and waving an undisputed commercial scepter over the South. By means of her railways and navigable streams, she sends out her *long arms* to the extreme South; and, with an avidity rarely equaled, grasps our gains and transfers them to herself—taxing us at every step—and depleting us as extensively as possible without actually destroying us. Meantime, the South remains passive—in a state of torpidity—making cotton bales for the North to manufacture, and constantly exerting ourselves to increase the production as much as possible. We have no ships in the foreign carrying trade, or very few indeed. No vessels enter Southern harbors (comparatively speaking) laden with the rich "merchandise" of foreign climes directly imported from those distant countries. We extend but little encouragement to the various mechanical arts, but buy most of our farming implements from the Northern people. Although Mississippi has within her limits an extensive seaboard, affording capacious and secure harbors, capable almost of sheltering the shipping of the world, still the blue waters of our harbors are unbroken by a single keel, save the diminutive fishing smacks which frequent those waters. Although nature hath prepared for us most beautiful positions for commercial cities, and pointed, with her unerring finger, to the advantages spread before our *blind eyes;* still, we have no seaboard cities, except so far as they exist in imagination, or are delineated *on paper,* or are shadowed forth in pompous resolutions emanating from disunion conventions! Why is this? Why are we so far behind in the great march of improvement? Simply because we have *failed to act* in obedience to the dictates of sound policy. Simply because we have been almost criminally neglectful of our own pecuniary interests. What should we do? What remedy have we?

Why, in the first place, let us withdraw one-third, or even one-half of our capital from agricultural operations, and invest it in the establishment of manufacturies of cotton. Thus, we will greatly reduce the production of the raw material; and, as a necessary consequence, greatly enhance the market price of our great staple. The business of manufacturing the common cotton fabrics can be as profitably conducted here in Mississippi as it can be in Massachusetts. This fact has been demonstrated by the humble history of the few manufacturies already operating in our State. It has been proven that the business of making cotton goods in Mississippi pays from 10 to 12 per cent. profit per annum on the investment. Now, suppose we had extensive establishments for producing common fabrics of cotton in every county of Mississippi, created by Southern capital, and owned and worked by our own people; we could clothe ourselves at a small expense, comparatively, and sell the Yankees our surplus cloth, and thus realize a profit, instead of buying for ourselves. Consider the enhanced price of cotton, consequent upon the reduced supply; calculate the profits of manufacturing at home; refer to the opportunity we would thus have of becoming stock raisers, and producers of the small grains and fruits which our climate and soil are capable of maturing; and who does not see, at a glance, how eminently advantageous and profitable such a system would be. Connected with this policy, let us encourage the mechanical arts. Let us fabricate here all of our carriages and wagons; all of our farming implements; every article of furniture required by our people; and thus secure to ourselves an accession of valuable citizens, those multiplied thousands of industrious, honorable, moral artisans, who are producers, instead of consumers, and who are valuable, indeed, to any community that can secure their presence. Let us sedulously cultivate the sentiment, so true in itself, that *labor is honorable and dignified*. Lastly, let us at once begin the business of direct importation and direct exportation, and thus keep at home the millions of dollars which we annually pay to the North. The business of direct importation and direct exportation would, of course, build up, as if by the wand of a magician, splendid Southern cities of commercial grandeur and opulence; and thus we might become the most happy, prosperous, wealthy and intelligent people upon whom the sun has ever smiled. All this we should do—not in spitefulness—not in a spirit of envy—not with a view of breaking the ties of national Union—not with a design of engendering sectional animosity, but in obedience merely to the dictates of enlightened sectional policy, and in obedience to that universal principle, so well understood and acted upon by our Yankee friends, of consulting our own pecuniary interests, and adding to our general and individual pecuniary emoluments.

This is a fruitful topic. It might be spoken of in *volumes*. We have but glanced at it in the foregoing observations. After all, what we have penned, so far from being original suggestions, is but the recapitulation of self-evident propositions, suggesting themselves to every intelligent mind. It remains to be seen whether the South will awake from her ignoble slumber, and act for herself, or whether she will indolently remain inactive, and continue to be mere "hewers of wood and drawers of water," for the merchant princes of the North.

5. A SOUTHERN CONFERENCE [1]

(*Richmond Semi-weekly Examiner,* January 24, 1860)

The speech of the Commissioner from South Carolina, on Thursday, was a complete and able refutation of every vague, false and absurd rumor which was in circulation respecting the object of his mission.

The Legislature are now aware of the fact that our chivalrous, gallant and favorite Southern sister seeks from Virginia no immediate act of disunion nor any endorsement of measures of an impracticable and untimely character. Far from doing any of these things, whilst recapitulating through her Commissioner the many aggressions of the North by which the slave States have been insulted and stripped of their early power and influence, South Carolina now proposes to Virginia a plan for uniting the South and securing concert of action for our protection and defense, the wisdom, safety and practicability of which commends itself to the most conservative of the true and loyal of all parties.

Immediate, precipitate disunion, rash and suicidal from want of concert of action among the Southern States, is not what South Carolina desires at the hands of Virginia.

The lessons of experience taught by past events have not been lost upon her statesmen and people. Alive to dangers which surround us, painfully aware that for nearly half a century the work of sapping and mining the Constitutional rights of the Slave States has been insidiously,

---

[1] John Brown's raid at Harper's Ferry aroused the lower South to the need of immediate action in defense of its peculiar institution, and induced South Carolina and Mississippi to propose a conference of slave States for the formulation of a specific program of concurrent action. Each sent a special commissioner to urge Virginia's participation in the proposed conference. The correspondence, reports, and speeches of the South Carolina commissioner, C. G. Memminger, were published in *De Bow's Review,* XXIX, 751–771, and reprinted in Henry D. Capers, *Life and Times of C. G. Memminger* (Richmond, 1893). The official papers of the Mississippi commissioner, Peter B. Starke, were printed for distribution in a twenty-two page pamphlet bearing the title *Communication from the Hon. Peter B. Starke, as Commissioner to Virginia, to his Excellency, J. J. Pettus, with Accompanying Documents.*

yet constantly progressing, South Carolina now seeks the counsel and aid of Virginia as the leading Southern State. A feeling of reverence for the ancient and present greatness of the Old Dominion, mingled with a chivalrous desire to share the dangers which environ Virginia as a frontier State, prompted South Carolina to select Virginia, of all the slave States, as the first of the Southern Sovereignties to whom she sent her Commissioner.

She remembered, too, that in times gone by, but not forgotten, Virginia sent to South Carolina an Ambassador, on a mission of peace and sympathy, and that the Executive of this State then declared no soldier of the Federal Government should tread Virginia's soil in invading the Palmetto State.

In making an appeal to Virginia at this time, South Carolina doubtless remembered that as she, upon two memorable occasions, repealed the ordinances of her Conventions and the resolutions of her Legislature, at the earnest and respectful solicitation of Virginia, that we would now accede to her requests. Particularly does the mission of Col. MEMMINGER commend itself to the people of Virginia, from the fact that it looks to the protection of the interests of no particular Southern State, but to the welfare of every State where slavery exists.—Interested as we all are in the same species of property, menaced as we all are by the same dangers, the only difference between us being that some are frontier States and others not.—South Carolina, as she does not contemplate separate secession, has no interests or objects which are not in common with those of Virginia.

What South Carolina proposes at this time may, therefore, be briefly stated. She desires to secure concert and unity of action by the appointment or election by all the Southern States of delegates or Commissioners, who shall meet in Conference for the purpose of consultation and grave deliberation, and for the recommendation of measures, designed at once to unite the slave States, and also to take the necessary steps for the defense and protection of our common interests. To prevent that infirmity of purpose, vacillation, and impotency for effective action, which, for forty years, has resulted in disasters and sacrifices innumerable to the South, this Conference of Southern deputies is designed.—As a Conference, it does not contemplate final action. Its ordinances, provisions, and recommendations will be subject to the approval or disapproval of the Legislatures or people of all the Southern States.

Such a Conference would make patent a conclusion at which nearly every Southern man has long since arrived, which is, that the rights of the South are now so inadequately protected by the General Government that the people of the slave States must define and clearly set forth those measures of redress, indemnity and protection which the dominant party in the free States have again and again insultingly denied us.

To this Conference we should send statesmen of approved judgment and tried fidelity to the South; and such men, we hope and believe, are yet to be found in the Southern States.

Such a deliberative body would separate all great questions of vital importance to the South from ordinary matters of Federal legislation.— It would direct and concentrate the attention of the Southern people upon the deliberations of a body charged with the responsible duty of framing a Charter of Southern Rights as sacred as that of the "Barons of England." If the action of such a Conference met the approval of the Southern States, it would present an *ultimatum* to the free States which they would be required to as religiously respect as the Kings of England have respected the action of that famous old Conference at Runnymede. Why should not the South have her Magna Charta as plainly and strongly written as that by which the English people, without a disrupture of the Government, defined the powers and checked a monarch not half so lawless and aggressive as the Black Republican party has proved itself to be? Why should we not, ere it is too late, solemnly and deliberately designate to the North the exact limits and boundary of our forebearance and patience, and thus secure the existence of the only Union in which the South can remain with honor?

The advantage which the North possesses over the South, at this time, consists mainly in the thorough organization of that sectional party which menaces the Union with speedy dissolution. So thorough is the discipline and drill of this party, that it is able, for weeks together, to present an unbroken phalanx to the assaults of a divided and discordant South.—Ordinary party discipline at the South has not been able to procure the concert of action essential to the efficient defence of our rights and liberties. Elected with reference to other issues than those presented by the present fearful crisis, the Southern members of the National House of Representatives can unite in support of no efficient. man or measure.

We believe that in a conference of Southern delegates the requisite harmony and concert of action could be secured.

One of the recommendations of the Conference proposed by South

Carolina is, that, whilst the chances in favor of its accomplishing much good are very great, its recommendations and suggestions must meet the formal approval of the Southern States before they become binding or obligatory. The result of its labors, like those of the Convention which formed the Federal Constitution, must be submitted to either the people or the Legislatures of each of the slave States. Meeting and deliberating as the representatives of sovereign States, the action of a majority of the States will not bind the minority. Each State will express, in due form, its approval or disapproval of the action of the Conference, and those who shall not acquiesce in the wisdom of its recommendations will not be governed by them in any manner whatever.

To those who may be inquisitive with respect to the questions which will, in all probability, engage the attention of the Conference, we may venture to say, that all matters of interest to the South, growing out of sectional agitation, will be topics of legitimate discussion by the Conference.

A demand for the repeal of all laws passed by the free States nullifying those acts of Congress which have simply carried out the provisions of the Federal Constitution for the protection of the property of the South, would be considered by the Convention.

It would also secure concert of action upon the part of the Southern States with reference to the solution of the problem of Southern commercial independence by the encouragement of direct trade and domestic manufactures. To secure the success of such measures, unity of action among the Southern States is indispensable; for whilst one slave State favors commercial independence of the North, and the rest of the Southern States enrich the Abolition States by their trade, nothing of importance can be accomplished.

Many other questions of even greater importance would occupy the attention of the Conference; but we deem it unnecessary to enumerate them.

A Conference of the character desired by South Carolina would be an admirable initiatory step to sending Commissioners to the Northern States, charged with the grave task of presenting to them a Southern *ultimatum.*—Before the South can venture to say to the North, "Thus far shalt thou come, but no farther," it is indispensable to the success of our last effort to preserve our rights and honor within the Union that the South should agree upon some fixed, determined, matured plan of action.

How can this concert of action be secured better than by a Conference of delegates from the Southern States? It cannot be attained by legislative resolutions, for they would afford no opportunity for a comparison and reconciliation of conflicting views.

Regarding, therefore, the Conference proposed by South Carolina as the best as well as the most pacific means for securing united action upon the part of the Southern States, we earneastly recommend an immediate compliance with the request which South Carolina has just made of Virginia. She asks it in behalf of the whole South, and she appeals to Virginia as a State of whose fame and greatness all of her sister States of the South are justly proud. Reminding Virginia of the respect and reverence with which South Carolina has heretofore listened to her counsels, our well-beloved Southern sister asks us to provide a safe and effectual means for uniting the South in defence of common rights and against common dangers. This she asks, and in a manner so courteous, and through a Commissioner so prudent, able and discreet, as to disarm every prejudice.

If Virginia refuses to appoint delegates to confer with those from the other States of the South, when the object of the proposed Conference is the defence of violated rights and the protection of kindred interests, it will be a declaration, upon her part, that she does not desire concert of action upon the part of the Southern States. She will refuse to acquiesce in the only practical scheme of the day for uniting the South.

Standing at the head of the column of Southern States, the invasion of her own soil being the proximate cause of the impending crisis, is Virginia prepared to shrink from the position of leader in this last great plan for the preservation of the Union by the South's making a solemn appeal to the justice and conservatism of the North? Shall she say to South Carolina: "We refuse to aid you in your proposed call for a peaceful Conference of the slave States, although the design of it is to protect that institution in which we are most largely interested." For South Carolina asks, through her Commissioner, for nothing more than a Conference, an advisory body whose action must meet with the approval of each slave State before it can be binding. Surely the Legislature of Virginia will not deny to the people of the South this safe and judicious means for procuring harmony and concert of action.

We, therefore, appeal to the Legislature to make provision, without delay, for the appointment of delegates to the Conference of the slave States proposed by South Carolina.

6. THE TRUE REMEDIES

(*The Daily True Delta,* New Orleans, February 1, 1860)

The return of Senator Douglas to his place in the United States Senate after his protracted and severe illness, has been at once signalised by one of those patriotic constitutional movements with the inauguration of which his great name has been so often associated. He had scarcely taken his exalted place among his peers and rebuked the Iversons, the minor Clays and the Davises, of the body of which he is himself the ornament and the pride, than he promptly proposed a bill [1] which there is every reasonable expectation will become a law, and which will effectually for all future time provide means, efficient and reliable, for the apprehension and conviction of the abolition hordes upon the frontiers of the slave-holding states, who may in future attempt a renewal of depredations upon the property, slave or other, of their citizens, as has been systematically the case for years past. Mr. Douglas will not allow the South to be at the mercy of free state mobs, nor will he leave their stolen property to be recovered through the clumsy and deceitful operation of an unexecuted or partially enforced fugitive slave law; but nobly takes the crime and the criminals by the throat, and provides the means at the general charge and with perfect certainty of success of extirpating both. Douglas, ever true to the great principles of his life, in this his last movement to secure the safety and rights of the South, but not by truculent threats against or frothy denunciations of the Union, the great Western states-man has exhibited that practical statesmanship for which the truly great men of this republic have, on all great emergencies, been so distinguished, and a knowledge of which, in every civilized country, has led the inhabitants of all such to regard our political dissensions and disagreements, however serious in appearance, as of the most evanescent and paltry consequence in reality. It would be a gross miscalculation of the purpose of Stephen A. Douglas to suppose that with the success of the bill now proposed by him in the Federal Senate, for the greater security of the persons and property of citizens of the slave States from the designs, covert or overt, of conspirators in the free

[1] *Resolved,* That the Committee on the Judiciary be instructed to report a bill for the protection of each State and Territory of the Union against invasion by the authorities or inhabitants of any other State or Territory; and for the suppression and punishment of conspiracies or combinations in any State or Territory with intent to invade, assail, or molest the government, inhabitants, property, or institutions of any other State or Territory of the Union. *Cong. Globe,* 36 Cong., 1 Sess., I, 448.

states, he will be contented—far from it; he is too national in his views and character for that, and we believe it will not be long before he will, with equal promptitude and sagacity, devise a legal and constitutional mode to make the individual states respect the laws and the constitution, as he is now endeavoring to compel individual traitors to do. We are sure the intrepid senator of ever-faithful and loyal Illinois takes the view that the conductors of this journal have ever maintained, namely, that a failure upon the part of any state or states faithfully to respect and maintain the laws of Congress and the obligations of the federal Constitution, is a crime, not against another individual state or against several states, but a wanton, flagrant and treasonable defiance of all; and if such state or states cannot by means of their own inhabitants—that is, by the application of the legitimate power of the people therein—be compelled to conform their practices to the requirements of the constitutional pact, then we unhesitatingly declare our conviction that the great Western statesman will be found ready and willing to shape and sustain such national action as will compel the guilty to perform every duty and respect every obligation they have voluntarily bound themselves to do.

We are of those who believe the people of a state possess the unquestionable right to secede from this Union, whenever the compact of union to which she is a party is violated or the rights of its own people or of the people of any other state or states in the confederacy are infringed, invaded or overthrown; but while we can scarcely imagine and will not believe in the possibility of such an occurrence, we repudiate and repel the action of mere delegates of this or any other state representing very different matters and interests, to pledge the people or the country to any such dangerous and impracticable result. We also unhesitatingly protest against the assumption, that the failure of Massachusetts, New York, or Pennsylvania to carry out the requirements of a law of Congress, or fulfil a constitutional obligation affecting the pecuniary interests of the slave-holding states, is a cause for the secession of Virginia or South Carolina from the Union, any more than for New Jersey and Illinois, neither of which states are prepared to sanction a criminal and traitorous disregard of their most solemn and binding obligations upon the part of the commonwealths we have named, or any other members of the federal pact, whether such violation be directed against one description of property or another, or the particular institutions of any state or section of the Union. That the South has been deeply aggrieved and most atrociously wronged, by the action of many of the free states, in their legislative, executive, judicial departments, cannot be disputed if it can be forgiven or forgotten; but while the whole South has experienced the loss and suffered the specific injury, the crime itself is equally against the free states who do not sanction or approve but honorably denounce it; in a word, the grievance is local, the crime national, and the redress also should be national. If oaths will not bind the people of some states; if no obligation, however sacred, can command the respect and the fidelity of the people of particular states or sections; the mode of applying the corrective, whether it be by force or otherwise, is not by the abandonment of its rights and interests, not by a sacrifice of its place in the Union by any one state, or by several states, but by the united efforts of all loyal, faithful and compact-observing states against those which have proclaimed their hostility to their brethren by the blackest perjury and the most unpardonable crimes. The South, like every other important section of the confederacy, will fight in the Union, not out of it; the people of Illinois, represented by their greatest men, will not sever the fraternal ligaments which indissolubly bind them to Louisiana, because perjured traitors in other states violate the constitution and infract laws, but they tender, on the contrary, the whole power they possess as a sovereign and independent commonwealth, and as a member of this powerful confederacy, to compel, if need be, the enemies of the equality of each and all to abandon their course or suffer the pains and penalties their damnable treason and injustice provoke. Let traitors to the Union leave it; let the states of the North, which have wallowed in their infamous disregard of their sacred duties, preach disunion and secession; but the loyal and true should come more closely together, make common cause against the renegades and traitors, and compel them to act faithfully, honestly and justly, or be expelled from the Union they have disgraced and betrayed.

The South cannot abandon a Union which her industry, her enterprise and her fidelity have contributed so largely to make what it is, merely that some demagogue or other may be a president who dispairs of such distinction in the Union as its;[2] or for the gratification of those short-sighted few who foolishly imagine enormous wealth would flow to them especially from a calamity so dreadful. Let the violators of the laws of Congress and those who aim at the destruction of the constitution abandon the Union; not those who in all times have submitted to every privation to maintain its honor and perpetuate its power and

[2] Printer's error for "it is."

integrity. Neither should we forget, as we have already said, that a crime against the Union is not one to be resented by any one state or a few states, because although one or more may be the sufferers the whole is wronged; and whether the wrong consists in an actual theft, as the stealing a negro, or it be inflicted as Buchanan and his cabinet did it, by giving aid and comfort to the Abolitionists of Illinois against the constitutional party of that chivalrous state, it must be dealt with and punished by the whole Union as it exists under the constitution, and we regard it as quite equal to the undertaking.

Should Douglas be elected President of this Republic in November next, as we confidently believe, he will satisfy the friends and foes of equal and just government and of this democratic Union that under our constitution remedies exist for all exigencies and for the maintenance of the sovereign rights of every state, however situated, which belongs to this grand confederation.

7. NEW CONSTITUTIONAL GUARANTEES

(Richmond Whig and Public Advertiser, February 2, 1860)

The object of the proposed "Conference" of the Southern States, as explained by the able and distinguished Commissioner from South Carolina, is to demand of the Northern States new Constitutional guarantees for the protection and security of the rights of the South.— In other words, amendments to the Constitution are to be proposed— such amendments, too, as there is no probability of obtaining, as Col. Memminger himself frankly admits; and yet, if these amendments are not granted by the Northern States, the Southern States will forthwith secede from the Union.

As for ourselves, we have already expressed our opposition to the objects of the South Carolina Commissioner. We want no conference at present looking to a dissolution of the Federal Union, nor do we want any tampering or tinkering with the Federal Constitution. We concur with the Louisville Journal, that no new Constitutional guarantees are required, or can be obtained, or would be of any sort of value, if procured. The whole thing, therefore, according to our judgment, is simply and palpably a mere excuse for disunion. It is the flimsy pretext with which to cover over a great moral and national wrong in distinct and present contemplation.

God and our fathers have already given to the American people the most perfect provision for the protection of human right and liberty that the world has ever seen. The Federal Government, representing the sovereignty of the nation, and the State governments, representing the sovereignty of each state, in that wondrous combination which Divine and human wisdom have concurred in producing, present a more real and effectual guard against oppression, while all the legitimate purposes of government are fully provided for, than was ever effected before by any division of power between separate States of the realm.

This provision is not a mere paper constitution. It is a real and substantive thing, the result of our actual condition and history. It is a "power ordained of God" most manifestly, for His Providence brought it into being, and the highest human wisdom has gratefully accepted the blessing and sought with assiduous care to guard the inestimable treasure.

The principle of this glorious provision is that the Federal Government can execute its own laws by its own sovereign authority, while its jurisdiction is restricted to a limited range of subjects. The State governments by an equal sovereignty execute their laws over a much larger range of the ordinary subjects of legislation. Thus each government is in the constant and habitual exercise of sovereign power. In ordinary governments there is no resource against oppression but individual resistance, or the irregular, feeble, and injurious expedient of conspiracy and rebellion. But in the American constitution the attempted oppression of the stronger central government can be met at once and effectually by the organized resistance of an actual working government, just as sovereign and just as legitimate as the usurping power. The theoretical right of every man to maintain his liberty and to resist oppression is thus clothed with all the sanctity of a national act, and armed with all the power of a prepared and legitimate government. And this is the very highest guarantee and protection that human right and liberty can have.

Human wisdom cannot get beyond this. You cannot invent a system that will work itself smoothly along without ever calling in aid human responsibility. The "ultima ratio" is the necessary condition of all right.—The perfection of our system is that it clothes that condition with effective and salutary power.

The fathers of the Republic understood all this very well, and therefore upon the first flagrant instance of unconstitutional and oppressive legislation by the Federal Government, the States of Virginia and Kentucky, in 1798-9, at once announced their determination to exercise their sovereign authority in resistance to that legislation; and they called upon the other State governments to do the same thing. This determination was accompanied with this plain and distinct declaration:— "That the General Assembly of Virginia doth unequivocally express a firm resolution to maintain and defend the Constitution of the United States, and the Constitution of this State against every aggression, either foreign or domestic."

These men of nerve and intellect knew very well the stern arbitrament to which they were appealing for the maintenance of their liberties, and they knew that that arbitrament was the ultimate and only sanction of all human right. But they just as well understood and fully appreciated the persuasive and effective power of that *"ultima ratio,"* when applied by sovereign States and working governments.

A generation later the amateur statesman of South Carolina took up these same resolutions and put upon them the fanciful and notable interpretation of PEACEABLE NULLIFICATION AND PEACEABLE SECESSION. Gen. Jackson battered the former of these notions so unmercifully that both have been out of countenance ever since.

Now the same men are trying to delude the South into a demand for "constitutional guarantees." What are these and what will they be worth?

Has not experience amply demonstrated that all the mere written checks and balances of the Constitution have been easily and constantly overborne by popular majorities? Only the great conservative feature of the independent sovereignty of the Federal and of the State Governments remains in its integrity and in its power.

Do the South Carolina gentlemen mean that the Constitution must fasten down the country in marble rigidity to its present condition of progress and population? That the whole subject of slavery shall be taken away from the State governments, none being allowed in future either to adopt or to abolish it; and that the representation in Congress shall be divided with arithmetical equality between the two sections? If the claim has any distinct meaning at all, this absurdity must be the bright conception.

But even such an impracticable arrangement, if it could be effected, would be no security against a storm of popular fanaticism, or against the easy and convenient process of purchasing a few recusant Senators. The real security at last is in the power and integrity of the respective State Governments. This is all that we need as men capable of freedom and of self-government. The present cry for further constitutional protection is more delusive and far more childish than the exploded conceit of peacable nullification. Its only design is to allure the South into a position which will precipitate disunion.

We therefore appeal to the members of the Virginia Legislature, without distinction of party, to beware how they take a step in so fatal a direction. We throw out to them a warning in time, and we hope they may have sagacity and patriotism enough to heed it.

8. ARE THEY DISGUSTED, OR AFRAID?

(*The Savannah Republican,* February 8, 1860)

There is a numerous class of politicians and political dabblers in the South, interspersed here and there with a goodly number of Editors, who go into a sort of hysterical spasm whenever the name of the *Union* is mentioned. At the slightest allusion to the talismanic word, they throw themselves into all sorts of curious distortions, and a strange sort of shudder—resembling somewhat the physical demonstrations peculiar to the Shaking Quakers—is visible from their heads to their toes, penetrating bone and marrow and every member of their political bodies. The world has for some time looked on and pitied their agonies from so simple a cause. It was indeed cruel to talk of such things in view of the disastrous nervous effects that were sure to follow.

But there is no limit to "man's inhumanity to man." Not content with these heart-rending sufferings of the poor afflicted souls, some fiend in human shape has recently added fuel to the flame by the invention of another obnoxious word, and placing it in immediate juxtaposition with the original source of the aforesaid lamentable result. A *"Constitutional Union"* is now talked of—a still more horrid monster, conjured up from the infernal deep to harass the souls and imbitter the probation of the tender-hearted and susceptible patriots. We refrain from any further allusion to the heart-rending effects of this new persecution. It is the last pound that breaks the camel's back, the last pang to an already unutterable despair. Is there no one that can induce, by imprecations, threats, prayers, or in any other human way, these cruel ministers of pain to cease their remorseless work!

But seriously: this extreme repugnance to sentiments of attachment for the Union, is one of the ominous signs of the times. It either proves a settled disloyalty to the government under which we live, or a fear of the patriotic sentiment, as inimical to certain political plans that have been concocted for the future. We are inclined to think that both hypotheses are established by the evidences before us. Why should any good patriot object to a Union party, and especially to one that is pledged to guaranty and preserve inviolate the constitutional rights of every section and member of the confederacy? Is there no necessity for such an organization? If there be not, then the daily recitals of wrongs and injustice that are rung into our ears, are a delusion and a lie. We are told by nine-tenths of the presses and politicians of the South that our rights have been trampled upon, that the Union is in danger of dissolution, that the government has failed, and the constitution set at nought; whilst some, considering the system created by our fathers no longer worth preserving, on account of these abuses, are casting about for a radical change of affairs, and southern independence. This is the startling state of things that is daily rung in our ears and held up for our mournful contemplation; and yet, who has had control of the government—who the management of our foreign and domestic relations—who the absolute direction of all political affairs—while this harvest of woe was maturing for the country? Will some one answer that question? We have section against section, arrayed in deadly strife; the sentiments of mutual respect, love, and brotherhood supplanted by mutual contempt, hatred, and alienation, while the country trembles and totters under the influence of the strife—and yet we are told that there is no need of anything new; the same propelling influences that have driven us to the brink of the precipice, will, by some wonderful feat of moral mechanics, reverse its action and drive us back from the peril! Is such the principle upon which rational men guide the actions of their daily lives and manage the machinery of their private interests? We think not. To our mind, the prospect looks unpromising indeed.

The present is no time for reproaches; nor would we be understood as writing in any such spirit. We speak simply truth, solemn, incontrovertible truth; and we beg our readers of every name to place it in the balance and give it the weight that is due. We have no war to make upon Democrats. Where they are wrong, our highest aim should be to show them their error; where they are right, it is our firm determination, to the extent of our humble ability, to stand by and uphold them in their patriotic endeavors to sustain the truth and the Union.—But there are some truths to which no man can shut his eyes, except such as are resolved to be blind. Nothing can be more evident to our own mind than that the Charleston Convention is destined to result either in disgraceful failure or in a triumph that will prostrate the South, and overthrow every principle and right for which she has contended in the ten years' struggle that is about to close. It cannot be otherwise; and there is something alarming in the fact that some of her own sons, who love her less than they do party and place, are now engaged in preparing the minds of her people for the sacrifice. The altar is erected, the worshippers at the shrine of Mammon are standing eagerly around —is the South prepared to surrender peaceably as the victim? We hope not, and our voice shall not cease to be heard, in solemn, earnest protest against so foul a prostitution and wrong. We do not address ourselves to the politicians and placemen of the South; they are both deaf and soulless. To the *people* we would appeal, and arouse them, if possible to the defense of their honor, their rights, and their firesides. We cannot believe that they are to be bartered away for a mess of pottage, and to give their sanction to the bargain.

As before stated, we belong to no political party, and have nothing but the best interest of our common country to direct our course in the future. We are not afraid to be called a Democrat, when that party shall place itself in a position to secure our confidence; nor shall we hesitate to oppose it with all the energy at our command, when we believe its triumphs are freighted with disaster to our section, or peril to the Union. On the other hand, we know little or nothing of the rumored movements for the organization of a new party. If such a project be on foot, it must come squarely up to our standard of constitutional right, to secure our respect and support. On the other hand, it is our firm conviction—and we have had of late the very best opportunities for forming a correct opinion—that, organized as the Demcratic party is at present, without the slightest agreement on the most vital questions of national concern, divided as to men, and promising the overthrow of all principle in the coming nomination, it presents no security either for the rights of the South or the peace of the country.

We see no cheering prospect of the successful formation of a new party at the present time; but could such a thing be done, on a footing that shall guaranty the rights of every section and put down disunion agitation at the south and anti-slavery agitation at the north, it appears to us that it would be the duty of every patriot in the land to bid it God speed and give it a helping hand. Heaven knows the country has suffered long enough from contention and strife, and it is equally evident that existing parties have been looked to long enough for the remedy, and looked to in vain. What promises have we for the future that have not utterly failed in the past?

9. Causes and Effects

(The New Orleans Bee, February 9, 1860)

It is generally supposed that the defeat of Mr. SHERMAN [1] for Speaker of the House of Representatives foreshadows that of Mr. SEWARD before the Black Republican (so called) National Convention. We have very little doubt that the one event will follow the other, though we question somewhat the correlation of cause and effect. True it is that Mr. SHERMAN lost the Speakership, because in endorsing the Helper book [2] he manifested anti-slavery sentiments in the most odious and ultra form. Equally true is it that WM. H. SEWARD has forfeited his strong hold upon Black Republican sympathies, and will probably be set aside for some more available exponent of anti-slavery sentiments, chiefly because that wily politician for once mistook the temper of the people, and blurted out practical abolition in his Rochester speech [3] in its most offensive shape. Yet it is quite possible—nay, extremely likely—that SHERMAN would now occupy the Speaker's chair in the House, and that SEWARD would be in the safe line of precedents for the Presidential nomination, but for the Harper's Ferry raid. That abortive effort at an outbreak has done more to injure the ultra Black Republicans, their doctrines and champions, than any other possible event. It aroused so universal a feeling of indignation among all who were not irretrievably committed to the wild and destructive theories of a GARRISON, a PHILIPS and a CHEEVER, as fairly to overwhelm those imprudent party leaders who had prematurely exposed the ultimate designs and inevitable tendencies of Black Republicans. To this cause do we chiefly ascribe the compulsory withdrawal of SHERMAN after two months' ineffectual efforts to elect him. No candidate holding extreme sectional opinions could have been chosen Speaker in the condition of the public mind superinduced by the Harper's Ferry affair. To the same cause do we impute the comparative decline of WM. H. SEWARD. He will not be the nominee of the anti-slavery party, because they will not dare to encounter certain defeat under a standard-bearer who has initiated the doctrine of a perpetual and irrepressible conflict between the North and the South.

[1] John Sherman of Ohio. Representative, 1856–1861; Senator, 1861–1877, 1881–1897; Secretary of the Treasury, 1877–1881; Secretary of State, 1897–1898.

[2] See *Cong. Globe,* 36 Cong., I Sess., I, 16.

[3] *The Irrepressible Conflict,* delivered at Rochester, Oct. 25, 1858; *The Works of William H. Seward,* Geo. E. Baker, ed., IV, 289–302.

From these developments it would appear that the wicked and atrocious experiment of JOHN BROWN, though resulting disastrously for himself and his accomplices, may be productive of great ultimate benefit to the South and to the Union. One of its earliest and most palpable effects has been at the North to terrify every anti-slavery man who is not actually blinded and besotted by sectional fanaticism, and to strengthen conservative citizens of that section in their determination to use every possible endeavor to crush out the foul, hateful and mischievous spirit of abolition. On the one hand the rank and file of the Black Republicans, in their dread of a reaction against them, are repudiating JOHN BROWN and his principles, and assuring the South that beyond a repugnance to the extension of slavery, they bear no animosity whatever to our section of the Union. On the other hand, the mass of those truly national and praiseworthy men who have steadfastly combated fanaticism, avail themselves of the opportunity to demonstrate the inevitable consequences of sectional feuds; to show that the attempt of BROWN and his associates at Harper's Ferry was the legitimate result of the tenets and teachings of Black Republicanism, and to warn the North against the fatal error it has so long cherished. Thus, we fully believe, the effect at the North has been to compel Black Republicanism materially to moderate its tone and its demands, and at the same time to invigorate and encourage the brave and patriotic spirits who have heretofore striven against the heresy of abolitionism, and in favor of the rights of the South.

With us we can chronicle some things even more gratifying. The South, for almost the first time in her history, has felt the necessity of a union of all her sons in a firm, temperate, but unyielding demand for the recognition of her constitutional prerogatives. While there are extremists at the South, just as there are at the North; while we have amongst us those who are clamorous for disunion, just as in the North there are those who will be satisfied with nothing short of the immediate abolition of slavery, the great body of our people occupy a position at once calm and dignified. They ask for the enjoyment of their indefeasible rights—for nothing more, nor will they be contented with anything less. The South is a unit in this respect. A still more important consequence is visible in the determination of the South to build up her own domestic industry; to depend less on the North; to cease, as far as is practicable, from nourishing and sustaining her foes; to strive to foster the spirit of self-help, self-improvement and commercial independence. Thus while the South will eventually be released from the shackles of utter dependence on the North and will become self-sustaining, she will administer a wholesome and well-merited rebuke to fanatics and incendiaries in the only way in which it can be sensibly felt. When the North is made to appreciate the value of Southern friendship by the losses and the sufferings consequent upon its forfeiture, we may reasonably hope that interest, if not fraternal concord, will admonish that section of the expediency of letting us alone.

10. The Constitutional Union Party

(Daily Chronicle and Sentinel, Augusta, February 13, 1860)

We think the formation of such a party is a necessity of the times, and while we regret, we are not surprised at, the opposition it meets with. Besides being opposed by *disunionists per se,* by men North and South who agree in nothing else save calling the Union a covenant with Hell, it also meets the opposition of numbers of the Republicans and Democrats, *not* disunionists, but who, as partisans, fear the success of the movement, and the overthrow of their own organizations. The best thing these men can do is to join the new party, and go in on the first *spring flood.*

Seriously, we pity the man who cannot, in a time like this, conquer his prejudices, his antipathies, his party feeling, and give himself, heart and hand to his country. That country has need of him—it needs all the patriotism and all the courage it can enlist to save it from destruction. Bad men have ruled too long, bad men have *recklessly,* to say the least, if not with positive evil intent, rushed the old Ship of State far out of her Constitutional course, and now, in the wild waste of waters, the tempest and the darkness are upon her, and the white waves are wreathing themselves, angrily as serpents, upon the terrible breakers just ahead. In such a crisis, in such thick-gathering gloom, who will not lend a hand to right the old ship, and to save her? In such a time, who will not cease the miserable cry of the spoiler, and join in one more strong endeavor to rescue the ark of the covenant, and to give peace and security and prosperity to our beloved land? Then, away with the doubter, away with the scorner, away with him who will not see the danger, or, who seeing, will not work to avert it.

But what kind of a Union party shall we have—upon what basis shall it be organized? These are important questions, not only as affecting the success of the party, but as to its real worth to the country, should it prove successful. Of course, if it is to follow in the beaten track of the old parties—if it is to be a mere shifting, halting, ambiguous, delphic concern—it will prove of no advantage to the country, whatever it be to its own camp followers. Such a party the country does not need—it wants anything else. We love this Union sincerely; it is a sentiment with us, that has grown with us from our youth, and strengthened with our manhood. But we love justice.—We do not favor a Union party, organized upon generalities, and with the simple battle-cry of the Constitution and the Laws. We want specialities—we want nobody deceived, and nobody cheated. We want all the elements which are to compose the party to come in upon terms of perfect equality, and we want all to have a full and fair understanding of the bond of Union—of the grounds upon which we will administer the government, if we can get possession. We shall join in no cry of the Union, the Union, for the sake of the Union *only,* nor for the sake of party ascendancy. We wish to preserve this Union for the sake of the blessings it has conferred, and for those we hope it may still continue to confer upon our children and our children's children. With all those who may seek to enter the organization, we hope bygones may be bygones. "Let the dead bury their dead." Let no names and distinctions heretofore known among us be a hindrance to any one conscientiously seeking the salvation of his country. Let us meet as equals and friends, to overthrow those who in willfulness or ignorance have brought us to the brink of the precipice.

But what shall be the basis of the new party? In the first place it must be truly a Union party, standing on middle ground between the extremists of each section, rebuking the fanaticism of the North and the ultraism of the South. Its great aim must be to preserve the Union of these States, its becoming in fact as well as in name a *Constitutional* party. Not simply by unmeaning declarations of fealty to the Constitution, because all parties say that, but something more. The bond of Union must include an unequivocal pledge to maintain and enforce the laws, especially the fugitive slave law of Congress, and an *unconditional repeal of all State laws* which practically nullify the act of Congress, or hinder its enforcement.—In addition the party must commit itself plainly to the decision of the Supreme Judicial tribunal of the land, which declares that the *only* right of Congress over the question of slavery in the Territories is the *right* coupled with the *duty* of extending to the owner adequate protection for his property, whenever the same becomes necessary. It must set its face determinedly against the *unconstitutional* heresy which clothes the creature, (the Territorial

Legislature) with more power than the Creator (Congress) itself possesses, and under the specious plea of popular sovereignty, surrenders the constitutional rights of the citizens to the arbitrament of those who are not sovereigns. This doctrine of popular sovereignty is only another name for freesoil, and its advocates, *wherever found* are freesoilers at heart, and only deterred by *fear* from so declaring themselves.

The party which, in good faith and without evasion, adopts the platform above set forth, will become the *real* "Constitutional Union Party" of the country, whatever may be its *name*. And to such a party we confidently hope the entire Opposition of Georgia and the South may be rallied, with a majority of the Democracy also. Such a party, *with the right leaders,* we believe, can carry enough votes in the Northern States to elect its candidates for the Presidency and Vice Presidency. "Principles, *not* men" was once a rallying cry—we prefer principles *and* men, for there is frequently as much in the men as in the principles and it is as much a party *duty* to use all honorable means for success, as to maintain good principles. For of what avail can principles ever be, unless you so organize your forces as to secure their successful enforcement? Our opinion then is, that to be *successful,* a Southern man should be the Presidential candidate, with a Central State man for the Vice Presidency. Let this not alarm our Union friends at the North—we do not *demand* the first choice, but we think success depends on it, and therefore, we ask it as a concession from those who become our Northern allies.

It may be said that we are *ultra* as to the platform—that we ask too much. We think not, and we think this the most opportune time we ever saw to insist upon a *full* and *final settlement.* Is there one conscientious, honest, reflecting man in the North who will say we are not *justly* entitled to an absolute enforcement of the Fugitive Slave Law? That we are not *justly* entitled, under the decision of our own highest Court, to protection for our property of all kinds? If so, let him speak and give his reasons. We claim to be conservative, Union-loving, law-abiding—that has been always the character of this paper, and therefore we hope our language may be heeded by our Northern friends.

It may be asked then, what ultraism and what fanaticism do we propose to fight—from what save the country? We answer that we oppose, and we wish the Union party to oppose, on the one hand that fanaticism at the North which refuses enforcement of the law, and declares no more slave States shall be admitted, and on the other, that ultraism at the South which declares for disunion in the event a Republican is elected. We oppose both of these, and we would save the country from the infatuated rule or ruin policy of those who preach such doctrines.

11. The Appointments of the "Conservative, Old Line Whig," Black Republican Speaker

(Richmond Semi-weekly Examiner, February 14, 1860)

The formation of the committees of the House is an admirable commentary on the conservative, anti-sectional character which the Opposition friends of Pennington [1] in the South have been so kind as to give him. His union with the Black Republicans—his continued, zealous and unhesitating service in their ranks—his nomination and election by that party—his refusal to vote for a South American or a Southern old line Whig, could not convince the leading Opposition press in Virginia that he was any other than a true, patriotic, Union-loving, anti-sectional conservative. The people, we trust, need no further evidence to convince *them* that he is not only in full affiliation with the bitter enemies of the South, but that his election is another evidence of the power of those enemies, and a dangerous and offensive attack upon the interests and rights of the people of the slave-holding States. The Black Republicans know, appreciate and reward him. Let the people of the South understand, and take warning. They have nothing to expect but conflict. The House of Representatives is presided over by their uncompromising foe, and he has not been slow to show his hatred, nor has he bungled in the execution of his allotted task. Sherman and Grow [2] and Hickman [3] evidently planned it, and he hastened to its execution—not as if he was hired by wages alone, but as if he was called to a labor of love. He has finished the first part of his work. No fault can be found with its completeness, or with the fidelity of the laborer. It is but a foretaste of what the South has to hope from power placed in the hands of "conservative, old line Whig, Union-loving" men turned Black Republicans. "This thing is done in

[1] William Pennington, Whig Representative from New Jersey, 1859–1861. He was elected Speaker of the House after a deadlock of several weeks had demonstrated that the House could not be organized until the Republican candidate, John Sherman, withdrew from the contest.

[2] Galusha A. Grow, who introduced his free homestead bill at the beginning of each session for ten years until it became a law in 1862. Appointed Chairman of the Committee on Territories by Speaker Pennington.

[3] John Hickman, elected to the 36th Congress as a Douglas Democrat, and to the 37th Congress as a Republican.

the green tree. What will be done in the dry?"—Let us look at the formation of the important committees by this Speaker. Let us judge him by his principles carried into action; not "by what he calls himself," nor by what newspaper editors say of him. His election was followed by filling the House with Freesoil subordinate officers. This was done by himself and his Black Republican associates. Let us see how he acted of himself, on his own responsibility, at the bidding of his hidden advisers. At the head of the first and most important committee, he places the most noted leader of the strictest sectional party—the endorser of HELPER—JOHN SHERMAN. He and four other Northern men constitute the majority of the Committee of Ways and Means, and the Southern minority of the committee is headed by the notorious HENRY WINTER DAVIS, who is as bad as the worst Northern Freesoiler. This committee has a controlling influence over the taxation of the people, and it is so constituted as to devise, and plan and secure the greatest injustice to the Southern people in the Confederacy.—This is the first example of this man's equal love of all sections and of his love of justice. The next—the Committee on Commerce, whose task it will be to provide for discriminations against Southern industry and in favor of Northern—has a majority of two-thirds Northern men, headed by the Black Republican WASHBURNE,[4] of Illinois, with a minority of three Southern men.—The Committee on Elections has a majority of Northern men, and the Committee and the Southern minority have at their head Mr. GILMER,[5] of North Carolina, who has the reputation of being as near in thought and feeling like unto Mr. HENRY WINTER DAVIS as any man living in the South with any pretense to the possession of a conscience can be. Mr. H. W. DAVIS's seat is contested, and this committee reports on it.—The Committee on the Judiciary, second only in general importance to that of Ways and Means, has seven Northern men and three Southern. The Northern men are all either Black Republicans, or Anti-Lecompton Democrats, headed by the rancorous enemy of the South, HICKMAN, and the three Southern men have amongst them the anti-Southern, Northern-leaning NELSON,[6] of Tennessee. An excellent chance there will be here for devising means to evade the Dred Scott decision, and rendering of no avail the Fugitive Slave Law, if such can be accomplished by any legislative jugglery. The Committee on Foreign Affairs is composed of five Northern men

[4] Elihu Benjamin Washburne, Whig-Republican Representative, 1853–1871.
[5] John A Gilmer, Whig-American Representative from North Carolina, 1857–1861.
[6] Thomas A. R. Nelson, Union Representative from Tennessee, 1859–1861.

and four Southern. In memory of the patriotic prayer, put up in the late war with Mexico, that our enemies should welcome our citizen soldiery "with bloody hands to hospitable graves," the noted THOMAS CORWIN,[7] the Black Republican author of this traitorous piece of blasphemy, is put at the head of this committee.

Out of twenty important committees, eighteen are presided over by Northern Chairmen—all the eighteen are Black Republicans, we believe, save two, these two are BRIGGS [8] and HASKIN,[9] who are rewarded for their desertion of the Democracy and efficient service rendered to the Black Republicans. Of the two Southern Chairmen of Committees, one is GILMER—who has sailed under the same flag with HENRY WINTER DAVIS so long—the other is ETHERIDGE, of Tennessee, both of whom are thus rewarded for their desertion of the South, and their persistent efforts to defeat a union of the South Americans [10] with the Democracy in their long and luckless struggle with the Black Republican assailants of the South. To no man from the South, who has the confidence of the Southern people, who has shown any disposition to resist Northern aggression, has he shown favor or given prominent position. To no man North, out of the ranks of the Black Republicans, has he given power, unless he purchased his reward by base desertion of his professed principles and party, and added to his infamy the degradation of supporting this said PENNINGTON for the office he now holds. These are the evidences of his unselfish purity, of his anti-sectional feeling, of his "Old-line Whig" conservatism, of his love of the Union. He gives all power to one section—he places that power in the hands of the most embittered sectional party in that section—he rewards no man from the South who has not signalized his disregard of Southern rights by aiding, directly or indirectly, in his own personal elevation. He had not the common feeling of kindness and generosity, even of good taste, to extend the common courtesy to his Democratic or old-line Whig opponents, BOCOCK [11] and SMITH,[12] a complimentary appointment, even as first on an unimportant committee.

We submit, now, to the judgment of the conservative people of this

[7] Representative from Ohio; Minister to Mexico during Lincoln's administration.
[8] George Briggs, American Representative from New York City.
[9] John B. Haskin, Democratic Representative from New York.
[10] The term *South Americans* designates southern members of the Know-Nothing or American party.
[11] Thomas S. Bocock, Democratic Representative from Virginia, 1857–1861; Speaker of the House in the Confederate Congress, 1862.
[12] William Smith, Governor of Virginia, 1845–1848, 1863; Representative in Congress, 1853–1861.

Union, North and South, whether an official position in this country was ever filled by a man whose action proved him to be more thoroughly sectional, a more embittered and bigoted enemy of the South, or a more unvarying and unscrupulous partizan? Let other cause be found for rejoicing in the South than this man's election. Let us see other reason to abate our vigilance, and to stay our dread and hate of freesoil aggressions than can be found in this last victory of Black Republican representatives. Let not the North hear any voice from the South save of wrath and regret at this fatal achievement of the enemies of the Constitution and the South.

12. A Consistent Democracy

(*Daily Courier,* Louisville, February 22, 1860)

The resolutions adopted by the Democracy of Alabama have been condemned by some inconsiderate and unthinking Democrats even, in the Southern States, as unadvised, rash, and dangerous. An attempt has been made in certain quarters to create the impression that this convention did not reflect the sentiments of the gallant Democracy of that most loyal of States—that it was controlled and managed by fire eaters, secessionists, disunionists *per se*. Nothing could be more unjust. The convention was duly and properly called; the delegates were selected after due and sufficient notice; the meeting was largely attended; the committee on resolutions, consisting of two members from each Congressional district, selected by the delegates from the districts respectively, made a unanimous report, and the report was almost unanimously adopted. That the resolutions adopted by this convention fairly represent the views and opinions and wishes of the party in that State, cannot be reasonably questioned.

Nor have the Democracy of Alabama taken their position without having fairly and fully counted the cost. Their action was not unadvised. They did not pass resolutions and announce their determination to the world thoughtlessly, or in a mere spirit of spite or bravado. They but re-affirmed their old platforms and planted themselves anew in their old foot prints. No new principle was enunciated; no new plank interpolated; no new tests of party fealty incorporated; even old principles were not re-asserted in new or uncertain language. The old landmarks of the party were observed and adhered to. All honor to the consistent Alabama Democracy!

In 1848, their State Convention passed the following resolutions, among others:

That the opinion advanced and maintained by some, that the people of a Territory, acquired by common toil, suffering, blood, and treasure of the people of all the States, can, in any other event than in forming a constitution preparatory to admittance as a State into the Union, lawfully or constitutionally prevent any citizen from any such State from removing to or settling in such Territory [with his property], be it slave property or otherwise, is a restriction as indefensible in principle and as dangerous in practice as if such restrictions were imposed by [act of] Congress.

That it is the duty of the General Government, by all proper legislation, to secure [That the treaty of cession should contain a clause securing] an entry into those Territories (referring to the Territories acquired from Mexico) to all the citizens of the United States, together with their property of every description, and that the same should remain protected by the United States while the Territories are under its authority.[1]

In 1856, they adopted the following resolution:

The unqualified right of the people of the slaveholding States to the protection of their property in the States, in the Territories, and in the wilderness in which Territorial governments are as yet unorganized. The Democratic platform is based on the recognition, not of one, but of both these principles; and when efforts are made to separate these two questions, the Democratic party, resting upon its platform, says: we cannot compromise either proposition, but stand united upon both.

The resolutions adopted by the last State Convention enunciate the same principles in almost the same language, nothing omitted, nothing added. But the 10th resolution adopted by the last convention, is the one upon which the strongest opposition is based. Men whose real objection is to the doctrines avowed in the preceding resolutions, make the one instructing the delegates to withdraw from the Charleston Convention in a certain contingency the scapegoat upon which to heap all the sins they find in the action of the meeting. That resolution reads as follows:

That our delegates to the Charleston Convention are hereby expressly instructed to insist that said convention shall adopt a platform of principles

---

[1] These resolutions, like those of 1860, were written by William L. Yancey. The bracketed interpolations are inserted by the present editor to show the variance of the *Courier's* quotation from the text as printed by Yancey in *Substance of the Speech made by Hon. W. L. Yancey in the Democratic Meeting at Marion, Perry County, May 19, 1860.* See also "Platform of the Alabama Democracy, adopted in State Convention, February, 1848," in *Important Political Pamphlet for the Campaign of 1860*, pp. 9–10.

recognizing distinctly the rights of the South as asserted in the foregoing resolutions; and if said convention shall refuse to adopt in substance the propositions in the preceding resolutions, prior to nominating candidates, our delegates to said convention are hereby positively instructed to withdraw therefrom.

And what is wrong in this? The Democracy of Alabama have adhered firmly to their principles; they have often proclaimed them; they believe they are right; they are Democrats because they understand these principles to be those of that party; is it not right that they should stand by these principles now, firmly and regardless of consequences? If these principles are rejected at Charleston, they cannot as honorable men, remain in a convention which has repudiated their platform, and endorsed different views. To do so, would be to plead guilty to a charge of inconsistency, hypocrisy, and dishonesty. To do this, would be to admit that not principles, but the spoils of successful party conflicts, is the incentive to action and the object of their struggles. If they were honest in adopting their resolutions, they were right in demanding that they shall be recognized at Charleston. But the instructing resolution is not unprecedented. A similar one was adopted by the same Democracy in 1856. The language is scarcely different. The instructing resolution of 1856, is as follows:

That if said National Convention shall refuse to adopt the proposition embraced in the foregoing resolutions, our delegates to said Convention are hereby positively instructed to withdraw therefrom.[2]

We may regard the platform and resolutions of the recent Convention at Montgomery as expressive of the deliberate and fully formed convictions of the Democracy of Alabama—convictions heretofore expressed, since re-affirmed, honestly entertained, and by which they will adhere unwaveringly. They deserve honor for their consistency and firmness, and the thanks of the people of the South for the correct and patriotic stand they have taken.

13. The Territorial Rights of the South "Barren Abstractions"—
No Territory

(*The Charleston Mercury,* February 28, 1860)

In noticing yesterday the Montgomery *Advertiser,* we mentioned grounds on which the Partisans and Unionists of the South strive to

[2] For the platform of the Alabama Democracy, January, 1856, see Appendix II.

belittle the right of the Southern people to colonize common territory, and to have adequate protection with their property. Admitting them to be, as alleged, abstractions, we adduced the unanswerable argument of Mr. ALEXANDER H. STEPHENS himself to show that the people of the South should "be prepared to assert them themselves, as their fathers did, at any hazard, though there be nothing at stake but their honor." We deny, however, that they are abstractions. The assertion is sustained by two false premises. The first, that there exists *no territory* into which the Southern people can go with slave property; the second, that were there ever so much territory adapted to slave labor, the South has *no population* to spare for colonizing. We shall notice to-day the first of these, and endeavor to point out that both in the past and for the future the assertion is the merest concoction of self-stultified politicians, in pursuit of plausible pretexts for surrendering what it is inconvenient for Party men and Unionists to maintain.

The right to have property protected in the territory is not a mere abstraction without application or practical value. In the past there are instances where the people of the Southern States might have colonized and brought new slave States into the Union had the principle been recognized, and the Government, the trustee of the Southern States, exercised its appropriate powers to make good for the slaveholder the guarantees of the Constitution. It has been the great question for ten years. When the gold mines of California were discovered, slaveholders at the South saw that, with their command of labor, it would be easy at a moderate outlay to make fortunes digging gold. The inducements to go there were great, and there was no lack of inclination on their part. But, to make the emigration profitable, it was necessary that the property of Southern settlers should be safe, otherwise it was plainly a hazardous enterprise, neither wise nor feasible. Few were reckless enough to stake property, the accumulation of years, in a struggle with active prejudices amongst a mixed population, where for them the law was a dead letter through the hostile indifference of the General Government, whose duty it was, by the fundamental law of its existence, to afford adequate protection—executive, legislative and judicial—to the property of every man, of whatever sort, without discrimination. Had the people of the Southern States been satisfied they would have received fair play and equal protection at the hands of the Government, they would have gone to California with their slaves. They would have made good with their strong arms and stout hearts, with revolver and bowie-knife, any minor deficiency attributable to the

condition of the country. California would probably now have been
a Slave State in the Union. But such was not the case. The Government
was notoriously unwilling to do its duty. It sought popularity with the
stronger and more determined North by sacrificing the rights of the
South. It even went so far as at once to preclude the emigration of
slave-holders by inaugurating Squatter Sovereignty for the control of
the entire territory in the first handful of Northern settlers. An officer
of the United States army was used to effect the purpose. It got them
to adopt an Anti-Slavery Constitution, prohibiting the holding of
slaves in California. It effectually prevented the experiment of Southern men introducing their slaves into the diggings. And California
was brought into the Union as a Freesoil State. Without affording the
South an opportunity to colonise.

What has been the policy pursued in Kansas? Has that territory had
a fair chance of becoming a Slave State? Has the principle of equal
protection to slave property been carried out by the Government there
in any of its departments? On the contrary, has not every appliance
been used to thwart the South and expel or prohibit her sons from
colonizing there? Have not the chief executive officers of the Territorial Government, appointed by the President of the United States,
been from the beginning successively Northern Freesoilers, whose
whole influence has been exerted, either openly or secretly, to exclude
the South? While impunity in license was given to abolition ruffians
and Northern disturbers of the public peace of the JOHN BROWN school,
the army of the United States was used to check the vindication of
Southern Rights unprotected by the Government. Have not the officers of justice, time and again, quashed indictments against the per-
turbers of the security of Southern men and Southern property—
murderers, incendiaries and negro thieves, &c.? Finally did not Congress, after the Southern settlers had made an astonishing struggle
against all the influences and odds opposed—after they had achieved a
victory, adopting a Pro-Slavery Constitution by a duly authorized Convention of the inhabitants of the territory—did not the Congress of the
General Government reject the application—under whatever flimsy
pretexts—yet in reality, because it was contrary to the universal Northern creed of "No More Slave States," that Kansas should come in
under the Lecompton Constitution? In our opinion, had the principle
of equal protection to Southern men and Southern property been rigor-
ously observed by the General Government, both California and Kansas would undoubtedly have come into the Union as Slave States. The

South lost those States for the lack of proper assertion of this great principle.⌋

We know that it is easy for politicians, now that the opportunity is lost, to assert, without positive proof to rebut the statement, that Kansas could not have been made a Slave State. But there are many facts that point in a different direction, rendering the question one that has at least two sides in the argument. Kansas lies back of the Slave State of Missouri. It was accessible only through Missouri. The counties of Missouri where slavery was strongest and slaves were most numerous, were contiguous to Kansas, The hemp culture there was exceedingly profitable and the negroes were healthy and prolific. The lands of Kansas were similar in soil and climate to these counties, and, of course, much cheaper. Without a political crusade, the natural emigration would have been Southern. Had slave property been protected, the non-slave-holders of the North, with their fanaticism, would not have sought contact with slaveholders. They would not have gone there. They went there by encouragement, and, to a large extent, for the purpose of expelling Southern institutions, which were taking root, and might have flourished, but for the hostilely indifferent course of the Government, and its failure to afford the protection to which all people are entitled from their GOVERNMENT.

So much for the past. But it is maintained that, however this may have been once, it is not so now. The South has now no interests whatever to subserve in insisting on any right in any territories on this continent. All questions, therefore, concerning such territories are merely speculative. In the Union, Nebraska and Washington Territories are too cold. Utah and New Mexico are too barren and arid. The Indian Territories belong to the Indians. Out of the Union, Central America, although nearer than California, is too distant. Mexico is forbidden fruit to us; and Cuba, if she comes to us at all, it will be as a slave community, and the question relative to our rights in new territories will have no bearing upon her. Thus, all the territories on the continent are quite beyond the sphere of Southern occupation or civilization; and all talk about the rights of the South as regards any such territories, is sheer nonsense.

Now, if these views be correct, the first remark which will strike any reflecting mind is, that the Southern people must be a most singular and remarkable people. Every other people in the world would have some interest in territories belonging to them, or in those around them. With every other people, expansion would be a blessing. They alone are to be unrestricted and uninjured by being prohibited from their own territories, and being kept out of all neighboring territories which may be placed under their common Government. The Southern people must be most unfortunately and extraordinarily situated in regard to the quality of the territories by which they are surrounded, and their civilization must be strange indeed that it has no use for extension. *Prima facie* evidence is emphatically against the *dictum* that there is *no territory* into which the Southern people can go.

But let us examine, by other than vague assertion, these views, and see whether the territorial rights of the South are without practical value for the future. The Indian Territory lies contiguous to Arkansas on the west. It is a large, rich and beautiful country, and will, unquestionably, ere long be opened to colonization from the States. Applications have already been made, as we have been assured, for leave to settle there by the Southerners expelled from Kansas. No one doubts but that the Indians will be removed to the more western locations of other tribes, and that the Anglo-Saxon will occupy the land in their stead. When that territory is opened, the principle of protection to slave property by the General Government will have a local habitation and a practical application which the most unwilling devotee of Democratic official success and the Union will be able neither to gainsay nor ignore. With the South failing sternly to assert and maintain her territorial rights in the Union, and the continuance of the Union, there is not a shadow of doubt as to the destiny of the Indian Territory— *one or more Freesoil Anti-Slavery States.* If the principle and right of protection now surrendered by the indifference of Party men or Union-savers at the South, in order to patch up a hollow truce with the Freesoil Democracy at the North and by their co-operation secure a party triumph, destitute of principle, and damaging to all hopes of Southern expansion, can the South hereafter, with any show of consistency or moral force, resurrect her dead rights? No; the principle will be lost, and we shall fail to secure that important territory. It will be snatched from us by Freesoil recruits, backed in their inroads by the General Government in the hands of Freesoilers.

Senator SEWARD, in the United States Senate, asserted that the tone of the debate on the part of Northern Senators went to "show that if the State of Texas should be divided into four States hereafter, and they should come here (to Congress) all as Free States, those States will come into the Union as Free States." "And if, unhappily, any such States should come as Slave States, the question will then arise whether

it is wise and expedient, and just and right, to establish Slave States."
These remarks show how SEWARD's thoughts are running and his
hopes. Are we to fold our arms and see the predictions of this arch
enemy fulfilled, without an effort to establish those rights on which
our expansion, our power, our interests and civilization depend?

Is it, too, beyond the bounds of possibility that the mines of Arizona
might be valuable to the South, and sufficiently attractive to allure the
slaveholder if he has the prospect of security? We have heard of companies already organized in Texas for that purpose. At any rate, it
is cowardly and suicidal to determine that because there is just now
no territory we care to occupy, that, therefore, our rights, which may
be vital and invaluable, should be yielded to a hostile sectional sentiment at the North.

New Mexico, it is asserted, is too barren and arid for Southern occupation or settlement. Admit this to be true, although it has localities
as rich as any in the Mississippi valley, is the surface of the soil, by
agriculture, the only source of wealth to man? The richest portions
of the world by its mines, are generally the poorest for the purposes of
agriculture. Now, New Mexico, like Arizona, teems with mineral
resources. Two centuries ago its silver mines were worked profitably,
and were never, we believe, discontinued until Anarchy sprung up in
New Mexico, in the name of Liberty. The whole country is unex-
plored. It is like California, when first acquired. Who anticipated the
vast resources of California by her mines of gold and quicksilver, when
it was first acquired? They lay hid from the ignorant and lazy Span-
iard, or more lazy Indian, and would have been hidden forever, but for
the enterprise and sagacity of the Anglo-American. But the other day,
Southern men said of Kansas what is said of New Mexico, that it was
worth nothing to the South; but already veins of gold are discovered
in this territory which may make it as rich as California in its mineral
resources. There is no vocation in the world in which slavery can be
more useful and profitable than in mining. The mines of Mexico were
the original cause of African slavery. We submit, is it wise, in our
present condition of ignorance of the resources of New Mexico, to
jump to the conclusion that the South can have no interest in its territories, and therefore shall waive or abandon her right of colonizing
them? Is it not the plain dictate of prudence and duty to insist on our
constitutional rights with respect to them, as affirmed by the highest
tribunals of judicature in the land, and to drop all party association
with those who deny them?

We frequently talk of the future glories of our republican destiny on the continent, and of the spread of our civilization and free institutions over Mexico and the Tropics. Already have we absorbed two of her States, Texas and California. Is it expected that our onward march is to stop here? Is it not more probable and more philosophic to suppose that, as in the past, so in the future, the Anglo-Saxon race will, in the course of years, occupy and absorb the whole of that splendid but ill-peopled country, and to remove by gradual process, before them, the worthless mongrel races that now inhabit and curse the land? And in the accomplishment of this destiny is there a Southern man so bold as to say, the people of the South with their slave property are to consent to total exclusion, or to pitch their tents, by sufferance, only along those narrow strips of inhospitable country where the white man cannot live, and where contact with squatterdom cannot reach us? Is all the rest to be given up to the aspiring, enterprising and indomitable people of the Northern States? Is this the conclusion of those who make light of the principle of equal protection to slave property as an "abstraction"? Is this the grand finale for the South in the future, to which they would have our acquiescence for the sake of promoting somebody to the Presidency, and many others to many other places? Is it for this that the value of the Union and our duty to our sister States is invoked? We tell them the South repudiates such a prospect. Our people will never sit still and see themselves excluded from all expansion, to please the North. These questions have to be decided. In the decision of the institutions to be established on this continent, the territorial rights of the people of the Southern States are of vital import. They will never consent to yield by ignoring them before the denial of the stronger section. They will repudiate those who give such counsels.

The North has hitherto been opposed to the territorial extension of the United States. This has been a policy enforced on the Union by the South. It was a wise policy so long as the territories acquired were free to the colonization of all sections of the Union equally. But if we are now to give the North to understand that the South considers herself as having no interest in any future territory acquired from Mexico, and that therefore we will ignore and surrender our right to colonize any portion of them;—in other words, that we practically assent to the Wilmot Proviso being enforced in them, in the shape of Squatter Sovereignty—how long will Mexico remain a fruit unswallowed by the North? If there is a terrestrial paradise on earth, it is Mexico. It will not, and in our judgment it ought not, to remain useless to the rest of the world, with its vast capacities in the hands of a weak and semi-barbarous people, retrograding to savagism every day. It will as certainly be colonized and appropriated by the Anglo-Saxon American as the seasons roll on. Bordering on the Southern States, the natural course of extension would cover it by the enterprising population of the South. Whether this shall be the result, however, or not, is it wisdom—is it good practical statesmanship, for the South to proclaim in advance, that Mexico is "forbidden fruit" to her; and by her party affiliations, lift to power those who declare that she shall have none of it? If we could make Mexico also "forbidden fruit" to the North, there might be some plausibility in this abnegation policy. But the North has the majority in the Senate and the House of Representatives in Congress. They can pluck and eat the "forbidden fruit" just when they please; for Mexico stands helpless and ready for absorption by the United States. Is it meant that Mexico shall be "forbidden fruit" to the South but not to the North—and that, by our consent, the North shall stretch forth around the Southern States in boundless expansion, whilst the South shall remain stationary, with a daily increasing weakness and helplessness, from her comparative inferiority? It is exactly that which the Abolitionists first broached in Congress when California was admitted into the Union. Are those agitating a speculative question merely, who maintain that the Southern people owe it to themselves, and owe it to the integrity of the Constitution, to vindicate in the elections for the Executive of the United States, as well as for the Legislature, the rights of the South in our territories, present and future, as solemnly announced by the Supreme Court of the United States? Whose policy is the most speculative—that of those who endeavor to show that the people of the South have no interest in any of the territories on this continent, within the Union or without it, and therefore ought dumbly to acquiesce in the denial of their right to colonize them equally with the people of the North—or that of those who maintain that the South has interests in all such territories, and ought to maintain her rights with respect to them by all the legitimate means the Constitution of the United States prescribes? To us the former policy appears to rest upon nothing but the most speculative and baseless assumptions. If true statesmanship consists in the practical, it is just no statesmanship at all. It inculcates that nothing exists, and therefore we must do nothing. The latter policy, on the contrary, rests on facts and rights which notoriously exist, and inculcates decided action to enforce them. It is, therefore, eminently practical. Nor are they singular in the opinion that the territorial question is a great *practical question.* The whole North is agitated by it. The Northern people are by no means prone to pursue mere abstractions. They know that on this question rests in a large degree their future mastering ascendancy in the Union. They will rejoice to learn that what they consider so vital to their sectional domination over the South, is considered in the South as a mere abstract matter, not worthy the consideration of Southern statesmanship. They will hail such demonstrations as the most flaunting signals of surrender. Having all the power, they need but one thing to complete their self-complacency; and that is, to know that their power will not at all be embarrassed by those silly abstractions called principles.

14. THEORY AND PRACTICE

(*The New Orleans Bee,* March 5, 1860)

The issue of protection to slavery in the Territories, and a Congressional slave code, which is so warmly agitated by the Southern portion of the Administration Democracy, really seems to us destitute of any prominent practical bearing; while the opinions of Mr. DOUGLAS, which are deemed absolutely heretical, and at war with the dearest interests of the South, are justly viewed by many as innocent abstractions. Let us glance for a moment at this subject by the light of reason and experience, and see what can be made of it.

We are told, for instance, that the protection of Congress is indispensable in order that slavery may be planted in various portions of the territory of the United States. Against this view it is alleged that slavery is essentially dependent upon soil and climate; that it may be transplanted, but cannot be made to thrive where its labor will be less profitable than that of the white man. Hence, human effort, while it may force slavery into northern latitudes, cannot possibly keep it there. Certainly these opinions appear to be sustained as well by observation as by argument. It is now pretty generally admitted that Kansas, if left to herself, would never have been a slaveholding State. Those whose ardent desire is to extend the institutions of the South would doubtless have endeavored to graft slavery upon Kansas, but it would have languished and finally disappeared, just as in the neighboring State of Missouri the institution is now languishing, and is doomed unquestionably to eventual extinction.

But suppose slavery were free to go wherever it pleased; suppose Congressional protection were extended to it throughout the Territories of the United States, would the spread of the institution be greatly promoted? We doubt it. The existing Territories are Nebraska, New Mexico, and that vast expanse extending between Kansas and Utah. With the exception of New Mexico, much the larger portion of this region is north of the old Missouri Compromise line. The climate is for the most part exceedingly cold and ungenial, and the soil rugged and imperfectly adapted to cultivation. Slave labor could not be rendered remunerative in those latitudes, and though it might be carried thither it would prove but a sickly exotic. The home of the black race is within or near the Tropics. There he luxuriates in life and vigor, and there he may be usefully employed in a species of toil which to him is natural and healthy, though it would be insupportable and even deadly to the white man. We have cited Missouri as an illustration of the impossibility of maintaining slavery in a land unsuited to it. In that commonwealth a formidable emancipation party now exists, and its efforts cooperating with individual interests, will ere long drain Missouri of her servile population. In Maryland a similar disposition begins to prevail, and nothing save the insane violence and folly of the Abolitionists has retarded the growth and influence of this feeling in Virginia and Kentucky. Men, under the stimulus of excitement, will for a while persist in acting in opposition to their obvious interests; but this cannot last long. We even now perceive that while the frontier slave States are professedly denouncing Northern sectionalism with the utmost fury, they are sedulously engaged in ridding themselves of their slaves as rapidly as possible, by transferring them to an extreme Southern market.

This reflection conducts us to another branch of the topic. Granting that Congress acceded to the prayer of the Southern Democracy; admitting that a slave code and protection to slavery in the Territories flourished in full and undisputed vigor, we should like the philosophers and political economists to inform us where the slaves are to come from, that the various Territories may be peopled by them. How stands the case at present? Every negro that is taken from Virginia or Kentucky to the cotton and sugar States of the South commands a price far exceeding his value at home, because his labor is more essential and more profitable in Louisiana, Texas, and Mississippi than it can possibly be in the Northern slave States. So true is this that there is a constant exodus of slaves from the latter. The demand for slave labor throughout the cotton belt is enormous and constantly increasing. As the culture of that great staple yearly extends, so is the necessity of field hands more strongly experienced. Hence the regular and rapid enhancement in their value. Cotton, too, continues to command handsome remunerative prices, because, immense as is the crop, it does not exceed the demand. The four and a half millions of bales which this year will be brought to market will not do more than supply the wants of Europe and America, and if, as is not unlikely, the production next year should reach five millions, the only effect will be to stimulate manufactures without lowering the price of the article. Meanwhile, negroes will be in constant demand. Every new plantation opened; every acre of virgin soil planted with cotton increases the necessity for slave labor, and augments its value. Is it not readily seen that this condition of affairs must ultimately tend to empty the Northern slave States, and to concentrate the servile population in the cotton growing region? Do not the exorbitant prices now paid for negroes show that, vast as is the supply, it is hardly equal to the perpetually increasing want? And if such be the case—if there are scarcely negroes enough to perform the work required of them in the existing slave States, where is the new supply to come from which would go to people the Territories, in the event that they were thrown open to slavery? Is it not clear that we have not more slaves than are needed for Southern plantations; and that if we undertake to discover new fields for their labor, we should, as an essential prerequisite, provide the means for a fresh supply? Is there anybody so verdant as to imagine that while this Union lasts, Congress will ever consent to reopen the slave trade? Of what possible use then is it to discuss questions as practically unavailable, as some of the theological problems on which the early Christian fathers were wont to indite elaborate folios of learned speculation?

15. Virginia Refuses to Confer with Her Southern Sister States

(*The Charleston Mercury,* March 10, 1860)

For the last ten years the people of South Carolina have thought that a dissolution of the Union afforded the only adequate remedy to check Northern aggressions upon the South, and to secure Southern institutions and civilization from the fierce and increasing assaults of that inimical section. In '51 the State was divided between those who, after the failure of Virginia and other States following her lead, to resist at all hazards the adoption of Squatter-Sovereignty in California, favored the separate secession of South Carolina from the Union, and those who proposed to wait for co-operate action of several Southern States. The developments of the last year roused the people of the South to the dangers that menace them; and the Legislature of South Carolina adopted, by a unanimous vote, a preamble and resolutions. These stated her right of secession, and her reason for [not] exercising it, to be a deference to the position of other Southern States with whom she was desirous to act in concert. Measures of defense and security seemed necessary; and South Carolina invited a conference for comparison of opinions and the consideration of remedies, that by discussion and the canvass of suggestions, the States of the South might select and enforce whatever measure would be efficient to release us from the present condition of continued harassment, growing inferiority, and increasing peril. An especial Commissioner was sent to Virginia to solicit her co-operation and leadership in this calm and cautious method of getting the Southern States to address themselves in earnest to the solution of their present and portending difficulties. The matter has been fairly and ably presented and pressed upon the Legislature of Virginia. It has been urged upon that body, day after day, as a Union measure for rallying the South to check the North, through fear of the consequences of Southern unanimity looking to action. But, after many weeks, the telegraph announces that, by a vote of two-thirds, the proposition, even to *consider* remedies in concerted action, is refused. Virginia will not or cannot lead the South, either in determining upon or enforcing the remedy against the evils that are upon us.

Virginia is truly Southern in her feelings and sympathies. There is doubtless a party in that State who see the dangers and are ready to meet them in time and by adequate action; but this party is too weak to inaugurate any measure of real resistance. There are influences, associations, and disabilities, which will ever prevent that State from moving in the van of the South. And if this mission has failed in its prime object, it has at least accomplished a good purpose in showing where the Southern people are to look for measures of redemption.

We have heretofore repeatedly expressed an opinion which we now reiterate. In the contest forced upon us by the North, the South proper —the necessarily Slave South—has labored under two fatal errors: First, in relying upon any party of the North as able to protect us; and second, in relying upon the Frontier Southern States—Slave States at convenience—to lead the van of our resistance, and to bear the brunt of the conflict.

When we do save ourselves—when we do establish firmly and in peace the institution of slavery at the South—it will be by acting independently of both these allies. The pro-slavery party of the North has gone down for the want of sufficient support at the South. On each and every occasion of appealing to the Union sentiment to kill off the enemies of our constitutional rights, they have been made to cut the figure of the credulous or designing man who cried "wolf, wolf," without reason. We have not been prompt to defend our interests or safety, and our tame conduct belying their predictions in our behalf have put them at the mercy of the enemy. Instead of fighting our battle so as to strengthen and assist these friends, we have made fools of them, calling upon them to fight for us, while we idly threaten without striking a blow to save them from destruction or give triumph to our just cause. Had we relied upon ourselves and fought our own battle these twenty years, there would be no lack of true friends—not half-faced enemies —now.

And what right have we to expect Virginia, Maryland, Kentucky, Missouri, to bear the brunt of the struggle in which we are much more vitally interested, with fewer inducements to postponement and inaction? What reason have we to expect either of them to take the initiative in our defense? They may live and thrive without slavery; and with them slavery or its abolishment is a question of expediency—a choice of different instrumentalities of prosperity. To us the institution is indispensable. We must maintain ourselves in the contest, or be utterly destroyed; and it is, so far as we are concerned, vain and cowardly to look to the Frontier States to lead the South to the recovery of her independence and security. The Slave South proper—the Cotton States—must look to themselves alone for defense.

This refusal of Virginia will have the effect of inspiring the Black Republican party with confidence in the submissive spirit of resistance, and greatly tend to remove fear of a dissolution of the Union. In our opinion it insures the election of a Black Republican to the Presidency. To resist this, two of the Cotton States, Alabama and Mississippi, have pledged themselves. South Carolina is ready to co-operate with them. These States will constitute a nucleus around which several others will rally. We trust that hereafter Virginia will not be looked to for leadership. It is a false position to assign her, situated as she is, and her truest and ablest men are ready to acknowledge the fact and urge other States to move. Virginia will always be found to follow the South, to which she really and truly belongs. In December, 1857, a distinguished Virginian, who has profoundly studied the subject, Mr. EDMUND RUFFIN, discussed this very matter in De Bow's *Review*.[1] We cannot better close this article than by citing his opinion. The following is the passage:

"The opposers of further submission to wrongs, and consequent advocates for secession, in the more Southern States, have been looking to the great State of Virginia to lead in the movement, in which case the large majority of the more Southern States would follow immediately, and all others of the slaveholding States soon after. But, for reasons which ought to be manifest to every thinking man, a border State, as Virginia, or Maryland, or Kentucky, would be after the general separation, never will, and scarcely can take the first step in the actual deliberate movement of secession. There will always be in States thus situated, at least a minority, timid, and also numerous enough to paralyze the will and strength of the majority. And such is the case now in Virginia, even though a large majority of the citizens are most earnestly opposed to longer submission to Northern wrongs. The proper and perfectly safe and peaceable course to bring about the secession and subsequent confederation of all the slaveholding States (excepting Delaware perhaps) will be for Virginia, and all the other of the Northern tier of the slaveholding States, with North Carolina and Tennessee, *not* to move at first, or as early as the more Southern States. Whenever the evils inflicted under the present Union, and the usurpations and oppressions by the Northern States are deemed no longer tolerable (if that time has not already arrived), if five or six only of the more Southern States adjoining each other, acting in concert, shall declare their independence of, and secession from, the present Federal Government, the movement will be perfectly safe from the danger of producing individual conflicts and border feuds, as well as from attack or war from the Northern States, or the still remaining Federal Power. There could be no border feuds, because the people and their magistrates, or leaders on both sides of the new (and but temporary) line of separation, would be alike in interests and sentiments. And if the government or people of the Northern States should be so insane as to make war, and attempt to march an army to coerce or conquer the seceding States, there would be to these an impregnable barrier of protection afforded in the common feeling and friendship, and the position of the slaveholding and (as yet) non-seceding States. And within a few months, or as early as the plan of government of the new Southern confederacy would be determined on and organized, and the power of the already separated States would be consolidated,

[1] *De Bow's Review*, XXIII, 605–607.

the time would have arrived for the final and practical settlement of the great question—the question which would have been growing more and more intense in interest as to the subsequent course of the non-seceding and slaveholding States. This question is, would they follow the course and share the fortunes of their friends, or remain in the power, now more than doubled for their injury, of their opponents and worst enemies? Whether the first seceding States were ten or but five in number, they would be equally and perfectly safe from Northern hostility or attack. And whether five or ten in number, their secession would equally leave the non-seceding and slaveholding States in a help-less and hopeless minority in their then political connection, and at the mercy of a hostile, malignant, and remorseless majority of their enemies. If now, when the Southern States in the present confederacy number fifteen, to sixteen non-slaveholding States, their rights are trodden down, and their dearest interests are in the course of being gradually but certainly destroyed by their barely more numerous co-States, what will be their prospect for defense or safety when they shall number but five or ten to sixteen hostile Northern States? Scarcely would a year elapse, or the requisite legal formalities be complied with, before the present provisions of the Federal Constitution, which authorize slave representation, and protect slave property, would be an-nulled, and when other enactments would make the complete destruc-tion of the institution of slavery but a question of time. Would Virginia and North Carolina, or Kentucky and Missouri, wait for this certain consummation? Certainly they will not, unless they are already pre-pared to submit to this extreme measure of outrage and spoliation. As soon as these middle-ground States could act through their legislatures, they would undoubtedly and necessarily determine to unite with their more Southern sister States in their common cause and political con-nection. Not only would all these named States so act, both from prefer-ence and necessity, but Maryland also. For, if this State were separated from political connection and friendship with Virginia and the other more Southern States, the commerce of Baltimore would be ruined, and with it the great commercial interests, as well as the property in slaves of that State. Unless the people of Maryland are prepared to make these sacrifices, immediate or remote, for the benefit of remain-ing united with the Northern States, ready indeed to submit to certain ruin, they will as certainly concur in and follow the seceding move-ment, as will the more Southern people.

"In this manner, without risk of war or bloodshed, the separation of our present Union with our worst enemies may be effected, and the consequent construction of a Southern and slaveholding confederacy. Then, freed from the hostile and incendiary action of our now fellow-citizens and 'brethren' of the North, the people of the South will be well able to guard against them either as foreigners or (if they prefer that character) as enemies. Slave property, by being then duly guarded and protected, will become even more secure in the northern border counties of Virginia and Maryland, than now in their southern frontiers. Freed from longer paying millions every year of legal tribute to the North, through the machinery of tariffs, banks, and other commercial privileges (as in the fishery bounties, exclusive coast navigation and bounties to lines of ocean steamers), the Southern States would soon rise to the high position of economical, commercial, and political prosperity, which would be the certain result of retaining the products of their industry and wealth for their own use and benefit. On the other hand, if things continue as they are, the outside pressure of fanaticism, and its secret incendiary action, operating more and more to render property in slaves unsafe, will continue to cause (as has long been the case) and to increase the removal of the slave population from the border slaveholding States until these will lose all, and ceasing to be slaveholding, must consequently become more and more assimilated to the North in sentiment and policy. On this account, every year that shall pass before the secession movement is made, will serve to depress still lower the property and slavery interests, and the power for resistance and self-protection of the border slaveholding states. If these States are to be successfully defended in the possession of their property, their political rights, and everything dear to free men, or if they are to be preserved as a future integral portion, and the border bulwark of a Southern confederacy, it must be secured by the more Southern States seceding first, and speedily."

16. FAILURE OF THE SOUTHERN CONFERENCE

(*Daily Chronicle and Sentinel,* Augusta, March 14, 1860)

Virginia has emphatically refused to go into the Convention of Southern States, proposed by South Carolina, and particularly urged upon the attention of the Old Dominion by a commissioner appointed for that purpose. Thus the last hope of the conference is gone, Virginia's refusal being emphatic, two thirds against it. And so Carolina, Mississippi, and perhaps Alabama, will be left alone to carry the scheme through.

What is the reason that Virginia and the majority of her Southern sisters will not be represented in this proposed Convention, and what is likely to be the effect? There could be no reasonable objection to a Convention of the Southern States, held for the purpose of devising ways and means to restore harmony between the sections, and thus preserve the Union of the States in peace. There could be no objection to a peaceable and lawful assemblage of good citizens, taking counsel together for the perpetuity of our institutions, and our common government. But we fear the reason why this movement of South Carolina has been condemned and discountenanced by the South, is that the Southern people instinctively felt it was a scheme not of union, but of disunion; a movement, not to connect the ties which bind us together as States, but rather seeking dismemberment. The South would not go into the Conference, because she felt satisfied that it was designed to precipitate us into revolution *without sufficient cause*. The South is not ready to dissolve the Union yet, nor is the South by any means ready or prepared to declare for dissolution, merely on account of the election of a Republican President, and *therefore* she would not go into the Conference.

This refusal of the South to go into the proposed conference, as we understand it, is a rebuke, and we think a deserved rebuke, of those who are seeking the disruption of the government without cause. We do not mean to say that the design of the Convention, and of those who proposed it, was disunion, but the people believed that to be the design, and that was the sole reason of its falling through. Let our hot-bloods take warning from this lesson. Let them learn that, however loud the press and the politicians may clamor for a re-organization of the government, the people will not heed them—they will not dissolve until they see good reason for it.

Now, what effect will this refusal of Virginia and the other States have? It will be important, and we fear disastrous. Already the Charleston *Mercury* declares its conviction that it will result in the election of SEWARD to the Presidency. And why? Because it will serve to convince the North that the South will *never* consent to dissolve the Union; and remove from the minds of Northern men all fears upon the subject. Just as always happens, this failure in an impractical and foolish plan works the South harm, and harm alone. The *Mercury* and its class of politicians say that disunion will probably now be precipitated, because the Southern people will take no steps to avert it by concert of action, and thus the North becomes emboldened to go forward in its mad career.

Well, who is to blame if the North, from this action of the Southern States, arrives at the conclusion that the Union is stronger than slavery? The *Mercury* throws the blame upon Virginia and her conservative sisters, because they will not act. But not upon Virginia, nor upon the great mass of conservative Southern citizens can that blame rightly rest. No, it is justly chargeable upon those who have so much zeal with so little discretion; upon those who have taken in the beginning a false position, and one to which no reflecting man ought to think the South could ever be brought. One great source of our troubles comes from these people who go off half-cocked, and will not listen to reason.

We would not speak harshly of such people—perhaps it is an inherent defect in their natures, and they cannot help it. They, in South Carolina and elsewhere, as we know full well, are noble, chivalrous, honorable people, but they seem to lack ballast. Would that heaven might vouchsafe to us, if not less zeal, at least more wisdom, prudence and moderation, less fiery eloquence and denunciatory oratory, and more plain, old-fashioned common sense. Would that these ultra men might come to see, and know, and understand once for all, that every attempt of theirs to lead the South into a false position must fail, and that every such failure works to the injury not only of those who make the attempt, but to the injury of the whole South. "Offences must needs come, but woe to them through whom the offence cometh."

17. POLITICAL AFFAIRS NORTH

(*New Orleans Daily Crescent,* March 16, 1860)

It will be no holiday sport for the nominee of the Charleston Convention, though he be the only one man who has any chance of overcoming Black Republicanism, to defeat that motley but most thoroughly drilled organization, which, though made up of the rags, shreds, and patches of all parties, is united on the one great issue of opposition to the South. Black Republicanism sustained injury, it is true, from the revulsion occasioned by the intemperate John Brown demonstration, which was in accordance with its tenets, but was too violent and premature to be politic, and shocked the sensibilities of the weak brethren who had not yet come to a stern conscientious conviction of the desperate and inevitable nature of the irrepressible conflict.

These sensitive members gave evidence of a rebellious spirit which broke out in Union meetings and kindred demonstrations, the effect of which has been, we fear, to give an undue and unwise confidence to opponents of Abolitionism. How have the astute leaders of Black Republicanism comported themselves to bring the rebels back beneath their dark banner? With the utmost wisdom. Too shrewd to attempt to whip them back into the traces by abuse and denunciation, they have adopted a conciliatory tone, "sinking the nigger" as much as possible from his unpopular eminence in their platform, and cunningly resuscitating old questions that have now scarcely the importance of side issues, which they adroitly advance as the principles they are battling for, and in which they know the rebels must sympathize with them, however strongly they may decline to swallow John Brown. They keep John Brown as far out of sight as possible, knowing that those who endorse him will still cherish him, and that he is obnoxious to those whom they wish to circumvent.

The speech of Senator Seward, the great arch-plotter of Abolitionism, is a patent example of this sort of political finesse by which he and his fellows are striving to win back into the fold and unite on the presidential contest all who were shocked from the ranks by the bloody business of Harper's Ferry. Seward obtruded nothing that could startle the nerves of the most sensitive of the seceders. He played traitor to John Brown, his most illustrious disciple, and bamboozled the "Unionists" in the most scientific style. No doubt most of them are now convinced that Black Republicans generally, and Seward particularly, are now quite as much against the John Brown method of operation as themselves are, and that they were rather hasty in denouncing the party as a whole. That it was with them after all, and that they were with it and are with it, and will not be compromising their late position by seeing it through the Presidential contest.

It is thus that popular sentiment is being managed and controlled to the end, and, meanwhile, secret electioneering work is not neglected, but is being reduced to the perfection of political management that will result in a most thorough organization of the Black Republican forces in readiness for the day of battle. We have now before us a copy of a secret circular, issued by the Black Republican Central Committee, which is composed of three members of the Senate of the United States and six members of the House. It calls for the organization of clubs in every town, village and city of the North. The circular, signed by the committee, states, "We address you as one known personally, or by information, to the committee as a friend to the cause, and ask an early reply to this communication, with such information from time to time as you may think proper." The circular especially solicits contributions of money from every friendly voter—a sort of political "St. Peter's pence"—which is to be collected and forwarded by the "friends of the cause" to whom the circular is addressed, and which sets forth that "the Republican party must rely upon the voluntary contributions of its friends." This enginery is to be put at work especially in the doubtful States, where they hope to buy up or whip in a majority to carry the day for a sectional President.

Of course the whole South is safe for the nominee of the Charleston Convention, and most of the Northern States for him whom that of Chicago may select for standard-bearer; but those doubtful States of the North are essential to the success of either. In these the battle will be fought, and it will be no holiday conflict. No labor and no expense will be spared by the Black Republicans, and hence we say that it will be no light work to defeat them, and the man who does, must be he who already has the greatest number of firm and avowed friends and supporters in those States, and not a man scarcely known outside of his own district, who may be taken up and "put through with a rush and a hooray," simply because he is the nominee of the Charleston Convention. We believe that the only man who has this essential popularity, this ready-made strength in those Northern States which we have the best chance of carrying, and which we must carry to insure success, is Judge Douglas. We believe that a vote sufficient to give him the thirty-four Northern electoral ballots is already cut and dried, and that it is exceedingly doubtful in what direction that vote will fall if he is not the nominee to claim it. It is quite as likely that it will be directed to the Chicago nominee as to the one commissioned at Charleston. We shall see; but we do not look to it with a calm, philosophical curiosity, for we cannot, and no one can, be oblivious to the fact that the coming Presidential election is a test trial of strength between sectionalism and nationalism.

18. Passage of the Homestead Bill

(*Richmond Whig and Public Advertiser,* March 19, 1860)

The passage of the Homestead Bill in the House of Representatives at Washington, by an overwhelming majority—by a vote of 115 to 66

—is an ominous event in the history of the country.[1] That bill is based upon the unjust, loose, radical, revolutionary principle of Agrarianism, and is, therefore, at war with the political and social rights of the people, and absolutely infamous in its character. It is the bantling of the great Democratic demagogue from Tennessee, who disgraces a seat in the United States Senate. It was begotten by the notorious Andy Johnson, and adopted by the united Republicans and Democrats of the North. Every Republican in the House voted for it, and every Northern Democrat in the House voted for it, too, except Montgomery, of Pennsylvania; and there was, also, one *Southern* Democrat who voted for it, Craig, of Missouri, while many of them *dodged,* including several members from Virginia. Never was there a more odious and iniquitous bill passed by any deliberative body on earth.

It provides that any person who is the head of a family, or who has arrived at the age of twenty-one years, and is a citizen of the United States, or who shall have filed his intention to become such, shall be entitled to enter free of cost, one hundred and sixty acres of the public lands upon which the said person may have filed a pre-emption claim, or which may, at the time the application is made, be subject to pre-emption, at one dollar and a quarter or less per acre, or eighty acres at two dollars and a half per acre. No certificate is to be given or patent to be issued until after the expiration of five years from the date of said entry; and, on payment of ten dollars, the rights secured by the actual settlers shall issue to the heirs and devisees. The lands thus acquired are in no case to become liable to the satisfaction of debts contracted prior to the issuing of the patent.

Thus, under the provisions of this Homestead Bill, the public lands, comprising over one thousand millions of acres, and belonging equally to *all* the States, are *given* away to all manner of persons, and for the exclusive benefit of the Northern States. They are given not only to native born citizens, but to *all* persons who may file a declaration of their intention to become citizens at a future day—thus embracing in the terms and benefits of the grant the hundreds of thousands of foreigners, who annually land upon our shores. And thus goes the vast and magnificent public domain, to the strengthening and enriching of the Northern States at the expense of the Southern, Virginia included.

Do not all intelligent Southern men now see the justice and wisdom

[1] The bill was defeated in the Senate by a vote of 31 to 26. For the text of the bill and the vote in the Senate, see *Cong. Globe,* 36 Cong., 1 Sess., III, 1999. This bill was endorsed by the Republican National Convention at Chicago, *Proceedings of the First Three Republican National Conventions* . . . , p. 132.

of the policy of an *equal* distribution of the public lands among *all* the States, for which the Whigs of the Union have so long and so vainly contended, and which the Democrats have opposed with such fatal pertinacity? For long years we have admonished the people of Virginia and the South that, unless they accepted the policy of *equal* distribution, these lands would all be squandered, in the course of a few years, for the benefit of the Northwestern States. What, a short while ago, was only prophecy, is now a startling reality. These lands, in which *all* the States, Southern as well as Northern, Virginia as well as Illinois, have an equal interest, are now granted, *free of cost,* to all the vagabonds of all nations and all climes, and for the express purpose of building up the North at the expense of the South! Virginia, though loaded down with taxes, and "groaning" under the weight of her burden, is thus robbed and swindled of her just rights in the public domain, in consequence of the *scruples* of Southern Democrats and the rapacity of Northern Democrats and Republicans combined.—If Virginia could obtain her rightful share of those public lands, her public debt, now amounting to thirty-five or forty millions of dollars, would be soon wiped out, and all her projected improvements completed, without the necessity of levying a cent of tax upon her citizens. But, great is Democracy; and Democracy forbids her taking her share of the public lands, because Democracy thinks *equal* distribution among all the States *unconstitutional!* And yet, this same Democracy considers *unequal, partial, one-sided* distribution altogether constitutional—altogether right—altogether wise—altogether proper—altogether patriotic. These lands may all be squandered upon the Northern States, for the purpose of building up, strengthening, and enriching our Northern enemies, and *Democracy* issues no protest and utters no complaint. But, when it is proposed, in a spirit of strict justice and impartiality, to allow Virginia and the other Southern States to participate in the advantages and benefits of this "common fund" of all the States, *Democracy* flies into a furious passion, and swears that such a proposition is unconstitutional and wrong, and cannot for a moment be tolerated.

And yet, these are the men—these scrupulous, conscientious Democrats—who profess such ardent devotion to the rights and interests of the South, and who would forthwith dissolve the Union, because the Yankees are in the habit of stealing from us a few negroes. And these same men stand silently by and let the public lands, worth millions and hundreds of millions of dollars, and half of the whole amount belonging to the South, by a title as clear and unquestionable as that by which

Southern men hold their negroes—let all these lands, we say, be taken from them by the North, and given away, for the purpose of enhancing the prosperity and power of the Northern section of the Union. While the Southern Democracy stand silently by, and permit this great outrage to be perpetrated upon Virginia and the South, the Northern Democracy are actively aiding and abetting in it—all of them, except one, having voted for the Homestead Bill, which was voted for, also, by one *Southern* Democrat. Now, it makes no difference whether the North steals our negroes, or appropriates to its own exclusive use our lands—the outrage is as great in the one instance as the other. Indeed, it is much greater in the case of the public lands, for the reason that these lands are worth infinitely more money than all the negroes that have been, or ever will be stolen. And yet, these Southern Democrats are ready to break up the Union, and plunge the country into civil war, on account of the North stealing a negro, and are yet as submissive as spaniels in the presence of its grand larceny of the public lands, which belong in common to all the States, the Southern as well as the Northern. And thus, are these political reprobates always straining at a gnat, and swallowing a camel.

In conclusion, we invoke our readers to reflect upon the character of this Homestead Bill, and its inevitable effect upon the rights and interests of Virginia and the South. We, also, invite them to remember that all the Northern Democrats in Congress, but one, voted for it; and that the Southern Democracy are justly responsible for it, on account of having opposed an equal distribution of the public lands, among all the States, as recommended and advocated by the Whig party.

19. THE POSITION OF THE SOUTHERN OPPOSITION

(*Republican Banner,* Nashville, March 29, 1860)

We have often enough, and explicitly enough stated what we understood to be the leading idea upon which the Southern Opposition desire to go into the Presidential canvass, and that idea is a cessation of the slavery controversy. Without such a prerequisite, a fair, open and straightforward national contest is out of the question. With the subject of slavery as an issue between the two controlling parties, and no alternative left to the opponents of both but a choice of evils, the contest necessarily becomes purely sectional. It is unnecessary to remain long in doubt as to what must inevitably result. No one but disunionists can look to the issue with anything else than horror. The people of the

South surely can expect to gain nothing by it. They have gained nothing thus far from this slavery contest—not even an abstraction. Majorities must rule, and minorities must submit, or resort to revolution. The persistent agitation of the question has forced nearly the whole American people to take sides. The general acquiescence which followed the Compromise of 1850, and which the Democratic party solemnly pledged itself to perpetuate, was wantonly disturbed by that party, in violation of that pledge, by the repeal of the Missouri Compromise and the attempt to force upon the people of Kansas a constitution which they did not approve. This policy inaugurated a renewal of the controversy, and built up a sectional party in the North, with opposition to slavery extension as the leading article of its creed, which has become complete master of the field, and is now regarded and styled by that Democratic party, whose policy spoke it into existence, as a "triumphant enemy." This is what the Democratic party, with its slavery agitation hobby, has done for the South and the country. It has developed and arrayed against the Southern institutions the prevailing sentiments of a majority of the States of the Union. And now it persists in keeping the "triumphant enemy," which it has thus invoked, in the field, fighting the South. If the destruction of the Union was the avowed object, this would be the policy that would necessarily be adopted. It cannot result otherwise.

If any right of the Southern States was imperilled—if any guaranty of the Constitution was sought to be vitiated—we would be the last to seek a cessation of hostilities. But no one will undertake to say that there is any cause for this controversy, any practical issue in which the rights of the South are involved. It is merely a war of opinions and words—a discussion upon abstract principles from which no advantage can be gained by either side, and the worst results must inevitably ensue to both.

It is time the *people* of both the North and the South should look at this subject without their party glasses—with a naked, patriotic eye. They will then see two parties occupying the front ground, the cohesive element in both of which, as far as ideas are concerned, is a sectional question. They will see that without this sectional cement both parties would disintegrate and become powerless. They will see the principal ingredient in this patent political glue is their own sectional prejudices, upon which they have permitted the political tricksters of the day to draw *ad libitum*. They will see that they have been drawn into an unnecessary and unholy contest, in the decision of which, in the abstract, they have really no stake, but the pursuit of which threatens to undo all the work of our revolutionary fathers and the patriotic statesmen who followed them.

We say the *people* of both the North and South should at once set about thinking for themselves upon this subject. They should do so as patriots—as men anxious to perpetuate our institutions as they have been handed down to us. But more especially should the people of the South arouse themselves. With them one of two evils must inevitably result from a persistence in this slavery agitation. Whenever the issue is made a practical one they must calculate upon finding themselves in a minority in the Union. They will then be called upon to submit to the majority, or resort to disunion. It is idle to attempt to blink the fact that the sentiment of every free State in the Union is against slavery. It has always been so and we fear it always will be so. But in the formation of our government that sentiment compromised, as did other conflicting ideas, and opposition to slavery in the free States, until aroused by the diabolical arts of demagogues, was latent and acquiescent. The harmonious working of the machinery of government can never be secured until this question is again put to rest. It is therefore clearly the duty of men of all parties to turn their faces against useless agitation. It is not only the duty, but pre-eminently the interest of the people of the South.

Democrats in the South and Republicans in the North, though they may by such a course destroy their respective party organizations, will secure a boon worth more than all parties—a harmonious Union. The North does not hope to convert the South—neither does the South hope to convert the North. We have no doubt a majority of both sections prefer the Union as it is, the Constitution unchanged, the laws enforced, and the courts respected, to either the agitation of this sectional issue, or a dissolution of the government. They have to choose between these alternatives. Those who are for perpetuating this sectional contest, knowing that neither section will ever submit to the extreme views of the other, and that the worst of consequences must result, will act with the Democratic party of the South or the Republican party of the North. Those who are for renouncing this sectional controversy, in which neither party has a practical issue at stake, will act with the party which declares itself in favor of a cessation of the slavery discussion, for the Union, the Constitution, and the Enforcement of the Laws.

For ourself, we unhesitatingly choose the latter. We are willing to sacrifice abstract political views upon minor questions in supporting a ticket nominated upon and pledged to such a policy. We regard it as a paramount duty to so act as to secure the UNION against the perils of a sectional contest, first, and to defer the settlement of subordinate questions until that object is accomplished. We believe that *in the Union* and *under the Constitution,* the rights of all sections are secure, and therefore, our platform and our policy is true both to the Union and the sections. It is a platform for the whole country, and the only one now before the country, or likely to be put before the country by the respective party conventions, upon which a Union man can consistently place himself—and therefore the only one that is NATIONAL.

20. SOUTH AND NORTH

(*The Charleston Mercury,* March 31, 1860)

There is not, probably, in the whole political world, a more contemptible course of policy than that which now characterizes a considerable portion of the South. The Supreme Court of the United States having rendered it impossible for any man but a born or self-made fool to doubt the rights of the South in our territories, and it being perfectly apparent that the Northern people (Squatter Sovereignty Democrats and Black Republicans), despite the Constitution, intend to nullify and defeat these rights—the self-seekers, office aspirants and submissionists of the South are striving, by all sorts of pretexts and falsities, to reconcile the Southern people to their passive surrender. When Kansas was the theatre of contention, the same people were busy with the same policy. ROBERT J. WALKER [1] got up the isothermal line by which he proved that slavery was totally unsuited to Kansas. It was too far north, although lying broadside by the richest tobacco counties of Missouri; and the vast majority of the population being opposed to slavery, of course the will of the people ought to be obeyed. It turns out now, not only that Kansas is a fine hemp and tobacco country, but abounding in mines which may make it the rival of California in the production of gold. Having turned Kansas over to the North, they are now busy, with the same tactics, to induce the Southern people to surrender to the North the rest of our Territories, present and future.

And with what brazen effrontery—with what dexterous sophistries—is this traitorous policy towards the South defended and recom-

[1] Senator from Mississippi, 1836–1845; Secretary of the Treasury, 1845–1849; Governor of Kansas in 1857.

mended! How base and hypocritical are their professions of confidence in the Northern people, in their fidelity to the Constitution and the rights of the South in the matter of Southern slavery; and with what heroic devotion do they vaunt of the power of the South in the Union, and her noble adequacy for her protection! Thus, by belittling the interests of the South in our territories on the one hand, and magnifying the Union on the other—by ignoring the *past* aggressions of the North, and falsifying everything bearing on the *present,* they propose to quell the rising spirit of the South, and induce her to acquiesce in the plunder of [2] the North of all our territories. How different is the course of things at the North! There, right or wrong in their policy, no mistake rests on its tendency. It is true to the North. Crowds follow Senator DOUGLAS wherever he goes, as the legislative conqueror of Kansas for the North, and their cunning and faithful leader for future domination in our territories. Mr. SEWARD leaves New York for Europe; and thousands in steamboats, with music, flags and shoutings, escort him down the bay. He boldly declares that the emancipation of our slaves must be accomplished by the General Government, and he reigns a prince in their affections. To keep out or drive out the Southern people from our territories, is the grand basis of parties at the North. No man dares insult the intelligence of the Northern people by maintaining their insignificancy. No man ventures to wound their pride by belittling their vast conquests over the South in our common territories. The battle is fought and won by the North, is the haughty boast of all. They are now only to follow up and secure their victory, and all our vast territories will be theirs. Apology for Southern slavery seldom drops from their lips. Love for "the glorious Union," when spoken of in connection with the institutions of the South, seldom pollutes, by its hypocrisies, their frank antipathy. No admiration for those who have struggled, in obedience to the Constitution, against their sectional hate and ambition, graces their oratory. These are cast aside with scorn; and right on, consistently, unswervingly, they move to the consummation of their sectional rule and aggrandizement. We may not respect the faithlessness to the Constitution which governs this policy; but we cannot but respect the courage—the openness—the manliness—with which it is pursued; whilst, from the very bottom of our hearts we regard, with a loathing, abhorrence, and contempt, utterly inexpressible, the base self-seeking and treacherous submissionists of the South who seek to make her its victims.

[2] Error for "by."

21. THE DEMOCRATIC PARTY

(*The Charleston Mercury,* April 16, 1860)

The Democratic party, as a party, based upon principles, is dead. It exists now, only as a powerful faction. It has not one single principle common to its members North and South. It has degenerated into a mere political organization, variously united, to obtain power and place. On every living issue deemed vital to the South, the Northern members, as a body, are against the South, and agree, substantially, with the Consolidationists and Black Republicans. And this result, the South herself has produced by her weakness and timidity. She has now no other alternative, but to raise up the lifeless body of the Democratic party, by restoring to it living principles, and putting it into power, or to dissolve the Union. To stand in her present position in the Union, is to be in the broad road to inevitable ruin, helpless and hopeless.

The South owes it to herself, to rebuild the Democratic party. It was founded by her, and its great achievements are monuments to her fame and honor. Resting upon the sovereignty of the States, and the plain grants of the Constitution, it is capable not only of governing beneficially these United States, but the whole continent of North America. Nay, more. Its great principles of confederation and justice, may fold the whole world in its embraces. No antagonism, no sectionalism can exist, under its wise and restricted operations of government, because it exercises no power over interests which are not common and general to all the States and sections over which it rules. Abuses cannot be permanent, because they cannot be partial. Where all portions of a vast country are equally to be affected by the operations of a Government, the interests of all afford a sure guarantee against abuses or misrule. Such is the Democratic party, as founded in '98 and '99 by the Virginia and Kentucky Resolutions. But it is now overthrown by Centralism and Consolidation. Like the British Parliament, Congress is omnipotent. That great sectional interest, the institution of slavery—the last and the most deadly to reach—is swept into the vortex of Federal jurisdiction; and the two great portions of the Union, stand apart in stern sectional defiance and hostility. The timid and faithless expedient of concession to encroachments, has whipped out, one by one, all the limitations of the Constitution; and forced upon the South the alternative of rebuilding the Democratic party, and making it triumphant, or of submitting to or resisting a Government without limitations on its powers, in the hands of a hostile section. Experience teaches, that the South must reverse her course. She must be done with the progressive and accumulative folly of compromises and concessions. Firmness is the dictate of necessity. She must cease fraternization with any who deny her essential rights, and the great principles of the Democratic party. She must insist upon a plain acknowledgment of the rights of the States, restoring to practical efficiency the confederative features of the Constitution, and upon a rigid adherence to the plain letter of the Constitution, and an abstinence from the exercise of all doubtful powers, in administering the Government. False pretenders to Democracy at the North—false on the taxing and appropriating powers of the Government, and false on the great matter of the rights of the States in our common Territories—conquered by federalism, and swallowed up by sectionalism, can form no portion of the Democratic party. To act with them, the South must consent to abandon principles, and thus become coadjutors of a mere faction for federal offices and honors; or she must stand herself, and compel all who accept of her affiliation to stand, on the great principles of the Democratic party. In this way alone, can the Democratic party be restored again to life. By this way alone, can the South be true to herself, and to the great mission of preserving the Constitution, which Providence seems to have committed to her charge.

If Northern Democrats will not join her in resuscitating the Democratic party—if they are fataly bent on assisting to set up a consolidated sectional despotism in the Union, over the South, then what business have they in the counsels of the South? Let them go and elect Mr. SEWARD or Mr. DOUGLAS to the Presidency. Let them in the North seek only Northern political associates. The South cannot possibly be benefited in any way by their association. If she is to be set upon by the sectional power of the North, let her at least preserve her self-respect by not contributing, by her affiliation and co-operation, to her own persecution or downfall. A victory with such allies will be the most disastrous of overthrows, because it will establish the enemy in her midst and paralyze her for any efforts at extrication and redemption. But, if the Democrats of the North are not entirely forgetful of their interests, principles, and policy, nor ignorant of the vast benefits our Union confers upon their section of the Union; if they still have existing within them any respect for justice and the Constitution, and that love of liberty which made them one with the South in founding the Democratic party, they will join the South in the effort to restore it to life. So far as the Territorial question is concerned, Messrs. FITCH, BIGLER, BRIGHT and GWIN, of the Senate, and Mr. WOOD, of New York, and others of the Democratic party of the North, have earnestly pressed upon the South to pursue this policy.[1]

But a mere agreement upon principles, whilst it will breathe into it the breath of life, will not restore the Democratic party to a mastery of the Union. Something more must be done. The South must prepare for action. She must plainly make it known to her confederates in the Union that at the next Presidential election the question is not only a Democratic or Black Republican President, but union or disunion. *"In hoc signo vinces."* It would have conquered us peace long ago, but for our ignorance or pusillanimity. It will do it now, if believed at the North. At all events, it is the only and last alternative by which the Democratic party, with living principles, can be restored to power. It is the sole hope of saving the Union, consistent with the salvation of the South.

22. THE ATTITUDE OF THE SOUTH

(*The Daily Delta,* New Orleans, May 2, 1860)

The disruption of the Charleston Convention is a catastrophe which, however much its necessity may be deplored by those who hoped for united and harmonious action, must be regarded as the natural and justifiable consequence of the arrogant pretensions set up by the Northern delegations to govern the Convention in its choice of a nominee, and to impose upon it a platform of principles which would be rejected by every Southern State.

The course pursued by the Southern delegations justifies the confidence reposed in them by their constituents. It is the logical culmination of the principles universally avowed by the Southern Democracy, as well as an inevitable political necessity. Submission to the rule of the sectional majority of the Convention would have been the death of the Southern Democracy. It would have been as fatal to the vitality of the Democratic party, as a party of principle, and as the defender of Southern rights and interests, as submission to Black Republican domination would be fatal to the equality of the South in the Union and under the Constitution.

[1] Senators Graham N. Fitch of Indiana, William Bigler of New York, Jesse D. Bright of Indiana, William M. Gwin of California; and Fernando Wood, Democratic Mayor of New York City, 1855–1857, 1861–1862.

The Southern delegates to the Convention have seen the inseparable connection existing betwen the logic of the Union and the logic of the Democratic party. They have heard the Southern people, the Southern press, and Southern politicians, proclaim that a sectionalization of the Federal Government would be not only a good reason, but a peremptory reason, for severing the connection between the North and the South. They have thought, and justly thought, that for much stronger reasons, the sectionalization of the Democratic party demands a separation of the Southern Democracy from the Democratic party.

There is no need for them to entertain any doubts of the manner in which their constituents will receive the news of their action. They will not be required to defend their course or justify their acts before a disappointed or unsympathizing people. The demonstrations of joy exhibited by the Charlestonians, the congratulations offered to the seceding delegates for their manly and determined course, their firm and impressive attitude, are only premonitory indications of the electrical effect which the receipt of the intelligence will produce throughout the South. There can be no doubt that the Southern Democracy, with the rare exceptions of timorous and trembling conservatism, embraced within even the most progressive of parties, or the perhaps more numerous exceptions of spoils-hunting and office-seeking partisans which afflict every party, will enthusiastically indorse and sustain the action of their representatives at Charleston. Only submission to the tyranny of the sectional majority by the acceptance of a platform utterly opposed to every principle of Southern and State Rights Democracy would have placed them in the position of culprits before the South and forced them to the task of an onerous and impracticable defense.

We hope that the Southern delegations will stand firm, and make no concession involving the smallest sacrifice of principle. As Ex-Governor Mouton,[1] the Nestor of the Louisiana Democracy, very justly said: "If we are to fight the Black Republicans, in company with the Northern Democracy, we must fight them with the same weapons and exhibit the same front." It is perfectly plain that if the two sections differ on a question which is a vital question, and which involves cardinal and fundamental principles, they no longer belong to the same party. They are, in fact, two parties, distinctly marked and widely separated. To go into an election in company would be a mockery and a farce; but an adjournment of an inevitable conflict, in which the longer the

---

[1] Alexander Mouton, Governor of Louisiana, 1842–1846; President of the Louisiana State Convention which voted the State out of the Union, January, 1861.

issue is deferred, the more certain becomes defeat and subjugation to the South.

23. THE NEW COMPROMISE—GRAND "ULTIMATUM OF THE SOUTH"

(*The Charleston Mercury,* May 3, 1860)

We suppose that there was not a man, in or out of the Charleston Convention, who did not anticipate the proposal of a new compromise on the rights of the States in the Territories, as a necessary consequence of the withdrawal of the Cotton States from the Convention. The Southern people have been so often cheated by words in the shape of compromises, that, of course, it would be presumed that they could be cheated again. Accordingly, after the close of the twelfth ballot for President had taken place, and the Convention was about to adjourn, Mr. HOWARD, of Tennessee, announced that the Tennessee, Kentucky, and Virginia delegates, had agreed on a resolution, which was presented to them by the delegation from New York, as follows:

Resolved, That the citizens of the United States have an equal right to settle with their property in the Territories of the United States; and that, under the decision of the Supreme Court of the United States, which we recognize as the correct exposition of the Constitution of the United States, neither the right of persons nor property can be *destroyed* by Congressional or Territorial legislation.

He proposed to offer the resolution, whenever the proper opportunity occurred, *as the ultimatum of the South.*

Our readers will understand the true purpose of this *"ultimatum of the South,"* when they remember, that no party at the North has contended that "the right of persons or property can be *destroyed* by Congressional or Territorial legislation." The Abolitionists at the North contend that there can be no property in slaves, and that, therefore, there is none to destroy. The resolution does not use the word slave or slavery. It does not recognize the right of property in slaves. Thus, therefore, the most rabid Abolitionist might vote for the resolution. But, again, it does not touch the question of Squatter Sovereignty. Mr. DOUGLAS never contended that a Territorial Legislature could *"destroy slave property."* He admits that there is property in slaves; but he asserts that a Territorial Legislature, by "unfriendly legislation" (by taxation, for instance) can prevent slaves from *entering* a Territory, whilst by failing to legislate for the protection of slave property, it might be exposed to such hazards as will effectually exclude it from a Territory. Slave property, like property in obscene prints or opium, or ardent spirits, may be subjected to a heavy license law or discriminating taxation, by which it can be prevented from entering a Territory. This is the position of Squatter Sovereignty. When, therefore, the resolution offered by Mr. HOWARD affirms that "neither the right of persons nor property can be *destroyed* by Congressional or Territorial legislation"—every Squatter Sovereignty adherent in the Convention can vote for it. It does not touch their heresy, nor is it intended to touch it. The resolution is the old device of deceiving those who are willing to be deceived. The reference to the *Dred Scott* case is equally evasive— "That under the decision of the Supreme Court of the United States, *which we recognize as the correct exposition of the Constitution of the United States.*" But what is the exposition of the Constitution of the United States this decision has made? The Squatter Sovereignty Democrats contend that it has made no exposition condemning their heresy. If this is so, the recognition of its expositions commits them to no denial of Squatter Sovereignty; and they manifest what they suppose the decision determines when they say in the words following in the resolution, that "neither the rights of persons nor property can *be destroyed* by Congressional or Territorial legislation." Even WILLIAM H. SEWARD, and the whole Black Republican party, could vote for this resolution. They contend that Congress can, by its legislation, prevent slavery from entering a Territory; but they do not claim the power in Congress to *"destroy"* it. The Southern Delegates in the Convention present, as their patriotic and triumphant *ultimatum,* what every Black Republican and Squatter Sovereignty Democrat in the whole Union may support. That is, certainly, a most remarkable way of vindicating the rights of the South! And when do they propose to present this august *"ultimatum?"* Why, after the nomination of President and Vice President of the United States is completed. By a resolution, which they voted for, the Convention determined that no nomination for President or Vice President should be made until the Convention had first settled the platform of principles upon which the nomination should rest. The Convention, after six days' agitation and debate, has adopted the platform upon which it proposes to put its nominees. That platform is Squatter Sovereignty. The resolutions, affirming the rights of the South, have been rejected; and now, after both platform and nomination shall be completed—and not before—these heroic vindicators of the rights of the South propose to introduce into the Convention the miserable cheat invented by New York *"as the ultimatum of the South."* Suppose that this *ultimatum* was rejected (of which, however, there is not the slightest probability), what would they do? Go out of the Convention? The Convention will go out itself; for, having accomplished by their aid all it came to do (made a platform and nominated candidates on it for the Presidency), of course it will adjourn. The only danger is, that the Convention, having finished its business, may adjourn without considering the grand *"ultimatum of the South,"* and thus get out before the delegates from Virginia, Tennessee and Kentucky. There may yet be a pretty race.

24. The Charleston Convention and Its Consequences

(*The Daily South Carolinian,* Columbia, May 6, 1860)

The split in the Charleston Convention has resulted, as our readers already know, in the division of the old time-honored Democratic party. Sprung from the State Rights school of Mr. Jefferson, it is the only national party that has ever dared to meet at all the consolidation party of the Union. The overthrow of a national bank, a disconnection of the Government with grand schemes of internal improvements, a reduction of the protective tariff system, the expansion of our territorial limits, and the annexation of both slaveholding and non-slaveholding communities to the confederacy. Its progress has recently received a shock from which it may never recover; but if it does, we hope it will be under such auspices that it will again rise to power with a banner of principles floating proudly above it. Eight of the Southern States have now raised the standard around which all who desire its regeneracy upon principle, should now rally. They call not upon the Southern States alone, but upon all who recognize the equal rights of all the States in the common Territories of the Union. Their shibboleth is "equal rights," and with this battle cry, they intend to go forth to battle in every State of the Union. They go forth with an appeal not to a section, but to the entire Union. Those who imagine they see in it, either with fear or favor, a foreshadow, or rather a design, of disunion, are mistaken. They might, with as much propriety, call the Constitution which binds the States together an instrument of disunion. The Richmond Convention will meet one week in advance of the Baltimore

Convention.[1] The majority platform, or one similar to it, will be presented, and candidates for the Presidency and Vice Presidency put upon it. Between this and the time of its meeting, the Chicago Convention and the Baltimore Union Convention will each have entered the contest, with their respective principles announced and their candidates proclaimed. The Richmond Convention will thus have the benefit of their action. The delegates from the Southern States that withdrew have referred their action back to their respective constituencies. They have done that which exceeded the object of their appointment, and they will appeal to those who appointed them to give them the sanction of their approval through another State Convention. By a notice from the Chairman of the Democratic Central Committee of the State, it will be seen that a meeting of the Committee has been called. This Committee will then determine upon the time of the Convention, and issue a call for District and Parish meetings for appointing delegates to another State Democratic Convention. That it will be warmly seconded by all who participated in and favored the State Democratic Convention of April, we have no doubt. We are also satisfied that there will be many to join in now who did not disapprove of the Convention policy in itself, but were deterred from participating in it by the many unfounded and unjust rumors raised and circulated by some who opposed the April movement. The propriety of the policy has been vindicated. More than once during the course of the late National Convention, the vote of South Carolina turned the scales. But for the vote of our committeeman, Col. Preston, who labored for days with the other members of the Committee on Platform, the Cincinnati Platform would not have been voted down, as the majority against it was only one. The Richmond Convention meets to vindicate a principle in which every lover of the Constitution is deeply interested. It should be sustained with warmth and zeal. Let the people of the States whose delegates withdrew, second their action with earnestness, and not only will North Carolina, Virginia, Tennessee, Kentucky, Maryland, and Missouri, but California, Oregon, Pennsylvania, New York, and some of the Northwestern States, march into line and unite their columns at Richmond with those of the Constitutional Democracy of the States that have locked shields in this contest for the equal Territorial rights of every section of the Union.

[1] The delegations which withdrew from the Charleston Convention organized at Military Hall as the *Democratic Constitutional Convention*. When the rump convention adjourned without making nominations and with a motion pending to reconsider the platform, this convention adjourned to meet at Richmond on the second Monday in June.

25. [FALSE GRATULATIONS]

(*The Kentucky Statesman*, Lexington, May 8, 1860)

It is difficult to reconcile the exultant gratification of the southern opposition [1] at the dissensions which threaten the future concentration of the democratic vote of the country upon a single Presidential candidate with a dutiful loyalty to the South and a proper hostility to Black Republicanism. It is manifest, beyond the shadow of a doubt, that the Democratic party is the only organization which stands between the Republicans and the public offices of the Government. Divisions in the Democratic party, and all that tends to break its harmony or impair its strength, enhances the chance of the Republicans. Yet the Abolitionists of the North did not receive the news of the dissensions at Charleston, with more expressions of joy nor exult over the split in that Convention with more deep-felt delight than did the oppositionists of Kentucky. There seems to be a common bond of sympathy between these factions, which leads each to prefer the success of the other to the further ascendancy of Democracy. We would scorn to appeal for sympathy to our opponents here in the troubles which now threaten our party, and through its defeat, in our opinion, imperil our confederacy. We do not protest against their affiliation with the free-soilers and anti-slavery men of the North. Their hostility to Democratic men and measures, their intense and implacable hatred to Democracy, and their untiring efforts to break down the Democratic party, are all legitimate and natural. Not a murmur should escape the lips of a Democrat, and no cry for quarter should be heard in the Democratic camp. But we have the right to demand of these opponents that, they should avow their affiliation, that they should admit the inevitable consequences of their course and assume the responsibilities of the position they take. And this responsibility they will be compelled to meet before the people of Kentucky. Let them avow their sympathy with the Republicans, and let them come out boldly and manfully, and say that, they prefer the election of Seward or Bates or McLean to that of any southern Democrat. Such is the meaning of their present exultations. They cannot rejoice at the prospect of Democratic defeat, and at the same time disavow all affiliation with the Abolitionists. They cannot herald with joy and shouts of triumph, the defeat of Democratic candidates in the free States and withhold their sympathy from

---

[1] This alludes to that element, styling itself Constitutional Unionist, which soon afterward put the Bell-Everett ticket into the field.

their victorious Republican competitors. They cannot rejoice at the disruption of the Charleston Convention and foretell with deep gratification, the overthrow of the Democratic party, without at the same time espousing the Republican cause, and confessing their desire for its success. Every Democratic defeat at the North and every word of dissension in the Democratic convention enures to the benefit of Republicanism. The southern opposition, when expressing pleasure at Democratic discomfiture, at the same time exhibit a desire for Republican success. They cannot escape the dilemma. The political forces of the country are too well organized, and the issue too well defined. Then we say to them rejoice, exult and shout as loudly and long as you will, but don't attempt to conceal your sympathy with the Abolition party of the North. Laugh and chuckle as you will at our misfortunes, ring your peals of victory in our ears, and proclaim your heartfelt joy, but don't stultify yourselves and insult the intelligence of the reader by denying that you prefer the selection of a Republican to a Democratic President. Rejoice, but rejoice as becomes intelligent men, understanding the consequences of the events which elicit your utterances of gratification and willing [ness] to espouse the triumphant cause before the people. In a word, exult as much as you may over Democratic defeats, and we, for one, will not murmur a word of complaint if you at the same time avow, like men, your sympathy with Republicanism, and your desire that the Government shall be tranferred to the hands of the anti-slavery party.

It is vile nonsense, the merest folly to talk about a third party. It is insulting to the intelligence of the American people to attempt to organize any party which shall ignore the slavery question. That issue must be met and settled. The cry of "Union" will not rally a corporal's guard, unless upon a platform in which this question is met in every phase, and all its issues, clearly and explicitly enunciated.—It is no part of patriotism to shut the eye to present dangers; conservatism does not turn its back upon disturbing questions which demand adjustment. True patriotism meets with intelligence the exigencies of the times, and conservatism grapples with threatening difficulties. The subject of domestic slavery now overshadows every other issue in American politics, and its consideration cannot be escaped in the pending national canvass. The coming Presidential election will turn upon that question, and it is quite time all men had determined their course. All the "Conservatives" of the land cannot quiet the troubled sea of politics. The rallying cry of Union will fall unheard in the tumult.

All attempts to raise up a third party to the issue, any effort to intervene a power between the great contestants and arrest the trial of strength, will be vain and fruitless. The hope, possibly honestly indulged by some, that a new party can be organized to wrest the Government from both the contending parties, will be illusory and worse than illusory. It may turn the scale of victory but nothing more.

The Baltimore Convention and its action will scarce exert a perceptible influence upon the political fortunes of the country.—Its candidates will not contend for the prize. It may distract the southern forces and weaken the combination of southern States now so important to their safety.—It may determine the victory between the great contending parties, but there its influence will end.

The third party movement has derived no strength from the threatening dissensions in the Democratic party. It may add to the trouble, and yet further divide the forces of the South, but nothing that has occurred or that it can accomplish, will enure to its advantage. It is but a Hessian band of intruders, capable of annoying the contending armies, but not esteemed by either worth the price at which it holds its alliance.

26. WHERE WE STAND

(*Richmond Enquirer,* May 8, 1860)

The present position of the Democratic party, in view of the complications which have lately arisen in the councils of their representatives, requires the utmost moderation of temper and firmness of purpose to prevent the final catastrophe of party disorganization.

A brief review of the occurrences which have led, step by step, to the present crisis, will materially assist towards eliciting a prudent course of action, likely to maintain party organization without the sacrifice of constitutional principle.

A little more than twelve months ago, the fact was fully developed, that a large portion of the Northern Democracy had accepted, and were ready to insist on an interpretation of the Cincinnati platform altogether at variance with the interpretation understood and acted on by the Southern Democracy. Thus a direct conflict of opinion was produced. On the one hand it was insisted that the Cincinnati platform recognized the uncontrolled power of each territorial legislature to establish or abolish the right of property in slaves in the respective territories of the Union. On the other hand, it was insisted that the just interpretation of the platform on this point recognized the right of slave property in the territories as an existing right guaranteed by the Constitution, and that the power which Congress could exercise, either immediately or through its delegates, the territorial legislative assemblies, was the power coupled with the duty to protect such existing rights of persons and property.

Here, as in every similar instance of difference, many political leaders and presses were ready with suggestions of compromise. We thought then, what we know now, that this was a case in which both principle and policy precluded all middle ground of compromise. Indeed, we saw but one possible ground of compromise—that which suggested the re-enactment of the Cincinnati platform without any reference whatever to the point of disputed interpretation. Such a compromise as this, we were utterly unwilling to adopt. We foresaw that its adoption would result in nothing less than the demoralization of the party through the perpetration of a double deception. We foresaw, too, that even were such deception possible, it could only be made practicable through the nomination for the Presidency of some man either too timid or too dishonest to avow his opinions on the point at issue. Altogether, we recognized the policy of compromise as too equivocal to be honest, too timid to be prudent, too selfish to be safe.

Regarding, then, the doctrine of federal protection to persons and property in the territories, as made imperative by the Constitution, and as furnishing the only just and logical interpretation of the Cincinnati platform; we did not hesitate to place at the head of the editorial column of the "Richmond Enquirer" that exposition of principles, which has floated ever since at our masthead.[1] Nor have we spared an effort to inculcate the fact that the maintenance of this banner of constitutional principle is inseparable from the integrity of the Democratic party.

---

[1] Cardinal Democratic principles on the slavery question:

Absolute non-interference by the General Government; to introduce or to exclude slaves, in any of the territories of the Union.

No federal Slave Code. No Congressional discrimination in favor of slave property in the territories, and no Congressional discrimination against it.

Whenever in any of the territories the safety of slave persons or the right of slave property, or the right or safety of any description of persons or property, is unconstitutionally assailed, it is the power and duty of Congress, not less than of any and every other Department of the General Government, to exercise its proper functions, for the security of equal protection to the rights and safety of every species of persons and property.

The full and unimpaired right of popular sovereignty, entitling the people of each Territory, on application for their admission as a new State into the Union, to enact their own State Constitution, by a fair and full reference to a popular vote, without force, fraud or Federal dictation, and by such Constitution to provide for the maintenance or the prohibition of the institution of slavery as to them may seem best.

Unceasingly—at every juncture, in season and out of season—we have urged this view of the matter by every argument of principle and policy which we could discover or expound.

We felt confident that the Democracy of Virginia would sustain us in this position. Nay, we knew that we were touching a chord to which the Democracy of every Southern State would respond.

In neither point have we been mistaken.—Every Southern State has recognized the issue as vital to its own rights and to the interests of the Democratic party. Five Southern States have regarded the necessity before them as so urgent that they have peremptorily instructed their delegates to withdraw from a National Convention whenever a majority should refuse to sanction this doctrine of equal protection.—Nor have Southern Democrats found themselves sectionalized in the struggle. The two Pacific States have yielded an active and undivided support to the same doctrine. And throughout the North a strong body of conservative Democrats have rallied under the same banner, and elected delegate after delegate to the National Convention to maintain the same doctrine. The Democracy of New York, acting through their district conventions, have elected a full delegation unanimous in their support of the constitutional platform,[2] and a large minority of the delegates elected by the State Convention of New York have given the same platform a support—silent only because their hands were tied by the unit system.[3] A majority of the Pennsylvania and New Jersey delegations are now ready to co-operate with us. So are delegates from different New England States. And even in the Northwest—in the very State of the great expounder and champion of the opposite doctrine—a body of conservative Democrats have taken their stand and erected their platform on the basis of Federal protection to slave property in the Territories.

Such is the diagram, by which it is effectually demonstrated that at this moment an overwhelming majority of the Democratic party are firmly united under the same banner of constitutional principle which has floated so long at the masthead of the Richmond "Enquirer." Every other test yet applied furnishes the same solution of the political problem which now agitates the Union.

When the partisans of the respective doctrines of territorial sovereignty and Federal protection drew the dividing line at Charleston—

[2] Fernando Wood delegation, not admitted at Charleston.
[3] Dean Richmond delegation, admitted at Charleston, composed of forty Douglas and thirty anti-Douglas delegates, but casting a solid Douglas vote of thirty-five under the unit rule.

on the one hand we saw the doctrine of equal protection boldly and unequivocally pronounced. On the other side, the doctrine of territorial sovereignty was not even reduced to writing. Among all the resolutions offered to or acted on by the Convention, not one can be found declaring, either in direct terms or by implication, the doctrine that a territorial Legislature may abolish slavery, or even denying the duty of the Federal Government to protect slave persons and slave property in the territories.

Virtually admitting that the present assertion of the doctrine of territorial sovereignty was incompatible with the integrity of the Democratic party, the advocates of that doctrine only asked that the question might be submitted for further judicial decision, and pledged themselves to abide such decision.

This was, we are free to admit, something more than a concession of weakness. It was honestly intended as an effort at conciliation, and as such considered and respected by those to whom it was tendered. Still its acceptance was impossible. The advocates of equal protection were obliged to adhere to their original position. If their doctrine had any validity at all, it was a necessary part of the Constitution, which might be asserted or enforced by judicial sanction, but which no action of the Federal Judiciary was competent to impair. Moreover, the omission to assert the doctrine of equal protection would practically result in the negation of that doctrine, and thus, on grounds of policy as well as of principle, the compromise tendered was equally unacceptable.

Nevertheless, it is clearly apparent that the proposal for compromise received a support in the Convention much larger than could possibly have been secured for the doctrine of territorial sovereignty.

Even with this advantage against the advocates of equal protection, the test of Democratic strength was overwhelmingly in their favor. On the first trial of strength, a majority of all the States pronounced in favor of the direct assertion of the doctrine of equal protection.—On the first trial of strength,[4] fifteen out of the nineteen States (more than three-fourths) which cast their [electoral] votes for the Democratic ticket in 1856, pronounced the same decision. On the first trial of strength, fifteen out of the seventeen States (more than five-sixths) which gave Democratic majorities in 1856, pronounced the same decision. On the first trial of strength, 116 of the 174 electoral votes (two-

---

[4] Vote on question to recommit platform. *Proceedings of the Conventions at Charleston and Baltimore*, p. 89.

thirds) cast for the Democratic ticket in 1856, pronounced the same decision.

And even on the last delusive trial, when 122 electoral votes, which no enthusiast expects to see cast for the Democratic ticket next fall were thrown into the scale; and when 15 votes from New York were thrown against the wish of 30 delegates from the same State, under an arbitrary enforcement of the unit system; even then the operation of the doctrine of equal protection was refused only by a vote of 165 to 138.[5]

Thus, on every test, it is manifest that an overwhelming majority of the effective strength of the Democratic party has pronounced in favor of the open assertion of the doctrine of equal protection by the Federal Government to persons and property in the Territories. The final omission, then, of the National Convention to assert this doctrine at Baltimore, will entail the following results: 1st. The doctrine of protection will be defeated as absolutely by being ignored, as though it were absolutely negatived; 2d. The opposite doctrine of territorial sovereignty will be virtually established; 3d. The will of the majority of the party will be openly disregarded; 4th. The inevitable dismemberment of the party.

This general view of the question is rendered more apposite by peculiar circumstances. In obedience to the positive instructions of their respective constituencies, delegates from five Southern States have already withdrawn from the National Convention, in consequence of the refusal of that Convention to assert a vital principle of constitutional right.[6] Delegates from five [7] other Southern States have followed the example, deeming it inexpedient as well as improper on principle, to leave the co-laborers isolated in a step unavoidable to them, and taken for the maintenance of a principle common to the interests, the affections, the duty of all.

We have no desire nor intention at this time to arouse jealousies or awaken conflicts by criticisms applied to the course of those delegates who coincided in principle with the retiring delegates and yet have omitted or delayed to co-operate in their action. It may be that their course was the most prudent which could be adopted under the circumstances, and that furnishes now the only hope of the ultimate re-

---

[5] Vote by which the main minority report was substituted for the majority report.

[6] Alabama, Mississippi, Florida, Louisiana, Texas. Winston of Alabama, and Jones and McHatton of Louisiana withdrew under protest.

[7] Four only unless Fisher of Virginia be included: South Carolina, Georgia, Arkansas, Delaware.

union of the party on a basis of constitutional principle. We know that there are men in each of the Southern delegations which still remain in the National Convention as loyal to principle and as devoted to the rights and interests of the South as any son of the South who has retired from the National Convention in vindication of national principle and Southern honor. We know that these men have acted from loyal motives, nor do we presume to say that their action has been either improper or imprudent. As we have said before, we deem it possible, nay probable, that in pursuing a different course from that adopted by a number of their associates, they have only taken a precaution which will result in pledging the whole Democratic party to the maintenance of that principle of Constitutional right which they deem essential.

Admitting all this, we still vindicate, without reservation or exception, the action of those delegates who have retired from the Convention. Their action was right—right in principle and expedient in policy. When delegates were instructed by their constituencies to withdraw from the Convention in a certain contingency—on the happening of that contingency they had no choice. And when they withdrew from the Convention—it was due to them, due to their constituencies, due to loyalty and to principle, that they should not be left isolated in the position to which their imperative duty had assigned them. Had they refused to obey instructions, or, after obedience, had they been left isolated by their associates, the principles for which they contend would have fallen to the ground. All honor, then, to the retiring delegates! Whatever credit may be attributable to other soldiers in the battle of constitutional right, these cavaliers who *par excellence* have assumed the post of danger, maintain a claim to national gratitude, second to that of none of their peers.

As to the ultimate action to be adopted at Baltimore, we see but two alternatives presented to the Democratic party. The doctrine of protection in the territories must be finally rejected or accepted. If it is rejected, as we have already indicated, its rejection will involve the dismemberment of the Democratic party, and a separate nomination of a Democratic candidate on the platform of constitutional protection will inevitably ensue. If it is rejected, then the rejection must be unequivocal. If the delegates who now compose the Convention are willing to yield the point—if they are willing to tolerate the doctrine of territorial sovereignty, then, by all means, let the issue be presented in the most tangible form—by the nomination of Stephen A. Douglas. Mr. Douglas has taken his position in a fair and open manner. It is unjust to him, and unfair to the host of friends who sustain him and his doctrine, that any compromise candidate shall be allowed to steal his thunder. Much as we oppose his doctrine of territorial government, we would infinitely prefer to see him elected on the honestly avowed platform of territorial sovereignty, rather than witness the election of a man who shall consent to go before the people on a platform speaking one sentiment at the North and another at the South.

We are convinced that the large majority of the Southern Democracy will be satisfied with no candidate who does not openly avow the doctrine of constitutional protection in the Territories. The Southern Democracy are naturally averse to any precipitate action.—They will calmly await the action of the Baltimore Convention. Let that Convention adopt, to the full extent, in their platform, the great doctrine of the equal rights of the sovereign States; and they will support any candidate who can stand on that platform. And if the Baltimore Convention shall proceed to name a candidate without asserting the doctrine of equal protection, then the candidate himself, whoever he may be, will be required to inscribe, with his own hand, on the banner of the party, the doctrine which the Democracy of seventeen States have already pronounced to be essential. On no other terms can he unite the support of the Democratic party.

With these views we respectfully, but earnestly, appeal to the Convention that will assemble in Richmond on the 11th June next, to take no decided action until they shall be informed of the measures adopted by the Baltimore Convention on the 18th June. As matters now stand, the question of a platform is still open, and we yet trust that the Democratic Baltimore Convention will see the vital importance of adopting a platform that will meet the views of the Richmond Convention, and thus secure the harmonious and united action of the Democracy of every section of the confederacy.

27. THE TENNESSEE PLATFORM

(*Nashville Union and American,* May 10, 1860)

One of the most eloquent and appropriate speeches made during the sitting of the Convention at Charleston was that made by Col. JNO. K. HOWARD, of this State, when he presented the resolution that had been assented to by the Virginia, Kentucky, and Tennessee delegations as a fair basis for the settlement of the difficulties which threatened a total disruption of the Convention. On Monday afternoon the

States of Alabama, Mississippi, Louisiana, Texas, Florida and portions of Arkansas and Delaware withdrew. On Friday morning the delegates from South Carolina, Georgia and the remaining delegates, except two, from Arkansas retired. The delegations from Virginia, Kentucky, North Carolina and Tennessee had been in consultation the night previous. The work of secession had extended further than any member of the Convention had anticipated. Upon the withdrawal of the delegates from South Carolina and Georgia, the delegations from Virginia, Kentucky and Tennessee asked leave to withdraw for further consultation. They met and agreed upon the resolution presented by Mr. HOWARD. During their absence from the hall Mr. McCOOK, of Ohio, had introduced a resolution to proceed to balloting for a candidate, and upon that the previous question had been called, cutting off all amendments and debate. This was the state of the proceedings when the delegates who had withdrawn for consultation returned. The most intense feeling was manifest as to what would be the course of the great conservative and preservative Southern Democratic States. For it was announced that if they withdrew, New York, New Jersey and a large part of Pennsylvania, with probable portions of Massachusetts, Connecticut, Maryland and Missouri would retire, and thus occasion a final dissolution of the Convention. Although other business was then under consideration, by general consent, Mr. HOWARD was permitted to read for information the resolution which had been agreed upon by Kentucky and Tennessee, and to which Virginia gave her assent. Mr. HOWARD prefaced the introduction of his resolution with an eloquent appeal to the justice and patriotism of the Convention, and beautifully alluded to the past of Tennessee in the cabinet and on the battle-field. His allusion to the noble stand which the Democracy of Tennessee had always taken in favor of the Constitution, and the firmness with which they had resisted the surges of fanaticism, and the efforts of passion elicited rapturous applause. We have already published Mr. HOWARD's resolution, but as it is destined, in our opinion, to become the object of very general comment before the re-assembling of the Convention on the 18th of June, we re-publish it:

> *Resolved,* That the citizens of the United States have an equal right to settle with their property in the Territories; and that, under the decision of the Supreme Court, which we recognise as the correct exposition of the Constitution, neither the right of persons nor property can be destroyed or impaired by Congressional or Territorial legislation.

This resolution is still pending and will undoubtedly be brought up for the consideration and action of the convention at Baltimore. We invite to it the unimpassioned deliberation of the whole South. It does not demand a slave code, and yet it declares in a sufficiently emphatic manner to make it acceptable to the Democracy of Virginia, Kentucky and Tennessee, that "neither the right of persons nor property can be destroyed or impaired by Congressional or Territorial legislation."

The *States and Union* thus speaks of it:

Under the Tennessee platform, the slaveholder is free to go into the Territories with his property. He may claim the same protection from his government that it is bound to afford him anywhere else within its jurisdiction. Its hands are bound not to injure him, nor can the Territorial authorities discriminate against him or his property. Ought not this satisfy all parties desirous of harmony? . . . It will be seen that wise and temperate counsels will in the end prevail, and the Democratic party may be united upon principles at once just and fraternal.

The Chicago *Herald* defining its position on the present difficulties of our party says:

There were two platforms before the Convention. The States of Virginia, Tennessee and Kentucky put forward a *compromise* proposition, which was *never voted upon*. The Convention then adjourned to Baltimore, to take time to consider the matter. Now our purpose is this:—We really *mean* to consider it, and to advise the Illinois Democracy to accept this compromise, and then to nominate whom they please, and we will help to elect him. We are for a fair *compromise*. We are for peace and success.

We also ask for this resolution the calm consideration of the Southern Democracy. Although it was not acted upon by the Convention, it was understood that the Democracy of the Northwest were not unwilling to grant the correctness of the premises assumed in that resolution. We repeat in the language of the *Union and States,* "Ought not this to satisfy all parties desirous of harmony?" Already have the various organs of the several prominent aspirants commenced a course of aspersion and detraction which will lead to evil and only evil. This internecine war about men must cease. Better, a thousand times better, that Mr. DOUGLAS, Mr. HUNTER,[1] Mr. DAVIS, and the rest of them should never be heard of again than that the discussion of their personal claims should cause a dissolution of the Democratic party. We

[1] Robert M. T. Hunter, Senator from Virginia, 1847–1861. Secretary of State in the Confederacy.

have our preferences as deeply seated as those of other men. We believe that Gov. JOHNSON is as true a statesman as is spoken of, as capable, and by far the most available, but because we may not succeed in securing the nomination of our favorite we shall not endeavor to rend the party in twain. We honestly and earnestly believe that the nomination of Judge DOUGLAS at this time would make the judicious grieve. So with Mr. DAVIS or Mr. HUNTER. But because we thus believe and have the frankness to say so, we are not to be ranked as "free-soilers" or "traitorous disunionists." A little less passion and a little more judgment and the Democracy will yet survive its present dissensions and stand ready and able to drive in disgrace the Black Republican hosts from the field of battle.

28. THE TRUE ISSUE

(*The Daily True Delta,* New Orleans, May 10, 1860)

Our readers must be by this time pretty familiar with the exact issue which is before the South, and which was made the pretense for the secession of the delegations or fragments of delegations of some half-dozen of States, mainly of the minor orders, from the National Democratic Convention and from the National Democratic party, they have undertaken to divide and to destroy. The real cause for the secession was the certainty which confronted the bolters that the nomination of Stephen A. Douglas could not be defeated, nor, if nominated, his election prevented; hence they had no other resource, the jobbers and schemers, who have so long controlled the imbecility and corruption of the Federal Government, than to retire into fitting obscurity, accompanied by the execration and contempt of the country, or to bolt the Convention, set up some creature of their own for President, and each for himself, and the Devil for all, make the best terms possible with the enemies of democracy among the crowd of mongrel aspirants for national supremacy the breaking up of the Democratic party has emboldened to take the field. But the bolters at Charleston felt that some excuse for their treason to the party whose generosity they had all enjoyed, and whose confidence they were meditating so foully to abuse, must be advanced, and they accordingly took issue upon the readoption of the Cincinnati platform, alleging that it sanctioned the popular sovereignty heresy, which they insisted, aye these very men who were the authors of what they term a disgrace and a huge wrong to the South, insisted should be repudiated and denounced, otherwise they would break up the Convention and destroy the great conservative party of the Union, which alone stands or can successfully stand between the South and her implacable foes.

Two sets of political schemers combined in this movement—one, the more powerful and artful of the two, was the Bright, Buchanan, Slidell, Ike Cook and Fernando Wood free corps, of which Mouton of this State was honored with the leadership, and whose aim was place at any price, regardless of principles or consequences; the other wing, or the fanatical branch, was marshalled by Yancey, of Alabama, and had Jeff. Davis and the fire-eaters generally in the background.

Davis for some time past had been studiously conciliating the first branch of these corps, and, in the hope of getting a nomination for the presidency from them somehow or other, was not disinclined to trail after the lead of such a leash of beauties as Ike Cook, John Slidell and Fernando Wood. Before the Convention met it had been agreed between these high contracting parties, and not objected to by the partisans of the score of other equally eligible aspirants for executive honors, that somehow or other Douglas must be defeated, when each schemer hoped his own chance might come up then; but the backbone was wanting when the final tug came, and only the wretched rump, whose discordant proceedings on the last day of their being together we laid before our readers yesterday, had the nerve and the effrontery to present themselves as seceders from the ranks of the Democracy. Bound together by no tie other than hope of individual success and enrichment from the accidents of the desperate game they were playing against their country, the result of their disgraceful bolt might easily have been foreseen, for it happened as every one anticipated— eventuating in a general scramble as to whom should be preferred for the honors they impudently assumed the authority to dispense. A portion of the Louisiana delegation early received a hint from their director to edge out of the body where it was manifest he had rather a slim hold; but the vigilant of Avoyelles, who had a role of his own to get through with, seemed to regard such hints as not in the bond, and tenaciously clung to his post, even after the last mark of the fugitive Bayard's form was visible upon the soft cushioned chair he so dignifiedly and apparently so innocently occupied.

But Mouton, the tenacious bolter from the regular Convention, was not entirely alone in his glory, for Yancey, the loquacious, the consistent Yancey, the original Squatter Sovereignty man, Cass, Douglas, and all others to the contrary notwithstanding, stood up like a veritable fire eater, apparently none the worse for not being immersed in that floral shower the beauty of Charleston had, by orders, been at such pains to accumulate in the galleries of the hall in which the National Convention assembled, to drown the champion of disunion in, when the happy moment arrived which was to witness the final overthrow of this old Republic Washington, Jefferson and Jackson vainly labored to create, consolidate and perpetuate. Yancey, the author of the now famous or infamous Squatter Sovereignty heresy, as he and his fire-eating confederates style it, was there cheek-by-jowl by the ex-governor of poor unconscious Louisiana, where people have just about as much idea of giving up the Union as they have to turn infidels and defy their Maker.

These innocents could not destroy the Union as they speedily discovered; but they, nevertheless, chuckled with delight at their success at doing the next thing to it—destroying the great party, which alone has the power, the vitality, and the prestige to keep it together. That the destruction of the Union was the grand aim of the Yanceys and the Moutons of the bolters there can be no doubt; they were acting on a foregone conclusion, and were not animated by calculations of plunder like the Ike Cook, John Slidell, and Fernando Wood Company, which was in the same venture with them. Both Yancey and Mouton, as we have said, made the reproduction of the popular sovereignty doctrine by the National Convention, the excuse for their departure from the Democratic party and the disruption of the National Convention. Let us now, then, examine history a little in regard to the origin of this doctrine, the faithful maintenance of which has ostensibly brought upon the great statesman of the Union so much of obloquy and unpopularity in the South. Let us examine whether popular sovereignty be of Northern or of Southern birth, a creation of those hostile to slavery or a well-matured principle which, fairly carried out, must secure to the slave States their real strength and their legitimate influence in the confederacy. To do this, at the risk of being considered prolix, we shall take our readers with us in an examination of a historical work, in which justice is done impartially and fairly, it cannot be denied, in apportioning the credit of the authorship of the Squatter Sovereignty creed. The work we refer to is "Benton's Thirty Years' View," and the chapter is the one hundred and seventy-eighth. Speaking of the presidential nomination of the year 1848, and of the Democratic convention and platform, that deceased statesman thus discourseth: "The construction of the platform, or party political creed for the campaign, was next entered upon, and one was produced, interminably long, and long since forgotten. The value of all such constructions may be seen in comparing what was then adopted, or rejected as political test, with what has since been equally rejected or adopted for the same purpose. *For example* (the italics are ours), *the principle of Squatter Sovereignty, that is to say, the right of the inhabitants of the* TERRITORIES *to decide the question of slavery for themselves, was then repudiated, and by a vote virtually unanimous; it is since adopted by a vote equally unanimous. Mr. Yancey of Alabama, submitted this resolution as an article of Democratic faith to be inserted in the creed, to wit:*

"THAT THE DOCTRINE OF NON-INTERFERENCE WITH THE RIGHTS OF PROPERTY OF ANY PORTION OF THIS CONFEDERATION, BE IT IN THE STATES OR THE TERRITORIES, BY ANY OTHER THAN THE PARTIES INTERESTED IN THEM, IS THE TRUE REPUBLICAN DOCTRINE RECOGNIZED BY THIS BODY," that is by the National Democratic Convention which nominated Lewis Cass, of Michigan, for President, and William O. Butler, of Kentucky, for Vice President.

In 1848, Mr. Yancey, of Alabama, and the supporters of extreme Southern views in the same body, sought ineffectually to engraft on the platform of the national democracy, for the preservation of the most cherished interest of the South, a principle for the maintenance of which now the same Mr. Yancey and his supporters of 1848 denounce the fearless Stephen A. Douglas, bolt from the National Convention, and labor, with all their might and their malice, to annihilate the Democratic party as a national omnipotent party organization. Do such men imagine the people to be insane, that they will follow their lead; or so steeped in corruption that they will listlessly witness the destruction of their government and dismemberment of their glorious Union under such dictation? On the contrary, these disturbers of the public peace, these conspirators against the integrity of the Republic, these aspiring and plotting demagogues will discover that the people are not the fools or the madmen they take them for, and that they know the true patriot from the impudent pretender and imposter, Stephen A. Douglas from the Slidells, the Yanceys and the lower herd who bay at their heels and decry in impotent ravings his universal popularity with his countrymen.

29. SHALL THE SOUTH BE UNITED?

(Richmond Semi-weekly Examiner, May 11, 1860)

In our issue of yesterday, we stated briefly the action, and the ground of action, of Virginia and the border States of the South in the late Charleston Convention. We stated that by remaining in the Convention they had secured two principles of the greatest importance to the South and to the Democratic party, and, by consequence, to the Union. The one of these was the adoption of a rule of nominations by which the strength of the whole South was to be so counted as that their dissent from any nomination would amount to a veto.[1] This, it is obvious, will secure the nomination of a sound man, if the South can agree among themselves as to who *is* a sound man. The other principle gained was the recognition, by a distinct pledge, of those composing a majority of the Convention, that the Tennessee Resolution should be adopted. That resolution is as follows:

Resolved, That all citizens of the United States have an equal right to settle with their property in the Territories, and that under the decisions of the Supreme Court, which we recognize as an exposition of the Constitution, neither their rights of person or property can be destroyed or impaired by Congress.

This, which brings in the full force of the Dred Scott decision, repudiates Squatter Sovereignty and fixes the rights of the South on an impregnable basis. Those rights, thus secured by a rule which gives the South the control of the nomination, and an acknowledgment of a great principle, seem to us as containing all that it was necessary to demand of the North. For this reason we approve cordially of what Virginia did, and do not well see what else she could have done without error. We trust that on a calm review of the whole subject the seceding States will come to the same conclusion, and will unite with the Border States in Convention at Baltimore, and there secure for themselves, by action, the advantages that have been secured for them in principle.

We see that one of the papers representing the views of the seceders argues that if they return to the Convention at Baltimore, they will, in some, if not most, cases be met there by contested delegates from their States; and that as these will be Douglas Democrats, they will be admitted in such mode as to insult the retiring seceders. Now this re-

---

[1] That two-thirds of the vote in the Electoral College rather than two-thirds of the vote represented in the convention was required for a nomination.

sult we do not anticipate. We are very sure it will not take place in Virginia; and we cannot imagine that if the delegations of other States have not been deemed to have forfeited the confidence of their constituents, that any attempt will be made to supersede them. But if it shall be, and shall prove successful, it will demonstrate that an opposition to the extreme Southern movement is to be made at home; which will be disastrous not only to the interests of the Democratic party, but to the slavery system of civilization. It must be admitted by the warmest advocates of Southern rights, that an explosion within our limits would rend us to atoms, whilst we may safely challenge outside pressure. In other words, we must be united to command respect to ourselves or safety to our society.

Suppose they shall not unite, but run an independent candidate as advised. With four candidates thus in the field, to wit: the Baltimore nominee, their candidate, the Whig or Opposition candidate, and the Chicago nominee, the election, of course, goes to Congress—the Whig will be dropped as lowest, and the seceding States must then elect between their own candidate, the Baltimore nominee and the Black Republican. In that event a Squatter Sovereignty man may, and most probably will, as the candidate of the Baltimore Convention, be submitted to their choice; and the question will be,—if their own man fails, as undoubtedly he will—whether these States will reject the Baltimore nominee, and thereby secure the election of the Chicago nominee: and so *create* the very state of things, on the *happening* of which they are pledged to disunion. It is just in that view of the future that we contemplate *this* crisis: how far the South will be held justified in the opinion of the world and in the sight of heaven for involving not the Union, but themselves, in a civil war upon the occurrence of an event which they could have prevented by the exercise of moderation, and by the use of means which are deemed abundantly sufficient by States at least as much interested as themselves in the institutions they seek to uphold. The action of the border States assures us that they think enough has been conceded to keep the Democratic party still united, and to give the South such a check upon it as to sustain their rights. These States now appeal to the seceders not to break up, and send new delegations, but they appeal to the seceding delegations themselves to come back and fight for their rights upon principles which must unite the South, because the border States are committed to it.

The invitation to fill vacancies cannot be construed into an invitation to appoint new delegations. It was issued for the sole purpose of securing complete delegations from each State in order that the South might have the benefit of her full strength. We have reason to know that it was worded expressly with the purpose of avoiding any opinion as to whether the voting of any delegation in whole or in part created vacancies.

30. SHALL WE BE REPRESENTED IN BALTIMORE?

(*Weekly Montgomery Confederation*, May 12, 1860)

We presume that our readers have long ago been made familiar with the proceedings of the regular National Democratic Convention, and also with those of the seceding organization. In consequence of the inability of the former to make a nomination without complete delegations from every State, and with a desire to give the unrepresented States time to send delegates to the Convention, Mr. RUSSELL, a very prominent Virginia politician, and delegate from that State, offered a resolution to the effect that the Convention should adjourn to reassemble in Baltimore on the 18th of June next. This move was hailed with intense delight by the whole Convention. All of the members saw plainly the impossibility of making a nomination until all of the unrepresented States were fully represented in the Convention, and therefore looked upon the resolution of Mr. RUSSELL as a matter of vast moment and importance. By an adjournment to Baltimore sufficient time could be afforded to the people of the Southern States for deliberation and reflection. They could perceive the propriety of being represented in the Baltimore Convention.

Our only hope for the preservation of this Government and the perpetuity of our interests is centered solely in the organization of the National Democracy. If Southern men prefer disunion and the establishment of a Southern Confederacy, then let them send their delegations to the city of Richmond, and carry out the wild and dangerous schemes which some of the seceders have inaugurated.

The issue of Union and Disunion is now upon us. By having ourselves represented in the city of Baltimore, we will be evincing a deep and serious concern in the welfare of our country, and the protection of our own Southern section; but by refusing to send a representation to that city we shall at once declare ourselves as willing and eager for a dissolution of this Union. To a man of candor and reflection it is evidently apparent that we are now in the midst of circumstances that are trying, serious and distressful. The latest intelligence from the city of New York furnishes us with an announcement of the decline of State stocks, and of the terrible and fearful apprehension that is consequent upon it.

It becomes necessary now for the Southern States to be represented in a National Convention if they are desirous of keeping the Union together and protecting their own property. It is not in the power of any man to predict who will be the nominee of the Baltimore Convention. In all human probability it may be a Southern man. But this is a matter of but little importance when the Union and the rights of our people are at stake. No man should be desirous of a dissolution of this Confederacy over an abstract principle, and, in all truth, we do not believe the honest masses of the country would ever submit to such a thing. The Cincinnati platform, which is indeed the sum and substance of the minority report, met, in 1856, the hearty response of every Democrat in the Union, and now it receives the curses of a few over-ardent seceders. The Northern Democrats asked for the adoption of the minority report, because upon it they had fought, in 1856, a good and victorious battle. They thought that in 1860 with the same platform and a true man, either from the North or South, victory would again perch upon their pole.—We ask now the people of the South, are they willing to break up this government because the Cincinnati platform has been adopted by the National Convention? On this platform the Northern Democrats expect to fight for the rights of the South. We Democrats of the South have not [sic] angry conflicts to engage in—we have no bonfires to build, nor much stump speaking and the like to make. Democracy always rides triumphant over the Southern States. But in the North, where there is a mighty and serious conflict going on between the Democrats and the Black Republicans—the very worst enemies of our country—we think it would be wrong for the Southern people to spurn these men who are standing up for our institutions, and achieving victory after victory over the whole combined forces of the Black Republicans. Unfortunately some of our Southern citizens have become so intensely fire-eating as to disregard all this friendship that Northern Democrats exhibit, and even go so far as to stigmatize them as traitors and incendiaries. This should not be so. With these men our Southern Democrats should affiliate. We should send a delegation to Baltimore, and harmonise upon some good and loyal Democrat as our standard bearer, and go forth then to crush fanaticism North and South. We are no lover of the Union when we find that our rights are not secure within it; but, now, we find not a right impaired, or even a probability of it, and, therefore, we think it our duty to the South and our duty to the country to suggest the propriety of the Southern States being represented in the regular National Democratic Convention.

We hope now that the people of the South will consider well this subject before making up an opinion. It is a matter of serious concern to every well-wisher of his country. All will admit that we are now placed in a condition the most unexpected and alarming, and by the exercise of a little coolness and self-possession we are obliged to learn how to accommodate ourselves to it.

The news that stocks had fallen in New York, and that Virginia, Tennessee, Kentucky, and other border States, were being seriously affected by this, will aid in opening the eyes of some men who have not given this matter as much reflection as it deserves.

31. The Prospects

(*Nashville Union and American,* May 15, 1860)

In a recent article we stated that the feelings of the delegates towards Mr. Douglas were intensified by the action of the Charleston Convention. We said that his friends were more determined in their devotion; his opponents more steadfast in their opposition. The tone of our exchanges fully corroborates what we then said. We had earnestly hoped that this strife about men would cease and that the leading Democratic papers in the North and in the South would no longer be organs of men but become organs of the party. That they would express a willingness to see the claims of prominent aspirants ignored rather than see the party divided and defeated. But in this reasonable hope we have thus far been disappointed. With the Douglas men the cry is, *aut Cæsar aut nullus,* Douglas or nobody. A directly antagonistic sentiment is expressed by the seceders. There is then but little prospect of a reconciliation between the two without an unexpected change of feeling. But there is a large portion of the Southern Democracy still represented in the convention, and they claim to have some rights which should not be totally disregarded. They do not demand a slave code, and they will resist all efforts to force upon the Northern Democracy a candidate of that school. Having such opinions, they feel that they have a right to reason with the Democracy of the North as to what is best to be done for the preservation and perpetuity of the party, believing that thereupon depend the preservation and perpetuity of the Union. This portion of the Southern Democracy, of which we profess to be a part, have seen with deep regret the attempts of leading Northern Democratic papers to brand the entire Democracy of the South as Disunionists and Secessionists. We are boldly and defiantly told that the democracy of the North and West have made up their minds, and they will not surrender another inch. We are rather insultingly informed that thousands of good Democrats in the free States are becoming convinced "that no dependence can be put in Southern honor, or Southern consistency." We respectfully submit that this is neither the language to use nor the spirit to manifest in order to restore harmony. The delegates from Minnesota who voted for Gov. JOHNSON [1] at Charleston have been publicly denounced in Cincinnati, by an Ohio delegate, as "two traitors, who sold themselves for money." "We had their daguerreotypes taken," said the speaker, Mr. WARD, "and you can see them in the rogues gallery." Such language we find reported, without dissent, in the DOUGLAS organ of that city. Inflammatory appeals are made to the Northern Democracy calculated to excite their passions and unfit them for consultation with their friends as to what is best for the common good. From rank to rank the command flies "stand firm." Suppose the Democracy of Virginia, North Carolina, Kentucky and Tennessee, follow the example of the Democracy in the North, and send forth the word "stand firm." The trip to Baltimore will be a trip neither of pleasure nor profit. There must be a spirit of conciliation and the sooner the better. We disclaim for the Democracy of Tennessee any intention or desire to force upon the Northern Democracy any Southern extremist. They will oppose the nomination of such an one. Having said this much, we have a word to say against the policy of nominating Mr. DOUGLAS. We know that in doing so we render ourselves liable to be denounced in certain quarters as Disunion, Secession, Yancey-ites. With many, opposition to DOUGLAS and Yanceyism are synonomous. What we have to say is in a spirit of kindness, certainly with no intention to produce further irritation. We respectfully ask what claim has Mr. DOUGLAS upon the gratitude of the Democracy of the nation which should make the necessity of its recognition superior to the success and existence of the party? Grant, if you please, all that is claimed for him by his warmest admirers, and yet he stands like every other Democrat in this broad land of ours. He has no exclusive privileges. If there are any rights involved, with becoming modesty, those rights belong to the South. Again and again and again, for more than a quarter of a

[1] Andrew Johnson of Tennessee.

century have the South yielded the nomination to the North and have supported with the zeal of devotees during all that time, with but one exception, a Northern man. Is the South because of her minority in the Convention never again to have a Presidential nomination? Her longer exclusion would be both unjust and unwise. Let the Democracy of the free States make their selection among Southern men and we shall be content, or if we must of necessity have a Northern man let those Southern Democrats who adhere to the National Convention indicate who that Northern man shall be. In either event we can pledge an undivided South for the nominee; otherwise, we cannot.

The fact that Mr. Douglas received a bare majority of the electoral vote does not affect the two-thirds rule. He at no time received two-thirds of the votes that were actually cast, and if he had done so, it would not have been just to those Southern Democrats who remained, to take advantage of the action of the Seceders, and force upon those remaining a candidate unacceptable to them. Comparisons among friends are at all times unpleasant; hence we do not intend to institute any. But for the purpose of a correct understanding, let us analyze the vote. Mr. Douglas on four different ballots received 152½ votes. Only 10½ of those votes came from the South.[2] He received only 45½ votes from reliable Northern Democratic States: Rhode Island 4, Connecticut 6, New Jersey 2, Pennsylvania 9½, Illinois 11, Indiana 13; and from those States there were 22½ votes cast against him. So that from these and the remaining reliable Democratic States, including California, Oregon, and the entire South, Mr. Douglas received only 56 votes, or but little over one-sixth of the vote of the convention. While there were cast against him in these reliable Democratic States, the seceding States included, one hundred and thirty-nine votes, or thirteen less than a majority of the whole vote. In the doubtful and positive anti-Democratic States he received 97 of his 152½ votes, or nearly two-thirds of the vote he received was from exceedingly doubtful or positively anti-Democratic States.

We know that Mr. Douglas' friends in the height of their ardor claim as certain for him Maine, New Hampshire, New York, Ohio and the entire Northwest. But we have but one way to judge of the future and that is by the past. We have no disposition to under-rate Mr. Douglas' strength but we ask his zealous supporters that they do not

[2] Eleven and one-half: Maryland 4, Virginia 1, North Carolina 1, Missouri 4½, Tennessee 1.

over-rate it before they, in terms of defiance, nail his flag to the mast. Let us not be unthoughtful of results.

32. [*The Charleston Mercury* AND THE RICHMOND CONVENTION]

(*Richmond Enquirer,* May 18, 1860)

The Charleston "Mercury" misconceiving the reasons that induced the "Enquirer" to request the Richmond Convention to suspend action until after the meeting of the Baltimore Convention, asks us the following question:

"We beg leave respectfully to ask the Richmond "Enquirer," under the action of the Charleston Convention and of the non-seceding Southern delegates in that Convention, can it be reasonably supposed that the Richmond Convention will pause in their action a single hour on account of anything that the Baltimore Convention may do or fail to do?"

In answering our respected contemporary, that we *would have* the Richmond Convention pause and await the action of the Baltimore Convention, we would assign some of the reasons that influence our judgment in giving that advice.

It will not be a matter of any importance whether the nominations to be made at Richmond be precedent or antecedent [*sic*] to the Baltimore Convention, but it will be a matter of very great importance to have the whole South cordially and harmoniously united, upon a platform of principles, and with candidates in whom all confide. It will be found impossible for all the States who concur in the majority report to send delegates to Richmond. The State of Virginia fully and cordially concurs in that platform, and yet the short period of time between the adjournment at Charleston and the 11th of June, will prevent the appointment of delegates; and whether or not those already appointed will meet the Southern States we are unable to say, but whether they do or do not, we wish it distinctly understood, that the Democratic party of Virginia, so far as we have been able to ascertain its sentiments, desires most earnestly to participate in the action of the Southern States.

Virginia may not be represented in the Richmond Convention, and if represented by her present delegates they will not feel themselves competent to concur in nominations made by a Convention other than that to which they have been accredited.

There are other Southern States similarly situated. The time between adjournment at Charleston and the 11th of June, was not sufficient for county meetings, to appoint delegates to a State Convention, without which there could have been no harmony. Virginia, therefore, may be ostracised from the councils of the South by definite action being had in Richmond of the 11th prox.

But should the Richmond Convention when it meets, adopt the majority platform, and then await the action of the Baltimore Convention, the South can be united, either in Baltimore or upon nominations made by delegates from all the Southern States. We feel confident that unless a satisfactory platform is *first* agreed upon at Baltimore, *all* of the Southern States will withdraw.

Should the Richmond Convention nominate a ticket upon the majority platform, and the Baltimore Convention make different nominations, but upon the same platform, much confusion would ensue, and difficulties as embarrassing might arise as any that now beset the party. But by awaiting until the Baltimore Convention has finally acted, all these difficulties may be obviated.

We have also advised the Southern States to send the delegates appointed to the Richmond Convention as delegates to the Baltimore Convention. We advised this not from any desire or hope that they will be satisfied with any platform less than that they demanded at Charleston, but that their voice and influence may aid in obtaining the rights of the South from a united Democracy. We regard the rights of the Southern States as paramount to all parties, and above the advancement of any man; we desire to obtain those rights as a means to preserve this Union; and we believe the best means to secure this end, is for the Southern States once more to meet in the councils of the National Democracy, and make one more effort for justice and right. If that last effort is unsuccessful, the attempt will not be without its benefit; it will have removed all suspicion of factiousness; it will have shown the South as endeavoring by every fair means to preserve the organization of the party, and it will prove that the disruption of the party was made only after every effort at justice and right had twice failed, and when every doubt as to the object and end of a majority of the Convention was removed. By again uniting with the Democracy at Baltimore, all questions of representing or misrepresenting the popular sentiment of the Southern States will be finally settled. No man will doubt that the seceding delegations represented the sentiments of their States if they again appear in Convention, accredited to demand the same platform, and again instructed to withdraw if it be refused.

We have no doubt of this now, but there are many Democrats who have been induced to believe that the Southern States were misrepresented by the seceding delegations. The settlement of even this question will be worth the return of the Southern delegations to Baltimore.

The importance that attaches to the dismemberment of the Democratic party, demands that no slight cause should be allowed to produce consequences so fatal to the Union. The return of the Southern delegations to the Baltimore Convention may secure all the rights of the South and preserve the party in efficiency to protect those rights by success before the people. But by hasty and ill-advised action at Richmond, the rights of the South may not only be imperilled before the people, but would, in our opinion, be destroyed by the success of the Republican Party.

We are at a loss to discover in what way the rights of the South would be imperilled by the Southern delegates meeting at Baltimore, and seeking once more to obtain their rights from a Convention of the National Democracy. We still entertain the hope that some portion of the Northern Democracy will be disposed to do the South full justice when the Convention re-assembles at Baltimore; and with this hope, and unable to see any ill consequences that can result from the re-union of the Southern States, we have advised their return. We are actuated to this from the belief that the National Democracy will not be indifferent to the claim of right and justice, but that the Convention will retrace its fatal steps at Charleston, and will be again united on principle. We desire to preserve the efficiency and organization of the Democratic party, as well as to secure from that party the rights of the South. When convinced that the rights of the South will not be respected by the National Democracy, we shall be among the first to quit the organization, and to look for our preservation to the "might which slumbers in the peasant's arm" throughout the Southern States.

We appeal to the Southern States not to withdraw their voice and influence from the Border Slave States, but to unite again in the councils of the party, and seek that justice which is common alike to the farming as [sic] to the planting slave States. These are some of the reasons that induce us to appeal to the Southern States to "pause" until the Baltimore Convention has acted, and for these reasons we hope the Southern States will reappoint the seceding delegates to Richmond and to Baltimore, and thus carry out the wise advice of the chairman of the Georgia delegation, which felt themselves compelled to withdraw from the Charleston Convention.

33. State of Parties in the Union

(Richmond Semi-weekly Examiner, May 18, 1860)

It is impossible for any observer, however deeply interested, at this time to predict the result of present political movements in the United States. One thing is certain, the crisis is pregnant with such consequences and productive of such excitement that it cannot endure. If pressing difficulties are not overcome by judicious and prompt action, the Gordian knot will be cut by the people. Neither public sentiment nor public interests will admit of protracted discussion, nor procrastinated conflict. Those who have forced this fierce struggle on the people must solve the dangerous enigmas which they have propounded, or they will be speedily dismissed from public position and confidence.— We trust we are in no bad temper towards any party in this Confederacy. Some we certainly condemn with all the sincerity of hostile conviction. Some actions of those to whom we are more friendly we cannot approve, and the evil consequences of those actions we are anxious to avert. But as we are fully convinced that interests, the most vital, are dependent upon the wise action of the contesting parties in the political organization of which we are an humble member, we have endeavored to bring to the consideration of these controversies a calm temper and a liberal spirit. Our view of the proper course to be pursued was given long ago, and very often repeated. It failed to have the effect we desired on many, both in the North and South, who had the destinies of our party, and, we believe, of the country, in their hands. The controversies of the different and contending sections of our party were carried to Charleston, and failed to obtain a satisfactory settlement there. Their decision has been postponed, and the controversialists appeal at no distant day for a final hearing before the most authoritative tribunal known to our polity. The contestants had an appeal to CAESAR, and they have made it. What judgment they will receive we have no authority nor power to predict.

In common with the whole people of the Union, we have a deep interest and as deep a feeling as to the mode and character of this decision. The people have a right to demand a prompt and just decision of those long canvassed and perplexing matters which have produced such distraction in their counsels, and have menaced every interest in the country with dangers so alarming and extensive. Let those who have thrust them upon the country so sternly, and at a time so inauspicious, relieve the community from the anxiety incident to so ominous and perilous a conflict.

The most potent and conservative political engine in this land has been threatened with destruction, and has been paralyzed at least for a time. Around it were clustered the hopes of thousands of citizens whose all was, and is, staked upon the destruction and overthrow of the aggressive sectional majority which is still threatening the most precious rights and interests of the country with oppression and ruin. The time-honored policy of the great Democratic party of the country has been sternly (and, possibly, not very considerately) condemned. It is the duty of those who have undertaken to set aside and supersede this trusted political agency to bring something before the country which shall relieve it from the sharp and trying anxiety this movement has brought upon it. The exigency cannot be ignored. The anxious hopes and reasonable fears of an endangered people demand and are entitled to an explicit and prompt relief.

The enemies of the Constitution and the assailants of the rights and property of the South have possession of the largest and most potent branch of the legislature of the country. They have the control of the local legislatures and recognized authorities in a majority of the States of this Confederacy. By the action of those who have paralyzed the Democracy, they have now at their command the most efficient and best disciplined, as well as numerically the strongest popular political organization in the Union. The Democracy and the Black Republicans were, a few weeks since, the solitary stable partizan organizations existing in this Union with power to direct the legislation and political action of the Confederacy. The Black Republican party is still existing, and existing in full vigor and vitality. Where is the Democratic party, and what is its condition? Virginia and a few large slaveholding States in the Union have secured to that party a short space for consideration—an opportunity for concentrating its distracted energies and girding itself for its last and most decisive battle in defense of right, justice, and the Constitution and Union of these States. Who have the power to reunite and strengthen that mighty political power? Two portions of the country have at their command the means of arraying, disciplining and leading that great popular agency to a victory more decisive and beneficial than it has yet won.

The Northern States have a deeper interest in this conflict than any portion of the people of the Union. They have a stronger reason for removing distracting questions that afflict this organization than any others. Let this conservative organization be broken, and they and theirs are in the hands of the Philistines. They and their property are given over to a power which hates peace and revels and lives in constant revolution and disturbance.

What concession is demanded of them now? Is there any they cannot grant? We think not. We admit that the pressure of such demands as have been made upon them was not required by any exigency, even by any real necessity. But let them remember that the people who are struggling with them against their aggressors in the North have been robbed, pillaged and insulted in this Union by free State majorities.— That not only their rights of property, but their property itself, are subjects of constant and open and extensive spoliation. They cannot wonder that people so circumstanced and so wronged should be very jealous, and even over-exacting in demanding the fullest acknowledgment of their rights. The demands may be pressed unwisely and needlessly, but much must be granted to a wronged and persecuted people.

The South has not now, or at any time, demanded anything more than an acknowledgment of what it, and most conservative men in the United States, consider an established right.—Such demands should not be refused on slight grounds at any time, and certainly not when such refusal ensures the triumph of a corrupt and tyrannous party.

There is another party which can reunite the Democracy and secure the defeat of the Freesoilers. The Southern seceding Democrats may again rally the popular party of the Union, and secure a triumph over the enemies of the Constitution and their section. They have made, unwisely in our judgment, a needless issue with those whose aid is essential to the maintenance of the sole power which can prevent the actual existing government of these States from being administered to the loss and damage of Southern rights and property. The action of Virginia and other border slave States has secured them an opportuniy of again fighting for their rights and the Constitution inside of the Democratic organization. Pride of opinion may keep weak men or passionate men in a state of antagonism to this party. But patriotism and every incentive of interest, as well as mandate of duty, would seem to urge a combination with the conservative Democratic elements in the next Presidential canvass. How they will accomplish this great and patriotic result, we have no right to advise or press upon them. But we, and the people of the frontier slave States, who are to feel the first and most severe effects of civil commotion and an anti-slavery war, have a right to ask that their condition should be considered and their fortunes regarded. The union of these States with the other slaveholding States is no matter of doubt, no question of probability. The State of Virginia is bound by every social, political and moral bond to the other slave States of this Confederacy. Their fortunes cannot be sundered. This largest and leading slave State has striven, and is still striving, to protect and defend the rights and property of her sister States in the Union. She has appealed to the conservative men of both sections to make one more effort to overthrow the fanatical and corrupt hordes, who are striving to make the Government and the Union "a den of thieves."—Will the men of the South reject her counsels and· contemn her appeal in this their hour of extremity? We trust not. We hope to see the Baltimore Convention solve these perplexing difficulties. With the aid of the patriotism, wisdom and power of the whole slaveholding States, we are confident that such a result can be achieved.

34. THE CHICAGO NOMINATION

(*The New Orleans Bee,* May 21, 1860)

The action of the Black Republican Convention on the Presidential question has confirmed singularly and opportunely the remarks made in our last issue on the influence of conservative views upon the party politics of the day. The Democratic National Convention tacitly acknowledged this influence by strenuously resisting, even to a partial disruption of its strength, the efforts of the extreme South to force upon it the recognition and endorsement of a sectional platform. It was likewise felt in the conduct of the Union Convention, which contented itself by simply proclaiming obedience to the Constitution and the laws as the test and touchstone of political fealty. Finally, the Black Republicans of Chicago, although avowedly a sectional faction, based upon a single prominent idea—that of the limitation of slavery—have been so directly subjected to the same potent agency as to promulgate a programme of principles which, with few exceptions, would apply quite as readily to one portion of the country as another. Instead of breathing hatred and persecution against the South—instead of classing slavery with polygamy, and resolving upon the annihilation of both as twin relics of barbarism, the Black Republicans denounce forays like that of JOHN BROWN in emphatic language, disclaim the slightest intention of interfering with the institutions of the South, and confine the assertion of their peculiar tenets to the denial of the duty of Congress to protect slavery, and to the expression of an opinion in favor of the immediate admission of Kansas into the Union. These are striking evidences of the power of popular sentiment in moderating the frantic zeal of faction.

It is, however, in the choice of a Presidential candidate that the Black Republicans have furnished a signal manifestation of their determination to avoid extremes. Having before them WM. H. SEWARD, beyond all doubt the AJAX TELAMON of the party; the man who gave it being and breath; who nurtured its sickly infancy and fostered it with earnest solicitude until it attained its present formidable proportions; who dared boldly and bravely in the face of an assembled multitude to avow its ultimate purposes; who originated the axiom of the existence of an irrepressible conflict between slavery and freedom; who is the head and front of Black Republicanism; who in the United States Senate is ever its cool, watchful, wary, sagacious, bland, keen and indefatigable advocate; who, in fine, by his talent, his position, his high standing, and his prolonged services has ever been deemed pre-eminently worthy the most exalted honors his party can bestow, they have thrust him aside to make room for ABRAHAM LINCOLN, of Illinois. In thus acting, Black Republicanism has evinced base ingratitude, but crafty and prudent policy. It has treated its founder most vilely, but it has added materially to its own prospects of success.

We predicted long ago the defeat of SEWARD in the Chicago Convention. We saw that he was opposed by two redoubtable antagonists— first, the conservative element of his party, and next, the power and influence of the West. The former combated his claims because his candidature would frighten off all who were not fully committed to the ultra doctrines of the party. The latter considered that he was decidedly weak in the West, and could not carry any of the doubtful States. The two influences combined proved sufficient to effect his overthrow. But the Chicago Convention did not complete its work when it eliminated SEWARD. The subsequent nomination of LINCOLN was a master stroke of political craft. Mr. LINCOLN belongs to the moderate wing of the Black Republicans. He was formerly a Whig member of Congress, and then but slightly tinctured with anti-slavery notions. On the dissolution of the Whig party, he joined the ranks of the Black Republicans, and took a prominent position in that party. He rendered himself particularly conspicuous by the zeal and ability he displayed in the canvass last year for U. S. Senator from Illinois, when he and DOUGLAS traveled throughout the State, addressing the people alternately. Although DOUGLAS triumphed, he had confessedly in LINCOLN a foeman worthy of his steel, and ever since that memorable struggle the Black Republican sheets of the West and Northwest have placed LINCOLN on the list of aspirants for the Chicago nomination. He is a man of agreeable manners, a ready and forcible speaker, self-made and self-taught, and personally popular among the hardy sons of the West.

Another controlling motive for the choice of the Convention is to be found in local influence. The Black Republicans know that the doubtful States are Pennsylvania, Illinois and Indiana. SEWARD would have been beaten thirty thousand votes in the first, and could not possibly have carried either of the others. LINCOLN will undoubtedly prove a powerful candidate in Illinois and Indiana, and will run in Pennsylvania at least as well as any other Black Republican. His strength, in short, is in the debatable States. Anbody can receive the electoral votes of Massachusetts and Vermont, while New York would not be more certain for SEWARD than for LINCOLN; but there are votes which must be had to secure the success of the candidate, and those votes are cast precisely by those States where LINCOLN is best known and most popular. Hence his nomination. We regard him as a formidable competitor for the Presidency, and as at present advised, we consider that should the Democrats reunite at Baltimore, the nomination of LINCOLN will impose on them the necessity of looking to the West for an opponent. We should not be surprised to see DOUGLAS pitted once more upon a broader field against his ancient foe.

35. THE RICHMOND ENQUIRER AND THE RICHMOND CONVENTION

(*The Charleston Mercury,* May 23, 1860)

The Richmond *Enquirer* persists in its counsel, that the Richmond Convention shall await the action of the Baltimore Convention. One reason for this counsel is, that there is not time for sending Delegates to the Richmond Convention by the 11th of June, when the Richmond Convention is to meet; and yet, in the very columns of its editorial, there is the report of a meeting of the people in Barbour county, held on the 10th May, requesting their Delegates to the Charleston Convention to attend the Richmond Convention, "to participate in such *preparatory* action as may be deemed advisable in *advance* of the meeting of the Convention at *Baltimore.*" Could not the people of Barbour county, in the Northwest of Virginia, have, on this occasion, appointed Delegates to the Richmond Convention? and cannot the people of Virginia, by one month later, send Delegates, if they think proper, to this Convention? We cannot doubt it. The instructions of the people of Barbour county, to their Delegates of the Baltimore Convention show the reason they do not act. It is not for want of time, but of disposition.

Another objection urged by our contemporary against the independent action of the Richmond Convention, is, that after nominating for the Presidency a man true to the South at Richmond, the Baltimore Convention may nominate another, and thus the South will be divided between two candidates equally faithful to the South.

We think the *Enquirer* may dismiss from its patriotic anxieties all such romantic anticipations. The Squatter Sovereignty element—domineering in Charleston—will by no means be weaker in Baltimore from the new recruits invited into it from the South, by the Virginia delegation, and the nomination of Mr. LINCOLN, of Illinois, as the Presidential candidate of the Black Republicans. No man can be nominated at Baltimore *faithful to himself, and on a platform faithful to the rights of the South;* but if such an event takes place, the *Enquirer* may be assured that there will be no division in the South in supporting him. If the Baltimore Convention will not nominate the candidate of the Richmond Convention, nothing is easier than to withdraw the Richmond candidate. The same fidelity to the rights of the South which will have occasioned his nomination, will commend his withdrawal from the canvass; whilst his nomination at Richmond will *go further than any other course* to produce the nomination of a proper candidate at Baltimore.

As an inducement for the Richmond Convention to wait on the Baltimore Convention, the *Enquirer* says: "We feel confident that, unless a satisfactory platform is *first* agreed upon at Baltimore, all of the Southern States will withdraw."

Now, perhaps, our contemporary does not know that the platform adopted by the Charleston Convention was followed by a motion to reconsider, and this motion was laid on the table. The matter of the platform is thus, according to the parliamentary rules adopted by the Convention, *incapable of further consideration.* No propositions with respect to it can be entertained by the Convention, but by *unanimous* consent. The Convention, then, after thus settling its platform, went into a ballot for the nomination of a Presidential candidate to represent it. This is the order of the Convention when it adjourned, and must be renewed when the Convention meets at Baltimore. Now, is there the ghost of a chance that the DOUGLAS delegates will *unanimously* assent that the balloting shall cease, and that the platform adopted, which is just as they want it to be, shall be revised and changed? The *Enquirer's* buoyant faith says, yes!

But if all the DOUGLAS Delegates were unanimously to consent that the platform shall be revised to suit the rejected demands of the seceding Delegates, is it probable that *"a satisfactory platform"* will be adopted by the Baltimore Convention? It is a part of the history of the Charleston Convention, that a platform may be perfectly *satisfactory* to Virginia, Tennessee and Kentucky, but not at all *satisfactory* to Alabama, Mississippi and South Carolina. The Richmond *Enquirer,* with great force, has shown that the Tennessee Resolution, declared in the Charleston Convention as "the *ultimatum* of the South," to which the former States assented, is utterly inadequate and fallacious as regards the rights of the South. Now, what security have the Cotton States that anything better will be offered by the Baltimore Convention? We cannot expect the Freesoil States, to grant more than the Southern States shall demand. Would not the seceding States only go into the Baltimore Convention, to be cheated by words, or be compelled to withdraw again? And if they withdrew on a platform which Virginia, Tennessee and Kentucky affirms to be "satisfactory," how can these States withdraw with them, from the Baltimore Convention? They could not, and would not withdraw; and if the Cotton States withdrew, there would be an angry contest and division raised in the South itself—the *very thing the enemies of the South would desire to produce.* For such a purpose, we doubt not the Northern delegates in the Baltimore Convention might consent to any alteration in their platform, which, whilst it leaves them free on the hustings and in Congress, to advocate and enforce their policy of Squatter Sovereignty, would paralyse the South by divisions. We frankly say to the *Enquirer,* that although he may "feel confident," we do not—that the Baltimore Convention will agree upon a platform *satisfactory to the Cotton States*—and that, if it is not satisfactory to *them,* that "all the Southern States will withdraw." The Convention will agree to a platform satisfactory to the *Frontier States,* and they will not withdraw from the Baltimore Convention. In our judgment, the worst thing which can befall the South, is bickerings and contests amongst ourselves. The union of the Democratic party, demoralized as it is, into an organization hostile to the South, is of little moment, compared with the union of the South. If the seceding States in the Richmond Convention act in subordination to the Baltimore Convention, they will be cheated and disgraced; or the South must be enfeebled by exasperated divisions. Now, there is division on a mere matter of policy. The Frontier States remain in the Baltimore Convention, hoping to have the rights of the South yet acknowledged by that Convention. The Cotton States have tried fairly and patiently to have them acknowledged by the Charleston Convention, and, despairing of any agreement upon the essential rights of the South, they have seceded, and now call another Convention to enforce them. Let both parties of the South, without collision, pursue their respective courses, to maintain the rights of the South. If agreeing in principle, they will soon agree in policy. The course of consistency, dignity, and peace, it appears to us, requires that the seceding States shall carry out their purposes at Richmond, without any regard whatever to the Baltimore Convention.

36. THE WASHINGTON ABORTION

(*Daily Chronicle and Sentinel,* Augusta, May 24, 1860)

There was a wailing, a cry of anguish, startling the night, and the doctors were called. When the great party died at Charleston beyond hope of resurrection, the doctors in Washington city began the work to galvanize the body into new life. They labored night and day, for many days and nights together, and reports flew thick and fast all over the land, of the remarkable efforts they were making, and the great success which would probably crown their labors. Day after day the Telegraph informed us of the all-healing address which was to be issued from headquarters to call the "wandering sinners home." The worthies labored sorely, and after great travail we have at last The Address. A miserable, abortive failure it is, and its parents will scarcely own it. It fell still-born everywhere, and the patient, long-suffering public acknowledges itself *sold*.

This address, which we shall preserve for our curiosity shop, after all the drumming and persuasion that could be brought to bear, has received the signatures of eighteen members and Senators, and of one *myth* J. R. Morrison. It calls upon the seceding delegates, to go back to the Baltimore Convention, to make one more effort to obtain the right platform, and holds out a delusive hope that such may be obtained. These immortal signers were perhaps influenced by a sincere desire to restore harmony, and to revivify the dead body—perhaps not. We think it more probable that they considered it *good policy* to pretend such a thing, for they ought to know that it can never be accomplished. What these gentlemen would consider a *good platform* we do not positively know, and very likely they could not agree themselves. It is probable that the two Senators from Virginia, the two from Arkansas, Senator SLIDELL, Senator TOOMBS, and Representatives GARNETT, REAGAN, LOVE and JONES, would accept the New York-Tennessee resolution—the remaining signers would possibly insist upon the Charleston majority platform.

There is no possible chance for re-union and harmony as proposed, and doubtless many of those who signed the address felt satisfied of the fact. If the seceding delegates were not actuated by a determination to sustain sound principles, which we will not charge, they *know* that they have ruined themselves if they do not now insist upon them. But in the first place, many of the seceding delegates *will not* go back to Baltimore, upon any sort of Congressional assurances, because they feel it would be a humiliation, because they believe the door is closed, and there is no chance to re-open the platform question so as to be allowed to get their principles again before the Convention. In the next place, if willing to go back, it is very doubtful whether the Convention would allow them, for it requested the States to supply vacancies on account of this secession, and the train-bands of DOUGLAS are already at work in the seceding States, under orders from the "Little Squatter," to fill these vacancies with his tools. But they will have to send *bogus* delegates from Geogria, and the other seceding States, for it is now reduced to a dead certainty that the Milledgeville Convention will send no DOUGLAS delegate to Baltimore. His adherents will have to get up a Rump Convention if *they* send any delegates from Georgia.

Admitting, however, that the seceding delegates return, that they are received, and that the platform question is reconsidered, which, according to parliamentary law, cannot be done, what change is to be made in the Charleston platform? Suppose the South accept the New York resolution, that is not acceptable to Mr. DOUGLAS and Mr. STEPHENS; and the *Constitutionalist* says:

"Let none deceive themselves with the hope of concession from the North, for the New York resolutions, which the Chairman of the Georgia delegation refers to, were not the voice of the State delegation, and the Virginia ultimatum was the Tennessee resolution which was let die unnoticed. We think that *compromise and argument was exhausted at Charleston.*"

So, if the South should consent to accept the resolution the Douglasites will not give it to her, though they might very well afford to do it for the sake of the nominee; because that resolution does not meet the issue, and even under it, there still remains the position of Judge DOUGLAS, and of Mr. STEPHENS too, that slavery is *solely dependent upon the local law,* and that simple non-action on the part of the Territories would legally *free the slave,* because he is *free* everywhere except where the *law enslaves him.* But Judge DOUGLAS, who has declared "the people of a Territory, while in a territorial condition, have the inherent power and right, through their Legislature, to exclude slavery by positive enactment," has, last week in the Senate, made his declaration of war against the South and seceders, holding that he and his positions have been endorsed by a majority of the Charleston Convention, and he never will surrender, and he is backed up by many powerful names in Georgia and the South, including JOHNSON,[1] STEPHENS, FORSYTH, CLINGMAN [2] & Co.

There then seems little hope of even the passage of the New York resolution; but, were it passed, will the seceding delegates accept it? We believe some few of them would, but as it is manifestly a cheat and a humbug and has been denounced as such by the Richmond *Enquirer,* the Charleston *Mercury,* Mr. YANCEY and others, it *will not* be accepted if tendered. A majority of the Constitutional Democracy will insist on the majority platform, and they will be backed, before the adjourned Convention meets, by the substantial endorsement, *by vote under oath,* of *all* the Democratic Senators save two or three, or four at most. Can the majority platform be passed at Baltimore? The signers of the address hold out a hope of that kind, on the ground that there was a majority of delegates in the Charleston Convention for it, (or at least for something better suited to this market than the minority platform,) if they had only been allowed to vote *per capita.* Well, how is this to be remedied at Baltimore? If the seceding delegates return they will stand as before, and the *rule of the Convention* will remain as before, which provides only that the vote of those States be cast as a unit, whose State Convention instructed, requested, or *provided* for such action. Can the rule be reversed, and every delegate allowed to cast his vote as he pleases? Not without the consent of DOUGLAS and his friends. There were only two States (Georgia and New Jersey,) which had any difficulty at Charleston on this point. New Jersey was allowed by the Convention to divide her vote—so a change of the rule will not affect her. Pennsylvania was not trammeled at all. The DOUGLAS men would vote

---

[1] Herschel V. Johnson of Georgia.
[2] Thomas L. Clingman, Non-Interventionist Senator from North Carolina, 1847–1861.

for Georgia to divide her vote, but that, with the same delegates, only makes against the majority platform. The difficulty then will be only in New York and Indiana, and is anybody so superlatively foolish as to suppose that the DOUGLAS men (in a clear majority) will rescind the rule, even if it could be reached by parliamentary usage, in face of the declaration that a part of the New York delegates will abandon him if they can, but who are now bound to him by the unit rule?

Suppose, although it is not a supposable case, that the majority platform be adopted at Baltimore, what then? Why a secession of the North instead of the South; because the DOUGLAS men never will surrender, and Senator PUGH has lately said in his place that "he did not think a single delegate from Ohio, or even a *Democrat* in the State, would have voted for the majority platform." [3] This is the spirit of the Squatter Sovereignty men of the North.

So then it is an utterly futile and hopeless task to re-organize, re-unite and harmonize the disintegrated Democratic party, unless this is to be done by a total abandonment of all principle, for the sake of plunder, and that, under existing circumstances must *insure* a Waterloo defeat. No, sensible people might as well make up their minds to the fact that the Democratic party is dissolved forever, that new organizations must take place, and that henceforth, till the final decisive battle, there are three great parties in the country. Those who agree in principle, must and will unite in effective organization. The Republicans, at least during this campaign, maintaining their prohibitory dogma and their revolutionary tendencies, will fight a hard battle. Those who maintain the dangerous heresy, call it whatsoever specious name you will—non-intervention, Squatter Sovereignty, or Popular Sovereignty—that the people of the organized Territories are sovereign to exclude slavery, and by non-action, unfriendly legislation, or positive Territorial statute, to destroy or impair the rights of the Southern emigrant in and to his *lawful property,* and that the Federal Government has no power to protect the citizen against such illegal confiscation, will rally to the call of the Little Giant of the Northwest. And those who oppose both these organizations, their dogmas, their aims and tendencies, and who seek to perpetuate the union of these States by maintaining the rights of each sovereignty, and the equality of all citizens, will constitute the great Constitutional party of the country.

The first is entirely a sectional organization, having scarcely a name South of Mason & Dixon's line, and its leading dogma can never again

[3] *Cong. Globe,* 36 Cong., 1 Sess., III, 1968.

be law, until the "final analysis of Liberty" be reached. The second is also a sectional organization, having the same aims as the first, and what is alarming, having an organization powerful in character and ability, but not numerically strong, in our own midst. Both are public enemies, and their existence is a standing threat against the peace of the country, the constitutional rights of a minority, and the perpetuity of the government itself. They must be defeated; and first, the war must commence against those who are among us and of us. Then unfurl our banner, stand firmly by the right and the Constitution, yield not an inch, crush out the advocates of inequality at home, and call upon the true, the faithful, the constitutional, the fraternal everywhere, to stand with us by the *written law,* and we must eventually prevail.

37. LINCOLN AND DOUGLAS

(*Daily Courier,* Louisville, May 26, 1860)

Mr. Lincoln has accepted the Presidential nomination tendered him by the Black Republicans. Whatever may be the result of future Conventions held by other parties, we know now who is to lead on the formidable, well-drilled, and hopeful hosts of the main body of those who are warring upon the institution of slavery. The "irrepressible conflict," despite our wishes, our hopes, our struggles to arrest or postpone it, is now upon us. A million and a half of votes, controlled and managed by able, adroit, ambitious, and, in too many instances, unprincipled leaders, flushed with the prospects of victory, animated by the hope of immediate reward, all united in one compact and thorough political organization, are now in the field. Their success must be secured by the cooperation and united exertion of the friends of the institution of slavery, of those who will stand by the Constitutional rights of all sections, of the true patriots North and South who will abide by the compact our fathers made, of all who would perpetuate the Federal Union, preserve the liberties of the people, and maintain the independence of the States.

We may regret it, we may wilfully shut our eyes to the fact, we may be deaf, if we can, to the mutterings of the coming storm, but we had as well attempt by deprecatory appeals to the elements to change the course of the hurricane or to still the rage of the winds as to try to evade the issue tendered us, to pretermit its discussion or to escape its consequences. Neither is it the part of wisdom, of patriotism, of honor, nor of safety. The minor wing of the Opposition, not a party, without an organization, destitute of a hope, its future not penetrated by one ray of light, feeble, fickle, changeable as the moon, may claim that the "solution of the slavery question cannot be reached by popular agitation," that "parties cannot honestly agree respecting it," that "the people cannot," and thus found a pretext for "pretermitting" any expression of opinion on this absorbing, controlling, "irrepressible issue." But the conflict yet goes on. The major wing of the Opposition, struggling for power, with the control of the Government almost in its reach, catering to the passions and to the prejudices of the ignorant, feeding the fires of fanaticism and madness, with the Constitution, fraternity, and equality on their lips, are pressing on to the extinguishment of slavery, though to reach this end it be necessary to trample under foot the Constitution, to invade the sovereignty of the States, to violate the rights of individuals, to dissolve the Union, to inaugurate strife, anarchy, and civil war.

If the friends of the South, of the Constitution, of the American Union, of civil and religious liberty, will consent to immolate their prejudices, their preferences, their individual opinions on matters of lesser importance on the altar of patriotism, and agree to unite against a common enemy for the common good, Black Republicanism may be overthrown, the sectionalists may be defeated, and the consequences of the triumph of the party of which Mr. Lincoln is the representative and leader, from the contemplation of which the mind shrinks appalled, may be averted. This cannot be done by cowardly attempts at evasion, by concessions, by abandement [sic] of principle, and by a surrender of rights. It may be all wrong, useless, even dangerous, for the masses to "agitate" any question about which they cannot agree. It might be better if the people would consent to give up the consideration of questions affecting their interests or their rights, and leave all such matters to the superior judgment and greater patriotism of such statesmen as Bell and Everett, as modestly proposed by the Louisville Journal; but the Black Republicans will not give up their capital, and the men of the South will not give up their rights and abandon their principles—the one will not submit their pretentions, nor the other their honor and safety, to the arbitrament even of statesmen and patriots whose antecedents cannot be any guarantee to either party to the controversy, and whose present position might justly subject them to suspicion. On one hand is the Black Republican party, on the other is all those who will maintain at all hazards and to any extent the Constitutional rights of the citizens of the slaveholding States. No pretermitting of opinions, no evasions, no dodge, will relieve parties, factions, organizations, or individuals from the responsibility of determining what those rights are; and when this point is settled, the only other question is, whether they shall be guaranteed or withheld. In such a contest, involving such interests, there can be no neutrality. Every freeman must array himself upon one side or the other.

Mr. Lincoln is the candidate of the Black Republicans. In his behalf a thousand presses are laboring, and to bring about his election forces are being drilled, means and munitions of war collected, and all the appliances, ordinary and extraordinary, known to politicians are being brought into requisition. The only course consistent with the honor and dignity of the threatened States, the only hope of safety, is to meet the issue presented at Chicago, frankly, squarely, and unequivocally, and to make an honest and manly appeal to the intelligence, the good sense, the interest, and the patriotism of the country. Any other course must not only lead to defeat, but would entail dishonor.

Mr. Lincoln is before us. How is he to be opposed? "Shall Mr. Douglas be nominated, who only differs from Mr. Lincoln as to *which* has the power to exclude a portion of the citizens of the United States from all the advantages of emigration to the new Territories, Congress or the inchoate people? Both acknowledge the theory or false premise of anti-slavery, viz: that negro subordination, or so-called slavery, cannot exist without positive enactment—that it is created by municipal regulation or the *lex loci,* hence that it is not a thing existing in nature, but unnatural, and if so, it must be wrong—an evil, and then follows all the logical sequences of the anti-slaveryites, even down to John Brownism. What sort of a fight can we make with an adversary while we allow his premises? If Mr. Lincoln believes that "slavery is an evil," we do not see how he could consistently be less an anti-slavery man than he is, for he declares he would vote for a Fugitive Slave Law, and for every other right which he believed the South entitled to under the Constitution, though it conflicted never so much with his own prejudices. He even goes so far as to say in one of his speeches (and he drives this point home upon Mr. Douglas with tremendous power) that if he believed that the Dred Scott decision properly construed the Constitution, and that Southern men had the right to take their "slaves" into the new Territories in defiance of the will of Congress, he would not only favor it, but he would, if in Congress, vote to enact such laws for the protection of slave property in the Territories as to make the right practical. He says he thinks he would be no less than a perjured man, after taking the oath to support the Constitution, if he believed, as Mr. Douglas does, that Southern men had the right to go into a Territory with their "slaves," and then he should refuse to vote for such laws as would give vitality to that right. We know that such sentiments as these will not fail to command respect even from Mr. Lincoln's opponents, and we are free to confess that we know of no arguments with which to oppose them, except to strike at the very foundation of the whole superstructure of fraud and delusion which anti-slaveryism has erected. Mr. Lincoln's doctrines are the most subtle and dangerous form of anti-slaveryism, and if we do not have a candidate who is opposed to them, why, there can in reality be no fight. True, we may have a sham battle to determine who is to have the offices and the emoluments; but we shall not be a whit nearer settling disputed principles. Men of sense, who never fight except when they are in earnest, we feel sure, can have no stomach for such a Presidential contest, and they will either look on, or retire from the field in disgust. To nominate Douglas is at once and in advance to give up the fight.

38. POLITICAL PROBABILITIES

(*The New Orleans Bee,* May 30, 1860)

In estimating the probabilities of a reunion of the divided segments of the Democracy, it is important to bear in mind several important facts. There is a double dissension pervading the ranks—one arising from a difference of principle, the other having reference to personal animosities. With respect to the first, it is well understood that for some years a small, but not utterly uninfluential, band of Southern Democrats have assumed extreme opinions on the slavery question, and have steadily required from the Democracy such acknowledgments of doctrine as could not be reasonably expected. In default of these concessions, this faction has invariably threatened rebellion and disorganization. Latterly the numerical feebleness of the ultra wing has been considerably strengthened by accessions from the ranks of the Southern Democracy—so much so, indeed, that at the meeting of the Charleston Convention they proclaimed their immutable adherence to a platform embodying their views, and when the decision of the majority was announced against them they threw up their commissions and bolted. This political faction is composed of two distinct elements—one revolutionary and radical, the other more moderate and less exacting. The one will accept nothing short of the formal recognition of its principles; the other would be contented with a compromise. One would infinitely rather break up the Democratic party than surrender a jot or tittle of its demands; the other would be willing to yield something for the sake of harmony, a united party, and the prospect of a triumph. It is evident, therefore, that in the existing schism, the radical element may be expected to reject all overtures of reconciliation unless accompanied by the explicit recognition of its creed, while the conservative element will strain every effort to get back to the Convention, or so to influence its counsels as to afford a decent pretext for patching up a peace. We may consequently expect that unless the Baltimore Convention should give way, and surrender at discretion to the Seceders, a portion of them, probably confined to the States of South Carolina, Mississippi, Texas, and possibly Arkansas, will maintain their independent attitude, and place in nomination those who may be considered the most fitting exponents of their political faith. We may add that this fraction of the Seceders desire probably in their secret souls that the feud should remain unhealed, as they are at heart disunionists, and conceive that the disintegration of the Democratic party would be an infallible initiative to the wished-for consummation.

Should, however, such a contingency be possible as the settlement of the question of the platform, there lies behind another fruitful source of discord, another *teterrima causa belli*. It is the question of men. The North, in a great measure, and a part at least of the South, have declared in emphatic terms their preference for DOUGLAS. The Seceders, together with a number of those who refused to abandon the Convention, are inflexibly opposed to him. The quarrel has assumed proportions far beyond the mere personal rivalry of two or more favorite candidates. The advocates and the opponents of DOUGLAS assail each other with inconceivable fury and spite. They wage against one another a more deadly warfare than against Black Republicanism. In fact the mutual hatred and malignant recrimination have gone so far that, with all our experience of Democratic elasticity, we are unable to perceive how either wing would tolerate the triumph of the other. Suppose for instance that DOUGLAS should be nominated by the Baltimore Convention, we have not the shadow of a doubt that his violent Democratic adversaries, especially in the South, would endeavor to ruin his chance of success, by starting another candidate. Suppose DOUGLAS to be rejected by the Convention. It appears to us equally certain that his ardent friends would run him as an independent nominee in every

State where they possess sufficient strength to get up an electoral ticket. There would indeed be one way of cutting the Gordian knot, viz: for Senator Douglas to withdraw from the contest; but this, we fancy, he feels little inclined to do, since he is the unquestionable choice of a majority of the Democratic party; and besides if he were magnanimous enough to desire to immolate himself for the sake of the party, we apprehend that his leaders would not suffer him to commit political suicide.

Thus we are compelled to acknowledge that the Democratic party is in a dangerous and perplexing situation, with but a gloomy prospect of extrication from its embarrassments. The schism at Charleston, whether preconcerted or not, has proved a fatal error. It has engendered a world of strife and ill-feeling utterly inimical to any cordial reconciliation hereafter. The very fact of the existence of so terrible a split is the most convincing evidence of the progressive denationalization of the Democracy. Sectionalism has corrupted it and destroyed its cohesiveness. Even the attractions of power and office are incapable of resisting the centrifugal influences of Northern fanaticism and Southern sectionalism. Everybody with half an eye can behold these influences at work. Why, even in the Senate of the United States we have Douglas attacking Davis and defending himself, and Davis and Benjamin [1] abusing Douglas and his doctrines, and Pugh vindicating the Little Giant. In other words, Democrats, men professing to belong to the same party, are squabbling over theories, and angrily denouncing one another as recreant to Democratic principles. From all of which the impartial reader will wisely conclude that there can be no homogeneity of principle among them. If, with so formidable a foe in the field, Democracy cannot heal its dissensions, but must needs enfeeble itself by intestine strife, does it not demonstrate how wholly unworthy it is of the confidence of the country.

We believe, nevertheless, that there is a national and Union sentiment among the people which will finally crush out brawling faction. We hold with a Northern journal that the political party which, in the present Presidential contest, places itself in harmony with this rising sentiment of national life, will be the one that will secure predominance during this generation, just as Jeffersonian republicanism and Jacksonian democracy, respectively, secured it during the past sixty years. The leaders of the Democratic organization might effect this

---

[1] Judah P. Benjamin, Whig Senator from Louisiana, 1853–1859; Conservative Senator, 1859–1861.

glorious object, but have they enough of intrinsic vigor and strength, enough of self-sacrificing spirit, to throw aside abstractions, bury their personal quarrels, stick to a national platform, and bring forward a national man?

39. HARMONIZE THE DEMOCRACY

(Richmond Semi-weekly Examiner, June 1, 1860)

From the general tone of the Democratic press, and the proceedings of numerous public meetings throughout the country, there is manifested the most earnest and patriotic desire for the re-establishment of harmony in the ranks of the Democracy. This is as it should be, and, to hopeful minds, is a sure augury that the great party which has so long battled successfully for the Constitution and for State Rights will not now disband in face of danger more threatening to the true principles of republican government, and to the future peace of the Confederacy, than it has heretofore encountered. Under whatever specious disguise, or artful concealment of their real designs, the Black Republicans have taken the field in the approaching Presidential contest, it is obvious from their newspapers, their platforms at various times, and the speeches of their representative men, that their policy is as subversive of the true character of the Government, as the style of their speeches and writings is insulting to the people of the South, upon whose rights and feelings it is their special mission to make war. With such an enemy in front, already marshalled for the struggle which is to be decisive of the fate of the sacred compact of Union, and perhaps also of the Union itself, it would be nothing less than a national calamity for the Democratic party to break up and scatter its forces. How the opposing elements into which the Charleston Convention dissolved are to be reconciled, is a question of difficult solution. How they cannot be, seems to us obvious enough, and the present crisis in the fortunes of the Democracy imposes a most serious responsibility upon the Convention of seceders which assembles in Richmond on the 11th inst.

Harmony cannot be restored if that Convention should insist upon engrafting the doctrine of Congressional intervention in Territorial matters upon the national platform; nor if it should proceed to nominate a ticket (without regard to the probable action of the adjourned Convention to meet in Baltimore on the 18th) embodying the extreme views of Mr. YANCEY and his followers; much less, should it also sympathize with that gentleman's known hostility to the Union, and with the policy of re-opening the African slave trade. We go as far as the farthest in asserting the constitutional rights of the South on all proper occasions, and whenever a reasonable prospect appears of doing so successfully. But we are not willing, at a time when there is no absolute necessity therefor, and no practical good to result therefrom, to take a position that, however just, is for the time untenable, except at a cost greater than the value of the thing sought to be attained. We are equally averse to proclaim as an indispensable condition to future co-operation with the Northern Democracy, the present assertion in the party platform of principles which can have no application to the existing state of affairs. The all sufficient reason for this position on our part is, that if the opposite be taken, consistency would compel us to maintain it not only to the irreparable disruption of the Democratic party, in case the demands were rejected, but pursuing principles to their ultimate consequences, even to a dissolution of the Union, should the occasion arise for their application and the government failed to make it. We trust, therefore, that a spirit of wise moderation will rule the counsels of the Richmond Convention—that they will studiously abstain from every act and declaration calculated to widen the breach between themselves and the non-seceding portion of the Charleston Convention—and as one step in the right direction, that they will not nominate a ticket until after the Baltimore Convention shall have met and acted. We, moreover, respectfully suggest that all those whose official connection with the National Convention at Charleston was not dissolved by their acting under instructions from their State Conventions, adjourn from Richmond to Baltimore, and unite with the delegates there in restoring harmony, by forbearing to press extreme measures upon the Convention, and by patriotically sacrificing personal predilections and prejudices to the one great end of preserving the national character of the Democratic party, and bringing out a ticket that can beat the Black Republicans.

40. THE ADDRESS OF NINETEEN MEMBERS OF CONGRESS

(Richmond Semi-weekly Examiner, June 1, 1860)

Nineteen members of Congress (says the Charleston *Mercury*) out of seventy or eighty, from the South, have put out the address which we publish in our columns to-day. It purports to be addressed to "the National Democracy;" but, in reality, it is addressed to the seceding delegates from the Charleston Convention. It proposes to the seceding delegates that they shall

return to the adjourned Convention to meet at Baltimore, and shall abandon
the Richmond Convention.

*   *   *

The proposition, in our judgment, is as insulting as it is impertinent. It is
not only a proposition to eat up their words, but to swallow themselves, and
to leave nothing behind them but the stench of disgrace and infamy. How
honorable men could make such a proposition to others, is only possible, we
suppose, in the reeking atmosphere of Washington.

But the proposition is not only insulting; it is impossible in performance.
These gentlemen must know that in two States, at least, the contingency of
their delegates leaving the Convention was anticipated, and that they were
instructed to withdraw from it. Their duty is discharged. Their commission
is ended, and they are no longer delegates.

The above extracts from the Montgomery (Ala.) *Weekly Mail* may
be taken as a fair sample of the reasoning by which the re-union of the
Democratic party is to be first denounced and then rendered an impossibility. Every effort to unite a party formed purely for temporary
purposes, to secure an election of good officers and the temporary administration of Government, is treated as a question effecting a revolution in the confederacy, or the reconstruction of the political system of
the country. The country is not looking to the revision of the Constitution or to the inauguration of a new form of Government through
the agency of the Democratic party, or to make either by the nomination or election of a candidate for the Presidency. The people had no
such objects in forming the Democratic party; they had no such design in calling the members of the party into general convention; they
never looked with any such view to the election of delegates to Charleston, or to their re-assembling at Baltimore. Their object in the creation
and regulation of the party was to control and regulate the administration of the Government under the Constitution and in the Union.
When the federative system failed, or the Government was incapable
of being made to fulfil its purposes and perform its functions, then the
people, and not a party, were to be appealed to to remedy the ills of a
country, the political institutions of which were too defective to promote their happiness or protect their interests.

The difference between us and the Southern seceders is, that they
look to a difference on every question affecting our rights as a reason
for breaking up a mere party organization. Now, we consider that the
causes for forming and maintaining party organizations are limited in
number and not very great in extent. A party is but a mere piece of

machinery to aid in directing the actual temporary movements of the officials of government. The party has nothing to do with the construction or demolition of the political system established by the people. It is only to be destroyed, in our judgment, when one can be formed better calculated to direct the action of the acting officers of government. When evils so severe and dangerous come upon the country as to demand the destruction of government or the adoption of revolutionary measures, then other and new agencies are to be called into being by the popular will. Party associations and all the regular agencies of an established polity are certain to be set aside in such a contingency. Do the seceders consider this such a crisis? We conceive not. Their action does not show that they do. They propose to break up the Democratic party organization and to form a new one, with what view? Why, to contend for the election of a President and Vice President. They design to influence the action of a government elected, maintained, paid, and controlled by the present Northern and Southern States, possessed of identically the same powers, conferred by the same charter, as those under which the present Administration acts. They pretend not to seek for a new limitation of powers for the Executive; they design to make no change in the fundamental law, or in the relation of sections; to put no additional restraint on the power of the majority, nor in any manner to give one particle of additional security to persons or property, other than can be obtained by the election of patriotic men to executive and legislative offices entertaining sound views on constitutional questions and animated by a devotion to the maintenance of the just rights of citizens and States. This is their design in forming a new party.—They design to do nothing more by their party revolution than to affect the administration of the Government to be elected for the four years of its existence. They design to create no new safeguards for liberty—no new defenses for rights of property—no new guarantees for State sovereignty. They intend to try, through a new party, to get possession of the Federal Government and its patronage and power. They have no design beyond this; they avow none, and in good faith they can have no ulterior and unexplained purposes beyond these—the election of the Government officers and the direction of their practical action during their terms of office. They cannot, in honesty, be attempting to break up a party organization by their secession for the covert purpose of electing a worse set of officials, to necessitate a social and political war, without announcing their object to the people.

If we are right, and the object of forming and preserving the Democratic and other party organizations is to secure the election of officers and the control of their conduct, it is obvious that the views which separate party friends must have a direct and almost exclusive reference to attaining these objects. Now, do the advocates of this continued war in the Democratic party—those opponents of any reconciliation between its dissatisfied sections—hope, design, or wish to accomplish, these objects through the disruption of the old, or formation of the new party?—Every man who reads, or can make a common arithmetical calculation, knows they do not. Then, we say, as far as the direction of the action of government is concerned, and securing the purposes for which alone the creation of the party organization is either required or justified, this movement has no apparent reason to support it. And we are confirmed in the opinion by the needless and unprovoked incivility with which the discussion is conducted by the extremists on both sides.

We come now to consider the obstacles presented in the articles we quote to a reunion of the Democratic delegations. First, it objects that the seceding delegations cannot appear in the Baltimore Convention without eating "their own words." Now, if the Convention had finished its work—if the questions of policy and principle had been really and definitely settled—if the Convention were over, passed, gone, and its work perfected, there would be some reason for this. But not only every politician, but every man of full age, who has not had a custodian appointed by the courts to take care of him and his affairs, knows that not one act of the Democratic Convention which assembled in Charleston on the 23d of May [April] last, has one particle of authority attached to it, no motion that was passed, not one resolution that was adopted, not one principle that was announced, is as yet a part of the acts of that Convention. It is a body now in being, its action purposely undetermined, its session deliberately and considerately continued, its decisions wisely and properly unannounced, because they were not made.

The recess taken by the Convention for more than a month was to give men of common opinions on public affairs an opportunity of conferring together and devising some means of concentrating the energies of the true friends of the constitutional rights of the States and property-holding citizens. We say, in all kindness, to the editors of the *Mail* and the *Mercury* that they can afford to reason, and dispense with such phrases as "impertinent," and "insulting," and "insolent," and "base," to a proposition made by such men as have signed the address to the Democracy of the country. Although these gentlemen happen to hold position assigned them by enlightened constituencies of their several States, they are not necessarily to be vituperated even by the petulant and corrupt little office hunters who never expect to get office under an administration in which one of them has influence. The editors of the *Mail* and the Charleston *Mercury* belong to a different and higher class than the wretched creatures who creep into small offices by treason to men and neighborhoods, whose weapons of offence are loathsome vituperation and transparent mendacity, and whose labor of love is to do the dirty works of service which honest men can scarcely believe is ever performed. The editors of the *Mail* and *Mercury* have no reason to assail others who are really as deeply interested as they in the maintenance of Southern rights, and who have proved by a life-long action that they are as true to the South, and as good republicans and surely as tolerant gentlemen as they.

The recommendation of the nineteen may not accord with the views of those who seek to sever the Democratic party because it is the "strongest ligature which binds the Union," but it does accord with the feeling, sentiment and objects of those who wish that the government shall be controlled by friends of the South, and not by Black Republicans. It will meet the approval of those who wish the people to be called directly to meet the issues with their Northern assailants, and not to be drawn to it by indirection and without preparation.

41. THE DELEGATIONS FROM THE SECEDING STATES AT BALTIMORE

(*Daily Courier,* Louisville, June 9, 1860)

Every State in the Union was represented at Charleston. The Convention was full. At a certain stage of the proceedings, the representatives of several of the States saw proper to withdraw. After doing so, they met together to consult as to the proper course for them to pursue. They passed resolutions expressive of their views on the questions in issue before the country, and adjourned.

Their withdrawal from the Convention then in session certainly cannot be held to have excluded them from any future Democratic Convention to which they may be sent; nor from the adjourned session of the Charleston Convention, particularly if they, on their return to their constituents, be again accredited as representatives. South Carolina has refused to participate in several National Democratic Conventions; yet South Carolina Democrats have not been read out of the party, nor have their delegates been excluded from subsequent Conventions. If the Democracy of South Carolina could refuse to take any part in, or to be bound by, the proceedings of one Convention, without excluding them from the pale of the party, or losing their right to representation in subsequent Conventions, surely their delegates could withdraw from such a body without surrendering the rights of those they represented.

The delegation from Alabama, for instance, were instructed in positive terms to pursue a certain course. Knowing that such instructions had been given, by the body which appointed them, they were admitted into the Charleston Convention as Democrats, no voice being raised against their recognition. Did those delegates cease to be Democrats in carrying out their instructions in their letter and spirit? If they did not represent a *Democratic* constituency, they were not entitled to seats in the National Convention; if their constituents were Democrats then, they are Democrats now, having committed no offense, and been convicted of no crime, since the 23d of April; if the constituency are Democratic, as was admitted by the admission of the Alabama delegation at Charleston, they have a right to be heard at Baltimore, through their regularly accredited agents.

The withdrawal of the Alabama delegates made it necessary for the Democracy of that State to take such action as they thought proper. How should they act? The party had an organized existence in the State. They were in the habit of meeting in State and District Conventions to nominate candidates for the various offices to be filled. They met in State Convention and selected their delegates to Charleston. The Convention at Charleston, after excluding the Wood delegates from New York because they were not regularly accredited, admitted, without objection, the Alabama delegates who were selected by the regular organization of their own State. The organization is an active and efficient one; and the Democrats of Alabama could only act through it.—They have done so. When their representatives went home, and reported what they had done, the Executive Committee of the State, appointed by the State Convention which elected the delegates to Charleston, by the authority vested in them by special resolution, called a new State Convention to determine whether they would be represented at Baltimore, and, if so, by whom. No proceeding was ever more regular. The authority of the last Alabama State Convention was recognized by the National Convention in the prompt ad-

mission of the delegates appointed by it; if it had the right to select
representatives to Charleston, it unquestionably was authorized to
name a State Executive Committee, and define its powers and duties;
and, this granted, that Committee not only had the authority to call
a new State Convention, but the special action of the power by which
it was created made it obligatory upon its members to do so.

The Convention thus called, met at Montgomery, on the 4th inst.,
and appointed delegates to both Richmond and Baltimore. We believe
they indorsed the course of their representatives at Charleston, and
reappointed and accredited anew a majority of them to Baltimore.
They will go there, in obedience to the will of those who selected them,
the only representatives of the Democracy of the State of Alabama.
No delegation will be known or recognized but those coming in
through the front door, representing a regular organization, and
chosen in accordance with the established rules and usages of the
party in the State from which they came.

There will be a bogus delegation at Baltimore from Alabama. They
will represent no organization. They will not have the semblance of
regularity. The meeting by which they were appointed, met, not upon
the call of any executive committee, not at the instance of any one
authorized to speak for the party, but upon the invitation of a few
men acting only for themselves.[1] At best, it was only a mass meeting
of men claiming to be Democrats. As such, delegates appointed at it
will have no right to appear in a regularly-called Convention consisting
of the representatives of State organizations. Their position will not be
as good as that of the rejected New York delegation, nor of the rejected Illinois delegation, for both of the latter were appointed by
what had some claim to being a regular organization. The bogus
delegates from Alabama cannot even plead that the Convention by
which they were appointed was called by those who pretended to have
any other than their individual authority for what they did. It is as
though, after the Executive Committee of Kentucky had called our last
State Convention, half a dozen men from Henry and Campbell counties had taken it upon themselves to order another Convention. Of
course nobody would have advocated the admission of delegates selected by the unauthorized and illegitimate body which might have

[1] The call for this convention was issued by Forsyth, Seibels, and Winston through the
columns of the Montgomery *Confederation*, Mobile *Register*, and Huntsville *Advocate*. The
convention met at Montgomery, June 4, and was attended by delegates from twenty-eight
of the fifty-two counties in the State. It endorsed popular sovereignty, appointed a contesting delegation to the Baltimore Convention, and instructed it to vote for Douglas.

assembled under the latter call, in preference to those chosen by the regular Convention.

But the only hope of the Douglasites—their only hope to secure a majority-vote for their favorite and then to break up the Convention without a nomination—is in the admission of the bogus, and the rejection of the regular and legitimate, delegates from Alabama and her sister States. The New York delegation, holding their seats by virtue of the regularity of the organization they represent, dare not sustain the political gamblers who look to this desperate chance for success. No one regarding the future of the party will dare reject the regular delegates. They will be admitted. Their admission seals the fate of the plotters against the peace and welfare of the party.

42. SUMNER'S STATISTICS

(*New Orleans Daily Crescent*, June 15, 1860)

Mr. Charles Sumner, in his recent tirade in the Senate,[1] undertook to demonstrate the malign influence of slavery by citing the inferiority of the South in the respects of population, wealth, colleges, newspapers, and everything else. Some of his assertions were true and some false. But none of them, whether true or false, served in any degree to establish his proposition that the institution of slavery in the Southern States is an obstacle in the way of civilization, or wealth, or the general happiness and contentment of the people.

Very true is it that the North has grown in population more rapidly than the South. But can Mr. Sumner account for it in no other way than because of slavery? He could, easily enough, if he chose. But Mr. Sumner is one of those logicians who never states an argument fairly. He states only such facts as favor *his* side of the question, but coolly ignores such as would damage him. Because the South has not grown in population as fast as the North, *ergo,* according to Mr. Sumner, it is slavery alone that has done it. The argument is just as unfair as if we were to assert that Sumner is a viler abolitionist than Fessenden because the initial letter of his name is S, while that of the latter is not.

The North has increased in population more rapidly than the South for two reasons. One is the heavy annual immigration of foreigners, most of whom settle in the Northern and North-western States; and the other is the unjust, one-sided and partial policy of the Federal Government. Until a year or two ago the immigration to this country

[1] "The Barbarism of Slavery," delivered in the Senate, June 4, 1860, and distributed as a campaign document by the Congressional Republican Committee.

was very great—reaching, some years, the high figure of half a million of people. It takes but a few years of such immigration to give a decided preponderance of numbers to the section in which they may settle. When Mr. Sumner talks about the excess of Northern over Southern representatives in the lower House of Congress, he ought to recollect that enough foreigners to constitute a constituency for four or five additional representatives come to this country this year.

These foreigners settle mainly in the North-western States. Doubtless, Mr. Sumner will argue that it is slavery that keeps them from the South. But this is not true, in the sense which Mr. Sumner would have the people understand it. These immigrants can go to Illinois, Iowa, Minnesota, Wisconsin, etc., and buy rich and productive Government lands for a mere trifle—never over one dollar and a quarter an acre. They can buy no such lands in the South at that price. Moreover, it is a general law of emigration, as we have shown in a previous article, that people follow the parallels of latitude. Germans and Irishmen, coming to this country, settle down where the climate is the nearest approach to that which they left behind. In the Southern cities we find a great many Spaniards, Italians, and emigrants from the south of France; but we find them very rarely in the cities of the North.

In addition to this, we think it can be easily shown, though not within the narrow limits of a newspaper article, that the whole policy of the Federal Government, from the beginning has been to build up and enrich the North at Southern expense. In this business that monster engine, a high Protective Tariff, has been the chief instrument. It has enabled the North to do nearly all the importing and exporting business of the country, with immense profit. Besides the Tariff, we have fishing bounties, and navigation laws, and the giving away the public lands, millions of acres at a time, all of which tend to aggrandize the Northern section of the Union.

But, even admitting, for the sake of argument, that Mr. Sumner's assertion is correct—that it is slavery which has prevented the South from keeping pace with the North in the matter of population—Mr. Sumner has yet to prove, to make his argument against slavery a valid one, that a dense population is desirable. There are many people who will consider it the strongest sort of argument *in favor of slavery,* if it can be shown to have the effect of preventing a dense population. It is undeniable that where large masses of people are assembled together in circumscribed limits, there is not only more crime and lawlessness, but more actual suffering for the common necessaries of life. We read

every day of such suffering, and sometimes of starvation itself, in the
dense communities of the North—rarely, if ever, in the sparsely settled
sections of the South. Is it the policy of Mr. Sumner to crowd people
together until population encroaches upon the means of subsistence,
and there is a constant struggle for bread? Everybody will admit that
that policy is best which secures the greatest average amount of happiness and comfort to each citizen—everybody, we mean, except such
sentimental and transubstantial philosophers as Mr. Sumner, whose
chief delight seems to be to make people miserable instead of happy.
And if a dense population has the effect of reducing the average of that
happiness, and that density is the result of the absence of slavery, then
the circumstance becomes an argument in favor of the institution rather
than against it.

But while the South may not have advanced with the rapidity that
the North has—so far as population is concerned—yet there is no other
region on earth where such progress has been made. Mr. Sumner calls
slavery a "blight" and a "curse." But, under the influence of this "blight"
and "curse," what are the facts in regard to the development of the
Southern States?

In 1790 the population of the slave States was less than two millions.
In 1850 it was nearly ten millions. The blight and the curse of slavery
produced this result.

In 1800 there were about one million slaves in the South. Now, there
are about four millions. One would suppose, to read Sumner's speech,
that the "chains" and the "lash" and the "bloodhounds" of slaveholders
would soon extirpate the African race in the South altogether. Instead
of that they have *quadrupled* in number since the beginning of the
present century.

In 1820 the exports of Southern productions were thirty-eight millions
of dollars in value. In 1859 they were two hundred and twenty-two
millions.

In 1824 the export of cotton was worth twenty-two millions. In 1859
it was worth one hundred and sixty-one millions.

Of the *total* exports of the Union at the present day, those of the South
constitute *eighty per cent*. Four-fifths of the surplus wealth of the country
is the product of the States of the South.

With these figures before our eyes—taken from official sources—
Mr. Charles Sumner may rail at slavery, and call it a blight and a curse
as much as he chooses. People who have any desire to know better,
understand the true facts of the case—and they will set Mr. Charles

Sumner down, not as a fool, because he is no fool, but simply as a pestilent knave and low demagogue, who, from the meanest of motives, is trying to create sectional hatred in the country, and to subject one portion of the Republic to the political domination and tyranny of the other.

43. The Result of Unwise Action, or an Erroneous Nomination by the Baltimore Convention

(*Richmond Semi-weekly Examiner,* June 19, 1860)

We have already expressed our views as to the propriety of admitting the delegations from the Southern Democratic States which have been recently in session in this city to a full participation in the proceedings of the adjourned Convention to meet in Baltimore. All our reflections confirm and strengthen us in that opinion. We see nothing but mischief to the party and country to result from an effort to reject them. The party once broken now, is and must be sectionalized. It may be made a strong organization for Southern defense, but will not and cannot be made an efficient agent in controlling the action, limiting the expenditures, or directing in any manner the administration of the Federal Government. It may have some limited power of resistance in the Union, but its usefulness will result from the readiness with which it may be used for purposes of attack or defense in case of collision with the power of the federal majority, when there will be necessity to dissolve the Union. The party once sundered at Baltimore, the Northern Democracy becomes the weakest of all parties in the Union. The Baltimore Union Convention nominees and the Seceding Democrats will fight it out in the Southern States. The Black Republicans will sweep the North, if the abolitionists do not disorganize them. Whoever wins, the Northern Democracy goes down never to rise, unless the present Democratic party shall be preserved. We have heard some absurd assertions, that when the fragment of the Baltimore Convention shall reject the delegation from the South and drive out the non-seceding slave States—that they can nominate a candidate after rejecting the majority platform and the Tennessee resolution, and carry the election, too. This opinion is based on the idea, we hear, that Mr. Douglas can carry the North, when the delegates at Baltimore shall refuse to make him the nominee without a two-thirds vote, and carry it so entirely as not to require a Southern electoral vote. Now, if the Northern Democracy have any such thought, or any disposition to act on it, the whole matter is ended, and LINCOLN is elected; and, for ourselves, we will rejoice at it. That may possibly rouse the South. Mr. Douglas and his men have had a fair chance before the country and the Convention. He must get his nomination fairly through the action of the Democracy in Convention on the terms agreed to in the past and confirmed by the action of the most recent Democratic assemblage, or he will be execrated by every honest man in the land. His nomination at any time in the last two years would have been an unfortunate one, and his election at the best most doubtful. And this would have been the case if his nomination had been made by two-thirds of a full Convention, and the bitterness of his present quarrel with the extreme Southern Democratic States could have been avoided. But his election by the people, or by the House of Representatives, will be simply impossible, should he come before the country on his own motion or as the nominee of a fragment of the Democratic Convention. In the face of these facts his peculiar friends, South and North, are stimulating the quarrel between the Northern and Southern Democrats. It certainly is no concern of ours, but he is about to be crushed between the upper and nether mill-stones of rash friends and of foes who are arrayed in the garb of friends. We say that it behooves every friend of Democracy, and of every candidate who desires to be elected, to take the last chance now presented of uniting and consolidating the strength of the only party which can save the country from Freesoil tyranny. Those who please may talk about going before a Black Republican Congress for an election; everybody knows what that means—to take the chances of buying a vote, or making a corrupt arrangement, and to ensure what is the certain, final result, absolute submission to anti-slavery domination. Say what they may, this is to be the result of an appeal from the people to Congress. If this catastrophe is to be avoided, it must be by an election by the people, and this cannot be secured, as everybody knows, unless the Southern Democratic vote is cast in mass, or very nearly in mass, for the most prominent opponent of the Chicago nominees.

All this bluster about severing the Democratic party, and beating LINCOLN and electing a Southern or Northern conservative man by the people, is mere stuff, and every man of sense knows it when he hears it, and almost all know it when they say it. There is no man in the United States who can offend and throw off fifty conservative electoral votes and beat the Black Republicans. Desperate politicians make desperate boasts, and more desperate efforts, to retrieve fallen fortunes or to make new ones. But the people desire that the next

election shall be made in such a manner as to secure the country against
the ruinous consequences of corrupt and fanatical tyranny. The people
are neither gaming, speculating nor seeking to get control of money
or patronage. They have great interests at stake—a posterity to care for,
a country and a grand polity to preserve and improve. They will not
see with patience, or pass by with impunity, the acts of those who put
these to hazard for the petty purposes of electing a man to office, or for
the equally little cause of maintaining consistency on an immaterial
question. The Union is in danger, that is something; the chance of
severing the Southern people into hostile parties is imminent, and that
is greatly more. The possibility—nay, the probability—of subjecting
the Southern minority of property-holders in this great Confederacy to
the domination of a government ruled by the enemies of their section
and the destroyers of all rights of property in slaves, is imminent, and,
we believe, will be unavoidable, if the Baltimore Convention hearkens
to the counsel of those who desire and are striving to drive off the
Democracies of the cotton States.

44. Disappointed

(*The New Orleans Bee,* June 25, 1860)

The counsels of Black Republicanism are guided by two distinct sets
of spirits. A portion, and probably the larger, studiously seek to keep
ultraism in the background, affect a temperate assertion of their tenets,
profess kindness and fraternal attachment to the Union, and talk lov-
ingly of the misguided and deluded South. Their object is clearly to
enlist the sympathies and the votes of that numerous body of Northern
citizens who, while cherishing an inherent dislike of slavery as an institution, have no idea whatever of committing themselves to an organized crusade against the South. Mr. SUMNER's speech plays the mischief with the calculations of these politic and wary leaders. Its broad
assertions of the barbarism of slavery; of its pernicious effects on the
morals and intellect of the South; of the duty of all men to co-operate
in endeavoring to extirpate it—albeit sophistical, one-sided and fallacious
to the last degree, constitute dogmas and tenets of as radical and revolutionary a character as any professed by WENDELL PHILLIPS or GARRI-
SON. All who accept the conclusions proclaimed by SUMNER must cease
to be classed as Black Republicans, and can be considered hereafter
simply as rabid Abolitionists. Now this is precisely what the politicians
we have referred to wish to avoid. Mr. SUMNER's speech is to them dis-

tasteful and unseasonable; and accordingly we find that presses such as the New York *Courier and Enquirer,* the *Times* and the *Tribune* say as little as possible of it, allude to it in reticent and gingerly language, and strive to induce their readers to forget that CHARLES SUMNER has returned to the Senate, and has delivered the most ultra, uncompromising abolition speech ever uttered in that body.

Perhaps the efforts to cover up and conceal this premature exposition of Black Republican doctrine might have succeeded but for the existence of another faction in the same party, which has no notion whatever of suffering SUMNER's resplendent light to be hid beneath a bushel.

The Black Republican party are sorely perplexed with Senator SUMNER's recent terrific onslaught on slavery. He has given them more than they bargained for, and especially at a time when they were solicitous of assuming an appearance of extraordinary moderation and conservatism. The leaders of Black Republicanism were foremost in greeting Mr. SUMNER's return to the United States Senate, and hailed that auspicious event as the harbinger of an eloquent and elaborate effort in behalf of their principles. They did not, however, anticipate, and were consequently unprepared for the virulent, unconditional and intensely abolition attack upon the institution of slavery itself with which their favorite regaled the Senate on the first suitable opportunity. The Black Republicans had forgotten that Mr. SUMNER believed he had a debt to pay; that as he was unable or unwilling to requite in kind the treatment he had received from a Southern man, he was determined to ventilate his resentment in the only practicable way, by unpacking his heart with words, and by a fell catalogue of curses upon slavery, its promoters and upholders almost equal in comprehensiveness of imprecation to the Papal bull against VICTOR EMANUEL. Mr. SUMNER, it seems, sacrificed policy to the burning thirst of revenge. He did not regard the interests of Black Republicanism half as much as the vehement and irresistible desire to abuse the South and slavery. Hence his speech, which, as the painfully concocted product of years of research, of much meditation quickened and stimulated by a revengeful spirit, and of a predetermined intention to regard the subject from but one point of view, was necessarily specious and at times eloquent, went far beyond the wishes or expectations of the Freesoil party.

Massachusetts, the fanatical element of Black Republicanism, is particularly prolific. Consequently no sooner had SUMNER's effusion seen the light than resolutions were submitted to the Legislature of Massachusetts, then in session, extolling it to the skies, and declaring emphatically that it embodied and expressed the genuine principles of Republicanism. These resolutions were passed after some debate, and now stand forth as the deliberate endorsement of the rankest and foulest abolition doctrines by the General Assembly of the Commonwealth of Massachusetts. We notice, too, that in other States, such as Illinois, New Hampshire and Ohio, the Black Republican sheets, in their paroxysms of delight at SUMNER's wrathful diatribes, accept the speech and hail it as a truthful representation of the opinions of the party. Thus it happens that the enthusiasm of the small fry defeats the profoundly crafty tactics of the leaders, and has led to an untimely acknowledgment of the real objects and designs of anti-slavery.

We are not sorry for this. It may be hereafter discovered that Mr. SUMNER has quite unconsciously rendered a service to the South. He has planted the Black Republican faith upon the only true platform—hostility to slavery in all its forms. By stripping it of false pretenses and hypocritical assurances; by enabling all men of all parties to discern its character, and its necessary and inevitable tendencies, he has furnished an opportunity rarely enjoyed by the thoughtful and patriotic people of the North to examine dispassionately into the principles avowed by leading politicians of that section, and now laid bare and made visible by one of their most prominent champions. The people of the slaveholding States will henceforth act with their eyes wide open. They can now have no excuse for further affiliation with Black Republicanism. Mr. SUMNER has told them it means abolition.

45. THE CONVENTION

(The Wilmington Journal, June 28, 1860)

In April last, the Democratic National Convention met in the City of Charleston. Its ranks were full. From the Atlantic to the Pacific, from the Saint Lawrence to the Rio Grande, no State was unrepresented, hardly a seat was vacant. Of the six hundred and six delegates present, a compact body representing between one hundred and twenty and one hundred and thirty electoral votes went for "Douglas or nobody," and for Douglas with *his* interpretation of the Cincinnati platform, or not at all. By adroit management this minority of the Convention obtained control of its organization and were able to appear with a clear majority of voting strength, although largely outnumbered on the floor of the house. This was done by the operation of the rule that each delegate should vote separately, unless where the Convention of his

State had otherwise directed or provided; but that where such Convention had so directed or provided, the vote of each State should be cast as a unit.—The *effect* of this adroit manœuvre was that in *every* State where there was an anti-Douglas minority, the voice of such minority was suppressed; while, in every State where there was a Douglas minority, such minority was allowed to poll its full strength. In New York the voice of fourteen electoral votes was suppressed. In North Carolina and Virginia, even the one or two votes that the Douglas men could rally had its full bearing. The ten Douglas votes of Pennsylvania were counted, although a minority. The five anti-Douglas votes of Indiana were suppressed, although bearing as large a proportion to the Indiana delegation as the ten Douglas votes did to the Pennsylvania delegation.

This was the position of things at Charleston. It shows the adroitness and unscrupulousness of the Douglas managers—it does *not* prove, as asserted by Mr. Douglas and his supporters, that he or his platform ever received a *bona fide* endorsement at the hands of the members of the Charleston Convention. Tricks of this kind neither make nor indicate public opinion.

As the first week of the Charleston Convention wore on, it began to be apparent that the fictitious power thus obtained was to be used with the utmost rigor, and when on Monday of the second week the crisis did arrive, it was not until the Southern delegates had exhausted every effort to obtain such concession on the question of platform as was essential to their own honor, and due to the rights and interests of their section—such concession too as the managers for Judge Douglas might easily and fairly have granted—such concession as they *ought* to have granted, and *would* have granted had their object been harmony, or had they not considered the rights and interests of the Democratic party altogether secondary to the promotion of that gentleman. And we take occasion here to say that although the delegates from North Carolina were not originally Douglas men, yet they went to Charleston without any pledge, and generally without any serious committal against him. On any reasonable and fair platform we were prepared to go for Judge Douglas at any moment when our vote might have sufficed to nominate him. But his wire-workers at Charleston would concede nothing, and when we use the word "concede," we wish it distinctly understood that no one asked for or wished for anything in addition to or in advance of the Cincinnati platform.—With that the whole South was and is perfectly satisfied. The object of the Southern and other constitutional delegates was simply to obtain such a recognition of the true intent and meaning of that platform as would prevent future difficulties and misconstructions. And many of us were willing for harmony sake to be satisfied with a lower standard of construction than we had originally insisted upon. But no proposal would be listened to by the Douglas managers.

Let us here remark, that all along we had the highest respect for the character, abilities and past services of Judge Douglas, but that we could not accept him with the Cincinnati platform unexplained, because, to do so, would be to accept and endorse his interpretation of it, to which we could not consent. There may have been those who made war upon Judge Douglas. To that war, one way or another, North Carolina was no party. We may have regretted the unfriendly relations existing between the President and Judge Douglas, or between the friends of the President and those of the Senator from Illinois. We are not the apologists of the President, nor are we the defamers of Judge Douglas. We think the Democratic party and its principles matters of far greater moment than either of these gentlemen, or than one hundred of them; yes, five hundred, or any other number. We think that the rights of the masses of a great party—the dominant party in a Union of thirty-three States, containing thirty millions of people, are become cheap enough when one man can say—such and such are *my* notions, and unless the Convention agrees to these notions, I will not consent to be nominated, and then his friends come into the Convention to work all tricks, determined to swerve the principles and sacrifice the rights of the party to this *one man*. When this became apparent, there *did* arise for the first time strong anti-Douglas feeling at the South, as resenting this dictation on the part of Judge Douglas' friends, with whose movements it was impossible not to connect that gentleman himself.

Not even when eight of her Southern sisters left her at Charleston —left the Convention there,—did North Carolina cease her efforts at reconciliation—cease to labor for harmony. She conferred with the remaining Southern States—with the seceding States, and with what were supposed to be the more conservative Northern States, with the view of arriving at and agreeing upon some basis on which all could stand, and upon which the seceding delegations could return to their places in the Convention, and the unity of the body be restored. Then first was it found that the Douglas leaders were *opposed* to the restoration of that unity—were opposed to the return of those withdrawing States; for the first time, indeed, was it found that *any body* could be opposed to the restoration of the unity and nationality of the Convention. *Why* this opposition on the part of the Douglas managers might easily have been surmised at Charleston—it was made perfectly apparent at Baltimore. Indeed, rather over-zealous Douglas men let the secret out on the cars, that the object was to "fix up" Douglas delegations from all those States and oust the regular ones.

The result of these plans became apparent at Baltimore. With the numerical, and, still more, the voting power of the Convention largely in their hands, owing to the operation of the unit rule and the withdrawal of fifty-two Southern delegates, the Douglas managers determined to carry things with a high hand, and they *did* so. Their tone had become reckless, defiant, domineering. They were evidently determined to exclude the regularly appointed delegates from the Southern States, and fill their places with creatures of their own, as per programme, and they *did* so, in the cases of Alabama, Louisiana and Arkansas. They failed to get up any showing from Mississippi, Texas, South Carolina or Florida—indeed, no application was made from either of these two last named States.[1]

Among other incidents, all pointing in the same direction, we may allude to the cases of Mr. Hallett, from Massachusetts, and Mr. Clardy, from Missouri.[2] These were regular delegates from their respective districts—were unable to attend at Charleston, but did attend at Baltimore —they notified their substitutes of their inability to attend in the first instance, and of their ability to attend in the second. The principals *did* attend at Baltimore, and are ousted to make way for their substitutes— need we add that the principals are *not* Douglas men, but that the substitutes *are?* But this instance of injustice, however gross, is only individual in its character, and would not of itself justify decided action. The cases of the States of Alabama, Louisiana and Arkansas are more grave in character, as they involve the rights and principles of party organization in sovereign States.

The regular delegates from Alabama had been originally sent to Charleston by the Democratic State Convention. Of the regularity of that appointment no question had been raised. When the adjournment

---

[1] The South Carolina delegation did not go to Baltimore. The Louisiana delegation was in Baltimore, but did not apply for admission to the convention.

[2] Hallett, author of the *Cincinnati Platform*, was unable to attend the Charleston Convention because of the death of Mrs. Hallett. Clardy's case was similar. Both members were present when the convention re-assembled at Baltimore, having received tickets of admission from Chairman Cushing, but were expelled by vote of the convention.

took place at Charleston, the Democratic State Executive Committee called together a new State Convention which was largely attended, which re-accredited the former delegates to the National Convention. These delegates appeared at Baltimore with the credentials of the regular Democratic organization of the State of Alabama, while the contestants who were admitted were wholly outside of the Democratic organization of Alabama, and might as well have been picked up in the streets of Baltimore for any authority they had or were entitled to, so far as the Democracy of Alabama is concerned. If Mr. Yancey indeed be a disunionist, as asserted, we do not sympathise with his views. He denies it, and however it may be, it is for the people who send him to judge about his fitness as their representative.—The regularly organized Democracy of Alabama have *twice* accredited the delegation of which Mr. Yancey is a member. The Convention assumed to disregard the decision of the sovereign State of Alabama, and to receive and set up *bogus* and unauthorized delegates to represent her.

The same was the case with Louisiana. The case of Arkansas is fully as bad, though differing in kind, as it presumes to do what a State only can do—instruct how its vote shall be cast. We would refer for a fuller account of these matters to the very able report of Gov. Stevens [3] in to-day's paper.

If these things were done to Alabama, Louisiana, Arkansas—to the members from Massachusetts and Missouri, what security could delegations from North Carolina, Virginia, or elsewhere, feel that their turn might not come next? That if it suited the wishes of the dominant majority their seats might not be given to some parties whose views might be more acceptable. No wonder the *bogus* delegates from Alabama and Louisiana were a "unit for Douglas"—they were sent for on purpose. The rights of individuals and of States were alike violated—made subservient to the ambition of one man. State Sovereignty was set at naught in what ought to be its chosen sanctuary—all avowals of principle were made to bend in accordance with the expressed views of that one man. Was it any wonder that a division should occur in a body so irregularly constituted, or that the truly National Democracy of a majority of the States, preferring to have their action free from such extraneous influences, should have resumed their sessions at the Hall of

[3] *Minority Report of Mr. Stephens, Delegate from Oregon, Showing the Grounds upon Which the Regular Southern Delegations Were Entitled to Seats in the Convention at the Front Street Theatre, Baltimore.* Published as a campaign document by the National Democratic Executive Committee.

the Maryland Institute, where the distinguished presiding officer, Hon. Caleb Cushing, continued to preside over a truly National Convention. A national platform was soon adopted and national nominations promptly made. We have placed these nominations at our head. We will do our best for their success.

The sense of obligation during these trying days at Baltimore was actually painful. The great majority of our delegation felt that but one course was honorably open for them, and that they pursued. They do not attack any who differ from them—they simply ask a fair and candid examination of their own course.

In speaking apparently on behalf of the majority of the delegation, we do so with no more authority than a knowledge of the facts and a community of feeling seem to permit; but for what we say we distinctly state that we alone are responsible. To those of our brother delegates who differed from us at Baltimore we have none but friendly feelings—we seek no controversy with any of the few Democrats who may prefer Judge Douglas after the events that have occurred. We have stated our own case. We now counsel harmony.

It will be seen that the attempt to bribe Alabama by placing Senator Fitzpatrick [4] on the Douglas ticket has failed. Mr. Fitzpatrick *declines*. Whether Herschel V. Johnson accepts or not, Georgia will maintain her rights.

46. NATIONAL CONVENTIONS

(*The Charleston Mercury,* July 10, 1860)

The Richmond *Examiner* and other papers have put forth strong commentaries on the late Democratic Convention held at Charleston, and finally acting at Baltimore. They denounce it, for its unfairness and trickery; and on this ground, justify their opposition to its nominees. On the other hand, Mr. Douglas and his friends claim his nomination for the Presidency, as the legitimate fruit of the regular organization and action of the Democratic party in Convention.

Now, it appears to us, that both sides in this controversy are right, and both wrong. Douglas and his friends are right in affirming that they were in possession of the regular organization of the Democratic party in Convention; but they are wrong in maintaining that, therefore,

---

[4] Benjamin Fitzpatrick, Governor of Alabama, 1842–1845; United States Senator, 1848–1849, 1853–1861.

their frauds and trickeries ought to be tolerated. And the wronged portion of the Democratic party are right in refusing to submit to the frauds of the majority in the Charleston and Baltimore Convention; but they are wrong in denying that this Convention was the Convention of the Democratic party.

The truth is that party Conventions, got up to nominate candidates for the Presidency and Vice Presidency of the United States, are, more or less, fraudulent in their incipiency and practices. Their object is to set aside or supersede the regular action of the Constitution in electing the President and Vice President of the United States. The people have very little to do with them. Here in South Carolina, after a call which excluded all who were not in favor of the State being represented in the Charleston Convention—with but thin meetings of the people—we saw the delegates appointed by them immediately assume to represent the people of the State. Again: As such Conventions are party Conventions, to nominate candidates to be supported by the party, it is clear that the power in making the nominations should be in proportion to the ability to vote for them. States that have no power to vote for nominees should not control the nomination. This is absurd—monstrous. Those States which have the ability to vote for the nominees should have the power to make the nominations. This could be easily determined by taking the relative strength of the Democratic party in the different States, as *developed in the preceding elections of members of Congress,* and giving them that strength in the Convention. This would approach fairness. But to give States which notoriously cannot give a single Democratic vote in the Presidential election the same party power in nominating the candidates of the party as those which are certain to vote for the nominees, is manifestly the grossest injustice. Here is the great vice of all Conventions held hitherto to nominate candidates for the Presidency. Let this be rectified in the way we have stated, and then the advantages obtained by Mr. DOUGLAS' adherents in the late Conventions could not exist. All the States may vote as units; but they could not bring with them, in nominating candidates for the Presidency in a Democratic Convention, the whole strength of the Black Republican party as well as their own. After the late Conventions in Charleston and Baltimore, the Southern States, we trust, will never again consent to go into any Conventions organized upon such loose and unjust principles. National Conventions are abolished, or they will be reformed. The abuses at Charleston and Baltimore are the natural fruits of their vicious organizations.

47. The Cry of Disunion

(*Richmond Enquirer,* July 10, 1860)

The effort now being made to attach odium to Mr. Yancey, and through him unpopularity to Mr. Breckinridge, shows how little the people of the North understand the political sentiments of the great mass of the Southern people. Never was any State more ably represented, or her interest more gallantly defended, than was Alabama by her gifted son, Wm. L. Yancey. Every sentiment of his speech at Charleston, and his noble defence of his State at Baltimore, finds a response in the Democracy of Virginia, and all the unmerited abuse that folly levels at his head but endears him to the Southern people and renders his influence greater and more controlling.

The charge of disunionist, now so frequently made against Mr. Yancey and through him directed at the supporters of Breckinridge and Lane, is so supremely ridiculous and silly that it reflects more upon the good sense of those who make it, than injury upon those against whom it is levelled. With just and equal rights to every State, there will be no disunionists in any section; but a denial of the benefits and equality designed by the Constitution, will make disunionists in every section. We have respect enough for the manliness and courage of the Northern people to believe that a successful refusal of their just rights would make them as much disunionists as we know such refusal will create at the South.

Resistance to wrong and injury—to tyranny, whether of one man or eighteen millions—is the cherished birth-right of every citizen of the Federal Union. A penny on the pound of tea was an abstraction utterly insignificant and worthless when compared with the consequences of a war of seven years, and expense of millions of treasure, and the loss of thousands of lives; and yet that penny created an independent people, and built up a nation, now one of the first powers of the world. Disunion in '76 had not more enemies nor less friends, because of its insignificant penny abstraction cause; nor will disunionists in 1861 be deterred by the tory cry of Union, when a majority of the States have authoritatively pronounced for "the irrepressible conflict" against the rights, interests, property and lives of the minority.

If the Southern States are to be ruined by "missiles" hurled by the hands of Lincoln and his followers, not from Illinois against Kentucky, but from Washington City, with the power and patronage of the Federal Government, against the institutions and lives of the people of the Southern States, it will be a matter of small consequence whether that ruin follow the effort at independence or comes as the natural consequence of a servile submission to Black Republican rule. Mr. Yancey, as the advocate of disunion without cause, would be powerless, but as the bold and powerful champion of the rights, property and lives of the Southern people, even with the cause created by an abstraction, would prove a most powerful Moses to the second exodus.

Upon the accession of Lincoln to power, we would apprehend no direct act of violence against negro property, but by the use of federal office, contracts, power and patronage, the building up in every Southern State of a Black Republican party, the ally and stipendiary of Northern fanaticism, to become in a few short years the open advocates of abolition, the confiscation of negro property by emancipation sudden or gradual, and eventually the ruin of every Southern State by the destruction of negro labor. By gradual and insidious approach, under the fostering hand of federal power, Abolitionism will grow up in every border Southern State, converting them into free States, then into "cities of refuge" for runaway negroes from the gulf States. No act of violence may ever be committed, no servile war waged, and yet the ruin and degradation of Virginia will be as fully and as fatally accomplished as though bloodshed and rapine ravished the land. There are no consequences that can follow, even forcible disunion, more disastrous to the future prosperity of the people of Virginia, than will be this sowing the seeds of discord and division, of emancipation and abolitionism by Northern hands, to be cultivated and harvested by the people of Virginia.

If Mr. Yancey is a disunionist to avert these sad consequences, there will be no odium in the charge; on the contrary, the best and noblest men of the Southern States will rally around the gallant Alabamian, to avert consequences so calamitous to the peace and prosperity of the Southern States.

The supporters of Mr. Brenckinridge are no more disunionists, because Mr. Yancey may be so considered, than are the friends of Mr. Douglas slave-traders because Mr. Gaulding, or some such man, advocated the slave trade unrebuked in the Douglas Convention. The only Georgian present in the Douglas Convention advocated the slave trade in a labored and silly effort for nearly one hour, unrebuked by any delegate; and yet we are not uncharitable enough to charge the slave trade upon Mr. Douglas, because of the folly of his Georgia supporter.

These are reflections which address themselves to the supporters of Mr. Douglas in Virginia, and to all those who advocate two tickets—Douglas and Johnson, Breckinridge and Lane—in every State.

The running of two tickets in Virginia has other consequences equally serious. It divides and distracts the Southern people, and, by the division, and the animosities which it will excite, encourages the fanaticism of the North. It matters not how true to Southern rights and Southern interests the supporters of Mr. Douglas may be, the very act of separation from the great body of their friends, neighbors and associates of the South, and the adoption of the silly slogan *"disunion,"* towards their fellow citizens of the South, will give them the character of *submissionists,* which will cause them to be regarded by the North as the pioneers of Black Republicanism in the South. In vain will they point to the record of Mr. Douglas as justification against the suspicions they will have excited at the South, and the hopes they will have encouraged at the North.

48. A Constitutional Union

(North Carolina Standard, Raleigh, July 11, 1860)

North Carolina has been for the space of seventy years a member of the federal Union. She entered this great sisterhood of States after mature deliberation. She did so believing she would thereby best promote her own interests, and more effectually than in any other situation protect herself from encroachments by foreign States. Strong in her own arm and in her own determined purpose to maintain the right under all circumstances, she was nevertheless not unmindful of the fact that in union there would be strength beyond that which any individual State could possess. During this long period she has been faithful to all her Constitutional obligations; and on the other hand, while her rights as a slaveholding State have not always been as fully respected and maintained as they should have been, yet no deliberate wrong has been put upon her, and none of her vital interests have been assailed or threatened by the common government. When her co-States of the South have complained of unjust tariff laws, or protested against the encroachments of the non-slaveholding States upon their rights in the common territories, she has sympathized with them in these complaints and protests; but when they have nullified the laws, or taken steps to dissolve their relations with the other States, she has mildly but firmly interposed to prevent the calamitous consequences which would flow from nullification and disunion. She has never been either a nullifying or a disunion State, and she is not so now. Some great cause must move her—some great wrong must either be inflicted or must overshadow her, before she will seriously contemplate by her own act a severance of the Union. She feels that while Virginia, and Tennessee, and Maryland, and Kentucky are safe in the Union she will be safe also; and that her honor, as sensitive and as untarnished as theirs, has been confided to her own keeping, and not to that of South Carolina, Alabama, and Mississippi. She is a bread-stuff rather than a "cotton State." Her interests are central among the southern States, relying as she does for protection not more on the slaveholding States south of her than on those of the north and west. She is not so much of a "cotton State" as to be ready just now to pitch into the vortex of disunion and revolution. She will not rush into this vortex herself, and she will hold others back, if she can.

During this long period of seventy years, North Carolina has enjoyed almost uninterrupted repose. The battles rendered necessary by a just regard for the honor of the country, have been fought elsewhere than on her soil. Her people are now contented, prosperous, and happy. Her fields smile with plenty, and the hum of industry is heard in all her workshops. Her credit in the money market is equal to the best. Her internal improvements are progressing, and prospering as they progress. Her Common School system is the best in all the Southern States. Her slave property is secure. No menace even is uttered against her, save by the more radical portion of the black Republicans. The national Democrats of the non-slaveholding States have defended and are defending her rights as a slaveholding State both in Congress and before their fellow-citizens.

In a word, no reason exists why North Carolina should contemplate at this time a dissolution of the Union.

While we would surrender no right of our State, and while we would preserve her honor untarnished among her sisters, yet disunion is one of the last things to be thought of. Disunion would be fraternal strife, civil and servile war, murder, arson, pillage, robbery, and fire and blood through long and cruel years. It would unsettle all business, diminish the value of all property, put the lives of both sexes and all ages in peril, and launch the States on a sea of scenes which no eye has scanned and no navigator sounded. It would bring debt, and misrule, and oppressive taxes, to be followed, perhaps, by the military rule of titled tyrants. It would wrench apart the tenderly entwined affections of millions of hearts, making it a crime in the North to have been born in the South, and a crime in the South to have been born in the North. It would convert the great body of the conservative men of the North, who are now our friends, into either deadly enemies or indifferent spectators of our intestine struggles, which would increase in intensity until law, order, justice, and civil rule would be forgotten or unknown. We repeat, there is no good cause *now* for dissolving the Union. The cause may arise, but let us not hasten to make or meet it.—Who desires it now? Who would cause it? Who would "precipitate the States" into bloodshed and revolution? Who would darken the stars that now flash in the flag of the Union? Who, without cause and for no sufficient reason, would have war instead of peace, discord in the place of concord, and all the calamities which must result from the dissolution of a government such as ours? If such a man exists, let him stand forth to be blasted by the indignant maledictions of patriotic millions. Voices from the past, voices innumerable in the present, appeal to us not to peril rashly our Constitutional Union. From all battle-fields where Southern blood has mingled with Northern blood beneath one common and glorious banner; from the shores of Delaware, over whose breaking ice, on that stormy night, pressed the weary and bleeding feet of those two thousand soldiers, the only, the forlorn, the last hope of great WASHINGTON himself; from the kingdoms of the earth, in which the down-trodden millions struggle beneath the iron hoof of despotism, casting longing and hopeful glances towards this, the first, as it may be the last great experiment of self-government among men; from the whole civilized world, interested in our material prosperity and in the progress and happiness of man, there comes up to us with thundering sound—and over all of it, and ringing through all of it as with the blast of a trumpet, the spirit-voice of the immortal Jackson, speaking from his record and from his whole military and civil life—"THE FEDERAL UNION—IT MUST AND SHALL BE PRESERVED!" Preserved, not as a consolidated, aggressive, usurping Union, but as a *Constitutional* Union, protecting all equally, and dispensing its benefits and blessings as much to one section as another. Let us cling to such a Union as "the mariner clings to his last plank when night and the tempest close around him." As long as the Constitution is preserved inviolate we shall have nothing to fear. It will be time enough when that instrument, which is the bond of the Union, shall have been broken, or its spirit disregarded, to dissolve existing relations and provide new guards for future security.

49. The Country Wants Peace, and the Country Must Have
Peace—An Appeal to All Lovers of the Union of All
Sections and Parties

(Daily Nashville Patriot, July 25, 1860)

It cannot be doubted that the pending struggle for the Presidency involves the fate of the Union, either immediate or proximate; and the sooner the people come to realize the fact, the better. Our present purpose is to review the attitude of the parties to the contest, as briefly as may be, and to suggest a practical exit from impending dangers and difficulties.

It is palpable to the least observant that the acerbity of feeling which prevails among a large portion of the people of the two sections of the country, has grown out of the agitation of the question relating to the institution of domestic slavery in what are denominated the Southern States. This agitation, as can be easily shown by tracing its history, in its inception and generally throughout its continuance up to the present moment, was and is intended more to subserve the interests of mere politicians than to advance the true interest and prosperity of the country or to answer a positive demand of the people of either section. Really but twice in our career as a united government under our present constitution has the question been presented in a shape involving practical results under circumstances of excitement and well-grounded alarm. Those two occasions were the application of Missouri for admission as a State in 1820 and the application of California and the simultaneous disposition of the territories acquired from Mexico, in 1850. On those two occasions the issues were practical and the popular excitement and apprehension and alarm were real and well-founded. The STATESMEN of those days succeeded in settling the differences in both instances peacefully and to the satisfaction of the people of both sections. In 1852, the two great antagonistic parties, the Whig and Democratic, each having distinguished representatives who were engaged in the last great pacification, each participating in the great achievement and sharing alike the glory of saving the Union from dissolution, solemnly agreed that the legislation of 1850 was just to both sections and ought to be a finality. Of course, there were malcontents both in the North and the South, but the great masses of the people everywhere were satisfied with the adjustment, and were in a majority so overwhelming that

the opponents of the adjustment, except a squad of chronic abolitionists who voted for John P. Hale,[1] dared not show their faces in
any quarter. Indeed so perfectly content were the great masses of the
people with the settlement of 1850 that the chief topic of debate between the adherents of Mr. Pierce and General Scott was as to which
was the better friend of the measures through which the settlement
was effected, and which was most likely to prove reliable in adhering to them and perpetuating the peace so happily restored to the
country. Here, then—leaving out of view all disputes upon the subject anterior to 1850—we have a standpoint of safety, of peace, of
satisfaction, of concord behind which we need not go to trace the immediate source of present danger.

But, notwithstanding, both the then existing parties had voluntarily
placed themselves under bonds to keep the peace on this question, had
given solemn pledges in their national party conventions to hold that
peace final and sacred, it was ruthlessly broken up by one of the parties.
The act was not demanded by either section of the Union—it was not
necessary to secure the rights of the people in either section. We speak
now only of the act of thrusting the subject upon the country—the act
of resurrecting the tomahawk which had been buried. It was unnecessary, it was uncalled for, it was cruel; it displayed a faithlessness to
pledges, a recklessness of the public peace and a disregard of the public
weal, that is without a parallel in the annals of the country. Without
going into detail, it is sufficient now to say that its immediate effect
was to shiver the Whig party into fragments. It created from nonentity
a huge organization, now known as the Republican party, based on the
single idea of hostility to the extension of slavery. It was an application
of blazing brands to dry stubble, and the fire which it kindled swept
over the Northern States with such energy as to carry almost everything before it. The House of Representatives in the Congress in which
the subject was thus introduced, consisted of 159 Democrats, 71 Whigs,
and 4 Freesoilers; in the next one returned by the people the Democrats
had dwindled down to 83, while the Freesoilers, under the name of
Republicans had increased from 4 to 108. In 1856, this party of Free-
soilers put forward its candidates for President and Vice President, on
a platform of hostility to slavery extension, both selected from non-
slaveholding States, not having an electoral ticket in any of the slaveholding States, and obtained a popular vote of one million three hun-

[1] John Parker Hale, Anti-Slavery Senator from New Hampshire, 1847–1853, 1855–1865;
Free Soil candidate for the presidency, 1852.

dred and forty-one thousand five hundred and fourteen, in an aggregate of four million and fifty-four thousand.

This extraordinary state of things at the North, marked by great bitterness of feeling in that section towards the most important domestic institution in the South, aroused an opposite antagonistic feeling here. All remember how intense was the excitement which prevailed everywhere throughout that campaign—how it was argued in all the assemblies of the people that the issue has [sic] at length come direct between the two sections, and the South was urged to unite as one man against this great Northern party which carried destruction to Southern rights and institutions in its pathway. And though there was a middle party endeavoring to stay the advancing legions of both, which sought to overthrow both, and to restore the country once more to peace, it was overwhelmed in the turbulence of the hour, and was able to count but one State in the entire Union as a supporter. For some time the contest between the enraged sections was in doubt, and steps were taken by State Executives in the South for a dissolution of the Union, in the event of the election of the Republican candidate. Majorities in all the Southern States, save one, did unite on the democratic candidate, and, with the aid of five of the Northern States, he triumphed. The contest thus came within five States in the North, including California on the Pacific—within four in the North proper—and one in the South of being a united North against a united South. Thus was the verge of sectionalism pure and unrelieved, reached in 1856. No true lover of his country and of its union and its peace and safety can desire to see it go nearer than that.

The interval between the canvas of 1856 and the present has been devoted by the party managers of the two sectional parties to diligent efforts to complete the work of uniting the sections against each other. The Republicans, seeking power with an unholy lust, know that scarcely less than a united North will suffice them, and hence they are straining every nerve to bring about that result. On the other hand, an element of the South, desperate and reckless, desiring a dissolution of the Union, have bent their energies to bring about the result labored for by the Republicans, though with a far different motive. We have heretofore exposed the diabolical machinations of these men in these columns, and shown, by irrefragable proof, the scope of their design and the means to be used for its accomplishment. They have so far succeeded as to cleave the democratic party into two impotent parts, and are now urging a union of the South upon Mr. BRECKINRIDGE. The

Northern Democracy, in the mass, are against the Southern wing of the party as directly and unalterably as they could possibly be upon the slavery question. They have as their champion, the man who, above all others, is responsible for reopening the box, so happily sealed in 1850, out of which all this strife has sprung. And lastly the FILLMORE men of 1856, still seeing the inevitable catastrophe approaching, are striving to beat back the maddened elements on both sides.

Having thus stated the attitude of the parties to the contest we proceed to offer some suggestions which should command the thoughtful attention of patriotic men of all parties and sections. It must be borne in mind that the contest of 1860, is vastly different from that of 1856. The Republicans stand in solid phalanx, as in 1856; the Democrats, then only a plurality, are now divided into two factions, irreconcilable amongst themselves, and wholly powerless so long as they are divided. The Union men, Mr. BELL taking the place of Mr. FILLMORE in 1856, are still standing firmly out against sectionalism everywhere and advocating peace. This state of things among the opponents of Republicanism must give that party the greatest advantages. It renews their hopes and strengthens their courage, enlists their enthusiasm and encourages them to put forth their utmost energies. If they succeed, we are clear in the conviction that it will lead to a direct attempt to dissolve the government. Though we do not believe that such an event, of itself, would be a justifiable cause for breaking up the Union, we have no sort of doubt that the attempt would be made, and that it would be so serious in its nature as to result in incalculable evil to both sections of the country. We can see nothing but evil and disaster in it. And whether they were successful in inaugurating an administration or not, nothing but strife and contention and confusion and bad feeling would come out of it. Peace, that which is most necessary, could not be hoped for. This our Southern readers already know, and the Republicans had as well be convinced of it first as last.

On the other hand it is impossible for either faction of the democratic party to elect its candidate, as parties now stand. This proposition admits of no manner of question. But let us grant that by a united South, a thing utterly impracticable, Mr. DOUGLAS could be elected over Mr. LINCOLN. It would be upon a very close struggle, and instead of breaking down the Republican party it would tend only to cement its forces and bring them out in still sterner array for the contest of 1864. Besides, his administration, on the basis of a fallacious doctrine of popular sovereignty, and devoted, as it would certainly be, to an effort to engraft that doctrine as the settled policy of the government, would only continue and aggravate an unprofitable strife, which is the very disease which now afflicts us.

In the next place, granting for the purpose of this argument, that Mr. BRECKINRIDGE could, by a complete union of the Southern electoral vote, triumph over Mr. LINCOLN, what would be the most favorable results that could be anticipated? He would, unquestionably, go into office as the exponent and embodiment of the views of the ultraists of the extreme South, at least it would be so held by the Republicans and the DOUGLAS democracy. His support by conservative Southern men could not release him from the influence of the Southern disunionists. The entire body of the Northern DOUGLAS democracy would certainly array themselves in opposition to him, and upon the issue of Congressional protection coöperate, for all practical purposes, with the Republicans to make that opposition effectual. There is not probably half a dozen Congressional districts in all the Northern States, which, upon the issue of protection to slavery in the territories, would return members in favor of such a measure. The attempt, under such circumstances, would necessarily prove a failure. This would have the effect to give the Republicans a permanent ascendency in the House, and possibly in the Senate, before the expiration of his term. This would, of course, still further inflame the Southern mind, and render still more confident and determined the great Northern anti-slavery party. The people would then be prepared to meet the final issue between the North and the South, and the speedy dissolution of the Government. The most, therefore, that could be expected or reasonably hoped for from the election of Mr. BRECKINRIDGE would be a prolongation of the struggle. Instead of securing the coveted boon of peace, the only thing that can save us as a nation of united people, his administration would be but a continuation of the turmoil with increased bitterness, and to place reconciliation out of the question. There is no candid man of intelligence of any party who will deny that all the tendencies and probabilities are as we have stated them, in relation to the Republican and two Democratic candidates.

Lastly, we have Mr. BELL. Unlike all three of the others, each of whom is directly mixed up, in his political history and personal schemes, with this agitation, Mr. BELL has let no opportunity pass, in an active public career covering the entire period of strife to within something over a year past, without doing all in his power, consistent with the constitution and the principles of State equality, to discountenance and quiet agitation on this subject. His course has been marked from the outset by a desire to promote peace and concord. He has never proved untrue to any section, but all his antecedents are elevated, national and conservative. By the circumstances of his nomination he is placed before the people in opposition to the extremists of the South and to the sectionalists of the North. His election would be not only the nominal defeat of both, but it would be an emphatic declaration on the part of the people, that on an issue between the North and the South, involving the fate of the Union, they were prepared to stand by, uphold and defend the Union on the basis of the Constitution and the Laws of the land. On what other ground can the Union continue? On what other can we have peace? On what other can the dangers which threaten to engulf us in ruin be averted? Cannot the friends of the Union, on the basis named, forget, for a time, party feeling and lay aside party prejudice? Cannot the conservative people of all parties and sections sacrifice, for the time being, something of past party recollections and love, to the impulses of a noble and generous patriotism and to the obligations it imposes? We do not ask the support of the disunionists, nor of the fanatical abolitionists; but we appeal to the true-hearted lovers of the Union everywhere to unite with us in crushing both—in our effort to extract the deadly fang which is rapidly penetrating to the vitals of the body politic. If done at all, it must be effectually done. It will not do to content ourselves with sending the election to the House of Representatives in Congress. In that case the work would be only half done. The sentence of condemnation upon the enemies of our repose must come from the PEOPLE. From politicians, who have brought the trouble upon us, we can hope for but little. If it could be made reasonably manifest that the great conservative States, such as Virginia, North Carolina, Tennessee, Kentucky, Missouri, &c., in the South, would go for BELL and EVERETT, we are convinced that the corresponding conservative States of the North would unite with us in decisive majorities in a declaration of attachment to the Union and the equal and just rights of all the States under the Constitution. By this means, the vote of LINCOLN would be reduced to a few States, and the power and prestige of his party would be broken and its ranks scattered forever; while the disunionists, South, would be forced to hide their heads in very shame.— Thus, and thus only, can peace be restored to a land distracted and torn. Thus would the election of Mr. BELL be peace. His administration would set its whole power against a renewal of the slavery agitation, and its energies be directed into other channels of governmental econ-

omy, now long neglected. Thus would we heed and be benefited by
the farewell warning of WASHINGTON, and thus would we obliterate
parties based on "geographical discriminations."

What true and loyal and conservative democrat of the South or the
North can object? Its effect would be to deprive them of power for one
term. On questions of national policy they may still differ with Mr.
BELL. Having shut out the sectional controversy and re-instated the
goddess of Peace in the National temple, we could afford to differ on
questions of national economy. And the probability is that parties would
soon be reorganized, one being for and the other against the administration, exclusively on those questions. Thus would the foundation be
laid for broad and national parties. Thus the scattered democracy might
be again re-united, and the country again be divided into parties of great
national principles.

Is it not worthy of an effort? Can any man suggest a more practicable and effectual exit from our present difficulties and dangers? We ask
that the PEOPLE, independently of leaders and politicians, take the subject under their thoughtful consideration, and answer at the ballot-box
to their consciences and to posterity.

50. THE UNION

(*The Charleston Mercury,* July 25, 1860)

The Union of the Constitution, we presume nearly all men in the
South, desire to be perpetuated. It is the bond of our fathers, and as
their children we will maintain it. But do the dangers and agitations
which now shake the United States, arise from the Union of the Constitution? If it does, then the work of our fathers is most inadequate
to our times. We maintain that these dangers and agitations are the
result, not of the Constitution they transmitted to us, but of its overthrow. The Union it established does not exist. Usurpation and encroachment have drawn into the vortex of Federal power, interests
which were never intended, by the Constitution, to be embraced in its
operations. The General Government, under the sectional predominance
and policy of the North, has become omnipotent in the laying and appropriation of the taxes; and now stretches its authority over slavery
in the South. The Constitution, under such usurpations of power, is
virtually abolished—and the Union it established is virtually dissolved.
Hence the dissatisfaction in the South and the conflict between the
North and the South, which must end either in the Union of the Con-

stitution being restored, or in the South being destroyed by the sectional despotism of the North under the auspices of another Union, established by power on the one side and subjection on the other. Nor is the test of the true condition of the South very far off. The elections next fall must settle the question of Northern predominance—of a complete sectional despotism over the South, or of yet another chance for Southern deliverance. As things now are, the probability is that the Black Republicans will sweep the North, and command the Electoral College in the Presidential election. Now, in such a condition of things, is it truthful—is it politic in the South to deal in professions of devotion to the Union? Will they prepare the people of the South to resist the sectional despotism of the Black Republican party? With a full knowledge of the fatal effects to the South, of the possession and control of the Federal Government by the Black Republicans and Abolitionists of the North, do not such professions inevitably tend to a submission to their rule? Ought not the people of the South, rather, to be aroused to a full sense of the perils which hang over them, and be prepared to meet them, and to control their own destinies? What is now the Union?

1. It is a Union with the Northern States.

2. It is a Union with the Northern States, who have nullified the Constitution in the Fugitive Slave Laws.

3. It is a Union with the Northern States, who for twenty years, have kept up in Congress an agitation against Southern slavery.

4. It is a Union with the Northern States, who have determined to exclude the Southern people from settling, with their slaves, in any of the Territory of the United States.

6. [*Sic*] It is a Union with the Northern States, who have organized their *sectional* power, to rule and govern the Southern States, as their interest, ambition or fanaticism shall require.

7. It is a Union with the Northern States, who have overthrown the Union of the Constitution, and have substituted in its stead a Union having their despotic power the sole criterion of its terms and limitations.

8. It is a Union with the Northern States, in which a party predominates whose vital *principle* is hostility to African slavery in the South and whose *policy* it is to extinguish it.

9. It is a Union with Tariff plunderers, who, by the Tariff Laws of the Federal Government, appropriate the property of the Southern people to their use, and make them their tributaries.

10. It is a Union with Treasury plunderers, who, by unconstitutional appropriations, drain the Treasury of the United States for their sectional enrichment and aggrandisement.

11. Briefly, it is a Union on the part of the South with her bitterest revilers, haters, oppressors and enemies.

Now, that any man in the South, who realizes the truth of the above positions, can *love* or *reverence* the Union, *as it exists*—is an utter impossibility. Lying lips may utter praise—and a cowardly heart may refrain its murmurs:—but the meanest political slave must hate a despotism which scourges and threatens to destroy him. Love and hate, are not under our control. God has so constituted the human heart that we *can* love only *what is lovely*—and we must hate what is morally *wrong and detestable*. We do not wish to judge others harshly, but it does appear to us that no one in the South can *love* or *reverence* the Union *as it exists,* but one who is at heart an Abolitionist. Many may tolerate it, under the hope of reforming it. Many may remember and love it, as it was in past days of usefulness and glory, when it was the Union of the Constitution. But now,—as it is *now without* the Constitution—*with* its furious sectionalism, and its anti-slavery fanaticism and policy at the North—the only feelings in the South which it can rationally inspire, are those of distrust, fear, contempt or hate. If you have still hopes of reforming it, and of again reinstating the Union of the Constitution—say so; but to accomplish your object, you must *condemn the Union as it is.* If it is worthy of your devotion—why reform it? What are all your opposition and complaints, but hypocritical ravings, for factious ends?

51. The Presidential Election—Its Probable Result—Its Moral Influence

(*The Daily South Carolinian,* Columbia, August 3, 1860)

The result of the Presidential struggle is no longer one of much doubt or uncertainty. Take State by State, and make whatever calculations we may, based upon the relative strength of parties, as indicated by recent elections, and as they will probably vote, owing to existing divisions, and we can arrive at no other conclusion than that Lincoln is to be the next President of the United States, if the Southern States permit it. For years the agitation of this slavery question has been conducted with spirit and energy by Northern politicians. They have enlisted in their behalf the sympathy and aid of a portion of the Northern pulpit; they have leagued and allied with those who have sought to foster hot-house interests by pecuniary aid abstracted from duties on a foreign commerce created and sustained by the great agricultural interests of the country; they have received in their motley and hungry ranks the political refugees of all the other parties; and now, with ranks swollen to proportions sufficient to achieve victory, they are ready to seize upon the Government. What is their first and strongest idea, that which has brought to them three-fourths of their strength? It is the idea of Abolitionism; it is the idea which furnishes the actors for every manifestation of hostility to the rights and institutions of the South; it is at the bottom of every raid upon the South; it incites to the murder of her citizens, whether at home, amid the quiet of domestic life, or in neighboring States demanding the restoration of property stolen away by those who covenanted to respect it and to restore it; it is the idea which furnishes an insult for every column of the *Congressional Globe;* it is an idea that is restless and active; that has a reality in view, and is working night and day for its accomplishment. We must weigh the consequences of this party's success not by the words of their leaders. They would blind us from a perception of their aim by all manner of soothing terms. We may actually believe them when they protest that they themselves intend no open and direct hostility to the South; we may concede to them all this, and yet it should not lull the South into repose, or cause her to dismiss a single apprehension. The same hand that plants the seed does not always reap the harvest; the same hand that fashions the dagger does not always use it. But if, through the instrumentality of this party, ideas be disseminated in the Northern mind, and if these sowers of the seeds, whose fruits are well known, meet with Northern support, why need the South wait to ascertain that the harvesters will be approved? There never was a revolution that was not preceded by the disseminators of the ideas of which it was but a logical result. And if we see the Northern mind receiving with approval the ideas of hostility everywhere promulgated by the Republican leaders, we may rest assured that if they be not resisted now, they will present themselves to the South, not as abstract ideas, resting but lightly upon the surface of the Northern mind, but as ideas fully developed and fully matured; ideas deeply rooted and deeply imbedded; ideas active and bristling with terrible designs and as ready for bloody and forcible realities as ever characterized the ideas of the French revolution. We have already had some of the forward offshoots of this growing crop, and if we await until their full maturity, their resistance will be a still more difficult problem for Southern solution. If, then, this party succeeds, and succeeds upon such ideas as these, can any one calculate its moral influence upon the enemies of the South at the North, and its disastrous influence upon the spirit of the South? These ideas have been gradually developing themselves, notwithstanding the opposition of a strong party at the North and against the influences and patronage of the Federal Government. When this party of patriots is destroyed, and when the power of the Government shall be cast against us; when the President shall promulgate these ideas from the Federal Capital, and proscribe every man who dares to raise his voice in favor of the constitutional rights of the South and for the equality of the States of the Union; when every voice raised for Southern defense shall be hissed at as the voice of a traitor and factionist, and frowned upon by the ruling powers of a Government for which the South is called upon to shed her blood and to expend her wealth when its honor is to be vindicated or safety preserved; when the Senate and the House shall swarm with Sumners and Lovejoys, who study their language that they may excel in abusive epithets—can the South, then, in the Union, hope for safety? Can she hope for peace? We have hoped with those who have indulged hope most pertinaciously. We have watched, admired and applauded the gallant battles which Northern men have made for the constitutional rights of the South. We have seen our friends successful here and there, but the triumph was always short. While we have sometimes seen our friends successful—we have yet to see the first instance of any Senator or Representative who became conspicuous in abusing the South, that was not returned by his constituents. Is this fact not instructive? It will be so with this Presidential election. Let the South submit to it, and her very remonstrances will be construed then, as they are now, and as they were during our colonial existence, into threats intended to intimidate the North, and every appeal to a Northern sense of justice will be drowned by counter-appeals to Northern courage and stubbornness; and these very remonstrances will only be made use of to array against us a still stronger hostile public sentiment. The instances are few where the minority's remonstrances have not been construed into arrogance and factiousness, and even in its powerless condition been accused of imperiousness and insolence, that greater burdens might be heaped upon it. Senator Seward in his last speech said to the North, "The elections have demonstrated that you have the power to elect your President and take control of the Government—it now remains," says he, "to be decided if you have the firmness to use it." Under such appeals, the North will not have the courage to disengage itself from the shackles with which this Republican party has bound it, and is hurrying it onto the consummation of its designs. Even now, if we remain silent, some Northern Representative rises and offers an insult, hoping and knowing that some Southern Representative will repel it, and furnish by his reply, based upon the patriotic sentiment of loyalty to the constitutional rights of his section, capital with which to inflame the Northern mind. Even now, the surest tenure a Northern man can hold upon a seat in the Federal Legislature, is that which he obtains through active discharge of the office of Southern crimination. Until now, the seats of Senators and Representatives from the Northern States have become so many pieces in a grand battery, from which malignant denunciation is heaped upon the South. The same causes will operate a like result in the administrative department. The surest tenure upon it which any Republican occupant could have, would be derived from the institution of measures of hostility to the South. Then when the South remonstrated, the popular sentiment of the North would be appealed to, to sustain a President whom the South was trying to bully and force into terms. And as this party has advanced from one *idea* of hostility to another; from the same causes, when in power, it will advance from one *act* of hostility to another, in each advancement sustaining itself by an appeal to Northern support to protect it from Southern imperiousness, until the ruin of the South will have been accomplished. Then, as now, we shall have a party in the South proclaiming that those who remonstrate are responsible for all the troubles. It is not simply opposition to the Democratic party that has rallied such a formidable support to the Republican nominees—it is hostility to the South. If it were hostility to the Democratic party and not to the South, why are Bell and Everett, and Douglas and Johnson, received with so little favor that they cannot now claim one single Northern State? If the object of the North was simply, as some say, to take the Government out of Democratic hands, why are these two tickets received with so little Northern favor? No, the ticket that alone commends itself to the North, and that will probably receive its almost united electoral votes, is that which is not only hostile to the Democracy but to the South. And these middle ground tickets, now supported by so many Southern men, without any prospect of success, seem to be pushed forward with the poor prospect that they will paralyze the only party that has boldly met this hostile organization, and by dividing the South, demoralize her in her efforts to defend herself in the Union, and, by demoralizing her, strengthen her enemies, and force upon her the alternative of disunion or a submission in which each year she will be summoned to a lower abasement of her pride and manhood. Of the alternatives, we cannot but believe that the South should choose disunion. We do not lightly esteem the benefits of the Union or the evils of disunion. We are ready to weigh heavily the consequences of national rivalry, jealousy and distrust. France and England illustrate it. We would still choose disunion, believing that these causes will entail expensive Governments, standing armies and large navies upon each section, to protect their frontiers and their commerce, but we would choose it, believing that all of these evils are preferable to the inferiority to which Republican rule would sink the South. We advocate resistance, not because we see such a bright future in disunion, but because we see such abasement in a Union so administered.

52. THE PRESIDENTIAL ELECTION AND UNION SAVERS

(*The Charleston Mercury*, August 4, 1860)

1. The Presidential election turns upon a single fact. If the Northern people, believe that the Southern people will dissolve their connection with them, should the Black Republican party succeed in electing LINCOLN to the Presidency—LINCOLN *will be defeated*. Should they, on the contrary, believe, that the Southern people will submit to Black Republican domination by the election of LINCOLN to the Presidency—LINCOLN *will be elected*.

2. There is but one way, by which the people of the North can be convinced, that the people of the South will not submit to Black Republican domination by the election of LINCOLN; and that is, *by their union against him*. Everything, therefore, which tends to disunite the South, aids the election of LINCOLN.

3. The only party in the South, standing simply on the sectional rights of the South, and opposed to the sectional policy of Black Republicanism in the North, is the party which supports BRECKINRIDGE and LANE for the Presidency; and this party commands the immense majority of the Southern people.

4. Those who oppose this party in the South, do all in their power, to satisfy the Northern people that the Southern people will submit to Black Republican domination, by the election of LINCOLN to the

Presidency. They, therefore, powerfully aid his election *in the North*.

5. The Union-savers in the South are especially the most efficient allies of the Black Republican party. By assailing, with disunionism, their brethren of the South who support BRECKINRIDGE and LANE, instead of joining them to maintain the rights of the South, they manifest a greater regard for the Union than for the rights of the South. This is all the Black Republican party want, of any ally at the South.

6. That the Union is stronger than slavery in the South, is an axiom of the Black Republican party. Their success, in grasping the power of the General Government, rests upon it. All movements in the South tending to show that their axiom is true, is a most efficient co-operation with them, and nerves and stimulates their progress and power at the North.

7. If the above positions be true, then the Union-savers in the South and the Black Republicans are one in their policy; which is, to subject the people of the South to Black Republican domination, by the election of LINCOLN to the Presidency.

We have no doubt of the truth of the above positions; but we by no means intend to charge that those in the South who are upholding for the Presidency Mr. BELL or Mr. DOUGLAS, under the cry of Unionism, realize their true position. Many of the leaders, in this senseless cry, do prefer the destruction of slavery to the destruction of the Union, but the greater part of their supporters are led away by false professions—and an imperfect view of the designs of the Black Republicans —or exaggerated representations of the value of the Union, and the dangers to the South from its dissolution. Time is, however, rapidly sifting out the truth, from the dust of falsehood by which it has been concealed. The assimilation of all parties at the North against the South is showing its development. Squatter Sovereignty, Unionism, and Black Republicanism, are approaching one common fusion. The progress of sectionalism at the North for sectional aggrandisement can only be arrested by the union of the South in defense of her rights. Cannot the Union-savers of the South see that, by their silly policy, they are driving the two great sections of the Union into collision; and that thus the very object they profess to have at heart—the preservation of the Union—will be defeated? Let them join the great majority of the people of the South in the maintenance of their rights, by the election of BRECKINRIDGE and LANE to the Presidency—with the alternative (made manifest by their co-operation) of Union or disunion, plainly presented to the North—and the Union will be safe, as the result of this Presidential election. Does not fidelity to the Union, as well as to the South, require this policy?

53. THE CONDITION OF AFFAIRS

(*Louisville Daily Journal*, August 13, 1860)

The Black Republican organs of the North undertake to make light of the idea that any of the people of the South seriously contemplate dissolving the Union in the event of Mr. Lincoln's election. Most assuredly a good many of them do seriously contemplate it, and they are even now trying to effect Lincoln's election in order to carry out their plan. We are not disposed to urge this fact upon the Republicans as what should at all influence their course in the canvass or in the election; but we are inclined to dwell upon it as a matter to be weighed and duly heeded by those who are not of the Republican party. It is all natural enough for Lincoln's own party to think and say that they will elect him if they can, be the consequence to the Union or the world what it may; but other parties may well be expected to do whatever *they* can, consistently with principle, to avert a fearful catastrophe. If the Republicans were to elect their candidate, we should labor as earnestly as any of them, and we have no doubt far more earnestly than most of them, to preserve the Union; but we can see no reason why patriots should seek to place the Republic or be willing to see it placed in any such deplorable exigency. We do not want to see the Union brought into direful perils simply to have the privilege of engaging in a doubtful conflict in its behalf.

The Republican leaders think or pretend to think that what is said in the Southern presses about the dissolution of the Union is mere empty bluster intended to frighten the North and influence its political action. We can calmly assure them, that, as a general thing, the fact is far otherwise. Most of the Southern organs, instead of telling more than the truth upon this subject, tell less. We have had many hundreds of private letters within the last few weeks, all informing us of a settled and widely-extended purpose to break up the Union if a Republican shall be elected to the Presidency, and very many of them bearing testimony that the fire-eating Democracy want Lincoln elected in order that their conspiracy may be executed at once. We admit that the conspirators are mad, but such madness "rules the hour."

We had a private letter yesterday from a political friend in Alabama, who writes, "I know that arrangements are made, in the event of Lincoln's election, to light up the fires of civil war." We had another letter from an Alabama gentlemen, enclosing a list of subscribers for our paper, who says, "there is probably no use in sounding the alarm, but I may say that it is within my personal knowledge that a concerted blow will be struck for the dismemberment of the Union if Lincoln be elected." We had a letter from a highly respectable Georgian, also enclosing us a list of names of subscribers, who says, "the North professes to think we are not in earnest, but, as sure as there is a God in heaven, a powerful movement will be made to prevent the inauguration of Mr. Lincoln over a united Republic." A few days ago we saw a highly intelligent Bell and Everett elector from one of the extreme States of the South, who informed us that he had just passed through Mississippi, and, that he happened to have peculiar means of becoming acquainted with what was going on in that State. He said to us that it was the fixed determination of the fire-eaters there, in case Lincoln should be elected, to strike all the laws of United States dead within the limits of Mississippi; and he added that troops, even now, are secretly drilling in preparation for the anticipated crisis. He fully agreed with us as to the character of the treason he spoke of, but said that there could not be the shadow of a doubt of its extent and power.

Now the Yancey men, who contemplate this treason, broke up the Democratic party at Charleston and Baltimore for no other purpose under heaven than that Lincoln might be elected and an opportunity thus afforded them for inaugurating their projected rebellion and revolution. And they are now getting up Breckinridge tickets in all the Northern States, not because they have the slightest hope or desire of carrying any one of those States, but simply to cause them all to go for Lincoln through the creation of divisions in the ranks of those by whom alone he could by even the remotest possibility be defeated. Well, as we said before, we do not invoke the Republicans to desert Mr. Lincoln because his election would be the signal of a Southern insurrection; they can give just as much thought and just as little to that consideration as they please; but we do earnestly appeal to Northern men who are not Republicans to oppose by all legitimate means the accomplishment of the atrocious purposes of the Southern traitors. These traitors are diligently at work through their agents and followers in all the non-slaveholding States to elect Lincoln, without which they cannot hope to dissolve the Union; and we appeal to our friends in the non-slaveholding States, we appeal to all, who, not being Republicans, are still the friends of the Union, to work diligently to defeat Lincoln in those States. While Breckinridge tickets are got up through all the Northern States simply to give those States to Lincoln, the Black Republican organs, understanding the purpose, encourage and foster those tickets, praise them upon all occasions, and exaggerate the strength of the faction that supports them; and we therefore, as patriots, as friends of the country, call upon our brother patriots of the North to resist the accomplishment of the common object of the Black Republicans and Disunionists, by resorting to every legitimate means for carrying the Northern States against Lincoln.

We do not ask men to sacrifice their principles, we do not ask them to vote against the convictions of their own judgments, but we do ask them to serve their country as effectively as possible in this day of her utmost need. It is our hope, our desire, we may add our expectation, to elect Bell and Everett to the Presidency and Vice Presidency. The result of the late election in Kentucky, viewed in connection with other recent events, gives certain evidence to those who understand the condition of things throughout the South, that the whole or nearly the whole of the Southern States can and will be carried in November for Bell and Everett. What is chiefly wanted now by the friends of the Union, the Constitution, and the Enforcement of the Laws, is that Lincoln may not be elected by the people through the concentration of one whole section, and the larger section, of the country upon him. If this result can be prevented, and the election devolved upon Congress, most certainly neither Lincoln nor Breckinridge will be elected; and there is good reason to believe that Bell will be. Thus the great need of our friends is that as many Northern States as possible shall be wrested from the Republicans. It matters little how they go, so they *don't go for Lincoln*. Let this be prevented, and all will be well. And it must be prevented, or fearful disasters may be the consequence. Let the work be done honestly, but certainly.

We hear much from the Black Republican organs in regard to the evils of an election of President by the House of Representatives. We are aware that those evils are not merely imaginary. We should heartily rejoice if a just and patriotic and national election could be effected by the people. But most surely we should regard the election of a truly national President by the House, even in the midst of a raging conflict of parties, as an incomparably less evil than the election of a President by one section of the country, who should be utterly and deeply obnoxious to every State and county and district and precinct of the other section. If any of the Northern States can be carried for Mr. Bell, in the country's name let it be done, and we shall most earnestly rejoice thereat; but, if they cannot be carried for Bell, let them not be carried for Lincoln.

54. THE TRUE POLICY EVERYWHERE—NO FUSION

(Weekly Montgomery Confederation, August 17, 1860)

The Staunton *Vindicator* says that nothing is now left for the friends of Douglas in Virginia "but to proceed to organize the National Democracy, and marching forth in the right, to fight the battle through, and either fall or triumph in defense of the honor and integrity of the National party and their candidates, Douglas and Johnson."

Thus speaks the great organ of the Tenth Legion Democracy of the old Dominion; and it speaks well. We trust such will be the policy in *every State* of the Union. No alliance, no combination, no union, no *sympathy* with the seceders and disunionists, the sectional disorganizers, on the part of the National Democracy supporting Douglas and Johnson at no time, no place, and under no circumstances. The disruptionists, led by Yancey, Rhett & Co., have deliberately left the great Democratic party of the Union. Not only so, but they assembled their faction, organized *another party,* as they avowed, upon the *debris*— ruins—of the National Democracy, and to *counteract its policy,* (so said Mr. Rhett, who leads the forces in South Carolina,) and nominated a ticket for the Presidency and Vice Presidency; a ticket that they call *National* in one section of the Union (as in the Northern part of Alabama, and the Northern and Middle States generally;) *sectional* in another, (as in South Carolina;) *"States' Rights Constitutional"* in another, (as here about Montgomery—see Mr. Judge's letter,) and the *Union* Democratic party in others. Such is the piebald concern that the old line, true blue State rights National Democracy—with but *one and the same name* from Maine to California and Oregon—are invited to join, in such localities *only* where the disunionists think themselves in a minority, and no hope of success without them!

But however all this might be overlooked or disregarded; have the National Democrats supporting Mr. Douglas *no self-respect?* Will they get upon their knees, and crawl into the counsels of men who have applied to them every possible form of opprobrious epithet of which the language is capable? Shall we cordially take the political hand of men who have denounced us as no better than abolitionists and free-soilers; who have expressed a preference for even Lincoln over Judge

Douglas, who has done more *for* the South against the abolitionists than all the Rhetts and Yanceys in christendom? Who have denounced our Convention as a conclave of "Squatters" without authority—a "Rump Convention," to which no allegiance is due by the Democracy, and where no Southern man could go with honor? Who have tried to heap upon us every species of ridicule and contempt, branding us as submissionists and traitors, and thus rendering us, if they could, *socially,* as well as politically, odious among our neighbors and countrymen?

No. The Douglas men that would join them would be proving themselves the fit recipients of all the odium and abuse that has been heaped upon them. Let us *forever* stand aloof, at least in a state of armed neutrality, from such an intolerant and proscriptive set of Jacobin conspirators. They have no lot or part with us. We wish to rally and preserve the Democracy and perpetuate its ascendancy, in order to save the Confederacy formed by our revolutionary fathers, and transmit it to our children. *They,* on the contrary, are trying to *disrupt* and *defeat* the Democracy, in order that a Black Republican may be elected, that the Union may be dissolved and that they, the leaders, may be put at the head of a Southern Confederacy.

Between *such men* and the National Democracy supporting Douglas and Johnson, there is and *can be no sympathy whatever.* We repudiate both the doctrines they teach and the men whom they put forth to disseminate them. We seek not *their* alliance and scorn their wooings. We have no doubt, now, that the recent elections have disclosed their utter imbecility, and inability to carry scarcely a single Southern State, that the National Democrats would be welcomed as marvelously clever fellows, if they would only "help me Cassius or I sink." But Cassius is going to let this Caesar sink this time certain and sure.

We hope, therefore, for the honor and respect of the party, that our friends in Virginia will not commit the great folly—the *crime,* of uniting their forces with the disorganizers of the Richmond Convention—the supporters of Breckinridge and Lane. If they do we hope, from the depths of our soul, that the ticket may be as disastrously beaten as it has just been in Kentucky. But we have no fear of it. We have every confidence that the National Democracy, of the Old Dominion, will preserve the organization of the party untarnished by any coalition with the sectional and disunion faction supporting the Breckinridge, Yancey and Rhett ticket. These men and their representatives, were declared to be outside of the party at Baltimore, and we hope no effort will be made to get them back. *The people* will rally to our standard sooner or later, and leave these disorganizers where they have ever mostly been, at home.

55. Mr. Lincoln—Mr. Seward's Speech

(*Louisville Daily Journal,* August 22, 1860)

There are in the non-slaveholding States a great many men, old Whigs and others, who, being moderate and conservative in their feelings, have stood aloof from both the Republican and Democratic organizations, and who, deeming perhaps that in their States the Union candidates for the Presidency and Vice Presidency lack strength, seem to be in doubt as to the course which it is their duty, as lovers of their country, to pursue in the present canvass and in the coming election. Calm and conscientious in their views and purposes, they have no other desire than to do what is best for the great interests of the Republic. To all such we would address an earnest exhortation that they do everything in their power to prevent the triumph of any mere sectional party, for such a triumph, we solemnly believe, would be a fearful if not a fatal calamity to the nation. No such triumph was ever achieved in our land, and God grant that none ever may be.

We have a favorable opinion of the personal and even the political integrity of Abraham Lincoln, but he is, as the whole nation knows, a sectional candidate and only a sectional candidate. He is recognized as such at the North, and he is justly denounced as such at the South. We all remember, that, in his great contest with Mr. Dougles in which he so ably sustained himself, he assumed and boldly enforced the position that the conflict between the sections must necessarily go on until the whole domain of the United States shall be free territory, or the whole slave territory. It was this doctrine, which Mr. Seward, sometime afterwards, enunciated in a modified and somewhat mitigated form in his famous Rochester speech, which created such a profound sensation throughout the Southern portion of the Republic. And there is reason to believe that Mr. Lincoln still entertains the views to which he gave such vehement utterance in 1858, and that they have probably been strengthened and rendered even more violent since by the wild and powerful and raging partizan influences by which he is now continually surrounded. Mr. Seward is universally recognized as the ablest expositor and most distinguished embodiment of the principles of the party that supports Mr. Lincoln as its candidate, and when he undertakes to state publicly Mr. L.'s position his statements may well be regarded as authentic. Well, here is a brief extract from a speech made in Boston by Mr. Seward on the 13th inst.:

What a commentary upon the wisdom of man is given in this single fact, that fifteen years only after the death of John Quincy Adams, the people of the United States, who hurled him from power and from place, are calling to the head of the nation, to the very seat from which he was expelled, Abraham Lincoln, whose claim to that seat is that he confesses the obligation of that higher law which the Sage of Quincy proclaimed, and that he avows himself, for weal or woe, for life or death, a soldier on the side of freedom in the irrepressible conflict between freedom and slavery. This, gentlemen, is my simple confession. I desire now only to say to you that you have arrived at the last stage of this conflict before you reach the triumph which is to inaugurate this great policy into the Government of the United States. You will bear yourselves manfully. It behooves you, solid men of Boston, if you are here—and if the solid men are not here, then the lighter men of Massachusetts —to bear onward and forward, first in the ranks, the flag of freedom.

We call upon the conservative men of the North, those who would have peace and harmony restored to this fearfully agitated Republic, to mark well these words of the great Free Soil Senator. The country is told that Mr. Lincoln's sole claim in the estimation of his supporters to the high seat he aspires to is that he confesses his obligation to "the higher law," that he holds himself bound by an anti-slavery law in his own soul above the laws and the constitution of the United States and independent of them, that he considers himself at liberty to trample all the statutes of the land and the decisions of all the tribunals of the land under his feet when they are at variance with his own private judgment and sense of right, and that he avows himself, for weal or woe, for life or death, a soldier, or in other words an active and professional fighter, in the conflict that must be kept up between freedom and slavery until the one or the other shall be annihilated throughout the country. If these views, publicly and boldly ascribed to Abraham Lincoln by his own and his party's greatest champion, and unquestionably in strict keeping with the doctrines put forth by him in his Illinois campaign, are entertained by him, as assuredly there is every reason to believe they are, we ask whether any conservative men of the North, any who have not yielded themselves utterly up to the control of sectional passion, any who look anxiously forward for brighter and better days for the Republic, can, under any circumstances or for any conceivable reasons, reconcile themselves to his support.

But Mr. Lincoln has not left to Mr. Seward or to any other distinguished friend or friends the whole work of speaking for him at
the present time. No, he has very recently spoken for himself and he
is probably ready to do so with his characteristic boldness upon all
occasions. A few nights ago, when a great army of his political friends
gathered before his house in the city of his residence, he made them
a brief address, in which he said:

I am profoundly grateful for this manifestation of your feelings. I am
grateful because it is a tribute which can be paid to no man. It is a testimony
which, four years hence, you will pay to the next man who is the representative of the truth on the questions which now agitate the public mind.
(Cheers.) It is an evidence that you will fight for this cause then, as you now
fight for it, and even stronger than you now fight, although I may be dead
and gone. (Cheers.)

These in truth were words of fearful import. We have supposed that
hundreds of thousands, if not a majority, of those who contemplate
voting for Mr. Lincoln, look forward to his election as an event that
may terminate the unhappy sectional strife that agitates the country,
or at least contribute to its termination. We have hoped that few who
are truly the friends of the Union, devoted to its permanence and its
prosperity, are taking part in the agitation with the design or the expectation that it shall extend beyond the election and inauguration
of the next President to disturb and threaten the peace of the nation
at the end of another four years. But such, alas, is the expectation of
the Republican candidate for the Presidency, and he proclaims it, not
in a tone of sorrow and regret, but with a shout of unconcealed exulta-
tion, echoed back, by the triumphant shouts of his myriad hearers.
He proclaims in the language of triumph, that, four years hence, the
Black Republicans of the North, in the midst of such agitations as now
convulse the public mind, will be gathering together to hail the next
Black Republican candidate for the Presidency, and he predicts that
years and years hence, when he himself may be dead and gone, they
will fight on in the great sectional conflict with even more violence
than they are fighting to-day.

We beseech, you, O ye conservative men of the North, to mark these
things well. Ponder deeply the declarations of the Republican candidate for the Presidency and the declarations of his greatest champion,
to say nothing of the declarations of the numberless fierce and intemperate organs and orators that support him. If you would have peace

instead of strife and commotion reign throughout the land, if you would have a country worth living in and dying for, if you would not have the rage of brethren so protracted and exasperated that it can never be quenched but in the blood of brethren, we appeal to you to use every honorable and patriotic exertion to prevent the election of Abraham Lincoln to the Presidency of the United States.

56. SOMETHING FOR ALL PATRIOTS TO READ AND PONDER

(*Daily Nashville Patriot,* September 19, 1860)

If the eye of any one who loves party more than his country, or who believes that a separation of the Union on Mason and Dixon's line would promote the interests or well-being of the people of either section, should rest upon these lines, he had as well lay aside the paper. We are not addressing him just now. But we trust that all patriots of every name and party and station and section will read this article and ponder it well.

The Presidential campaign of 1860, is now more than half over. There are four candidates still in the field. Three of them stand in opposition to the fourth. That far, at least, they are united, conceding to each all that it claims for itself. That fourth one represents a party which stands out boldly before all mankind as a great sectional fact. Whatever may be thought of its principles—whether its doctrines are sound, or its aims wicked or charitable its existence is unquestionably a sectional fact. The universal Southern mind is in antagonism to the Republican party and its candidate. He cannot and will not receive support in any of the Southern States. That is settled beyond all question or controversy. The Union was not made on any sectional basis, nor can it be prolonged on such a basis. It was entered into upon the idea of a community of interests among all the States, each one making some sacrifice of a minor interest to secure the incomparably greater one of Union. And that is the way in which it will have to be continued. No one State could have its exclusive way in the beginning, and no one section can have its exclusive way now. If such attempt is pushed to extremity, the Union must come to a speedy and disastrous termination. Though nothing in the past would justify separation—would justify the giving up of the Constitution and the Union which constitute our nationality, our glory and our power—yet there is a point in all public affairs which might render such a course not only justifiable, but necessary. The erroneous construction of the nature of our compact of

Union has given rise to a brood of vagaries, asserting the right of peaceable secession, which are worse than nonsense. So long as the Federal Constitution exists and preserves its binding effect, we are one people —one confederation of States—united and inseparable. There is one way—and but one, true and logical—by which the obligations of that instrument, that ligature of Union, can be broken and destroyed, and that is by Revolution. The right of revolution—the *ultima ratio gentium* —nobody, at any time ever denied. It is a part of the history of all peoples—it never was denied, cannot be now and never will be. It is this autocratic idea that a portion of the united people having one set of interests or one set of opinions—whether practical or abstract—must have their own way to the exclusion of the other portion having a different set of interests or opinions, that breeds revolution—that justifies revolution—that makes revolution necessary. But only when pressed to extremity, and when every other mode of redress has failed. Then it becomes just in the sight of earth and Heaven. No diligent observer has failed to see that our Republic is now engaged in an alarmingly swift race for this revolutionary goal. Four years ago the Republican party came before the American people declaring that it would have its own way; and was defeated. To-day it rallies to the contest with the same determination, and with increased ardor and with its legions under better discipline. It may succeed. Let the true-hearted patriot pause and ponder that subjunctive proposition—it may succeed. Its leaders tell us they desire success that they may show the South—the anti-Republican States—that they mean no harm to them, but that all their intents are entirely charitable. That is an exhibition, however, for which the South has little or no desire. But we shall see.

Since 1856, there has a party sprung up in the South, the counterpart of the Republicans of the North. That was the natural and almost necessary product of this. The contact of 1856 was simply an act of procreation, and gestation has been regular, healthful and prompt. This Southern antagonistic party would fail of its mission—would be untrue to its paternity—if it did not also seek to have its own way. We shall not inquire in this place, whether we have transposed the real progenitor. It is enough for us to know that they occupy these relations and that they are marching respectively on their proper mission—that of ultimate revolution—and that unless they are checked such will be their goal. Does any intelligent citizen dispute this? If he does, we only ask him to read the speeches of the Republican champions, and then turn to those of the new Southern party, for which we have such a variety of names that we cannot be sure of the right one. The former tell us that if the latter triumph and continue to triumph, all the North will be overrun with slaves; while the latter tell us if the former succeed the South will be reduced to a state of vassalage, and that horrors will be enacted in comparison with which Milton's vision of hell is but a sorry piece of moonshine. What does this mean? What is the English of it, if it is not simply that the Northern and Southern States cannot live together in the same Union? It can signify nothing else; and that is but another expression for revolution; and that, too, not justifiable or necessary.

The great, overruling question for all those whom we are now addressing, the patriotic men of all parties, is therefore, whether this fatal and fearful result can be averted, and if so, how? By the side of it all others sink into insignificance. On one side of the balance is placed the Union, and on the other all minor questions of party and policy. Without the one the other would be nothing. The Union may exist without parties, but without the Union, there can be no parties. To hold party higher than the union is, therefore, preposterous. Our first duty, then, is to avert revolution by defeating these great sectional parties that are urging us to it. Such a defeat can only be accomplished by a union of all who desire a continuance of the Union on the basis of the constitution. If it is desirable to avert revolution, such a union is desirable. As an effective party organization the Republican is by far the stronger of the two sectional parties. The Southern extremists have not a shadow of ground to hope for an election before the people —but the Republicans have—not because of absolute numbers, but because of the divisions of their opponents. They do not hold a majority vote in the country, and cannot possibly elect by their own numbers. Their sole chance is in the divisions of those who are opposed to them. To show the truth of this assumption let us inspect the facts. The following was the vote of 1856.

Mr. Buchanan received 1,838,169
Mr. Fremont   "   1,341,264
Mr. Fillmore   "   874,534

Thus in a total vote of 4,053,967, the Republicans polled less than one-third, leaving a clear *majority* against them of 1,371,439, or about two to one. Calculating the increase on the rate exhibited in the two last elections, the total vote the present year will be, in round numbers 5,150,000. There has nothing occurred since 1856 in the North to strengthen the Republican cause, but on the contrary developments have been made well calculated to weaken it. The ultra positions assumed by its most conspicuous leaders have tended to alienate the more conservative men of that section from their standard. Their only source of increased power is in the fact of the opposing have-your-own-way party in the South. And granting that this sectional antagonism has given them increased strength and compactness, and allowing them one-half the entire increase of the popular vote, which is quite as liberal as any of them will claim, their vote next November cannot exceed one million nine hundred thousand, scarcely two-fifths of the aggregate vote cast. We have taken some pains to estimate the probable vote at the approaching election, on the basis of that of 1856, in connection with subsequent developments, the division in the democratic ranks, and the *present* state of feeling throughout the country, and give the following, in round numbers, as the probable result:

Mr. Lincoln will receive	1,900,000
Mr. Breckinridge "	850,000
Mr. Douglas "	1,000,000
Mr. Bell "	1,400,000
Total	5,150,000

If our assumed increase on the aggregate popular vote of 1856, shall prove nearly correct, the actual result would not probably vary materially from these figures were the election to take place to-day. But it should be borne in mind that Mr. LINCOLN's less than two-fifths might be so disposed in the States, as to carry a majority in the electoral colleges, and thus elect him, not by a majority, but by a minority. And hereupon arises the only possibility of his success. So far as Mr. BRECKINRIDGE and Mr. DOUGLAS are concerned, neither can hope for election —and while the former will obtain a less actual popular vote, he will receive a larger electoral vote. Mr. BELL's vote is the strongest of the three, and will continue to increase up till the election—but whether it shall be sufficient to elect him is certainly doubtful, if the friends of BRECKINRIDGE *and* DOUGLAS continue their mad warfare. But with a union of the true national, conservative sentiment on Mr. BELL his triumph would be placed beyond question, and both the sectional parties prostrated.

Can this be effected? The politicians have tried their hand upon it, and have failed. From them we can expect nothing further in that direction, and the matter is now wholly in the hands of the people. It is for them to do all that may be done for the safety of themselves and their country. If they will but rise to the importance of the great occasion, they can and will restore peace to a land distracted and endangered. It is to them we now appeal. Do they want revolution with its terrible consequences? Do they still prefer to cling to party names and party leaders while the Republic is imperiled? Will they close their eyes to the real dangers that encompass them and theirs, and still persist in aiding to bring on the catastrophe? They have followed the politicians until they have approached nearly the precipice, will they then leap into the vortex of revolution of their own will and heart? Or will they rather abandon their leaders for their own safety and the preservation of their country? That is the question, and the only significant question now to be decided; we ask them to take it and answer it as becomes intelligent, independent, patriotic freemen.

We have this to say, in conclusion: If the people shall neglect the high and solemn duty now imposed upon them; if they permit the machinations of the enemies of the Union to prevail by their divisions, on them be the responsibility. If they allow a minority to precipitate them into a revolution, unnecessary and unjustifiable, they will be held as criminals to history and posterity. We now denounce in advance all trouble, all strife, all revolution, all blood that may immediately issue out of the pending election as unnecessary, unholy, unpatriotic. It will be brought about by minorities and not by the majority; and upon the shoulders of the aiders and abettors be the burden and the toil.

57. THE FUSION CHEAT

(*The Daily True Delta,* New Orleans, October 4, 1860)

The Breckinridgers are about these times very strong on the fusion swindle. They think it peculiarly hard that, holding, as they mainly do, the democratic organization of the several Southern states in their hands, there should be any such disagreement as would lead to their being dispossessed, and accordingly we find in Virginia, Tennessee and even in Louisiana wires being judiciously placed to secure the bolters and disorganisers from the fate that is sure to overtake them. In the fore front of the councilors of the scheme are, of course, the old party hack journals that have lived a life of lazy ignorance upon the democracy for the last quarter of a century; overlaying its principles and keeping in the background and upon the lowest seats every one not sunk in the lowest political meanness and corruption, and permanently and especially warring upon every young, active, talented and fairly aspiring man who would not submit to the degradation of upholding them and their cliques. We have seen how it has been here in Louisiana, and the practice which has prevailed here is a fair representation of what has prevailed in every other southern state, and indeed for that matter, in every state in the Union. In New England there was the combination of Caleb Cushing, Butler and the rotten Boston Post confederation which, contemptible in everything but their knowledge of how to dwarf a great party into manageable proportions for their own purposes, have well nigh eliminated democracy from the Yankee states, and what they have accomplished for it in the eastern section, the Buchanans, the Van Burens, the Schells, the Croswells, the Bradys, the O'Connors, the Butterworths, the Caggers, the Biglers, and a host of equal and lesser schemers, have done for it in the middle states. In the west the Brights, the Fitches, the Pettits, the Rices, the Gwins, and the enormous corps of jobbers subordinate to them, but co-operating and dividing with them in the contract system, have brought things to a similar pass as in the other sections, and consequently we can well understand how desperately they are put to it to accomplish the defeat of the Douglas, who will terminate their peculations and jobbery, and at the same time, if possible, keep up such an organization in the states they are endeavoring to seduce and debauch as will leave them in continued control. This is the whole secret of the propositions to fuse, which they are trying to humbug some soft-headed Douglas men into acceptance of; but the political scoundrelism which sanctions such compacts in other sections cannot succeed in the south, and it glads our heart to see how the true men of Tennessee regard it. Led on by the Appeal of Memphis and the Evening Democrat, of the uncompromising Carrol, of Nashville, the truly national democracy repel the insidious appeals of the Nashville clique backed by Senator Johnson, who, in his blind and precipitate clutchings at the presidency, seems to have lost sight of that good, sound common sense which he must have had when he left the workshop of the honest mechanic to become a leading and unwelcome politician among the Yancey aristocrats. Nicholson is dictating his *rôle* to him, and his present adhesion to the instructions of that old placeman and astute politician is just as certain to lay him politically cold as if old death with his scythe had touched his physical vitality. This the plebian Johnson, as the Yanceyites used to regard him before the dazzle of the presidency made the ex-governor forget the democracy and go over to the enemy, ought to know, just as he ought to remember, also, that no man ever betrayed the people and was forgiven.

The course of the true democracy in this contest, and the subsequent ones which will originate in it, is plain. They ought to make no combinations with the avowed enemies of the national integrity, north or south, east or west, because there can never be an honorable compromise of principle; nor can the loyal and disloyal, any more than oil and water, harmoniously meet and mingle. The momentary loss of party supremacy in the individual states is of vastly inferior importance to the maintenance intact of great principles of government; and should the nation be destined to such a calamity as the defeat of Douglas and the election of Lincoln, as the Yanceyites desire, the adherents of the democratic constitutional candidate can bear up against the defeat, and re-organize under more fortunate auspices. The result will, at all events, demonstrate the absurdity of galvanizing into momentary life extinct factions, and thus compel all to unite in one national organization in harmony with the great mass of the people everywhere, and in accordance with their well-understood ideas of republican government. The sloughing off of the unsound adhesions to democracy may work momentary mischief, but the mischief will be permanent and incurable if the national democracy, under an absurd supposition that party compactness by a diseased cohesion is preferable to a rigid adherence to principle, consent to any compromise or fusion with those between whom and themselves there is now an impassable gulf. If the Yanceyites desire to keep the democratic party united and healthy, let them retire their dummy candidate from the presumptuous position they have drawn him into accepting; otherwise, we are sure, no reliable national man will ever consent to a fusion or to such a combination as will return to the senate of the United States the Slidells, Fitzpatricks, Iversons, Brights, Fitches, Greens, Gwins, Rices, Lanes and Biglers, who are now hanging by the eyelids before the people.

58. An Appeal to Non-Slaveholders

(The Kentucky Statesman, Lexington, October 5, 1860)

The great lever by which the abolitionists hope to extirpate slavery in the States, is the aid of non-slaveholding citizens in the South.

They hope and propose to array one class of our citizens against the other, limit the defense of slavery to those pecuniarily interested, and thereby eradicate it. We constantly meet with appeals of this character in the Abolition press, and hear it from the mouths of the great missionaries of the anti-slavery cause. They address themselves to the laboring men of the South, undertake to convince them that slavery degrades labor and prostitutes the social status of the laborer. They attempt to prove that the poorer classes thrive and prosper more in free communities than when they are forced to compete with slave labor. These are the arguments and these the appeals by which the Abolitionists expect to build up a party in the South to aid them in the work of aggression upon slave property.

We regret to notice the Opposition men of the South taking up the argument and employing the same appeal. We constantly meet the reply to our arguments on the subject of the rights of the South in the Territories, that "you own no slaves, why do you care?" If we assail the record of John Bell as a Southern man, an Oppositionist responds, "you have no slaves to lose." We met this rejoinder in a public discussion we had the honor of conducting with a distinguished gentleman in an adjoining county. When unable to defend Mr. Bell's record, he replied that John Bell owned more negroes than we. Doubtless this is true. But has a Kentucky voter no right to enquire whether a Presidential candidate is true to the rights of the South because he cannot count his slaves by the hundred? We notice again that Mr. Soulé [1] recently in a speech in Louisiana desired to know what interest the non-slaveholders in his audience had in the question whether slaves were permitted to go into the Territories or not. He illustrated the falseness of the clamor (as he alleged) made by the Southern men for the right touching slave property, by an anecdote of Judge Porter's. The Judge was accosted in the Harrison campaign by an Irishman who deplored the ruin in which the South was about to be overwhelmed. "What's the matter," said the Judge. "Oh," replied Pat, "they are going to elect Gen. Harrison President, and he is an Abolitionist and will take away our slaves!" "How many have you got," asked the Judge. "None," replied Pat. "Well, I have more than a hundred," added Judge Porter, "and if I can trust him, I think, Pat, you can afford to do the same." And this, said Mr. Soulé, is the condition of the Pats of the present day.

[1] Pierre Soulé, Senator from Louisiana, 1847, 1849–1853; Minister to Spain, 1853–1855.

Here is an undisguised attempt to array in hostile positions the slave-holder and the non-slaveholding Southern men; to wrest from slavery all its defenders, save those pecuniarily interested in slave property; to make emancipationists and Abolitionists of all who do not own slaves. Mr. Soulé appeals to non-slaveholders, and urges them not to inquire into the record of any candidate on the slavery question, for, says he, "you have no interest in the subject." He adopted the anti-slavery appeal, and would convince non-slaveholders that they are not interested in the extension and protection of slavery.

We can say to these gentlemen that their appeal is vain. The interest felt by the non-slaveholders of the South in this question is not prompted by dollars and cents. Their zeal for their social institutions does not rest upon a pecuniary calculation, nor does it arise from an apprehension of loss of property. It is educational and deep seated. They believe slavery to be right and socially beneficial. Instead of de-grading labor and destroying its reward, they believe it elevates and enhances labor. Its effect is felt in society and brings a condition of public sentiment, taste and life entirely congenial to their idea and feelings. They cannot be swerved by such appeals, and every such argu-ment will be repelled with indignation. The strongest pro-slavery men in this State are those who do not own one dollar of slave property. Go to the mountains and find there thousands of as true Southern men as tread the soil of the cotton States, yet comparatively few own slaves. They are sturdy yeomen who cultivate the soil, tend their own crops; but if need be, would stand to their section till the last one of them fell. Tell these men that they have no right to look into Bell's record; tell them that it is of no importance to them to enquire where Douglas squatter sovereignty will lead; tell them that none but the master of many slaves has any right to ask whether a Presidential candidate is sound on the slavery question, or whether a given measure will operate inimically to the South; in a word, tell them that an Abolitionist is good enough for them, and stand up, if you can, Mr. Soulé, against their indignant rebuke. Such men will spurn the sordid motives to which you appeal, and hurl back your insidious argument with scorn. No men in Kentucky examine more closely the records of Presidential candidates, and none will reject a record tainted with abolitionism more promptly than the non-slaveholders. We would rather trust them than a thousand John Bells.

59. How Far Are We Apart?

(Daily Chronicle and Sentinel, Augusta, October 10, 1860)

We have long thought that there was vastly too much bitterness and exasperation and rancor in the party politics of America. But especially is there too much now between the different parties in the South. We are brethren, and while we differ, each should allow to the other that honesty and sincerity and patriotism which it claims for itself. There is not this day such an essential difference between the Bell and Breckinridge and Douglas men of Georgia as should alienate them from one another in view of a common cause and a common danger. It is true that we do differ somewhat in principle, and *vastly in policy,* in this emergency. The Bell men honestly believe that the election of Mr. Bell will secure the South in every essential right and interest in this confederacy, and that it will restore that harmony and good feeling between the unhappily embittered sections, without which the Union of the States is not an object of paramount desire. Our Breckinridge friends, on the other hand, just as sincerely believe that the only road to Southern security in the Union and to permanent peace lies through the election of their ticket, which alone, as they think, fairly meets the issue tendered by the hostile Republicans. And still the Douglas men, with equal honesty, believe that the election of Mr. Douglas will preserve the Union, and secure quiet and destroy slavery agitation, because such election will be a most emphatic endorsement of Congressional non-intervention with the whole question, leaving it to be settled by each Territory for itself, subject to the Constitution.

And, in fact, *we are all* really agreed and pledged, by the distinct platforms of Douglas and Breckinridge, and by the acquiescence of the Bell men in the laws, (for we are a party of law-abiding people,) that the people of the Territories shall settle slavery for themselves, subject to the Constitution. The trouble is, that the Bell and Breckinridge men hold that subject to the Constitution, the Territories have no *lawful authority* to exclude slavery nor slaveholders, while Mr. Douglas and his Northern supporters hold that the Territories *have* such lawful authority, and his supporters at the South, whether holding such doctrine or not, are content to let them *exercise* it. To the doctrine of Judge Douglas we, of the Bell party and the Breckinridge party, can never, and will never, assent, as a fundamental principle of party organization, or a fundamental rule of practice in the administration of the Government. We hold now, as always that the doctrine is totally indefensible, and, as Mr. TOOMBS says, that it is supported by neither reason nor authority. Upon this then, the BRECKINRIDGE and BELL men stand firmly together, and upon this we are both *forever* separated from the DOUGLAS party, as far as the poles asunder, unless the DOUGLAS party abandon the position.

As the BELL and BRECKINRIDGE men are a unit mainly as to this principle, and totally at variance with the DOUGLAS men, what other differences are there amongst us? There is almost nothing else divides us but the *best policy* to be pursued in order to defeat LINCOLN. For while we all have our own principles, which we hold tenaciously and will not surrender, yet most of us would be patriotic enough to forego a contest upon them at present, for a greater object—the defeat of LINCOLN. In the great battle States of the North the DOUGLAS and BRECKINRIDGE men do show a willingness to lay aside a contest about their distinctive doctrines, and to unite upon the BELL platform, the Union, the Constitution and the laws, however indistinct or inexpressive that may be—and for what purpose? Simply to prevent a great calamity, the election of a sectional President. The danger is more menacing to us of the South than to our brethren of the North, for they are not directly interested in any property which the Republicans war against—they have no immediate and vital interests in jeopardy— they are in no danger. Why then should not we unite, who have all at stake, when our cordial union is *the thing necessary* to nerve the arms of our Northern friends for victory? Why may we not put away, for this time at least, our dissensions, in *face* of the danger which threatens us more than the North?

We *are* all willing enough to unite, but each party desires the other two to unite with it, on its platform and for its candidates. Mr. DOUGLAS of course is entirely out of the question in the South—his doctrines are odious and himself unpopular in the highest degree. And still it is surely not the interest or the policy of the other two parties to declare and wage war upon him and his, in face of *the fact* that without his aid North, we are powerless to defeat a greater enemy. While the BELL men and the BRECKINRIDGE men are opposed to DOUGLAS and his doctrines, *they are the natural allies of each other,* for they agree mainly on principle, and that principle is strong in the hearts of the Southern people, and is right. Agreeing thus, we are dividing our forces on men, and on matters of policy, and on unmanly prejudices. We have ever accorded to Mr. BRECKINRIDGE the highest praise as a citizen and as a public man. We never doubted that he was honest, faithful and true—and we think no calm, unprejudiced supporter of his can fail to accord as much to Mr. BELL. We have fought each other, because *each* clearly saw that *the other* was the *only opponent*. It is time this unnatural contest was ended. This deplorable bitterness should cease. We are all but human—with the frailties common to humanity, and no doubt each one of us has much to regret in the past of this short conflict. It is time we came together, upon the strongest man.

The vote of the South for either BELL or BRECKINRIDGE, is a distinct declaration on our part *against* the Wilmot Proviso and Squatter or Popular Sovereignty, or whatever it may be called, and in favor of equal protection to the slaveholder and every other property holder in the Territories. Mr. BELL's record is clear on all these points—it is sound, constitutional, Southern and national. Mr. BRECKINRIDGE's is not so much so, but his platform and the interpretation thereof by his Southern friends is quite as much as could be reasonably expected for the time. The *policy* of making a distinct party on that platform, at this juncture, we have always deplored, and have thought it was *the duty* of the seceders to have united with us from the beginning, either by accepting our ticket, or by dividing the ticket. This *policy* it is, mainly, which has made the BRECKINRIDGE party an *embarrassment* in the contest, and the best that can be done, under the circumstances, at this late day, is *for the people,* the honest BRECKINRIDGE voters, seeing their leaders will not harmonize, and that *they* are powerless in their present position, to come out like men and vote for JOHN BELL. We doubt not there are thousands of them who will do so, because they can do nothing effectual, as they are, and they are only dividing friends who should be united.

60. THE TERRORS OF SUBMISSION

(*The Charleston Mercury,* October 11, 1860)

A few days since we endeavored to show that the pictures of ruin and desolation to the South, which the submissionists to Black Republican domination were so continually drawing, to "fright us from our propriety," were unreal and false. We propose now to reverse the picture, and to show what will probably be the consequences of a submission of the Southern States, to the rule of Abolitionism at Washington, in the persons of Messrs. LINCOLN and HAMLIN, should they be elected to the Presidency and Vice-Presidency of the United States.

1. The first effect of the submission of the South, to the installation of Abolitionists in the offices of President and Vice-President of the United States, must be a powerful consolidation of the strength of the Abolition party at the North. Success generally strengthens. If, after all the threats of resistance and disunion, made in Congress and out of Congress, the Southern States sink down into acquiescence, the demoralization of the South will be complete. Add the patronage resulting from the control of ninety-four thousand offices, and the expenditure of eighty millions of money annually, and they must be irresistible in controlling the General Government.

2. To plunder the South for the benefit of the North, by a new Protective Tariff, will be one of their first measures of Northern sectional dominion; and, on the other hand, to exhaust the treasury by sectional schemes of appropriation, will be a congenial policy.

3. Immediate danger will be brought to slavery, in all the Frontier States. When a party is enthroned at Washington, in the Executive and Legislative departments of the Government, whose creed it is, to repeal the Fugitive Slave Laws, the *under*-ground railroad, will become an *over*-ground railroad. The tenure of slave property will be felt to be weakened; and the slaves will be sent down to the Cotton States for sale, and the Frontier States *enter on the policy of making themselves Free States*.

4. With the control of the Government of the United States, and an organized and triumphant North to sustain them, the Abolitionists will renew their operations upon the South with increased courage. The thousands in every country, who look up to power, and make gain out of the future, will come out in support of the Abolition Government. The BROWNLOWS and BOTTS', in the South, will multiply. They will organize; and from being a Union Party, to support an Abolition Government, they will become, like the Government they support, Abolitionists. They will have an Abolition Party in the South, of Southern men. The contest for slavery will no longer be one between the North and the South. It will be in the South, between the people of the South.

5. If, in our present position of power and unitedness, we have the raid of JOHN BROWN—and twenty towns burned down in Texas in one year, by abolitionists—what will be the measures of insurrection and incendiarism, which must follow our notorious and abject prostration to Abolition rule at Washington, with all the patronage of the Federal Government, and a Union organization in the South to support it?

Secret conspiracy, and its attendant horrors, with rumors of horrors, will hover over every portion of the South; while, in the language of the Black Republican patriarch—GIDDINGS—they "will laugh at your calamities, and mock when your fear cometh."

6. Already there is uneasiness throughout the South, as to the stability of its institution of slavery. But with a submission to the rule of Abolitionists at Washington, thousands of slaveholders will despair of the institution. While the condition of things in the Frontier States will force their slaves on the markets of the Cotton States, the timid in the Cotton States, will also sell their slaves. The general distrust, must affect purchasers. The consequence must be, slave property must be greatly depreciated. We see advertisements for the sale of slaves in some of the Cotton States, for the simple object of getting rid of them; and we know that standing orders for the purchase of slaves in this market have been withdrawn, on account of an anticipated decline of value from the political condition of the country.

7. We suppose, that taking in view all these things, it is not extravagant to estimate, that the submission of the South to the administration of the Federal Government under Messrs. LINCOLN and HAMLIN, must reduce the value of slaves in the South, one hundred dollars each. It is computed that there are four millions, three hundred thousand, slaves in the United States. Here, therefore, is a loss to the Southern people of four hundred and thirty millions of dollars, on their slaves alone. Of course, real estate of all kinds must partake also in the depreciation of slaves.

8. Slave property is the foundation of all property in the South. When security in this is shaken, all other property partakes of its instability. Banks, stocks, bonds, must be influenced. Timid men will sell out and leave the South. Confusion, distrust and pressure must reign.

9. Before Messrs. LINCOLN and HAMLIN can be installed in Washington, as President and Vice-President of the United States, the Southern States can dissolve peaceably (we know what we say) their Union with the North. Mr. LINCOLN and his Abolition cohorts, will have no South to reign over. Their game would be blocked. The foundation of their organization would be taken away; and, left to the tender mercies of a baffled, furious and troubled North, they would be cursed and crushed, as the flagitious cause of the disasters around them. But if we submit, and do not dissolve our union with the North, we make the triumph of our Abolition enemies complete, and enable them to consolidate and wield the power of the North, for our destruction.

10. If the South once submits to the rule of Abolitionists by the General Government, there is, probably, an end of all peaceful separation of the Union. We can only escape the ruin they meditate for the South, by war. Armed with the power of the General Government, and their organizations at the North, they will have no respect for our courage or energy, and they will use the sword for our subjection. If there is any man in the South who believes that we must separate from the North, we appeal to his humanity, in case Mr. LINCOLN is elected, to dissolve our connection with the North, before the 4th of March next.

11. The ruin of the South, by the emancipation of her slaves, is not like the ruin of any other people. It is not a mere loss of liberty, like the Italians under the BOURBONS. It is not heavy taxation, which must still leave the means of living, or otherwise taxation defeats itself. But it is the loss of liberty, property, home, country—everything that makes life worth having. And this loss will probably take place under circumstances of suffering and horror, unsurpassed in the history of nations. We must preserve our liberties and institutions, under penalties greater than those which impend over any people in the world.

12. Lastly, we conclude this brief statement of the terrors of submission, by declaring, that in our opinion, they are ten-fold greater even than the supposed terrors of disunion.

61. MORAL OF THE OCTOBER ELECTIONS

(*Nashville Union and American,* October 12, 1860)

The elections recently held in Pennsylvania, Ohio, and Indiana were looked to with the deepest anxiety by every Southern patriot. Whatever may be the bitterness existing between parties in the South, it cannot be denied that they were united in a concurrent and common hope that the Old Keystone State would prove true to her ancient fame and overthrow the Black Republicans on last Tuesday. It mattered little which one of the three antagonistic parties shared most liberally and largely in the honors of the hoped for triumph. That was not the question. Like the allied forces at Sebastopol, hereditary and rival foes, with the exception of part of the BELL and DOUGLAS factions, were seen, side by side and shoulder to shoulder, advancing, amid the tumult of action to the intrenchments of the enemy. They were cheered on by the entire Southern hosts, who themselves are engaged at home in local feuds and most strange encounter. Their cause, as against the Black Republicans, is, or ought to be, a common cause. Disguise it as you may, misrepresent or smother the common sentiment of the South as interested parties may choose to do, it is the cause of "the Constitution and the equality of the States," which the gallant BRECKINRIDGE truly says are "the symbols of everlasting union." Let LINCOLN be elected and Black Republican rule once established, and he is infatuated who will deny that the equality of the States is virtually crushed out.

Whatever effect the election of Mr. BELL or DOUGLAS might have, this will undoubtedly be the result of the triumph of a candidate who has not even a ticket in one-half the States of the Confederacy. Can any true Southern man calmly contemplate such a result without horror and the deepest humiliation? If he does not feel humiliated for himself he must feel so for his children's sake. If this be so, has the South lost her manhood? Is she so weak, imbecile and distracted that her sons cannot unite and strike one good, strong, healthy blow for her independence and equality before this election shall forever decide her fate and consign her to the condition virtually of an inferior province in the Union, or drive her to revolution and anarchy? Every true Southern patriot will say, "strike the blow." What can be done then? There is no resource left than to unite upon one ticket, than for all the Southern States to decide upon casting a united vote for one candidate in this contest, and thus present an unbroken front to our sectional oppressors. It is true we may not carry the election even with the united vote of the South, without the aid of some of the larger Northern States. But we may teach our enemies to beware of us. We may give them to understand that we are not so weak, divided and degenerated that we are ready to surrender to their insolent, tyrannical and insulting demands and purposes without resistance, first by every constitutional means within our power, and if it must be, by every means that honest men and patriots may adopt to save themselves from degradation and dishonor. Perchance seeing our determination and cordial union, some of the Northern States may come to our assistance in time and preserve us from the dread dilemma of submission to sectional domination, or, in the very last resort, resistance to unconstitutional oppression. It will not do in a crisis like this, to hide our heads in the sand, like the poor ostrich, and dream that there is no peril surrounding us because we have wilfully shut our eyes to it. There *is* danger and the South might as well look it manfully in the face. We are on the brink of a precipice, steep and dangerous. We are beset by perils that every truly enlightened and wise man does not fail to recognize. If not, what mean these unprecedented majorities in three of the great central Northern States for those who are seeking to crush out the life-blood from our section? If LINCOLN should be elected, where will be the man so disloyal to his section as to accept a commission bearing his seal? And if not, where will be Federal authority in the Southern States? We say nothing of the threats of South Carolina, the resolves of Alabama, or the purposes of Mississippi. We speak only of the inevitable consequences of LIN-COLN's election. Mr. BELL's most distinguished Elector has denounced, in advance, the man who would degrade himself by accepting a Federal office under LINCOLN. The sentiment of Col. PEYTON [1] undoubtedly finds a very general response in the Southern heart. No man can accept a position under such an Administration without bringing personal odium upon himself, and, in many localities, the tone of opinion will drive him from the community, into the wilderness or among his more congenial associates, the Black Republicans.

Is it not time that the South pause and take her reckoning? Is it not time to dispel prejudice and party animosities among ourselves and unite upon some one of the candidates, to show at least to the world that we are conscious of the dangers by which we are environed? And in so doing, we should discard mere personal and party preferences, and obey the unerring sentiment of our section, by yielding our support to the candidates who most fully and emphatically embody the general Southern sentiment, and who are the most acceptable to a majority of the South. If we determine on a united South, as we must now do, if we are true to ourselves, it is but just and reasonable that the majority of those, seeking to be united, should control the choice. Such a union is impractical unless we thus defer to the prevailing sentiment. Not only so, but the leader chosen to face the approaching hordes of Black Republicanism must bear upon his banner, written in unmistakable language, avowed and emphatic opposition to the claims of our enemies. The siren song of "no agitation," the policy of ignoring the great, vital issues about which Black Republican war upon us will not do in the face of a bold, energetic, triumphant enemy. We must let them feel that we know our rights, and knowing dare maintain them. It will not do for the South, in this trying emergency to take a candidate who in all the great battles between the sections has voted side by side with those who are now coming with such dreadful pace upon us. Such a policy would be regarded by our enemies as an act of timidity, a con-

[1] Bailie Peyton, Presidential Elector from Tennessee on the Bell-Everett ticket.

cession of our principles through fear of them. Instead of driving them back, such a policy would but urge them on, and invite further aggression.

It has now been demonstrated that it is most consummate folly to talk about the Northern strength of either BELL or DOUGLAS. Neither of them can now claim, without doing violence to public intelligence, the least show of strength in the Northern States. Mr. BRECKINRIDGE can rally to his support the whole strength of the Southern States. The late elections in Delaware, Florida, and Mississippi demonstrate, beyond question, his strength and popularity. The observation of every man, in his own section confirms this proposition. If either DOUGLAS or BELL were withdrawn singly, BRECKINRIDGE would sweep every Southern State by overwhelming majorities over his remaining competitor.

We have thrown out these suggestions for the consideration of the masses. If they are worth anything, if they are available to unite us, we can at least do that, and save the honor of the South, even if all else be lost.

62. THE ELECTIONS

(The Daily True Delta, New Orleans, October 12, 1860)

The complexion of the news of the elections on Tuesday, placed before our readers this morning, seems to vary little from that of Wednesday evening, and consists of nothing more than a general declaration by the reporter for the associated press that Indiana, Ohio, and Pennsylvania have gone by various majorities for the abolitionists. We shall accept this report as correct, subject to such modifications and explanations as the future may furnish, and, in doing so, we shall not attempt to disguise the real importance and seriousness of the condition of political affairs it reveals. We cannot, however, accept the result of the elections just held as decisive of anything, save the utter mischievousness of running Mr. Bell as a presidential candidate; for, however much democratic divisions may inspire hopes of some electoral success in the south, it is made painfully apparent that his running can have no other possible effect than to enable the foes of the Union, north and south, so to co-operate as to defeat the only candidate having the prestige of a great name, a spotless record and a powerful political organization to sustain him. We do not doubt the honesty of the intention which we are sure animates Mr. Bell and the mass of his supporters, nor question their patriotic disposition in the event of their electoral strength

being necessary or requisite for the election of Douglas to give it to
him freely, frankly and ungrudgingly; but as true Union men they
must now see clearly that under no possible circumstances can Mr.
Bell obtain a single northern state, and that consequently the only effect of his running will be to divide the strength of the national parties
and make those who regard the maintenance of the Union as above all
other considerations antagonistic to each other. That the administration
has done all in its power to bring about the disasters just recorded there
can be no doubt, and that it will up to the last incessantly endeavor to
secure the election of Lincoln there cannot be a question. Is it not the
part of common prudence, then, to take into consideration whether it
is not better to withdraw the Union candidate, who is unconquerably
weak in a national point of view, and combine all the conservative elements upon him who brings popular strength to our common cause,
and who, if elected, will have the great conservative elements of the
whole nation united to support his administration? The retention of
Breckinridge in the field will of course be persisted in, because the object of his candidacy was not the defeat of the deadly enemies of the
south, but the destruction of the Union democracy, which his running,
combined with the administration's secret and open hostility, it is hoped
will effect; therefore, it seems to us, if the good sense and patriotism
which we believe animate the main body of Mr. Bell's friends, are in
the ascendant, that he will be withdrawn, and the field thus made more
manageable against the disunionists who apparently unconnected work
assiduously to a common end.

The south is now rapidly drifting into the fatal embrace of her most
implacable enemies. The insanity or the malignancy of her prominent
public men has impelled them to assume the position which, of all
others, will be most fatal to her political importance and strength as an
integral section of the confederacy. They have sought to separate her,
not from the north, with which perhaps it is not of much consequence
to maintain alliance, but from the west, and in pursuit of the most selfish purposes, and the gratification of the meanest vindictiveness, have
repelled the offer of fraternization with it, without which, in the future, we can neither have political strength nor national consideration.
We are not of those who believe that Lincoln, as president, will either
overthrow our constitutional rights, or conspire against our DOMESTIC
institutions; we neither believe he has the capacity to do the one, nor
the motive to attempt the other; but so far as the south can be dwarfed,
cramped and shut in from healthy intercourse with the world, and such

profitable expansion of her territory as the natural order of things, under an able and protective administration of the government must take place, the abolition president will use the whole power of the country against it. Should, after his election, the governments of England and France dictate to Spain the emancipation of her slaves, does any southern man possessing one ray of common sense suppose that Lincoln would protest against such action, or interpose a single obstacle to the fulfilment of a purpose he has been—if chosen at all—elected to fulfil? That his election to the presidency will be taken advantage of by the governments we have above named for the purpose indicated we conscientiously believe, and it is in this way, and not by the immediate adverse legislation of Congress, the abolition party and abolition administration will proceed. To such a course of policy where will the efficient opposition be found, when we have provoked the democracy of the west, and repelled their brotherly intentions and good will? Shall we find it among the Caleb Cushings of New England, the Schells, the Bradys and the Creswells of New York, the Buchanans and Biglers of Pennsylvania, and the Brights, Rices and other senatorial jobbers of the free states? The election of Lincoln will be the death knell of the political and social prosperity of the south, it will forever put an end to an equality of representation in the cabinet, in foreign countries and in domestic administration generally; it will forever preclude the formation and admission into the Union of another slave state, and it will prevent the acquisition of territory subject to the condition that it may be devoted to slave-labor. This the seceders from the national democracy no doubt comprehend as clearly and thoroughly as we do; and this condition of political affairs the genuine nullifiers among them doubtless above all things desire to bring about, in the fallacious hope that it will lead to a separation of the states and a southern confederacy. In this hope, however, they miserably deceive and dupe themselves, for there exists in the south neither the disposition, the wish, nor the immediate motive to take any such step; and when at some future day it may be admitted by all as the only remedy for grievances become too intolerable for endurance, the power of accomplishing it will have passed away, and we shall be compelled to submit with what resignation we may to the steady adverse encroachments of an insidious enemy bent upon the overthrow of our most cherished institutions. Millions yet unborn will have reason to deplore the consequences of the conspiracy, if successful, which aims at the destruction of the great conservative democratic party, and among the first to deplore it will be those very men whose restless ambition led them to produce the state of affairs from which all subsequent evils have flown. It may not be yet too late to repair some of the evil done; is the patriotism of the people equal to the emergency?

63. THE LATE ELECTIONS

(*New Orleans Daily Crescent,* October 13, 1860)

There seems to be no longer any doubt of the result of the recent elections in Pennsylvania, Ohio, Indiana and Iowa. The Black Republicans have swept everything before them. They have gained—and it is as useless to deny the fact as it is painful to contemplate it—a decisive and overwhelming victory in each one of the above-named States.

Nor is it worth while to inquire into the causes which have produced the disastrous result. It is enough to say that the division and disruption of the Democratic party at Charleston is the principal one. That party was the strongest element of opposition to Black Republicanism in all the Northern States; and if they were powerless, when thoroughly united, to control the elections, still less could they be expected to do it after being broken to pieces, demoralized and disorganized at Charleston.

This general explanation will suffice to explain the late defeats in the Northern States. It is a waste of time to hunt up the dereliction or the apostacy of any party or any division of any party. It is the part of wisdom to look at things as they are, and to deal with events that are before us, and that are likely to occur. And the most prominent of these events is the certainty of Lincoln's election unless steps be immediately taken to concentrate the entire opposition to him upon one ticket in the Empire State of New York.

We say New York, because New York is now our only reliance. It is useless to talk about Pennsylvania, Indiana and Illinois. Pennsylvania, which gave a popular majority of one hundred and sixty-five thousand against Fremont in 1856, now goes for the representative of the same principles by a majority of over thirty thousand. Indiana, which gave nearly fifty thousand against Fremont, reverses her position and declares for sectionalism by fifteen thousand. We must now look to New York, whose electoral vote is sufficient of itself to turn the scale, to throw herself into the breach, and avert the dire calamity to the South and the Union of the triumph of a party justly obnoxious to the people of one-half of the Confederacy.

Will New York prove herself equal to the occasion? Will she now come forward, as the largest and most powerful State of the Union, and save us (and herself) from the consequences—social, political and commercial—of Lincoln's election? Will her chief city, built up to colossal proportions by the commerce of the whole Union, permit that Union to be endangered, if not destroyed, by the fanatical folly and madness of her own people? Are there not enough conservative men in the city and State, if they will only postpone their petty disputes and combine in solid mass, to save the State from the grasp of that party whose triumph will still further embitter the South—already fearfully exasperated—against the continuance of our Federal Union?

Whether this is so or not, one thing is certain—that New York is now our only hope of escape from the dangers that environ and the evils that threaten us. To New York alone the South now looks for effective resistance to the sectional foe. We undertake to say, in behalf of the people of the South of all parties, that New York is the only remaining hope of our people for deliverance from the evils that are impending over us.

So far as the South is concerned, we differ only in regard to candidates. Upon the common ground of hostility to Lincoln, there is no disagreement of opinion. We may vote for Mr. Bell, for Mr. Breckinridge, or Mr. Douglas—but the solid vote of the South will be against Lincoln. If Lincoln be elected, then, it will be by a sectional party and a sectional vote—and by a sectional party having as the basis of its organization a sentiment of hostility to a domestic institution of the South which in no respect concerns them. We will not undertake to say what will be the consequences of Lincoln's election. That the very mildest result would be to make the Union more objectionable, and to increase the number of positive and unconditional *disunionists,* no one will deny. New York has it in her power to avert that result. As the greatest member of the Confederacy, she can now strengthen or impair it as she may decide. Upon the great Empire State, alone, we repeat, the hopes of the South now rest for the preservation of the peace, the security, and it may be, the Union of the States.

64. To the Friends of the Constitution and the Union

(*Daily Nashville Patriot,* October 13, 1860)

The Presidental contest is rapidly approaching a termination. But twenty-four days more, and the field will be won or lost by the friends of the Constitution and the Union. Are they thoroughly alive to the importance of the struggle? Do they fully appreciate the momentous results which are suspended in the balance, and which but a slight weight may determine irrevocably against their peace and happiness, and the permanency of their government?

Since the adoption of the Federal constitution issues so grave as those now pending have never occupied the attention of the people. The crises through which the government has hitherto passed, subjecting it to severe tests, and calling forth into active exercise the wisdom, sagacity, and patriotism of leading statesmen of the times in which they occurred, fall far below the present in the imminence of the disasters which are threatened. The memorable controversies of 1820, 1832 and 1850, portentous as they were of evil, yet afforded grounds of compromise upon which the sections could meet, and harmonize. But now the unnecessary and wanton agitation of questions growing out of the institution of slavery—agitation commenced and kept up for the suicidal purpose of building up parties,—has precipitated upon the country the danger of consigning the administration of the government to a great sectional party organized in hostility to, and kept together by the pledge of war upon constitutional rights of an entire section of the Union. The aggressive spirit of anti-slavery fanaticism has been made too apparent for even the most confiding to doubt what will be its course when invested with the power and patronage of the government. Wherever it has had power, no constitutional barrier could impose restraint upon its action. It has claimed to be governed by a higher law than constitutions or human obligations; and mocked at their restrictions. Unwilling to await the development of its intentions in the administration of the government, we find States in the South prepared for taking such steps as shall sever their connection with a government administered under its influences, and leading men, and other organs of public sentiment, in a majority of the Southern States, declaring they will never submit. The issue may be avoided or postponed, perhaps indefinitely; but there is no ground for compromise. The friends of the Constitution and Union may, by coöperation, defeat the republicans, and thus avoid or postpone the issue, and give time for the sober second thought of the North to act; but, we repeat, there can be no compromise. The republicans must abandon their sectionalism and eschew their warfare upon constitutional rights of the South, or the South must either succumb or resist. The South cannot succumb— if she does so, she is lost. It is not probable that republicanism, flushed with success, would abandon its intentions. "War to the knife" must, therefore, ensue should a republican president be elected—a war of sections and kindred, fired by the fiercest and deadliest hate, ending in the destruction of the government, for the union could not survive the shock of such a conflict. The issue in this canvass, then,— the chief issue—is not whether slavery shall be kept out of the Territories or protected there by the general government; but whether this union shall be preserved or destroyed. We fear the great masses of the people, governed too much by party feelings, have not given the matter that serious consideration which it has deserved, and are scarcely conscious of the dangers, real dangers, which hover around them. We conjure them to dismiss party feelings and turn their thoughts to the question of preserving their government, and perpetuating the blessings which it has conferred upon them, when honestly administered. "We are in the midst of a revolution, bloodless as yet," but six months may not elapse before the sound of deadly conflict upon the field of battle startle you from the seeming security in which you repose. Awake, arise, act, before it be too late. There is now no time to give to doubt and hesitation. Prompt and efficient action is demanded. Will you, friends of the Constitution and the Union, in the few but supremely important days which precede the 6th of November, counsel together, and laying aside every sentiment and purpose but that of saving the country, combine your efforts for its salvation? An army invincible in serried array, if divided, a division here, and a regiment there, a battalion in one place and a company in another, acting independent of each other, loses its invincibility and may be cut up in detail, and overcome by an inferior force. This is the danger which threatens the defeat of the legions of the Constitution and Union army. They are all powerful in numbers, and unconquerable, when they stand together; but divided as they are amongst the supporters of BELL, and DOUGLAS and BRECKINRIDGE, they bid fair to be overwhelmed by the concentrated but inferior forces of Northern sectionalism. Shall this be their fate? Shall they, who have the power to save our institutions, fail, because they cannot sink issues of small importance before an overshadowing necessity? Oh, let not posterity reproach you for such weakness and imbecility; for recklessness so fatal. Sink all party disputations to the bottomless deep; let them be supplanted by nobler considerations, for the present; and when the enemy who is thundering at our doors, and undermining the citadel of our liberties, has been vanquished, there will be time enough to adjust questions of public policy of a nature less grave. Unite, and vigorously coöperating, shoulder to shoulder, for the remainder of the contest, save the Union, and then divide into parties if you choose. If we can but pass this crisis safely, the Republican party will be scattered. It cannot prolong its existence after another defeat. It will dissolve like the mists of the morning before the rays of the God of day; and the South may secure peace and repose.

65. False Issues on Which It Is Sought to Rest the Canvass for the Presidency

(*Richmond Semi-weekly Examiner,* October 26, 1860)

It has always been the habit of those who seek to obtain power, rather than to establish a wise policy and sound principles, by popular elections, to raise false issues and avoid the real questions before the people. In no contest that we remember has this policy been more persistently and recklessly pursued than by the opponents of State and Southern rights in this canvass.—The issues presented in this canvass are few, simple and distinct. Every man can see and the dullest can comprehend them.

In the progress of our Confederacy, from its infancy to its present maturity of power, the strength and weakness of the federative, limited system of our polity has been both developed and tested. The long struggle between those who thought the Federal Government too weak and those who sought to limit its powers has been continuous, and events have demonstrated that there was no need of strengthening, but much of restraining the powers of the general agent of the States. The opponents of the Democracy and of the rights of the States having tried to increase the power of the Federal Government, by direct legislation, by building up a system of monopolising class legislation, binding men and States to the support of the Federal agency by the bonds of a sordid pecuniary interest, have failed; and this failure has been caused by the conclusive conviction of the people that the agent of the Union —the Government of the Confederacy—had abundant strength of itself without adventitious and unconstitutional additions to its powers. The opposition to Democratic principles and popular and State rights, beaten on these old schemes, by the exposure of the weakness and mis-chievous tendency of their proposed policy, have been forced to desist from a direct advocacy of it. They seek, however, to attain their ends by a policy more indirect and circuitous, yet equally wrong and mischievous.

The development of our political and social system, and the rapid advance of our people in numbers and wealth and power, have demonstrated that the framers of our Union were most wise in limiting with great rigor the power of the General Government. The tendency of power is to centralization everywhere. Our Confederacy has proven no exception. Power has concentrated rapidly in the General Government located at Washington, and with that concentration of necessity the weakness of State authority, and the loss of individual right in the free citizen, have been almost contemporaneous, as they are natural and inevitable consequences. The concentration of power in the common Federal agent must weaken the powers of each State by every atom of power it absorbs. As long as that Government represents the will of the majority of all the people—is the agent of the powers of the people in mass—the rights of the free individual citizen are weakened and destroyed by the absorbing power of the numerical majority. That this has been the result of the past action of our political system, writers and observers of all parties must agree. The powers of the General Government have been enlarged—the power of resistance in the States through local authorities, or the separate popular sovereignty of each State have been disregarded and diminished. The political federative system is fast becoming a system giving efficiency to the consolidated power of numbers. A numerical majority is wielding the power of the General Government over, and in disregard of the will of many of the sovereign parties to the federative compact. These facts, we think, none will deny. Three, among numerous facts, demonstrate them beyond dispute. For more than thirty years a law of this Government excluded the property of the people of one-half of the States from the common Territory of the Union. This was done as legal investigation and the highest judicial authority concur in establishing in violation of the rights of the States and people, and in derogation of the Constitution of the United States. Next, no election for offices, even those exclusively local, and for the special service of the people of a separate State, is decided on grounds affecting the policy of the State; but such elections almost invariably are decided with a view to the relations candidates bear to some question or party of a general and Federal character. The third fact is this: The parties and Federal officers generally in this Union now denounce the right of conserving the political and social institutions of the people through the State authorities, and claim for the Federal Government the power of using its own will and discretion in conducting public affairs, even by coercing and subjugating the sovereign States of this Confederacy.

The power controlling this potent Federal agency, the Government, is now a sectional majority of the aggregate people of the United States.

The real issue of this canvass is not union or disunion; but the effort on the part of the State Rights Democracy is to limit and restrain the power of this Federal agent of the numerical sectional majority, and the effort of the opponents of the Democracy is to maintain the power of the Federal Government, even though it be the agent of a despotic sectional majority, and does seek to suppress the rightful independence and sovereignty of the separate States. These are the true and unquestionable issues in this canvass. It is nothing but the old contest between the friends of centralized, concentrated powers in the hands of a General Government, and the advocates of separate, distinct conservative powers, in the limiting Constitution and the sovereign State authorities.

The effort to make the issue of union or disunion, on the Presidential election, is utterly impracticable, and a mere trick to avoid the presentation of a true and vital issue to the people for their decision. The people, as a people, voting at the polls, can no more produce disunion directly, than we can by writing this article. The question is not and cannot be brought before the voters in this election. They cannot vote or even express their opinions on it. No candidate is running to be made President of a Union to dissolve it. Each candidate is seeking to become the chief man in the Union, to wield the powers legitimately belonging to its chief magistrate, and his fate and fortune, more than that of any citizen, is linked with the fate and perpetuity of the Union. The fear from a candidate, if he be elected, is not that he will try to dissolve the Union—the very creator and support of his power and consequence—but that he will seek to make the Government of the Union too powerful. Nor can the parties which seek to elect candidates even have in view, by electing the candidate it supports, such an object as a dissolution of the Union. These parties lie in different States, and are composed of citizens who seek to advance their own interests and carry out their purposes through the officers they seek to elect. Such parties can never seek by an election to destroy the legitimate power of the government they wish to control, direct and use. Such an idea is too preposterous to be seriously considered.

Why, then, it may be asked, is it sought to turn this canvass upon the question of disunion? The answer is easy. The advocates of enlarging and maintaining the Federal power of the sectional majority in this Union know that the people cannot be induced to part with the conservative, reserved rights of the States, or to consolidate the power of the Confederacy directly.—They seek, therefore, to raise a false issue, to alarm timid and peaceable men by making the preservation of the Union and the putting its power in their hands one and the same. They cannot prove, of course, that the election of BRECKINRIDGE will dissolve the Union; that they know is a folly and falsity too apparent and glaring to be publicly announced anywhere.—They cannot say that any principle or measure advocated by BRECKINRIDGE, or engrafted in the platform of principles on which he stands, tends or will be used to destroy the constitutional Union of these States. They know that he, his principles and policy are in the highest degree conservative. They know more—that if the government is administered on Democratic, State Rights principles that every citizen and all property will enjoy equal protection, and that the sovereignty and independence of the States will be ensured.

But the Opposition insist that the question of what shall be done in the event of a Black Republican election, is an issue in this canvass. We should like to know how it is or can be. If LINCOLN is not elected, then the question, of course, cannot arise. If he is elected, will a vote for BELL or DOUGLAS or BRECKINRIDGE have the least influence on the decision the people will make hereafter on the policy or propriety of submitting to Black Republican rule? Every one knows that it will not. The only officers voted for at this election are the President and Vice President. Now, elect LINCOLN and HAMLIN. Will the votes cast for BRECKINRIDGE, BELL or DOUGLAS confer any power of dissolving or preserving the Union on either of these men or their supporters? Will any vote be had in this election which can in any manner affect the power or will or intention of the people of the South to resist LINCOLN, or to submit to him? If so, will some good Union man show us how it will?

The great object of supporting a candidate against LINCOLN is to prevent any such question being proposed to the people for their consideration. The object of carrying this election against Black Republicans and Federalists is to put the Government in such hands, and to give it so conservative, just and protective a direction as to remove any temptation or motive to destroy the Union, to remove from the public policy and from the public mind all those wrongs, aggressions and insults which will make a union between the two sections hateful to either. The success of BRECKINRIDGE, standing on a platform securing equality and independence to each State and every citizen, may prevent all measures and movements hostile to the maintenance of a constitutional Union. A vote which in any manner weakens popular rights and State sovereignty and strengthens the power of the agent of the anti-slavery party, will sap the foundations and weaken the ligatures of this Union. This is the only danger to the Union, and this danger is one that will not be produced by BRECKINRIDGE and his supporters, but will be brought upon the country by those who are placing power in the hands of the Government of a sectional anti-slavery majority, arming that Government with constructive and unconstitutional power, and divesting people and States of the conservative power of controlling and resisting oppression and the despotism of numbers.—On those who enlarge the powers of government, not on those who seek to restrain them, on the advocates of Federal usurpation and not on its opponents, will rest the shame and sin of dissolution, when the scene of a dismembered Confederacy and a land covered with communities arrayed in bitter hate and civil war shall be presented to the world. When men at last are driven to repel violence by the sword, to right wrong by an appeal to the last bloody arbiter of human disputes, the conservative State Rights Democracy will be clear of the guilt of having evoked such a contest, and can point to the glorious history of their past management of public affairs, to their wise counsels and to their sound protective, conservative principles, and demand the approval of every wise and patriotic lover of freedom in this land.

66. [VOTE AGAINST SECTIONALISM]

(*Louisville Daily Journal,* October 30, 1860)

The advocates of the cause of the Union, fellow-citizens, have now concluded their argument in this remarkable canvass. It remains only for you to render your verdict at the polls. We have but a closing word to add.

We have shown, by undisputed facts and by unanswerable as well as unanswered reasonings upon those facts, 1, That the Seceding movement, at the head of which John C. Breckinridge in a moment of wild ambition consented to place himself and from the sheer blindness and tenacity of pride has since continued, was designed to bring about at once the election of the Republican candidate for the Presidency and the union of the South in overthrowing the government on the ground of his election; 2, That the necessary tendency of the Seceding move- ment is actually to bring about this double result; 3, That the origina- tors and leaders of the Seceding movement have resolved, if the election of the Republican candidate shall occur and a commanding vote be cast for the Seceding candidate in the South, to begin the work of overthrowing the government forthwith, in the hope and belief that the movement in question will have so inflamed and united the Southern people as to hurry them on into the pit of revolution pre- pared for them; and, 4, That even the defeat of the Republican can- didate, if it shall be attended by the triumph of his Seceding ally, will but lead the way to the beginning of the same work of national de- struction, under even more dangerous auspices, as soon as the con- trolling spirits of the Seceding movement can go through with the cun- ning mockery of demanding certain peremptory conditions of allegiance which they themselves acknowledge to be unattainable. We have shown that from these four leading established facts it follows irresistibly that the design of the Seceding movement is to unite the South with the view of destroying the Union as speedily as possible in any event of the pending election; in the event of the success of the Republican candidate, if he shall succeed, and, if not, then in the event of the rejection of the impossible conditions of allegiance to which we have referred—assuming always, be it observed, that the Seceding movement shall in the pending election unite the South in favor of the Seceding candidate. Finally, we have shown, that, as a corollary from this irresistible conclusion, the issue raised directly in the South by the Seceding movement is Union or Disunion whilst the same issue is raised indirectly by the Republican movement in the North, that, in other words, the Republican candidate and the Seceding candidate represent but different aspects of the single issue of Union or Disunion, the former presenting the negative phase of the issue, and the latter the positive. Wherefore, fellow-citizens, we have broadly and steadily pronounced the issue in the pending canvass everywhere to be Union or Disunion, and with equal earnestness have invoked the men of the North to defeat the Republican candidate and the men of the South to put down his Seceding accomplice. We now in all solemnity renew this invocation for the last time.

Men of the United States, defeat the Republican candidate and put down his Seceding accomplice, we implore you, as you love the Union and value the liberty which the Union enshrines. Rout both the Disunion candidates alike; the victory over one will be incomplete without the discomfiture of the other. Nay, such partial success will prove but an ultimate failure. If the Republican candidate alone shall be defeated, leaving his Seceding accomplice triumphant with a united South at his back, the unfeasible ultimatum of the Seceders, consisting of the repeal of the existing laws against the slave trade together with the establishment of intervention as the settled policy of the Federal Government, or some new ultimatum more specious but equally impractical, will be presented and rejected and the Union broken up before the administration of the government shall pass out of the hands of the revolutionists. The huge dense thunder-cloud of treason which now overcasts the national sky will still hang above us, spreading wider and growing blacker every instant. Perhaps the triumph of Disunion in the present election could not assume a more fatal shape than this. On the other hand, if the Seceding candidate alone shall be defeated, leaving his Republican accomplice triumphant with a united North at his back, the baffled Disunionists of the South, deriving fresh incentives from the supremacy of their Northern abettors, will recommence the strife with such augmented vigor and such increased advantages that ere another Presidential election shall draw near the Southern friends of the Union will be powerless, and, in the actual shock of that election, a united South will go down before a united and outnumbering North, and the government, though rescued now, will be lost and exterminated then. The vast thunder-cloud will grow lighter for the instant only to gather additional density and volume and break with more awful destruction upon our heads. This also would be the triumph of Disunion in a shape utterly fatal. But, men of the Union, defeat the Republican candidate and the Seceding candidate equally, rout Lincoln as well as Breckinridge and Breckinridge as well as Lincoln, and Disunion in both its aspects and in every shape will be vanquished and extinguished. Do this, and you will put an end to Disunion forever. Positive Disunion will be stifled and there will be no negative Disunion to restore it. Do this, and the frowning thunder-cloud will part not to discharge its red bolts of death but to melt into the sunlight of enduring peace. This and this only will constitute the triumph of the Union.

Citizens of the Union, will you not do this? Will you not achieve the triumph of the Union? Will you not, in this most tremendous crisis, trample upon the political sympathies and antipathies which fetter your patriotism, and lift up your voices and put forth your arms with an eye single to the preservation of your country? Will you not save the government? Will you not save your own liberty? Will you not save yourselves? Are you ready to set fire to the temple of freedom that Washington and his deathless compeers erected, and whose shining pillars, whilst they shelter and secure your liberties and your rights, blaze across the tumultuous ocean of human society as a beacon to the oppressed and struggling nations of the earth? As we write, your gaze, in common with that of the rest of the civilized world, is fixed with admiration and solicitude upon the efforts of the Italians under the heroic lead of Garibaldi to breast the waves of despotism, and guided alone by this beacon flaming from the citadel of your own freedom, to reach the haven of national independence. Are you prepared, whilst thus gazing with trembling anxiety upon the struggle of this gallant people for civil liberty, not only to put out the light that guides them, but to throw away the priceless boon for which they are struggling? Can you, *dare* you, as a free and Christian people, to say nothing of the guilt of national self-destruction involved in the act, take away the pillar of cloud by day and the pillar of fire by night from before this brave but subject people, and from before all other subject peoples on the globe, that their night shall be rayless, and, if their night ever end, their day without a compass or a sign? Are you willing with one deadly blow to destroy your own freedom and to quench the hope of freedom you have kindled in the bosom of your race? It cannot be.

Yet, men of the American Union, as you would escape this immeasurable wickedness and folly, the very thought of which causes you to shudder and recoil, we beseech you to crush out by your votes next Tuesday the foul and guilty heresy of Disunion in both its forms. In no other conceivable way can you escape the dire responsibility. In no other! If you would have your consciences and your names free from the ineffaceable and damning stain of liberticide, defeat the Republican candidate for the Presidency together with his Seceding accomplice, and bury the two in one common pit of ruin and of shame. It would be unmanly to deny that we await your decision with the most anxious and profound concern.

67. SECESSION

(The Daily Picayune, New Orleans, October 31, 1860)

When clouds obscure the heavens and winds have rendered the point to which his vessel has drifted uncertain, the prudent seaman avails himself of any opportunity to take an observation and learn his real bearings. Not less important is it, in the midst of the political storm that now sweeps over the land, for each elector to compare his present position with well-known landmarks, in order to see whether he is not drifting wide from sound principles and making a dangerous proximity to anarchy and confusion.

Insensibly, in time of ordinary quiet, all departures are made from the true principles that underlie the foundation of government. When passion is aroused, the fearless and defiant annunciation of even an indefensible and most dangerous doctrine, often passes with the multitude as a happy inspiration, and they are ready to grant it approval without the slightest examination.

Something of this is witnessed at the present moment in regard to the new idea of the present day, presented under the title of peaceful secession.

The public mind has become excited in view of the dangers, now real, that encompass the nation. The threats of encroachment upon the rights of a minority section of the Union, uttered with the earnestness of a wild fanaticism, are well calculated to arouse the most sluggish and trustful to anxiety, and to prompt the suspicious to measures of defense. Prosperity beyond example, increase in power and wealth beyond parallel, success in every department of individual and public life, but renders the shadow of coming evil the more noticeable and gives it the deeper gloom.

In casting about for a point of safety from the gathered storm, we are invited to seek peaceful secession. To avoid danger we are told quietly to withdraw from it. To overthrow the power of the North we are advised to secede peacefully from the Union and quietly, without fear of molestation from without, to set up for ourselves. No one dreams the North will consent to such an act. It is not, therefore, considered as a party to it.

If it were possible, what does this advice of peaceful secession involve? The surrender of all the common property of the States that comprise the Union; the abandonment of a joint interest in the public treasury, the navy, the national storehouses, the arsenals and manufactories of arms and munitions of war, and the entire public domain outside of organized States, is an essential element of such a secession. The very object of all the controversy between the free and slave sections of the Republic is, then, to be given up in order to escape the possible evils that continuance in the Union may ripen. This is the most intolerable of all possible submission. It is a base surrender, when holding an almost impregnable position, on the appearance of the enemy. To escape the possible creation of free States out of all the unoccupied territory of the United States, we are to abandon it to the quiet possession of freedom—give up all right even to vote, and remonstrate, and act to prevent such a consummation.

But it is said that after seceding we will call for a division of the joint property. But what power shall arbitrate between those now aliens to each other? Will the North, after the South has seceded, be any more willing to grant its just demands, than while it was an integral part of the Republic, with acknowledged rights and common interest? Will it generously give up what has been abandoned, sinking its hostility to slavery before a new birth of generosity to those, whom as brethren, it opposed? Or can that be expected from the arts of diplomacy out of the Union which could not be gained in it? No one dreams of such a conclusion. It is impracticable and impossible.

Then we will assert our rights with our swords, say the peaceful secessionists. Ah, but this is no longer peaceful. It is war, revolution, an appeal from the diplomacy of the Cabinet, from the voluntary justice of adversaries, to the might of the strong arm and the stout heart. Peaceful secession is a myth. It is a mere phrase to conceal the sad train of events that are inevitably to follow.

But whether a secession be peaceful or not, cannot depend solely upon the seceding party. Composed as this nation is of a series of equal States, if one break the compact and puts the General Government out of its territories, if its power be not there maintained, it falls to pieces of its own weight. Its strength consists not so much in armies and navies as in the acknowledged supremacy of the law. It is powerful in the States because it is hedged about by a species of reverence by public opinion. Those who desire to keep the fabric together must, therefore, in some shape resist secession of a single State. We have already seen how the government has met such defiance of its authority on two occasions at least, in both of which bloodshed would have followed, but for the adjustment of the difficulty before the first gun had been fired.

The States Rights men who framed the famous Kentucky and Virginia resolutions were far from originating this doctrine of peaceable secession of a single State or a series of States by their own will and without the consent of all parties to the federal compact.

That veteran defender of States rights, old Father Ritchie, who had such an influence upon the opinion of Virginia politicians of his time, and, we may add, upon the Democratic party of his time, wrote as follows in the Richmond Enquirer, of November 1, 1814:

No man, no association of men, no State, or set of States, has a right to withdraw itself from this Union of its own account. The same power which knit us together can unknit. The same formality which formed the links of the Union is necessary to dissolve it. The majority of States which formed the Union must consent to the withdrawal of any one branch of it. Until that consent has been obtained any attempt to dissolve the Union or distract the efficacy of its constitutional laws is treason—treason to all intents and purposes.

How far the leaders of the present day have departed from the doctrine of the fathers. How necessary to take an observation, lest we be seduced by false modern lights upon the rocks of destruction. Madison has placed his opinion on record on this point with all the explicitness and directness of which the English language is susceptible. The constitution, he said, could not be accepted conditionally; it must be unconditionally—without reserve.

Secession is, then, but a name for revolution. We have the right to revolutionize whenever the Government is no longer tolerable. But in that attempt we take all the consequences. We return to chaos again, if possible, to reconstruct government out of its confused elements.

With so much yet of hope before us—with such an army of allies on Northern soil, who if now borne down in the struggle will not give up the cause, this last, extreme remedy will not be rashly sought. Between us now and that terrible issue, lie a long period of civic battles, where the might of intellect, strong in the panoply of truth and justice, will do heroic devoirs for the South and a Constitutional Union.

68. What We Have to Look For

(*The Daily Delta,* New Orleans, November 1, 1860)

Mr. Yancey, in his speech on Monday night, very justly warned the Southern people against the danger of resting secure in the conviction that there are, in the South, no sympathizers with Black Republicanism. Whether or not there is any large number who entertain Black Republican principles at this moment, is not material. We rather incline to believe that the number of such persons must be small. But there are very many, as there must be very many in every community, who would yield to the pressure of a majority, to the allurements of office, to the seductions of power. These men, in a short time after Lincoln's election, should the South submit to his Administration, would fill the Federal offices, would wield all the influence of the Federal Government within the Southern States, and with their followers and friends would compose the Administration party. In other words, they would be the basis of a Black Republican organization, having more or less strength in every Southern State. This is the inevitable result of Lincoln's election should the South be deluded into submission. Nor does it require much sagacity to predict from which party the new organization will spring. No one can doubt that the election of Lincoln will precipitate upon the South an issue which must be speedily met. The question will then immediately arise, what course is the South to pursue? The division line between the party which places the rights of the South and the rights of the States above all Unions, and the party which considers the Union of more value than the preservation of Southern rights and the maintenance of Southern equality, will be run wide and deep. The party which insists on adhering to the Union, if it triumph in the South, must become the Administration party because the simple question and the only question will be, submission or opposition to the Black Republican Administration. From that party must come all the Federal office-holders. For the same principle which compels submission, demands the assistance of those who counsel submission, in carrying into operation throughout the South the whole machinery of the Federal Government. It would be absurd to say that it is the duty of the South to remain in the Union under Mr. Lincoln's Administration, and at the same time to say that it is the duty of Southern citizens to refuse office under Mr. Lincoln. It is, therefore, very evident that if the South submit, the instruments of the Black Republican Administration will be found ready made to its hands. We are conscious that the Bell party is composed mainly of persons who would sincerely and heartily repudiate the imputation of Abolition tendencies. We know also that many of them, after the election is over, and when the course of the South comes to be determined, will join the ranks of the Southern Rights

Party; but it must be clear to every reasoning mind that the logic of
principles, the logic of events, the pressure of circumstances, must force
a portion of the party with which they are now acting, into a position
of antagonism to the South, and of adhesion to Lincoln's Administration.

Does any one suppose that when this Black Republican party is
formed in every Southern State, it will be without followers and
sympathizers? He who imagines any such thing has read history to
little purpose. Even now distinguished men proclaim that the question
of Southern rights in the Territories is a mere abstraction; that it is
not worth contending for; that it never can be settled in our favor;
that it might as well be abandoned. And when that point is yielded,
precisely the same reasons can be urged to persuade an abandonment
of other rights, not less sacred, but much more intimately cherished.
Even now the very arguments of Helper's infamous book have been
reproduced in the South by the oratorical champion of one branch of
the Opposition and the newspaper representatives of the other branch.
Respectable leading journals of this city devote themselves to the task
of proving that the South is thriftless, lazy, poverty-stricken. Mr. Soulé,
preaching Douglasism to the people of Avoyelles,[1] declares that nobody but the slave-holder has an interest in the preservation of slavery.
Thus depriving the question of its sectional character, or rather of its
national character, and reducing it to a question, simply, of the maintenance of the peculiar rights of a privileged class. Thus endeavoring to
stimulate the jealousy of one portion of our population against another
portion, and preparing it for the reception of Abolition doctrines, and
disloyalty to Southern institutions. If these things are done now, they
would be done a thousand times more when the integrity of Southern
sentiment shall have been destroyed; when Southern spirit shall have
been broken; when Southern individuality shall have been annihilated
by submission to Black Republican domination and sectional despotism.

This is what we have to expect. This is what will surely come upon
us. We have been fighting against abolitionism at the North; and, as a
contest of sections within the Union, we have lost the battle. Let us
beware of the day when the struggle shall be transferred to our own
soil; when the slavery question shall cease to be a sectional question,
and shall become a domestic question; when the armies of our enemies
will be recruited from our own forces.

[1] A parish in Louisiana.

69. What Shall the South Carolina Legislature Do?

(*The Charleston Mercury,* November 3, 1860)

The issue before the country is the extinction of slavery. No man of common sense, who has observed the progress of events, and who is not prepared to surrender the institution, with the safety and independence of the South, can doubt that the time for action has come—now or never. The Southern States are now in the crisis of their fate; and, if we read aright the signs of the times, nothing is needed for our deliverance, but that the ball of revolution be set in motion. There is sufficient readiness among the people to make it entirely successful. Co-operation will follow the action of any State. The example of a forward movement only is requisite to unite Southern States in a common cause. Under these circumstances the Legislature of South Carolina is about to meet. It happens to assemble in advance of the Legislature of any other State. Being in session at this momentous juncture—the Legislature of that State which is most united in the policy of freeing the South from Black Republican domination—the eyes of the whole country, and most especially of the resistance party of the Southern States, is intently turned upon the conduct of this body. We have innumerable assurances that the men of action in each and all of the Southern States, earnestly desire South Carolina to exhibit promptitude and decision in this conjuncture. Other states are torn and divided, to a greater or less extent, by old party issues. South Carolina alone is not. Any practical move would enable the people of other States to rise above their past divisions, and lock shields on the broad ground of Southern security. The course of our Legislature will either greatly stimulate and strengthen, or unnerve the resistance elements of the whole South. A Convention is the point to which their attention will be chiefly directed.

The question of calling a Convention by our Legislature does not necessarily involve the question of separate or co-operative action. That is a question for the Convention when it assembles, under the circumstances which shall exist when it assembles. All desire the action of as many Southern States as possible, for the formation of a Southern Confederacy. But each should not delay and wait on the other. As these States are separate sovereignties, each must act separately; and whether one or the other acts first or last, we suppose is of no sort of consequence. What is really essential is this—that by the action of one or more States, there shall be the *reasonable probability* that a Southern Confederacy will be formed. We say *probability*,—because there is no certainty in the future of human affairs; and in the position in which the South will be placed by the election of an Abolitionist white man as President of the United States, and an Abolitionist colored man as Vice President of the United States, we should not hesitate, somewhat to venture. The existence of slavery is at stake. The evils of submission are too terrible for us to risk them, from vague fears of failure, or a jealous distrust of our sister Cotton States. We think, therefore, that the approaching Legislature should provide for the assembling of a Convention of the people of South Carolina, as soon as it is ascertained that Messrs. LINCOLN and HAMLIN will have a majority in the Electoral Colleges for President and Vice President of the United States. The only point of difficulty is as *to the time when the Convention shall assemble*. In our judgment, it should assemble *at the earliest possible time* consistent with the opportunity for co-operative action of other Southern States, which may, like ourselves, be determined not to submit to Black Republican domination at Washington. Delay is fatal, while our move will retard no willing State from co-operation. South Carolina, as a sovereign State, is bound to protect her people, but she should so act as to give the other Southern States the opportunity of joining in this policy. The Governors of Alabama, Mississippi and Georgia can act simultaneously. With this qualification, the *earliest time is the best,* for the following reasons:

1. Our great agricultural staples are going to market. The sooner we act, the more of these staples we will have on hand, to control the conduct of the people of the North and of foreign nations, to secure a peaceful result for our deliverance. Thousands at the North, and millions in Europe, need our Cotton to keep their looms in operation. Let us act, before we have parted with our agricultural productions for the season.

2. The commercial and financial interests of the South require that we should act speedily in settling our relations towards the North. Suspense is embarrassment and loss. Decision, with separation, will speedily open new sources of wealth and prosperity, and relieve the finances of the South through the establishment of new channels. In all changes of Government, respect should be had to all classes of the people, and the least possible loss be inflicted on any.

3. The moral effect of promptitude will be immense. Delay will dispirit our friends, and inspire confidence in our enemies. The evils

against which we are to provide are not the growth of yesterday. They have been gathering head for thirty years. We have tried, again and again, to avert them by compromise and submission. Submission has failed to avert them; and wise, prompt and resolute action is our last and only course for safety.

4. Black Republican rule at Washington will not commence until the 4th of March next—four short months. Before that time all that South Carolina or the other Southern States intend to do, should be done. The settlement of our relations towards the General Government, in consequence of our measures of protection, should be completed during the existing Administration.

5. It is exceedingly important, also, that our measures should be laid as soon as possible before *the present Congress.* The secession of one or more States from the Union must be communicated to the President of the United States. He has done all he could to arrest the sectional madness of the North. He knows that we are wronged and endangered by Black Republican ascendancy, and he will not, we have a right to suppose, lend himself to carry out their bloody policy.

6. By communication from the President of the United States, as well as by the withdrawal from Congress of the members of the seceding States, the question of the right of a State to secede from the Union, with the question of a Force Bill, must arise in Congress for action. The Representatives from the other Southern States will most probably be forced either to continue members of a body which orders the sword to be drawn against the seceding States, or they must leave it. They will most probably leave it; and thus the South will be brought together by action in Congress, even though they fail to co-operate at once by their State authorities. It will not be wise to pretermit either of these intrumentalities for the union and co-action of the Southern States; but, it is our opinion, that Congress is the best place to unite them. By prompt action, and through the question of secession in Congress, the agitations which must ensue, will not only tend to unite the Southern members of Congress, but to unite and stimulate State action in the States they represent.

We conclude, therefore, by urging the Legislature about to assemble, to provide for the calling a Convention, as soon as it is ascertained that Messrs. LINCOLN and HAMLIN have the majority in the Electoral Colleges for President and Vice President of the United States; and that this Convention shall assemble at the earliest day practicable, consistent with the knowledge of our course by our sister Southern

States. To this end we would respectfully suggest Nov. 22d and 23d as the day of election, and December 15th as the time of assembling the Convention of the people of South Carolina.

70. The State of the Union

(*The Daily Constitutionalist*, Augusta, November 3, 1860)

We believe that it is customary for Congress to convert itself into a committee of the whole on the state of the Union, and in that interesting condition, for its members to make speeches on every possible subject. With this illustrious precedent before us, let the following remarks ramble as they will, we cannot be charged with transcending our theme.

We have spent some little time and ink during the last few months, in the effort to prove that the country was in danger; and of all the remedies offered, ours was the best. We think so, and have said so, when it was very evident that all the promptings of ambition, power, influence and public favor, lured us the other way. We are well aware that we have been considered as mere alarmists, who sought to frighten the people into terms, and many of the American papers which first denounced us for such a course, have done us late, but honorable justice. Yet, while those who now think so absurdly, give us little credit in supposing that we deem fear a governing passion with our people, we can offer another consideration which should satisfy them that should we err now, we at least mean to be accurate. In the first place, it is now too late to influence this election by terror and rumor of war, for our country readers of the *Weekly* will see nothing more from our pen until after the election. Second: death-bed confessions are generally received as true, and yet with the late results in the North, resting with smothering weight upon our hopes, we would that we could reiterate with ten-fold emphasis, that there is danger in every breeze.

It is little matter of interest to calculate a result which the telegraph wires will report to us in a week, but still we will give some facts upon the present state of the Union, and some speculations on the future of our portion of it.

In the South, as every one knows, we are pretty well divided. Louisiana and Alabama are claimed for Douglas by many of his friends; Georgia is safe against Lincoln, and for the strongest of the three conservatives, we think, in her Legislature. South Carolina is for

BRECKINRIDGE, with perhaps Florida and Texas; and in the other southern States there is a triangular fight, with BELL and BRECKINRIDGE rather looked upon as the champions. Missouri we deem certain for DOUGLAS, now that the false report as to the defection of her Governor has been exposed. In the North, as we have said, the real battle rages. It is easy to be for the guaranteed rights of the South, when *in the South,* but when passion, gold, place and power combine with the stings of southern ingratitude to crush the faithful few in the North, we can judge of the sort of stuff of which such friends are made. In none of the northern States do we rely upon the BRECKINRIDGE vote. The strength of that party there is the Federal office holders, and they have felt perfectly free to vote as they please, (except for DOUGLAS,) since the organ of BUCHANAN in Washington city said, "between DOUGLAS and LINCOLN, we confess to a serene indifference"—confirmed as they were by the direct aid to LINCOLN in the Illinois Senatorial campaign.

Illinois is in danger from the same cause that carried Indiana against us, but the dark cloud which has lowered above New York, has at least showed a silver lining. We see it stated that LINCOLN, alarmed at the danger of immediate revolution at the South, has been so indiscreet as to say in advance of the election, and permit it to be published by TOM CORWIN and others, that he would, if elected, enforce the fugitive slave law and consent to the admission of new slave States into the Union. If this be true, the effect will be most damaging to his prospects with the Abolitionists; and should GERRET SMITH be able to draw off some fifty or sixty thousand votes in New York, the *fusion ticket* will carry that State, even were DICKINSON & Co., as active against it, as they are now cold and passive.

LINCOLN has also been denounced by a great Republican meeting in Philadelphia and GERRET SMITH endorsed.

It is hard to tell the result, for the Republican calculations may fail, in the face of the disasters they might lead to; and while it is only by their adherence to principle that we ask the National Democrats to do their whole duty, and not from hope of reward, still we think that there watches over this fair land, a Providence which "from seeming evil still enduces good;" and as the British loyalist prays "God save the Queen," so, from every patriot heart should well up the prayer, "God save our country."

If danger is to change into calamity, the hour is at hand, and it behooves wise men to look it in the face, and see if it be real, beyond the imminent danger from our own inflammable section; or only "men in buckram."

Granting that it would be very galling to be ruled by one of that party which we all love to hate, yet it is also very galling to be, as it were, forced out of the Union by such a party. If we could make *them* secede, it would please us much better.

There are various things to be considered. As Lincoln is generally considered a traitor to his country on principle, might not he become one to his party, when a national popularity should become more of an object than mere party strength? We believe that he would sacrifice his party, platform, and friends, to keep the Southern States in the Union, and the only question is, whether to permit such a deserter to reap the rewards of his treachery? Furthermore, we will have a decided majority in both branches of Congress, and the Supreme Court in our favor. Thus, with the President willing to sell out his principles for the poor boon of being permitted to keep his place—tied hand and foot, and impotent for evil, beyond the patronage which could scarcely be worse abused than it has been; with a House to whom the Covode men have set an illustrious example of watching the President, it does look a little doubtful, whether or not the South should back out from a Government which it has the power to control, and take fifteen States, or less with the peril of war, when it can command thirty-three States in peace.

It is well known that if the seceders had not bolted at Charleston, Douglas could not have been nominated, and Alexander H. Stephens would have been; and we fear that they may commit the same blunder now, of giving up the fight and running from a party, which may be nominally victorious by a minority vote, but really defeated and powerless.

If our old friends, the Democrats, and our new friends, the Americans, will only consent to let protection and squatter sovereignty lay still until we whip out the Black Republicans, we think that it would yet be easy to save the Government, and all our rights in it, and still keep a nice bone of contention to quarrel over, after we get Abolitionism abolished.

We confess that, after this fight with all the records of inconsistency to quote from, with the prestige of the old platform, power in the North, bolting opponents, the argument, the truth, the right on our side, an obnoxious Administration to make capital of, the Supreme Court to sustain our principles, and the great statesmen that the whole South once almost worshipped, to lead our host—if we fail to get at least a third of the votes of the South, we shall feel little inclined to try to reconstruct this, or build up another National party.

We believe in the right of secession, and do not find it in the Constitution but in the violation of that instrument and the law of might. But we must confess that we do not feel any particular evils resting upon us or our section of the Union, and if we can retaliate the insult of giving us an obnoxious President, (a thing for which we may more blame our own folly than *their* might,) by making him sit on a dunce-block for four years, and then kicking him and his party to perdition, we will feel pretty well satisfied.

Another great consideration in this canvass, is the vote. The only excuse for disunion, and the only reason that we deem the idea tolerable, is that the Constitution has been violated by the "personal liberty acts," and negro stealing mobs of the North, and that the election of a Black Republican will show that instead of fanaticism getting cool, it is growing worse, and, therefore, the sooner the South gets clear from them the better.

But should it turn out that LINCOLN is elected by less votes than FREMONT received in 1856, that cause will not exist.

We want it distinctly understood, that so long as a majority of the voters of the North stand by us—even if divided and thus defeated now—that we shall stand by them until our State says "come away."

We wish to make this proposition to our BRECKINRIDGE opponents, and will guarantee that all DOUGLAS men stand to it.

We request you to pass a resolution in this Legislature, (should LINCOLN be elected,) requesting the Governor to call a State convention, regardless of party.

Let the issue be endorsed upon the tickets for county delegates, "IMMEDIATE RESISTANCE," or "WAIT FOR A VIOLATION OF THE GEORGIA PLATFORM, OR THE CONSTITUTION, BY THE PRESIDENT OR CONGRESS." (We will all go out on the latter issue.) Let the matter be fairly debated, and let there be about a month to do it in; let your people refrain from "firing the southern heart" if they can; trusting to the deliberate valor of a great people rather than excited rage—pardon us if by fair statements of facts, we try to keep down excitement and promote wise and deliberate councils and, *let all men agree to abide the result.*

If a convention of our State decides to quit the Union, with other States, or by herself, with voice and arm will DOUGLAS men support her high decree, and under the banner of Georgia, as a "sovereign and independent State," we will, with you, defy the world in arms to force her back. If the verdict is to remain a while, let us all stay and get together for a great fight at the ballot box in 1864. This is fair, honorable, and just, and we ask, who will agree to it? If, after we agree to stay, a war should spring up between a sister State and the Government, we should be governed by the circumstances of the case —not noticing a mere insurrection, but backing the doctrine of secession in the case of a State acting by its legal majorities.

One word, in conclusion. If this threatened danger to our homes, our property, our people, and our honor, be averted by the kindness of a merciful God; if, again, we become great in the councils of our country, and Abolition preachers and fools become as of yore, the petitioners of Congress for disunion, let us all learn a lesson by the solemn and eventful past, and never divide our forces on the eve of battle; or permit hate, abstractions, lust of power, or any other thing, to become dearer than the good of this great, free land, and the rights of children yet unborn, to the glories and blessings of its future.

71. Cheap Self Government

(*The Daily True Delta,* New Orleans, November 3, 1860)

The standing argument and most powerful appeal of the nullifiers in favor of the division of these States, is the absurdly fallacious one that, separated, the cost of a southern administration of the government would be comparatively trifling, while the price of the importations of foreign merchandize would be greatly diminished in consequence of the absolute free trade that would then be established. This sordid appeal any one of ordinary intelligence can see is as destitute of weight as all the rest of the nonsense which is usually fulminated by the enemies of republican government; for, if absolute free trade were to prevail in the south on the separation of the states, as we have shown in reply to Yancey's harangue, one southern product, sugar, would soon cease to be numbered as a part of the agricultural wealth of Louisiana. Neither the disunionists or nullifiers of Virginia, South Carolina or Mississippi would consent to the payment of a bonus of forty per cent or more to the growers of a commodity, one-fifth of which, in all probability, they could not consume, merely to enrich Louisiana, but on the contrary, they would be found, as at present, doing their utmost to dispense with us and our products altogether, if compatible with their own convenience and interest. Nor could we blame them for so doing, were Louisiana to be so utterly destitute of sense as to place herself in their power, which, either within or without this Union, we are very sure her intelligent people will never do. But putting aside the matter of sugar, we should like one of those disorganizers like Yancey, or say, our eloquent, learned and profound free-trade friend, Slidell, who is a walking library, as we all know, upon all subjects, commercial included, how they propose to defray the expense of the southern government they are conspiring to create? If commerce is to be free as the air we breathe, as we think it ought to be whether the Union be dissolved or not, they, no doubt, have some other fiscal expedient, some other scheme in their budget, some ingenious contrivance other than direct or indirect taxation to maintain the standing army then necessary to protect us from "wide awake" invaders, from external filibusters, and marauders generally. We shall require, too, a navy, a federal judiciary, that is if the chivalry will condescend to take us into their happy and modest family, with a president, cabinet, diplomatic and consular corps and the usual expensive paraphernalia of government where the white mud-sills of society, mechanics, laborers and such like ungenteel trash, will be excluded from all voice, influence and participation in its administration. How then, we respectfully enquire of the disunionists, do they purpose to defray the cost of these expensive appurtenances to civilized society? They certainly do not contemplate raising taxes from poor white trash, their exchequer would surely shrink abashed from enrichment by contributions from any such ignoble source; then whence, we repeat, are the ways and means to be derived which the southern aristocracy will require to move the machine they are courting civil war and bloodshed to construct? Do they propose to impose direct taxation for the purpose; and if so, upon what description of property other than slaves and land, do they design to levy it? To protect our northern and western frontiers from the raids of our abolition enemies, to repel with dignity and efficiency the forays the restless and turbulent populations of the free states, bordering upon the new republic of the south, will undoubtedly then be constantly undertaking, will require at least a standing army of thirty or forty thousand men, to sustain which as many millions of dollars a year will be required. We do not stop to ask our nullifying masters of what description of force this army will be composed; nor whether they will accept the project of Chancellor Harper,[1] (we think it was) of South Carolina, who

[1] Chancellor William Harper of the Supreme Court of South Carolina. See *The Pro-Slavery Argument* (Philadelphia, 1852), pp. 79–82.

seriously advocated the embodying of fifty or sixty thousand slaves for
the purpose, which description of force at this time would cost the
new republic not more, at the outside, than say ninety millions of
dollars, a mere bagatelle for a purpose so patriotic and sublime as
cutting loose from the Northern mud-sills would admittedly be. If the
nigger army is difficult of organization, or if financial objections are
made to such a use of so large a quantity of agricultural muscle, perhaps the chivalry themselves—the large owners of slave property exclusively—will volunteer to compose the force, or adopt the French
system of conscription among themselves to sustain it. Common fellows, who are soiled by vulgar occupations, shop-keepers, tradesmen,
mechanics, editors and other human fry of unclean tendencies, ought
not to be allowed to aspire to places in the army raised for such exalted
ends; but on the contrary, its rank and file, subordinates and chief-
tains, should be like the Janizaries of the Turkish sultan of old, picked
for the purpose and pampered for the service. However this important
matter may finally be determined, the vulgar consideration of the cost
of the new enjoyment of southern government which is promised us
will intrude, and we again return to it and anxiously supplicate our
bolting friends to tell us how it is proposed to be met? The plan of
commencing the war by the confiscation of the property of all unpatriotic opponents of the new system is not a bad one; but as there
will be difficulty in clearly defining the guilt or innocence of parties,
we fear the amount realized will not go far in the event of actual
hostilities; therefore, "still harping on my daughter," we are greatly
exercised about the budget.

Our ancient friend Slidell will, we are sure, hasten to respond to our
wishes expressed above for more light on this rather murky prospect;
and as he has in matters of government everything at his fingers' ends,
knows Adam Smith, Say, Ricardo, Mill and all other writers on political economy and finance by heart, we know we do not expect too
much from the affectionate, good will he bears us, when we promise
our readers an elucidation of this knotty question from his pen that
will astonish the natives. At the same time let us disclaim in his behalf,
in advance, any intention of being himself in any way committed to
nullification or any thing of the sort in any manner involving any
personal responsibility, for which he will be our authority for stating,
he has no relish, at the same time, *should it succeed,* he desires it to be
understood he will, if his friends insist upon it, take the presidency,
secretaryship of state or the mission to France, provided he can have

the southern republic to do the handsome thing about Houmas, the Oregon war debt and the Tehuantepec affair. Our concern is not now, however, the claims personal of our modest and retiring friend, but the elucidation of the manner in which the Yanceyites propose to sustain the government they are engineering to impose upon us; therefore, laying the above random remarks before the country, we shall await our friend Slidell's communication upon the subject, before we hazard a decided opinion of our own.

72. What Is the True Issue?

(*The Daily Picayune,* New Orleans, November 4, 1860)

We are on the eve of a most important event. The result of the election just at hand may be fraught with momentous consequences. A determination is openly proclaimed in many quarters not to abide by the decision of a majority, if it secure a sectional triumph; and a great nation, blessed beyond all others in its basket and its store, but unfortunately torn by hostile and contending factions, seems on the very verge of revolution.

The gravity of the occasion suggests the inquiry, what is the extent of the wrongs suffered, that so arouse the fears and passions of men as to obliterate the influence of patriotism, and outweigh every consideration of public and private interest? What cause have men of the South to appeal to the god of battles for justice? On what issue is the determination made up to seek safety in a disruption of the government which has only shown an almost unlimited capacity for good?

Those who now strive to excite a tempest of popular passion, declare the election of the chief of a sectional party sufficient cause for resistance; but, as if conscious of the weakness of such an issue before a people reverencing constitutional forms of action and taught the duty of yielding to the voice of a majority, they triumphantly ask, in the manner of the most positive assertion, has not the constitution been often violated? Has not outrage followed on the heels of outrage, and forbearance but encouraged aggression, until honor, and manliness, and safety, are only to be maintained by resistance? Aroused to jealousy by the fact that the free States, if united in sentiment, can control the majority of numbers, in the House of Representatives and the Senate, and have in their power the distribution of the spoils of office and the direction of the policy of the government—excited beyond measure by the aggressive tendency of this Northern sectional party, that even now exults in the prospect of victory, and proclaims its irreconcilable hostility to slavery, they look back on the closed issues of the past, and all the bleeding wounds, cicatrized by time, open afresh. They seem to see but one continued series of assaults and weak defenses; one perpetual chain of concessions to be followed by those still more vital to the rights of the States, and these united in one bill of complaint are presented to the people, as an irresistible argument to stir them up to immediate and concerted resistance.

But can men of the South revive the strifes of the past to render the present issue with the North more strong? Is our cause of complaint so serious? Have the slave States been constantly suffering wrong, while possessing themselves in patience, always yielding yet never satisfying the grasping demands of the free States? Let us appeal to facts for a decision.

From the adoption of the constitution to the election of Martin Van Buren—from 1789 to 1841—a period of sixty-two years, a Southern man occupied the honored post of Chief Executive of the nation, with the exception of the single term of each of the two Adams' from Massachusetts.

During this period—that of nearly two generations—two-thirds of the foreign missions and the more important of domestic offices were enjoyed by Southern men.

From 1841 to 1860, but two Presidents have been elected—Harrison and Fillmore—who were not emphatically the choice of the South and really nominated and elected by the South. Of the six Presidents since 1841, three were Southern men.

It was the boast of Southern statesmen as late as ten years ago that the South had dictated the domestic policy of the nation. The purchase of Louisiana Territory was at the instigation of the South.

The annexation of Texas was conceived by Southern minds and achieved by Southern votes.

The war of 1812, from which the country emerged with so much glory, was voted and sustained by the South.

The war with Mexico, which added an empire in extent to the territory of the Republic, is due to the policy of men of the South, thus extending our Southern boundaries from the western limits of Texas to the Pacific Ocean. Of all this has the South reason to complain?

But our position is scarcely less improved in these series of years in regard to the question of slavery. If, under the operation of the laws of climate and production, slavery has been extinguished in that little patch of States denominated New England, in New York, Pennsylvania, and New Jersey, the purchase of the Territory of Louisiana has given us Louisiana, Arkansas and Missouri as slave States— a region of country much larger than that from which State sovereignty has eradicated human bondage.

The annexation of Texas, in 1845, devoted to slavery a territory equal to all New England, New York and New Jersey, and the acquisition of New Mexico by conquest, in which slavery has been established by territorial law, carries the institution two degrees above the line of the Missouri Compromise. Can we complain that the territorial limits of slavery have been circumscribed, or go back to this history of its extension to strengthen the catalogues of our grievances?

But, it is said, the perpetual agitation of this question in and out of Congress has driven the South to unjust concessions, every one of which should have been made the cause of resistance to the Federal Government; and that each as it followed the other in the order of succession increased the intolerance and aggressions of the free North. The Missouri Compromise was the first in order. If it was wrong, the South has to blame only itself; for it came from a representative of a slave State, and was supported by the almost unanimous vote of Southern delegates in both Houses of Congress. It was ratified again and again by the popular vote of the slave States, until it came to be regarded to have almost as binding a character as the constitution itself.

The next great struggle on the question of slavery resulted in the compromise bill of 1850. Here again the South gave birth to the act, and it was sustained, not only by the Southern vote in Congress, but was ratified by the people themselves. Georgia and Mississippi and South Carolina made the issue of resistance against it, and the people, with majorities unprecedented in any political contest, sustained the work of the noble patriots of that gloomy day. The South is then precluded by its own action from reopening the issues then settled and making them living questions at this time. Right or wrong, they belong to the dead past. A golden era of peace and general accord followed, until the elements of sectional strife were again let loose from their sealed cavern by the repeal of the Missouri Compromise and the Kansas and Nebraska bill.

Whether the South originated this act or not, it united in almost solid phalanx to sustain it, while the North was almost alone in opposition to the measure.

This reopened the agitations happily set at rest, and again plunged the country into an excitement which has resulted in the birth of a party that now stands avowedly sectional, openly aggressive, and by its doctrines, insults and defies the South. But it has to make a forward step to present a tangible issue that can be met only by a revolution. Its principles are dangerous if an attempt be made to put them in practice. No man with a Southern heart will defend its fanatical fury, or excuse its menacing attitude towards those States coequal with the free commonwealths. But can we look back upon the history of the past and find serious reason to complain, except it be of our own blindness and folly? Can we hope to strengthen the issue now proposed by accumulating with it the series of acts, or any one of them, alluded to in this brief sketch?

The very agitation of which we complain has in one respect accrued to our benefit. It has evolved the true principles on which the institution of slavery is based. It has convinced all Southern men of the moral right, the civil, social and political benefit of slavery. It has done more; it has modified the opinion of a large number of men in the free States, on this subject, and is gradually changing the opinion of the world—bringing it to regard slavery with more liberality.

The number of slaves has increased in a remarkable ratio, and today is stronger on the whole frontier line of the free States than it was ten, nay five years ago.

These notes of history cannot be denied, and when we meet the crisis created by the ballot of the nation about to be cast, let it be remembered that we have no cause to resist, except the unconstitutional, the weak, the untenable one of having lost our choice for the President of the Republic. The movement of demagogues and politicians to make this election, if adverse to the South, an opportunity for secession—which we have previously shown is but a word to mask the idea of revolution—is full of imminent peril to the South, not to the Union as we have been supposed to have asserted. Upon an issue so weak, to go into a contest which involves all the consequences of treason, the South must fail, for she cannot hope for accord among the citizens of any one State. The time may come when disunion, with all its consequences, must be chosen, but a failure now precludes future confidence in leaders or hope in resistance.

Let every Southern man feel it to be a duty he owes not simply to his country, but to his family and himself, to vote in the coming election so that he shall in no manner countenance the idea that his State or his parish is in favor of resisting the decision of the ballot. The home perils which a contrary course involve are of the most terrible character. Nations die a terrible death, just in proportion to their strength and vitality. If it be the destiny of the Union now to perish, none can estimate the throes of agony, the terrible scenes of distress, which will precede it. If the fires of civil war be kindled—and kindled they must be by any formidable movement in hostility to the Federal Government—they will burn until all is consumed that is perishable, and the land become a waste over which shall brood the silence of another and hopeless desolation.

73. [WHAT IS THE PERIL?]

(*Louisville Daily Journal,* November 8, 1860)

The intelligence now received at this point leaves no room for doubt that a clear majority of the whole number of Presidential Electors chosen by the people of the United States last Tuesday are Republicans and that accordingly the Electoral Colleges will on the day appointed by law choose Abraham Lincoln President. To all real intents and purposes Mr. Lincoln is at this moment the President elect of the United States. Mr. Lincoln's election is a fact accomplished.

We have prayed fervently against this event, and we have worked against it with every energy in our natures strained to the utmost; its occurrence fills us with sorrow and anxiety. We have deprecated it earnestly, and we now most sincerely deplore it. Yet we do not on account of it despair of our country; and least of all do we intend by reason of it to abandon her in any crisis the unhappy event may bring with it. And in this hopeful and dutiful resolution we know we have the sympathy and concurrence of every genuine patriot North or South. But how shall this resolution be carried into effect? In what manner can the true lovers of the country serve her most efficiently in this critical time? What ought patriots to do? It appears to us that the answer to this question is plain. Patriots ought to stand loyally and patiently in the Union under the Constitution and wield the might of the one and the checks and balances of the other to protect both. Why may this not be done? Why ought it not to be done?

What is the peril? And whence does it arise? The peril is, on the one hand, an infraction of the Constitution, and, on the other, a disruption of the Union, in anticipation of such infraction. It arises, in the first relation, from the deplorable event which occasions this inquiry, and, in the second, from the belief prevalent in a certain State or in certain States of the Union that the event under notice is a sure and infallible precursor of the infraction of the Constitution. Now, if it can be fairly shown that this event, grievous as it may be, is *not* an unerring precursor of the infraction of the Constitution, but, on the contrary, that the infraction of the Constitution in the mode anticipated cannot possibly follow the event, if the checks wisely provided by the Constitution itself shall be brought into exercise, why, then, the feasibility and the duty of protecting equally the Constitution and the Union in the one and under the other are of course perfectly manifest. And this can be fairly shown. It has been fairly shown time and again in the course of the last four or five months. We ourselves have shown it repeatedly. Indeed, the truth is a very apparent one.

We may in a day or two present this subject in a broader point of view, but for the moment we content ourselves with putting it practically in the briefest form. The first thing Mr. Lincoln will have to do after his inauguration is to appoint his Cabinet. But he can't do this without the concurrence of the Senate, which is politically opposed to him, and which clearly may so wield its discretion that the Constitution shall receive no detriment or reproach in this initial act of the new President. His next step will very probably turn out to be the appointment of ministers to foreign nations or home officers in some one or all of the Federal Departments. And here too the consent of the Senate is necessary and the same constitutional check may again be brought into salutary and efficient exercise. If, with a Cabinet of temperate views at his side, and with a full set of conservative representatives at home and abroad, which we have seen the Senate has the power to compel, he should proceed to recommend the enactment of an unconstitutional law adverse to slavery, and his political friends in either branch of the Legislature should introduce a bill pursuant to his recommendation, the branch in which the bill should be introduced, no matter which branch it might be, would reject it, since both branches are Anti-Republican. Here is the double check of the Senate and of the House of Representatives harmonizing in opposition to Mr. Lincoln's political views. No unconstitutional bill adverse to slavery could overcome this check and become a law. If it should, however, the barrier of the Judiciary rises next, as pure as the white summit of some snow-clad peak and as insurmountable. The Judiciary would declare the law void and it would be void. If, foiled at all these points, Mr. Lincoln should in some other direction commit high crimes and misdemeanors, the Anti-Republican House would impeach him, and the Anti-Republican Senate would try and convict him, which would be the last of him. Thus we see that Mr. Lincoln is on all sides at the mercy of his opponents sheltered in the forms of the Constitution. He is powerless for the evil apprehended at his hands. He could not infract the Constitution if he would. His election gives rise for the first time in our history on a considerable scale to one of the very exigencies contemplated by the framers of the government in the distribution of its powers and which these framers believed the distribution they made was entirely adequate to meet successfully. We believe they were not mistaken. At any rate we are willing to give their great handiwork a fair chance.

And we do not doubt that all other real friends of the country are also willing to do this. It is plainly the solemn duty of us all to do it. But it is not the whole of our solemn duty in this crisis. We must protect the Union as well as the Constitution, and, whilst wielding the checks of the one in its own defense, we must wield the might of the other for its own preservation. We must not only counteract Republicanism but quell disunionism; we must curb Yancey and Rhett at the same time that we check Lincoln and Seward, or as much sooner as the curb may be necessary. It is not enough to guard the Constitution against infraction; we must with equal vigilance guard the Union against disruption. The Union and the Constitution must be preserved. The maintenance of both intact is now the high task of American patriots. Let us invoke them to the vigorous performance of this task. We call on them in the name of duty and of interest alike to perform it. Not merely patriotism but religion summons them to the grand work. Let all obey with heart and hand. Union men of the South and of the North, comrades in the disastrous struggle of Tuesday, and in many another of equal fate, we appeal to you with special trust and pride in this emergency. We must not part. We again have lost the way, it is true, but we have still a country worthy of our love, and imploring our protection. By all the stirring memories of the past, by all the proud associations of the present, and by all the glorious hopes of the future, let us love her and protect her still. For such a country as ours it is sweet to fail. But we shall not fail another day.

74. What Shall Be Done?

(*The New Orleans Bee,* November 8, 1860)

The election of ABRAHAM LINCOLN is a fixed fact. The telegraph made known the disastrous result almost before the expiration of the day on which the contest took place. Nor can we say that the event created either marked surprise or consternation. Our citizens had been for some time prepared for intelligence adverse to their hopes. The triumphs of Black Republicanism in Pennsylvania, Ohio and Indiana last month portended too surely the catastrophe in November, to leave more than a feeble hope that by timely and powerful exertion it might be averted, and therefore when the public prints yesterday morning announced a Black Republican victory, they proclaimed what nine-tenths of the community had either openly anticipated or secretly apprehended.

We deem it superfluous at this conjecture to recapitulate the principal causes which have contributed to the defeat of the conservative party. Every one knows that apart from the intrinsic strength of the enemy, its ranks were reinforced by tens of thousands at the North whose sympathies with a national organization had been completely alienated by the protracted, envenomed and most unfortunate quarrel between the rival wings of the Democracy. It is not worth while again traveling over the history of that shameful feud, or discussing the question whether the friends of DOUGLAS or of BRECKINRIDGE most deserved censure. Our opinions on the subject have been repeatedly expressed; but in view of a misfortune common to the whole South, it is wholly unnecessary to persist in an irritating and now absolutely useless controversy.

The fact which stares us in the face, and which all of us, Bell, Douglas and Breckinridge men, have to consider, is LINCOLN's election. We have to look at this not as a subject of speculation, but as an event of actual occurrence. LINCOLN is chosen President, and whether with or without the consent and participation of the South, will be inaugurated on the 4th March, 1861. And what is equally to the purpose, LINCOLN has been chosen legally and constitutionally, without either fraud or violence, simply by the suffrages of an enormous majority of the people of the North. Against the manner of his election we do not exactly see what we can allege. It is true he was a sectional candidate; and equally true that with the exception of Missouri, Maryland and, to a slight extent, Kentucky and Virginia, he polled no Southern votes—but as neither the Constitution nor the laws compel a candidate to receive votes in every State, there can be no just ground for resistance or revolutionary movements on that score.

It may be said that the administration of a Black Republican President must necessarily be of an aggressive character towards the South; and that we should forestall so iniquitous a policy by withdrawing from the Union. This view of the subject is fallacious and extremely shallow. In the first place, we have no right to judge of LINCOLN by any thing but his acts, and these can only be appreciated after his inauguration. Secondly, the attempt to break up the Union, before awaiting a single overt act, or even the manifestation of the purpose of the President elect, would be unjustifiable, unprecedented and without the shadow of an excuse. Thirdly, disunion is an uncertain and a perilous remedy, to be invoked only in the last extremity, and as a refuge from wrongs more intolerable than the desperate means by which they are sought to be relieved. Have we yet suffered from such wrongs? Is it not utterly preposterous to pretend that we are cruelly outraged and oppressed? Where is the proof of these allegations? Let the fiery Secessionists adduce these, if they exist, or close their catalogue of fancied woes. Our wrongs are prospective rather than real, nor can they be inflicted so long as ABRAHAM LINCOLN is rendered practically powerless by an adverse Congress.

What we should do may, in our opinion, be summed up in a single word: WAIT. It will be time to fight LINCOLN with gunpowder and the sword, when we find either that constitutional resistance fails, or that he and his party are bent on our humiliation and destruction. We are for the Union so long as it is possible to preserve it. We are willing to go with Louisiana, but every good citizen is bound to use his best efforts to make Louisiana herself go right. A Southern journal—the Newbern (N. C.) *Progress*—in commenting on the probable consequences of LINCOLN's election, remarks:

If Lincoln be elected, of which all good men are fearfully apprehensive, there will be but two parties in the South after the conflict is over—one for union and one for disunion—and then it will be found what were the real objects of those who produced the trouble at Charleston in April last. It is needless for us to say that we shall be found battling for the Union as long as the Federal Government respects the rights of the citizens of North Carolina. Now is the time for all patriotic men to choose positions, for soon they must be found on the one side or the other—for the Union or against it.

We echo the sentiment. Let all patriots choose their position; let them resolve to stand by the Union as long as the Federal Government respects the rights of the citizens of Louisiana. We echo, too, the language of that staunch Democrat, Hon. JOHN S. MILLSON,[1] of Virginia, who, speaking of the election before his constituents at Norfolk, said; "Result as it might, in sixty days after it was over there would be no Bell, Douglas or Breckinridge party in the country. There would be but two—a party for the Union and one against the Union. He had sided, and would battle with the former!" And so will the Douglas and the Bell men, and a considerable proportion of the Breckinridge men. They will cordially sustain the Union so long as the North respects the constitutional rights of the South. Hence we say again, *let us wait!*

75. THE ELECTION RETURNS

(*Richmond Semi-weekly Examiner,* November 9, 1860)

It would seem that the sectional game has been fairly played out in the North. New York has gone for LINCOLN by a majority larger than she cast for FREMONT in 1856. Of the free States we see no reason to hope that the Black Republicans have lost more than two, and they amongst the smallest and weakest in political power—those on the Pacific. The solid, compact mass of free States has solemnly given its sanction and its political power to the anti-slavery policy of the Black Republicans.—The idle canvass prattle about Northern conservatism may now be dismissed. A party founded on the single sentiment, the exclusive feeling of hatred to African slavery, is now the controlling power in this Confederacy. Constitutional limitations on its powers are only such, in its creed, as its agents or itself shall recognize. It claims power for the Government which it will control, to construe the measure of its own authority, and to use the entire governmental power of this Confederacy to enforce its construction upon the people and States of this Union. No man can fail to see and know this who reads and understands what he reads. The fact is a great and a perilous truth. No clap trap about the Union, no details of private conversations of Northern men can alter it or weaken its force. It is here a present, living, mischievous fact. The Government of the Union is in the hands of the avowed enemies of one entire section. It is to be directed in hostility to the property of that section.

What is to be done, is the question that presses on every man, strive

[1] Representative from Virginia, 1851–1861.

to put it out of view as he may. Every citizen will have to look the difficulty calmly in the face, seek to avoid it as he will. Every State will have to consider and act on it, or it will have to make a more painful and difficult decision, whether it will or no. The distinct and unavoidable issue will be made up for those who seek to shrink from it by those who are anxious to have the disposal of the whole matter. Any Southern State can now easily take such action as will force every State to decide whether she will see a Federal force subjugating a sovereign people, or look on at the sad spectacle of a dismembered Union or an impotent and maimed Government. Nor can any State complain that these difficult questions have been prematurely forced upon its people without full notice.

No man need now annoy people with idle speculations as to how this matter might have been avoided, or whether the position of certain States was unwisely taken or no. The real, perplexing, perilous matter is here. How is it to be disposed of? Are one, or two, or three States to settle this grave matter on which the peace and union of all is dependent? They have the unquestioned power and right to do it. They have sought counsel and conference. Their request for a free and full conference was answered by a declaration from Virginia, and other States, that there was just then no need of consultation.[1] No such answer can be given now to the anxious people North and South. The Gulf States[2] are not asking counsel. They have striven, under the Constitution, to avert an evil which they proclaimed in advance would drive them to seek, through powers of their own, held of their own right, and through no consent of others, a remedy against the dangers which they apprehend from the domination of the Black Republican party. They announced that they should consider the election of a Black Republican President, by a purely sectional vote, indisputable evidence to them that their rights and honor and interests would not be protected, but would be endangered and sacrificed by submission to the rule of such government.

Their decision was not kept back, to be sprung upon their sister States suddenly and without notice. All men in every quarter knew their position. It has been freely canvassed and unceremoniously handled on every hustings and in every paper in this land. What will the other slaveholding States do now? Will they stand idly by to suffer

[1] Allusion is here made to the Atlanta Conference proposed by South Carolina and Mississippi following John Brown's raid.

[2] The term *Gulf States,* as ordinarily used in this connection, included South Carolina and Georgia.

this momentous issue to be disposed of by others, and then come dragged into a *melee* forced on them by others? We warn the people that the right and power of a State to bring this issue on the country is no subject for speculation now. Men may call it rebellion, treason, or whatever opprobrious name their own folly and bad taste may dispose them to use. The fact remains that a sovereign community has the right and power to make its own decision as to whether it will or will not remain under a particular form of government. Other governments may have the power to fight this community about it, but it will be a power, not a right—a fight, and not a pacific settlement of the difficulty. Whichever party is successful, the Union is broken, the relations of the contending communities are changed. Civil disturbance must come from such a collision.

We ask the people of Virginia calmly to reflect on the condition of affairs. They cannot dispose of the difficulty by saying that they will not make the election of Lincoln a cause of dissolution: that they will wait for an overt act of oppression. That would do if they were the only parties to the controversy. But there are other parties who have an equal right to decide these questions for themselves that Virginia has for herself. And they will decide it; and in their decision Virginia has a deep interest. Let the collision come when it will, Virginia will be a party to it. All the powers on earth cannot prevent it. Neither the Federal nor the State Government can prevent the people of Virginia taking part in the contest. How will she act?

We call the attention of the people to it. And we ask them to consider the question deliberately and at once. Consideration and action by them this present exigency demands and will have. Will they seek consultation and a union with the Southern slaveholding States? Or do they intend to stand aloof until a decision shall be forced upon them by a contest which they sought neither to avert nor direct? Will they again refuse to take counsel with their sister States of the South, and suffer a great convulsion to come upon them when they shall be found listless and unprepared? There is no time for delay. Let them take counsel with themselves at least.

76. A FEW REFLECTIONS ON SECESSION

(*The Daily Herald,* Wilmington, N. C. November 9, 1860)

It is thought by some persons that a dismemberment of our government is imminent, and almost inevitable; others are more sanguine as to the result of our present difficulties, but all agree that there is some cause for apprehension. The prevailing feeling seems to be rather one of dejection than of undue excitement, although the late exhibition in the city of Charleston, upon the receipt of the news indicating the election of Lincoln, furnishes a remarkable exception to the general sentiment, and, at the same time, indicates a most unfortunate and morbid state of feeling, and a total incapacity among those who would fain occupy the position of leaders in the movement for a separate government at the South.

The telegraph informed us yesterday that the news of Lincoln's election was received in Charleston with great rejoicing, and "long continued cheering for a Southern Confederacy!" Without discussing here the propriety, or the wisdom of secession, it may well be suggested that such conduct displays an utter inability to appreciate the importance of the step contemplated by the parties concerned, and partakes more of the character of the sports of a set of liberated school children, than of that more serious spirit which is supposed to govern men who are about to undertake a great, and terrible responsibility—a responsibility involving the destruction of the greatest and best government under the sun, without any reasonable prospect of establishing another as good in its stead, together with the probability of civil war, and a derangement, more or less, of the affairs of the civilized world. But it will not do to avoid a discussion of the question of secession now. It must be met. The more influential of those who favor the movement, are now, and have been for some time, engaged in familiarizing the public with the idea,—have been "firing the Southern heart, and instructing the Southern mind" [1] on the subject, and it has now become the imperative duty of every man who entertains a different view of the remedy to be sought by the South, to do all in his power to counteract the effect of these teachings, and to point out the consequences to which they lead. We do not propose to argue the *right* of secession. The ablest statesmen of the country have differed about that, although the weight of authority is greatly against it; but, admitting the right, there are other considerations which a good man, an honest man and a true patriot cannot disregard. There are a great many so-called *rights*, incident both to

[1] This allusion is to the letter of William L. Yancey to Joseph S. Slaughter, June 15, 1858, in which Yancey deprecated further attempts to preserve southern rights within the Union and said: "But if we could do as our fathers did, organize Committees of safety all over the Cotton States, (and it is only in them that we can hope for any effective movement) we shall fire the Southern heart—instruct the Southern mind—give courage to each other, and at the proper moment, by our organized, concerted action, we can precipitate the Cotton States into a revolution."

nations and to individuals, which it would be very unwise and impolitic to exercise. There is, too, a vast difference, sometimes, between a
legal and a moral right. And it is to the moral and the economical
aspect of secession we wish to look. Peaceable secession is an impossibility. The State that secedes must pass through a baptism of blood, in
which the garments of her surrounding sisters will be freely dipped,
although against their will. Self-defense, which is nature's first law, can
alone justify such a course on the part of any State, and the necessity
for self-defense does not exist. Any State that exercises the so called
right of secession, *under any circumstances,* does it at the expense of her
neighbors, and to that extent, inflicts upon them an injury; and this,
when not done in self-defense, nothing can justify. This principle un-
derlies all law human, and divine. And we are not begging the question in asserting that the necessity does not exist. The ostensible reason
for secession, and indeed, the only reason given, is the election of Lincoln, and it is admitted that he is powerless to do harm to the South
if he desired, inasmuch as he has neither judicial nor legislative power
to aid him. To confess this, and attempt to avoid it by anticipating his
future ability to do harm, is yielding the position entirely. And in involving other States in the consequences of secession, the injury is not
confined to the loss of some blood. The foundations of government
are broken up, nationality is destroyed, trade is ruined, the industrial
pursuits of the country are stopped, and universal distress, and bankruptcy follow. Is there anything, even in Lincoln's election, to justify
all this? It does seem as if our people are tempting the vengeance of
God by the madness of their conduct, and their total disregard of the
untold blessings he has poured upon us beyond all other people.

As a nation, we possess all the elements of greatness and power.

Peace smiles upon us from all quarters of the globe; a material prosperity, unparalleled in the annals of the world, surrounds us; our territory embraces almost the entire continent; we enjoy wide-spread intelligence, and universal plenty; we are happy, WE ARE FREE, and yet
—degrading thought—there are those among us, who, regardless of all,
would have us exchange these blessings for the expected benefits of a
Southern Confederacy!

Are the enlightened and conservative people of North Carolina desirous of the change? Do they wish, will they *submit,* to be dragged
into revolution and anarchy, and all to please the State of South Carolina, who, by her insufferable arrogance, and conceited self-importance,
has been a constant source of annoyance and disquietude to the whole

country, North and South, for the last thirty years? Will our people so far forget their independence, and their manhood, as blindly to follow the lead of that State into civil war? Where is the fraternal bond between us? Is it to be seen in the self-sufficiency and offensive air of superiority, which the people of that State have ever exhibited towards the people of this, in all their intercourse, of every kind, with us? We say unhesitatingly, that there are no two adjoining States in the Union, whose people have so little community of feeling as North and South Carolina; and no one State that owes less to another than the former to the latter,—but our people are charitable and generous to a fault, and in this is our danger, and against this *we* intend to struggle.

77. THE PRESIDENT-ELECT

(*New Orleans Daily Crescent,* November 12, 1860)

Abraham Lincoln is President elect of the United States. All the Northern States, with the exception of gallant and glorious New Jersey, have voted for him, and in most of them his majorities are very great. These majorities are more significant and suggestive than anything else—more so than the election itself—for they unmistakably indicate the hatred to the South which animates and controls the masses of the numerically strongest section of the Confederacy.

In emergencies of this kind it is the height of folly for men to strive to shut their eyes and stop their ears against stubborn facts. Especially is this proposition true in regard to the people of the threatened section. They, of all others, should look at the facts as they are, and should prepare themselves accordingly to meet whatever circumstances it is legitimately inferrable the future may have in store for them. They must, if they would pluck the flower of safety from the nettle of danger, neither be blind nor deaf nor inert. They must boldly, but deliberately, calmly and judiciously, meet whatever questions or dangers Northern abolition sectionalism may force upon them—and to meet them as they should be met, the sooner the proper steps are taken the better for all the parties to the controversy which seems to be unavoidable and imminent.

In a crisis like this there should be neither hesitation, vacillation or faltering. We should either submit quietly to Abolition domination, and do nothing, or we should go to work with resolution, prudence and inflexible determination. If we are going to submit, let us do so without any fuss or excitement. If we are going to fight, let us prepare for the conflict, while we have time, without ostentation or parade, and then go into the battle determined to preserve our liberties or perish in the attempt. If we are going to act at all, let us act forthwith; but, in the name of common propriety, let us have as little talk as possible, no matter which alternative is adopted.

Since the election of Lincoln most of the leading Northern Abolition papers have essayed the herculean task of reconciling the Southern people to his Presidential rule. Having succeeded to their heart's content in electing him—having villified and maligned the South through a long canvass, without measure or excuse—they now tell us that Mr. Lincoln is a very good man, a very amiable man; that he is not at all violent in his prejudices or partialities; that, on the contrary, he is a moderate, kindly-tempered, conservative man, and if we will only submit to his administration for a time, we will ascertain that he will make one of the best Presidents the South or the country ever had! "Will you walk into my parlor said the spider to the fly."

Now, as it is generally believed most things are possible, Mr. Lincoln may be all that these Abolition journals say he is. But, we do not believe a word they say. We are clearly convinced that they are telling falsehoods to deceive the people of the South, in order to carry out their own selfish and unpatriotic purposes the more easily. They know that, although Lincoln is elected to the Presidency, he is not yet President of the United States, and they are shrewd enough to know that grave doubts exist whether he ever will be. The chances are that he will not, unless the South is quieted; and if any such catastrophe happens, all their past labors and all their expected plunders and spoliations will elude their rapacious grasp. Hence the indecent and hypocritical haste with which they are attempting to conciliate the Southern people.

We propose to measure Mr. Lincoln by his own standard. None of his friends in this or any other latitude can object to such measurement. Mr. Lincoln is quite an old man, and we shall quote nothing against him which can be charged to the indiscretion of youth.

Some years ago the free negroes of Ohio presented Gov. Chase with a silver pitcher as a token of their affection for him. The ceremony of presentation took place in Cincinnati, and Abraham Lincoln was present. Mr. Lincoln was called upon, and made a speech. In that speech he said:

I embrace with pleasure this opportunity of declaring *my disapprobation* of that clause of the Constitution which denies to a portion of the colored people the right of suffrage.

True democracy makes no inquiry about the color of the skin, or place of nativity, or any other circumstance or condition. I regard, therefore, the *exclusion* of the colored people, as a body, from the elective franchise, as *incompatible* with true democratic principles.

Mr. Lincoln made a speech at Peoria, Illinois, on the 16th of October, 1854.[1] Here is an extract from that speech:

That no man is good enough to govern another man *without the* [*that*] *other's consent*. I say this is the leading principle—the SHEET-ANCHOR of American Republicanism [2]. . . the *master* not only governs the *slave* without his consent, but he governs him by a set of rules altogether different from those which he prescribes for himself. Allow all the governed an EQUAL VOICE IN THE GOVERNMENT, and that and that only, is self-government. (Howell's Life of Lincoln, page 279.)

On the 17th of June, 1858, Mr. Lincoln delivered a set speech at Springfield, Illinois.[3] Here is a paragraph from that speech:

We are now far into the fifth year since a policy was initiated, with the avowed object and confident promise of putting an end to slavery agitation. Under the operation of that policy, that agitation has not only not ceased, but has constantly augmented. In my opinion, it will not cease until a crisis shall have been reached and passed. A house divided against itself cannot stand. I believe this Government cannot endure permanently half slave and half free. I do not expect the Union to be dissolved; I do not expect the house to fall; but I do expect it will cease to be divided. It will become all one thing or all the other. Either the opponents of slavery will arrest the further spread of it, and place it where the public mind shall rest in the belief that it is in the course of ultimate extinction, or its advocates will push it forward until it shall become alike lawful in all the States, old as well as new, North as well as South.

Still later, in a speech at Chicago, July 10, 1858, we find Mr. Lincoln promulgating sentiments like these:

If I were in Congress, and a vote should come up on a question whether slavery should be prohibited in a new Territory, in spite of the Dred Scott decision, I would vote that it should.[4]

[1] *Life and Works of Abraham Lincoln*, Cent. ed., II, 248–249.
[2] "Republicanism" is not capitalized in the original. The editor may here have intended a deception.
[3] *Life and Works of Abraham Lincoln*, III, 35–36.
[4] *Ibid.*, 62.

All the foregoing extracts prove Mr. Lincoln to be a thorough radical Abolitionist, without exception or qualification; and in the last one he declared his willingness to violate his oath were he in Congress, sooner than allow slavery to exist in a Territory. If he was so anxious to perjure himself as a Congressman, it is barely possible he will be particularly scrupulous about his oath as President.

We have presented the above extracts, not with a view of stimulating excitement, but for the general information. We wish our people to be fully posted, so that when they act, they may act advisedly, and with full knowledge of every important matter pertaining to the past which has any bearing upon the present.

78. THE CRISIS

(*Daily Chronicle and Sentinel,* Augusta, November 13, 1860)

The crisis which has been so long looked forward to with apprehension by the patriot has at length arrived. A Northern geographical party, completely sectional in every aspect, and largely fanatic in its views and tendencies, has at length succeeded by the numerical force of majorities in electing a President and Vice President. Against all the warnings of the South, and the labors of conservative men in the North, the Republicans have persisted in electing their candidates. Of course this result, looked forward to by many, and by many others not believed possible, has created a profound sensation in the public mind of the South. It has aroused and exasperated our people, that their fellow-citizens in a common country should so far prove untrue to those principles of equality and justice, and those sentiments of patriotic loyalty and fraternity, without which it is impossible that this Republic should continue to exist.

After the close of our successful revolutionary struggle, the several States had widely diverse interests and feelings, but it was thought by the patriotic sages of that day that a more perfect Union should be entered into, for the purpose of common defense, and to strengthen the ties which necessarily existed already between those who had been engaged in a common cause. The Constitution of these United States was not the work of an hour, nor a day—it was formed after mature deliberation, by the wisest and best men of that day, and could never have been formed and entered into, except by constantly keeping in view the various interests of all sections, and providing for them justly, and in a spirit of conciliation and mutual good-will.

Alas that the day should ever come which sees the decay of those sentiments which actuated the framers of the Constitution. But it is apparent to all men that in place of brotherhood and equity, there is hatred, intolerance, fanaticism and defiance. It is truly deplorable that such a state of things exists, but as it does exist and that by the aggressive and sectional attitude of the North, maintained and exhibited to some extent for years, and now plainly marked by the election of candidates avowedly hostile to the rights, the honor, the interests, the peace, the safety, the tranquillity of one whole section of the Confederacy, it becomes the duty of the minority to consult wisely and well as to what is now their duty. That with the feelings manifested by the election of LINCOLN, and the feelings engendered on the other hand by that election, there can be no peace and good-will between the sections, unless a new order of things arises, seems to admit of no doubt. Without these feelings of mutual good-will and mutual forbearance, and without absolute justice to us on the part of the North, and a full and absolute carrying-out of the compact on her part in all particulars, and the absolute abstaining from every thing which jeopards our peace and security as a community, the Union has failed of the objects for which it was formed.

It is very plain that there is now to be a new order of things inaugurated. The North and the South must come fairly and squarely to understand one another, and to learn definitely what each will do. This is a matter which belongs to the people of each Sovereign State, and they will doubtless be called upon speedily to act—each State for itself. There is a community of interest and feeling between the fifteen Southern States, fully as great, perhaps greater, than existed between the original thirteen. The general tone of sentiment among us seems to be, and we think it eminently proper, that each State hold a Convention, and then appoint delegates to a general Convention of all the Southern States, so that they may act with unity and harmony if possible. And therefore, as we are all really one in interest and feeling, however much we may differ in judgment, we would plead for cordial unanimity, and sincere brotherhood among us, discarding all old issues, names and feelings.

Let us have no party spirit any longer, but let us all counsel and consult together for our own and our children's best interests, call a Convention and elect as delegates to it the wisest, and ablest, and best men we have in each county, and leave to them the consideration of the whole matter. Perish partyism, perish animosities, and let us all together [*sic*] now for our own beloved Georgia, the noble Empire State. Let us each and all cultivate a cordial regard for our great commonwealth, and avoid every thing which tends in the slightest degree to alienate us from one another. Let us have no strifes and dissensions any longer at home, but all unite for the great purpose of determining what is best to be done in this perilous time. We plead for unanimity among our people, and that is all. Whatever the calm judgment and matured wisdom of our State, in Convention assembled, shall determine upon, will receive our acquiescence, whether or not it conflicts with our own personal views of duty, interest, and necessity.

79. SUBMIT TO THE CONSTITUTION, BUT RESIST THE FIRST ATTEMPT TO ENFORCE THE PRINCIPLES OF THE REPUBLICAN PARTY

(*The Kentucky Statesman,* Lexington, November 13, 1860)

Pending the canvass just closed we repeatedly expressed the opinion that the election of Lincoln *per se,* under all the forms of law, ought not to be made the occasion of severing the present relations of the States and disrupting the confederacy. We assumed that position in full view of the movements which have been subsequently initiated, and now, with our most unwelcome expectations realized, we adhere to it. We would that Kentucky, by unanimous voice, could be induced thus to define her position. The attitude of our State demands at this juncture that her position be taken with great care; that our people be neither swayed by vain and senseless cries of "Union!" "Union!" nor be moved by what we must regard as a natural and just sympathy with our sister States of the South. Let Kentucky stand square up to the Union mark, but let her stand as firmly and boldly to the Constitution; let her be for the Union, but as firmly let her demand an observance of the Constitution. In a word, let her pledge no allegiance in advance to a union under a violated Constitution.

Our position seems to us right and susceptible of clear and brief statement. We do not receive the success of the Republican party as the "fate of war." It can not be regarded as the mere triumph of one man over another, or as the success of one political organization over a contending party. The verdict of the people on 6th of November can not be received and bowed to with the deference we are accustomed in this country to accord to the will of the majority. On the contrary, that verdict was wrong, radically, vitally wrong; it can not be reconciled with any reasonable hope of permanent union, nor can its enforcement be submitted to. The only hope of union is in the reversal of that verdict. The slave States can not and will never submit to the administration of the government upon the principles and policy as embodied in the platform of the Republican party. The principles enunciated in that instrument are directly opposed to the Constitution, are utterly subversive of the equality of the States, are destructive to all the rights of African slavery, and if enforced, must inevitably upturn our whole social system in the South and destroy the present Union. We flatly reject the cardinal idea of the Republican party, viz: the doctrine of an "Irrepressible Conflict," as antagonistic to the fundamental article of the compact of union between the States, and we hold that any attempt to employ the arm of the Federal Government upon either side of that "conflict" will and ought to divide the confederacy. The Southern States will not and ought not to submit to the inauguration of these Republican principles into the Federal administration, but should resist them even to the dissolution of the Union.

We, therefore, counsel acquiescence in Lincoln's election, or rather in the recent verdict of the people, upon the distinct and unequivocal expression of strong hope, if not belief, that no real attempt will be made to carry out the measures avowed by his party. If we believed that the Federal administration would and could now be used to carry out the aggressions of fanaticism against slavery, our voice would now be for resistance. But we cling yet to a hope for the Union.

We are now for submitting to the Constitution, and not to the carrying out of Republican principles. The South has never yet resisted the Constitution nor violated any of its provisions. Let us adhere to that position. Let us submit to the Constitution, under the forms of which Mr. Lincoln has been elected; but inasmuch as the Constitution does not compel us to submit to such infractions of its provisions as would degrade us, we would urge resistance to an attempted enforcement of Republican principles to the bitter end.

Our position is, then, briefly this: as partizans we opposed Lincoln because of the enunciation of his platform; as citizens we must measure our loyalty by his official acts. Then we would acquiesce in his inauguration and submit to his administration as long as he infracts none of the guarantees of the Constitution, but resist the moment he employs his official authority to carry out the purposes of the Republican party, submit to Lincoln, but resist the exponent of Republicanism. As an individual citizen duly elected, let him have our allegiance; but as the representative of the "Irrepressible Conflict" doctrine, never submit to his official authority. Let us do all the Constitution requires—only that and nothing more.

We are neither submissionists nor secessionist. We stand by the Constitution and advise no submission to its violation. Lincoln's election *per se* is not an infraction of any provision of the Constitution, and we submit; his attempt to carry out the avowed purposes of his party, to use the Federal authority on the side of free labor, in the irrepressible conflict, would be a violation of the Constitution, and when that is proposed we are for resistance to the death.

To our Southern friends we would appeal to postpone this resistance until the Republican platform is actually made the basis of Lincoln's official administration. Don't resist to the point of revolution a party platform, but await an attempt to enforce it by official acts. Let revolution come when the Constitution is trampled upon; let not resistance be predicated upon the purpose of even a successful party, to trample upon it. There is hope that Lincoln will not be so insane as to attempt to meet the purposes of his party, and there is stronger hope that he will not have the power to do it. Let us exhaust this hope, and when the proper time comes let us stand together. Let the Southern States, identified as they are in interest, act in concert. Wait, wait, wait, and if we fail to preserve the Union with a Constitution intact, then let us have a UNITED SOUTH.

80. THE CONSTITUTION—THE UNION—THE LAWS

(*New Orleans Daily Crescent,* November 13, 1860)

We have abated not one jot or tittle of our attachment to the "Constitution, the Union and the Enforcement of the Laws"—the proud and unexceptional motto of the party for which we battled during the long and exciting contest so recently closed. We occupy the same ground we have ever occupied. We have not changed in the slightest particular. Let the Constitution be enforced in all its integrity; let the laws of Congress, enacted in pursuance of its authority, be scrupulously and faithfully carried out; let the decisions of the supreme judicial tribunal of the land be respected and vindicated in all portions of the Confederacy; let a true and loyal obedience to the laws and the courts prevail everywhere in the North, South, East and West—and the Union will be in no danger of disruption from any cause, but will stand for ages an indestructible monument of the surpassing wisdom of our ancestors and the unvarying fidelity and patriotism of their descendants. \

But, we cannot say, and we have never said, that we were in favor of a Union to be maintained at the sacrifice of a violated Constitution, by a persistent refusal to obey the mandates of the Supreme Court, and by a general nullification of the laws of Congress, by the majority section, to oppress and outrage the minority portion of the confederacy. We have never been in favor of *such* a Union, and never shall be. The fathers of the Republic would have spurned such a confederation with as much loathing as they did the treason of Benedict Arnold. The Declaration of Independence itself says: "Whenever any form of government becomes destructive of these ends, (life, liberty and the pursuit of happiness) it is the right of the people to alter or to abolish it, and to institute a new government, laying its foundation on such principles, and organizing its powers in such form, as to them shall seem most likely to effect their safety and happiness." Higher authority than the above is not to be found in the history of the United States. The principle it enunciates constitutes the very corner stone of the temple of American liberty—of liberty everywhere. Wherever the principle is unrecognized, sheer and unadulterated despotism prevails. There is no such thing as civil and religious freedom where it is ignored. The right to change a government, or to utterly abolish it, and to establish a new government, is the inherent right of a free people; and when they are deprived of that right they are no longer free—not a whit more so than the serfs of Russia or the down-trodden millions of Austria.

The history of the Abolition or Black Republican party of the North is a history of repeated injuries and usurpations, all having in direct object the establishment of absolute tyranny over the slaveholding States. And all without the smallest warrant, excuse or justification. We have appealed to their generosity, justice and patriotism, but all without avail. From the beginning, we have only asked to be let alone in the enjoyment of our plain, inalienable rights, as explicitly guaranteed in our common organic law. We have never aggressed upon the North, nor sought to aggress upon the North. Yet every appeal and expostulation has only brought upon us renewed insults and augmented injuries. They have robbed us of our property, they have murdered our citizens while endeavoring to reclaim that property by lawful means, they have set at naught the decrees of the Supreme Court, they have invaded our States and killed our citizens, they have declared their unalterable determination to exclude us altogether from the Territories, they have nullified the laws of Congress, and finally they have capped the mighty pyramid of unfraternal enormities by electing Abraham Lincoln to the Chief Magistracy, on a platform and by a system which indicates nothing but the subjugation of the South and the complete ruin of her social, political and industrial institutions.

All these statements are not only true, but absolutely indisputable. The facts are well known and patent. Under these circumstances, in view of the dark record of the past, the threatening aspect of the present, and the very serious contingencies which the future holds forth, we submit and appeal to a candid and honorable world, whether the Southern people have not been astonishingly patient under gross provocation—whether they have not exhibited remarkable forbearance—whether they have not been long suffering, slow to anger and magnanimous, on numerous occasions where indignation was natural, and severe measures of retaliation justifiable? There can be no doubt on this point. For the sake of peace, for the sake of harmony, the South has compromised until she can compromise no farther, without she is willing to compromise away character, political equality, social and individual interest, and every right and franchise which freemen hold dear.

All the Northern States, with the exception of New Jersey, voted for Lincoln. As he is fully as odious to the South and just as dangerous to her institutions as William H. Seward would have been, the fact of his election, by an overwhelming majority, is full of portentous significance. It shows, beyond all question or peradventure, the unmixed sectional animosity with which an enormous majority of the Northern people regard us of the South. In connection with this, there is another fact, not as generally known as it ought to be, which we propose to lay before the Southern public. The Constitution of the country recognizes slaves as property; the laws of Congress recognize slaves as property; the decisions of the Supreme Court recognize slaves as property; and the constitution, the laws and the court declare that runaway slaves shall be restored to their owners. But how are the Constitution, the laws and the court regarded in nine great Northern States? Let us see. Here is a list of penalties prescribed by certain Northern Legislatures to such Southerners as venture to make legal endeavors to reclaim their property in those States:

	Fine	Inprisonment
In Maine	$1000	5 years
In Vermont	2000	15 years
In Massachusetts	5000	5 years
In Connecticut	5000	5 years
In Pennsylvania	1000	3 months
In Indiana	5000	15 years
In Michigan	1000	10 years
In Wisconsin	1000	2 years
In Iowa	1000	10 years

Every one of the above States, when they passed those laws, placed themselves beyond the pale of the Constitution, and virtually dissolved their connection with the Union! Yet no attempts have been made to force them to abide by the laws, and compel them to yield obedience to the stipulations of the general compact. Nothing of the sort. The outraging section appears to enjoy especial immunity; but let the cruelly aggrieved, the wantonly outraged and the causelessly robbed section presume to discuss the necessity of securing their own safety by resorting to their reserved, inalienable rights, and these violators of all laws, constitutions, unions and compacts, lift up their hands in holy horror and say that the Union must be preserved, the Constitution obeyed, and the laws enforced! The Devil can quote Scripture when it suits his infernal purposes; and so do the Black Republicans refer to the Constitution, the Union and the laws, when they contemplate some other scheme of wrong, outrage and spoliation.

Thus much to-day, by way of keeping our readers accurately posted. We shall refer to the subject, on proper occasions, hereafter.

81. MR. DOUGLAS' LETTER

(*New Orleans Daily Crescent,* November 15, 1860)

We published yesterday morning the letter of Senator Douglas in reply to an invitation signed by a large number of our citizens, without reference to party divisions, asking him to address the people of New Orleans "on the present condition of the affairs of our country" at such time as would comport with his convenience. The correspondence was handed in at too late an hour to admit of comment yesterday morning.

Senator Douglas gracefully acknowledges the compliment paid him, but declines to speak, giving good reasons for the declension. In this we think he acted wisely and judiciously. But, instead of a speech, he has written a long letter, which has, no doubt, been read by most of our citizens ere this. Upon that letter we propose commenting, touching some of its more salient points.

Senator Douglas is, of course, a strong Union man, and holds that the Constitution affords a remedy for every grievance. This was to be expected, for the Senator has reiterated the sentiment on numerous occasions during the late canvass. We do not question his sincerity, but we do most positively and absolutely deny the verity of his proposition. The Constitution affords no remedy for Southern grievances. To the Southern people the Constitution is as worthless as a piece of waste paper, so far as protection to the slavery interest is concerned. The Constitution authorizes slavery; the same instrument declares that fugitives shall be returned to their masters; Congress has passed laws in accordance therewith; and the decisions of the Supreme Court affirm and maintain the mandates of the Constitution and the laws of the National Legislature. Yet, if a slaveholder of the South, in pursuance of the rights guaranteed by this Constitution, these laws and these decisions, attempts to reclaim his servant, nine great Northern States, by express legislative enactment, have declared that he shall be fined from one to five thousand dollars, and imprisoned in the penitentiary from three months to fifteen years!

Now, here is direct nullification of the Constitution, the laws, and the decress of the Supreme Court, and an intolerable grievance to the South. Where is the remedy? Where the power to right the South? Where the authority to vindicate the Constitution? Where the might to enforce the decisions of the Court with a stern and strong hand? These laws have been in force for years. Some of them were in force during Gen. Pierce's administration. All of them have been in force during Mr. Buchanan's administration. As Gen. Pierce, with a Democratic Congress to back him, could not enforce respect to the Constitution, the laws and the Court; and as Mr. Buchanan, with a Democratic Senate and a Democratic House of Representatives to sustain him, when he went into office, failed utterly in the premises, the presumption is reasonable that the Constitution is powerless, when the rights of the South are in question, and that it has no remedies for any grievances, no matter how unjust and atrocious, that may be perpetrated upon us.

Senator Douglas says: "It is not pretended, so far as I am informed, that any *provision* of the Constitution has been violated in the recent election." Granted. But the *spirit* of the Constitution, the only valuable part of it, has been utterly violated and destroyed by the action of the Northern people in electing Abraham Lincoln. The Constitution was created "in order to form a more perfect Union, establish justice, insure domestic tranquillity, provide for the common defense, promote the general welfare," etc. Those were the objects for which it was formed—the sole and exclusive objects. Has the plighted faith of our forefathers been observed? Has the *spirit* of the instrument they created been maintained? No! Nine Northern States denounce fines and prison-houses upon all slaveholders who attempt to vindicate their rights under this very Constitution; and every Northern State, with a solitary exception, voted for Lincoln, after a protracted canvass, which was marked by every extreme of hatred and malevolence to the South, and a fanatical desire to subjugate her to the rule of those who proclaimed times innumerable that they would, sooner or later, utterly root out and destroy her social and industrial institutions. No violation! Nearly everything precious in spirit and meaning in the Constitution has been violated so often that the encroaching section only looks upon it as a means of carrying out schemes of wrong and oppression; and if they ever succeed in inaugurating the President elect, six months will not elapse before the District of Columbia, the forts, arsenals, navy yards, hospitals, custom-houses, post-offices, mints, magazines, dockyards, warehouses, lots and parcels of ground owned by the United States, will swarm with Abolition workmen and Abolition officials. This cannot be prevented, except by force; for section 8 of the Constitution confers upon the Government exclusive jurisdiction in such cases.

This would build up an Abolition party in our midst, disturb our "domestic tranquillity," and endanger our "general welfare," but as it would all be done without violating any *provision* of the Constitution, according to Senator Douglas it would be our duty to submit to it! If his theory be correct, we should submit, and keep on submitting, even if the incendiary's torch is in our dwellings and the assassin's knife at our throats, because we have the Constitution, the Supreme Court and a temporary majority in Congress on our side; and if all these should fail us, and a few scores of thousands of our people should be murdered, and a few hundred of our cities and villages be laid in ashes, we have the consolation of knowing that the distinguished Senator believes that such outrages, or similar ones, "would not only make the Southern people a unit, but would arouse and consolidate all the conservative elements of the North in firm and determined resistance, by overwhelming majorities."

"Make the Southern people a unit?" Senator Douglas! We admire you for your pluck, manhood and bravery, and have always, although differing politically, spoken a good word for you, as opportunity presented itself. We have the satisfaction of informing you that that portion of the South, which is the mainspring of the mighty time-piece of the earth's commerce, *is* a "unit," and that when it determines upon its course of action, as it shortly will, that it will move unitedly.

"Conservative elements of the North!" Why, Senator Douglas, we are astonished that *you* should make use of such an expression. You might as well say, "conservative elements" of Massachusetts. That State, on the 6th of the present month, rejected the pure, the wise, the peerless Edward Everett, by over seventy thousand majority [1]; and on the very same day, and within the very same hours, elected a Chief Magistrate by an overwhelming majority, who had presided over a meeting in Boston, and who, as presiding officer, made a speech in which he compared the execution of the felon and murderer John Brown to the martyrdom of the Apostle Paul! "Conservative elements," indeed! We want nothing to do with such conservatism, and the quicker we separate ourselves from it the safer it will be for us.

Senator Douglas speaks of the Constitution as the "supreme law" of the land. We have the high authority of Daniel Webster for saying that a bargain broken on one side is broken on all sides. A large number of Northern States, years ago, deliberately, wantonly, and causelessly violated the national compact, and released us from all obligations to them; and the result of the late election, all the circumstances considered, is the crowning point of violation on their part, which leaves scarcely any act of bad faith unperformed.

Again: Senator Douglas says, "Nothing has yet occurred to release any citizen from his oath of fidelity to the Constitution of the United States." Very few of our citizens have ever taken an oath to support the Constitution of the United States. All are true to Louisiana. All acknowledge the supreme sovereign authority of Louisiana; and when the day of trial comes, all will be found arrayed in serried phalanx on the side of Louisiana. "If this be treason, make the most of it."

In conclusion, we feel constrained to say that we never read anything from the pen of Senator Douglas which gave us so little satisfaction. It would have been better had he not said a word. The *rôle*

[1] Lincoln 106,533, Douglas 34,372, Breckinridge 5,939, Bell 22,331.

of pacificator does not suit his intellect, genius or temperament. He will fail signally if he attempts it. HENRY CLAY, were he alive and in health and strength, might do something in the way of reconciliation; but he is dead, and the places and the people which knew him and clung to him in adversity, only to throw him aside in sunshine and prosperity, will know him no more forever.

82. WHAT SHOULD GEORGIA DO?

(The Daily Constitutionalist, Augusta, November 16, 1860

The most inveterate and sanguine Unionist in Georgia, if he is an observant man, must read, in the signs of the times, the hopelessness of the Union cause, and the feebleness of the Union sentiment in this State. The differences between North and South have been growing more marked for years, and the mutual repulsion more radical, until not a single sympathy is left between the dominant influences in each section. Not even the banner of the stars and stripes excites the same thrill of patriotic emotion, alike in the heart of the northern Republican and the southern Secessionist. The former looks upon that flag as blurred by the stain of African slavery, for which he feels responsible as long as that flag waves over it, and that it is his duty to humanity and religion to obliterate the stigma. The latter looks upon it as the emblem of a gigantic power, soon to pass into the hands of that sworn enemy, and knows that African slavery, though panoplied by the Federal Constitution, is doomed to a war of extermination. All the powers of a Government which has so long sheltered it will be turned to its destruction. The only hope for its preservation, therefore, is out of the Union. A few more years of unquiet peace may be spared to it, because Black Republicans cannot yet get full possession of every department of the Government. But this affords to the South no reason for a moment's delay in seeking new guards for its future safety.

Such is the reasoning of cool-headed men in Georgia, who were a few days ago among the most conservative of Unionists. To them, therefore, any line of policy will commend itself, which is in the direction of preparation for the coming change. In this view the policy of retaliatory measures, as advocated by Gov. BROWN,[1] is entitled to con-

---

[1] The Georgia legislature assembled in regular session, November 8, 1860. Governor Joseph E. Brown, in his message to that body, recommended that it enact laws authorizing the seizure of property of any citizen of States responsible for loss incurred by Georgia's citizens, and providing a tax of 25 per cent on all goods from States which refused to repeal their so-called personal liberty laws. See Herbert Fielder, *A Sketch of the Life and Times and Speeches of Joseph E. Brown* (Springfield, 1883), pp. 168–169.

sideration and approval. The particular measures, themselves, recommended by him, are not in all respects politic or right, and one of them is especially reprehensible. That one is the repeal of so much of the Penal Code as gives protection within our borders to the "lives, liberty, and property of citizens of other States which have, by their legislation, practically nullified the Fugitive Slave Law."

Apart from the manifest unconstitutionality of such a proceeding, it would be obnoxious to the moral sense of the Christian world. It would introduce among us untold horrors of mob violence and brutal outrage upon unoffending people. It would put Georgia behind China, and on a par with savage tribes in barbarous cruelty to strangers. It would countenance atrocities as bloody as the massacre of Christians by the Druses in Syria. The proposition is sweeping in its terms, and would embrace men, women, and children. But the proposition is, no doubt, designed to frighten off the dangerous emissary of murder and robbery from the offending States—not to be literally enforced upon the innocent sojourners among us, thus indiscriminately put under the ban of outlawry.

For the retaliatory measure suggested in his message there should be more favor. The seizure of property by way of reprisal, and discriminating taxation as a penalty for bad faith, can be sustained on principles of justice, of reason, and of international law. But they are entitled to consideration, and will receive it from the people of Georgia, for a different purpose to that intimated in the message. The recommendations of the message are in a Union spirit, and with a view to preserve the Union. The Governor says:

It is believed that the legislation above recommended would tend to strengthen, rather than weaken the ties of Union between the States generally; as it would do much to destroy the sectional character of the controversy now pending between the free and slave States; and to narrow the issue to a contest between whole sections of the Union.

Too late! too late! is the plain, emphatic reply to this. The time was, when it was not patriotic to despair of the Republic. The time has come when the indulgence of hopes for its preservation is apt to delude the imagination and blind the judgment. The "ties of Union," if by the term is meant ties of fraternal sympathy, can never again be strengthened, for they no longer exist to bind the two sections together. They are broken—utterly sundered between portions of the South, and portions of the North. The antagonism amounts not simply to aversion, but to bitter disgust and hatred. While the Union lasts, as it may, for two, three, or four years longer, it will be a Union of necessity and of temporary convenience. It will continue only long enough to enable the southern States, whose people are resolved upon secession from it, to make such arrangements as a prudent, far-seeing, and practical people ought to make, for so radical a change in their political destinies.

The Governor proceeds:

The acknowledgment of the fact that one State has the power to protect herself against the unconstitutional and aggressive legislation of another, without the aid of the other sister States, and without disturbing her relations with them, not only destroys geographical lines of division, drawn across the Union, and localizes the controversy between individual States, but makes each State pay a more just regard to the rights of every other State, in view of the fact that she cannot look for protection in the wrong, from her other sister States of her own section of the Union, whose sense of justice as well as interest under the proposed legislation would prompt to a consummation of her bad faith, and her unconstitutional enactments.

Again, rises up the response: Too late! too late! What was once a hopeful prospect, and might have been achieved by the legislation suggested, is now a Utopian dream. In the patriotic views of His Excellency, the retaliatory legislation here urged would be operating as a depleting process, to cool the blood and relieve the frenzied brain of northern fanaticism, on the one hand; on the other, as an emollient plaster to soothe the fierce irritation of southern ultraism and disunion. The remedy might have made some impression a few years ago, when it was advocated in these columns and elsewhere in Georgia. But now the remedy comes too late. The disease is too deep seated. The election of Mr. LINCOLN to the Presidency, gives a tremendous onward impulse to anti-slavery sentiment. So far from the possibility of its being induced to recede, its steps are now nerved with new energy, and soon its arm will be clothed with the huge power of Executive patronage— a power that permeates through every nook and corner of the land— a power exercised not less by seductive persuasions than by the intimidations of authority—a power not felt alone in populous cities and at commercial points, where wealth and commerce concentrate—but felt along the far stretching highways of travel, and in remote recesses, wherever a government contract is to be awarded, or a government soldier is marched. What army, flushed with long wished for victory, after many years of toilsome struggle and reverses, ever stopped its onward march when on the very threshold of most tempting plunder?

Some of the southern States see, in the tremendous popular majorities which have elevated LINCOLN to the Presidency, the huge mountainous waves that are beating down on the South with resistless force, and if she supinely waits for the deluge, must engulph the whole social system of the South in the relentless waters of anti-slavery fanaticism. With them the question is, secession from the Union, and a self-defending, homogeneous southern Republic, or submission to the Union, and the fate of Jamaica and St. Domingo.

The conviction that this is the issue is ineradicable. No soothing words, or honeyed promises, from the lips of Mr. LINCOLN himself can up-root this conviction. He rides a wave he cannot control or guide to conservative results, even if so disposed. Or if he should, for his short term of office, check its destructive tendencies, this very restraint will give new strength to its pent up fury, and it will carry into the same office, four years hence, a man of more revolutionary ideas.

Whether these apprehensions be well or ill founded, is now of small practical consequence. They sufficiently possess the minds of a majority of the people in several southern States to render a dissolution of the Union inevitable. It is now a question only of time.

The Governor, in immediate connection with the last quoted sentence, says:

I am no disunionist *per se;* and would delight to contemplate our future glory as a nation, could I have the assurance that the Union, upon the basis of the Constitution, would be as durable as the hills and valleys embraced within the vast territorial limits of its jurisdiction. This cannot be the case, however, unless each section of the Union accords to every other section, the full measure of Constitutional rights.

The writer cordially responds to this sentiment. But how futile the hope that each section of the Union will accord to every other section the full measure of its Constitutional rights. Is it within the bounds of a reasonable hope that Massachusetts will do this—or Vermont, or Maine, or New York? In short, in what northern State are those indications even of a conservative element, potent enough to regain the surface, and counteract the dominant influence which has so recently overwhelmed it?

The retaliatory measures of the Governor will not now work as panaceas to restore the Union to healthful action, and re-unite its sundered ties. But they may so work to prevent further outrage upon the persons of our citizens traveling North, to reclaim their slaves; to prevent further depredations upon that species of property by the underground railroad.

This policy will operate in a way to diminish the dependency of our people upon northern looms, foundries, and workshops, and teach them the wisdom of encouraging their own artisans and mechanics. It will prepare our people for the great change which is ahead in their governmental affairs, and render them, whether for peace or for war, more self-reliant, more efficient, more prosperous.

Such results are not accomplished in a day, nor in a year. An individual involved in complicated business engagements cannot change his pursuits and his locality in that time without serious detriment. A man setting up in housekeeping requires time to make his arrangements, and to equip his establishment. A community, however small and homogeneous, requires time for thought and preparation in inaugurating an enterprise, however peaceful and unopposed, which may involve outlay of money, interruption of business connections, and new schemes of polity. How much more important, then, is time, deliberation, and the amplest preparation, to an agricultural people like those of Geogria, in the contemplation of the question of change of Government. There is no goad of necessity urging them to precipitate themselves out of the Union. The necessities that will force Georgia out of the Union are plainly foreshadowed in the distance, and can be contemplated in all their bearings. But they are not immediately at hand. They are at least two years off. Until the Black Republicans obtain control of the legislative departments of the Government, which they cannot do earlier than two years from the 4th of next March, no encroachment on the Constitutional rights of Georgia, as specified in her platform of 1850, is possible. Therefore, her honor and her obligations to her sister States, and to her own fame, do not require her secession short of that period. The precipitate action of South Carolina might drag her unprepared into disunion, but such conduct would meet with deserved protest from the best citizens of both States.

If she were ready to go out at an earlier day, we would not question the wisdom of her acting more promptly. If she were in a condition to secede to-morrow, and could do so without very great injury to important interests and investments, we would, from the reluctant convictions of our judgment, be an advocate for immediate secession. The hopelessness of preserving the Union has made disunionists, since the election, of thousands of Conservative and Union men. The necessities of the times, not of their seeking, but in despite of their solemn warnings and protests, have made it imperative with prudent men in the South, to seek new guards for their future security.

But immediate secession would be injurious to all, and disastrous to many interests in Georgia. Yet Georgia could secede with as little detriment to her immediate interests, and to her permanent prosperity, as any other southern State. The fact is they all require time and preparation for so important a step—the Cotton States not less than the border States. The precipitate rush of one State out of the Union, when no others were ready to join, or to follow, would be destructive to that State—injure her sister southern States—strengthen the cause of the common enemy, and give him an advantage not easily regained. In fact, a State so acting would defeat her own purposes, bring upon her people a lifetime of embarrassments and regrets, and render difficult the peaceful inauguration of a southern Republic, whether composed of five States or of fifteen, powerful and wise enough to be treated with as an equal by northern Republics, and by foreign monarchies, and rich enough to make treaties of commerce with her desirable to all nations.

83. THE TRUE POLICY

(*The New Orleans Bee,* November 19, 1860)

Most of those papers in the South which, during the late Presidential campaign, had assumed a conservative position, are now endeavoring to shape a course through the troublous period we have encountered which may possibly secure the rights of the South without entailing upon her the stern necessity of dissolving the Union. Among these journals we recognize the Savannah *Republican* as one of the most high-toned, patriotic and intelligent—loving the Union and desirous of perpetuating it, but loving the South and her claims to justice and fair treatment still more. In its number of the 14th inst., the *Republican* has an elaborate and well-considered article on the state of our federal relations and on the policy to be pursued. It begins by an enumeration of the facts of the case, which are, briefly, the election of LINCOLN as a purely sectional triumph; his election by a party whose leading sentiment and cardinal principle is opposition to slavery and the nullification by that party in most of the non-slaveholding States of a law providing for the surrender of fugitive slaves—a law which they openly acknowledge to be in accordance with an express constitutional provision. These are the positive, tangible, undeniable wrongs committed by the North upon the South. As it may be assumed that Mr. LINCOLN is better than his party, our contemporary proceeds to show, first, by authentic declarations from his organs, and next, by his own deliberate expressions of opinion, that Mr. LINCOLN is uncompromisingly hostile to the domestic institutions of the South. The evidence on the subject is recapitulated as follows:

To sum up the whole to a conclusion, we may reasonably regard it as settled, so far as Republican views and intentions can settle it, that the people of the South are living in sin and crime, that the Federal Government should outlaw the domestic institutions of one-half the States of the Union, and on all occasions where it is called on to legislate with regard to them, it should so legislate as will most effectually destroy them. The question whether or not the institution of slavery should be let alone and its existence or non-existence, everywhere, left to the laws of climate and production and the wishes of the people, has been decided against us. Nor is this state of things merely to last with Lincoln; we are told that a radical and permanent change in the policy of the Government with regard to slavery has been inaugurated, and that it is to be kept in operation until, through its agency, the institution shall have been swept entirely away. This is the promise, and they have the power to make it good. We take it for granted that they are honest in what they say. They may not have the power now, owing to the present constitution of the two houses of Congress, but it is evident that they have only to will it to accomplish every purpose within the next four years.

With such a prospect before them, the Southern States may well pause ere they consent to go on as they have hitherto done, trusting either to the conservatism of the North, or to the strength of party to neutralize Black Republican hatred. It is manifest that the South cannot possibly consent to dwell in the Union upon sufferance; the mere vassal and thrall of a party which aims at her ruin and degradation, and which only awaits a reinforcement to accomplish it under the forms of the Constitution. Such a state of practical servitude and submission, where all sense of equality would be lost, and where we should be placed at the mercy of a relentless master, would necessarily become perfectly intolerable. It is wholly impossible to remain as we are, because simple acquiescence in the existing state of things would encourage our foes and enfeeble ourselves. One of two remedies must be invoked: Either the South must separate from the North, or must receive such ample guarantees of security and immunity for the future, by a new and well-defined compact, as will dissipate all apprehension of a renewal of sectional conflict. Now there are hosts of honest, true-hearted Southerners who are loth to break up the Union, and will only consent to secede after it shall have been demonstrated that all other means of relief have proved futile; and that the South in justice to her own indefeasible privileges is compelled to resort to the paramount law of self-protection. If, therefore, the South can abide safely and honorably in the Union, there are few indeed who will not rejoice at the consummation.

But how can this be accomplished? How are we to persuade the North to forsake its oppressive and iniquitous policy, and to render equal justice to the weaker section of the confederacy? The Savannah *Republican* suggests a National Convention to be composed of three delegates from every State. This plan seems to us highly objectionable. We have learned from dear-bought experience to distrust National Conventions. The evils we are now deploring were to a great extent the result of the feuds and discords of a National Convention. Congress itself, which is practically a National Convention, presents a striking illustration of the irreconcilable contrariety of opinions, the hopeless jar and shock of antagonistic principles which such assemblages must inevitably engender. A National Convention such as is contemplated would prove a perfect bear-garden, wherein North and South would clamor, and quarrel, and combat. No! There is but one feasible mode of convincing the North that we are in earnest, and that the alternative of justice or disunion is before the country, and that is by a Southern Conference composed exclusively of delegates from all the slaveholding States. Such an assemblage would embody the ability, wisdom and patriotism of the South. The delegates would come together in a fraternal spirit; would dispassionately investigate the grave issues before them; determine precisely what legislative changes or constitutional amendments might be essential to the security of the South from future aggression, and draft a statement of grievances and bill of rights to be submitted to the North. Doing this, the South would occupy a position at once of calmness, power and dignity, as well as of conciliation. She would be in no wise responsible for consequences. She would claim her just rights as an indispensable condition of her further continuance in the Union. Failing to obtain them, she would then act with unanimity, and a resort to the extreme measure of separation would meet with no dissentient voice even from among the most conservative of her sons. This is the last solitary resource of those of us who still cling to the hope of preserving the Union.

84. STOP AND THINK—WHAT IS SECESSION?

(*Daily Nashville Patriot,* November 19, 1860)

The laws of the United States operate so gently and so seldom upon the people individually, that we are scarcely aware of their existence. But, at this juncture, we would appeal to every citizen to bear in mind that these laws are not addressed to the States, but to each individual person in the Union. For example, the United States Statute says to the citizen: "You shall not prevent or retard the transportation of the mails." Now, suppose Tennessee should pass an act forbidding the passage of United States mails through the State, and direct the issuance of process to arrest and stop the carriers, and to take the mail-bags away from them; and suppose a magistrate should, in obedience to the act, issue such a process, and a sheriff or other officer should arrest the carrier and seize his mail, what would follow? Would the United States government proceed against Tennessee? Not at all. The magistrate who issued the process, and the officer who executed it, would be indicted in the Circuit Court of the United States, and be brought to trial there. Do we flatter ourselves that the defendants could make a successful defense by pleading that they acted under the authority of the act of the Legislature? If so, we only deceive ourselves. The Court would inform us that the laws of the United States directing the transportation of the mails, and making it a crime to retard their progress, is supreme, and the act of the State Legislature forbidding it, void. The defendants would be convicted and fined. Now, how is the execution of this judgment of the Court to be prevented? It could not be done, except by the defendant himself or by the government of Tennessee. Let us suppose the marshal, armed with a writ of execution commanding him to make the fine out of the defendant's property, to come to make the money by seizing the defendant's horse. If the defendant resists the execution of the process, then he incurs the guilt of resisting the process and the laws of the United States; and for this he is indictable. Besides this, the marshal has the power, conferred on him by law, to summon a *posse* to assist him in seizing the horse. But suppose the people will not obey the summons, and thereby the marshal is prevented from executing the process of the courts; in that case the marshal reports the case to the proper department at Washington. The President is notified of the facts; and as he is sworn to see the laws executed, he will send an armed force to assist the marshal to make the money, and perform his duty. The defendant would find himself too weak to cope with the marshal thus assisted; and now nothing remains but to submit, or appeal to the Governor of the State to assist him in resisting the process, and the forces of the General Government. Then, suppose the Governor should raise a military force to prevent the execution of the process, the government of the United States and their armed forces are brought face to face, in a case in which the United States are clearly in the right, and we imagine that every one will concede that the right ought and must prevail.

Now, it may be said to all this: "Tennessee can find a remedy in this case by seceding from the Union." How? Suppose Tennessee, even by a convention, should solemnly declare herself out of the Union; but the government of the United States refuses to recognize the declaration of the convention, and turning aside from this act of Tennessee, still persists in enforcing the judgment against the defendant, pursuing him still, *as a private individual,* having no excuse for his resistance, and proceeds to enforce the judgment by military force? Either the State must at last acquiesce, or must oppose force by force. If she resorts to this alternative; still the United States will not proceed against the State; but, finding the people of the State with arms in their hands resisting the lawful authority of the Union, seize them and bring them to trial for treason, and punish them capitally. Blood is now shed, and it is said that this blood could never be appeased, but must beget a fatal hatred in the minds of the people against the government. Why? Would not every government, in the case supposed, shed the blood of the opposers of the law? Has not every government shed the blood of those who have incurred the guilt of doing what is forbidden under capital penalties? Could any government exist without this power? So, likewise, in a case where a citizen of one State sues and recovers a judgment in the Federal Courts against the citizen of another State. So, in the case of a fugitive slave, pursued under the act of Congress. So, in the execution of all constitutional laws of the Federal Government.

What does all this prove? It proves—that going out of the Union by solemn acts of State Legislatures or conventions does not absolve the individual citizen from the obligation to obey the laws of the Union, and notwithstanding the act of secession the individual still continues subject to the laws of the Union, and nothing can protect him from the penalties of the violated law, but the use of superior force. In all such cases the President's duty is plain. He is bound to execute the laws. He cannot, even, be relieved from it by an act of Congress, for Congress has no such power, and any act of the kind would be void. In any of the cases supposed, nothing short of an act of the whole people, in convention, can discharge the President from his obligation to enforce the national laws against all violators of them, and from employing the whole power with which he is invested by the Constitution and laws to discharge that duty.

Secession, therefore, by the people of a State, is a nullity in law, and every citizen of the State continues, in spite of secession, still a citizen of the Union, liable to the penalties of the laws of the Union; and every act of resistance to the laws of the government, either by one man or one hundred thousand is a crime, and can only be made innocent by the people of the United States, in convention. The contrary doctrine would give us a government without law, without order, without safety either for life, liberty or property—just no government at all. It will thus be seen that in the outset, the violation of the law by a single individual is simply a crime; if there be organized resistance to law by many it may be rebellion or nullification; and if by a State under the auspices of the Legislature, it is called secession. In principle and essence they are all the same, and in no form does the act free itself from the quality of criminality.

But it may be urged that if this view be accepted as correct, the people could have no recourse against oppression, and that they would be at once reduced to the yoke of any tyranny which government saw proper to impose. This is untrue, because the government belongs to the people and the laws are theirs. They have the power to alter, amend or repeal the laws at their will, in a constitutional and peaceful manner. If their agents or representatives have enacted laws distasteful to them, let them take the earliest opportunity to modify or abolish such distasteful enactments. They have the unobstructed power to redress all such grievances in peace. If it is still urged that obstinate and adverse majorities may rise up and prevent such redress, we reply, they must prove that by the effort. This is our duty here in Tennessee, and it is the duty of every State in the Union. We shall pursue this subject.

85. A Plea for the Union

(*The Kentucky Statesman,* Lexington, November 20, 1860)

Our plea is not addressed to the panic-striken Union-shriekers. We have no word of suggestion for those who propose in this hour of imminent peril, nothing beyond the Union resolves of county-town-meetings, and who are ready to impugn the loyalty of every proposition for action which is not interpolated with vehement professions of unqualified devotion to the Union. Such men are worse than drones in an emergency such as that with which we have to deal. But to the intelligent citizen who understands the true extent and character of the danger which threatens us, and would strike a blow in the right direction, we beg to submit a thought or two.

The people of the States of Mississippi, Alabama, Florida, Georgia and South Carolina have in every possible manner in which public sentiment can be expressed, in mass meeting, through their executive and legislative officers, through the addresses of leading men of all political parties, through the press, indicated a present determination to revolutionize the Government. We repeat that every avenue we have to the public sentiment of those States reveals to us a most appalling unanimity of feeling and opinion in favor of immediate secession from the Union. Steps are already being taken, and serious movements are now deliberately set on foot to sever their relations with the existing confederacy. That movement will accomplish its purpose if not arrested by influences beyond the border of States engaged. That powerful minority of anti-secession men to whom we have been directed so often, has not yet exhibited itself. We have as yet to note the first noticeable expression of opinion from any of the States we have named, in opposition to the revolution. Mr. A. H. Stevens [*i. e.,* Stephens], to whom so many eager eyes were turned, has virtually seconded the whole movement, only differing from the secessionists in a preliminary evolution of the forces.[1] There seems really to be no opposing minority in the cotton States; but if there is, it is manifestly powerless. He is a fool who doubts the settled purpose of these men, or questions that their resolution will be equal to the responsibility. They are in earnest,

---

[1] The debate between Stephens and Toombs before the Georgia legislature dealt primarily with the question of the process of secession. Toombs was afraid of a convention and urged the legislature to declare Georgia out of the Union. Stephens held that a state convention alone possessed the power to do so.

and will dissolve this Union before the 4th of March unless the border slave States arrest their lamentable movement.

We are not of those who say "let them go!" Nor are we of those who say, "whip them in!" We are for inducing them not to secede. We shudder at the thought of a dissolution of the confederacy, and would now labor to prevent it. The Union, the Constitution, the Government will not be worth the loyalty of the patriot when six, eight, or ten, States shall have over-ridden the law and proclaimed their separate sovereignty. Let us devise some mode by which the Union can be preserved intact. We think Kentucky, Virginia, Tennessee and Missouri can save the cause. How? certainly not by county or State Conventions; certainly not by extenuating the aggressions of the Republican party and pledging unqualified loyalty to the government administered on Lincoln's platform; certainly not by characterizing the action of the cotton States in harsh words of condemnation, and ignoring the wrongs which have impelled them to the step; certainly not by meaningless shrieks of Union and senseless denunciation of secession; all this does no good. If every man, woman and child in Kentucky were to assemble in one grand mass meeting, and with one acclaim resolve that secession is treason and the Union must and shall be preserved, secession would still go on, and the Union would as rapidly approach its dissolution. However much we may condemn the Southern secessionists as rash and wrong, let us not, at our own peril, mistake their character. Let us not commit the fatal folly of imagining that they are to be deterred by threats or frightened by the Opposition of Kentucky. On the contrary, let us at the earliest moment realize the fact that the more unqualifiedly Kentucky, Virginia and Tennessee pledge submission to Republican rule, the more determined will be the cotton States to assume their independence. But there is a mode whereby the cotton States can be induced to hear the appeal of the border States. Let us meet them in common council. Let us have a Southern convention, and let the slave States take counsel together as to the best mode of preserving their rights in the Union. We believe that if this proposition be made to the seceding States it will be acceded to and when once in convention we believe that such action can be determined on as will deter them from the step they now propose. By this Union of purpose and concentration of action the slave States have it in their power to coerce from Mr. Lincoln and from the Republican party a recognition of their rights and an abandonment of the unconstitutional designs of that organization. This can be shown to the cotton States; and with assurances of co-operation and support from their border friends, they will try it. It seems to us that the secession of five or six States at this time would be an act of egregious folly and gross ingratitude. Mr. Lincoln is absolutely at the mercy of the anti-Republicans in Congress. He can do literally nothing without their consent and acquiescence. They have it in their power to stop the machinery of government, to withhold supplies and vacate the public offices. He will be powerless for evil now as when a private citizen of Illinois, if the opposition to him is concentrated and well directed. All this advantage would be lost if the cotton States secede and withdraw their members. The non-seceding States would be left in a minority, without power to restrain Lincoln in any of his measures. What folly, then, to throw away such an advantage, and what injustice to abandon friends at such a time! Then let us meet these States in convention and appeal to them with these and other equally strong arguments. The Louisville *Journal,* a few days ago, appealed to Mr. Breckinridge to go South and to employ whatever influence he might have to restrain this movement. Won't the *Journal* now join us in an appeal to the Governor to appoint one or two leading and influential men from each of the three parties in Kentucky to meet similar delegates from all the Southern States in Convention, and there represent the true feeling of our State? If assent be not given to this proposition, then answer us, what on earth *do* you propose to do?

We believe that six or eight States will, on or before the 4th of March next, be virtually and formally without the Union, unless some action is taken to prevent it. We see nothing else to save the Union than a Southern Convention; and we believe that will. But the suggestion is our own, and for it we beg to say that neither the party we support nor any of its leading men, is in anywise responsible.

86. It Is the First Step Which Costs

(The Daily True Delta, New Orleans, November 20, 1860)

It is announced that Governor Thomas O. Moore has yielded before the pressure of Slidell and his rump retinue, and consented to the issuance of a proclamation convening the general assembly in extra session.[1] We were aware of the efforts being made by the leader of the secession

[1] The next regular session of the Louisiana legislature would not have begun until January 21, 1861. Governor Moore called an extra session to meet December 10, 1860. The session lasted three days only, during which time a convention bill and a $500,000 military appropriation bill were enacted.

jobbers at the Charleston convention to accomplish this object, and we feared that our weak, irresolute and easily persuaded executive would finally yield to incessant importunity, and thus lend himself to the disunion schemes of men who regard him only as a convenient and plastic tool in their hands. Under this impression we made no appeals to him on behalf of the great mass of our citizens who utterly repudiate all disorganising and revolutionary schemes for the redress of national or state grievances, nor yet in sympathy with the commerce of our city, which is being paralysed, and with those who conduct it, who are daily becoming conscious that ruin must soon overwhelm them.

What Governor Moore can imagine of good from an expensive proceeding like that of an extra session of the legislature, which, in any event, can only anticipate the regular session by three or four weeks, we are at a loss to conceive, as we are what he and those who dictate this course to him contemplate, unless indeed it be to add to the excitement, distrust and alarm already pervading the community, and which are involving every man of business to an extent of which the clearest-sighted and most sagacious cannot see the end or prepare for it. If Louisiana allows herself to be drawn into the wake of South Carolina, Florida and Mississippi on this occasion; if she follows the lead being prepared for her by men without principle, talents or patriotism, it will be well for her citizens of property, position and responsibility to wake up to what they seem utterly blind not to perceive is certain to befall them. It is all very well for agents of disunion constituents, for men deeply, perhaps immensely, indebted to northern houses, for capitalists with large sums of money unemployed and upon the look-out for sacrifices, for broken down and characterless politicians, and the large swarm of beggarly no-account people to be found in all large cities, to clamor for revolution and the wild license it allows to those who initiate or direct it while they happen to continue in the ascendant. But it is far otherwise with our banking, insurance and other institutions, with our merchants, traders and mechanics, with the industrious, hard-working, thrifty and law-abiding tens of thousands who constitute what is considered well ordered society, and to whose ears the howls of the disorderly, the clamors of the dissatisfied and the thunders of civil war carry nothing but the knell of prosperity, civil order and political freedom. Accustomed to great political excitement, many are utterly unable to comprehend the possibility of revolution, and to this habitude of thought must the apparent apathy now pervading the conservative masses of the south be ascribed. The vagaries of ignoble Catilines pass unheeded by the great body of this hitherto prosperous, contented and free people, and to this state of the popular mind, and not to real indifference to the maintenance of the laws, institutions and freedom of the nation, must the apparent unconcern witnessed be ascribed. That any portion of this highly intelligent and sensitively honorable population can share the sentiments daily proclaimed by persons announcing themselves ostentatiously as the enemies of this splendid and beneficent system of government under which we all live successful and free, we cannot believe, for we are utterly unable to comprehend how any but the most abandoned and wicked can desire the destruction, personally or pecuniarily, of his fellow-countrymen, however misguided, unjust or dishonest some, or a majority even, may have been; or how a really honest and upright man could stimulate political ill-will and state alienation with often no higher motive than springs from the suggestions of a dishonest intention to be thus enabled to escape from the payment of an honestly contracted obligation. Perhaps no member of this community has fewer ties to bind him to the inhabitants of the free states of this republic than the writer of these lines, or one who would be more prompt to advise the adoption of a rigorous course to compel them to do their duty according to the constitution and the laws; but rather than see a separation take place, tinctured, touched or contaminated by dishonesty, we would prefer that the waves of the Atlantic would overwhelm us all. We will never advocate or vote for a separation of this Union upon any ground less sufficient than will justify immediate revolution, and no pecuniary or sordid appeal, such as the organs new, old and hypothecated of disunionism are in the habit of addressing their few readers, will, we are sure, ever incline any honest or reflecting man to their standard. The reopening of the African slave trade, the consequential supersession of the white labor now employed mechanically and otherwise in these southern states, the repudiation of our just debts to the people of the free states, and other inducements of a similar character we daily hear and see addressed to the cupidity of men, cannot, we are convinced, seduce any good citizen from his duty to his state, the constitution, the laws and the Union! If the election of Mr. Lincoln is to be regarded as a just cause for a dissolution of this confederacy of peoples, before he has entered upon the discharge of his presidential duties, before he has proclaimed his views of public policy, or committed an overt act of treason, or even unfriendliness against the south or its institutions, and when it is known that a Senate and House of Representatives are opposed to him and his principles—that the Supreme court of the Union has judicially decided against, and will continue to decide against them—and that a million majority at least of the popular vote of the republic will be recorded against him; it follows that no stable government can ever exist on this continent again; for, it will not be reason or common sense, but the passions of men and the conspiracies of demagogues that will determine political conduct. No southern confederacy, certainly, can ever be formed with the consent of the people, if the reopening of the African slave trade, or the free trade ideas of Carolina prevail—for the first will be death to Virginia and the second to Louisiana—were the decision of the matter exclusively left with the agricultural slave-owners themselves, and the entire white population of the south, besides, excluded from a voice. These considerations ought to have suggested doubts to Governor Moore before he unwisely allowed himself to take his first step in the march of disunion.

87. To A. Lincoln, President-elect of the United States

(Daily Missouri Republican, St. Louis, November 21, 1860)

Sir: A little over two weeks have elapsed since, at the quadrennial election, provided for by the Constitution, you received a majority of the electoral votes for President. All that now remains is for the electors to meet in their several colleges, on the first Wednesday of next month, there to declare their votes for you, and on the 4th day of March next, to take upon yourself the administration of the Government of what may yet be termed *the United States.* You were elected by extraordinary means and influences. Fifteen of the States gave you their votes, and a majority of the electoral colleges. One State—New Jersey—with a decided majority of the people against you, yet gave you four votes, leaving three others to Mr. Douglas. Two more of those so-called Free States—California and Oregon—are in doubt, and one at least may have gone against you. Still, you are elected President by the forms of the Constitution, though little more than a third of the popular vote can be shown in your favor. You are, what is infinitely worse, a *Sectional* President, elected by Free States alone, on an issue made up to suit your case, and to accommodate the fanaticism of the peculiar elements composing the population of those States—elements of an extraordinary character, strongly and strangely intermingled, and representing the Puritan and the Infidel, in large bodies, and comprising the worst features of the intolerance of each class. Seizing hold of the Negro Question, with no hope of getting an electoral vote in any other State, and even when thus banded, meeting with the opposition, at home, of a million of Democrats, you have triumphed, and now behold the result.

Instead of finding, as has always been the case in former elections, a steady, if reluctant, acquiescence in the decision of the people at the polls, look at the condition of the country. When the gallant HARRY CLAY was stricken down and defeated in the race with POLK, God knows there was anguish and heartburnings at the result all over the land, but there was also a manly acquiescence on the part of his friends and the country. He had more ardent friends than any man who ever lived, and you were one of them, and they all yielded to the popular voice. And why? Because these States were not then divided by sectional lines—because appeals were not then made to the people of the Free States, as such, nor to those of the Slave States—because no such party then existed as the one of which you are now the representative —and because the battle was fought upon higher, nobler grounds, than any that have been presented by you in this contest.

But now look at the result of the late election. Little over two weeks have passed, and you find one State on the point of secession from the Union. You find another deliberating upon the course which honor and duty demands of her. You find the Legislatures of three States summoned to meet at unusual periods, to determine what course they shall adopt in this grave conjuncture of affairs. A show of military parade, the gathering of volunteers, the enrolling of minute men, the concentration of arms, and munitions of war—all these things are going on in all those States, with an energy which must satify you that they are in earnest. Meanwhile, the conservative States—Maryland, Virginia, North Carolina, Kentucky, Tennessee, and Missouri—are anxiously looking for the time when they can, by judicious action, restore peace to the Union. But be not deceived. Those States, while they are devoted to the Union—while they believe that ours is yet too good a Government to be destroyed now—will not stand idly by and see their sister States—bone of their bone and flesh of their flesh—trampled in the dust. They will not do it.

Need we ask you to look at the *other calamity* which this election has brought upon us—the total disruption of confidence between man and man—not in the South nor in the West alone, but in the East and the North—a calamity threatening bankruptcy to the whole country. Is it not an alarming crisis? And ought not something to be done

to stay its cruel, blasting effects? It may be said that you are powerless in this matter; that you are not yet even elected, and that you
will not take office, at the head, possibly, of a sundered Union, until the
4th of March next. Granted that this is true. Yet you must be aware
that some action on your part—some assurances from the free States
must be given, of a change in their relations towards the South and
the slave States, or all hope for a perpetuation of the Union is at an
end. You tell us that you are a conservative man, that your administration will be conducted with reference to the best interests of the
whole country—and you cite us to your speeches as enunciating the
principles upon which your official course will be based. So say all your
friends, Mr. LINCOLN. But we warn you that they will not satisfy
fifteen States of the Union now, nor in the future. They ask, and they
have a right to ask, new pledges and new guarantees. They ask, and
will continue to ask, that the Fugitive Slave Law shall be executed by
you with fidelity. The Constitution and the Law require it at your
hands. They ask, and they will insist upon, as preliminary to any adjustment of this question, that all laws passed by the free States, designed to avoid or prevent the execution of this law, shall be absolutely and unconditionally repealed, and that no acts, intended to
despoil the people of the Slave States of their property, shall ever be
passed. Mr. LINCOLN, in your own State, almost under your own eye,
a slave was last week rescued from the proper officers of the law, and
carried into Canada. Not only was the majesty of the law set at naught
by men who have just voted for you, but the owner of the slave was
insulted and abused by the mob. Think you, that outrages of this kind
will longer be submitted to? If you do, you are greatly mistaken. No
amount of force—not the whole North combined—can coerce the people of the Slave States to submit to these indignities—these constant,
repeated and open violations of the Constitution—any longer. The Free
States have nullified this law for years, and this is the cause of complaint, and for which the dissolution of the Union is now threatened—
not that your election affords ground for any such extreme act. We
warn you of the danger which menaces the country. The vast majority
of the People of the Slave States are true, loyal friends of the Union.
They will fight for it as long as it is worth preserving. They will not
give up hope, nor go out of the Union, until they are satisfied that the
rights of the South will not be respected by the North. They are in all
respects the equal of the North, and whether in or out of the Union
they will command respect.

Go to work, then, Mr. Lincoln, and counsel and insist upon the repeal of all these obnoxious laws, and avow your determination to execute the Fugitive Slave Law, and all may yet be well. Short of this, and in the present temper of the People, we see nothing but ruin and desolation to the whole country.

88. A General Survey

(*The Review,* Charlottesville, Va., November 23, 1860)

We have been speaking carefully since the election of Lincoln and the consequent excitement which has appeared at the South.—We felt ourselves so irritated by the sectional attitude and numerical tyranny of the North that we have at moments rejoiced in the fury of South Carolina, and said to ourselves, let the storm gather—let us appeal to the sword!

Undoubtedly the position of the North, viewed upon the most indulgent principles, cannot be guarded at all points from strong and just censure.

We have attempted to disabuse our minds of preconceived opinions, to take ourselves out of the present environment, and to look from a distance, with the calmness of a spectator, upon the events now transpiring.

If we commence at Massachusetts, we find the anti-slavery feeling strongest, the Republican party most violent. In New York, there is a perceptible moderation in the feeling. Pennsylvania and New Jersey are comparatively conservative. We then reach Maryland. Here we find a new opinion as regards Slavery. The people are not pro-slavery, and they are not anti-slavery. They have the institution, and they accept it as they find it. Still there is a Republican element. We find a public man like Henry Winter Davis.[1] We next reach Virginia. The feeling here is positive in favor of Slavery, but the State is decidedly for the Union and abiding the result of the Presidential election. When we reach South Carolina and Alabama, where we find more slaves, we encounter the most rabid pro-slavery sentiments. The African Slave Trade laws are nullified. They desire a dissolution of the Union on account of the Territorial question of Slavery.

Now we have followed a breadth of country of two thousand miles, and the sentiment on the Slavery question shades off with the precision

---

[1] Davis had been a Whig, and then a Know-Nothing. He cast the deciding vote for Pennington, Republican, for the speakership of the House, January 31, 1860, and from that time was regarded as a Republican by the southern-rights men. During the presidential campaign he had been the leader of the Constitutional Union party in Maryland.

and the regularity of the law of temperature. Give the latitude, and you can give the figure at which the negrometer stands. An opinion on Slavery is not an intelligent judgment; it is a prejudice. The bears in the North are white; the men are anti-slavery.—The bears in the South are black; the men are for the Slave Trade. There are also brown bears in Russia, and intermediate opinions of the Slavery question in Virginia and Kentucky.

It is idle for Mr. SEWARD to say, he knows he is right. It is idle for Mr. TOOMBS to say, he knows he is right. They each form their opinions according to the range of the thermometer, and the thermometer cannot settle accurately a moral question.

Even in Virginia the sentiment is graduated by the number of slaves in a county. Nottoway is very decided for the institution; Mason gives a respectable vote for LINCOLN. Even on the Gulf, the matter of interest asserts its sway in tempering the feeling, as decidedly as at the North. Louisiana, at the mouth of the Mississippi, is for the Union.

Who then is right? Which is right, the republican or the fire-eater? Is the idea of coercing a seceding State to remain in the Union, because LINCOLN has been *constitutionally* elected, or the idea of destroying the Constitution and the Government because LINCOLN has been elected— the right idea?

As we said, the Republicans, even from Northern standpoint, *cannot* stand entirely excused. We will just point to the nullification of the Fugitive Slave Law. Here is a patent and indefensible wrong. New Hampshire declares that the slave is, of right, absolutely a freeman. In Maine and Vermont he is free the moment he puts his foot on the soil. Other States delay and obstruct the execution of the law in various ways. Besides this, a large portion of the Republican party make war directly on the existence of the institution. They are for breaking it down by all methods. They endorsed JOHN BROWN.

On the other hand, not only the juries but the Federal judges, in South Carolina, have defeated the execution of the laws against the Slave Trade. Cargoes of slaves have been landed at various times in the South, and the community tolerates their purchase and their presence on the cotton plantations. South Carolina, also, has been steadily attempting to dismember the Union for thirty years. One of her representatives perpetrated the assault upon Mr. SUMNER. The extreme South also instituted the repeal of the Missouri Compromise, and carried through the iniquitous transactions in Kansas. They then admitted Oregon, but would not admit Kansas.

The position of Mr. LINCOLN, the actual head of the Republican party, is clearly with the more conservative element of that organization. He is explicitly for non-interference with the institution of Slavery where it exists. He is opposed to the abolition of Slavery in the District of Columbia, unless a majority of the people wish it abolished and compensation is made to the owners. He would consent to the admission of a Slave State. He is in favor of an efficient Fugitive Slave law. He is against negro suffrage. He recognizes the impossibility of abolishing Slavery except by natural causes, and the lapse of time.

This is the President of the United States—the executive branch of the Government.—The other departments of the Government are with the South—the Senate, the House of Representatives, and the Judiciary.

The question is, Under the circumstances shall we dissolve the Union on account of this election?

It was admitted that the conservative element of the country *could* have carried the election. A united Democratic party, without even the Bell party, would probably have succeeded. Instead of effecting a solid opposition, they put three candidates in the field.

It is also admitted, that the administration of Mr. BUCHANAN has been singularly unfortunate. It has excited the displeasure of all parties. Its unparalleled corruption, apart from the Slavery question, had arrayed against it an undoubted majority of the American people.—It is therefore true that thousands of the voters at the North sustained Mr. LINCOLN from mere dissatisfaction with the Democratic party. The Republican vote was made up in a very large proportion, not of sympathizers with Mr. SEWARD, but of enemies of Mr. BUCHANAN.

The question then comes back, What then shall be done?

Considering the whole thing, we are decidedly opposed to a dissolution of the Union. The attitude of South Carolina is not to be regarded for a moment. The present election is not the cause with South Carolina; it is merely the *occasion*. Mr. YANCEY and his party are merely seizing the opportunity to push matters as rapidly as possible. All we want is Time.

89. SIGNS OF THE TIMES

(*The New Orleans Bee,* November 23, 1860)

We know pretty well what are the views of at least a majority of the people of the cotton States. They are very generally in favor of secession, either immediate or eventual. In other words, while perhaps a minority would be disposed to do nothing, but remain quiet, accept the election of LINCOLN as an accomplished fact, constitutionally effected, and await aggression before proceeding to resistance, the remainder are resolved to bring matters between the North and South to a settlement—some thinking that the only mode of settling is by withdrawing from the Union, while others are willing to make a last effort by concerted Southern action to induce the North to abandon its iniquitous policy, and acknowledge our rights. These are the opinions prevalent in what are termed the extreme Southern States. There is no use in attempting to blink them. They are the open and avowed convictions of three-fourths of the citizens. The only manifest difference among them relates, as we have intimated, to the time of action, and the desire for the co-operation of all the slaveholding commonwealths.

In the frontier slave States, such as Maryland, Virginia, Kentucky, Tennessee and Missouri, the prevailing disposition is far more moderate. In Maryland, Kentucky and Missouri there are very few Disunionists; the press generally assuming the position that the election of ABRAHAM LINCOLN does not justify a resort to secession, and that the right arrogated by Southern States to retire from the Union is revolutionary, and not a peaceful remedy. Elsewhere we publish an extract from a letter written by Gov. MAGOFFIN, of Kentucky, which expresses the sentiments of the Breckinridge party of that State, and which will be deemed singularly conservative. The Bell and Douglas parties are, of course, for the preservation of the Union. Maryland agrees substantially with Kentucky. As for Missouri, we may readily imagine that a State in which LINCOLN received nearly eighteen thousand votes, has few sympathies with the Southern doctrines of State Rights. Virginia and Tennessee approach somewhat to the standard recognized in the cotton States; but they are far from displaying any of the spirit and ardor witnessed in South Carolina and Georgia. The Richmond *Enquirer,* which is the exponent of the dominant feelings of the citizens of the Old Dominion, without advocating secession, zealously maintains the rights of the South, and holds the Union can be saved only by certain concessions to be made by the North, such as the repeal of all laws impeding the enforcement of the Fugitive Slave law; the passage of laws to enable Southern men to carry their slaves in safety into Northern States, and to remove them thence; the repeal of the laws prohibiting the slave trade in the District of

Columbia, and the admission of Southerners with their property to equal rights in the Territories. In Tennessee the attachment to the Union is strong, yet a growing conviction exists that the present moment should be adopted for a definitive adjustment of the questions at issue between the North and South, and that their postponement will only aggravate the difficulty and render it insurmountable.

Such is a brief view of Southern ideas in reference to the unspeakably important topics which have taken form and substance since the election of ABRAHAM LINCOLN. If we turn to the North, we shall perceive various, but upon the whole unsatisfactory, developments. The comments of the Northern press upon Southern manifestations are sometimes temperate, sometimes full of taint [1] and defiance. Certain journals exult in Black Republican success, as a direct and splendid victory over the slave power, and speak of the South as if she lay prostrate at the feet of a conqueror. Others, however, adopt a less obnoxious tone, and endeavor to soothe the South by assurances of the conservatism of the President elect. Some sheets, such as the *Tribune,* mock and deride the South, yet deprecate any attempt to coerce a seceding State; while others, as the New York *Times,* avoid violent language, yet deny the right of secession and maintain the bounden duty of the President to put down by force any organized resistance to the laws of the United States. But we observe no evidence whatever of concession; no exhibition of the returning sense of justice; not the slightest disposition to meet the South in friendly conference, or to repeal the odious enactments of which she complains, or to take any practical step whatsoever calculated to convince that section that the North is willing to yield one jot to its demands. A single plan has been proposed by the *Times*—that of recompensing from the federal treasury the owners of fugitive slaves—and this project is inadmissible, because it does not touch the evil, nor render the Personal Liberty bills passed by the Northern States less a nullification of a solemn enactment of Congress, adopted in virtue of an imperative mandate of the Constitution.

We are forced reluctantly to the conclusion that there is little in the aspect which the North and South bear towards each other to justify the hope of a satisfactory arrangement. While the latter teems with complaints of injustice which the former scarcely listens to, much less agrees to redress, what well founded expectation can there be of concord, harmony and an unbroken confederacy?

[1] Error for "taunt."

90. The Policy of the Southern States

(Richmond Semi-weekly Examiner, November 27, 1860)

It is very evident that there are now but two parties in the Southern States—those whose first object is to obtain ample and solid security for the Southern minority against the action of the General Government and the Northern States, and those who are content to preserve the present political relations with the North without any additional security. While we know that a large majority of the Southern people belong to the first party, we are certain that their purposes may be defeated by their own imprudence or inaction, or equally easily by taking the counsels of those who really wish to do nothing.—There is not a man of sense in the community who does not know that the action of the General Government will hereafter be in obedience to the will of a sectional majority, carried out by sectional agents—members of a purely sectional and anti-slavery party. That this is not the Government which the Constitution authorizes none will dispute, and that to allow it to change its character thus will be a most hazardous experiment, even the most extreme submissionists admit. If this last is done, then we will have seen the whole civil polity of the Confederacy overthrown and revolutionized by a mere partizan election by a majority of voters, without the assent of the sovereign parties to the compact—without a direct and open appeal to the voters in the States to alter their laws; but a mere election of a man will be the actual destruction of the political institutions of the United States. Such a practice once inaugurated, such a principle once established, and every election will be a revolution. There will be, in reality, no Constitution or fundamental law. The whole framework of Government will be like the Cabinet of the President or the bills regulating the salaries of clerks and the appointment of officers about the Capitol, the subject of change every four years. Constitutional guarantees, always an unsafe dependence for a minority, where they are to be observed and executed by the majority only, will be even more worthless still, for they will lose even the value which their being part of what was designed to be a permanent Constitution had heretofore given them. Unless some security is now given to the people, not only against sectional oppression, but against the power of a party to revolutionize the Government, this Confederacy will be as unstable and as monarchical as any of the wretched attempts at Republics in South or Central America.

Constitutional securities, every one sees, are now only to be held at the will of a sectional majority. That that majority is a mere party, seeking to make its power permanent, and to wield the Government for its own advantage and profit, no one can dispute. Then, the will of this party, expressed every four years, is to fix the destinies of these States. The Southern minority is to depend for protection and safety upon voluntary provisions made by a sectional party majority every four years. The slaveholder and the man dependent upon the profits of slave labor is to look for the security and defense of both to the friendly provisions made by a party, whose only declared principle is hostility to slavery, and whose only known purpose is to put that institution "in course of ultimate extinction."

Now, we ask those who are seeking to preserve peace by urging people to be content with things as they are, and to make no stir in consequence of this election of LINCOLN, if they really expect to secure that poor respite from trouble and agitation they seek, by separating themselves from the other people of the South, and trusting affairs to the guidance of this party?—Even if this most shortsighted policy were practicable by Virginia, it most fortunately happens that neither the party whom they wish to trust nor the people whom they would distrust, will allow it to be attempted. The policy of inertia, the policy of trusting the enemies and distrusting the people of the South, is no longer practicable. It is one of those admirable pieces of political dexterity in accomplishing ruinous folly, which has finally made its own repetition impossible.

Those who have been patching up truces between sections have at last made the anti-slavery section strong enough to rule without the aid of the honest compromising friends of quiet, or the more mischievous friends of Northern power who dwell in the South. The peace which could be bought by yielding up territory, or granting away constitutional defenses, or giving an enlarged jurisdiction to the Federal agent of the Northern majority, is no longer to be preserved. The peace so dear to all, is now to be preserved by something provided for the South. We cannot assert that the securities and defenses essential to the South will be obtained by this or that means; but this we can say, that now the peace for which so much has been granted can only be preserved by furnishing these defenses and securities.

We are happy to know one thing, that in the part of the State we hear from most, and amongst the people with whom we have been thrown most, that men who were of all parties at the last election are of but one now. All with whom we have conversed agree in declaring that Virginia must go with the South, and that she must and will sustain the States of the South which shall secede.

We hear from all States of the South, and from all sections of this State, that this is the prevailing opinion. That the States which are most interested in slavery will take one of two courses, we suppose no man can doubt. Some will secede from the Union, others will adopt a system of State legislation which will make the relations between the citizens of Northern States and the people of those Southern States more hostile and as barren of profit as the relations between Great Britain and the United States were, which, under the embargo act preceding the War of 1812, made open war more tolerable to both people than the conflict of retaliatory legislation against trade. When such a temper prevails, and such a system of measures in which actual secession and laws, rendering the Union more unprofitable and irritating than actual dissolution are the only alternative policies in the minds of the majority of the Southern people, we imagine that reflecting men of both parties in the South will concur in the opinion that the only safety, as the only hope, of renewing any relations between the States of the two sections will be in uniting the South in some common policy. We see no other measure which can possibly attain the objects sought by those whose primary object is to maintain peaceable relations in the Union, or by those whose first purpose is to be secured against the mischievous rule of a sectional, anti-slavery party. We may quarrel over measures of detail, we may desire particular remedies, we may long for peace, we may shout for the present Union, but not one can be obtained as a solid, permanent political condition or measure until those States which intend to retain slavery shall be united in a common policy.

Those Southern States which design to take their destiny with the Northern States must make up their minds to sacrifice the institution of African slavery. That is the first purchase money they must pay for that alliance. In that Union LINCOLN's assertions will be undisputed truths—*it will not exist* "half slave and half free." *"It will be all one thing."* "Slavery (there) will be put in course of ultimate (and of rapid) extinction."

In the States which intend to retain slavery there must be a common policy, and to secure that there must be a union between them all in this struggle. If they wish to obtain the ends they have in view at the least sacrifice of private and public convenience, they should make a union in advance. They should let it be known at once that any collision between the General Government and a slave State will find them with the slave States. If they desire safety, that is their policy; if they desire a peaceable solution of these difficulties, an early union in demand for security is equally their policy.

91. Our Position

(The Florence Gazette, Florence, Ala., November 28, 1860)

No man who has intelligently reflected on the political condition of the country, says the Mobile Register, especially as developed in the Presidential canvass just closed, can resist the conclusion that the incompatibility of interests and views between the slaveholding and the non slaveholding States, or to adopt the phrase of the master spirit of abolitionism, the "irrepressible conflict," has at last come to a crisis which leaves but little, if any, hope to those who look upon this Federal Union as the master piece of human wisdom in the science of Government. Patriotic men have labored sedulously to devise some expedient by which a common government could still be made to work equitably for both sections; they have imagined that the principal subject of difference might be removed from the National Legislature and Administration wholly and forever, and the action of both strictly confined to matters on which the differences were not vital and irremediable; the result of the last Presidential election has demonstrated their error. Both the north and the south have cast an overwhelming vote for their respective sectional candidates, and the contest thus being purely sectional, the north as numerically the stronger section has gained the victory. The election of a President, of any party, is in itself a matter of but temporary importance, and affords, as we have often said, no valid ground for the dissolution of the Government; but the fact once clearly established, that henceforth and forever the north and the south would be arrayed as hostile sections in a contest which could end only by the subjugation of one or the other, and in which the weaker would rapidly become still weaker and the stronger gain strength—this fact once clearly established, as it has been by the last Presidential election, proves that the Union between those two sections has practically ceased to exist, and that its mere forms are but as the chain binding together deadly enemies sharing a common doom. "We should exhaust the last efforts at conciliation," those who have been taught to make reference for this Union almost a religion, will tell us.— True, and so we should. National dignity, and regard to the opinions of mankind, demand that the people of the South should do so while and before they take their station among the nations of the earth; but we should lack in candor to our readers were we to express any other conviction than that these efforts will be fruitless. Henceforth, then, the conservative feeling of peace-loving men must be directed less to the preservation of the Union, than to warding off the shock attendant upon its dissolution—to build up a new house while the one is being pulled down, so that we may not be shelterless even for a short space of time; or to use the same simile, to so pull down the house as not to be buried in its ruins. There are two ways in which we may proceed, and between them we honestly believe lies the only choice. One a mere hurrah movement, in which all the evils of revolution will be let loose, and the demons of anarchy will riot at will; in which frenzied appeals will take the place of reason, demagogues usurp the seats of statesman-ship, and secret leagues supersede constituted authority. The political fruits of such a revolution can be but fragmentary and incessantly changing combinations, amid which we should exhibit to the world the sad spectacle of the South American republics; its bearings upon individual and public prosperity need not be pointed out. The other way is to imitate the course of our forefathers, to proceed calmly, de-liberately, coolly, yet with a fixed object ever sternly in view, laying one stone for every one pulled down, so that we have at least a firm founda-tion laid for a new edifice ere the old one is razed to the ground. By such a course the worst evils attending so important a change will be essentially lessened, perhaps wholly removed, and the transition ef-fected without vital injury to any of our important interests. Whether it shall be the one or the other depends on the conservative men of the country. Other choice, we repeat, they have none. Inaction, or a stub-born refusal to recognize the duties of present, and blind devotion to a past which has ceased to be more than a historical idea, will inevitably give the control of the movement to those least able to make it end in good.

In the language of Governor Moore, in his admirable letter on this subject, the Convention, acting under such solemn responsibilities, is not the place "for either the timid or the rash. It should be composed of men of wisdom and experience—men who have the capacity to deter-mine what the honor of the State and the security of her people demand; and patriotism and moral courage sufficient to carry out their honest judgments." [1] To avoid either timidity or rashness in the steps which we take as an independent and sovereign people, every true Southern man should use his private and public influence. Co-operation with the other slaveholding States, at least the cotton States, is a vital necessity, but to insist on such co-operation as a *sine qua non* is unionism under a thin disguise, because every State making such a co-operation the condition of its own action, no decisive step could be taken by any of them. On the other hand, it is equally necessary to avoid rash and precipitate action, and therefore while the State should assume a decisive and determined attitude, so grave a step as isolated separation from the Union should not be taken with all the consequences it may involve, without a direct and final reference to the people who have to bear these consequences. Actuated by the desire to avoid either danger, insufficient action on the one hand and hot haste precipitation on the other, we have after anxious and mature consultation with former party friends as well as former party opponents, including prominent supporters of Mr. Breckinridge, determined to [recommend to] the people of Mobile the following propositions, embodying the views not only of those who acted with us in the last Presidential contest, but of intelligent and patriotic men of all parties, and forming a basis for a course of action in which all true lovers of their country, irrespective of parties, may be able to cordially participate.

First, that in our opinion the people of the State of Alabama, in Convention assembled, should declare and make known that the powers granted under the federal Constitution, being derived from the people of the United States, shall be resumed by them, the same having been perverted to our injury and oppression. And that Alabama shall declare herself a free and independent State, discharged of all connection with the federal government of these United States.

Second, that the people so in convention, after such declaration, shall make every effort to procure a union of Southern States, and to make such arrangements with the neighboring and other States as may secure to us our just share of the territory and property of the federal government, and with foreign nations for the acknowledgment and recognition of our independence by the nations of the earth.

Third, That in the event that the people of the State of Alabama, in

[1] Moore to Elmore, Phelan, and others, November 14, 1860, in William R. Smith, *The History and Debates of the Convention of the People of Alabama . . . 1861* (Montgomery, 1861), p. 17.

Convention assembled, determine to withdraw in co-operation with other Southern States, that then the action of the Convention shall be first. But if the Convention should determine to withdraw separately and without co-operation with the other Southern States, that such action shall be referred to a vote of the people at the ballot box.

92. THE POLICY OF SILENCE

(*New Orleans Daily Crescent,* November 28, 1860)

Some of the quasi-conservatives of the Northern States have been calling upon Lincoln to make an authoritative exposition of what will be his policy as President. They believe that if he will give assurances to the South that its Constitutional rights will be respected, it would go far to calm the Southern people and kindle within them a fresh flame of loyalty to the Government.

On the other hand, the Abolition papers promptly object to such a course on his part. They say that he is not yet President, and it will be time enough for him to indicate the tenor of his administrative policy after he has been duly installed in the Presidential chair. They declare that it will be proof of weakness and timidity, if the President elect yield to what they call "pro-slavery clamor," and declare his intentions, before he assumes the robes of office.

Mr. Lincoln has decided the question himself, and he has decided it in accordance with the advice of his Abolition allies. The other day a great celebration of their victory was had at Springfield, Illinois—the place of Lincoln's residence. The "coming man" was of course called on —of course made a speech. But, instead of giving any inkling of his policy, he was, in that respect, as mute as an oyster—what might be called eloquently silent. His discourse was full of stereotyped expressions of gratitude, of common-place verbiage, of meaningless platitudes. His friend, Trumbull, was rather more explicit—but even Trumbull failed to meet the issue, or to say anything that was positive and practical. An assurance that the rights of the South would be respected amounts to nothing, unless he had defined what those rights are, and the mode in which they are to be observed. People, North and South, differ widely in their construction of the Constitution, as affecting the rights of each section. And Trumbull, who is very far from being a fool, knowing this fact, knows also that his vague assurances are not worth the paper upon which they are printed, and that the South will derive no satisfaction whatever from their utterance. The time for evasion and subterfuge has passed, and the South wants a plain, positive, distinct recognition of what she conceives herself entitled to, and she will take nothing else. If she cannot get this in the Union, she wants to know it, and to know it at once.

But, the truth is, there is no need for Lincoln to declare his policy. We know well enough what is to be. The party that elected him would not have done so if they thought he would cheat them; and they had him sufficiently committed upon the record to be satisfied he would prove true to their doctrines. If Mr. Lincoln had gotten up and told the people that his Administration would protect the rights of the South as understood by the Southern people, he would have subjected himself to universal contempt, and made himself worthy of the brand of personal infamy and dishonor—because everybody knows that he was elected by a party organized upon the basis of hostility to those rights as universally understood by the Southern people.

Trumbull says that the rights of all shall be respected—but, how about the right which Southern men claim of going into Territories with their property? Does Trumbull concede this? If he does, he has been imposing upon his own people for many a long year. How about the right to recapture fugitive slaves—a right expressly guaranteed by the Constitution? Possibly they may concede this abstract right—but when they throw obstacles in the way which render the right worthless, it is an insult to the South to concede it. As well tell a man, condemned to imprisonment for life in our State Penitentiary, that he has a right to mine gold in California. How about the right which the South claims, to be free from oppressive duties and Government bounties to special Northern interests? How about the right to be free from John Brown raids, Abolition incendiaries burning our towns in Texas and elsewhere, and vagabond emissaries from the North instilling insurrectionary poison into the ears of our slaves? Does Trumbull mean these, when he talks about conceding the rights of the South? If he does, he has been guilty of hypocrisy heretofore, and if he does not, his declarations are utterly worthless and even positively offensive.

This is no time for clap-trap, and vague, indefinite generalizations. Words will not do. The South, so far as her political and social rights are concerned, cannot feed, like the chameleon, on air. It is a mockery for Lincoln or his friends to say her rights will be respected, when we know that *their* interpretation of our rights is exactly the reverse of *our own*. Compromises have failed to settle the questions in issue between us—expostulation and entreaty have done no good—a generous

forbearance on our part has been interpreted into fear and cowardice—
and now the catalogue of remedies is exhausted, with one exception
only. If anybody is in doubt of what that last remedy is, a few weeks
of time will soon tell the tale.

93. ARE THEY BLIND?

(*The New Orleans Bee,* November 28, 1860)

We are sorry to remark that in spite of the clearest and most convincing manifestations, the people of the North appear afflicted with tran-
scendental dubiety in respect to the earnestness and reality of Southern
movements. The numerous public meetings in the South; the determined expression of hostility to a further political connection with the
North; the evidences overwhelming and palpable of high-wrought excitement and invincible resolve—all seem lost upon them. If we are allowed to appreciate Northern feeling on the subject by the tone of its
press, we must conclude that a large majority of the people of that
section apprehend no serious peril to the Union. It is true they cannot
possibly overlook the demonstrations in South Carolina, or deny the
avowed secession movements in that State; but they continue to talk of
South Carolina as if she were a froward child, to be coaxed or chastised
into obedience, while they fancy, in their strange and unaccountable
incredulity, that Georgia, and Alabama, and Mississippi, and Florida,
and Texas, and Arkansas, and Louisiana are merely laboring under
temporary excitement, and have no well defined object in view. There
are journals which claim to be better informed respecting the existing
phases of Southern feeling. The New York *Herald* and the New York
Express approximate in their estimates to the true state of the case.
But these are only two out of hundreds. Even as able and usually well
posted a sheet as the New York *Times* fails fully to comprehend the
issue. The *Times* admits that the movement at the South is a popular
one—impressive on account of its unanimity and evident sincerity, and
important, by reason of its bearing upon the destinies, social and political, of our common country. It acknowledges, too, with some surprise,
that the movement encounters less opposition than was anticipated,
from what it terms "the conservative sentiment of the South." It confesses that the secession feeling appears to have control of the public
mind in all the cotton States, and in South Carolina it is unanimous.
And yet while conceding all these alarming tendencies, and deducing
from them discriminating and just conclusions, the *Times* displays the

shallowness of its knowledge by attaching immense importance to the speeches of ALEXANDER H. STEPHENS, and to a few Union meetings recently held in Georgia. This is a signal and striking illustration of the ignorance which pervades the North touching Southern sentiment. Even the more sagacious spirits who see the horizon darken and hear the thunder roll, refuse to admit that the storm is near, because it has not yet burst in violence over the welkin. Others less observant can see nothing more dangerous than a passing cloud, charged, it may be, with a little harmless heat lightning.

We hold it to be a duty of the Southern press, and especially of those papers which are usually deemed conservative, to point out to the North the gross error under which it is laboring. There are two capital and pernicious mistakes in the Northern mind—first, in supposing that the Southern movement is limited in extent, or simply effervescent and fugitive in character; and next, in imagining, as does the *Times,* that a quiescent do-nothing policy by the North will accomplish any good whatever. We, who have ardently loved the Union, who have clung to it persistently, and will still cling to it if we can do so without dishonor, we can assure the North that its ideas of the Southern secession movements are short-sighted and inaccurate. In the first place, this disunion proclivity is an epidemic in every one of the cotton States. Those citizens who were once wont to boast their unconditional attachment to the Union have disappeared. If there are any left, they are few in numbers, and indisposed to give free vent to their opinions. The only visible difference of sentiment among the people of the cotton States regards the timeliness of immediate action. South Carolina raises an unbroken voice for unconditional secession and separate State action. She will go out of the Union as soon as her constituted authorities have made the requisite preparations. Whether accompanied or followed by others, the Palmetto State will secede.

With regard to her sister States, let the people of the North fully understand that their dominant and unalterable position is that the question has to be settled, or the Union will be dissolved. We speak now of those citizens of the South who have generally been considered moderate. There are thousands amongst us who are ripe for a more violent and precipitate remedy, and who would be ready to-morrow to march out of the Union and leave the consequences to GOD. We believe, however, the majority favor joint action by the South; that they desire to see the South assemble in convention, and deliberate and act in common. They are willing, before taking the final step of severance, to give to the North a chance of conciliation; to allow it time for reflection and retrogression. If the North is really anxious to preserve the Union, the entire weight of responsibility is with her. She is the aggressor; we the aggrieved. Her State legislation; her predominant doctrines; her prevailing sentiments; her practical enforcement of a hideous fanaticism, as just evidenced in the election of LINCOLN; her persistent abuse of and assaults upon Southern institutions; her John Brown raids and Montgomery forays—all furnish damning proof that she is the aggressor. Let not the North delude itself with the fallacious impression that anything short of a radical revolution in her policy can or will postpone or avert the calamity of disunion. Let her be assured that the South is not swayed by a temporary gust of passion; that this is no partial movement in opposition to the opinions of the masses like the Nashville Convention of 1850. Woe to the Union if the North still remains blind to the tremendous auguries and portents around her! Woe to it, if having sown the wind, the North fails to see that she is reaping the whirlwind!

There is another point to be considered, and we take occasion to state that in setting forth the views of the South we are simply making known *facts*. There is no remedy for the evils complained of, save an entire change in Northern policy. The South does not look upon the triumph of LINCOLN, *per se,* with any special apprehension, but simply regards it as the crown and capstone of grievance, the last straw on the camel's back, the drop that causes the cup of bitterness to overflow. It denotes the foregone conclusion of the North, and is the entering wedge to the series of hostile measures of which the South will be the victim if she remains within the Union. Hence the solemn and unchangeable determination of her sons to have plenary guarantees of future safety and equality within the Union, or independence out of it. The South stands upon her reserved rights. She proposes nothing; she suggests nothing. It is for the North—if sufficiently impressed with the approaching danger, and solicitous to avert it—to tender justice, and nothing short of justice will content the South.

What we have written respecting Southern sentiment is sober truth, and we trust the North may so accept it. It is as certain as any future event that unless the North is prepared to discard sectionalism in every respect, to repeal its obnoxious laws, to secure to the South the peaceful and unmolested possession of her property, to acknowledge her absolute equality before the Constitution and the laws, the Confederacy of the States will not survive the fourth of March next.

94. THE REMEDY

(Nashville Union and American, December 1, 1860)

In all that we have written, connected with the present revolutionary condition of the Union, we have studiously and purposely avoided any discussion of the remedy for the just grievances of the South. We have assumed, what would be an insult to the intelligence of the Southern mind to doubt, that these grievances exist. We have not deemed it necessary to reproduce the volumes of insult and the long catalogue of aggressions that have been perpetrated by the North upon the South. This election of LINCOLN is not assumed to be an actual wrong in itself, but only the crowning and authoritative evidence that the series of outrages perpetrated upon our rights meet with the approval of a majority of the Northern people. It has been frequently pleaded that LINCOLN failed to receive a majority of the votes of the whole people, and therefore, that he is less dangerous and obnoxious to us. This is true. But it is a far more significant fact, because it exhibits the political power of the party that elected him, that he *did* receive a majority of the votes in every Northern State (including New Jersey by the recent returns); and that these States, in all of which he received overwhelming majorities, except in one or two small States, have the power, and will continue to have the power, to control the election of a President. It would, indeed, have been a far less bitter result to the South, if the President elect had stood on a platform conservative and broad enough to have controlled a sufficient number of votes in the slaveholding States to sum up a majority of the whole people of the Union. Therein lies the bitterness of the chalice commended to our lips; that the chief chosen by the Northern sectionalists could not even command one electoral vote in the Southern States, by reason of his determined and avowed hostility to our institutions. And he will therefore go into the Presidency a minority President, elected by an adroit marshaling of sectional hate, and by deliberately educating the Northern mind to this hostility, in the States who have thus usurped, under the cover of the Constitution, the entire Administration of the Federal Government. It is sufficient that the people of the Southern States recognize the wrongs and outrages they have suffered. We take it for granted that on this point the South is united. We find no respectable authority, no considerable portion of Southern men, certainly no true Southern men of intelligence, denying this patent fact. But the fact is different concerning the remedy. In some of the "cotton States" as they are designated in contradistinction to the more Northern slaveholding States, a sentiment almost united, and in South Carolina, entirely so, prevails. Secession is the remedy already determined on in the public mind, in several of these States. In all the States lying North of the cotton line a greater diversity of opinion exists. It is in deference to this acknowledged diversity that we have refrained from a discussion of the remedy. It is in deference to it that we favor the plan of a Southern Convention, where the calm and wise minds—the ablest, best and most patriotic men of the South may assemble, and after calmly surveying the field, may take counsel of each other and of their constituents, and resolve on the same remedy and a united action. Unity was never more essential to a people than to the South in our present condition. It is better that we should act with less wisdom, abstractly considered, than that we should be divided in our action. Any divided action must necessarily be feeble and inadequate, and must entail upon the South inconceivable evils. It is division and party strife that have thus far paralyzed every patriotic movement in the South, and have reduced us to the humiliation in which we now find ourselves. What Southern man is there now that would not prefer to see his most bitter political antagonist in the Presidential chair, under the old party designations, than to have witnessed the advent to power of this revolutionary party? If we could have given up our party prejudices before the election and united as one man, what a moral power might we not have exerted upon the Northern people! We might even, by this union, have convinced them that they could not try the mad experiment they have now ventured upon, and thus saved the South from the deep humiliation in which she is now placed and have saved our rights in the Union. It is idle to cry out that your party antagonist is alone responsible for this error. We were all wedded, perhaps too blindly wedded, to our party banners to agree before the election. We pass no judgment upon others, and do not wish to perpetuate the ignoble strife by throwing criminations at our opponents. It is the part of wisdom to heal up these criminations and prove mutually magnanimous and generous, by ascribing our division to party strife, and not by throwing all the blame upon our brother. We have our own opinion about the source of the error, and others may differ with us. But we will not offend any portion of our countrymen, at this juncture, by laying upon their shoulders the whole responsibility. We rather ascribe their errors to too great devotion to consistency, too much devotion to friends with whom they had formerly acted. The Southern people have magnanimity and patriotism enough to divide the censure and now unite for their country. Shall we perpetuate these animosities in the face of a foe that is perfectly consolidated, that has just harnessed on the tremendous powers of the Federal Government to strike us down? Is that man a patriot and a true Southern man, who, in the face of this mighty hostile force, continues to insist upon the ancient wrangles and enmities, continues to pour his batteries into those who are in the same cause with him, and continues to insist upon this fatal and weak division? It is now certain that these divisions have brought us to the verge of ruin, by deceiving our mutual enemies. These enemies have formed the erroneous conclusion, as we trust, that some of us were not loyal to our institutions, because we wrangled among ourselves. Is the South so fallen, so low and debased, that, seeing the effect her divisions have produced to strengthen her enemies and weaken her friends, she will continue this false and fatal system, and thus surrender, through sheer moral weakness, the very citadel of her strength? We trust not. May the Ruler of Nations avert so dire a calamity!

95. THE ARGUMENT IS EXHAUSTED—STAND BY YOUR ARMS!

(*The Daily Constitutionalist,* Augusta, December 1, 1860)

Such is the pet quotation of the day, and used in a thousand places that its author never dreamed of, and by many who have learned political phrases by rote.

The sentiment is, however, true, in a great degree, at this hour; and we would only change the invocation into the more appropriate words, *stand by your rights!*

We think that the very fact of argument being exhausted, should induce us to abandon the position of disputants and assume that of statesmen, whose rights are settled and understood by themselves, and who will no longer debate their rightfulness, but demand their full recognition.

The necessity, then, arises for us to consider how the argument has been exhausted, and the consequent necessity for upholding vested rights, even, if need be, by that last terrible resort, an appeal to arms.

Let us here remark, that bare assertions are not evidence, even when made by those immaculate oracles, politicians; and that he who flies into a rage at non-agreement with his unexplained views, is as absurd as the pedagogue who is amazed at the stupidity of the scholar, which it is *his business* to instruct.

Those who suppose that the South has gained nothing in the protracted "argument," are most strangely ignorant of their country's political history, for no sentiment on earth—not even the new born glories of Christianity—ever gained ground with such rapidity as the rightfulness of African slavery. Fresh from the storms of the revolution, the colonies were yet thrilling with indignation against everything that was fraught with memories of British tyrannny, and the African slave system shared the general detestation. Slaves first brought over to the tobacco and rice plantations, were pressed upon the already crowded market by the merchants of England, the remonstrances of our people were unheeded, and the effort to stop the flood tide of negroes, who were as wild and dangerous in the midst of civilizations as the Indians on its [*sic*] borders, were checked by the crown as an interference with trade. Thus it was that Georgia and Virginia entered the revolution to stop the influx of slaves, and emerged from it with their best statesmen prejudiced against the institution. The Abolitionist who fathers his creed upon JEFFERSON, WASHINGTON, and the sires of our country, but shows his ignorance of the times, which made great and true men oppose then, what they would love and cherish amid the events of to-day.

Twenty years ago, the owners of slaves thought it right to *excuse* themselves, under the plea that they had the slaves and could not dispose of them; in short, must make the best of an evil; and CLAY's plan of emancipation was hailed as inspiration by true men, not long ago.

Tell us not then, that it was folly to argue so long! The South did not understand her destiny, any more than the Constitution, when in 1820 she gaves the votes of her Representatives for the exclusion of slavery North of thirty-six degrees thirty minutes, and her faith grew into knowledge by slow but sure degrees. In 1850, the compromises were repeated upon a more definite basis, and after that long argument whose high debate shook all the land, the slavery question was declared settled. We lost empire and gained the recognition of a principle, but our real gain was the establishment of the Georgia platform, the support of all men to its fourth resolution, and the idea of *resistance unto dissolution,* then made a part of our State creed. But the argument of that day was not effectual, for the slavery question was not settled.

In 1854, after four years of debate, Democracy brought up her battery of southern mind, and following the lead of DOUGLAS, overthrew the forces of Abolitionism in the great victory on the Kansas act. Then, as in 1850, great men told us what they honestly thought, that the slavery question was "forever banished from the halls of Congress." But the throwing open the Territories to the South upon the principles of popular sovereignty and non-intervention, was as impotent to lay the spirit of discord, as had been the bartering of an empire for a right; and the vexed question did not leave the Capitol for an hour. Victors indeed we were, but the scattered forces of Abolitionism, joined with kindred elements, and the Black Republican party sprang up from the sown teeth of the dragon we had slain.

Our next plan was to pledge the people to the principles of 1854, by a solemn endorsement at the ballot box, and BUCHANAN and BRECKIN-RIDGE were sent to Washington, as exponents of the great peace idea. It is needless to say that the power of a chosen Administration did not banish the question, but that the integrity of the party was shaken, by disagreements between its great leaders.

In 1860, we tried all sorts of plans, from a party with a universal platform, to one with a sectional one. We attacked the enemy in front and flank by three divisions, and were all defeated in squads.

We are perfectly satisfied that we have exhausted the argument! We have gained advantages, and have brought up the entire South to esti-mate the value of her rights; but we are wearied of the interminable debate. We are convinced by the vote, that the number of the converts North does not bear a proper proportion to the length and energy of the sermon. We are all bound, as Democrats, to stop now, for we stand pledged to our platform, and that tells us to stop. Every Democrat, in 1856 and 1860, endorsed the declaration by his vote, that the principle of *non-intervention is* "the ONLY ONE on which the heart of the people can rely, in its determined conservatism to the Union."

That principle has been repudiated by the North, and voted down by the South, and the record of our votes declares that no principle now binds the popular heart to the Union.

Some persons desire to get up another National party, but we beg that our little wing be excused from the performance. Our party went into action with the old victorious banner of 1856 floating above them, and with its legions [*sic*] inscribed upon every door post in the land. The prestige of nationality, the power of name, the age and glory of its principles, the record of all great statesmen, save Mr. YANCEY and Mr. DAVIS, to sustain it—the great names of DOUGLAS and JOHNSON to give reputation—the worthy deeds of the one, and the love and respect for the other, to bind men to them; and the eloquence of both, with such aids as the voice of STEPHENS, to cheer our march. No party ever entered a campaign with such power of argument or force of intellect as we; and with the facts of the last month before us, why hope again! What glorious stones can be builded into a National fabric when these have crumbled? Do not try to rally again now that the foe have gained those batteries which fire gold and office; but you who have stood by DOUGLAS as the Nation's last hope, you who looked to hear the music of the Union rung from a happy BELL, you who looked for protection to BRECKINRIDGE, in a State which some of you do not consider *southern;* remember only, that we are all defeated together, and drop the wordy argument, and let us ACT.

All the action, however, should have distinct reference to the object to be accomplished. That object is simply to stand by our rights in every needful way, even by arms. To be true to rights, it is not needful to be extreme. While MURRILL, the great robber of the West, would not trust a new member of his band unless he had first outlawed himself by crime, it has never been necessary for a southern man by birth or adoption to officiate as hangman at the demise of an incendiary, or offer to fight any given number of northern men, in order to prove himself sound. All men who are conscious of their own devotion to home and country, may rest in quiet until the hour of action, and their worthy deeds shine just as bright, as bright as though heralded by a few months of preliminary boasting. Therefore we shall deem the man as true to his State, who obeys her by action, or non-action as he who scorns the authority of the local sovereignty, which he should die if need be, to uphold.

It is astonishing to witness the rage which inflames some of our friends; and still more so, to hear that our State is disgraced and dishonored. We repel with indignation the idea that spot or blemish can rest for a moment upon the proud escutcheon of Georgia, and we thank God that it never was in the power of any Government or State to humble the proud banner which bears up the arch of the Constitution on its folds. Where is the law on the statute books of the Union, to which the South did not give the assent of votes? Where the law on the books of a State which Georgia has commanded to be blotted out, and which stands there yet? Evils there are which our State will speedily right in one way or another, but no Yankee Governor or Congressman shall ever boast, with truth, that any power but our own volition could drive us out of the Union, or keep us in it.

Let us have no absurd gasconade or *ad captandum* arguments, for they do more harm than good. The boasts of deeds unperformed do not smell of sulphur, and thousands of good simple souls wonder why we do not spank the North like a bad baby, and make her behave in the Union.

An argument which only addresses itself to the pocket of the patriot, as a reward, will hardly influence southern men, since it has just failed to influence northern men as a punishment.

Therefore, let us not raise the cry of a disgraced and dishonored South, for secession would be but backing from a blow, not revenging it, and is not the final remedy if we have wrongs to punish.

Let us raise no cry of war and inevitable revolution, for we have failed to terrify the Abolitionists, and will find less plastic elements to bend here. Seek not to buy the people into virtue, by holding out calculations of which all the quantities are unknown.

Simply stand by our rights, and if the Union be not a safe ark for our tables of the law, we have timber and gold enough to make another. We know our rights, and they are all plainly laid down. We will have them, and all that is needful to do is to ask for them of the great partners of the Union firm, and quit doing business with those that refuse.

The resistance to which the State stands pledged, should be in exact proportion to the wrong complained of. If [we] resist at all, beyond remonstrance, we must get out of the Union to do it. We have heard of one county, a portion of whose citizens simply declare that the North has hurt our feelings, that we have no idea it intended to do it, and if we tell them of it they want [*sic*] to do it again. That position being impregnable, we will pass it by. We say that if we do not get all we desire by sending an ultimatum, (and it is rumored that one State has replied in the negative before it was sent,) then we must resist, and will have to secede before we can resist. The first thing to resist, is the influence, bribery and demoralising effect of a Black Republican Administration. It is not safe, as Mr. HILL has demonstrated, to trust eight hundred million of dollars worth of negroes in the hands of a power which says that we do not own the property, that the title under the Constitution is bad, and under the law of God still worse. So we must get out, to keep out or resist improper influence.

If we want retaliatory legislation to stop negro stealing, we must quit the Union to get it; for the Constitutional obligation of contracts and equality of citizenship, bars us while we remain with the North under it.

If we want a war of revenge, we must get out first, and get a Congress of our own, empowered to declare war and contract alliances.

If we want to raise an army and take possession of the Territories, we must first withdraw the delegated power to do so. If we are base enough to tie ourselves to England, the mother of Abolitionism, and wish to sit in her grand *pow-wows* side by side with a negro delegate from Canada, and be insulted, as Judge LONGSTREET was, we must first resume the power to make treaties.

The argument is exhausted, or has at least grown tiresome. Let us stand by our rights without fear or bravado.

Having failed to secure them in a Union where a controlling majority is against us, we must, as prudent men, seek new guards for future security.

96. DISUNION FOR EXISTING CAUSES

(*North Carolina Standard*, Raleigh, December 1, 1860)

A Confederacy or Union composed of the fifteen slaveholding States would, after a while, encounter some of the same difficulties which now beset the existing Union. The States south of us would produce and export cotton, while the middle or bread-stuff States would become deeply interested in manufactures. Foreigners from Europe and the North would pour into the latter, and push the slave population farther south. Manufacturers would demand and obtain protection, and free labor would contend with and root out slave labor in the middle States, until at length the latter could commence to agitate against the cotton States as the North is now agitating against us. As new regions towards the tropics should be acquired by the Southern Confederacy, and as the demand for cotton increased, the policy of re-opening the African slave trade would gain ground, and ultimately that trade would be established, and would be carried on openly under the Southern flag. This would be a death-blow to slavery in the middle States. It would at once reduce the price of our best slaves from twelve hundred to four hundred dollars, for the Southern planter would much prefer a barbarian at two hundred dollars to a civilized negro at five hundred. In addition to this, such a policy would expose the Southern Confederacy to the hazards of war with the Northern Confederacy and with European powers.

The two Confederacies, the Northern and the Southern, would meet as rivals at foreign courts and in foreign markets. Their ministers and merchants would partake of the spirit of the people at home, and they would cripple each other and involve themselves in endless and most injurious complications in their intercourse with foreign powers.— These foreign powers, stimulated by the hope of gain, and disliking us for our popular forms of government, would insinuate themselves into the very heart of our system—would foment jealousies between the two Confederacies, and lay one or the other under obligations to them for aid or mediation in the midst of strifes and wars; and the end would be *foreign influence* in all our councils, foreign manners in all our social walks, and *foreign gold* in the hands of unscrupulous demagogues as the price of some portion of their country's liberties.

In case of separation party spirit, the excesses of which are now so obvious and injurious, would rage with tenfold heat. There would be parties in each Confederacy against each; there would be parties opposed to and in favor of foreign influence; there would be parties advocating dictatorial powers in the central governments and parties advocating the largest liberty or least restraint; there would be parties advocating and parties opposing the acquisition of more territory; there would be parties siding with the great body of people, and parties endeavoring to grasp exclusive privileges for the few at the expense of the many. In the midst of all this war would most probably be waged along the lines of the two Confederacies—war interrupted only by hollow truces, or by compromises made but never intended to be observed, or by mediations at the hands of foreign powers. Of course as the result of all this industry would languish, trade would be obstructed, education would be neglected, internal improvements of all kinds would be arrested, and the morals of society would be injured. War would raise up standing armies, which would obstruct civil rule and eat out the substance of the people. This would be the case especially in the Southern States, where large armies would be necessary not only for defensive operations against the foreign Northern States, but to keep the slave population in subjection. The result would be *military despotism*. The Legislatures of the Southern States would have to sit perpetually or clothe their Governors with large discretionary powers. These powers would be abused, and the voice of law and the claims of justice would be unheard amid the alarms of war.—*Constitutional* liberty would no longer be the birthright of our people, but instead thereof we would have discretionary powers, martial law, military rule, oppressive taxation, perpetual contentions, and civil and servile war.

Such are some of the evils which would most probably result from

disunion for existing causes. Disunion at this time will certainly occasion war. If a peaceful separation in the last resort could be effected,
the two Confederacies, or any number of Confederacies *might* tread
their respective paths without engaging in mortal conflict. They *might*
at length re-unite in a new union on foundations more lasting than the
present; but if any one State shall secede, with the expectation of drawing other States after her, and if blood shall be shed, the beginning, the
middle, and the end will be civil war. The States thus forced out,
though they will sympathize with the State which committed them to
disunion against their will, and though they may stand by her and defend her in her extremity, yet they will dislike her and watch her as
an evil star in the new constellation. A violent separation would, therefore, sow the seeds of discord in the new Confederacy. It would commence its career with growing antagonisms in its members. It would be
a *forced* union which time would dissolve or passion fret to pieces.

There is only one evil greater than disunion, and that is the loss of
honor and Constitutional right. *That evil the people of the South will
never submit to.* Sooner than submit to it they would put their shoulders to the pillars, as Samson did, and tear down the temple, though
they themselves should perish in the ruins. But our honor as a people
is still untarnished—our Constitutional rights, so far as the federal government is concerned, are still untouched. If the federal government
should *attempt* even to tarnish the one or to deprive us of the other, we
for one would be ready to resist, and ready to dissolve the Union without regard to consequences. *But not now!*—the non-slaveholder says
not now!—the slaveholder, whose property civil war would involve in
imminent peril, says *not now!*—millions of our friends in the free
States say *not now!* If we *must* dissolve the Union, let us do it as one
people, and not by a bare majority. Let us wait until the people of the
State are more united on the subject than they are now. Depend upon
it our people are not submissionists. If their rights should be assailled
they will defend them. But if they should not be assailed, and if we
can preserve the government with safety and honor to ourselves, in the
name of all that is sacred let us do so.

97. IF THE UNION IS SAVED THE NORTH MUST SAVE IT

(*The Examiner,* Gallatin, Tenn., December 1, 1860)

The gloom which now hangs over the Union is the result of Northern fanatacism. The South has ever been loyal to the Union and has

always contributed two-thirds of the revenue which has supported the General Government, and this too when her representation in the halls of legislation is but little over one-half as much as the North. She has faithfully executed every law passed by Congress, and has furnished two soldiers to every one from the North, in all the Indian wars and in the war with Mexico. In the war of 1812, which was waged chiefly to protect New England shippers, the South furnished 18,000 more troops than the North. Yet with all this devotion to the Union, with all this loyalty to a common country, she is assailed by Northern fanatics as untrue to the vows she made when she became an integral portion of the Confederacy. Our plainest constitutional rights are denied us by direct legislation in many of the Northern States. The Constitution has ceased to be a barrier between Black Republicanism and its fiendish designs. A higher law has superseded its authority. This law has been carried so far that it is about rending the Government in twain. Every pillar of the temple trembles before the raging tempest. What must be done to avert the present calamity? This question is easily solved when we review the cause of the disaster which now threatens us. The cause must be removed before any cure can be effected. The North has forced this calamity upon us by her unceasing warfare upon the constitutional rights of the South. As she has inaugurated this "irrepressible conflict" between the two sections of the country, she must remove it. She must make amends for a violated law. She must rebuke fanaticism wherever it lifts its hideous front. She must demand that every State which has nullified the fugitive slave law or any other law protecting the interest of the South, should immediately repeal them. She should require the Northern States to enact laws compelling their officers and citizens to assist in the faithful execution of the fugitive slave law, and make it a penal offence for any of their citizens to encourage or assist any fugitive to escape from his master. They should pass laws giving full protection to slave property in the Territories, and should recognize slave property as on the same footing as any other species of property. These demands are all constitutional, and were contemplated by our fathers in forming the Constitution. The North must yield the substance of these demands, or there must be dissolution. He who would be willing to remain in the Union, if the North should solemnly refuse to concede to us our dearest rights, is already a slave. His chains are now forged, and he is ready to have them riveted upon his servile neck.

We repeat again, there must be a settlement, and the concessions must all come from the North. We have violated no obligation, either legal or moral towards them, and we have no overtures to make. We should make our demands in a spirit of kindness and conciliation, but at the same time with the firmness and dignity which so important a mission requires. If the South had any law upon her statute books inimical to Northern interest, we should urge its immediate repeal. We should be just ourselves before we could expect justice from others.

98. What True Conservatism Demands of the South

(The Daily South Carolinian, Columbia, December 2, 1860)

There never was a grosser misapplication of any term than that of "conservatism," as now used by a large number of individuals both North and South. When a Northern Republican catches the sound of a Southern submission voice, he calls it a "conservative" sound. When a Southern man deprecates the active measure now going forward to save the South from destruction, he contradictorily calls it conservatism. These men are misled, in the Northern instance, by their desire to conserve their power. In the Southern instance, they blindly yield to a sentiment which has grown upon them, and which prostrates them as mere worshippers at the feet of the Union idol. They reason not, they see not. Down upon their knees, with face in hands, and hands upon the ground, they will not see, they will not contemplate the dangers that threaten them—but can only shout "Union, Union," when their more practical and observant brethren shake them by the collar and warn them of inevitable ruin. And this they call "conservatism." There never was a grosser misapplication of a term. The spirit of conservatism is of all others the most practical and the least given to sentimentality. It is ever watchful, ever judicious, prompt to change or even destroy accustomed forms, when necessary, and always ready to remove rottenness, either to the extent of total subversion or total reconstruction. It is a spirit the least apt to cling to empty forms after the substance has departed. Yet this spirit, it is claimed, still admonishes acquiescence in the dangerous circumstances which now surround the South, and which have been growing up so unceasingly and steadfastly that even in 1832 Mr. Calhoun, with undisguised surprise, remonstrated with those who charged him with being too impatient and precipitate. From then to now, a false idea of conservatism has been crying against the precipitancy of those who would have preserved alike the spirit and the form of the now disintegrating Federal Government, and though with feeble articulation, since the spirit has passed away, yet it still clings to the putrid form. With all their senses enervated by the deadly effluvia of the corrupt form, many realize nothing of danger, but linger only over the beauty and comeliness that once dwelt there. And this they call the spirit of conservatism. Many of us may have stood too long around the old form, still hoping that constitutional life was not yet gone. But since it has hopelessly departed, it is dangerous to tarry near it. Every instinct of conservatism prompts us to get away from it as soon as possible. To linger is suicide and parricide. It is death to us, our country and its institutions. It is painful to see others yet hesitating, under the fatal delusion that there yet is hope. In the name of conservatism, they call upon us to make one more effort to revive the rotten carcass. But our conservatism prompts us to turn a deaf ear to their entreaties. They call upon us not to drag them from the infectious body, to remain yet a while with them, until they all can co-operate in departure. Our conservatism tells us that it is destruction to breathe longer the dangerous atmosphere; it tells us that those who wait are now under its weakening influence—that if we remain it will steal, too, upon our senses, and all of us will thus be involved in one common death. We cannot linger either in hope of new life, nor can we wait for all to co-operate. The penalty of death is affixed to either course, and the demands of a true, practical and unsentimental conservatism urges those who are ready, to get away each for himself by the shortest and speediest way. But we go further, not only is this the demand of the spirit of true conservatism—but the refusal to comply with it would be criminal. We are responsible for any idolatry we may be given to. This blind devotion, this obedience, not only to a sickly, but a deadly sentimentality, destroys our senses, and, if, under its influence, we fail to look calmly at surrounding events and thus are carried to fatal conclusions, the sin is our own. Such a recreancy to truth must bring its punishment on every nation whose people are guilty of it. It is this sentimentality—miscalled conservatism—that has arrayed opposition to every reformation or revolution, either religious or political, recorded on the pages of history. It behooves us all, then, to look at these grave issues of the day without regard to the associations of the past; sentimentality must be thrown aside as an unsafe pilot, and truth, reason and observation be accepted as our guides. Whatever decision they pronounce let us execute sternly, promptly and effectually. Let not the glories of the past divert us from, but rather stimulate us on to, the duties of the present. If the achievements of our fathers are objects around which our pride loves to linger, let us take care, lest by our own incompetency to meet the demands of the crisis, we disinherit our children of the same pleasure. Let us remember that their practical spirit of conservatism prompted them to sever forever the bands that united them to an oppressive mother country, and that this act of severance we cherish as the brightest in the history which they bequeathed us. They then asserted self-government as necessary to a conservation of their rights, and we are now invoked by the same spirit of conservation to dissolve our present political Union, in order to retain that inheritance of self-government.

99. DELAY

(*The Charleston Mercury,* December 3, 1860)

One of the ablest and most influential men in Mississippi, has been kind enough to send to a friend in this city, the proceedings of the people of Lowndes county, held at Columbus, on the 19th November. After various details, to show the encouraging state of things in Mississippi, he concludes his letter as follows:

The developments since I wrote you some days since, confirm me in the opinion that it is wisest for South Carolina to *act*—that co-operation will surely follow; and in a little while all the States of the South will be under a new government. *Delay is dangerous. It is the only policy our enemies have yet been able to suggest; and if they secure its adoption, their ultimate purpose will be accomplished.* This, believing in the imminency of the danger to the South, is the opinion of our people here; and while they feel great hesitation in suggesting any policy to South Carolina, they feel confident that this is the wisest course.

In our issue of Saturday our readers will see from our correspondent in Washington that this policy of delay is in full development in Washington, and, we doubt not, has been sent all over the Southern States by the agent of the Administration. We are to delay "until Virginia can be heard," according to the modest proposal of the Hon. Mr. GARNETT,[1] at the late Essex meeting. We are to delay, until we shall see whether their Personal Liberty Acts will not be repealed by the Legislatures of Northern States. We are to delay, until all the Southern States shall meet in Convention for conference. We are to delay, until Mr. LINCOLN's Administration shall show, by "overt acts," its hostility to

[1] Muscoe R. H. Garnett of Essex County, Virginia, Democratic Representative in Congress, 1855–1861.

the South. We propose briefly to take up these several causes for delay:

1. We are to delay, "that Virginia may be heard." Why should the Southern States delay any action of theirs, "that Virginia may be heard?" Did not Mississippi and South Carolina speak to Virginia last winter, through their Commissioners formally sent to her, and did Virginia heed their counsels? No. She rejected their proposal, simply, to hold a conference with them and the other Southern States. Virginia declined counselling with us, because her views of her interests differed from ours. She set up an alienation and separation from us, against our most earnest remonstrances and efforts; and if she now seeks to be heard by us, what is her object? Is it to aid us in our views of policy—to preserve our rights or save our institutions? Not at all. It is to defeat our policy by a Southern Convention, and to drag us along in subserviency to her views of her border interests. If we respectfully decline to delay in our course, that she "may be heard," we only treat her, as she has previously treated us. We will be very glad to hear her at all times; but to pause in the vindication of our rights, when, not nine months ago, she refused even to counsel with us for their preservation, would be the sheerest weakness and folly.

2. But what does Virginia propose that we should do? Why, that the Southern States should make another begging appeal to the Northern States, "*to preserve the guaranties of the Constitution.*" Suppose one man should deliberately violate a compact with another man, every year, for thirty years, and then should give him notice that he intended to kill him—what would be thought of the manhood or the wisdom of the poor oppressed devil, should he go to his oppressor, and beg him "once more" to observe "the guaranties of the Constitution" *with him?* Would not any unbiased observer, believe him to be an idiot? If such a "method of redress" was proposed by Virginia, after the Southern States had seceded from the Union, there might be some little reason in it, although the Northern States have shown that they are utterly incapable of observing any compact with any people. They would then, however, have a motive to recede from their aggressive and insulting course towards the South. But the South is to delay—she is to do nothing—she is not to secede—only beg. What does "delay" mean, under such circumstances, but submission, and the perpetuation of that "blessed Union" which Virginia would not venture even to disturb last winter, by the poor expedient of conference amongst the Southern States?

3. But we are to delay action further, to see if the Northern Legis-

latures will not repeal their Personal Liberty Laws. So far as the Cotton States are concerned, these laws, excepting in the insult they convey to the South, and the faithlessness they indicate in the North, are not of the slightest consequence. Few or none of our slaves are lost, by being carried away and protected from recapture in the Northern States. Nor to the frontier States, are they of much consequence. Their slaves are stolen and carried off—not by the agency of these Personal Liberty Laws—but by the combination of individuals in the Northern States. What are these acts as indications of the hostility and faithlessness of the Northern people towards the South (and they are nothing more), when compared with the mighty sectional despotism they have set up over the South in the election of Messrs. LINCOLN and HAMLIN to the Presidency and Vice-Presidency of the United States? Repeal that, and there would be something to invite delay. The real causes of dissatisfaction in the South with the North, are in the unjust taxation and expenditure of the taxes by the Government of the United States, and in the revolution the North has effected in this government, from a confederated republic, to a national sectional despotism. To prevent these evils, the South has already *delayed* thirty-five years. She is to "delay" longer, upon the mere speculation that the Northern States, without any inducement created by our action, may, in some eighteen months or two years, repeal their Personal Liberty Laws. What does such a policy mean, but submission?

4. The last motive for delay goes beyond the 4th of March next. It is that the Abolition Administration to be installed the 4th of March next, in Washington, has not yet made an "overt act" in the way of Abolitionism against the Southern States. Although you see your enemy load his rifle with the declared purpose of taking your life, you are to wait, as a wise expedient of defense, until he makes the "overt act"—shoots you. This is one of those glaring absurdities, which only such daring submissionists as BOTTS [2] and CRITTENDEN are capable of proposing. No ordinary man, can hope to comprehend its mysterious sublimities.

100. MEETING OF CONGRESS

(*New Orleans Daily Crescent,* December 3, 1860)

Congress meets to-day—probably the last national Congress that will ever assemble at Washington City. The session terminates by law on

---

[2] John Minor Botts of Virginia had vehemently denounced the Breckinridge forces as guilty of a conspiracy to break up the Union.

the 4th of March, but it would not greatly surprise us if it terminated much earlier than that time, so far at least as respects the Southern States and their Representatives. Unless we greatly mistake the signs of the times—unless we interpret incorrectly the steady development of the plan of secession, requiring time only for its consummation, several of the Southern States will be out of the Union before the session has half expired; and, of course, no Representative in either branch of Congress will remain there after his State shall have formally closed her connection with the Federal Government. Some of the South Carolina members, in anticipation of the future, have already declined to go to Washington at all, and have resigned their commissions as representatives of the people.

Probably the unhappiest man, this day, within the whole limits of the Union, is James Buchanan, the President of these nearly disunited States. In common with nine-tenths of the people of the North, he has been accustomed to regard the threats of withdrawal at the South as mere idle talk, which really amounted to nothing. He finds out, now, how much he is mistaken. He finds out that it is not mere idle talk on the part of the South, but a stern and inflexible determination. He finds out how terribly in earnest the South is, and with what confident step she marches to political independence. The difficulty which Mr. Buchanan has to confront is different from that which Gen. Jackson had to meet in 1832. Then, South Carolina proposed to stay in the Union, but at the same time to nullify the laws of the Union. She claimed the right to stay in the Union, and obey only such Federal laws as suited her, and disregard those that did not. Now, her attitude is changed. She is going to dissever her connection with the Central Government, and resume what she claims to be her original sovereignty as an independent State. This is the "lion in the path" which the Old Public Functionary has to meet, and which we are warranted in believing, from his conduct in the past, has made the Functionary bitterly curse the hour when, thirty years ago, he fixed his eye upon what was then the glittering prize of the Presidency.

That Mr. Buchanan will, in his message to be delivered to Congress to-day, take ground against the right of secession on the part of a State, we confidently predict. That he will plead with the people of the South —entreat them to forego their purpose of independence—beg them to remain in the Union and take another chance of subduing the anti-slavery element of the North—we have no manner of doubt. The old sing-song cry of "compromise, compromise," will again be raised. The traditions of the past, the glories of the revolutionary war, the experiment of self-government, the spectacle we will make before the other nations of the world if the Union be dissolved, the taunts and reproaches they will cast at us—all these will be invoked to "plead trumpet tongued" for Southern forbearance. But James Buchanan will now learn that the day of sentiment and clap-trap has gone by, and that revolutions, once commenced, rarely go backwards. He is now in a position where a bold man and a brave man and an honest and conscientious man might make his mark upon the times, and live in history. Without reference to old party antagonisms, we may say that such is not our estimate of the President—but we shall make haste to do him ample justice, if, in his message, he shall give us cause to reverse our judgment.

The Congress which meets to-day will, of course, be occupied mainly, if not exclusively, with the political affairs of the people. Little, if any, of ordinary routine legislation will be attended to. The peaceful revolution now going on dwarfs everything else. It is the grand, salient, conspicuous and absorbing topic of the times; and neither Congress nor the people will have any heart for other and inferior issues. That there will be stormy debates, violent political harangues, exciting scenes and untimely exhibitions of bad temper, we have every reason to dread— but if our voice can reach the ear of Southern representatives, we would counsel them to a mild but firm bearing, a calm demeanor, and a patient but yet fearless assertion of their rights and their remedies.

It is hardly within the range of probability that there can be any present adjustment of our troubles. There may be politicians, South as well as North, who will make the attempt—but the people of the South are in advance of the politicians, and their potential voice must and will be obeyed. They have come to the conclusion that they have at least [1] been driven to the wall, and it is a question now of life or death ——of political and personal independence, or of perpetual serfdom and vassalage. The issue has to be met sooner or later, and it had as well be met now and be done with it. If the madmen who have gained control of the ship of state are determined to run her upon the breakers and dash her to pieces, the South can, as a last resort, take to the long-boat and save her people from the wreck.

[1] Error for "last."

101. [BORDER STATE CONVENTION]

(*Louisville Daily Journal,* December 4, 1860)

The Douglas Democracy of Kentucky have called what they style a "Democratic State Union Convention" to assemble in Louisville on the Eighth of next January. The object of this Convention, as defined in the Call, is "the maintenance of the Federal Union, on the basis of non-intervention by Congress with slavery in the Territories, and the faithful enforcement of existing laws for the protection and surrender of slave property, without let or hindrance by the laws or authorities of non-slaveholding States." Such is the solution which one wing of the Democracy in Kentucky proposes for the existing troubles. The other wing declares through its organs in favor of a Southern Convention on the basis of an ultimate demand for new guarantees of the constitutional rights of the South. The Douglas Democracy presents the dogma non-intervention as the only expedient by which the Union can be maintained, whilst the Breckinridge Democracy holds out in like manner the formal offering of a Southern ultimatum by the united South and the formal acceptance of the ultimatum by the North. And in this matter, undoubtedly, both wings of the Kentucky Democracy are moving in the line prescribed or sanctioned by their respective allies elsewhere; in other words, the movements under consideration foreshadow the schemes of the Douglas Democracy and the Breckinridge Democracy respectively as integral parties. The movements, accordingly, may be treated as authoritative.

We thus have before us the devices which the two wings of the Democracy tender for the salvation of the country in this formidable crisis. In our opinion, the device of neither, however conscientiously designed, is adapted to promote the pacification and the permanency of the Union; but directly the contrary. We will give our reasons for this opinion in as narrow a compass as possible.

The first reason we shall bring forward applies equally to both devices. We conceive that an indispensable condition of all measures directed honestly to the accommodation of our present sectional difficulties is *a foundation sufficiently broad to admit the patriotic members of every party without distinction.* It appears to us that the indispensableness of this condition is self-evident. But the devices in question set this condition flatly at defiance. They are alike founded on mere party bases, of which, by a moral necessity, each excludes not only the adherents of the other, but the large and influential body of conservatives that rejects fellowship with either on such contracted terms. As respects the Douglas device, this fact is apparent at a glance. The device is simply the Douglas platform in the late eventful canvass, dragged up by the corners from the depths of confusion into which the disastrous issue of that struggle has plunged the country. It professes to be nothing else. The same thing is true substantially as respects the Breckinridge device. The notion of submitting a Southern ultimatum to the North by the united South, though not for obvious reasons incorporated into the Breckinridge platform, constituted notoriously the principal incentive of the Breckinridge Democracry in the Border Slave States throughout the recent canvass. The Breckinridge leaders in Kentucky especially made no concealment during the canvass of their desire to range the Border States politically by the side of the Cotton States *in order to bring about what they called indifferently an "understanding" or a "settlement" or an "agreement" with the North which should define the terms whereon alone the South would consent to remain in the Union.* The hope of executing this plan formed the chief motive which prompted the Breckinridge leaders here to work with desperation for "*a united South,*" and unquestionably the general recognition of the fact contributed most powerfully to the defeat of their desperate efforts. The device they now put forth, therefore, is merely an attempt to carry out the plan above-mentioned, notwithstanding the defeat of their efforts in the late canvass to unite the South for this very purpose. Like the device of the Douglas man, it is the naked reproduction of a party basis.

Our objection to these partisan devices, however, goes deeper than this. We will next consider the two devices separately. And first the Breckinridge device.

A Southern Convention or a Convention of all the slaveholding States on the basis of an ultimate demand for new guarantees of the rights of the South under the Constitution must of course either agree or disagree with respect to the nature and extent of the ultimatum to be laid before the North. If the Convention disagrees, not only does the device fall to the ground at once, but the spectacle of a South divided on what the entire movement assumes to be a question vital to the safety and honor of the Southern people is presented to instigate the fanatics and to mislead the conservatives of the North. The event will be accepted by the Northern zealots as a confession of inherent and incurable weakness on the part of the South, and even our best friends in the North will feel their respect for Southern steadiness and resoluteness considerably lessened. The South, consequently, will stand humiliated in the presence of the North, and the possibility of Federal aggression will be increased while the power of averting it by peaceable means will be proportionately diminished. All this will follow unavoidably if the Convention disagrees on the cardinal point in hand. And who does not perceive that the Convention must necessarily disagree on this point? Who believes that Missouri and Tennessee and Kentucky and Virginia and Maryland and North Carolina and Louisiana will at this time agree to any measure that will be satisfactory to South Carolina and the States affiliated with her in the treasonable enterprise of a Southern Confederacy? Surely no one who reflects dispassionately. In the face of certain, imminent, and intolerable aggression, the slaveholding States would beyond dispute present a united front to the aggressor, in whatever form or quarter he might appear, and herein lies their real security. But in view of a danger which is uncertain, remote, and impalpable, concerning which the widest and most radical diversity of opinion exists among patriots devoted equally to the constitutional rights of the slaveholding States, and when there is a prevailing opinion even in the South that the States which manifest a determination to rush into the indisputable horrors of revolution professedly to escape this vague danger are using it as the mere occasion for the execution of a settled purpose to destroy the government, a united South on the basis of any formal measure of defense is an utter impossibility. It is the dream of an enthusiast or the snare of a traitor.

But suppose that the Convention agrees. Admit, for the sake of the argument, that the seven States mentioned above consent to the ultimatum urged by South Carolina and her allies. Concede that the dream of our Breckinridge friends is realized. Grant that the South stands united on the basis dictated to her by the States now apparently treading the verge of revolution. Would the North accept the ultimatum thus submitted? He who fancies that the North would accept the ultimatum knows little of the temper of the times in which he lives. Most unquestionably the North would reject the ultimatum. The state of public feeling in both sections of the country puts any other result entirely out of the question. Rather than accept the ultimatum the North without doubt would assent to the peaceable withdrawal of the solid South from the Union. Certainly the ultimatum would not be accepted. Then what would follow? The answer is clear. The South, standing united on the ultimatum, and pledged to dissolve the Union in the event of the rejection of the ultimatum, would have nothing to do but either to recede from her declared resolution or to carry it out at all hazards. And her impetuous pride of spirit, and union of her people effected beforehand on the basis of Disunion in this contingency, and the fierce and eager instigation of the Cotton States, would render it easy for her to go forward, but difficult to recede. She would not recede. She would not be allowed to recede. She would be slidden with hardly an effort into the abyss of Disunion.

Suppose, however, that the North or the representatives of the North should accept the ultimatum. Allow that the agreement is ratified. What additional security would the bargain afford the South in reality? If the North can't be trusted to observe the Constitution how could the North be trusted to comply with the terms of a loose popular transaction of this character? Would the gloss of Rhett and Yancey and Toombs and their confederates be more unmistakable or more sacred than the text of Madison and Hamilton and Jefferson and their illustrious compeers? Could the people of the North be fairly expected to recognize the obligation to fulfil such a pact as higher and more binding than the obligation to obey the organic law of the Union? What, indeed, would prevent the people of the North from rescinding the act of their representatives at the earliest feasible moment? Not law; for the settlement, even if it should attain the dignity of law, would be repealable by a bare majority, no matter whence obtained. Not good faith; for the people of no section of the country are bound in good faith not to revoke in proper form a law, which they believe to be derogatory to their honor or inconsistent with the Constitution. Not fear of the consequences; for the American people, without distinction of geographical lines, spurn intimidation with contempt. If law, good faith, and fear of the consequences, could stamp any agreement between the North and the South with sovereign validity, assuredly the Missouri Compromise would have been held inviolable on every side; but the Missouri Compromise was repealed by the South without compunction. It is now quite too late in our history to set up the claim of sacredness in behalf of any popular or legislative compact whatever between the sections. There is and can be no true sacredness in such expedients. The best of them are devoid of salutary force.

Will it be pretended that the arrangement under notice, or any other arrangement of the sort in the least degree practicable at the present time, would possess a more potent sanction than the Missouri Compromise possessed? If so, whence would that sanction flow? From the equity of the arrangement? The Missouri Compromise was conceived by its authors to be laid in justice. From the calamity the arrangement would serve to ward off? The Missouri Compromise was currently believed to have prevented the overthrow of the government. From the peace the arrangement would promise to secure? The Missouri Compromise had in the general estimation actually secured the unbroken peace of the nation for upwards of a quarter of a century. From the names of the statesmen that would be likely to negotiate the arrangement? The Missouri Compromise was concluded under the auspices of Monroe and Adams and Clay and King and Crawford and Sergeant and Calhoun and Eustis and Wirt and Holmes and Lowndes and Baldwin and Pinckney and Southard and a host of other proud names belonging to the North and the South; the arrangement we are considering, if it should be concluded, would be illustrated by the names of Yancey and Seward and Rhett and Sumner and Keitt [1] and Burlingame [2] and Toombs and Hale and Wise and Wilson [3] and others of the like quality of renown. It is unnecessary to press the inquiry. Beyond all question the Missouri Compromise was clothed with a mightier sanction than any other compromise that has ever marked our history or ever will mark it.

Yet the Missouri Compromise was abrogated unreluctantly by one section against the vehement protest of the other. Ay, the Missouri Compromise was abrogated; and, in a little more than six years after the date of its abrogation, the question it was designed to put to rest for ever has returned to plague the nation *with redoubled violence and malignity*. The net result of the Missouri Compromise is the original difficulty plus the aggravations springing from the essential invalidity of the measure. After the lapse of forty years, the evil, inflamed by the remedy, confronts us anew. Is it probable that a fresh application of the same description of remedy under circumstances particularly untoward would be more effectual for good or less effectual for ill? On the contrary, is it not plain that, whilst a new remedy of this species would be much inferior to the old one in validity, its rescission or infringement would be the signal, not for local turbulence and frenzy merely, but for the concerted, irresistible, and uncontrollable disruption

---

[1] Lawrence M. Keitt, Representative from South Carolina, 1853–1861.

[2] Anson Burlingame, American-Republican Representative from Massachussetts, 1855–1861.

[3] Henry Wilson, Republican Senator from Massachusetts, 1855–1873; Vice-President of the United States, 1873–1875.

of the Confederacy? Is it not perfectly manifest, that, with the South united on a basis of Disunion in a specified contingency, the agitators of the Cotton States and the enemies of the Union everywhere else would not rest until they had brought the contingency to pass in some form or other, with the view of consummating the cherished scheme of their lives? And isn't it equally clear that the happening of this contingency in any manner would bring on the consummation of their atrocious scheme? No thinking or observing man can doubt it. The remedy, therefore, would bind up the peace and existence of the Union in a frail bargain subsisting at the mercy of the deadly enemies of both. It would hand over the life and destiny of the Model Republic of the World to the keeping of Yancey and his fellow-conspirators.

Wherefore, we should condemn strongly the arrangement contemplated by the Breckinridge Democracy if the North would agree to it. In our judgment, the arrangement is pernicious in tendency and false in principle. Unless the people of the United States, like the Bourbons, "forget nothing and learn nothing," the era of such arrangements is passed. Experience has shown not simply their futility but their mischievousness. They have no power to subdue permanently or with wholesome effect the rage of sectional strife. Resembling ropes of flax cast upon a fire, they quell the flame for a time only to augment its fury in the end. Shouldering the weight of the Constitution itself, they have at most barely the validity of an ordinary law, repealable by the majority. So far as the public peace is concerned, therefore, the consequence of their adoption must be in the long run very much as if we had no organic law at all, but were living at the mere good pleasure and discretion of the majority. They are, in fact, conventional or majority Constitutions, usurping, as to the matter involved, the place of the genuine instrument, and gathering up in their own feeble stipulations the mighty interests confided by the people to the great fundamental law alone. Pausing at this point of our history, and calmly surveying the past, we own we can imagine no more fatal way of assailing the integrity of the Republic than by luring the people from the impregnable masonry of the Constitution to stand on the scaffolding of compromises which a single blow from the hand of the majority may at any moment precipitate into the red waves of revolution. And we believe that if the prominent actors in the passage of the Missouri Compromise were living to-day they would confess the same thing. It is at all events our own deliberate and settled conviction.

We, therefore, object to the Breckinridge device, 1, Because the arrangement to which the device looks forward is essentially wrong and practically destructive; 2, Because the arrangement, if it were as right and conservative as it is wrong and destructive, is totally impracticable; and, 3, Because the attempt to bring the arrangement about would by conspicuously dividing the Southern people fix the South in a false position towards the North. In short, and generally, we object to the Breckinridge device for the reason that in every point of view it is a measure hostile to the peace and permanency of the Union. We object to the Breckinridge device on one other important ground. The device leaves entirely out of the account the pregnant fact that Kentucky and her sister States of the Border, though slaveholding States, and as such allied closely with the true and legitimate interests of the Cotton States, have nevertheless a peculiar interest of their own as the central members of the Confederacy, and acknowledge no part or lot whatever in the unlawful and unpatriotic aspirations which now seem to inflame a por-tion of their Southern sisters. The Border Slave States are not strictly Southern; they are not Northern; THEY ARE CENTRAL: and, by virtue of this position, they have a most especial concern in the preservation of the Union. It is scarcely too much to say that their total prosperity as States and the entire welfare of their citizens individually are staked upon the existence of the Union as defined broadly in the Constitution. Disunion would be a very appalling calamity even to the States that appear to be so eager to precipitate it, but to Kentucky and the rest of the Border States it would be nothing less than civic death. The stakes of the two classes of communities in the Union although coincident are not equal. This fact the Breckinridge device ignores altogether, which we hold to be a very grave objection in addition to the conclusive objections we have unfolded above. But we pass from the separate consideration of the Breckinridge device.

As for the Douglas device, we have nothing to say now that we have not said a thousand times before. We think of it to-day precisely as we have thought of it always. A blemish in morals, a blunder in law, and an artifice in statesmanship, its obtrusion at this time by the Douglas party as the basis on which the friends of the Union must harmonize, if they harmonize at all, is or should be a subject of profound regret to every patriot in the land. We do not doubt that the apple of discord has been thrown amongst the Union men of the South with the best of motives, but the resulting dissension will be none the less real or lamentable on that account. Let the responsibility rest where it belongs. Challenged, as we are, to show cause why the Union men of Kentucky and of the

South are not bound in honor to surrender at discretion to the Douglas Democracy, we have no thought of flinching from the test. Neither duty nor self-respect would permit us to think of flinching. But here we must needs be somewhat brief.

The device of non-intervention or squatter-sovereignty is exhibited to the public in two aspects. One is the *right* as well as the *liberty* of the people of the Territories to govern themselves independently of the National Government; the other is the *liberty* of the people of the Territories to do this without the *right*. The first-mentioned is squatter-sovereignty proper; the last-mentioned is practical squatter-sovereignty. Mr. Douglas himself and the bulk of his followers everywhere hold the former; some few of his followers in the South hold only the latter; the Call for a "Democratic State Union Convention" pretermits completely the distinction between the two, thereby presumptively at least committing every man who shall participate in the Convention to the principle as well as the policy of squatter-sovereignty. And indeed it would not be easy to determine which is really the worse phase of the device. Squatter-sovereignty proper affirms an unconstitutional principle and offers to execute it; practical squatter-sovereignty denies the principle and offers to execute it. What the first gains in consistency it loses in unconstitutionality; what the last gains in constitutionality it loses in fidelity. The one is unconstitutional and the other is immoral. The two together make up the doctrine of absolute non-intervention. And this is the basis on which the Unionists of the South are modestly summoned to maintain the Union under penalty of being read out of their own party.

But it is said by the blind partisans of this most absurd and pestilent dogma that the National Government has heretofore in point of fact pursued generally the policy of non-intervention in the affairs of the Territories. So the National Government has done heretofore, and so doubtless it will continue to do hereafter; but it has never repudiated the *right* to intervene, if occasion should require intervention, or abdicated the *duty* to intervene in such event, which, in truth, it couldn't do if it would, for a government can no more throw off its duty than an individual can lay aside his moral accountability. If the National Government has seldom intervened actually in the affairs of the Territories, it is because the necessity for intervention has seldom actually occurred, not because the Government has not at all times recognized both the right to intervene in a suitable emergency and the obligation to exercise the right. To non-intervention as understood and practised by the National Government from its organization down to the present moment we heartily subscribe; but that is not absolute non-intervention. It is neither squatter-sovereignty proper nor practical squatter-sovereignty. It is far from either. It is nothing more or less than the constitutional supremacy of the National Government, manifested in a wise discretion, tempered generously by the spirit of our free institutions. With non-intervention of this order we have no quarrel; but with non-intervention that denies the constitutional supremacy of the National Government, or paralyzes its chief arm of protection in the presence of Territorial outrage and oppression, we have a mortal quarrel. The idea of presenting such a mixture of illegality and immorality as the only possible "basis" for "the maintenance of the Federal Union" is repugnant to every dictate of prudence, to every maxim of sound statesmanship, and to every unperverted instinct of loyalty. The folly of the idea is so excessive as to be almost criminal. We are told, however, that the doctrine of protection or non-intervention as we have described it is an *abstraction*. Not so. It is a living reality; it is and has ever been the established policy of the government. The doctrine of absolute non-intervention is an *abstraction,* and will never be anything else. It can't be reduced to practice. It is at vengeful war with the fitness of things. The question of actual intervention for protection, we admit, is not one of immediate moment; and nobody that we know of proposes to urge it. The question is quiet and no one thinks of raising it. A case has not occurred to disturb it. And we are entirely willing for the right to rest undisturbed with the case until events shall call the latter up. It is to be greatly regretted that the Douglas Democracy are not like-minded. They, however, are madly bent on agitating the question, case or no case. With these remarks we dismiss the separate consideration of the Douglas device for the present.

We have now touched rapidly upon the main reasons in support of the opinion we entertain that neither the Breckinridge device nor the Douglas device for preserving the Union in this exigency is adapted to the end avowed. These reasons, expressed summarily, are, 1, Impracticability; 2, Destructiveness of tendency; and, 3, Viciousness of principle. An enlightened public will agree with us that no measure against which these reasons can be justly brought is worthy of adoption. Whether we have brought these reasons against the measures in question justly or not, we leave an enlightened public to judge.

We, however, may be asked what measure, in our judgment, ought to be adopted, or what stand the conservatives of this noble Valley should take in the present conjuncture. We will, with becoming deference, anticipate the question, though the extreme length of this article precludes the smallest expansion of the suggestion we shall offer. Without preface or comment, therefore, but not without much deliberation, we suggest that a CONVENTION OF THE CENTRAL STATES OF THE UNION, *on the basis of the Constitution as interpreted by the Supreme Court in its formal decisions,* be held in this city on the Twenty-second of February next. And by the Central States of the Union, we mean Missouri, Kentucky, Tennessee, Virginia, Maryland, Delaware, New Jersey, Pennsylvania, Ohio, Indiana, and Illinois. These eleven States, linked together more or less closely in destiny as in position, constitute the real Keystone of the Arch of the Union, and it is equally their duty and their interest to lead off in some intelligent effort to bring order out of the present chaos of our politics. We believe it is in their power to lead off in a successful effort for this purpose. Believing thus, we venture respectfully to submit the foregoing suggestion. Men of the Central States! let us hear your response. And Heaven grant that it may be favorable. If there is not conservatism enough in the centre and heart of the Union to animate and control the rebellious extremities, then, indeed, we fear the days of the Republic are numbered.

102. THE REASON WHY

(*The New Orleans Bee,* December 5, 1860)

It may appear somewhat inexplicable to those who have not maturely considered the subject, that the people of the South should with so much seeming suddenness maintain the propriety of an energetic plan of resistance to Northern aggression even to the severance of the Union. There are persons who fail to perceive why the South, which, prior to the Presidential election, was by no means unanimously of opinion that the election of LINCOLN should be regarded as a legitimate cause for disunion, should now be almost universally in favor of proceeding to the last extremities in defense of her rights. A little reflection, however, will make this matter clear and intelligible.

During the recent Presidential canvass the South was buoyed up with the hope of defeating Black Republicanism. The assurances of the Northern national men had had the effect of persuading even against their better judgment a large number of our citizens that the cause of the South was not desperate, and that it was sustained at the North by a popular strength sufficient to overthrow Black Republicanism and its hosts. Impressed with this idea, it was entirely natural for the South to cling to the hope of preserving the Union. Believing either that LINCOLN would be beaten, or that even if chosen, his success would be a bare and barren victory, due rather to the dissensions of his competitors than to the popularity of his cause, the people of the South did not and could not anticipate the overwhelming anti-slavery demonstration which took place on the 6th of November last. It may be safely said that when they spoke of acquiescing in the election of LINCOLN, they either thought such a result highly improbable, or imagined that if it did occur, he would be so evidently the choice of a slender minority as to dispel all apprehensions of future danger from his administration.

But the result proved astounding. It showed the tremendous power and popularity of Black Republicanism. That dogma has carried every non-slaveholding State in the Union for LINCOLN; New Jersey itself, which was at first thought against him, having given him four out of seven electoral votes; while both California and Oregon—States in which it had been confidently believed Abolitionism had no local habitation—have pronounced in his behalf. The thousands of Southern citizens who had honestly and sincerely imagined Black Republican-ism to be far less potent, stood aghast at these developments. The facts and figures of the Presidential election, as they came gradually to be known, sapped, destroyed and annihilated their long cherished senti-ments of nationality. What could be alleged against such convincing and irrefragable proof of Northern unsoundness? With what shadow of reason could Southern men be advised to submit and await the possible events of the future when Abolitionism had swept every Northern commonwealth, and had even displayed unexpected and growing power in some of the slaveholding States themselves? Hence it is that but a few days had elapsed from the announcement of the result when, to the astonishment of many, the former strongest advo-cates of union and conservatism were found battling in the front ranks of Southern rights and secession.

There are circumstances connected with the election of LINCOLN which may not strike the casual reader, and yet to the reflecting mind are cogent evidences of a state of public opinion in the North emi-nently unfavorable to the prospect of a harmonious adjustment of dif-ficulties. One of these points has been alluded to by Dr. PALMER [1] in his masterly discourse on Thanksgiving Day. He observed, in speak-

1 Johnson, *The Life and Letters of Benjamin Morgan Palmer*, I, 211.

ing of the improbability of obtaining effective guarantees from the
North, that the people of that section were, almost to a man, anti-
slavery when they are not abolition. "A whole generation," said he,
"has been educated to look upon the system of slavery with abhorrence
as a national blot. They hope and look, and pray for its extinction
within a reasonable time, and cannot be satisfied unless things are
seen drawing to that conclusion. We, on the contrary, as its constituted
guardian, can demand nothing less than that it should be left open
to expansion, subject to no limitations save those of GOD and nature.
I fear the antagonism is too great, and the conscience of both parties
too deeply implicated, to allow such a composition of the strife." We
may add that it is precisely this fear which haunts the minds of the
citizens of the cotton States, and which has identified so many of them
with the revolutionary movements of the day. It is not the naked fact
of LINCOLN's election. That might have been tolerated, because it
might have been the product of an accident, a mere slipping in of a
candidate of one party running against three representatives of another party. It might have represented all the symptoms of a fortuitous
and transitory misfortune, which the South might have accepted without repining, simply because it offered no peril for the future. But as
it stands the Black Republican victory of November is the incontrovertible proof of a diseased and dangerous public opinion all over the
North, and a certain forerunner of further and more atrocious aggression. Moderate men, therefore—good men—men who have heretofore
clung steadfastly to the Union, believed in its perpetuity, and discountenanced even a thought of its dissolution, are now forced painfully, reluctantly, with sorrow and anguish, to the conclusion that it is
wholly impossible for the South tamely to tolerate the present, or indulge the slightest hope of an improvement in the future. They now
see clearly that there are but two alternatives before the South, provided she is not insensible to dishonor and disgrace—either a final
separation from the section which has oppressed and aggrieved her, or
a new compact under which her rights will be amply secured. The one
may take place, and still eventually prepare for the other.

103. THE PRESIDENT'S MESSAGE

(*New Orleans Daily Crescent,* December 6, 1860)

The very full telegraphic synopsis of the President's Message, which
we published yesterday, will be sufficient to give our readers an idea

of its general tenor and scope. It will be seen that our predictions with regard to it, made a few days ago, have been verified almost to the letter, and that we knew beforehand what the Old Public Functionary intended to say, almost as well as he knew it himself.

The President recognizes and admits the fact that South Carolina is on the eve of withdrawal from the Union. So far as we can discover, he expresses no positive opinion about the abstract right of a State to secede; but he asserts that the Constitution does not confer upon the Executive the power to coerce a seceding State into submission. The value of this admission is somewhat destroyed, however, by the instructions which he says he has issued to the officers in command of the forts and other public property, to repel any attempt on the part of the State to resume possession of such property as she has granted to the Federal Government. We do not know that such attempt will be made—but if it be, we are notified in advance that it will be resisted. Herein is the only contingency in which the President appears to think there is any likelihood of a violent collision between the Federal authorities and those of a seceding State.

But while the President expresses the opinion, individually entertained, that he has no power under the Constitution to compel a State to remain in the Union, he shifts the responsibility over to Congress, and says the occasion will probably soon arise when that body will have to decide this question for themselves. He thus argues that Congress *has not* the power! If it be his opinion that Congress has no such power, the suggestion that Congress will probably soon have to decide the question seems to us decidedly inappropriate and out of place. Why should he suggest to Congress to determine a point which he has just said Congress has no right to decide in the affirmative? It seems to us that Old Buck is particularly muddy and confused in treating this point, but we must make some allowance, we suppose, for the delicate and unusual position in which the Old Public Functionary—never remarkable for decision of character—now finds himself so suddenly and unexpectedly placed.

Dismissing this branch of the subject, the President proceeds to give us the old stereotyped jeremiad over the horrors of civil war, and the blessings of "our glorious Union." For further particulars, consult any Fourth-of-July oration delivered within the last seventy years.

Secession, he says, is the very last remedy—to be resorted to only when everything else fails. This is exactly what the South says, and has always said. We have tried everything else, and everything else has failed—and it is precisely because this "last resort" only will save us, that we have determined to employ it. The "ebb and flow" in public sentiment, which Old Buck relies on, is a nice thing to talk of on the eve of an overwhelming and unprecedented expression of public opinion, just one month ago, in every Northern State except one, in favor of a sectional administration of the Government, looking to the present domination and the eventual overthrow of the South, her institutions, her rights, and the honor of her people. The South recognizes the fact that what she proposes is, as the President says, a last resort. It is only because it is the last resort that she has now taken position upon it, and will stand or fall upon the justice of her cause.

But the Constitution can be amended, says Mr. Buchanan—and he goes on to suggest what those amendments should be. He says this has been done before, when defects were discovered in the organic law. We suppose the Old Public Functionary is not aware that times are not the same now as they were sixty years ago. Then there was no fanaticism such as now exists—no such hatred between the two sections—no small politicians and corrupt political gamblers and tricksters in the high places of the nation. But the very guaranties he wishes given, he admits, have already been decided to exist by the high authority of the Supreme Court; and he weakly supposes that the people of the North will concede these guaranties of their own free will and accord, if they are allowed to pass upon them as States, though they do not now recognize them as decided and established by the Supreme Court! In other words, the people of Massachusetts, who now refuse to recognize the decisions of the Court that property exists in slaves —that this property is entitled to protection in the Territories—and that a man is entitled to recover his fugitive slave in another State— the people of Massachusetts, he says, thus spurning the decision of the Court, will vote to establish these same doctrines if they can act upon them within their own State! Faith will remove mountains, Mr. President; but the faith necessary to believe this, would remove the Alps from the continent of Europe, transport them across the Atlantic ocean and the American continent, and pitch them into the Pacific off the coast of California. Moreover, if the door were once opened for amendments to the Constitution, there is no telling where it would stop. We might be pledged to the observance of a Constitution openly destructive of our equality and our rights. The present Constitution is good enough for us, and its provisions plain enough.

All we require is that those provisions be observed. And if Mr. Buchanan, instead of suggesting new amendments, had appealed to the North to observe the Constitution as it now is, he would have occupied a much more manly and defensible position. If he had counseled the North to abandon their misrepresentations of the Constitution, and their evasion and nullification of the laws passed in pursuance of its provisions, he would have done the correct thing, and have applied the proper remedy for the disease. These suggestions to amend a Constitution, which the South already considers ample for her protection, if proper observance be paid both to its letter and its spirit, will be rejected by every Southern State as only a pitiful trifling with the question.

For the rest, the President thinks that the time has not yet arrived for resistance—it never will arrive, in our opinion, so far as *he* is concerned—and that Lincoln's election is not, alone, sufficient provocation. The President forgets that it is not the mere fact of Lincoln's election which the South pleads in justification of her conduct. But this is something which is now outside of the question. The South has gone too far, and rightly so, for recession. And if nobody has any better plan for a solution of the difficulty than the President, the fact is apparent that it is farther from adjustment than ever.

104. New Lines of Sectionalism

(*The Daily Picayune,* New Orleans, December 8, 1860)

For twenty-five years, the North and the South have been diverging from each other, their former fraternal spirit gradually disappearing, until they now stand in the attitude of such fierce antagonism that the possibility of a longer existence of the present Government is a doubtful problem. Wearied by the experience of the past, and determined to rely upon themselves for the protection of their rights, they look to a future Confederacy, in which common institutions and sympathies shall furnish guarantees of peace and accord between all of its members.

The tendency of some of the measures suggested by the Governors of several Southern States, and not unfavorably received, though not finally adopted, is to create a new line of sectionalism that shall divide the slave States themselves. Even at this early stage of the present Southern movement, the germs of future controversy, growing out of conflicting interests, are plainly to be seen.

Though the existence of slavery is a common bond of union between what are usually denominated the Southern States, their interests are not entirely coincident. Virginia, Maryland, Kentucky, Tennessee and Missouri look to the cotton region for a market for their surplus black labor, while the introduction of manufacturing industry gives them a divergence from principles that the cotton growers consider vital to their highest prosperity.

The States now moving for immediate secession from the Federal Government suggest the necessity of prohibiting the introduction of slaves for sale within their limits from either of the frontier Commonwealths. They would hold them, by this prohibition, as a shield of defense against the aggression of a hostile North; and force them to maintain the institution of slavery from the sheer impossibility of getting rid of it.

Doubt and suspicion of the soundness of the people of these States on the Southern question, has long been manifested by the advocates of extreme action in the cotton region, which now have actually grown so decided as to incite the recommendation of really unfriendly legislation. Hostility to a proposed convention of all the slave Commonwealths to decide upon future concurrent action, arises from want of confidence in them, and a feeling that material differences of opinion already seriously divides the South.

In some quarters the fears of such disagreement are so strong, that in the event of separate State action producing the future necessity of a Southern Confederacy, the determination is openly uttered to admit no State outside of the cotton region to have any influence in moulding its character. The door is to be left open for the admission of the frontier States, but they are not to be invited to be actors in the formation of the new government.

On another point the commencement of future difficulties is apparent. South Carolina, Georgia, Alabama and Mississippi are free trade States. Already the manifestation of a future free trade policy, in any new confederation that may be established, is openly made. But Louisiana is scarcely prepared to abandon at once all duties upon foreign sugar. Her sugar planters are now protected by what is equivalent to $300 bonus on every $1000 worth of sugar raised. With this protection to her industry the sugar planters are growing exorbitantly rich. Material interests will doubtless weigh but little in restraining her resistance, but it is different when a new government is to be formed.

In case of the separation of the slave States from the Union, the frontier States will become manufacturing States. The iron interests of

Virginia and Tennessee would be sacrificed by a system of free trade, while other branches of manufacturing industry would be overwhelmed with certain ruin. The two great questions which for many years has disturbed the peace of the present Union are likely still to exist to harass the South, even after separate State action has been the cause of the dissolution of the present relations of the slave States.

We are in danger of creating a new line of sectionalism; of awakening an antagonism of feeling between the frontier and the Gulf States, and even finding, at least one of them, that would view with much discontent a majority in any new confederation consisting of a majority opposed to her interests.

The question then arises, if we are likely to get rid, by separate State action, of periodic agitation; if we can form a new government in which a happy accord between its confederate members will secure a long continued peace and prosperity. It will not take so long a time, in any new confederacy, for dissatisfaction, with a majority rule of free trade, or cotton States, to precipitate a new revolution. The example of secession from a strong government can much more easily be copied in one that must necessarily be held together by weaker bonds.

Nor is it difficult to suppose that the controversy, once aroused, would be as much more violent as the contending parties are the more nearly connected by many common sympathies. It is human nature to tolerate in strangers that which would not be endured from close friends.

The clear manifestation of causes and action tending to create a new line of sectionalism, more forcibly than any other argument, proves the absolute necessity for a general Southern convention, to compose present difficulties, or to direct the future course of the South.

It is unjust to the people of the border slave States to consider them less chivalrous, less devoted to the interests of the South, or less to be depended on than those of the Cotton States, in any great struggle to conserve common honor and protect common rights.—It is a selfish policy, and one hostile to success in the present great movement, to decry the patriotism or cast doubts upon fealty to home institutions of any citizen or any State because of a difference only in the mode of action to secure an object alike the interest and honor of all.

Any action that disregards the invitation of sister States to counsel together before the final steps be taken—to deliberate in view of the vast responsibilities of decisions to compose differences and comprise conflicting opinions—to nip in the bud the possibility of the scenes of the past twenty-five years being re-enacted more violently on a narrower stage—is unwise, not to say unpatriotic, and hostile to the true cause of the South.

A new confederacy, if the present Union be dissolved, it must be conceded, is a necessity. The history of the world proves the failure of governments embracing very small communities. Italy, broken into minute divisions, has for centuries been the prey of the strong and the victim of the bold, and the present reunion of her people under one government is hailed by the civilized world as the regeneration of that country, famous alike for its ancient glory and modern shame. But the advocates of separate State action and immediate secession are working to produce the same fate for the South, which for centuries has degraded and ruined the Italians, unless the way is provided for a reconstruction of a government with territory, population, resources and wealth that will command the respect of the world. But separate State action and reconstruction by a few only of the slave States promises to prevent that agreement which concurrent action of all the States only can effect. It is even now giving birth to a sectionalism between the South quite as fatal as that that now exists between non-slaveholding and slave States.

In the present crisis, the presentation of the dangers and difficulties of hasty action is a duty which true men owe to the South. To be silent, or to slur over what should be understood by every man, is the part of that quiet submission which will meet every disgrace rather than come up to the courage necessary to express an opinion. Where our State finally goes, we are prepared to go; but until she acts we should labor to show all the difficulties, all the dangers of following mere impulses instead of being guided by great principles and actual facts, and expose the necessary consequences of the unfriendly acts to sister slave States, that seem to have no weak endorsement in the outward expression of public opinion. The cause of the South is our cause; the success of our section, if conciliation cannot be effected on our own terms, has our earnest hopes.

105. Regard All the Consequences

(*The Daily True Delta,* New Orleans, December 9, 1860)

It is surprising to every one how the secession presses and orators should continue to harp upon the declaration, that no violence, no protracted disruption of trade, no inconvenience of civil war need be apprehended from the dissolution of the Union which they contemplate, have seemingly so much at heart, and are with so much activity, zeal and profusion of exhortation preparing the hearts of the people to expect. They tell us that the states which remain in the confederacy have no right to obstruct the withdrawal of those which have determined or are inclined to secede, and that consequently no danger of a hostile collision need be feared when the event they affect to desire is actually consummated. So far as this administration is concerned we believe the orators and presses of the disunionists are strictly correct in this assertion. We do not for an instant doubt that the movement to destroy the Union was determined on long since, anterior by months to the disruption of the democratic party at Charleston, which was a part of the programme, and that Buchanan, the president, and the members of his cabinet, actively or passively approved of the scheme and pledged their official cooperation to its success. Admitting all this, however, as we are constrained to do, does it therefore follow that after South Carolina and other states have actually separated themselves from the Union, have placed themselves beyond its pale by acts incompatible with its organic laws, and have done so by the connivance of Buchanan and his advisers, that no ground, no cause, no impelling motive for a recourse to arms will exist, or indeed is evitable? We think not, we are sure not. We hold that it is utterly impossible to have a peaceable dismemberment of the confederation. We do not stop to argue the question whether a state has the undoubted right to separate herself from her sister states or not; we will not raise a doubt or challenge controversy in relation to such matter; we will on the contrary concede it, still, is it not obvious that after her separation, she must either relinquish all pretension, all claim, all right to participate equally in the national property, public domain, improvements of all kinds, army, navy and appurtenances, etc., or prepare herself to vindicate her demands for her share by a resort to force? Will the free states abandon the supremacy they now claim over the territorial property of the Union? and can they be made to do so otherwise than by force successfully invoked? No one, we think, will contend they will; therefore is it not certain that to extort from them that which we all unite in considering our own just due, a recourse to force must be had, and a civil war thus inaugurated with all the uncertainties, doubts, difficulties, horror and destruction of life and property inseparable from appeals from reason to the arbitrament of the sword? We do not for a moment doubt the willingness of the mass of the people to test the question of right with the north by the invocation of the sword; nor shall we doubt their perfect ability, albeit greatly inferior, numerically, to the foe they will be obliged to encounter, to conquer a successful peace. All this we shall accept as the more warlike among our population would have us; but as the bayonet is certain, in the event of a separation, to be called into action, to reconcile differences, we wish the important fact to be borne in mind, so that no one shall be allowed at any future time to plead ignorance when called upon as to his share of any responsibility that may devolve upon him in such contingency. A peaceful destruction of this government never can take place, in our opinion; therefore it is that we censure the parties that are fanning into a flame the passions of the people, who are preparing their hearts for revolution, who are sharpening sword-blades, yet are delusively shouting peace, peace, where there is no peace. It is not any alarm South Carolina, in or out of the Union, can inspire, that distracts the nation at this moment, that sends our working men into the streets, that shuts up our workshops, that shakes public confidence, that involves in one mass of common ruin the monetary, commercial and trading classes of the republic. The orators of disunion may tell you, as they do, that the terror is only imaginary, the perturbation an illusion; but reflecting men will see in it what it really conveys, the universal consciousness that the country is on the eve of a fearful convulsion, and that it is only by a special interposition of Providence that it can escape these perturbations which have, in all ages, destroyed the liberties of men and drenched the earth with the blood of brethren. We do not for a moment suppose that even consequences so deplorable will restrain men so ardent in the cause of revolution as many of the public men of the south proclaim themselves; for, making allowances for much of the theatrical in the character of politicians by profession, can we doubt the sincerity of the Rhetts, the Toombses, the Yanceys and the Jeff. Davises, when they welcome, in exultant tones, the prospect of war with their countrymen for opponents; what we deprecate is the perpetual assurance given by them that no civil war can originate in their revolutionary schemes, and that all questions in dispute between disjointed fragments of this, at present, powerful republic, will be amicably, justly and satisfactorily adjusted, when they well know no such expectation is really entertained by them, or can ever be realized by the public. If they succeed in their plotting against the integrity of the Union, they have no idea upon earth that even the seaboard cotton states could be induced to form a confederacy together.

They know well that Texas has never ceased to regret the merging of her national existence in that of this republic; and that no thought prevails so universally in that state as that which pictures to its people a separation from it; so that if their machinations should succeed, one state, at least, that they have encouraged to share their plans, will disconnect herself from them the instant the Union is dismembered and it feels itself free to adopt some new course and enter upon a new career. If all these things can be accomplished without war, we shall rejoice.—Meantime, our readers will do well to prepare themselves for whatever may happen.

106. The President and the Union

(*The New Orleans Bee,* December 10, 1860)

The President in his annual message is evidently at considerable pains to conciliate both sections of the Republic. He is willing to admit many of the grievances complained of by the South, but insists upon the existence of a potent conservative spirit at the North. In his statement of Southern wrongs he is not always well informed. For instance, he cites as a prominent peril of the times the malign influence of Abolition agitation on the character and conduct of the slaves themselves, and appears to imagine that every Southern fireside is haunted with the dread of domestic insurrection. This is a great though probably unintentional exaggeration of fact. The influence of Black Republican aggression on the slaves themselves is far from constituting the most prominent of the iniquities to which the South is subject, as in reality our servile population are for the most part docile and obedient, and require no extraordinary restraint or coercion to keep them so.

Another error into which Mr. Buchanan falls, in common with many just and fair-minded men of the North, is the belief that the South has been moved to resistance chiefly by the adverse result of the Presidential contest. We are told with marked emphasis that Lincoln has been elected in strict conformity to the mandates of the Constitution and the provisions of the law. Now this is not denied, nor does the South profess to desire a separation exclusively or even chiefly on account of the success of the Black Republican nominee. That was but the crowning stroke to a protracted and wanton series of aggressions on the South; the last drop which caused the bitter cup to overflow; the final and fitting upshot to a long-continued policy of injustice and oppression. Lincoln's triumph is simply the practical manifestation of the popular dogma in the free States that slavery is a crime in the sight of GOD, to be reprobated by all honest citizens, and to be warred against by the combined moral influence and political power of the Government. The South, in the eyes of the North, is degraded and unworthy, because of the institution of servitude. She is hated by the North because she holds the black race in bondage. She is persecuted because fanatics have made unto themselves a peculiar code of ethics with which the South does not agree, because she knows it to be fallacious. It is self-evident that if one-half of the people of a country look upon the other half as in the perpetual commission of a heinous offense before GOD, and disseminate the doctrine that they are guilty of the grossest violation of civil, social and religious canons, the section deemed thus culpable must be regarded as inferior in every respect to the former. If the North is sincere she must inevitably abhor the South. If this is a sentiment compatible with the endurance of a Union avowedly founded on the most perfect political equality and social harmony and fraternity, then we must ignore the history of our revolutionary struggles, our efforts in behalf of a sound government, and our success in the formation of the Constitution of the United States.

That instrument was designed to guide and govern a homogeneous nation—homogeneous in the patrimony of a common country, a common ancestry, and an independence achieved at the point of the sword after years of sacrifice and struggle. The events of the last quarter of a century prove distinctly and undeniably that the people have ceased to be homogeneous. They are divided into two separate sections, no longer animated by feelings of brotherhood, but alienated by animosity and perpetual strife. It is true that both sections are still subjected to the control of the Constitution, and live nominally under the same government; but virtually they are two separate nationalities, differing materially in domestic institutions, manners, habits of thought, and other characteristics. Is it not clear that the word "Union" applied to such antagonisms is little more than a barren name? There is no longer a union of heart and feelings, of patriotism and nationality. The North inveighs against the South, and is barely restrained by some lingering respect for law, and perhaps by a regard for safety, from assailing it with brute force. As it is, she steals our slaves, denies us the right of traveling with them, resists our efforts to recover them when spirited away, foments insubordination and insurrection, and triumphantly proclaims a political platform the leading feature of which is hostility to slavery. The South in vain asserts her equality and demands her rights. Injustice and aggression have engendered their legitimate offspring—alienation and distrust. It would seem impossible for the two sections to live together harmoniously under one Government. Hence the honest conviction of thousands that peaceable separation, effected in good faith and with due observance of equal justice to both sections, is the best, and indeed the only resource left.

The President appears to place confidence in various specifics which he proposes for the cure of the disease in the body politic. The amendments suggested by him are not likely to be adopted, and if under the pressure of the emergncy or the pervading sense of self-interest the North could be induced to accede to them, would they not prove but a filmy cover of an ulcerous surface, while the corroding abscess still raged among the vitals of the patient? What is needed is the surgeon's knife to extirpate the canker of fanaticism from the Northern heart. It is one thing to compel a people by the overwhelming might of law to avoid injuring their neighbors, and quite another to sow within their hearts the seeds of brotherly love and charity by which they will be eternally restrained from trespassing on the rights of others.

Our readers will do us the justice to admit that we have been uniformly attached to the Union. We have clung to it undismayed by the silly outcry of "submissionist," or by unworthy insinuations of a lack of patriotic sympathy with the South. Even now we should heartily rejoice if the Union could be preserved with honor and dignity to our aggrieved and oppressed section. God grant that the means of consummating the wish may yet be found; but humanly speaking, we must say that we can see none.

107. The President's Message

(*Richmond Enquirer,* December 11, 1860)

We have hitherto abstained from commenting at any length on this extraordinary document. Had such a message been issued in the commencement of an executive administration, we should have felt it our duty at once to have taken part in the work of a careful examination and exposition of its contents. But recognizing it as the act of an executive on the eve of the relinquishment of power, and which, even in the midst of power, has already been renounced by every political party, and by none more decidedly than by the party which elevated it to power, recognizing, too, the now all important fact that the great political issues of the moment have placed our political relations far beyond the control of the action or inaction of any or all the branches of the General Government, bringing the sovereign States themselves face to face in the attitude of consultive deliberation or of national conflict; under these circumstances, we have seen little necessity, at this time, for long discussion on the subject of the President's message, since we have not considered it probable that the message can in any manner influence the only arbitrament to which federal relations, by the inevitable force of circumstances, are now referred, that of the tribunal of STATE ACTION.

On the other hand, however, we are not blind to the existence of an opinion, entertained and expressed by many whose opinions are well entitled to respect, that if the message shall have no other important effect, it may operate to influence State action itself, in some instances to precipitate, in others to embarrass. If this apprehension be well-founded, then, indeed it is very important that the intent of the President's message shall be thoroughly sifted and carefully examined, and that its more serious errors should be unsparingly exposed.—With a view to rendering some assistance in this work, we lay before our readers the following outline of comment:

WHAT IS THE INTENT?

When the President informs us that the present movement at the South is the result, not so much of the infringements of the Constitutional rights of Southern States by Northern Legislatures and the Federal Government, but principally of a pervading apprehension of servile insurrection at the South excited by popular agitation at the North; yet that unless Northern "State Legislatures will repeal their unconstitutional and obnoxious enactments, without unnecessary delay, it is impossible for any human power to save the Union."—When the President further asserts that the Congress of the United States has never, except *possibly* in one instance, and that forty years ago, invaded the Constitutional rights of the South; yet admits immediately afterwards that the Congress is at this moment actually withholding Constitutional protection from Southern property in the common Territories. When the President further asserts that it is practically as well as constitutionally impossible for a Territorial Legislature to exclude slavery from a Territory, yet admits that during the past twelve months a Territorial Legislature has maintained such a law on its statute book. When the President further informs us that his successor, elected under the pledge of solemn promises to exercise all his power and influence for the exclusion of slave property from the Territories, for the nullification of the fugitive slave law, and finally for the extinction of slavery in the United States, must yet be "necessarily conservative," and that for us to believe him capable of doing what he is pledged to do, "would be at war with every principle of justice and of Christian charity." When the President further informs us that secession is not an act of State sovereignty, but only of revolutionary resistance, justifiable *only* when the Federal Government shall be guilty of "a deliberate, palpable and dangerous exercise" of powers not granted by the Constitution; yet admits, immediately afterwards, that acts of State Governments, which the Federal Government is powerless to control, will also "justify revolutionary resistance to the Government of the Union." When the President still denies that such resistance will constitute an act of public war, carried on under the ægis of sovereignty; yet admits, that any attempt on the part of the Federal Government to suppress such an "insurrection" by force of arms, would constitute not only an act of public war, but one so extraordinary in its nature as to be incommensurate with the limited powers of the Federal Government. When the President further asserts that the Federal Executive is contsitutionally and practically armed with full power to enforce Federal laws, even in the face of State resistance; yet admits that Congress may not even pass laws necessary for the execution of these powers; and further admits that the mere action of individuals, taken in advance and independent of State action, the mere resignation of offices by Federal officials in a State, is of itself all-sufficient to paralyse the whole power of the Federal Executive and Judiciary within the State. When the President finally recommends to Congress a call for State action through a Convention of all the States, as the only means now available to preserve the Union, or prevent a conflict of arms among the States.—From all this maze of contradictions, it is impossible to deduce, with any certainty, the real intent and purpose of the President. We are necessarily driven to surmise, and to inference. The only result at which we are enabled to arive, is summed up in the following conclusions:

1st. The President has endeavored to keep himself uncommitted, in his executive capacity, to any line of conduct whatever in the event of

State resistance and now endeavors to furnish himself, by anticipation, with a pretext of justification or apology for any line of action or inaction which he may hereafter find it convenient to adopt.

2d. The President recognizes the fact that the General Government is powerless to control the existing crisis, and attempts to demonstrate that, although the Northern States have palpably violated the Constitution to the manifest oppression of the South, united State action in general convention may preclude the necessity for, and, in any event, ought to precede separate State action.

This last recommendation might be worthy of consideration, were it, at this time, at all practicable. But, apart from the fact that some of the Southern States have already determined on separate State action, it is sufficiently obvious that the tone and temper both of the Black Republican States and of their representatives in Congress, is such as to preclude the possibility of obtaining a call for a Federal Convention. In the first instance, at least, there are now but two alternatives presented to each Southern State—that of resistance by separate State action, and that of entire submission to anti-slavery outrage.

Apart from the mere juxtaposition of the President's self-contradictions, the message offers various instances urgently inviting criticism and correction. Of these we take the opportunity to point out a few:

CONGRESSIONAL ACTION

It sounds strangely in the ears of Southern men, this deliberate assertion on the part of the President of the United States: *"No single act has ever passed Congress, unless we may possibly except the Missouri Compromise, impairing, in the slightest degree, the rights of the South to their property in slaves."*

Has the President forgotten that, in 1845, an act exactly similar to the Missouri Compromise was applied to slavery in the Territories of the new State of Texas? that this act was reiterated in 1850, and has never been repealed by Congress?

Has the President forgotten that, in 1850, property in slaves was directly assailed in the District of Columbia, and has ever since been oppressed, under a disabling act of Congress? Has he forgotten, too, that in the same year, Congress and the President resorted to a combination of squatter-sovereignty, anarchy and military dictation, to exclude slave property from valuable employment in the gold mines of California? Has the President forgotten that, in 1854, Congress repealed a code of laws protecting slave property in Kansas and Nebraska, leaving such property to a great extent without legal protection?

Again. Does the President pretend that Congress may not impair the right of slave property by unfriendly inaction, as well as by hostile action? And is not slave property, at this moment, subjected to oppression through the act of an agent of Congress, whose usurpation of power is tolerated by Congress?

SOVEREIGN POWER

It tells sadly for the spread of the doctrine of popular government, when a President of the greatest republic ever known in the world gravely informs us, in a public document, that the powers to coin money, declare war, make peace, conclude treaties, regulate commerce, &c. *"embrace the very highest attributes of national sovereignty."*

Yet, Mr. Buchanan it seems, has never yet imagined, that in this country, the power to coin money, or to declare war is *not* a sovereign power.

Grotius indeed calls each of these a sovereign power. So does Vattel. So do all European, and too many American writers on public law. But, thank God, the philosophy of government, in this land of ours, has taken a giant's stride beyond all the imaginings of Grotius and Vattel, and all the other publicists combined. In effect and in law, throughout all these United States of America, the power to coin money is no more a sovereign power than is the power to issue a county magistrate's warrant, or to affix a notarial seal. Towering far above the power of peace and war, of coining money or regulating commerce, there is a governmental power which embraces the sole and peculiar attribute of supremacy. There is one sovereign power, and but one, and that power is the CONSTITUTION-MAKING POWER.

Sovereign power, one and inseparable, remains with the people of each State. They may separate and distribute at will the subordinate powers of national or municipal government, but, wherever placed, these powers still remain merely subsidiary and subordinate, and at all times subjected to that sovereign power which constituted and delegated, and may at any time withdraw or resume them.

Indeed, the President seems to have an inkling of this great truth, when he says:

"To the extent of the delegated powers, the Constitution of the

United States is as much a part of the Constitution of each State, and is as binding upon its people, as though it had been textually inserted therein."

Exactly. And the people of a state, assembled in Convention, may, at any time, abrogate their State Constitution, *in whole or in part*. This is sovereign power.

James Madison has, indeed, ably and conclusively demonstrated that there is a difference between this "federal clause" of each State Constitution, and every other clause, which must be considered whenever the question of abrogation or amendment shall arise. The President evidently misunderstands Mr. Madison's masterly exposition.

MR. MADISON'S DOCTRINE

It is with much regret that we see the President adopting, however unadvisedly, the wilful and wicked perversions which Federalist and Black Republican newspapers are now applying to the Virginia doctrine of States Rights, as expounded by James Madison.

A few words will suffice to explain and to vindicate this doctrine. Mr. Madison held that the difference between each State Government and the Federal Government consists in the fact that, while the State Government is the separate agent of one State, the Federal Government is the common agent of all the States. The sovereign people of each State, through their State Constitution, have created a State Government, and delegated to it certain municipal powers. The same sovereign people have, through the Federal Constitution, delegated to the Federal Government certain other municipal powers. That they may, at any time, or on any pretext, or without pretext, abrogate their State Constitution, dismiss their State Government and erect another in its place, none can deny, or has ever ventured to dispute. But the Federal Constitution embodies an element unknown to the State Constitution—the element of national *compact*.

No State, indeed, has parted with any attribute of her sovereignty. But each sovereign State, on entering the Union, did so, with the necessarily implied compact, that she would preserve the Union, so long as her associate States should respect the conditions of the compact, and so long as her people should not be subjected to intolerable oppression, constitutional or unconstitutional. This compact, however, is upheld by no guarantee, save that of the plighted faith of State Sovereignty.—The Sovereign States were subjected to the dictation of no common arbiter. In case of infraction of the Constitution or of oppression of any sort, real or supposed, each State, for herself, must be the judge of the infraction and of the mode and measure of redress. Each must judge for herself, and act for herself—responsible only before the great tribunal of nations. If one State shall say to the other States: "You have, through your State governments, or through our common federal agents, violated the Constitutional compact—or even, without violating express compacts, subjected my people to oppression —I so judge, and my mode and measure of redress is to absolve myself from this compact." In such case, the other States may say: "We have an equal right to judge; and our judgment is, that we have respected the compact, and have not oppressed your people. We judge, moreover, that you have sought a false pretext by which to dissolve the compact; that this is an act of bad faith towards us, and one to which we will not submit." Thus a conflict of judgment may arise among the Sovereign States, and when it so arises, it must be calmed by forbearance, on the one side, or on the other, or on both sides; or it must be settled by formal agreement among the States—or, it must result not in "revolution" in the narrow sense of the word; but in public war, formally declared by State Sovereignties and conducted according to the "*jus belli*" of nations.

This is the doctrine of James Madison, a doctrine which not only upholds the right of secession, but which claims for each Sovereign State the right to employ any mode or measure of redress—whether it be by secession from the Union or the bolder policy of appealing to arms and declaring war against other States to vindicate her right of sovereignty and equality in the Union.

To deduce from this, any denial of the entire sovereignty of a State, Mr. Buchanan must first resort to a perverted statement of its teachings. And we have already shown, that in order to prove any division or concession of State sovereignty, he must renounce the Democratic doctrine of sovereign right, and have recourse to another and a foreign doctrine which draws its teachings from the dogma of the divine right of Kings.

108. THE EFFECT OF THE MEETING OF CONGRESS, AND ATTENDING DEMONSTRATIONS ON THE COURSE OF THE SOUTHERN STATES

(*Richmond Semi-weekly Examiner,* December 11, 1860)

The country had no right to anticipate much from the assembling of Congress calculated to quiet the agitation which has been disturb-

ing the country since the first week in November.—The popular
action in the election of President and Vice President had driven the
citizens of the Southern States to look to the decision of their own
sovereignties in the exigency which that anti-slavery action of the
North combined with its past conduct and avowed policy to force
upon the country. The event which created the disturbance came in
the last months of the most conservative and friendly administration
which the South can hope ever to have while the North possesses its
present preponderance in the Union, and its consequent control over
the business and property of the slaveholding States. These States can
hardly hope for a better Constitution. They can never expect now a
Chief Magistrate from the North whose temper, interests and opinions
are more favorable to the rights and interests of their section than
those of Mr. BUCHANAN have been demonstrated to be. They cannot
expect a Congress less hostile to the South, under the present federal
system, than that now in session. It is very certain that the next will
not be. We know that a few additional Northern Democrats have
been elected to the next House, but we know that the additions to the
Senate have been against the South, and more will be made equally
hostile in a few months. We know, too, that many Southern delegations will not be in the next Congress. It is well known that there
is no constitutional limit as to the number of the members of the
Federal Judiciary, and that the increase of the number of districts,
and the appointment of members will be in the hands of Congress and
the anti-slavery Executive.

This was the prospect before the country when the Congress assembled. What has been done by the Congress or the Executive to
remove the just and well-grounded apprehension, the settled conviction, that they were to suffer added wrong from the incoming administration, which obtained so extensively throughout the Southern
States? We can see nothing calculated to have such an effect, but
much which must increase the apprehension, and force the Southern
States to accord with previous conviction. That Mr. BUCHANAN desired
most earnestly to restrain the mischievous and aggressive action of the
Northern people and their agents—that he sincerely sought to correct the dangerous and hostile operation which sectional injustice was
giving to the Government of the Confederacy—that he was anxious
both as a man and a patriot to devise some plan by which present
irritation could be allayed and anticipated wrong averted—we think no
man who is not blinded by excitement or prejudice can doubt. After

mature reflection and evident labor, he has been unable to do more than to draw a dark, but truthful picture of the desperate condition of the Southern States in this Confederacy, and to point them, as their sole remedy for wrongs, their sole hope of safety in the Union, to an appeal to the justice and mercy of their freesoil assailants, while in the Union, and to an appeal to arms, in rebellion, against the armed and legally constituted authority of the Confederacy to get out of it when their humble petitions shall be rejected. To hold their peace, lives, property and individual and political freedom by the precarious tenure of the mercy and justice of Freesoil majorities, is the lot assigned by a friendly Chief Magistrate to the people of the South in this Confederacy; and to secure these rights and privileges by an armed conflict with an organized government, when they shall be denied by that majority, encountering at once the hazard of battle and the halter of the hangman, is to be the ultimate and sole rightful resort of this oppressed section when it shall seek to obtain them otherwise than by the grant of the sectional majority which oppresses them. The advice to appeal to the States for an amended Constitution, and the denial of any right of independent State action to protect its oppressed people, and the assertion that such action is at war with the Constitution and revolutionary, conveys this idea and nothing else. The denial of the right to coerce the State residing in the Federal Government, while he claims for that Government the right to levy taxes on the persons and property of the people of the seceding State to support the Government they have abandoned, cannot alter the case. The Southern States are left no hope except in an appeal to the justice of the majority in the free States, or to arms in rebellion.

While we differ widely in opinion with Mr. BUCHANAN on the questions of right and on the remedial policy he recommends, we are far from designing to assail the sincerity and purity of his desire to quiet the country and to give security to the South. His purposes are doubtless good. They are, unhappily, inefficient and mischievous, in our view. They have failed to satisfy either of the contending parties. So far as Executive action has been had or indicated, it increases the necessity for the assembling of each Southern State, in its own sovereign capacity, to consider the dangers which menace them severally, and to devise for themselves some measure calculated to provide the security requisite to save their property and liberties.

The indications given to the country through Congress, we think, increases the necessity for the call of a convention of its citizens by each Southern State. From no Black Republican in Congress have we seen any indication of an intention to give even the slender and value-less protection to the South suggested by the President. His Message, so far as we have seen, has provoked nothing but censure and con-demnation from the ruling party in the North, so far as it affects really beneficially the interest of the South. No additional constitu-tional security will be given the South, and without the concurrence of a large portion of that party, and of the Black Republican Presi-dent elect, the South can have no hope of even the insufficient protec-tion devised by the President. The whole party now in the ascendent in the Union denies the right of State action opposing Federal ag-gression, and claims what Mr. BUCHANAN denies—the right of the Government to coerce a State back into the Union should one secede. The party thus will not grant the slender security Mr. BUCHANAN desires, and will not allow the State to place itself in a position to protect itself against the oppression of their agent—the Federal Gov-ernment. We refer our readers to the declarations of those leading Black Republicans who have spoken, and to the comments of the press of that party on this portion of the President's Message, to con-firm this statement.

In the House a committee has been appointed to consider and re-port on the condition of the Union. This committee consists of 33 members—one from each State.[1] There are on it 14 avowed Black Republicans, if Howard, of Michigan, belongs, as we believe, to that party. From the South the notorious H. W. DAVIS, whose Black Re-publican proclivities and anti-State-Rights sentiments are notorious in the Union, is one; NELSON, of Tennessee, another.—And the com-plexion of the majority of that committee renders it certain that no security for the South, even approaching that suggested by Mr. BUCHANAN, will ever receive a favorable consideration from it. The hope even of this illusory provision will be stifled in the process of conception, and never have the opportunity of being lost and destroyed by the Congress.

The only effect of these abortive efforts at Executive and Congres-sional adjustments will be to drag on the time until the two sections are brought face to face on another issue demanding more decision of action. The secession of several of the Southern States from the Union is now a matter of almost absolute certainty. When this event or those events occur, the separate States will be called on to act. Congress and

[1] *Cong. Globe*, 36 Cong., 2 Sess., I, 22.

the Federal Government will be out of the question as mediators; they must either be spectators of the efforts of the States to reconcile the parties to the Federal compact, or they must occupy the more offensive and dangerous position of assailants of the seceding States. When these events occur, the States of the South ought to be in Convention, each within its own limits.—If they desire to mediate between the two parties, if they desire to prevent the coercion of sovereign States by the Federal Government, if they desire to decide definitely and authoritatively on their own relations to the sections or to the Government, they should be in the only position which can enable them to speak each for herself as a sovereign community.

But there is now danger of a sudden collision all over the South. There is not a Southern State which may not be called on suddenly to play a part in a scene in which all the physical resources it can command will be necessary. We think it highly important that each State should have a strong internal State organization. That the people in each county should be prepared to call at once into action a strong force, capable of acting either as a police, or forming the nucleus of armed force to support the State authority and to maintain its independence.

109. THE UNION-SAVING COMMITTEE

(*New Orleans Daily Crescent*, December 11, 1860)

Mr. Speaker Pennington, of the House of Representatives, has appointed the Union-saving Committee of thirty-three—one from each State—as provided for by the resolution of Mr. Boteler of Virginia, and their names are announced to the public.[1] This committee, ostensibly, is "to consider questions connected with the perilous condition of the country." This is the object of the movement, as it appears upon the surface. The *real* object is to patch up a sort of compromise or adjustment, with a view of luring the South back into a Union which she has firmly made up her mind to abandon. It is, in short, a Union-saving expedient, a dodge, a plot set on foot to entrap the

[1] Boteler's resolution was adopted on the second day of the session by a vote of 145 to 38. The Committee included four members who had voted against it: Tappan of New Hampshire, Morse of Maine, Howard of Michigan, and Washburne of Wisconsin. Ohio gave ten of the thirty-eight votes against the Committee, and Corwin of that State was made Chairman. The Committee was composed of sixteen Republicans, ten Douglas Democrats, two Constitutional Unionists, and five Breckinridge Democrats, of whom Hawkins of Florida and Boyce of South Carolina refused to serve. The Journal of Proceedings and the several Reports from the Special Committee may be found in *House Reports*, 36 Cong., 2 Sess., I, Rpt. 31.

South once more into submission, which is but another name for dishonor and disgrace. Such, we know, was not the motive which prompted Mr. Boteler to move the resolution—but that such would be its effect, if Southern Representatives had not made up their minds to have nothing to do with it, we have not the shadow of a doubt.

When we say "Southern Representatives" we mean those who represent the sentiment of the South—a sentiment almost unanimous for withdrawal. There are members upon this committee who have been chosen by Southern constituencies—but they are not representatives of Southern sentiment, if, for any reason, they yield one jot or tittle to the demands of Northern fanaticism, on the miserable pretext of "saving the Union."

Look at the names upon the committee. Whom has the Speaker selected: Millson, of Virginia, an avowed Union man; Davis, of Maryland—a Union-at-any-price man, and a semi-Black Republican; Winslow of North Carolina, an easy-going old gentleman, with no decided political tendencies, one way or another; Boyce, of South Carolina—less of a disunionist, perhaps, than any of his delegation; Nelson, of Tennessee, who made, at the last session, a regular spread-eagle, Fourth of July speech, circulated at the North by thousands, as evidence of Southern sentiment; Houston, of Alabama, Taylor, of Louisiana, Rust, of Arkansas, Phelps, of Missouri, and Hamilton,[2] of Texas—all supporters of Douglas at the last election. The friends of Breckinridge have no representatives upon the committee, except from States like Florida, Mississippi, etc., where no other sort of a man could be found. The Bell men are graciously accorded two representatives only.

Without any disrespect to those gentlemen, we may ask if anybody believes that Mr. Hamilton, of Texas, and Mr. Taylor, of Louisiana, represent the predominant public sentiment of these two States? [3] If they are for unconditional submission—if they are for compromise even—they do not correctly represent the people. Mr. Pennington, obviously, has framed the committee with a view to a Union-saving report. It was for this reason, no doubt, that Mr. Hawkins, of Florida—

---

[2] John Smith Phelps and Andrew J. Hamilton remained loyal to the Union and were appointed military governors of Arkansas and Texas, respectively. Thomas Nelson also remained in Congress after Tennessee seceded, but was captured and imprisoned by the authorities of the Confederacy.

[3] Miles Taylor was Chairman of the Douglas Democratic National Campaign Committee and had coined the slogan, "Thank God no disunionists support Stephen A. Douglas." Louisiana gave the following vote in the election: Douglas 7,625, Breckinridge 22,681, and Bell 20,204; Texas gave to Breckinridge 47,548 and to Bell 15,438.

who, being the only representative of that State, was obliged to be chosen—asked to be excused from a service for which, he foresaw, he would have no heart. And when the report is made, it will appear for what precise object the committee was framed, even if there be a doubt of it at present.

The whole thing will come to nothing. The day for compromises is gone. The experiment, however, will be harmless, and therefore let them go ahead. As well attempt to bring to life an Egyptian mummy, thousands of years dead, as to restore the Union upon its former foundations. The soul of the Union is dead, and now let its body be buried.

110. The Congressional Committee

(*The Daily True Delta,* New Orleans, December 13, 1860)

The disunionists are very much distressed because, in the appointment of the national congressional committee, several well-known, faithful, able, fearless and independent supporters of national democracy and genuine state-rights were selected over rampant disunionists, or the time-serving tools of conspiring demagogues. The names of Houston, of Alabama; Hamilton, of Texas; Miles Tayor, of Louisiana; Rust, of Arkansas, sound unwelcomely and harshly upon the ears of the enemies of the Union, and the hirelings of the traffickers in treason, without the remotest intention of sharing its risks, are, of course, loud in their censures and fluent in their impotent abuse of them. It may be asked what can the congressional committee as constituted, or however constituted, do in the present condition of the states? Can it compel the traitors in the free states to respect the laws and their constitutional duties? Can it make the abolition fanatics of to-day, or the Caleb Cushings, and Biglers, and Dixes and Van Burens, and others of similar kidney of the past, repent of the evil they have done, retrace their dishonorable and perfidious courses, and study in the future better how to respect their allegiance to the government, their duty to the confederacy, and their oaths to the constitution? Can it substitute common sense, sound views and veritable patriotism for the schemes of demagogues, the plots of factionists and the pretences of pseudo patriots? And if none of these things can be reached and attained by it, of what use is it, and how can such true southern men as Rust, Taylor, Houston and Hamilton benefit their country by sharing its work and dividing its labors? In answer to these, and all such objections, we respond, that at no past period was there ever presented to the faithful supporters and defenders of republican government so favorable an opportunity for admonishing bad men of their misdeeds, suggesting their corrective and indicating the mode, the manner and the time of doing it; and at the same time, also, to establish the folly, the futility, aye, the insanity of seeking in a dissolution of the government, an efficient remedy for southern grievances.

The selection of the four gentlemen named above as members of the committee of Congress is an indication upon the part of the black republican majority of the House of Representatives that they are at last brought to bay, and that they will no longer be tolerated either in Washington, or in their respective states in their infamous work of violating the laws and subverting the constitution. We know Mr. Taylor's views upon the issue now dividing the nation; we know how earnestly, sincerely and steadily he deplored the infidelity of the present administration and its predecessor to the plainest dictates of duty, to the obvious requirements of their obligations as servants of the people in their persistent declination of the issue presented by the abolitionists in their habitually wicked and treasonable opposition to the enforcement of the fugitive slave law. He deplored Buchanan's cowardice, and like all good men mourned the degeneracy of the times when two administrations—both under the complete control of men boasting extreme devotion to southern rights, duty and honor—disgracefully allowed the laws to be violated and defied, and their officers trampled upon and maltreated; as if, instead of bringing the authors of the treason to justice, they encouraged outrage with the purpose and design at some subsequent period of making their own infidelity to duty the principal pretext for the destruction of the government they had sworn to uphold and were honored and paid to maintain in all its integrity. Miles Taylor would not then, any more than now, counsel a withdrawal from a Union by those states which had committed no crime against its sovereignty, its authority and its laws; on the contrary, he would invoke the whole power of the confederacy to crush abolition, sedition and treason, and if there had to be secession he would make the commonwealths that had erred through perversity, obstinacy or prepense disloyalty, withdraw.—Miles Taylor, no more than any other upright, independent and conscientious man, can see why the South should abandon its just claims to its equal share of the national domain and other national property, merely because the Cushings of Massachusetts, the Van Burens of New York, the Biglers of Pennsylvania, or the Brights of Indiana, and other similar demagogues and tricksters of free states, have prostituted legislation in these places to the injury of the south, the defiance of the laws and the disregard of the constitution. He, on the contrary, would employ the whole force of this united government if necessary, to enforce the laws in these and all other states; and if by so doing Massachusetts or others deemed themselves aggrieved, they might withdraw in welcome. Mr. Taylor claims for his section all that her fidelity and devotion to the federal pact entitles her to demand and exact; but he will never, we are confident, be found supporting propositions for state secession at a wanton sacrifice of all the interests, material and moral, we of the south have, in the perpetuation of its institutions, ever faithfully labored to uphold, strengthen and perpetuate. If the fanatical states of treason-breeding New England, if Pennsylvania, Ohio and others of the middle and western states persist in disregarding and violating their constitutional duties, Miles Taylor would invoke the whole power of the republic to coerce them, at no matter what cost of blood and treasure, into respect for their duties; and if then they should still remain contumacious and rebellious, and dissolution of the Union was the only remedy for the incurable vices of those states, he would expel them, not withdraw ourselves from the Union. In this the faithful and able representative of the 2d congressional district of Louisiana differs from the brawling herd of place-hunters and the numerous brood of demagogues who seem to fancy themselves will be all great and powerful upon the ruins of their country; for Mr. Taylor has no desire for office and required the most powerful appeals of his constituents to allow himself to be elected to his present most responsible position in the great emergencies of these times. He does honor to Louisiana, and as a member of the congressional committee will not disappoint the hopes of the south.

III. The Policy of Aggression

(*New Orleans Daily Crescent,* December 14, 1860)

It is a mistake to suppose that it is the mere election of Lincoln, without regard to anything else, that has driven the States of the South into their present position of resistance, and their present determination to seek that safety and security out of the Union which they have been unable to obtain within it. The election of Lincoln is merely the confirmation of a purpose which the South had hoped would be abandoned by the opponents of slavery in the North. It is a declaration that they mean to carry out their aggressive and destructive policy, weakening the institution at every point where it can be assailed either by legislation or by violence, until, in the brutal language of Charles Sumner, "it dies like a poisoned rat in its hole." The election of Lincoln seals this purpose—pledges the party anew to it—reiterates the intention of the party to destroy slavery, if not boldly, at least by indirect and slow approaches; and, in short, is not so much an act of outrage itself as in the policy which it foreshadows, and the evil omen it brings to the South touching her future prosperity and security.

The New York Tribune, therefore, and other journals, which charge that we are like the people of South America and Mexico, who attempt to overturn the Government every time they are beaten in an election, misrepresent the true facts of the case. It is *not* because we have been beaten in the election that we are for resistance. But it is because self-defense, which is the first law of nature, no less than a just spirit of resentment towards a party which, in its sectional organization, is violative of the spirit of the Constitution, require that we should prepare for resistance before, by submission, the shackles will be so firmly bound upon us that we can never remove them.

That we do not misrepresent the purposes of this Republican Party in the future, let the following extract from one of its leading organs, the New York Independent, amply attest:

Let no opponent of slavery imagine that this is a time to rest from his labors. The Republican triumph, while it is an effective blow to the slave-power that has so long domineered at Washington, falls far short of the demolition of slavery. The gigantic iniquity still stands; hostile to the spirit of the Constitution and the known policy of its framers; hostile to the whole genius of our free institutions; hostile to every principle and precept of Christianity; an organized, unmitigated system of wickedness; but nevertheless *organized* by the laws of Southern States, and upheld, in face of the Christian sentiment of the age, by political, financial and commercial interests both at the South and at the North. While that SYSTEM stands, we cannot let it alone.

Here we have a distinct declaration that the work of the party is just begun—that this is not the time for them to "rest from their labors"—that the "demolition of slavery" is not yet accomplished, and the mission of the party is to produce that result. There can be no mistaking the language of this leading, widely-circulated and influential organ of the Abolition party. Whatever Corwin [1] and other so-called "conservatives" may say, there is not the shadow of a doubt that the policy of the party will be bold and aggressive. It cannot stop where it is without falling to pieces. If it hesitates it dies. Organized upon a sentiment of hostility to slavery, and for the purpose of accomplishing its destruction, the moment it recedes from its position it loses the confidence of its supporters, and perishes forever. This is well known to its leaders, and hence the doctrine of the irrepressible conflict. This party, odious as it is in its principles, would excite the contempt even of the South if it abandoned those principles at the very moment of victory, unless they were abandoned from patriotic impulses—and this we cannot expect from an organization which illustrates its "patriotism" by openly organizing a crusade against the people, the property, the rights and the honor of one-half of the confederacy.

When, therefore, the Independent says that the party *"cannot* let slavery alone," it means simply that it *will* not let it alone—that it does not intend to let it alone—that its object is to labor for its "demolition"—that it is a "gigantic iniquity" which must be removed from the nation. Where they cannot atack it in the States they will attack it at every other point they can reach. They will set fire to all the surrounding buildings in the hope that some spark may catch, and everything be destroyed in a general conflagration. They will undermine the pillars of the institution, and then wait quietly for the whole edifice to tumble. We know that there are many of this party who have no such purpose—who would shrink from the consequences of their own acts could they clearly foresee them. But they do not represent the spirit of the party—its animus, and its soul. The leaders have not only proclaimed their present and their ultimate objects, but they are gradually educating the people up to their own designs. Many will turn back appalled when they discover the true state of the case; but when hatred of slavery becomes, as it is now fast becoming, a part of the religion of the Northern people, we can look for no other result than perpetual war upon it, looking, in the language of the Independent, to its eventual "demolition."

It is the consciousness of this fact, and not the mere, naked election

---

[1] Ex-Governor and United States Senator from Ohio, Secretary of the Treasury under Fillmore. Corwin was hated in the South because of his bitter opposition to the Mexican War.

of Lincoln to the Presidency, which has caused the South to assume her present attitude. If we were to make war upon any social institution of the North, and attempt to destroy it under the forms of law even, and the North should fail to resist, they would be justly taunted as cowards and cravens. If it were an institution possessing a money value, it would make the case even worse for them. How they can complain of the South for doing precisely what they would themselves do if our positions were reversed, is something yet to be explained— but, complain or not, the fiat has gone forth; and the South, having had fair warning that she is to be subjugated, dishonored, and robbed *within* the Union, has no remedy left except to place herself beyond the reach of that Union which is to be used for such unholy purposes.

112. Vain Hopes

(*The New Orleans Bee,* December 14, 1860)

The political charlatans of the North and the patriotic but mistaken public men of the border slave States appear to outvie each other in efforts to discover a remedy for existing evils. They do not perceive that the wound inflicted by the North upon the South is essentially incurable. They think, on the contrary, it may be plastered, and bandaged, and dressed in some sort of fashion and will do very well. The Union is broken in two, but the political doctors fancy that the ruptured extremities can be readily brought together, and that by the aid of the world-renowned "compromise" machine, the integrity of the fractured parts may be completely restored. Without further figure of speech, let us say that we hardly know whether to smile or sigh over the innumerable devices resorted to by members of Congress to save the Union. With just about as much hope of success might they expect to breathe life into a corpse, or look for green leaves, bright flowers, and savory fruit from the blackened and withered trunk of a blasted tree, as imagine that the Union may yet be preserved. This *might* have been done a few months ago. The Union might have received a new lease of life, had the Abolition party been overwhelmingly defeated in the recent contest; but after its signal triumph to seek to bolster up the Union is as fruitless a task as would be the attempt to teach Garrison moderation, Sumner national patriotism, and Wilson the feelings and instincts of a gentleman.

And yet Northern and semi-Southern Congressmen persevere in their well-meant, but useless exertions. One thinks the Union may be saved by incorporating certain amendments in the Constitution, forgetting the impracticability of obtaining the consent of two-thirds of Congress, and the subsequent acquiescence of three-fourths of the State Legislatures. Another proposes the reapplication of the Missouri Compromise line, together with a new provision formally recognizing the right of Southern men to carry their property into the Territories, and to be entitled to protection. A third thinks the object aimed at would be accomplished by banishing the slavery question from Congress—as if the legislative department of the Government could be compelled to confine free discussion to particular subjects, and to exclude others from the wide range of debate. A fourth insists upon a reference of the entire topic to a special committee consisting of one member from each State, and indulges in the chimerical expectation that the members will agree upon some acceptable mode of arrangement. A fifth plainly and honestly confesses that he sees no immediate method of settling the difficulty, but hopes that delay may cool public sentiment at the South, and perhaps effect a radical change.

The inutility of these various plans is sufficiently obvious in the South, though they may seem invested with a certain measure of plausibility to those who propose them. There are two insurmountable obstacles to any theory of compromise with a view of effecting a reconciliation. These are, first, the unwillingness of the North to concede any thing substantial, and secondly, the determination of the South to carry out its policy of a separate nationality. Nothing can be more certain than that the dominant party in the country, viz: The Black Republican—will take no step backwards. A few of their organs, terrified at the prospect of a dissolution of the Union, have talked timidly of repealing Personal [Liberty] bills, and of offering guarantees of future respect for Southern rights, but nothing has been achieved. In the Vermont Legislature an attempt was made to repeal the Personal Liberty act of that State, but the bill to that effect was rejected by a vote of two to one—the Legislature, for the sake of appearances, referring the subject to a committee of investigation prior to adjournment. Meanwhile, a considerable number of Black Republican sheets have openly declared that the policy of the party shall suffer no change, and that its avowed principle of regarding and treating slavery as a sectional institution to which a majority of the people are opposed, shall be steadfastly maintained. This is the prevailing sentiment of the Northern anti-slavery men, and even admitting that there are among them persons disposed to treat the South with some degree of consideration, it is manifest that their influence would be totally unavailing with the mass of the party, and that no recognition of our rights which the South could for a moment entertain will ever be extorted from the faction which has elected ABRAHAM LINCOLN.

But the grand, overwhelming objection to these feeble and fruitless projects is the absolute impossibility of revolutionizing Northern opinion in relation to slavery. Without a change of heart, radical and thorough, all guarantees which might be offered are not worth the paper on which they would be inscribed. As long as slavery is looked upon by the North with abhorrence; as long as the South is regarded as a mere slave-breeding and slave-driving community; as long as false and pernicious theories are cherished respecting the inherent equality and rights of every human being, there can be no satisfactory political union between the two sections. If one-half the people believe the other half to be deeply dyed in iniquity; to be daily and hourly in the perpetration of the most atrocious moral offense, and at the same time knowing them to be their countrymen and fellow-citizens, conceive themselves authorized and in some sort constrained to lecture them, to abuse them, to employ all possible means to break up their institutions, and to take from them what the Northern half consider property unrighteously held, or no property at all, how can two such antagonistic nationalities dwell together in fraternal concord under the same government? Is not the thing clearly impossible? Has not the experiment been tried for more than seventy years, and have not the final results demonstrated its failure? The feelings, customs, mode of thought and education of the two sections, are discrepant and often antagonistic. The North and South are heterogeneous and are better apart. Were we foreign to the North, that section would treat us as our Government now treats Mexico or England—abstaining from interference in the internal policy of a country with which we have nothing to do, and with which we are at peace. As it is, we are persuaded that while the South continues a part of the American confederacy, there is no power which can prevent her progressive degradation, humiliation and spoliation by the victorious North. We are doomed if we proclaim not our political independence.

113. PUBLIC SENTIMENT

(*The New Orleans Bee,* December 17, 1860)

It may and doubtless must appear singular to many persons that so extraordinary and rapid a change of sentiment in regard to the Union should have taken place in a city as proverbial for its staunch nationality as was wont to be New Orleans. But we here have simply been subjected to the same wonderful process of transformation which is visible all over the South. If prior to the election of Lincoln the majority of our citizens were warmly attached to the Union, and believed sincerely that a Black Republican triumph would not justify a separation of the States, it was because they could not possibly imagine that such an event would be followed by a violent and almost unparalleled revolution in public opinion. The result of the contest of the 6th November was scarcely made [known] ere thousands of citizens who had previously proclaimed themselves conservatives hastened to rally under the standard of Secession, while prominent among them were men who, a few days previous, had been uncompromising advocates of the "Constitution, the Union and the Enforcement of the Laws." It was evident, indeed, that amid all the lip service professed for the Union, there had dwelt in the hearts of Southerners a tacit determination to regard the election of LINCOLN as proof of a settled and immutable policy of hostility and aggression by the North towards the South, and to refuse further political affiliation with those who by that act should declare themselves our enemies. In no other way can we account for the perfect whirlwind of public feeling which swept everything before it, either utterly annihilating conservatism and nationality, or reducing to impotence the few who still ventured to make a timid appeal in behalf of the Union.

We ourselves were slow to give away. For very many years we had been attached to a party which had ever claimed the proud distinction of sustaining the Union and the Constitution. We knew that popular opinion in Louisiana had been invariably against schemes of secession and ultra State Rights doctrines, and in all honesty we were far from anticipating the terrific explosion which succeeded the announcement of LINCOLN's success. We thought for a while that the perturbation of the political elements would gradually subside, and that the voice of calm reason and friendly expostulation would again be heard. We underestimated the strength of Southern feeling, and the irresistible excitement produced by the conviction of the hatred of the South by the North. In times like these men are more apt to be guided by emotion than by unimpassioned logic. They behold the evil nearing them; they see it advancing with gigantic strides, and they naturally and instinctively look around for the swiftest and surest means of repelling its approach. The secession movement which sprung up in Louisiana almost simultaneously with the vibration of the telegraphic wires as they flashed upon us the catastrophe of the first Tuesday in November, grew too fast from the gristle of infancy to the firmness and well knit proportions of manhood, to warrant the faintest hope of retarding its progress. We became satisfied of the impossibility of turning back the overpowering tide of resistance. All that could be done by moderate, dispassionate, patriotic and experienced men was to go with the current, endeavoring to subdue its boiling and seething energies, and direct it into channels where it might flow without danger of inundation and mischief.

At this period it is entirely safe to declare that there exists no Union party in Louisiana, and that New Orleans, formerly the most conservative portion of the State, is now the hot-bed of Secession. Doubtless there are thousands amongst us who, with that lingering love of country which, even when she proves a heartless stepmother, becomes a noble infirmity, to be viewed with sympathy instead of censure, regard the existing crisis with extreme solicitude and painful apprehension, and anticipate the final separation of the North and South with feelings akin to those they would experience at witnessing some crushing national calamity. We are not free from emotions assimilating these, and which, in spite of our better judgment, fill our hearts with regret at the prospect of disunion. But we are satisfied that there is scarcely a hope of a remedy. The South has assumed a position from which she cannot and will not recede. It is universally acknowledged even by the few who still profess to care for the Union, that the sole hope of its preservation is based upon the possibility of securing from the North the most ample and satisfactory guarantees of future safety and equality. Now there is no impartial citizen who pays any attention to the general tone and temper of the Northern exponents of public sentiment but must perceive that, with isolated and inconsiderable exceptions, the Northern people have no idea whatsoever of making any material concessions to the South. Many of their statesmen are unwilling or incompetent to appreciate the proximity of disunion; and those of them who are better informed are either indisposed to redress our grievances, or proffer mere palliatives and temporizing expedients, such as are unworthy even of consideration. Under these circumstances it may be easily understood how the former lovers of the Union now despair of its preservation. All they can do, and all indeed for which they are striving, is concert of action between the several States of the South; so that, if possible, we may not wander away, each like a flying meteor, from the central sphere, without settled aim or object, but may unite our strength and influence, and organize ourselves into a political Confederation possessing power, prodigality of resources, and dignity of position in the eyes of the world. Whether this or the theory of separate action be deemed most expedient, we hold the advocates of both to be equally honest and sincere, and that the question should be argued in neither a captious nor a dogmatic and dictatorial spirit.

114. AN EVENTFUL DAY

(*New Orleans Daily Crescent,* December 17, 1860)

To-day will be an eventful day in the history of this nation. To-day the Convention of South Carolina will meet, a Convention assembled but for one single purpose—that of declaring South Carolina no longer one of the States of the Union. That such will be her action some-time during the present week, we are not permitted to entertain a shadow of doubt.

Thus, then, one of the pillars which sustains the national edifice is about to be removed, to be quickly followed by others. South Carolina only precedes, by a few weeks, five or six of her former sisters in the Confederacy. What South Carolina does to-day will be done, very soon, by every one of the Gulf States, and eventually, in all probability, by every Southern State.

What makes the circumstance more significant is the fact that the State which to-day makes her preparations to leave the Union is one of the original thirteen. She was one of those which helped to form the Union, when the Union was first devised. Naturally, she would be regarded as more attached to it than a State subsequently admitted. She does not leave the Union now because she is any the less attached to the Union which our fathers made than she was in the beginning. It is because the present Union is *not* the Union that our fathers made. It is because the Union has been perverted from its original purposes—because it has become an engine of oppression, in-

stead of a dispenser of blessings—because it is a Union of force instead of one of friendship and love. It is for this that South Carolina
determines to seek that safety and security and peace outside of the
Union, which she has vainly attempted to obtain within it. It is appropriate, then, that the first State to leave should be one which was
an original party to the compact—that the lead of her Southern sisters
should be taken by a Commonwealth which was also one of the
leaders in the formation of the original Union.

From thirteen States, comparatively small in population and weak
in resources, we have grown in less than a century to be a nation of
thirty-three States, extending from the Lakes of the North to the
Southern Gulf, and from one ocean to the other, across the whole
North American Continent. We have become a great nation; and we
had the prospect, under a peaceful and just Government, of becoming
one of the greatest, if not the very greatest, upon the face of the globe.
That these prospects should have to be given up is something which
no patriotic American can think of without a feeling of sadness and
sorrow—but that they will be given up, firmly and unflinchingly,
there remains not a vestige of doubt. The Southern people, driven
to the wall, have no remedy but that of political independence. Forbearance has not only ceased to be a virtue, but has become absolute
cowardice. And that forbearance has even been interpreted as cowardice by the very people for whose sake we have so long forborne.

The nation, indeed, may have grown too fast. It may have become,
too suddenly, one of the great powers of the earth. In the physical
world, that which soonest reaches maturity soonest decays. Our free
institutions, our broad and smiling land, our great natural advantages,
have made a mighty nation of us too soon, perhaps. Less than a century is a short life, even for a Republic. But the causes that underlie
the destruction of all Governments—the discontent, and the reluctant
obedience and loyalty of large masses of the people—have been operating among us for many years. From the time that the central Government of all the States began to usurp powers not delegated to it in
the common bond of the Constitution—legislating for the benefit of
classes and sections, and the consequent oppression and injury of the
rest—taking upon itself the supervision of the respective States as to
their domestic institutions—claiming all powers that the most latitu-
dinous construction of the Constitution could suggest—from this time
the seeds of dissolution and decay were planted. And their first fruits
we shall to-day see in a State which was one of the battle-fields of the

Revolution, and which is as determined now to resist tyranny at home as she was to repel the tyranny which came across the ocean when we were colonies of Great Britain. The sort of liberty which South Carolina wants, she helped to wrest from the mother country, and is equally ready to wrest from the oppressor at home.

The events of this week, then, will satisfy those at the North who have been blind to Southern sentiment how great an error they have made. They thought at first that South Carolina was blustering, and would soon get over her sacred passion. After a while they concluded that South Carolina was in earnest—but that she would be solitary and alone in leaving the Union. Presently they discovered that the same causes which impelled one Southern State to withdraw were operating in all of them. And when popular manifestations, legislative assemblies, the public press and the voices of leading statesmen, told them that the Southern States had a cause, and that while one only might lead, others would eagerly follow, the North then awoke from her dream, and the whole truth now flashes upon them. Commissioners may be sent to the South—as New York city proposes—men like Fillmore and Bronson, whom the South loves and respects—but it is too late. The North had fair warning before the election. The evil cannot be repaired now that the warning has been unheeded, and the threat of Northern domination insolently flung in our faces. Louisiana, in common with the other Gulf States, to-day sends greeting to her Palmetto sister, and will be but little behind her in the new struggle for political equality and independence which our manhood and our honor compel us to make.

115. Are We Ready for Revolution?

(*Republican Banner,* Nashville, December 18, 1860)

The Revolutionists assume that the general Government is, as they assert, a contract, and as some of the parties to that contract have violated or disregarded some of its obligations, the other parties to it have the right to regard the contract as at an end, and the Government established by it as dissolved. Thirty-three men own as many houses, inhabited by themselves, their wives, their children, and their servants. These thirty-three houses were built by their respective fathers, and are enclosed by the same common outward walls, and covered by the same roof. The demolition of any one of them will involve the destruction of all of them, by destroying the common outward walls, and the common roof, and will bring distress and suffering upon the owners and inhabitants of all. What would be thought of the moral conduct of the owner of any one of these houses, who should insist upon his right to pull down his own house, and thereby endanger the safety of all the other houses, and bring ruin and misery on the owners and inmates of all the others, upon the ground that the contract under which his father and the father's of the other owners had erected them, had, by the owners of some of the houses, been violated? To be sure he might urge that the house was his own, and he had the right either to let it stand or pull it down, as his own judgment should dictate. Would not the owners of the other thirty-two houses have the right to answer him, that right, reason and sound morals required him so to use his own house as not to inflict an injury upon them, and if he persisted in the demolition of his own house, and thereby brought ruin and misery upon the others, their wives, children and servants, would he not be guilty of the perpetration of a great wrong against them? If the owners of the other fourteen houses, standing immediately adjoining his, had always been his friends—had never violated or disregarded the contract of their fathers—and were greater sufferers from the alledged violation of the contract by others than he was, and if the demolition by him of his house would injure them and theirs as much or more than the alledged violations of the contract, would not the moral wrong to those fourteen be greatly aggravated? Would it not be, indeed, without palliation? And if he had refused to hold any conference or consultation with those owners who had suffered as much or more than himself, before he proceeded to his act of destruction, would not insult be added to the great moral wrong he inflicted upon them? Yet, that is exactly what South Carolina proposes to do, with the exception that it is a Government with which are bound up the destinies of thirty-three States, and the lives, liberties, property, business, prosperity and happiness and religion of thirty-one million of men, women and children, instead of a house, which she means to destroy. All right and morals, all reason and justice, all laws and constitutions, condemn the act. "Society is, indeed," said Burke, "a contract." Subordinate contracts for objects of mere ocasional interest may be dissolved at pleasure. But the State ought not to be considered as nothing better than a partnership agreement in a trade of pepper and coffee, calico or tobacco, or some other such low concern, to be taken up for a little temporary interest, and to be dissolved by the fancy of the parties. It is to be looked on with other reverence, because it is

not a partnership in things subservient only to the gross animal existence, of a temporary and perishable nature. It is a partnership in all
science; a partnership in all art; a partnership in every virtue, and in
all perfection. As the ends of such a partnership cannot be obtained
in many generations, it becomes a partnership not only between those
who are living, but between those who are dead and those who are
to be born. Each contract of each particular state is but a clause in
the great primeval contract of eternal society, linking the lower with
the higher natures, connecting the visible and invisible world, according to a fixed compact, sanctioned by the inviolable oath, which holds
all physical and all moral natures, each in their appointed place. This
law is not subject to the will of those, who, by an obligation above
them, and infinitely superior, are bound to submit their will to that
law. The municipal corporations of that universal kingdom are not
morally at liberty, at their pleasure, and on their speculations of a
contingent improvement, wholly to separate and tear assunder the
bands of their subordinate community, and to dissolve it into an un-
social, uncivil, unconnected chaos of elementary principles. It is the
first and supreme necessity only—a necessity that is not chosen, but
chooses; a necessity paramount to deliberation, that admits no discussion, and demands no evidence—which alone can justify a resort
to anarchy. This necessity is no exception to the rule; because this necessity itself is a part, too, of that moral and physical disposition of
things to which man must be obedient by consent or force. But, if that
which is only submission to necessity should be made the object of
choice, the law is broken, nature is disobeyed, and the rebellious are
outlawed, cast forth, and exiled from this world of reason, and order,
and peace, and virtue, and fruitful penitence, into the antagonistic
world of madness, discord, vice, confusion, and unavailing sorrow.
The first of the Revolutionary earthquake has shaken the country
from the Atlantic to the Pacific—from the Lakes to the Gulf—from
its centre to its circumference—destroyed all confidence and credit—
closed the vaults of most of the Banks—depreciated the value of the
stocks of the general Government some ten per cent., and of State
securities some twenty per cent.—reduced the values of slaves in some
parts of the South at least one-fifth, and all other property in a greater
or less degree—paralyzed all business and deprived the producers of
their usual ready market for their products. What will be the effect
of the inward march of the revolution over Government, general and
State? And who is responsible for all these evils, and yet greater evils

to come? The Abolition parsons of New England and their deluded followers, there and elsewhere in the North, and the revolutionary leaders of South Carolina, and their disciples elsewhere, who have, for thirty years, schemed and labored for the disruption of the government of the Union.

116. NEGOTIATION—NOT LEGISLATION

(Richmond Enquirer, December 18, 1860)

The troubles which prevail at present, involving the continuance of the Union and the peace of the country, belong not to the province of legislation and are not to be a[l]leviated by any emo[l]lients that Congress and its committees can contrive.

A vicious public sentiment has poisoned Congress as well as Northern society, and no remedy which does not reach the great producing cause, can be expected to furnish any relief whatever. We have never expected Congress or its Crisis Committee to restore peace. The most that Congress can do is the passage of Union resolutions, what Carlyle would call "beautifullest sheet-lightning," but no thunder-bolt to rive and split the upas tree of fanatacism.

Negotiation, and not legislation, alone can restore peace; the States, as parties to the Constitution, must be brought into direct negotiation, with the ultimatum of separation distinctly and unmistakably tendered by South Carolina, as an earnest of what will certainly result from a failure of pacific negotiations. The effort to refer the matter to Federal Legislation, is a cunningly devised resort to preserve the form of the Government, which all men see has already, to all intents and purposes, gone to pieces; it is an effort to preserve an organized power, to attempt coercion in the name of the Federal Government, but really on behalf of the Northern States; it is an attempt to involve all men at the North in the conflict that must soon convulse the country, and to array the Northern conservatives against the Southern States, by holding up the form of the Federal Government, as the object to which each citizen owes allegiance, in a conflict with a revolting State. Hence, all coercionists are looking to Congress for relief, hoping to maintain a power which shall combine all the Northern States against any seceding State. In this they will find themselves disappointed. Individuals throughout the North have for several weeks been in decided opposition to any attempt at coercion; they have, in many cases, tendered their aid and services to South Carolina in anticipation of any attempt at subjugation. The North is divided, and will become the scene of civil war should their mad folly induce them to attempt an assault upon any State.

Legislation might as well, then, abandon all efforts at the restoration of peace. The cause of quarrel is beyond its province and cannot be reached by any of its remedies. The most that Congress can do is to provide quickly for bringing the States into direct communication with each other. Congress should second the efforts of the President to preserve the peace, by immediately taking such steps as may be necessary to hand over to the authorities of the seceding States the forts, &c., that may be situated within their limits. There is hope as long as the peace is preserved. And had the President precipitated a collision by attempting to strengthen Fort Moultrie, he would have been held directly responsible before man and God for involving his country in the horrors of civil war. He has acted wisely and prudently, and if peace cannot be preserved except by abandoning the forts at Charleston, the President had far better issue orders to the commanding officer to deliver up the forts rather than have them taken by assault and the country involved in civil war.

This matter comes home to Virginia, in the disposition of Fortress Monroe. Shall the fortress remain in the hands of our enemies?—a depot for troops, arms and munitions of war for the subjugation of the people of Virginia. These are questions which to the people of Virginia are becoming more and more important as the 4th of March approaches—and which we fear must be determined by a bloody conflict, unless the present administration shall preserve the peace by depriving the Federal Government of all power to attempt coercion. Should Mr. Buchanan deliver over to the States all the forts, &c., situated within them, thus depriving the Black Republicans of all means of provoking a conflict—the States will, by negotiation among themselves, adjust all differences, and final reunion may result from the negotiation. But to deliver over to Lincoln the defenses of the States is to offer to him opportunities of aggression, and to aid in producing civil war. It is the duty of every patriot to embarrass the new administration at every point; to deprive those who have produced the present state of affairs of all means to further involve the country in civil war. The inauguration should be prevented by Maryland, and, if necessary, Virginia should aid her. All financial aid should be withheld; the army and navy should be so distributed according to the birth place and predilections of officers, that the Federal Government, emasculated and shorn of power, may be unable to involve the country in civil war. The financial depression will be a sufficient incentive to the States to quietly harmonize and adjust matters; and, in restoring peace, the power of the Federal Government would be restored.

Negotiation should be commenced immediately, and by the *Northern States*. They should invite conference and provide for all the States uniting in consultation. If the Northern people really desire the preservation of the Union, let them move in this matter of negotiation; let them say to Mr. Lincoln, remain away from Washington city; you shall not precipitate civil war, by presenting yourself to an outraged people; remain at home until the States have restored peace by calm negotiation. And, if Mr. Lincoln should then attempt to be inaugurated, let the consequences be on his head and those of his friends who may come to witness the scene.

The States can alone remedy the evils that now threaten the country with ruin. If they will act promptly they may restore peace and union; but every day of delay, not only postpones peace, but tends to civil war.

117. Hopes Doomed to Disappointment

(*Richmond Semi-weekly Examiner,* December 18, 1860)

We have been much surprised at the varying expressions of hope and despair which we see in the newspapers on the reception of the daily news from Washington. If politicians, Presidents or Congressmen could have quelled the present popular agitation or quieted discontent, it would have been done long ago. The evil was aggravated by Congress, but was far above its control. The mischief rules the Northern power which rules Congress, and will rule the Government. The men who but await the 4th of March to seize on the power and gain the processes, to get which are the true sources of disturbances, are the men whose agency is the only means of giving even the delusive hopes of peace through the Government. To make even a pretended effort to satisfy the South, those men must dissolve their party, resist those from whom they hold their positions, and, in the face of the country, abandon at once the principles and objects of their organization. Their bond of Union, their weapons of defense, their tenure of political power and of social position, are all summed up in one intelligible, practical policy—*it is to make this Government an agent to repress and extinguish African slavery.* The men whose hopes and political existence are dependent upon a zealous and energetic support of this policy, are the men who must co-operate with slave-holders even to enable Congress to send forth the valueless indication of a disposition to attempt to devise the worthless deception of a possible legislative compromise of a difficulty which the sovereign popular authorities of the different States will find it difficult to cope with. And yet it is by the vague givings-out from members of Congress, who have no connection with this potent party, that the hopes and fears of men are raised and depressed.

Every reasoning man must see that hopes from Government action, so far as permanent quiet is concerned, are futile. The nature of the evil, the very constitution of Congress, forbid men to hope for a solution of these difficulties through that agent. The recent election settled the power of Government over the public disturbances. It has not now, and it will not have, the trust or respect of the men whose dangers and whose wrongs cause disquiet. But the action of Congress and the Executive have confirmed what reason and the election made sufficiently clear.

The Executive recommends to Congress and the people, as the sole means of satisfying the discontented and securing the endangered, remedies which Congress cannot grant, and which will, if granted by the Freesoil Legislatures of the North, put fetters on the people and representatives of the ruling party in that section.—Thus he sends the question before another tribunal, because the Government has not power to adjust it. But the action of Congress has been still more disheartening to those who hoped for peace through it. The first and only move came, most unhappily for the compromisers, from the endangered and assailed section.[1] What wanted Black Republicanism more to strengthen and confirm it in its purposes? Nothing. The cry for peace came in advance of the combat from the wronged and the endangered. The shout for mercy and justice came from Harper's Ferry, the scene of Black Republican atrocity, sent up to the endorsers of HELPER and the agents of JOHN BROWN's sympathizers. And how

---

[1] Boteler of Virginia introduced the resolution proposing the Committee of Thirty-three, Powell of Kentucky proposed the Committee of Thirteen, and Crittenden of Kentucky introduced the famous resolutions about which the whole effort at conciliation centered.

acted the stern, inflexible agents of anti-slavery on the proposition? They granted a committee to consider it, to be appointed by a member of their party; and he did the work admirably. Out of thirty-three, he appointed fifteen known anti-slavery men. When he came South he took men from that section at war with the sentiment and feeling of the discontented people; men, whenever he could get them, who thought, and acted on the idea that the South had no wrongs to complain of or apprehend—DAVIS, NELSON, MILLSON, &c.—who see no danger in Black Republican ascendency. And yet, it is on the action and words of this committee that men, otherwise rational, have been actually founding hopes.

Still another demonstration, more conclusive against looking towards the Federal Government with the least hope, has been given. In the Senate the Black Republican party has either made no move on this absorbing question,[2] or when it has, has but given indication of a firm adherence to its policy, and of resolve to enforce it even by arms. In the House of Representatives, the party has kept silence, refused to give the least sign of ruth or change of purpose. The South appears begging, entreating, craving the boon of justice and mercy; their inexorable foe pursues its ordinary avocations, goes on with the routine of business, and calmly awaits the hour when it shall wield the Government and inaugurate with authority and plenary power its declared policy.

There is nothing in these constant watchings and prayings over Congressional movements but shame, sorrow and humiliation for the South. Nothing can come from it but the bitterness of disappointment, rendered more torturing by the memory of the weakness which brought it on us. The Congress could not stop the meetings of the sovereign States; it cannot stop their action; it will now scarce have weight or consideration in the conventions of the South. The politicians in their sphere have failed. Power over the people's affairs and destiny has passed from them. The sovereign authority in this Confederation, long dormant, has been awakened.—Sovereignties will be in counsel in a few weeks. Their Federal agents may go on with their ordinary business. They have no control over what the sovereign States choose to do. Elements too powerful for them are at work. The people of the South will scarcely hear or read the proceedings of the Committee

---

[2] The Powell resolution creating the Committee of Thirteen was not approved by the Senate until December 18.

of Thirty-Three. If it choose to employ its time resolving or sitting, we suppose nobody will care.

118. Is There a Mode of Settlement?

(The Daily True Delta, New Orleans, December 18, 1860)

The question is perpetually put to us by correspondents whether, in our opinion, there is a possible way of extricating the country from the dangers in which it is involved by fanatical conspirators on one side, and disappointed and designing demagogues in combination with its chronic and consistent foes on the other; and if so, whether we think Congress will be able to accomplish it? Those who propound these questions entirely forget our persistent discrimination between the steadfast and consistent disunionists of South Carolina, Alabama and Mississippi, and such people as the Clingmans, the Iversons, the Fitzpatricks and the John Slidells, would lead in their train.[1] The former are sincere, frank, bold and resolved men, whatever many of the mere rampant and extravagant of their pseudo-leaders may be, and with them now, as heretofore, the destruction of this Union is, of all political catastrophes, that upon which their hearts are most firmly set. Until the present they were unfortunate in always finding opponents of their designs sufficiently powerful to defeat them in the administration of the government; but Buchanan and his surroundings encouraged, abetted, and perhaps, stimulated their disposition, and now, without apprehension of obstruction or hindrance from them, they will, we are sure, undertake to go out of the Union and set up for themselves. But Texas, which has taken advantage also of the opening Buchanan has provided for the destruction of the government he was sworn to uphold, is operated upon by very different feelings from those which animate South Carolina and those states which she leads, for, grievously disappointed at the poor results which followed to her from the merging of her independence in the federal Union, and animated by great expectations from European alliances which her public men fancy will enable her greatly to extend her present territorial limits—indeed, at once to prolong them to the Pacific, and as far on her south-western frontiers as may be desirable

[1] Clingman, Iverson, and Slidell were United States Senators from North Carolina, Georgia, and Louisiana, respectively. Fitzpatrick was the Ex-Governor of Alabama, who had refused the nomination for the vice-presidency on the Douglas ticket.

—she is now ready to cut adrift from a connection which has ceased to give her that assurance of future development and greatness she had been led to promise herself from its formation. Besides, Texas has every reason to expect from both England and France encouragement and support in the early annexation of Mexico, if not Central America also, to her present territory, so that by means of an unlimited supply of cheap labor from the east, which at small cost and with great safety, could then be transported across the Pacific, would enable her to compete in the yield of cotton and tropical productions with the southern states of our North America and the West Indian Islands besides.

We will not stop to examine the correctness of this view or these calculations; it will be sufficient for our present purpose to say that they are entertained and believed to be realisable by men of the most enlarged views and deep reflection in our sister state, although having very little in common with the considerations which animate the Wigfalls [2] and chance medley speculating politicians, who now float like foam on the wave of popular opinion among our neighboring brethren. From two sides, then, may we confidently consider the Union to be in imminent peril; namely, from the honest and determined disunionists we have alluded to as controlling Mississippi, Alabama, South Carolina, and from Texas, because of the brilliant future a disconnection from us so gorgeously presents. This is apparent to all. In view, then, of this exact condition of affairs, we do not see how a withdrawal of these states from the confederacy can possibly be prevented, least of all when the affairs of the general government are in control of men notoriously hostile to the Union, and the chief magistrate himself, with treasonable activity and zeal, is doing all in his power to facilitate it. Besides, we must continually bear in mind that the genuine secessionists aim at the dissolution of the Union not because of any actual wrong done them by the free states, for, as Iverson frankly stated, the cotton states are not affected by personal liberty bills or the enforcement of the fugitive slave law, those only hurt the border states, and they unanimously decline to accept a dissolution of the Union as the remedy for the wrongs to which they are subject and from which they suffer.

To reconcile, then, the states we have enumerated to a continuance in the Union, by any conciliatory proceeding of Congress, we frankly confess we consider almost impossible—save, perhaps, in the

[2] United States Senator from Texas.

event of the other slave states adopting a general scheme of settlement, and employing their whole power with them to induce them to accede to it. Nor does it appear to us an easy matter for Congress to undertake; for, apart from what we have stated as to the real intentions of the seceding states, it must be obvious to every one that save in the exclusion of the slave question from Congress, now and for all future time, and leaving it in the territories of the Union to be determined as those to be affected by it deem right and proper —nothing can be done. The fugitive slave law is a good and sufficient measure as far as it goes, as good as any new law that can be passed, and if it cannot be enforced by moral means neither can any compact looking to similar results ever command respect or its mandates obedience, in the absence of the employment of force to give it validity. This force it was the duty of President Buchanan and his immediate predecessor to have employed, even if the streets of Boston had been dyed in blood, or the fields of those states which defied the laws and violated the constitution had been crimsoned in the gore of their rebellious citizens. No compact will be binding in the absence of the needful power to enforce its stipulations; and that neither Pierce or Buchanan enforced the fugitive slave law, is proof either that they connived at the violation of the laws, or were aiming at the production of a state of affairs which would render a dissolution of the Union inevitable. Men determined to do wrong will not listen to justice or change their purposes by appeals to their reason, their interests, or their patriotism.

119. What Co-operation Is

(*The Daily Picayune,* New Orleans, December 20, 1860)

The movement effectually to protect the rights of the South begins to assume a definite shape, and the result of the steps taken are now distinctly visible in all parts of the Union.

Congress, though attempting to devise means for conciliation, is too slow to meet the wishes of the people, at least at the South, even if it be possible that any good result can be secured by its action. Whether, with the best intentions and the most liberal feelings, any propositions emanating from that body can now calm the storm and restore confidence, is very problematical, for the South is not willing, after so many mere temporary conciliations, again to trust to terms yielded under the pressure of necessity.

We have believed, and still believe, that constitutional amendments, rendering unnecessary platform definitions of Southern rights, or executive constructions of the constitution, would be the only terms upon which peace can be restored to the States, and the Union be preserved. The way to obtain this adjustment of present troubles is conceded to be difficult—nay, impossible—without a returning sense of justice at the North. A revolution is necessary there, in the public mind, such as has been produced at the South, to secure such a result—one which, through a love for the Union and an appreciation of the blessings about to be lost, will secure as decided a feeling of self-sacrifice as is now to be seen in the slave States.

For united Southern action we have persistently struggled, in order to precipitate this revolution in Northern sentiment and action, which a sense of immediate danger has set in motion in the South. It would be to disregard all facts, to deny that signs of that revolution in popular feeling are now visible, not alone in the great commercial centres, but in all quarters of the non-slaveholding States. Though it lack that thoroughness and irresistible character which may justly be deemed necessary to concede, as constitutional amendments, that upon which we may rely as a final settlement of all controversy, the fact that the commercial capitals are aroused to the degree to overwhelm all opposition, that States begin to question the friendliness and justice of their sectional legislation, and that the Government, which all revere, is admitted to be tottering to its foundations, are not to be ignored as indications of what may be possible when proposed action becomes a reality that is felt as well as feared.

To convince the North of the certainty that no patched up adjustments will now effect peace; to bring that number of States to act together, which shall solemnly proclaim not only a Union lost, but a government for all its States overthrown, unless the constitution itself be construed and made definite in its utterances in regard to the rights of the States and the relation of the institution of slavery to the General Government, the respective States and the Territories, is the object and aim of State coöperation.

We need not now allude to our grievances, nor endeavor to make out a case for resistance. The occasion of a sectional political triumph has been seized to bring the long contention to an issue; and it must be a final one. This is the feeling of the entire South, not alone of the Gulf States, the first to move though the least aggrieved. The border States express the same determination while they urge a pause, and entreat admission to our counsels; and we throw away the strength of the South while we expend zeal and labor only for separate State action.

United State action, or, in other words, coöperation of the Southern States with each other, is sought, not simply to acquire a more powerful influence on the Northern States, but for the protection of the South itself. If no concessions are obtained, and a withdrawal of the South, as many fully believe, becomes an inevitable necessity, the union of the South, once secured, saves us from the terrible convulsion which all revolutions inflict. It arrests the shock and panic which the disruption of civil relations and usual forms of administration, even when only threatened, produce. It restores confidence that we shall not, though we break away from the Union, be without a Union binding together the seceding States, or a Government like that from which we have withdrawn.

There is another consideration that is potent with those seeking State coöperation. Withdrawing separately from the present Union, the States leave behind them the public property, the national domain, and all common interests, the very objects to secure which we have risen in resistance to the sectional majority laying claim to undivided enjoyment. If the States, similar in institutions, necessarily subject to the same destiny, and willing to make a common cause with the cotton growing commonwealths, come together with one purpose, the line forming their northern border will be above all that territory which, from its climate, its soil and productions, is adapted to the extension of slavery. Our Western frontier will then outlie upon the North and the East of a large portion of this territory. It will be at the control of the united South, and we can scarcely fail to secure its occupation even if no division can be amicably effected. More than this, we absolutely carry with us not only a Southern confederacy, which will not be the work of time but will be effected by the very act of secession, but the District of Columbia, with all the millions of national property within its limits. Stop here a moment and observe the moral force of a united South and the invincible position it occupies. It holds the mouth of the Mississippi and has the keys to the commerce of the entire Mississippi and Ohio valley. It possesses the District of Columbia with the archives of the Government and all its offices and organization. It abuts upon Mexico on the east and north, with which it is in direct communication. It commands the navigation of the Gulf of Mexico, and holds the entrance into the territory of that distracted State. More than we demand in the Union, is thus already in the possession of a United South the instant a secession is consummated. Is not this worth a contest? Call you an effort to obtain this a submission? Why here is the only effective platform for resistance.

The question is not to save the Union; that is worth an effort before the last step be taken, and the South, united, is in a position to make herself heard and listened to with respect; but to secure to the slave States when secession comes if it be necessary, the objects for which the struggle commenced. It was for equal rights in the Territories the South determined to make a stand; not to abandon them; nor to submit to bold robbery by the North; and in carrying out the project of resistance, shall we by separate State action, by throwing off all connection with each other while allegiance to the General Government is withdrawn, give up all the rights we were to defend? Well may extreme factionists of the North look with complacency upon Southern secession that leaves them the seat of Government, the Treasury, the control of the navy and army, and the public domain uncontested. These are the positions taken by the friends of coöperation. There is no coöperation of the South sought with the view of acquiescing in the administration of Lincoln, or acquiring a hollow peace that may be broken as soon as the contest ceases. There is no trust in the reaction of Northern sentiment that shall only repeal personal liberty bills and annul hostile and unfriendly legislation. The work that shall give confidence must be a reconstruction of the constitution, and the alternative is a united secession of the South.

Nor do we consider that the immediate secession of one or more States prevents this coöperation. The necessity of a Southern convention, or congress, all immediate secessionists admit. The difference between them and coöperationists is on a point of time only. When a Southern convention is called, as called it undoubtedly will be, are the border States to be shut out if they have not seceded, or, will those who may have seceded before the coöperating States meet in convention, take no interest and stand aloof from the deliberation? A conference must be had, and we do not consider coöperation to have failed if one or more States go out at once.

120. THE TIMES CHANGE

(New Orleans Daily Crescent, December 20, 1860)

When Virginia was invaded by John Brown, her citizens murdered, and their slaves vainly approached with a view to a servile
insurrection, the circumstance produced a profound sensation, not in
that State alone, but throughout the South. It was one of the first
fruits of the irrepressible conflict, which was to make the States of
the Union all "free." Although the soil of Virginia only was invaded,
the other Southern States felt that it was a blow aimed at them all
alike. It was intended as the beginning of a crusade against slavery
all through the South, to be ended only with the utter extermination
of the institution wherever it existed.

Two of the other Southern States—South Carolina and Mississippi
—indignant at the outrage, and sympathising with Virginia, appointed
Commissioners to that State to tender the aid of the States they
represented in repelling all similar incursions in the future, and to get
the consent of Virginia to enter a convention of all the States of the
South. These Commissioners were received and treated with characteristic hospitality and kindness; but the suggestion of concert of action
among the States of the South was respectfully declined. Virginia, not
from any lack of appreciation of the indignity offered her, nor from
any want of fealty to the rights and institutions of the South, but from
a conviction that there was then no necessity for the step proposed,
declined going into the conference proposed by her Southern sisters.

In one view of the case, the action of Virginia was undoubtedly
right. Under the theory of our Government—a theory, however, which
has been woefully perverted in its practical application—each State is
a sovereign power in respect of all matters of internal concern. Each
State is the judge and arbiter of her own rights, her own wrongs, and
her own remedies, in all things outside of the few delegated powers
held by the Federal Government. Virginia, with none but the kindest
feelings for her sister States which had proffered their aid and their
sympathy, yet held that she was able to take care of herself, as well
against hostile and revolutionary incursions like that of John Brown,
as against any present or threatened usurpation by the Federal Government upon the reserved rights of the States, or any encroachment
upon that sovereignty which, as an independent Commonwealth, she
had ever claimed.

But, is there not an inconsistency in the present appeal of the Border States for a conference, when the proposition for a conference, made by at least two of the Cotton States, has already been rejected? It may be answered that the circumstances of the case are now different. This is true—but the difference is all in favor of the present position of the States of the extreme South. The case is made only the stronger in our favor by the different phase of affairs at the present time. *Then,* it was only proposed to consult together about the John Brown outrage, and the mode of preventing such things in future—and this was something legitimately within the jurisdiction of *all* the slave-holding States of the South. An attack upon the institution of slavery anywhere, was an attack upon it everywhere. It was an institution common to all the Southern States, and for this reason those States might properly consult together to guard against forcible and violent raids, like that of John Brown. But, in the present crisis, we are to determine another matter altogether. We are not to concert measures to protect slavery *in* the Union, but we are simply to decide whether to remain in the Union or to go out of it. And this is something which cannot now be done by the united action of all the Southern States—even were it Constitutional so to do, as we showed yesterday that it was not. It can be properly done in no other way than by the separate action of each State, acting upon her own responsibility, and in her capacity as an independent political sovereign.

No man who admits the doctrine of State rights and State sovereignty, can consistently favor the plan of coöperation, or can consistently oppose the duty and the necessity of separate State action. It has ever been the boast and the pride of the Southern States to assert their sovereignty, and to claim it as the safe-guard of their rights. Whatsoever powers were yielded to the Federal Government were in no respect intended to impair the sovereignty of the States individually. Virginia and Kentucky, by resolutions which have become specially noted in the political annals of the country, have been among the foremost States to assert and uphold this doctrine.

Now, then, a sovereign State must properly go out of the Union *as such*. A poor exhibition of sovereignty would it be for the States to league together, as if they were petty dependencies, instead of free and independent communities. The States asserted their sovereignty when they were weak, and each one decided for herself whether she would go into the Union or not. Now that they are strong, are they any the less proud of their sovereignty, or any the less tenacious of their reserved rights? If they were bold and independent when they were feeble in population and resources, shall they be the reverse now, when they are strong and powerful?

No. The States must go out of the Union, if they go out at all, precisely as they went in—one by one. Each State determined for herself, and at different periods of time, whether she would become a member of the Federal Union—and each State must now determine for herself whether she will stay in or not. For, disguise it as you may, this is the naked issue. There is none other. The issue is whether to stay in the Union, and become abject submissionists to Northern domination, and kissers of the rod that smites us, or to resume the rights granted to the Federal Government for good purposes, but perverted by that Government to purposes most unholy and infamous. Any side issue, anything, in short, which complicates the matter, no matter whether so intended or not, leads to submission. And submission, in our deliberate opinion, is, but another name for dishonor and disgrace.

121. The Position of the Cotton States

(*Daily Courier,* Louisville, December 20, 1860)

Those in the border Slave States who are willing to give up everything that freemen should hold dear, to maintain the existing Union, and, if that cannot be done, desire to fasten these States on as the tail of the Northern Confederacy, complain bitterly of what they call the precipitancy of the Cotton States, and are indignant because the latter do not wait for Kentucky and Missouri to inaugurate some movement for the preservation of their property and make a demand for the protection of the rights guaranted to them and their citizens by the Constitution.

And when the people are told that the border Slave States lose ten times as many negroes, and suffer ten times as many inconveniences, through the hostility of the Northern people to their institutions, as the Cotton States do, and that, for this reason, the latter should at least bear with the few wrongs inflicted upon them, until those who suffer so much more, and who stand between them and danger, should feel it their duty and interest to act, it is not without effect. And this is the favorite argument of the submissionists here:—that Kentucky and the border Slave States suffer more seriously than South Carolina and the Cotton States from the Abolitionized North;

that they are between the latter and danger; and that the "precipitancy" of the States now in the act of withdrawing from the Union does not arise from any apprehensions of danger, but is founded upon a treasonable purpose to break up the Union, to promote which they make LINCOLN's election the pretext and occasion.

If it is true that Kentucky loses more negroes, and is in a more exposed position than South Carolina, it is unquestionably equally true that the latter, in common with the other slaveholding States, has been wronged, insulted, injured, and attempted to be degraded from her equality in the Union. This cannot be controverted by any advocate for the North, nor denied by any apologist for the conduct of the people of the Free States. And being true, it is of itself a refutation of the position assumed by the Southern men with Northern principles, who so offensively complain because the Cotton States do not see proper to wait for the border States, which are so slow in moving; for the principle is the same, and the indignity quite as great, whether the property involved is valued at one cent or one dollar, at one dollar or one million; and the principle once conceded, and the indignity once submitted to, the one cannot easily be regained, nor the other well resented. If Kentucky has a right to withdraw from the Union, or to resist oppression by the Federal Government or wrong doing by the States, to save all her negroes, South Carolina has the same right, neither more nor less, to act in her sovereign capacity for the protection of the property of her citizens, though the loss of but a single slave is involved. In either event, it rests with the State in question to act or not to act, as her people think wise, proper, or necessary.

But the people of the Cotton States are influenced not alone by the principle involved, for that might be saved by a solemn and formal protest; not alone by the value of the property that may be lost through the nullification of the Fugitive Slave Law, for that would not equal the cost of the civil war with which they are threatened; not alone by the attempts that have been made to incite their slaves to insurrection and murder, nor by similar attempts with which they are menaced; not alone by that sense of insecurity which they are told by Northern men prevails throughout their length and breadth; but they see that their submission now to all the wrongs they have suffered, all the indignities that have been offered them, all the injustice that has been done them, all the bad faith of which they have been the victims, all indorsed and made their own by enough of the people of the Free States to choose a President—to the "irrepressible conflict" with their institutions and rights proclaimed long since by individuals and now made the policy of the Federal Government by the voice of the people—to be deprived of their rights in the common property of all the States, of their equality in the Confederacy, and of all the benefits secured to them by the Constitution, to which the principles of the Black Republican party are indirectly antagonistic,—their submission to these things now, if submission were possible, they know, must be followed in a few years with other evils of greater magnitude than these, from the contemplation of which the mind recoils horror-struck—evils the border States might escape, but from which they could not flee.

In the Union we see no reason to hope that the war on slavery will ever cease.—The settled hostility of the Northern people must become stronger with each year. The present dominant party in the Free States, based upon the single idea of opposition to the extension, spread, or existence of slavery, now numbering in its rank nearly two millions of voters, will become more powerful as the sentiment upon which it is founded gains strength and intensity. It has now secured the President. In two years more at most it will have both Houses of Congress. Then the Supreme Court will be reorganized; and Mr. TRUMBULL's [1] recent by-authority boast that we shall have "no more Dred Scott decisions" will be made good.

Anti-slavery is progressive and aggressive. As it gains in strength, its determination to extirpate the object of its hate from the country becomes more fixed and irradicable [sic]. The effect of this warfare is seen in Delaware, now almost free, and felt in the border counties of the border Slave States. The operations of the Underground railroad and the certainty of escape when once the line is passed, take from 1,500 to 2,000 slaves from this State alone each year. This loss principally falls on the border counties and the tier back of them. As this property becomes more and more insecure, holders sell it to those living further South. How long under present auspices will it be before that portion of this State lying on the Ohio river will be practically "free territory?" Kenton county, the second most populous in the State, had, in 1858, less than six hundred slaves; Campbell county, directly opposite Cincinnati, Ohio, has less than two hundred; Mason county, both wealthy and populous, had in 1840, 3,785 slaves, in 1843, 4,992, now scarcely 3,000; Jefferson county hasn't as many slaves as

[1] U. S. Senator Lyman Trumbull of Illinois.

were in it ten years ago. If this perpetual warfare is kept up ten years longer, by a party strong enough to control the legislation of the adjoining States, and backed by Personal Liberty Bills and such legal "aid and comfort," the time is not far distant when the counties in Kentucky bordering on the Ohio river will have no slaves in them; and the same remark is true in regard to the border counties in Missouri, Virginia, and Maryland. Already St. Louis, in Missouri, is Abolitionized, and Wheeling, in Virginia, is no better.

If the present Union, with no *efficient* provisions for the protection of Southern rights and property, is maintained, we can easily see where the "irrepressible conflict," as far as Kentucky and the border States are concerned, will end. The slaves now in them will be gradually sold to the farmers and planters of the Cotton States; and almost imperceptibly they will thus rid themselves of property, to hold which would require eternal vigilance and a constant conflict with fanaticism and folly and madness. *The "border" will be transferred to the States South of us.*

And then what? Anti-slavery will not be content to rest. The war will be transferred to the States where slavery will then prevail. Partial success will have but emboldened those whose prejudices and passions and partly their ignorance now impel them to demand the extinction of slave property. The war will be transferred to the Cotton States; but in them slave labor is not only of itself indispensable, but there are no States South of them to which their negroes can be sold. The people of Kentucky can, if they are not disposed to fight for their rights, get rid of their property without loss. Should the border line be transferred to the Northern boundary of the Cotton States, there will be no retreat for slavery. Hemmed in by long exclusion from the Territories, by Free States on two sides, and the ocean on the others, it will be a war of life and death, sooner or later terminating in a repetition of all the horrors of St. Domingo, at one fell swoop making the rich and prosperous States whose exports constitute the wealth of the nation an uninhabited and habitless desert!

The Cotton States, justified by the circumstances attending and preceding the triumph of Black Republicanism, and in view of the declaration of war made on them and their property, owe it to their own citizens and the world to secure themselves now against a calamity which the continued possession of the Federal Government for a few years by the Black Republican, or anti-slavery, party will make more than possible.

122. Difficulties and Dangers

(Daily Chronicle and Sentinel, Augusta, December 22, 1860)

It cannot be truthfully denied that there are many and great difficulties in the way of a final and satisfactory adjustment of the impending troubles between the North and the South. It were simply
the most besotted ignorance, the most criminal indifference, which
could induce any to shut their eyes to these difficulties. We repeat
that the difficulties are between *the people* of the North and South—
not between the South and the General Government, for we have no
serious ground of complaint against the Government. The danger is
in the spirit and temper of the two sections. And while, just now, the
prospect of adjustment seems brighter than heretofore, it is well that
we be careful not to deceive any one, and not to be deceived ourselves.

Times change, and men with them. Two weeks ago we estimated
the vote in our January Convention as probably 169 for immediate
secession, to 132 against it. A great change has occurred since then,
and now we have scarcely a doubt that the immediate secessionists will
be defeated at the January election. We do not believe, from present
indications, that 140 immediate secessionists can possibly be elected
to the Convention, unless some great and unforeseen revulsion takes
place. By immediate secessionists we mean those who are pledged to
carry Georgia out of the Union as soon as the Convention meets,
without waiting to make any further attempt at adjustment of our
troubles. Many of these designed to take Georgia out by the action of
the Legislature, and to make her the leader in the secession movement; but they were defeated by the sober-minded and cautious. Should
they be again defeated by the people on the second day of January,
it will be indeed a great popular triumph—a triumph of reason over
passion, of prudence over rashness, of calm reflection over excited
prejudice.

But herein is one of the greatest dangers of the times—the danger
arising from the probable misapprehension of the true state of public
sentiment in Georgia. It is well known that as Georgia goes, so goes
the South. Calm, self-possessed, moderate and just, her course will
determine the course of most of the slaveholding States. For this cause
it is all-important that nobody shall mistake the position of our Empire State, nobody here or at the North. It may prove a fatal, an irretrievably fatal error, should the conservatism of this State, as it is likely

to be manifested in the January election, be misconstrued into *sub-mission,* or a delay designed eventually to lead to submission. We feel it incumbent upon this journal, which is now, as it has always been, the exponent and the representative of the prudent, cautious, reflecting portion of the community—of that class which is known by its acts as the great conservative body in the State—to state fully and frankly the danger of imagining that this January election will exhibit a triumph of Union for the sake of the Union.

Nothing can well be farther from the truth. Georgia will indulge no threats, will use no menace, will attempt no bullying. But, relying upon the righteousness of her cause, the manliness of her people, the power of her resources, her position and her renown, she will simply demand that which is honorable to concede, and accept what it is honorable to accept. It is beneath her own dignity, it is impolitic, and it is unjust to her confederates, to employ gasconade—she will only ask for justice, for security and for peace—for a final cessation of slavery agitation, upon terms which it can be no disgrace to grant, and less than which will be unsatisfactory to her people, hazardous to her interests, and dishonoring to her fair name. She will make an earnest and an honest effort at adjustment, beseeching her sisters of like interest to join with her—should her reasonable demands be granted, she will maintain the Union of our fathers, should they be rejected, she will then take such steps (in co-operation with her sister slave States) as may be dictated by Honor, Wisdom and Patriotism.

A very large portion of the Northern people, from various causes, social, political, religious, economic, have become hostile to African slavery. It may well become them now, in the face of the great peril that threatens, to reconsider their opinions, to form clearer conclusions as to the thing as it actually exists, and *juster* conclusions as to their duties as good citizens. For, above all other things, it is patent this day to every careful observer that the North regards *the Union as a matter of value to them.* Regard slavery in any light you may, it is a matter of grave moment for you to consider, whether comity, good-fellowship, fraternity, and, above all, *interest,* (though we dislike to appeal to such a sordid motive) do not require you to bury your prejudices against that which does not immediately concern you, and to do justice to your equals in the Confederacy.

The *name of slavery* is perhaps really the most repugnant thing connected with the institution. The words slavery, bondage, property in man, are perhaps unpleasant to you; but does it become men, sensible men, to allow foolish prejudices against *names,* to outweigh the *value* of *things?* Let slavery be repugnant as it may to you who live afar off, and know nothing of it, the question now is, forced upon you by your own folly and wickedness, will you sacrifice the value of the Union to you, will you deny justice to your confederates, will you continue your maddening warfare, will you persist in continual harassment, will you still maintain a position which makes a whole section uneasy and restless from a feeling of insecurity, rather than like men conquer your insane prejudices and do your whole duty? We warn you now, calmly and kindly, that you retrace your steps—not from fear, for we scorn to appeal to that—but from a just regard to sacred obligations.

And, above all things, we conjure you, men of the North, not to mistake Georgia's position, and Georgia's determination. It has been taken deliberately, and we think wisely; it will be maintained firmly and persistently to the end, with all the means the God of Nature has given us. That position and determination, sure and unmistakable, is, that we must have equality, justice, fraternity, peace, in the Union, or we shall, however reluctantly, be forced by a sublime sense of the obligations we owe ourselves, our children, our civilization, our social existence, our security and our happiness, *to conquer peace and independence.*

123. A POSSIBLE FUTURE

(*The New Orleans Bee,* December 22, 1860)

The Washington correspondent of the Cincinnati *Enquirer* in a late letter touches slightly a point which has received considerable attention at the South. The writer says:

Private letters received in this city from distinguished Southern politicians hold out one hope for the reuniting of the Union after secession has taken place, and making it stronger and firmer than ever; that is, the reconstruction of the Government upon such principles as will make all the States co-equal, at the bottom of which lies the right of the master to his property, wherever he may take it, and an equality in the tariff laws, or more plainly speaking, free trade.

This idea is by no means unplausible. It is absolutely certain that in less than ninety days nearly all, if not all, the cotton States will have withdrawn from the Union. Whether their policy will be regarded as wise and judicious or as hasty and reprehensible, is not germane to the question. We are alluding to a state of fact which, as far as human foresight can discern, will positively exist within a few weeks. Moreover, although we cannot predict with so much of an apparent certainty that the frontier slave States, such as Maryland, Virginia, Kentucky, Missouri and Tennessee, will unite with the South in the secession movement, the daily development of public opinion in those commonwealths justifies the belief that they will ultimately imitate the conduct and share the fortunes of the cotton growing States. The result will be eventually that probably in six months every slaveholding State, with the possible exception of Missouri, will combine under a single government, republican in form, and with a Constitution assimilating in all its best features the instrument which has hitherto united the several States of the Confederacy. He must be but a superficial observer of human motives and actions who can take any other view of the future than this. South Carolina has seceded, and her single example will prove more irresistibly contagious than ten thousand appeals from the public men of the South. Already has the intelligence thrilled to the heart of the community, and stirred the secession fever to a fiercer paroxysm than ever.   .

When once the South shall have displayed its independence, and the determined assertion of its rights, we hazard little in saying that the effect upon the North will be tremendous. That section thus far has been rendered just sufficiently uneasy to indulge in wearisome platitudes about the Union, and to address warm appeals to the South to pause and await the future. When, however, the act which the North hardly seems yet to anticipate shall have been consummated; when the South shall be completely cut off from the North; when New England, the Middle States and the Northwest are left to mourn a Union dissevered by their folly and wickedness, and are compelled to confront the frightful commercial calamities which must ensue, and the progressive decadence to which they will be exposed, we may feel well assured that the insane fanaticism which has proved the prolific fountain of the evils present and prospective under which the country labors, will be utterly discarded. This will be no temporary and transient victory of sound principles over the reckless and destructive tenets of abolition, but it will be a crushing, overwhelming and enduring triumph. The South now rejects all proffers of compromise because she knows they are the mere offspring of alarm and financial distress, and because she has abundant cause to fear that her consent would be construed into timidity and a base surrender of right, and that Black Republicanism would soon revive from its seeming humiliation. But when experience will have demonstrated the manifest dependence of Northern industry upon Southern agricultural labor, and the impossibility of high Northern prosperity without Southern co-operation, we may not unreasonably expect such propositions for a new compact emanating from the North as the South may regard with deliberation, and may possibly accept.

It is to our knowledge that a large proportion of the citizens of New Orleans, who, though heretofore proud of their nationality, are now ardent advocates of secession, are greatly influenced in the decision they have reached by this very idea of forming at some future period another and a better Union, upon a basis of complete equality, and with inviolable constitutional guarantees. The reconstruction of the Government hereafter is by no means a chimerical notion—especially if the Federal powers throw no insuperable obstacles in the way, by an insane effort at coercion. If the Southern States are left to the peaceable exercise of their sovereignty, there will be no insurmountable objection to another Union. Such a consummation will materially depend upon the changes which events may bring about in the feelings and convictions of the people of the non-slaveholding States. If they resolve once and forever to put down Abolition, and to respect the South, it may be that the Providence which is now separating us will bring us together once more in a more durable compact, and under happier auspices.

124. Co-operation

(The New Orleans Bee, December 24, 1860)

We are decidedly in favor of a united South. Nay, we hold that the Southern States must combine with a view of exhibiting consolidated strength, and of blending their resources for support and defense. No single State could possibly long maintain an independent existence without grinding her citizens to the earth by a weight of intolerable taxation. If, therefore, a community of feeling and principle, a common object and a common destiny failed to admonish the Southern States of the necessity of union, this object would be attained by the irresistible impulse of a common interest. The Southern States which secede must come together under a confederated government.

Hence the question of co-operation and concert of action among the several slaveholding commonwealths scarcely admits of discussion. None oppose it, at the proper time and in the proper manner. All are satisfied that the various States which contemplate secession must deliberate together, and agree upon a system of government and an organic law which each alike will bind itself to respect and obey. But there exists a difference of opinion touching the mode and manner of co-operation. One portion of the community contend that this can only be effected by the several States after they have seceded; that it is a logical absurdity for States within the Union to seek concert of action with States outside of the Union, and that after secession this paramount object may be easily and expeditiously accomplished. The other portion are desirous that co-operation and mutual consultation should precede secession; and some of them appear to indulge a hope that the final resort may possibly be averted by the adoption of their views. As we observed in a former article, we entertain no doubts whatever of the entire good faith and sincerity of both parties, and deem it unwise as well as ungenerous to fling reproaches in the teeth of honest Southern men because they fail to appreciate conclusions which have been reached by other Southern men, equally honest and patriotic. The point at issue is a legitimate one, which may be fairly and fully discussed in a spirit of entire candor and moderation, and without the slightest admixture of personal or sectional feeling.

If concert of action among all the Southern States were practicable, we should willingly give our sanction to the project; but with respect to Louisiana it must prove wholly impracticable and impossible. Just look at the movements in progress among the Gulf States. Here is South Carolina, to begin with, no longer part and parcel of the American Confederacy. Being out of the Union, we of Louisiana cannot lawfully and constitutionally enter into compacts or agreements with her, so long as we continue to recognize the Constitution and laws of the United States. We are and will remain under another government until our Convention shall assemble, and shall formally dissolve further connection with the American Union. We really, then, have no right to consult South Carolina. Next comes Florida. The delegates to the Convention of that State were elected on the 22d inst., and the Convention itself will meet on the 3d January next. Florida will be out of the Union in less than two weeks. Georgia holds her election for delegates on the 3d January, and her Convention meets on the 18th. The predominant policy of Georgia is secession. There is an effort now making in the State to organize a co-operation party; but it will fail of achieving any thing substantial. Mississippi has chosen an immense majority of separate secession delegates, and her Convention meets on Monday next. She will undoubtedly follow the example of South Carolina. Alabama votes to-day for delegates, and her Convention will assemble on the 7th January. The public sentiment of that State is overwhelming in favor of immediate secession.

With respect to Louisiana, we do not choose our delegates until the 7th January, while our Convention is not convoked until the 23d of the same month. Consequently, so far as human foresight extends, we may say that when Louisiana proceeds to deliberate on the policy she will pursue, South Carolina, Florida, Georgia, Alabama and Mississippi will have severed themselves from the Union. With what States is Louisiana to co-operate, and seek concert of action? Must she leave her five sisters—her associates and co-laborers in the production of the great agricultural staple of the South, and linked together by identically the same interests—must she desert them in the critical period of their fate, to join the border slave States and chaffer and haggle with the North for new compromises and concessions? Is this a policy becoming the dignity and self-respect of Louisiana? Would it be just towards those cotton States which have already assumed their independence? We can understand the position of those who support co-operation because they still hope to preserve the Union. There are such amongst us, and we respect their convictions while thinking them erroneous. But how men professing to be Secessionists still proclaim themselves opposed to separate State action is something so paradoxical that it may well puzzle the shrewdest understanding. If the policy of united action were submitted as an original proposition preceding actual secession on the part of any Southern State whatever, the argument in its behalf would be a potent one; but as nothing of the sort has been essayed, as seven or eight States have provided for the resumption of their sovereignty at an early day, and by separate action, the scheme of co-operation is divested of those features which would otherwise recommend it. It cannot be carried into effect so as to embrace the entire South. It cannot, therefore, bind the South. It cannot affect States which will not be in the Union at the time the experiment would be made. Hence we cannot conscientiously recommend it.

But there is a species of co-operation which would not be amenable to the objections urged against the theory we have been considering. It is embodied in the annexed passage from a letter of the Hon. T. R. [R.] Cobb, brother of the late Secretary of the Treasury:

The greater the number of States which *retire together* from the Union—the more dignity and moral weight will the movement have. *Any haste in one State to move in advance of the others* (though not so intended) *will have or be construed into an appearance of a disregard to the will and action of others.* And while I am free to admit that each State must act for herself and resume, by her own independent will, her delegated authority, yet I conceive that it is possible and *highly desirable* that *all* of them should assign some *common day* for such resumption. In the mean time proper steps might be taken not only to secure harmonious action, but to provide for a future confederacy.[1]

A similar view has been very recently put forth by Senator Toombs, of Georgia, in a letter to the citizens of Danburg, who had requested him to address a public meeting at that place. He distinctly favors a simultaneous period for the secession of the cotton States, saying, "we ought not to divide on this point," and that we should not delay longer than the 4th March, next. To co-operate in the time of withdrawing from the Union, so that adequate preparation may be made for the exigency, is undoubtedly desirable, and is a very different thing from the species of co-operation proposed by its supporters in New Orleans.

125. The Proposed Settlement

(*Montgomery Daily Post,* December 24, 1860)

It will be seen that the Hon. Robert Toombs and Hon. T. R. R. Cobb, as well as others of the most prominent statesmen and uncompromising-resistance-men of Georgia, and of other Southern States, are contemplating the possible settlement of existing difficulties between the North and the South, by such amendments to the Constitution as may be necessary to secure the rights of the South in the Union; and in the event of these amendments not being sanctioned by a sufficient portion of the North, then for the Southern States to withdraw from the Union.[2] This would seem to be a very feasible proposition, and it is true to say, that it is ably sustained by the distinguished gentlemen that approve it. And so far as the policy of withholding final action for the present is concerned, in order to concentrate and harmonize public sentiment in the South, we think it both practical

---

[1] Thomas R. R. Cobb to the Editor of the *Federal Union*, December, 1860, in *The Savannah Republican*, December 20, 1860.

[2] See Robert Toombs to E. B. Pullin and others, December 13, 1860, in American Historical Association, *Annual Report, 1911*, II, 519–520; and Robert Toombs to the People of Georgia, December 23, 1860, *ibid.*, 525.

and prudent; but as to the final settlement of the question between the two sections of the Union, we have many misgivings. Suppose the North should agree to these amendments to the Constitution, what assurance have we that they would observe them any longer than it suited their purposes to do so? The present Constitution is not essentially deficient, but it has been maliciously violated; the laws that have been enacted under it are not materially inefficient, but they have been shamefully disregarded. Now, what assurance have we that additional clauses in the Constitution would not share the same fate at the hands of misguided fanatics, who are governed more by higher law doctrines than by the Constitution and laws of their country? It is no difficult matter to make Constitutions, but to have them observed is quite another matter. If the present Constitution had been adhered to, we apprehend the present difficulties never would have occurred; but it will be said that sufficient penalties should be attached to insure the observance of it. Now, let us see if this is likely to succeed. To incite servile insurrections is already recognized as a criminal offense, and the most severe penalties are imposed upon the instigator; but still they continue to occur. To abduct a slave is already declared a violation of the Constitution and of the supreme law of the land, still the underground railroad continues in operation, and even on the other hand, to traffic in African slaves is declared piracy. Yet we are well aware that to a considerable extent the trade has been continued. Now, we would not be understood as insisting that a perfect Constitution must be adopted, and a perfect observance of it secured. These are things that imperfect beings can never attain to; but unless the government can be accommodated to the general sentiments of the people, it cannot expect to command respectful observance at their hands. One man, for instance, regards slavery as a moral wrong; another as a moral and religious evil, and a third as a moral, social, religious and political curse. Hence, no matter what the Constitution may enjoin, no matter what the law may declare, it is not to be expected that men will sacrifice their moral sensibilities, or what they consider their religious duties and obligation, in order to comply with the requirements of political governments. Before the rights and institutions of the South can be safe in the hands of Northern men, entertaining views hostile to slavery, they must be re-educated; they must learn to look upon our domestic institutions through a different angle of vision; they must be taught to regard it as we do—as a moral, social and political blessing, and not as a curse; otherwise no constitutional provision and no enactments of law, will induce them to observe it as we think they should. Without a material re-action in public sentiment upon the slavery question, we entertain but little hope of a permanent settlement of it by any constitutional form in the Union.

126. THE FORCE POLICY

(The Kentucky Statesman, Lexington, December 25, 1860)

The prepared speech of Senator Wade, delivered in the Senate on Monday last, the remarks of Senator Hale,[1] on Mr. Crittenden's resolutions, the tone of the whole Republican press and other indications, develop, as we think, very clearly the policy of the incoming administration. The right of secession is denied and scoffed at, and in all quarters a bold determination expressed to maintain the entirety and supremacy of the Federal Government by physical force. It is now clearly foreshadowed that the new Republican administration will refuse to recognize the movements of the Cotton States, will decline to treat with them and will steadily push the question to a hostile solution. Rather than permit the Union to be dismembered, they will crush the country in civil war. Force is to be employed to coerce the seceding States into submission, and steel and lead are to be the arguments employed. This issue Kentucky will be speedily called upon to meet.

We can not mistake Kentucky feeling on this subject when the Federal Government shall undertake to use bayonet and cannon to subjugate six or eight slave States to the Administration of Mr. Lincoln on the Chicago platform; we do not hesitate to believe that Kentucky, indignant and united, will take her position along with the section to which she belongs, and present her face to the enemy. In such a dread contingency we shall hear no more of party, but will only know each other as freemen and Kentuckians, impelled by a common sentiment and united by a common interest and one destiny. In such an emergency we should scorn to appeal to party feeling, and spurn the attempt to draw party lines. Old Kentucky! would be the cry, and in her defense of her honor and her cause, men would rally oblivious of old associations.

But Kentucky should at once and promptly meet this issue. We regard this "Force policy" of the Republicans as the most dangerous enunciation, the most fearful issue possible to conceive. To acquiesce in it is to become subjugated provinces, to await its inauguration is to

[1] *Cong. Globe,* 36 Cong., 2 Sess., I, 115–116.

subject the country to the most fearful war ever undertaken. It would be a war of devastation and extermination, bloody, terrible and awful beyond any the world has known. But to accept the issue promptly is to avert both results. Let the border States unhesitatingly announce that upon such an issue they will stand a unit with the South, and the Republicans may be deterred from presenting such an issue. Resistance then and immediate avowal of a purpose to resist by the border States is the best policy for peace, for the Union, and for our honor and liberties. War would be the death knell of Union now or reconstruction hereafter. Boldness and firmness at this juncture by Kentucky, Virginia, Tennessee and Maryland will do more to save the Union, avert civil war and secure our rights, than any position we could take.

127. A NATIONAL CONVENTION

(*Louisville Daily Journal,* December 27, 1860)

Pursuant to the promise we made in our paper of Tuesday, we publish to-day the forcible and eloquent remarks of Senator Crittenden in explanation of his joint resolution, which we append to the remarks.[1] We need not commend both to the attention of our readers.

The public has doubtless observed that the plan of Senator Crittenden, whilst it has met with greater favor in Congress than any other integral plan, is likely to fall short of the favor requisite under the Constitution for the proposing of amendments to that instrument. In fact, there would seem to be no reasonable likelihood whatever that two-thirds of both Houses of Congress will be brought to concur in proposing the amendments embraced in Mr. Crittenden's resolution; and, if not in proposing these amendments, then certainly not in proposing any others. This puts an end to the attempt of Congress to pacify the country. The attempt has proved a failure.

Nor is the cause of this effect at all obscure. Congress is composed for the most part of men who think more of office than they do of their country. In other words, Congress, generally speaking, is a body of mere politicians. It is of the nature of politicians to dare nothing for the public good. Hence, the present Congress has dared nothing and consequently done nothing for the peace and preservation of the Union. What remains?

We answer, EVERYTHING; for, though politicians are very potent in

[1] *Cong. Globe,* 36 Cong., 2 Sess., I, 112–114.

raising popular discontents, they are to be counted as nothing in the work of allaying the turmoil they have evoked. This work belongs pre-eminently to the PEOPLE, and they alone can perform it. But they have not yet even undertaken it. We believe the time has come for the people to take hold of the work.

How shall they do it? Our readers know that we have thus far steadily opposed the demand for new guarantees on the part of the slaveholding States at the present time, because we believed that the necessity for such guarantees was not sufficiently clear and imperative either to assure the harmony of the South in making the demand or to justify the undoubted hazards of its rejection by the North. In accordance with this belief, we have endeavored to rally the friends of the Union in the South under the banner of the Constitution as it is, without additional guarantees or expositions, leaving extraordinary measures of redress to the time, if it should ever come, when our constitutional rights should be actually assailed or abandoned by the Federal Government. We have called on the conservatives of the South to stand firmly by the Constitution without gloss or alteration, and, secure in the ample ability of the slaveholding States to protect themselves in any emergency, await calmly the development of Mr. Lincoln's policy. But we have called in vain. Our endeavor has been ineffectual. The unconciliatory bearing of the Republican leaders in Congress renders the further prosecution of the endeavor worse than ineffectual. We relinquish it.

But we do not relinquish our hope for the Union. Far from it. We but yield to the conviction that the present unhappy derangement of our political system is so deep-seated and so pervading that nothing less than a revision and amendment of the Constitution will correct the disorder. We yield to this conviction most reluctantly, and only after a close and patient and anxious survey of the whole question in all its momentous bearings. The course of events both at the North and at the South has forced the conviction upon us. We accept it reluctantly but without fear of the issue. Our faith in the preservation of the Union is unshaken. The American people, when fairly appealed to, are incapable of suffering the Union to perish. Let them be fairly appealed to without unnecessary delay.

There are but two constitutional modes by which this appeal can be made; namely, 1, The proposing of amendments to the Constitution by two-thirds of both Houses of Congress, and, 2, The calling of a Constitutional National Convention by Congress on the application of the Legislatures of two-thirds of the several States. The first mode, as we have seen, has been tried unavailingly. The second, in our judgment, is perfectly feasible, and preferable to the first on many other grounds, which we need not specify at present. There remains, to be sure, the revolutionary mode of calling a National Convention by Congress without the application of two-thirds of the States or of any other number of them, which, we believe, has been introduced into the Senate at Washington,[2] but which obviously nothing save the direst national extremity could excuse. It appears to us that the present national extremity would hardly justify the adoption of this mode. The stain of inceptive unconstitutionality might fatally discredit the entire movement.

We think the true mode of initiating this great appeal to the American people is for the Legislatures of the various States approving it to apply immediately or as soon as possible to Congress to call a National Convention for proposing amendments to the Constitution. This mode is constitutional and at the same time practicable. Let Kentucky or Virginia or any other State lead off in the movement, and she will unquestionably be followed by the requisite number of her sister States. We at any rate are persuaded that the movement should be promptly initiated in some form or other. The failure of the Committees of Pacification in Congress to agree upon any plan of adjustment, taken in connection with the inflexible and defiant port of the Republican leaders, gives a totally different and far more threatening aspect to a crisis grave and formidable enough at best. It puts a new and sadder face on affairs. The people of the United States must come together and heal this breach, or the breach will swallow up the Union.

For ourselves, believing that the highest welfare of Kentucky and of every other State of the Confederacy is bound up indissolubly in the perpetuation of the Union on terms of equal justice to all, we shall never cease to labor with our whole strength for the perpetuation of the Union on this everduring [sic] basis; and, assuredly, if we know our own hearts, no pride of opinion, no political passion or prejudice, no fear of censure or of calumny, no hope of fortune or of applause, shall stand for an instant in the path of our labor. We are ready cheerfully to make any and every honorable sacrifice for the perpetuation of the

---

[2] Lane of Oregon presented a resolution in the Senate, December 18, requesting a convention of southern states, instructing the Executive Department to refrain from a force policy, and providing for a national convention. *Cong. Globe,* 36 Cong., 2 Sess., I, 112. A similar resolution presented by Burch of California in the Committee of Thirty-Three was defeated by a vote of 13–16. *Journal of the Committee of Thirty-Three,* p. 39.

Union. And so we confidently believe are the masses of the American people. Let them at all events have a fair chance to decide the solemn question for themselves.

We shall to-morrow recur to the subject of a National Convention.

128. THE LAST HOPE OF THE UNION

(*The Kentucky Statesman,* Lexington, December 28, 1860)

The failure of the Senate Committee of Thirteen, appointed under Gov. Powell's resolution, to concur in any report presenting a basis for the peaceful adjustment of our political difficulties, was received in Washington on Saturday last as the end of all negotiations and the sure precursor of inevitable dissolution. To the action of that Committee attached the last lingering hope of Union, and when its proceedings were eagerly sought and announced, the gloom and despair was manifested in the countenances of all. We have never witnessed a gloomier day in Washington. The most sanguine and hopeful seemed at last to yield the cause before clung to with great tenacity.

The announcement of the dissolution of this Committee without making a report will doubtless precipitate prompt and energetic measures in the Southern States for secession. It will be received by the country as the end of negotiations and compromise, and the signal for action. A disruption will now be received as unavoidable, and all parties will now look to their own safety and interest.

This Committee of Thirteen was composed of six Democrats, six Republicans, and one Southern Oppositionist, Mr. Crittenden. It was manifest that a majority report if [not] approved by the Republicans would be worthless, because it was only by their votes the proposed measures could be carried through Congress, and ultimately carried through the State Legislatures. Hence, by a rule, the Committee was divided into two classes, Republicans and Opposition men, and no report allowed to be made unless supported by a majority of each class.

The Crittenden Amendments were submitted by their author, and it is said were urged with great fervor and eloquence. The Southern men agreed to stand by them as a compromise, but the Republicans voted in a body unanimously against every solitary one of these resolutions, *seriatim*. The ayes and nays were taken and no Republicans crossed the line to vote for a single measure proposed by Mr. Crittenden. The Committee then ordered the Chairman to report the facts to the Senate.

Thus have the Republicans once more distinctly and unequivocally announced that they will not yield a solitary plank or splinter of the Chicago platform. They evince a mulish, stubborn, obstinate, sullen mood, callous to consequences and utterly impervious to all the appeals of the country for peace and justice. They intend to administer the Government on the Chicago platform, recognize no secession of any State, and avow their purpose to enforce the laws in all the thirty-three States regardless of the consequences. This is the question we have now to meet. Submission or Resistance is the issue. We have written RESISTANCE on our flag. We trust there will not be a submissionist found in Kentucky.

129. SOUTH CAROLINA AND HER SISTERS OF THE SOUTH

(*The New Orleans Bee,* December 28, 1860)

The telegraphic dispatches from the Charleston Convention [1] published yesterday place the question of co-operation in the proper light. The body representing the sovereignty of South Carolina, having declared by solemn ordinance the withdrawal of the State from the Union, proceeds forthwith to endeavor to secure concerted and concurrent action from the other States of the South. In the first place, a favorable report was made on the proposition to send Commissioners to the slaveholding States,[2] with a view doubtless of apprising them formally and officially of the action of South Carolina. In the next place, a highly important ordinance was offered by Mr. RHETT, and referred to the appropriate committee, providing amongst other measures for a Convention of the seceding slave States, to arrange for the formation of a Southern Confederacy—Montgomery (Alabama) being indicated as the most suitable location for its session.[3] We entertain little or no doubt of the passage of this measure.

Much invective and reproach has been lavished on the Palmetto State for taking independent action on the question of secession, with-

---

[1] An epidemic of small-pox had caused the convention to adjourn from Columbia to Charleston.

[2] The resolution providing for interstate commissioners was introduced into the convention on December 19, and referred to the Committee on Relations with Slave-holding States. That committee did not report until December 31, and commissioners were not elected until January 2, 1861.

[3] The interstate commissioners appointed by the convention, at a meeting on January 3, agreed upon the first Monday in February as a proper date to propose for a Southern Convention. The proposal of Montgomery as the most suitable location probably originated in the Alabama state convention. See Smith, *The History and Debates of the Convention of the People of Alabama . . . 1861,* pp. 78–80.

out consulting with any of her sister commonwealths of the South. But it should be borne in mind that South Carolina had proclaimed months before the result of the Presidential contest that she would consider the election of LINCOLN a legitimate cause for secession. Her conduct was the direct and inevitable sequence of her principles. Moreover, it was requisite that some State should take the initiative; and certainly that position appertained peculiarly to South Carolina, as for years she had been most prominent, emphatic and unconditional in her hostility to and denunciation of the abolition proclivities of the North. It was clear and evident that South Carolina would be foremost in the movement, and that she could not afford to await the tardy deliberation, and perhaps tardier action of the other States of the South.

Nevertheless we see that having deliberately cut herself loose from the Union, South Carolina hastens to recognize her geographical, political and social relations to the other States of the South, and exhibits an entire willingness and even an anxiety to affiliate with them on the basis of a Confederation and a common Constitution. In proportion as each State resumes its individual sovereignty, it will form a league of friendship and fraternity with South Carolina, until, in the course of a few weeks or months, the seceding commonwealths will be sufficiently numerous to form articles of confederation, and combine together for purposes of mutual protection and defense, and of good government. This, as we understand it, is the theory of co-operation universally maintained by the supporters of separate State action. It strikes us as being far more practicable, and more expeditious than any other plan, and likewise as leading to positive and tangible results. If, for example, the partisans of united action were to prevail, it might happen that months would be wasted in fruitless appeals to the border States; and, in the interim, the administration of LINCOLN would be in active existence, and the States professing their determination to resist his sway would be necessarily quietly submitting to it. Nay, the procrastination which would attend these propositions for a Southern Conference and their discussion, and possible rejection by some of the States, would so strengthen the arm of the Federal Government as to render it well nigh impossible for such States as might eventually determine on secession to carry their policy into effect without encountering a vigorous effort at coercion. We need not add that this would be the precursor to a sanguinary and protracted war.

For these among many reasons we conceive that South Carolina has pursued a judicious course, and one that will tend to a speedy and effective combination among the States favoring secession.

130. PROSPECT OF CONCILIATION

(*The New Orleans Bee*, December 29, 1860)

There are a few singularly hopeful and sanguine spirits at the South who really believe that if we are but patient, and long-suffering and forbearing, the North will do us full justice. We should rejoice at the possibility of an adjustment of difficulties within the Union, but every day's experience and observation satisfy us that expectations of this kind are absolutely futile. Shortly after the assembling of Congress it was thought that propositions of a character to content the South would be adopted as the basis of a satisfactory settlement. We have seen how groundless were these hopes. Propositions were, indeed, presented, but only to be rejected. The tender consciences of the Black Republicans debarred them even from entertaining the conciliatory resolutions submitted by the venerable JOHN J. CRITTENDEN.[1] The solemn farce of the Committee of Thirty-Three is nearly played out, and the majority of anti-slavery fanatics on that committee manifest inflexible opposition to every effort at compromise.[2] In the Senate MR. WADE's speech [3] is a portentous indication, as well of Abolition indisposition to yield any thing to Southern demands, as of Abolition willingness to employ coercion, if it can be possibly invoked.

Such are the developments in Congress, whence alone can properly emanate all overtures for the restoration of harmony and good feeling. If we extend our examination to the Black Republican press, even a fiercer spirit of opposition may be discerned. It is useless to consult the conservative sheets of the North, as they are powerless, and moreover represent the minority alone. To the Black Republican organs must we look for a correct expression of the dominant public sentiment of that section. We honestly acknowledge that we can find in these journals no evidences whatever of a disposition to yield one

---

[1] The Crittenden Resolutions had been defeated in the Committee of Thirteen, the Republican members voting against them in their entirety. *Journal of the Committee of Thirteen*, pp. 4–6.

[2] The Nelson and Taylor resolutions had been defeated in the Committee of Thirty-Three by a solid Republican vote. *Journal of the Committee of Thirty-Three*, pp. 3–9.

[3] *Cong. Globe*, 36 Cong., 2 Sess., I, 99–104.

jot or tittle of opposition to slavery. We have before us at this moment multiplied proofs of their persistance in the odious sectional platform upon which LINCOLN was elected. Nay, this triumphant partisan himself will not budge an inch. We have the assurances of his home organ, the Springfield *Journal,* that he has no compromises to make, that he regards secession as treason, and that he will use the entire power of the Government to put it down. Another authoritative sheet says "it is enabled to state, in the most positive terms," that Mr. LINCOLN is utterly opposed to any concession or compromise that shall yield one iota of the position occupied by the Republican party on the subject of slavery in the Territories, and that he stands now, as he stood in May last, when he accepted the nomination for Presidency—square on the "Chicago platform." Does this bear the aspect of conciliation? Is this an inducement to the South to postpone action, and to hope in returning justice?

Let us look a little farther. THURLOW WEED, of the Albany *Evening Journal,* ventured some days ago to hand out a flag of truce, and to propose certain concessions to the South. They were received with a shout of reprobation by the Black Republican prints. Nevertheless Mr. WEED went to Springfield, and had a personal interview with the President elect, striving doubtless to impress upon Mr. LINCOLN's mind the expediency of adopting a conciliatory course. His success may be appreciated from the statement since made in his own paper that ABRAHAM LINCOLN is determined to require from all the States an enforcement of the laws and obedience to the Constitution, and that he continues earnest and inflexible in his devotion to the principles and sympathies of the Republicans.

Most, if not all other journals of the Black Republican stripe hold language equally decided. The New York *Courier and Enquirer* of the 22d instant says "secession is rebellion, and all rebels are traitors to the government under which they live." And again: "Why should we hesitate to call upon the rebels in South Carolina and elsewhere to bear in mind that halters are being prepared for traitors?" And yet again, speaking of the people of South Carolina:

We disown them. They are no longer our brethren, but a band of rebels and traitors, pledged to pull down the fairest temple of liberty ever raised by human hands; and it is a duty which the Executive owes to his oath of office and the Constitution—to our country and to the whole civilized world—to give notice to the fools and madmen of South Carolina that the slightest resistance to the laws of the United States or any attempt to interfere with her forts, arsenals, or property of any kind, will inevitably be met with prompt and severe public chastisement.

And so on, through a column of tirade, in which the advocates of secession are perpetually denounced as "rebels" and "traitors." The *Tribune*—though we will do that sheet the justice to say that it is opposed to coercion—is earnest and emphatic in repudiating the slightest concession to the South. Here is a specimen from a long article in its issue of the 24th instant:

Our clear duty is to check the extension of slavery. We have still a vast region of almost uninhabited territory yet to be made into States, and on that soil should never be impressed the foot-print of a bondman. We owe it to generations of men yet unborn. We have no right to leave the question to be settled by the contingency of climate, or the accident of any existing or possible circumstance. One unvarying law, as stable and inevitable as the great law of nature, must be applied to it all, and for all time—THE TERRITORIES MUST BE FREE.

Is it possible, then, for us to yield one inch on this question? Never! We believe in the great doctrine of the Federal Constitution; we believe in the principles of our fathers; we are not willing to compromise with an evil, that it may spread and live forever, which they only tolerated for a season, in the hope that it would speedily perish; and we want peace. "We want peace, and not panic," and therefore we can make no compromise and yield no concession which is to be a perpetual plague to us, and to those who come after us an inheritance of perpetual political strife, to end, sooner or later, in a struggle more terrible than any civil war the world has ever witnessed. The real settlement of the question is now begun, let it be fully accomplished, and not again be put off to a future day.

We have culled these samples of Northern opinion almost haphazard. Other journals, such as the *Times, Commercial Advertiser*, the Republican organs in Boston, Philadelphia, Cincinnati, Chicago, &c., all breathe the same spirit. When in the midst of a most dangerous crisis—the work of disunion having already begun—the Lincoln organs unanimously cry "no concession, no compromise," how ineffably absurd is it on the part of any Southern man to think of preserving the Union by a salutary and radical change of Northern sentiment. Our only resource is independence.

131. DISUNION

(The Daily Constitutionalist, Augusta, December 30, 1860)

This is the last time we can address our readers of the *Weekly Constitutionalist,* before they are called upon to decide that issue which involves FREEDOM or SERVITUDE to us and our children, and which issue should alone be written—"Victory or Death."

Oh, that when young men ask the daughters of the land for song, they would sing the *Marseillaise* hymn; and that the old and the waiting would learn wisdom of the girls and young children; for the blue cockade of secession contrasts with many dark or golden tresses, and the lonely, golden star of Georgia shines bright amid the robes of little boys and girls, just old enough to lisp of—Mother, God, and Liberty.

From the great popular heart, however, the anxious question is, "Watchman what of the night?" and while we cannot reply, "Day is breaking, and all is well," yet Revolution twines her crimson wings with the snowy plumes of peace, and both look on, as the great veil of the future slowly lifts upon the second act of the drama of the West.

The stage is yet dim, and the characters shadowy; but the scenes are those of Southern Empire, and the figure plainest seen is Hope.

But dramatic rhetoric does not satisfy the questioning heart, and the varied question is, "What of Georgia?" The answer is, *she will secede before the 4th of March 1861.*

There is no majority in Georgia for secession; but every county meeting, save two or three, has resolved as the sense of its members, and the faith of its nominees for delegates, that disunion is either a necessity now, or will be on the refusal of new guarantees, and even the most conservative will reluctantly vote for immediate secession, because the Abolitionists are not base enough to ask them to delay.

Commercial relations will force Georgia out, for she cannot afford to have a string of custom houses on her Alabama, Florida, South Carolina, and perhaps Tennessee frontiers, and kindred and fraternity forbid that we should remain aliens and strangers amid those glorious sisters, which have begun to embroider *Independence* upon the robes of their empire.

We are told that in all our contests with the North, until this last disastrous one, the South has uniformly been victorious; victors in

1820, victors (it was said) in 1850, victors (in truth) in 1852, victors in 1854, and in 1856, besides innumerable great or less contests scattered over the bosom of the past forty years. Let us grant it all, grant the victories and forget how many such victories would be worse than defeat; but before we thank GOD for such success, let the solemn question be answered, WHY WERE WE ASSAILED? Was it the purpose of the "more perfect Union," which our fathers sealed in blood, that we should be an eternal target, warding off with fear and trembling, the shafts of a relentless foe, that foe our brothers? Were we ever the aggressors, and have they not always been?

It is true that we have escaped annihilation in a series of conflicts, from each and all of which the Constitution should have been our shield; but each one of these fratricidal blows would have been fatal had it succeeded. Like convicts on the wheel, we have contented ourselves with avoiding the "mercy stroke" which was intended to finish us, and put up each time the piteous petition—oh, say you won't do it again! The war is against us and defeat is ruin; this day we are defeated, and we must seek the embattled heights of southern independence, or be captives in the next battle on the plains of the Union.

It is truly said that the South has never yet been disgraced and ruined. That is true; but with fair notice that the Abolitionists intend to do it, and have just received the power to do it, shall we wait till they do it? Does it become us to stay and court dishonor?

Perhaps the most absurd, and yet universal argument against us, is the Psalm to the Stars and Stripes. Strange that "sensible" men can find no evidence of the value of the Union, save a flag, a few graves and some facts of past history! Stranger still when we remember that there is no copyright on the flag to prevent our having one like it; that the graves, worthy to be "The Delphic vales, the pilgrim shrines, the Meccas of the mind," are on southern soil, and that it is a task for our school children now to remember those historic memories of glory, which are *all* our own.

We are referred to the growth of this country, as evidence of the value of our Government; but emigrants came when there was no Government at all, and its rapid spread is hardly commensurate with the triumphs of Saxon blood, under the cross of St. George, against old empires, Thugs, Asiatic cholera, and the spotted, striped, creeping, and miasmatic death in Bengal.

We are told that the Federal Government has done no wrong. Granted; but it is as well to recollect that it has never been more than the paid agent of the States, powerless for harm; and as our old servant has taken service under Abolitionism, we simply discharge him, with a good character and a recommendation to the new master.

Those avoid the issue who say we quarrel with the Government. We do not; but our partner States have sinned, and they, or we, shall quit the firm.

It is said, by our ablest opponents, that we have only two causes of complaint, to-wit: The Territorial question, and the fugitive slave law. That is not true, for it is probable we will abandon the Territories, and are able to let a million or two a year be stolen from us in slaves. It is the northern heart which we complain of, and no marriage bond can be sacred enough to make us cling to a termagant that don't love us.

It is said to be the extreme of folly to resist evils before they come, but we are accorded permission to get ready to resist. Exactly! And our idea is to form a Southern Union, get armies, navies, treaties, etc. etc., so when an attempt is made to abolish slavery, we will be ready to resist.

The Georgia platform is pled. That never was right, for it held the Federal Government accountable, instead of the States, and ignored State rights. It is said the North threatens but dares not act. Well, it is certainly the first time that a big crowd was afraid to attack a little one, and if it is all bluster, let us go South out of the cold and let them bluster by themselves. "They lack the power!" Ah, indeed! and who found that out? They will, by the secession of cotton States, have every department of the government by March, and with all the power that *is,* they are probably satisfied. "Lincoln tied!" so is the devil, but his chain is long enough to let him walk over hell, earth, and heaven, (*vide* Job).

"The South will have the whole military power of the Government to aid her," in defense of her Constitutional rights, says a great man; and of that "whole military power," Abe Lincoln is Commander-in-Chief!

"Pray don't *precipitate* things," cries one and another, and where was ever recorded more calm deliberation, than is seen in the call of the South Carolina and Georgia State conventions?

But there are disunionists, *per-se!* Yes, and all honor to the men who braved the howl of "treason," by being the first to say so. Traitors let them be called, but *such* was Washington.

The last hope is exhausted, and Toombs did violence to his own feelings, that he might demonstrate the hopelessness of Constitutional amendments, by the votes of Republican Senators. Abolitionism will not even listen to that old sage of the Union, Crittenden, and it tells us as plain as it can talk—"there is no compromise."

The following is a statement of the entire vote cast in the United States, after separating and distributing the fusion ticket:

Popular Vote

Lincoln,	1,786,480
Douglas,	1,354,428
Breckinridge,	784,896
Bell,	605,801

The Douglas vote being almost double that of Breckinridge, and the popular vote against Lincoln, nearly a million.

The causes which led to the election of Lincoln have been most minutely enquired into, to show that it is not an Abolition triumph.

Breckinridge men in the North voted for him, for dislike to the great opponent of the Administration. Douglas men voted for Lincoln, because they feared Breckinridge would get in the House; Bell men, because they hated Democracy. Foreigners and others, because of the fusion with Americans. Pennsylvanians, on the tariff on iron, and other manufacturers for other tariff interests. New Englanders, for the homestead measure, and ten thousand lesser causes were at work. Yet all these things but demonstrate two great truths: first, that a Government which cannot prevent such *accidents,* is worthless; second, that whoever may have been the first choice of our northern brothers, the second choice was generally an Abolitionist.

We are told that interest will compel the North to do right, but have before demonstrated that it is religious zeal which impels them against interest; and the fact of the committee of thirteen in the Senate, of thirty-three in the House, refusing all compromise even now while their constituents are out of work and bread, proves the desperate tenacity of fanaticism.

But we cannot expect these legislators now elect, to do right, in State or Congress, but wait for the ballot box to speak! It has just spoken.

Let us be unanimous! Certainly, and who keeps us from it?

We will not be able to control fanaticism—it is said—even if we separate from it. That may be so, but we can make the incendiary get a passport, and the peddler and drummer pay duty at the gates of the land.

We can open our ports to the world, and not longer feed the beast which wants to eat us. We can risk our lives upon the chances of glorious battle and if slaves we must be, we at least, can avoid the mockery of being called their brothers.

Some say the border States are frightened; if they are, let them sell their negroes cheap and turn Abolitionists.

But we will lose their sympathy if we do not consult them! We intend to consult, as soon as we get free enough to do it without perjury. Was the Confederacy formed before or after the war of the revolution began?

The brightest idea however is, that slavery cannot extend South, for the Indians, Creoles, Spaniards, *et sic de similibus,* would be in the way as lords, proprietors of the soil, opposed to slavery, and therefore we are stopped that way. It is conceded that slavery must expand; or to use the elegant wish of the northern Senator, "the viper will sting itself to death." It was never expected to expand North; deserts, free States and oceans, bar it West and East; we are now informed that it can't go South, therefore it seems to us that the premises are not true, or we are in a bad predicament, and the continued Union does not aid it a particle.

It is the old argument which was laughed at in the case of Florida, Louisiana, New Mexico, California, and Missouri, for the dominant race will supplant all others, and slavery will expand South to Brazil and from her till stopped by snow. It may be an evil, but like cholera, no power can check it but frost.

The British press informs us—and unkindly it is repeated by the Georgia born—that England lets us alone now only from fear of our National greatness, but will no longer respect the MONROE doctrine after we divide. Such is the argument to scare us from independence!

Take heed, oh men of the South, how you shrink from your destiny; for, when the children of Israel, terrified by the report of the spies that there were "giants in the land," shrunk back from the fords of Jordan and the hills of Canaan, they were led back, and for forty years strewed the desert with their graves. JOSHUA and CALEB alone said, "we are able to take it"; and they alone of all that myriad host lived to go over—the one to dwell in the fertile vales of Hebron, then his own; the other, to die with his people around him, amid the hills of God.

Let those, however, who would shrink from giants, remember, before us we have but the world of aliens to oppose; behind us, the world still stands in arms, and our own Government is chief conspirator. The alternative is not peace at all, but other nations, or other nations and our own.

We cannot get Cuba if we go out of the Union. Perhaps not, but we have an excellent opportunity to lose what we have got by staying in the Union.

We will save ourselves and look out that England does not get Cuba.

If slavery is only respected because the North lends it her countenance, its credentials are very bad, and the sooner we earn it a better reputation, the better we shall do.

It is a fact that England had some thoughts about freeing slaves in Texas at the time she became free, but the whole course of British statesmanship only shows their sublime ignorance of the slavery question, and slavery must stand in spite of England and the North, its only bulwark being truth and the sword.

Let us hear no more then of the craven voices which croak of the future.

Grant that the world is opposed to us and our property rights, grant that the tariff, the slave trade, the banks, the mouths of the Mississippi, may be difficulties yet unsettled; but the deck of the Union ship is on fire behind us, and whether there be sharks in the ocean of the Future or not, we must leap and swim, supported by truth and guided by the stars.

We would be glad to argue at length each of the positions taken against us; but time will not permit. It has simply been our purpose to give a key to every door in the "Doubting Castle," which the foes of secession use to imprison thought.

In conclusion, we are happy to be able to inform our readers, that Georgia is committed to disunion, on the failure of new guarantees —a respectable minority of the counties having decided for immediate secession—and all amendments to the Constitution having been refused, we can entertain no doubt of her being out of the Union by the 4th of March, 1861.

Then alone, or with others, she will still be GEORGIA—

"Forever strong in conscious might,
Her pillared flag in faith unfurled,
And her star still shining in steady light,
On the very evening of the world."

132. A Few Reflections on Coercion

(The Daily Herald, Wilmington, N. C., January 3, 1861)

Some weeks ago we wrote an article, which we had the satisfaction to see copied extensively in the papers of the country, under the caption "A Few Reflections on Secession." In that article we refrained from any discussion of the right of secession, and confined ourself entirely to a consideration of its consequences. We said then, that peaceable secession was an impossibility, and we believe our prediction will prove true.

We propose to say something to-day about "coercion" which is the correlative of secession. To our mind it is becoming more and more apparent every day, that in spite of the efforts of moderate men, both at the North and at the South, the present contest is rapidly culminating in a war, in which the *whole* North, will be arrayed against the *whole* South. The news from Washington and the North reveals, more plainly each day, the fact that there is a growing unanimity in that portion of the country, in favor of enforcing the federal laws. The Black Republicans are a unit on the subject, and the conservative men there, with few exceptions, while deprecating Lincoln's election, can see no other course to pursue. The secessionists of the South are a unit for immediate resistance, and the more moderate men here, while they deprecate the course of South Carolina, will never agree to have the troops of a Black Republican administration garrisoned on Southern soil, to awe the people into submission. Coercion means civil war, and, though we have been educated in the Federal school of politics, and do not believe in the right of secession, we would never, as a Southern man, suffer a Southern State to be driven into subjection by armed force, as long as we could stagger under a musket. We have argued and protested against secession, we have denounced our friends for being disunionists, we have done our utmost, in a feeble way, to prevent the present deplorable state of affairs, but we should be recreant to our nature, and our name, and should dishonor the blood which flows in our veins, and which was freely shed to establish American Independence, if we hesitated to beat back the armed aggressor, come from what quarter he may. We have no argument to offer against coercion except the argument of the sword. We hope it will not be attempted. We *believe* it will. We *know* it will fail. We believe an attempt will soon be made to blockade the ports of the seceding States. An attempt may also be made to garrison all Southern forts. If so, it will be, and ought to be resisted. It will not do for Mr. Buchanan to place troops in these forts for Mr. Lincoln's benefit. If this civil war is to be inaugurated—and there can now be but little doubt of it—the Southern people ought to be prepared for it as much as is possible. We regret that Mr. Bledsoe's amendment to the Military Bill, proposing a million instead of three hundred thousand dollars for the purchase of arms &c., was defeated in our Legislature. We hope the amount appropriated for that purpose will be more than $300,000. These piddling appropriations have been the ruin of our Internal Improvement system, and have generally been caused by demagoging politicians, who did not dare to be decently liberal, for fear of unpopularity.

It is hardly necessary for us to say that we deeply lament the necessity for expressing such views as these, but lamentations and regrets furnish no remedy for the evil with which we are threatened. We are satisfied that the *argument* on this matter is exhausted. We have used it freely, as long as it could be used effectually, and we now await the issue of events. The same honest motive which has actuated us in our cause, heretofore, impels us to the utterance of these sentiments, and will always govern us in the expression of our opinions as a public journalist. Events march so rapidly, and changes develop themselves in such quick succession, that a course of action which might have been proper a week ago, would be unwise and injurious to-day, or a week hence. We have little regard for any man who is fickle in his opinions, or cowardly in giving utterance to them; but we have less for him who stupidly adheres to a blind and unyielding prejudice, or violently advocates a useless and impracticable theory.

133. COERCION

(*The Review,* Charlottesville, Va., January 4, 1861)

We are among those who believe that the United States is a government, and not a league. We regard the Constitution as a fundamental national law, and not as a treaty. We consider that we are citizens of the United States, and owe an allegiance to the Federal

Government. Any resistance to the Federal authority we regard as rebellion.

We moreover love the United States. We revere that magnificent government which, formed with so much difficulty, and by so many compromises, has thrown over us its shield for seventy years, and raised us to our present dominion and greatness. It is to us the palladium of civil liberty at home, and in the world. We do not regard the Union as having been oppressive to one section or the other. We do not regard the South or the North as having dominated over the other section, or taken to itself the main benefits of the Confederation. The influence of the National Government seems to us in nearly all things to have been beneficent and enabling to all the States of the Union.—So far from considering that an irreconcilable conflict exists between the sections of the country, we esteem the welfare of each to be bound up with that of the other, and the interests to be co-ordinate and conjunctive.

When the Gulf States complain that the existing imposts of the country have built up the North to their impoverishment, we have argued that the Tariff, if it benefited Pennsylvania and Massachusetts, did not *injure* South Carolina and Georgia. That even if it was unjust to South Carolina and Georgia, it was equally onerous against Illinois, Indiana, Ohio, Michigan, and nearly all of the non-slaveholding States. And this will appear when South Carolina undertakes to establish a revenue system of her own, for she will find that she will have to levy at least three dollars of taxes on her people to one that she has paid in the present Union. It was necessary that the United States should have manufactories somewhere, and if Pennsylvania and Connecticut and Massachusetts were the best points to locate them, the existence of those manufactories, while it specially benefited these particular States, generally benefited the whole country, just as the existence of the great city of New York, or the city of New Orleans, appreciates the value of property throughout the Union.

On the other hand the staples of the South have been poured into the lap of the North, in return for the manufactured articles which they have sent us.

So important do we regard the Union, so much do we cherish it, that the pulling down of its splendid columns is to us like the fall of the paternal walls and roof, and the demolition of all the most endearing emblems of home. We know that we shall never find any other such country. We know that we shall never see any other such flag. We know we shall never stand up as proudly and as exultant under any other nationality.

Therefore, with our views of the nature of the government, and with these affections towards the Union, under any ordinary circumstances, the feeling at the South in favor of resisting the impetus and intemperate action of South Carolina, would extort from us the most hearty and unqualified sympathy.

Even as the matter stands, we entertain towards South Carolina the most bitter resentment. We feel that she has not only precipitately thrown down the bulwarks of the Union, and inaugurated on her own responsibility revolution and anarchy; but she has done so with the full knowledge—aye, the intention—to hold Virginia and the border States between her and the Storm, and to carry out her caprices, regardless of these border States, while relying on them.

But—however it has been done—an issue has been made. The subjection of South Carolina or any seceding State, in consequence of their determination not to submit to the policy of the Republicans, is a blow at the entire South—subjection to all. We are, thenceforth, humiliated. We are conquered. We could not hold up our heads in that Union any more. We would meet a Northern man as the Saxon met the Norman.

Our fellow-countrymen at the North can undertake to preserve this Union with the sword, if they shall deem it wise. They may consider South Carolina, Alabama, or Mississippi, as in a state of secession or rebellion. The naked fact is, that, at the South, upon any display of force, whether belonging to the political school of Mr. CALHOUN or Mr. WEBSTER, every sword will leap from its scabbard from the mouth of the Susquehanna to those of the Mississippi.

Is there any man at the North who loves the Union? As one loving it equally as well, we implore him to utter that word no more. The Southern people will stake all upon war, if war must come; and if the superior numbers of the North expect to *subdue* fifteen Southern States, with a population of eight millions of whites, of undoubted courage, they may fairly rely upon war.

Numbers—numbers of the people of Virginia—who are outraged by the insulting attitude of South Carolina—nevertheless, see that it is best, in the matter of the forts, to even bear with it—for the sake of the future.

The heart of Virginia yearns towards the Union. If the Northern people feel an interest in the Union, let them co-operate to pluck it from the present fearful peril. Every word of menace in a northern paper—every threat and taunt from the Republican leaders—swells and deepens the tide of Secession. We do not expect anything of the New York *Tribune:* why does the New York *Times,* the *Courier* and *Enquirer,* the Springfield *Republican,* use words of bitterness? If they are determined against all adjustment, if civil war is inevitable in their view, it were still in better taste on their part and ours, to draw the sword in silence.

If this question is to be referred to a National Convention—when each party will have had the great element of *Time*—no invective and no blood had better intervene.

After that, if the Northern people think proper—and in the meantime they can get ready—if there is no adjustment, the war can commence.

We think it a great misfortune that there is not at present a calm interchange of opinion between the Northern and Southern press. There is not the slightest occasion for any exasperation of language. Let us behave with courtesy.

One word, and we are done: The Northern press rest their uncompromising opposition to such an adjustment as the Missouri Compromise line, on their conscientious objections to extending slavery. Any adjustment of this question between the North and the South would contain a provision against the reopening of the African Slave Trade. Therefore the number of slaves, would not be (materially) increased by allowing it to go to the territories. Slavery would be diffused, but not increased. Or rather it *would shift its location.* Missouri, Kentucky, &c., would in process of time, become *free,* and their slaves would go to the Cotton States, and the new Slave Territories. —Each new slave territory would drain a border State; the area of slavery would not really be enlarged.

On the other hand, if the South has no outlet for its slaves, in the process of time, it would become Africanized. The tide of emigration from the border States might be even arrested, and Slavery *fastened* where under the principle of expansion, it would otherwise cease.

Now, does any fair-minded anti-slavery man desire this? Does he wish to overwhelm the South with a slave, or free, negro population?

At all events, under such a view of the case, is the position of the

South on this question, a singular one? Does it not, even in the eyes of an anti-slavery man give great force to their claim of "equality" in the territories—even supposing slavery a great evil? Is it the mission of the United States government to dam up slavery, until the South is submerged?

134. SOUTH CAROLINA

(Daily Courier, Louisville, January 10, 1861)

South Carolina is the object of the bitterest and most persistent attacks of those among us in the border Slave States, whose innate and ineradicable hatred of our peculiar institution prompts them to whatever may embarrass or complicate the movements of the people of the South at this terrible crisis in their affairs.

That noble little State, so fruitful of great statesmen, and heroic and immortal soldiers—the hot-bed of chivalry and generous achievements—the home of domestic virtues and private worth, the very faults of whose people arise from an excess of the sentiments and impulses most honorable in human nature—that State, because she was the first to do that in which her sisters are hastening to join her, is sought to be made odious to the people of the country; and to this end her institutions are libelled, her citizens calumniated, her purposes misrepresented, her actions distorted, and all that the finest wit or the coarsest ribaldry, the most skillful and delicate perversion or the most absurd and palpable falsehood, the most unwarrantable and criminal suppression of facts or the most industrious circulation of unfounded and maglignantly false rumors and reports can accomplish, is done to affect public sentiment and destroy the influence of an example which appeals alike to the sympathies and to the interest of the Southern people.

We need enter on no defense of South Carolina. She may have erred; but she at least has erred on the side of safety. She may have been precipitate; but when equality, independence, and liberty are at stake, it is better to strike too soon, than to wait until it is in vain to strike at all. She may not have suffered as much up to this time as Kentucky has; but it is undeniable that she has more to risk in the future. She has nearly twice as many negroes as this State; and while our people might gradually get rid of their slaves by selling them to the States South of us, South Carolina must keep hers, because she cannot find a market for them; and to part with them would be to convert her vast plantations into barren wastes and dreary deserts; white labor may produce corn, and wheat, and cattle, and mules, and horses; but African slavery is indispensable to the production of cotton.—South Carolina did not consult her sister States before withdrawing from the Union; but she has asked consultations and conferences in regard to interests common to all, in times past, and they have refused to meet her, and some of them have treated her with positive indignity: she would not have rejected overtures for a conference with such States, but she could not again propose one.

Acting not rashly, but with due reflection, in view of all the facts, and with a proper regard for the consequences, the people of South Carolina, appealing to God and the civilized world for the rectitude of their intentions and the justice of their conduct, and pledging to each other their lives, fortunes, and sacred honors, have formally and solemnly repealed the act by which they became one of the United States of North America and proclaimed themselves free and independent.

This important ordinance bears date, December 20th, 1860.

South Carolina, having been the first to take this important step, is kept in view by the enemies of a Southern Confederacy to the exclusion of the other States that are joined in a common cause with her, for the purpose of making the impression that she is alone; that she is actuated purely by factious motives and revolutionary considerations; that she is trying to "drag" the other States into the movement, and that she, small in extent and with an inconsiderable population, may be easily dragooned into obedience by the Federal Government.

The idea which it is thus endeavored to convey is equally false and mischievous.

South Carolina was the first to withdraw, but she is not alone. *In thirty days from the date of her ordinance of secession Florida, Alabama, Mississippi, and Georgia will have passed similar ordinances.* She deserves no more censure, no more abuse, no bitterer denunciation, than these States do. Their action and hers will be the same. When she is singled out for attack it is but to divert the public mind from the magnitude of the movement she is engaged in, and thus to deceive our people in regard to the nature of the crisis. And this is neither patriotic nor just to our people.

135. To A. Lincoln, President Elect of the United States:

(*Daily Missouri Republican,* St. Louis, January 14, 1861)

Gloom pervades the country—despair of a settlement of the differences between the North and the South is taking deep root in the minds of the People. Those who were sanguine a month ago that the good sense of the leaders of opposing sections would work out a peaceful and satisfactory solution of questions which in themselves ought to be adjusted in a day's time, now begin to give up in despair, and to look to the consequences of a disruption of the Union and civil war. Brave men though they be, as all Americans are, they yet do not contemplate the alternative without shuddering and abhorrence. It is no ordinary thing to look at such an array as this country will present if instant measures are not taken to prevent a resort to arms. Men who are now tranquil and even indifferent—men who, in the quietude of their homes, rest under the delusion that these questions are to receive an amicable solution—will, when aroused to the dread reality of the clash of arms, be as prompt to resist coercion of the slave States as any citizen of any one of the Cotton States. Blood ought not to be—must not be—shed, if patriotism and love of country can prevent it. The Governor of Virginia, in a manly, noble message, has said to Virginia, and to the country, that no hostile army designed to coerce any one of her sister States, shall set foot upon or pass over Virginia soil without meeting with resistance. That sentence is, of itself, indicative of the determination of fifteen States of the Union, and they will find hundreds of thousands of supporters in the Free States. We of Missouri have always held close relations to Illinois. We see each other every day—we administer to each other's wants— we buy each other's products—we intermarry with each other, and cultivate the most kindly social feelings: think you, sir, it will be a pleasant sight to see people holding these relations arming for the deadly strife—the carnage and destruction which is to follow civil war? And yet, no man who looks at public affairs as they now stand, can avoid any other conclusion than that, unless there is a speedy and final settlement of these difficulties the country, must be deluged with blood. South Carolina, Alabama, Mississippi and Florida have declared their separation from, and independence of the United States. Two other States, Louisiana and Georgia, will soon follow.[1] Thus,

[1] The Georgia Convention did not assemble until January 16; that of Louisiana not until January 23.

six States have virtually gone out of the Union—so far as their own action is concerned—hastily, without sufficient cause as we believe, but still they have assumed an attitude of independence of the Government of the United States—and what is to be done? To attempt to coerce them back, by military force, will bring ruin upon every State in this Union. One-half of your own State will resist any attempt to organize or march an army for the subjugation of Mississippi, or any one of the revolting States, and Kentucky and Tennessee, when the worst comes to the worst, will again become "dark and bloody ground," before they will suffer their soil to be polluted by the tread of armed hosts marching to the slaughter of their neighbors and friends and kinsmen in the Southern States.

You, Mr. Lincoln, have it in your power to stop all this disorder and possible civil war.—Upon you will rest the responsibility if it be not done. You have only to say the word, and two weeks need not elapse before all these difficulties may be healed, and harmony and fraternity are restored. It will not do to say that you are not President, or that it will be presumption in you to move before you are sworn into office. Men of good impulses are moved to do whatever is right, whenever and wherever the occasion arises. You claim to be, and we concede that you are, a Patriot, and that you desire to restore the harmony and the prosperity of these States. We doubt not that you would sacrifice your life, if by so doing you could bring back these States to the condition in which they were six months ago. Can it be regarded as a very great sacrifice, then, when you are asked to advise your political friends at Washington, in Congress, to give up their opposition to the measure of adjustment known as the Crittenden proposition. A word from you is sufficient for that purpose, and as you have said that you are willing to do anything that is honorable to secure a restoration of fraternal relations between States, why not do it now, before men become more exasperated than they are, and when settlement is yet possible?

Mr. Lincoln—the people of St. Louis spoke trumpet-tongued, two days ago, in favor of the Union, and of the adjustment of all difficulties on the basis of the Crittenden proposition. Your own political friends took no part in that meeting. We commend the resolutions then and there adopted to your consideration. You will note, if you read them, that they are no common expressions of opinion, but that every word was well weighed before it was adopted. Had you been present, and witnessed the calmness, the decision and the fixedness of purpose which marked every countenance, you would have seen that they were in earnest. So far, Missouri has shown less of bravado, less of intemperate action, than any other State in the Union; and she has a right to ask, and she does ask, that you will interpose with your friends to put a stop to all these troubles between the North and the South, and which, if not adjusted, will lead inevitably to civil war—in which fifteen States will have to be subjugated before the shadow of peace can be restored. Will you do it?

136. SEWARD ON THE CRISIS

(*The New Orleans Bee,* January 15, 1861)

The brief abstract published of the speech of Senator SEWARD [1] has produced some little sensation, and excited a notable amount of discussion. It is entirely evident that Mr. Seward reflects the views of the President elect, whose Secretary of State he has consented to become. Hence the opinions expressed by the shrewd and sagacious Senator from New York on the existing crisis really merit more than passing attention. Besides, SEWARD is the foremost man of the Black Republican party, and probably commands a larger share of influence in the non-slaveholding States than any other politician. Though not seated on the throne, he is the power behind the throne, greater perhaps than the occupant himself. Few men surpass him in ability or in that bland and oily demeanor with which crafty statesmen are wont to veil their inmost thoughts. So successfully does Mr. SEWARD wear the drapery of polished manners and moderation of language, that while he is equally dreaded and distrusted by the South, he has constantly maintained friendly relations with Southern Congressmen.

When Mr. SEWARD preaches conciliation, it is incumbent on the South to watch him closely. Curt and meagre as is the summary of his remarks, we think it betrays his usual characteristics. He is anxious for Congress to redress, if it can, any real grievances of the offended States. Very magnanimous, but with important qualifications! If Congress can, it should do so and so, and if the grievances are real, they ought to be redressed. In the ample margin which SEWARD furnished, it will be hard indeed if he cannot evade responsibility, either upon the score of the inability of Congress to grant what may be demanded, or because the alleged grievances will be said not to exist. After settling these desiderata, which may be done summarily, as just indicated, Mr.

[1] See *Cong. Globe,* 36 Cong., 2 Sess., I, 341–344.

SEWARD is for supplying the President with all the means necessary to maintain the Union. Of course this is the essence and staple of Black Republican harangues. They are all intensely Unionish. The Southern States have nothing to complain of; they are froward and rebellious children; they must be kept in the Union—that is, in obedience to the supremacy of Black Republicanism, peaceably or forcibly as the case may be. In Black Republican political philosophy there is no such thing as the recognition of our Federal Government as a compact. Whatever it may have been at the period of its formation, it is now simply the sway of the majority over the minority. So let the South beware how she cherishes any chimerical notions of the right to withdraw from a violated compact. The Black Republican dogma of the perpetuity and imperishability of the Union carries with it the right to resort to coercion for its enforcement. To send armies and navies to fight the South is the practical meaning of Mr. SEWARD's desire to maintain the Union.

But it is only fair to give the Senator credit for a spirit of compromise. Unlike the most truculent of the Black Republicans, he is willing to do something. Let us see the extent of his generosity. In the first place, he will not object to the repeal of the Personal Liberty bills. Extraordinary condescension, especially when it is remembered that Congress has no jurisdiction whatever over the States which have passed these bills, and therefore, that Mr. SEWARD simply expresses his individual sanction of their repeal. Next, he is absolutely disposed to vote for an amendment to the Constitution that Congress should never have the power to abolish slavery within the States. What a boon to the South! What a wonderful spirit of concession is herein displayed! The Black Republicans promise to bind themselves not to abolish slavery in the Southern States. They will steal our slaves, and abuse us with frantic violence; they will fight us with the tremendous and almost omnipotent engine of public opinion, but they will abstain from passing an act to abolish slavery. The South should certainly evince eternal gratitude to Senator SEWARD for such amazing liberality. Finally, he will support any law by which forays and raids of Abolitionists upon the slave States may be hereafter prevented. This is the merest flammery. No law can prevent misguided fanatics and zealots from putting their own necks in peril, and jeoparding the safety of the South by attempted invasion and insurrection. A reform in public sentiment is the sole available remedy, and of this specific Senator SEWARD does not and cannot promise us a particle. His compromises are therefore utterly valueless. Not one of them, nor all of them together meet the case, or would for a moment induce the South to retrace her course. Senator SEWARD's smooth tone of conciliation, and apparently expansive patriotism mean nothing tangible, and afford no prospect of reconciliation. His speech is sublimated Black Republicanism under a flimsy disguise of kindness and sympathy for the South.

137. FUNDAMENTAL PRINCIPLES INVOLVED

(*The Daily Picayune,* New Orleans, January 15, 1861)

The Northern journals come freighted with threatenings to bring back the seceding States into the Union by force. Senators in Congress of the Republican side talk of it as a high duty, and public gatherings of their partisans endorse the sentiment. Governors of Northern States make it a leading topic of their official messages, and here and there a bellicose member of some State Legislature, or a blazing patriot in some town meeting, calls upon the Northern States to put themselves on a war footing at once, to organize State armies with a lavish disregard of the cost, to be tendered to the federal authorities "to maintain the Government."

The favorite form of expression in which these resolves are clothed is, that it is the first and highest duty "to maintain the Union." But a Union upheld by a war, which is made necessary by the revolting of many large and powerful States from an unfriendly and oppressive Government, is condemned at once by the act. When armies and fleets are employed to keep a confederation of States together, it is a mockery to send them forth as messengers of union. It is for the subjugation of the minority section to the will of the majority, and every element which makes it a circle of consenting States in a harmonious Union disappears under the crushing process. To talk of war, therefore, as the means of perpetuating a Union is a mockery. It might perpetuate a Government, but that Government will cease to be a federative one, and will contain within itself essential traits of a military despotism—the retention, by superior force, of an unwilling people in political bondage, to a Government which they had unanimously risen to throw off. The Government so established, if such a monstrous thing could ever be established, would have no principles remaining in common with those which make the true theory of the constitution of the present Government, a departure from which has brought on the present convulsion. A war to "maintain the Union" is simply, therefore, a war to extinguish the Union, and to maintain a Government such as was never contemplated by any of the States which compose it, and which would not be tolerated by any State now, if there were a question of creating or·restoring a Government.

The clamor for dealing with these grave issues by the sword is so intolerably aggressive in spirit and in purpose that its effect is seen in the rallying the most hesitating of the border slave States into a common cause with each other to proclaim unflinching opposition to such sentiments, and a unanimous determination that no such attempt shall be made without being resisted to the last extremity, on the first step, and on the borders of the first invaded State.

Suppose it granted, that in point of logic, under the forms of the existing constitution, the right of secession does not exist; that one State cannot secede, nor two States, nor five nor six, nor any number of States. What then? Are these awful issues to be treated on naked considerations of power, or technical considerations of jurisdiction only? If we must yield to all governments because they are established and because they have the forms of regularity, and can make out a good paper title, the American Revolution was a crime, and the Boston port bill, by which Great Britain undertook to punish Massachusetts for interrupting the payment of duties on tea, was a lawful exercise of the power to collect revenue.

What has been reasoned before—in behalf of the right of self-protection against an oppressive government—will be reasoned again; what has been done before, to maintain that right, will be done again, subject to the same invincible rule of human conduct, as set forth in the Declaration of Independence—that "mankind are more disposed to suffer, while evils are sufferable, than to right themselves by abolishing the forms to which they are accustomed."

If the action of the Southern States be indeed what these Northerners describe it, altogether revolutionary, what then? The magnitude and unanimity of the movement lifts it above any possible association with rebellion, for an accomplished rebellion is a successful revolution, and what revolution could be more perfectly completed than this promises to be within a few days—in all its forms—than it is already, studied in the point of view in which public law looks upon the change of government. Five of the cotton States have already formally abolished the whole machinery of federal authority within their limits, and displaced all the federal officers. The federal forts and arsenals, with a few exceptions, are occupied by State troops. Each State has its own separate government organized, and its people are arming for State protection. In a few weeks they will probably have a provisional government for the whole; and that government will be accepted by three millions of people. There will then be no vestige of the federal authority left within their borders, except a few soldiers in some beleaguered fortress.

Now, a confederacy thus formed and a government thus created make an established State as completely as though independence had been won by ten years of battle. The principle of State sovereignty will have carried the country in a few weeks to a consummation which under a consolidated State or a despotic government would have been effected only through sore travails and with infinite internal disorders. No disorders need be apprehended with these, except from without; and such a development of popular will and the sovereign energy of State organization would clearly place any external invader in the wrong. No theory of the rights of government other than that which impelled the conduct of George III in the last century, and Francis Joseph of Austria in this, would justify an invasion to overthrow a government established principally among themselves by three millions of people, in their separate but concurrent communities, for their own security and happiness.

That invasion would be one for reconquest of a country as completely independent before the world as the Dutch Republics were after they had expelled the Spanish troops, and much more so than any of the feeble South American Republics were when the Governments of Europe took them into the society of nations. If, then, as these violent men at the North assume, secession is rebellion and rebellion must be put down; were it not better to consider that a rebellion, if they be pleased so to call it, which is so widespread, thoroughly organized, and sustained, and accomplished, makes a revolution which must be encountered by a war for conquest, as distinctly as though it were a foreign country they propose to overrun.

We say nothing here of the costs and chances and direful consequences of such an unnatural war. These will doubtless have their full weight in the councils of the real people of the North, when the fact of the actual formation of a complete and harmonious Southern Government calls upon them to consider as well the state of the whole country and the true relations of the dissevered parts to each other, as to take out of the hands of the political managers, whose violence now seems to threaten implacable and undying war, the power to attempt the fulfillment of such purposes. The main fact to be considered by them, and at the North, is that from present demonstrations there will be presented to them a new government, erected by a people of the same language and blood, in the exercise of the indestructible right of all communities to provide for their own safety and happiness. They must determine whether they will go to war, interminable and hopeless war, to subvert it. If not, will they accept it, as the basis of a re-arrangement of rights and securities under a new confederation, to embrace the whole? Or, acknowledging the necessity which denounces the separation, undertake to live in peace between friendly and coterminous, if divided, governments.

It is the earnest prayer of all hearts—not fired to frenzy by passionate partisanship—that so terrible a choice, among these alternatives, may not be made—for subjugation by war, rather than negotiation for peace. The signs are not favorable, but they are not decisive. Selfish politicians, bellicose preachers, angry partisans and an incendiary press, have uttered a great deal of fiery and threatening talk, but the point of a full knowledge of the position and inflexible purposes of the people of the South is not yet reached by the controlling masses who will have to fight, and to pay, against the judgment and conscience of multitudes—against the instincts and interests of still more.

The steady advance of action in the South towards concentration and absolute unanimity, on every essential point in these disputes, and upon resistance to the attempt to close them by the sword, and the mighty considerations with which it appeals to the undivided American sentiment in behalf of the natural right of communities to self-government, to the precedents of our own history, our own treatment of other separate States, and our own recorded assertions of the principles of public law; and to the concessions which their justice has extorted, in our own day, from the mightiest sovereigns in Europe, ought to be our absolute security against the employment of any invading force whatever, the immediate tender of a satisfactory plan for a perfect reunion, or the recognition of separate independence.

Whether such wise counsels prevail at the North or not, foreign Governments will look only to the fact that a Government is established. If it have only a provisional Government, as in the case of mere insurrectionists, that is a sufficient dominion *de facto* for admitting the carrying on of commerce under the authorities in possession of the control of the local affairs. A Southern Government, fully organized and supported by the whole body of its own people, could not be excluded from intercourse with the rest of the world by the Mexican process of giving notice of the right of recovery to be used hereafter. Neither England nor France is to be prevented from seeking supplies indispensable to their own convenience and subsistence by such new fulminations of obsolete doctrines.

But this involves too many considerations to be treated in an article which has already grown under the pen to the length of *this*.

138. CAPTURE OF THE SOUTHERN FORTS

(*The Daily Picayune,* New Orleans, January 17, 1861)

The capture of the arsenals and fortified places of the United States, within the limits of the Southern States by the people and Government of those States, has given rise to an amount of Northern indignation wholly disproportioned to the gravity of the offence, viewed even in the light of a filibustering exploit. If it had been the foray of a lawless mob, for purposes of robbery and rapine, it could not have been visited with a greater amount of vindictive denunciation. The pious loyalty—which slept sweetly over the murderous raid of John Brown, or only roused itself to the utterance of a jibe, or to amuse its lassitude with a sneering objurgation—is aghast with horror at the orderly and authorized occupation of forts and arsenals which cannot be used at all by the captors except in defence of the people or territory they were erected to defend. It will take but little reflection to set this matter right, with those, at least, whose opinions it concerns us to conciliate. Some of our people entertain doubts as to the propriety of the seizure, and numberless conservative thinking men, elsewhere succumbing before the wild ado of their press and politicians, look upon it as treasonable and felonious.

To understand the moral bearing of any act, it is necessary to view it in connection with the circumstances under which it was done. It will be asking little enough to beg our readers who may entertain doubts in this matter, to give to the consideration of a proceeding, which many think might be justified on the naked sovereignty of the actor over the premises, the advantage which even a criminal in the dock has a right to claim, of being judged by the circumstances of the case. Now, the main fact in the matter is that there is an imminent danger of a hostile collision between the North, represented in this issue by the general Government, and the South, represented, for the time being, by their State Governments. Who denies this? Who does not feel it? Whether the causes which may produce this collision be judged sufficient or not, whether the Southern position has been taken precipitately or upon sufficient consideration, it matters not; the main fact in the premises is the same—the imminency of hostile collision. Surely the North will not controvert this fact, whilst she desecrates the Senate with the vaporings of a seedy buffoon like Hale, or the air be vexed by the mouthings of a sentimental poltroon like Sumner. With here and there a bright exception, like jewels glittering in an Ethiop's ear, the Northern press is a dreary waste of hostile diatribe and threatening denunciation. The fact is so —collision is imminent.

This admitted, what in the name of all that is warning in history, or reasonable in prophecy, would any one have the people to do? Sit befogged and listless under frowning batteries till awakened by the alarms of war? This was not the way our revolutionary fathers did. As soon as the war with the mother country became imminent, they seized upon the forts and arsenals of the Government of Great Britain. The ease of the taking of Ticonderoga by Ethan Allen has become memorable from his challenge to the officer in charge to surrender, "in the name of the Great Jehovah and the Continental Congress." But this was not an isolated instance of the capture of Government property before the war was declared. The right was exercised wherever it could be; and Mr. Hale, when he gets back to New Hampshire, can visit, if he thinks fit, the site of a British arsenal so taken; and Mr. Seward, from the parade ground at West Point, can see the ruins of an old fort that met the same fate.

But let us come nearer our own times—last month is near enough we should think—for our purposes. The people of Pittsburg, in December last, imagined that the Government was about to send cannon to the South from the United States Arsenal there. Upon the rumor of such an intention they assembled in great masses and resolved that the cannon should not leave the city. If the Government had any purpose of sending cannon down the river, the menaces of the populace awed them into submission. The cannon were not sent. Now, these pieces of ordnance were not in use in Pittsburg. They were Government stores; and the people of Pittsburg did not know what use the United States designed making of them. But this they did know: that they were not to be employed against them; they were not to be used to coerce that city, to demolish her smoking foundries, to quell her teeming factories.

Contrast the two cases in view of the facts in each, and which is the greater crime, admitting for the sake of comparison both to be wrong? The United States holds her armories North under the duress of mobs. They are as much captured as the forts and arsenals of Louisiana. She cannot move them where the exigencies of the State, in the opinion of the Government, require them. The apprehension that in some way, or in some sort, they know not how, when or where, but certainly not against them or their firesides, they might be employed for or against a people who have as much right to them as they have, was enough to array a posse against their removal, which the Government could not or did not resist. In a practical point of view, the arsenal at Pittsburg was as truly captured as the arsenal at Baton Rouge, without any of the justifications which qualify or the order that characterized the seizure of the latter. And yet not a whimper is heard from one end of the North to the other, not a reproach, not a rebuke.

And all this was done before the seizing of the forts and arsenals of this State was mooted as a precautionary measure. Should the people of Louisiana, or could they, longer delay to take possession of such parcels of munitions as chanced to be within her jurisdiction, until the little that she had should be given to those who had already more than they wanted?

In a strategical view of the pending trouble, the captured places were of no use to the Government. They could not be held against the State in time of war. They were all inland and indefensible from land attack. They were eye-sores and irritations. They were depositories of munitions of destruction, which might be used against us, or removed to leave us naked to our enemies. Does the North want all? Does she require all the ships, and cannon, and stores, and munitions of war to subjugate us? If she does not mean that, she has no use for the things taken. In a few short months she will have her President, her Vice President, her Cabinet, her everything. Why, a generous enemy, instead of railing at the little the South has got, would divide the property held in common, and "after, fight" her.

It is the province of infatuation to view this matter in any other light than that which the time or the facts shed upon it. To consider it in the same spirit in which it would have been viewed a short twelve months past, we would have to bring back the *status quo* of the twelve months past. Would that we could roll back the wheel of time, retrace the many hours through which eighteen hundred and sixty, "like a foul and ugly witch," limped tediously away, that the people might behold the gulf into which fanaticism and sectional excesses were hurrying them! This can not be; but for the year to come, the North can act as she might have done, had she seen the end in the beginning of the last.

139. MR. SEWARD

(The Daily Picayune, New Orleans, January 20, 1861)

Mr. Seward is reported to have said, in his late speech in the U. S. Senate,[1] that whoever shall succeed in adjusting the constitution so as to bring peace to the country, and re-unite the States in the bonds of perpetual amity and concord, will win and deserve a greater renown than those who framed it. If the New York prophet believes in his own vaticination, it is but reasonable to suppose he is ambitious of reaping the fame he so glowingly depicts—for Mr. Seward is an ambitious man. Will he aspire to so great renown? Will he undertake the task? Will he indeed labor for its accomplishment in the spirit in which it can alone be obtained? Will he bring himself to the heroic task of throwing himself into the yawning chasm and, like a second Curtius, let the gaping wounds of his country close over his buried body if need be?

The South has regarded him as the arch-demon of an infernal throng. His genius has organized the vagrancies of fanaticism into a code of aggressive principles. He is the author of the pandects of the "higher law." For a long season he alone, of the locust horde of treasonable declaimers, was or even sought to be respectable. He is the leader, the maker, and the manager of the Northern party; for although he lost the nomination of the Chicago Convention, and for a time seemed overslaughed and laid aside, he recovered his position the moment the excitement of the occasion expired, and stands now confessedly the champion of the Republican forces and without a peer. For him to propose a settlement such as would be acceptable to the South, would be to invoke a storm of denunciation from the loose masses which his right hand shaped into a successful organization. Has he the courage to do it?

Mr. Seward knows better than any other man of his party what

[1] *Cong. Globe,* 36 Cong., 2 Sess., I, 341–344.

will be a satisfactory settlement of the troubles that are threatening the country. He knows well that in their adjustment he must approach the subject as though he had never spoken or given a vote upon it. It would be no dishonor to any man who claims to be a statesman to sacrifice his opinions, however sincerely entertained, to the safety of his country. It would only prove that he loves his country more than he does his opinions. He may well ask himself if his theory on any subject is worth the price of revolution, of civil war, and the dismemberment of an empire. Mr. Clay, on an occasion less momentous than the present, offered up the "American system," of which he was the father and the supporter, on the altar of peace. Mr. Clay lived to receive the homage of the Union for an act of devoted loyalty to the interests of his country. Mr. Seward will have to make the same sacrifice, encounter the same risks, buffet a ruder storm, encounter a wilder opposition. Has he the patriotism to do it?

Mr. Seward's sands are running low in the hour glass. But he has time enough, perhaps, to do great good. He may win the imperishable renown he predicts for those who shall heal a broken constitution, and bring back a bruised and scattered people. If he persists in a career which must inaugurate civil war, he can scarcely live to see the end of it. His waning years will be spent in the midst of convulsions which drown the voice of reason, and wars which waste a country he professes to love so much, with sword and brand. He will be harassed by the reflection that he, in a great measure, was the author of the desolation which he beholds. The blasted emblems of his country's prosperity will sear the eyeballs to look upon. His name will be held in execration by the wise and good. If, however, he should succeed in reconciling the differences which now distract us by just councils and amending the constitution so as to make it the guardian and protector of all the rights of all the people, and guarantee the equality of all the States in the Union, he will rescue his name from the political desperadoes who use it for purposes of evil. He will enjoy the satisfaction of being a public benefactor, reap the rich harvest of his own prophetic vision, and close his eyes upon his country's flag emblazoned with other stars and glowing with added light. Has he the wisdom to do it?

We expect nothing from fanatics. Their hearts are stone, their ears are deaf, their eyes are bleared, their breath is pestilence. When did unbridled fanaticism stop short of the stake? When was it sated short of desolation? Its incense is the odor of charring bodies: its revelry the blazing of sacked cities. It blesses the earthquake which swallows up the land; it chimes with the storm that wastes the sea; it consecrates the emissaries who carry firebrands into defenseless places. Not from such do we expect anything, hope anything, wish anything, or fear anything. But Mr. Seward is not a fanatic.

Neither have we anything to say to the soldiers of fortune, the swash bucklers of the abolition camp who hire their lances to the highest bidder, who snuff the spoils before the battle rages. They have nothing to hope from peace, nothing to lose from war. They care nothing for the country, deserve nothing from it and expect nothing from it but the offal of the slaughter. Mr. Seward knows this. He has seen a mercenary whom no one suspected of a sweet tooth, plot his overthrow in the Chicago Convention, because he did not, when Governor of New York, stow with good things a maw which seemed so meek to be so ravenous. He knows that his followers, except the fanatics who will devour him in turn when there is nothing else to prey upon, are composed of the venal of other parties who openly apostatised or secretly deserted their comrades as the tide of hope ebbed from the flow which attracted them to it. He knows they are ready to desert him as well, and will do it when the fortunes of their party wane, or when a pliant tool is needed to spoil the country for the sake of the distribution. Not from such has the country anything to hope. But Mr. Seward is not an adventurer.

Mr. Seward's position is one which enables him to inaugurate measures of pacification in the right quarter. He is too shrewd for a fanatic; above the temptations of an adventurer. He is ambitious, and he is able. Has he the heroism to embalm his name in the memory of posterity at the risk of martyrdom? Has he the patriotism to offer his theories on the altar of his country's peace? Has he the wisdom to devote his talents and great opportunities to the offices of pacification? We know what he is not; believe what he is; where will the sequel find him?

140. THE DIFFERENCE

(New Orleans Daily Crescent, January 21, 1861)

There is this difference between the Northern and Southern States, which illustrates the exact nature of the quarrel between the two sections: That, while the Southern States, in the Union, would have interposed no objection to the secession of any Northern State, the

Northern States, on the other hand, are thrown into a perfect paroxysm of rage at the mere whisper of an intention to secede, on the part of any State of the South.

Thus, if, at any time within the last ten years, Massachusetts had threatened to leave the Union, the idea, so far from being unpalatable to the South, would have been hailed with the liveliest demonstrations of joy and satisfaction. The South would have bid her go and go quickly, and have esteemed it a happy riddance. But, on the other hand, when any Southern State proposes to leave the Union, Massachusetts becomes intensely disgusted thereat, and considers herself very much insulted and scandalized.

Why is this? Why is it that the South is perfectly willing for the North to secede, while the reverse is true of the North, as respects the South? In social life, when two persons are together, and the presence of one is known to be distasteful to the other, the remedy of withdrawal is universally admitted. But, for the offending and offensive party to follow up the withdrawing party and insist upon forcing his company upon him, when he knows it to be irksome and hateful, is a breach of every canon of good manners and polite society.

When the North tells us that we have no right to withdraw from the Union, we answer that we are perfectly willing to stay in the Union if *they themselves* will withdraw! We will not question *their* right to secede, but, on the contrary, will concede it cheerfully. We would perhaps prefer this arrangement to the other. The South, which claims the right of secession for itself, is equally ready and willing to grant the same right to the North; and we will undertake to pledge the Southern States that if those of the North wish to secede from the Union, not only will no objection be raised, but, as to a large majority of them, the secession will be accounted a most fortunate and happy circumstance for us.

But, as the Northern States will *not* leave the Union, as in common decency they ought to do, seeing that they are so unhappy about the countenance the Union is supposed to give to the institution of slavery, there is no alternative to the South except to withdraw for herself. As it is manifestly impossible for the two sections to get along together in peace and harmony, and as the North, which might withdraw without objection, refuses to do so, we are driven to the necessity of withdrawing ourselves, painful as it appears to be to our loving and considerate friends and brethren of the States of the North.

But, why is there such objection made to the withdrawal of the

South? We are told by Abolition orators and organs that the South is a poor, miserable region—that most of the wealth, the enterprise, and the intelligence of the nation is in the North—that the Southern people, as was said by Sumner in the Senate, are identified with, and apologists for, an institution essentially "barbaric"—that our section is unable to support a mail system, and that we are pensioners, to that extent, of the Federal Government—that we are, in short, a semi-civilized, God-forsaken people, a long ways behind the "great North" in the arts, in refinement, in education, in enterprise, and in everything else that constitutes what they call "civilization." One would suppose they would be eager to be relieved of association with a people of whom they have so poor an opinion. So far the contrary, however, they are, as we have before said, mortally offended at the bare idea of our dissolving with them our political connection.

There must be a reason for this, as there is for everything else, and the reason is plain enough. All that they say about the South is false, and, what is more, they know it to be false. They know that the South is the main prop and support of the Federal system. They know that it is Southern productions that constitute the surplus wealth of the nation, and enables us to import so largely from foreign countries. They know that it is their import trade that draws from the people's pockets sixty or seventy millions of dollars per annum, in the shape of duties, to be expended mainly in the North, and in the protection and encouragement of Northern interests. They know that it is the export of Southern productions, and the corresponding import of foreign goods, that gives profitable employment to their shipping. They know that the bulk of the duties is paid by the Southern people, though first collected at the North, and that, by the iniquitous operation of the Federal Government, these duties are mainly expended among the Northern people. They know that they can plunder and pillage the South, as long as they are in the same Union with us, by other means, such as fishing bounties, navigation laws, robberies of the public lands, and every other possible mode of injustice and peculation. They know that in the Union they can steal Southern property in slaves, without risking civil war, which would be certain to occur if such a thing were done from the independent South. And, above and beyond all this, is the Puritanic love of mean tyranny and cold-blooded, inexorable oppression, which the Union enables them to cherish and reduce to practice—coupled with the Pharisaical boast of "holier than thou," which they are constantly uttering as a reproach to the South—both of which feelings are innate in the descendants of the Pilgrims, and have become a part of their nature, which they could not get rid of it they wished.

These are the reasons why these people do not wish the South to secede from the Union. They are enraged at the prospect of being despoiled of the rich feast upon which they have so long fed and fattened, and which they were just getting ready to enjoy with still greater *goût* and gusto. They are mad as hornets because the prize slips them just as they are ready to grasp it. Their fruitless wailing and frantic rage only serve to confirm the South in her inflexible determination to break up an alliance which is as unnatural as it is, to us, oppressive and degrading.

141. NORTHERN SENTIMENT

(*The New Orleans Bee,* January 22, 1861)

The Northern journals received by mail afford us some inkling of the state of feeling in that section. There is nothing whatever in it to countenance the hope that the Southern States will be allowed without molestation to consummate the resumption of their independence. Whether Black Republicanism stifles the better and purer instincts of the North, or whether the commercial and pecuniary crisis consequent upon political agitation has blinded the sufferers to all sense of right and justice, we know not; but certain it is that, with few exceptions, the Northern press seems to consider secession as treason and rebellion, to be put down by the strong arm of the Federal Government. The quasi-Southern views put forth in the earlier part of the session by Mr. BUCHANAN, and the disposition at first manifested by him to offer no obstacle to the movements of South Carolina, created universal indignation throughout the non-slaveholding States; and even now when the President has greatly modified his tone, has called around him coercionists as his official advisers, and displays a marked leaning towards the North, there prevails considerable dissatisfaction because he does not proceed to send armies and navies to chastise the rebellious cotton States with fire and the sword. There is in fact among the people of the North a willful, or at all events a strange misconception of what is going on at the South. Although, like the dissolving views of a diorama, star after star is disappearing from the flag of the Union, they cannot be induced to believe that the South is in earnest. It is true that Florida followed South Carolina, that Mississippi next withdrew, that Alabama then seceded, and that Georgia has now abandoned the Union. Yet the North acts upon the presumption either that these renunciations are mere empty formalities, and may be easily recalled; or that they have been made against the wishes of immense numbers of the population of the seceding Commonwealths.

So limited is the understanding of Southern opinion that the North is wholly insensible to the truth that there is no Union party in some ten or more slaveholding States. It confounds Co-operationists with Unionists, and is possessed with the fallacious idea that because many high-minded and sincere Southerners believed it would be more expedient for the cotton States to act in concert than to withdraw separately, they are all anxious to preserve the Union, albeit at the price of submission to the administration of ABRAHAM LINCOLN. This is a wild and absolutely baseless notion. Seven-eighths of the Co-operationists are heartily in favor of secession; and, indeed, events have succeeded each other with such startling rapidity as nearly to annihilate whatever there might have been amongst them of opposition to earlier and decisive action. A more egregious error than that of supposing that there are any Union men *per se* in the cotton States cannot well be imagined. Whatever may be the policy of the North, let it dismiss the foolish notion that its Union theories have any friends in this quarter.

Meanwhile the Northern people continue to hold what they are pleased to style Union meetings. We have examined the proceedings of some of these assemblages, and perceive that they are little better than Black Republican gatherings, at which the South is treated to an unlimited amount of obloquy; States which are out of the Union are denounced as subject to the penalties of treason; States which are preparing to quit the Union are menaced with dire mischief, and offers of men and money for the laudable purpose of coercing the South are freely made. This is Black Republican exemplification of love of the Union. They appear to forget that the very term itself "Union" implies voluntary association, and that if any of the parties should be forced to maintain a compulsory compact, it would cease to be a Union, and would become a despotism wielded by the many over the few, and by the powerful over the feeble. Is it conceivable, indeed, that the Federal Government, at the instigation of Northern fanatics, could possibly regard the secession of ten, twelve or fourteen States—nearly half the Republic—as rebellion, and could undertake to whip them back into their former relations with the North? Such madness appears impossible. And yet, if the false and pernicious theory of treason and coercion is to be practically illustrated, it is beyond a doubt that the Government will have to direct its fleets and armies against most, if not all, the slaveholding confederacies. Under any circumstances some eight States will abandon their connection with the Union in a few weeks, while a resort to violence will inevitably add five or six more to the number. We must confess that whilst the North ignores these considerations, and insanely cries out for coercion, we cannot but think that when it once clearly perceives that it is only knitting and consolidating Southern Union, and driving the reluctant border States into a close alliance with us, it will relinquish its unwise, wicked and sanguinary schemes. If, however, this hope should prove futile, we of the South are forewarned, and will in time be forearmed.

142. THE MODERATION OF TYRANNY

(*The Daily Delta,* New Orleans, January 23, 1861)

Mr. Seward's late speech is said, by his admirers at the North, by superficial people at the South, to be characterized by a tone of peculiar moderation. Thence the Black Republicans argue that the South, convinced of the fallacy of her suspicions, ought to abandon her attitude of resistance—her idea of independence. Thence, the few at the South who still worship at the altar of Unionism infer that the extinct fires may be rekindled, and the falling temple be restored. The arch-leader of Black Republicanism has spoken. Words of lactaqueous moderation fall from his lips. In honied phrases he recommends forbearance and patience. The fanatical and arrogant majority at the North will probably not relish a style which is so antagonistic to their feelings. Many of them may not understand the philosophy which forms the foundation of Mr. Seward's theories. But that sagacious man is now, as he has always been, in advance of his followers in ideas, while he has seemed to lag behind them in expression. He knows that a show of moderation costs little, and may gain much. The opiate before the dagger gives certainty to the final blow. To lull the victim to sleep averts the danger of his dying struggles, and simplifies the work of dispatching him. Mr. Seward understands those truths. Hence nothing appeals to him so strongly as the dangers in which the country is now involved. Nothing, he considers, is so necessary as moderation. He appears to be, in short, a remarkably amiable enemy. But the bloodiest tyrants that have ever disgraced humanity have counterfeited an amiability which might shame even Black Republican competition. Moderation is the favorite device of despots. While Philip the Second was engaged in burning his subjects at the stake, plundering them of their property, destroying their towns, he was particularly fond of calling himself a "sovereign, clement, mild and debonair." After the Duke of Alva had, by one sweeping decree, condemned all the inhabitants of the Netherlands to death, he expressed the most unbounded astonishment that those ungrateful people should have repaid his extraordinary moderation with discontent and rebellion. It was true that liberty of conscience was suppressed, and an unlimited royal despotism introduced in place of the ancient charters of the Provinces, but the Government had conceded everything except freedom of religion and a limitation of the royal prerogative.

Mr. Seward and his Black Republican followers are just as amiable as Philip, just as moderate as Alva. They are astonished that the South should distrust them in spite of all their protestations of moderation, all their declarations of forbearance. It is true that they have violated all their Constitutional obligations, but they are quite ready to enforce on the South their own theories of Constitutional obligation. It is true they have broken their promise not to steal Southern slaves, but they are willing to promise not to steal them again. It is true that they have robbed the South of her rights in the Territories, but they are willing to allow her to exist without them. It is surely strange that in the face of such magnanimous offers, such amiable declarations, the South should persist in her resolution to withdraw from the Union. Mr. Seward is willing to concede everything except our rights—grant everything except what we ask. He disclaims any intention to interfere with us, except for the repression of slavery; he repudiates all idea of coercion, except for the enforcement of the Federal laws. After the present difficulties shall have been composed, after the controversy shall have been ended, after the questions at issue shall have been settled, he is ready to sanction the call of a Convention to amend the Constitution in accordance with the requirements of the situation, and the demands of justice. But he will not consent to this until the contest shall have been terminated either one way or the other; until the South shall have succeeded in establishing her independence of the North, or until the North shall have subjugated the South. That is to say, he will not permit any arrangement until an arrangement shall have become either impossible or unnecessary. This is the remedy which Mr. Seward offers for the evils afflicting his own section of the country; these are the concessions he tenders to the adverse section. The remedy is only an aggravation of the evil; the concessions are only a repetition of aggression.

143. THE CRITTENDEN COMPROMISE

(*Republican Banner,* Nashville, January 25, 1861)

The Resolutions [1] adopted by the General Assembly, published in our paper a few days since, define the position of Tennessee satisfactorily, as we believe, to the great mass of the people. They substantially adopt the CRITTENDEN COMPROMISE as a basis of adjustment of the pending issues between the North and South, and Tennessee will say to the people of the North, not in a spirit of blustering defiance and braggadocio, but firmly and calmly, and with a sincere and honest desire that this adjustment may be accepted—we demand nothing more—*we will accept of nothing less.* This settlement can be agreed upon by the people of both sections without the sacrifice of a principle or of any material interest. It would be acceptable, we believe, to a majority of the people in the seceding States, and the State of Tennessee could take no course better calculated to befriend and conserve the interests of those States than by maintaining such a position as will enable her, in conjunction with other Southern States, to negotiate the adoption of this compromise with the North. That the sympathies of Tennessee are emphatically Southern, no one will deny. She will take no course, in any event, calculated to militate against the interests of her Southern sisters. But the question for her to decide— and it is a question upon which hangs her own and the destiny of the South and the Union— is what course is most judicious, most patriotic, and best calculated to conserve the interests of her Southern sisters, and if possible preserve the Union? Upon this question there is a difference of opinion. Some are for precipitate secession. Others for maintaining our present attitude, prepared, when the time comes, to act as mediators upon the basis of the Crittenden adjustment. If the policy of the former party is pursued, we lose the advantage of our position as pacificators, and gain nothing that we could not gain at

---

[1] "Resolutions of the Legislature of the State of Tennessee, relative to the present Condition of National Affairs, and suggesting certain Amendments to the Constitution," in *House Mis. Docs.,* 36 Cong., 2 Sess., Doc. 27.

any future time, when it shall be demonstrated, as it unfortunately may be, that a settlement is impracticable. We are therefore opposed to hasty action. We do not think the friends of a fair and honorable settlement, in the seceding States, desire Tennessee to follow their example until all honorable endeavors to secure such a settlement are exhausted. Doubtless there are many in those States who do not desire a settlement—who prefer disunion and a Southern Confederacy to any reconstruction of the Government. There are a few, even in Tennessee, who sympathize with these disunionists *per se,* but they are very few, and thus far have been very modest in the avowal of such sentiments. Tennessee is emphatically a Union State, if the Union can be preserved upon terms of equality and justice, and is for making an attempt to preserve it before abandoning the hope. The difference of opinion among her people is merely as to the best policy to be pursued to accomplish a given end, at which all seem to be driving. We should rejoice to see this difference of opinion reconciled or compromised, so that we might all move in solid phalanx, and as a unit. It would add immensely to our influence in the crisis, and might, indeed, be the means of securing what, under existing circumstances, may not be attained—a perpetuation of the Government.

In confirmation of our opinion above expressed that the CRITTENDEN COMPROMISE will be acceptable to the seceding States, we call attention to the following extract from a leading editorial in a late number of the New Orleans *Bee,* a secession paper:

Of the various plans of adjustment called forth by the crisis, that of Mr. Crittenden is the only one that seems fully inspired by a sense of justice. It offers something tangible—something which the South could and probably would agree to take into consideration, and which the North, or that portion of it which boasts its nationality, might accept without the smallest sacrifice of dignity or right. Mr. Crittenden himself entertains such entire confidence in the validity of his scheme of settlement that he is anxious to submit it to the ordeal of popular suffrage. Now, the Black Republicans boast that the people of the North are with them. We believe that with the possible exception of a few of the New England States, there is not a non-slaveholding Commonwealth of which the people would not accept the Crittenden amendments by an overwhelming majority. Give them but a chance to do so, and our firm conviction is that they would record a sentence of condemnation against Black Republicanism such as it has never yet received.

144. THE CONVENTION

(*The Review,* Charlottesville, Va., January 25, 1861)

Would the people of Albemarle desire a dissolution of the Union *per se?* Do they desire it for its own sake?

There are two things to be considered by our people in deciding whether our great country shall be dismembered and broken down: the first is the point of *honor:* the second is the point of *interest.* The question of honor is paramount to all others. If the Northern people, or rather the Republicans, will not concede *equality* to Virginia as a member of this Confederacy, we for one are for disunion—and shut our eyes to the consequences. Let our slaves be lost; let our fields be desolated; let our blood flow; never—*never,* with our consent, shall the free, proud spirit of this Commonwealth be humbled—never shall this brave people yield that most precious of all earthly possessions— their feeling of *self-respect.* There is a habit of speaking derisively of going to war for *an idea*—an abstraction—something which you cannot see. This is precisely the point on which we would go to war. An idea is exactly the thing that we would fight for. It is for ideas that all the great contests of the world have taken place. The Revolution of 1688 in England, and the execution of Charles I., was for an idea. The French Revolution was for an idea. Our resistance to Great Britain was for an idea.

The people who will not fight for ideas will never retain the spirit to fight for anything.—Life loses its highest meaning when opinions become matters of indifference.

It is the reproduction of the old fallacy, that it does not matter what a man believes; it is only his acts that are to be looked to. But a false belief necessarily begets wrong actions.—A man's belief *is the man.* That which is in his mind flowers and becomes manifest in his daily life. A man who believes wrong may in his outward life appear to act well; but the whole is a *counterfeit,* resembling the true thing, yet essentially base and worthless. Such a man is a villain for all the smooth and specious covering that he puts upon his actions.

Therefore, we say, for this *idea* of State honor—for this abstract principle of not bating her just claims upon threats of coercion—we would convulse this Union from centre to circumference. When that equitable *ultimatum* which the South should demand has been determined on by our people—there let our feet be planted, and let us stand like a rock.

When we come to the other matter to which we have referred, the question of *interest*—here our public men begin to divide. There is a large class who love the Union, who see in it innumerable advantages and blessings—who believe that its destruction will bring ruin on many, if not all, of the States—and who earnestly desire its salvation and perpetuity. There is another class, who see in it nothing but injury and oppression to the South—who regard it as a great incubus upon our industrial interests—as the source and origin of all the evils that afflict us as a political body. These *desire* the dissolution of the Union. When some message comes upon the telegraph, announcing something favorable to peace, they question it and are disturbed at it. When there is a prospect of a collision at some fort—or when they hear of a violent coercion speech from a Republican, they tell it with undisguised happiness, and say that we must get away from them as quickly as possible.

Nothing will satisfy these gentlemen. Their demands rise with the prospects of a settlement. We were conversing with one of them— a distinguished name in the State—recently in Richmond. He assured us very oracularly that all hope was over. That they would yield nothing. We ventured to refer to the CRITTENDEN resolutions; "Oh, they—he wouldn't touch them—they wouldn't do at all." We mildly suggested, that we saw Mr. HUNTER had expressed his willingness to vote for them.—"The fact is," said our distinguished friend—a leading member of the CALHOUN school—"the fact is, it is the general opinion, that Mr. HUNTER has shown by his recent speech that he is *not equal to rising to the exigencies of the times.*" We said, that we observed that Senator DAVIS, of Mississippi, had expressed his willingness to sustain the resolutions. "The fact is," said our distinguished friend, "the general opinion is, that Mr. DAVIS also has fallen short of the exigencies of the times." We refrained from pushing him any further by adding that Senator Toombs was also not fully up to "the exigencies of the times."

This is the feeling. Such men as HUNTER and DAVIS are behind the revolution. So of Gov. WISE, we suppose. *No settlement is wanted.*

Which of the two classes of men, thus decided, should be sent to the Virginia Convention? A Unionist at heart, or a Disunionist at heart? The man who will vote for the secession of Virginia, as the last resort—but would be pleased to see peace restored; or the man

who would take Virginia out of the Union the first opportunity—
and would rather deplore the reconstruction of the old fabric?

There are persons who either believe, or profess to believe, that the
material and social advancement of the South would be best promoted
by an independent, slaveholding Confederacy—even if our just claims
are admitted by the North. Such, we hope and believe, are few in
number. We presume that the great mass of our people are animated
by the desire to restore and maintain this great Republic, in all its
integrity, if it can be done consistently with our rights and our honor.
Having this common object in view, they are divided, as upon all
other questions, as to the means by which it can best be accomplished.
We have distinctly and emphatically indicated what method appears
to us to present the most feasible hope of adjustment—a Border State
Convention. In this view we are sustained by many of the wisest
and most patriotic men of this and neighboring States. Ex-President
Tyler has declared for it; [1] Gov. Magoffin, of Kentucky, recommends
it in his message; [2] we have reason to think that Maryland favors it,
and that Missouri and Tennessee will cordially unite in carrying it
out. Others think that a National Convention offers a better mode of
securing to the South the Constitutional amendments which we are
entitled to, and which we are determined to have if we remain in the
Union. We will cheerfully lend our efforts to further this scheme if it
is promptly taken up and meets encouragement North and South.
There is a third class who urge that the only method by which the
Southern States can impress upon our Northern brethren the necessity of concession, is by immediate secession, and by presenting an undivided front. They allege that this attitude will be so imposing from
its strength and its determination, that the North will not only give
up all idea of coercion, but will be compelled to yield all our demands in order to bring us again into the Confederacy. So specious
is this argument that it has had vast weight in this community, and
has converted numbers of conservative, Union-loving men into regular
fire-eating secessionists. We propose to examine briefly the validity of
this position.

The Northern mind has been trained for two generations to look

------

[1] Lyon Gardiner Tyler, *The Letters and Times of Tylers* (Richmond, 1885), II, 579.
[2] In pursuance of Governor Magoffin's message, the Kentucky legislature applied to
Congress for a National Convention, January 25, 1861. See "Resolutions of the Legislature
of Kentucky, applying for a Call of a Convention for proposing Amendments to the Constitution of the United States," *House Ex. Docs.*, 36 Cong., 2 Sess., Doc. 55, p. 2.

upon slavery as a great moral, social and political evil. In an abstract point of view, nothing to them could be more unjust, or more injurious to the country; and upon this idea has been built up a great party, which at length, has gotten the reins of government in its hands. Whilst all this has been going on, they have never, as a people, ceased to remember that the question is not an abstract one. They recognize the fact that it has ever been protected by the Constitution of the United States, and that we of the South are alone responsible for any sin that they conceive to exist in the institution. They have never wished to make war upon it in the States where it is recognized, and have never dared to oppose its introduction into the Territories, except by *professedly* Constitutional means. In this view of the case, suppose this Union to be dissolved, and the North thus to be released from all *obligation* to *recognize* the existence of slavery. Does any one suppose that they would ever deliberately place themselves in the position of *establishing* slavery by a direct act of their own; that looking upon this holding and trafficking in slaves as a sin, they would vote to take this sin on their conscience, by uniting in a Constitution that legalized and protected it? He knows but little of the Northern mind who supposes that anything but the requirements of an existing Government and law could make them be participants in what would, to them, be crime to establish. We pronounce, then, emphatically that there can be no such thing as a reconstruction, if the fifteen Southern States dissolve their connection with this Union.

Again: imagine this dissolution to have taken place. Of course we come forward to claim our share of the general property. We must have a division of the public domain; we must have the city of Washington with its numerous and costly public buildings, as lying within the area of the Southern Confederacy; we must have the fortifications in the Florida Keys, which command the navigation of the Gulf of Mexico; we must have the right to establish strict police regulations on the Mississippi river. Does any one suppose that all or any one of these things will be yielded by the North? We deliberately dissolve our connection with the General Government, and leave it, in their opinion, a just claim to this property, and an army and navy to defend that claim. The result will be, that they will make no war on us, but we will be forced to make war on them; or else ignominiously resign all our just and equitable claims.

Such are the inevitable consequences of a general secession of the

Southern States. We say all this that the public may clearly know what is before them when they are called upon to act.

It is with unutterable grief that we can sit down to the contemplation of the destruction of all the fond anticipations, all the grand conceptions based upon this great experiment of popular government.

To us there is more involved in this question than the mere destruction of our material prosperity. With the dismemberment of this Confederacy, which has, in the brief space of eighty years, become already the asylum of all oppressed nations, perishes the brightest beacon to struggling freedom that the world has ever seen. Pause, then, fellow countrymen, before you dash all these hopes to the ground.—Do not, we implore you, give up this brilliant promise until all honorable efforts are exhausted.

For our part, we are prepared calmly to accept all the "woes unnumbered" consequent upon a separation, before we will submit to any degradation. We say now that these questions must be finally settled. They must be settled by constitutional amendments, securing the rights of the South. If all the means which have been indicated fail to secure this settlement and these rights, then, and not till then, let us renounce all allegiance to the American Union and the American flag.

145. THE FEDERAL COMMISSIONERS

(*Richmond Enquirer*, January 25, 1861)

The appointment by the Legislature of a Board of Commissioners charged with the duty of the inception of a new adjustment of federal relations, on the "basis" of the "Crittenden Resolutions," affords a rare instance of nondescript legislation.

After issuing a call for a State Convention to deliberate on the subject of federal adjustment, our General Assembly, in its wisdom, has seen fit to forestall the deliberations of the Convention, not only by laying down a "basis" of adjustment, but by providing the ways and means of its ultimate adoption.

After doing their utmost to tie the hands of the Convention, by requiring that their action shall, in certain contingencies, be limited merely to the office of *recommending* measures for popular adoption or rejection, the Legislature makes bold not only to express the opinion that the people of Virginia are prepared to submit to anti-slavery oppression, but to take important action and to recommend similar action on the part of other States, in pursuance of this opinion.

While the United States Senate is occupied in passing resolutions of coercion, and while Northern States are eagerly tendering men and money to the Federal Government to be employed in the subjection of Southern States [1]—while the whole North, with the Federal Government to aid them, is advancing as fast as possible in active aggression—the General Assembly deputes a commissioner charged to urge upon the Southern States the expediency of abstaining from acts of open resistance to a system of coercion.[2] We hardly imagine a task more repugnant to a public officer's known views and disposition, than that which has been assigned to Judge John Robertson. We venture to predict that the officer will be found altogether unwilling to perform the task allotted to him, and that this conference with the authorities of South Carolina and Florida will result in something very different from the programme of temporizing submission intended by the action of the General Assembly.

Again: The Commissioners, while furnished with a scheme of adjustment, on a "basis" of submission to be tendered to the Northern States, are to offer it on several conditions, to wit:—1st. Its adoption by the State Convention. 2d. Its adoption by the Southern States generally, since, in the event that "all effort to reconcile the unhappy differences existing between the two sections shall prove abortive, then every consideration of honor and interest demands that Virginia shall unite her destinies with the slaveholding States."

See, then, the long list of conditions, each of which is necessary to an adjustment on the proposed "basis."

1st. Northern and Southern States must respond to the call for

---

[1] "Resolutions of the Legislature of the State of Ohio, on the State of the Republic," *House Mis. Docs.*, 36 Cong., 2 Sess., Doc. 18; "Resolutions of the Legislature of the State of Maine relating to Existing National Affairs," *ibid.*, Doc. 26; "Joint Resolutions of the Legislature of the State of Minnesota on the State of the Union," *ibid.*, Doc. 33; "Resolutions of the Legislature of the State of Pennsylvania relative to the Maintenance of the Constitution and Union," *ibid.*, Doc. 24; "Joint Resolutions of the Legislature of the State of Michigan, relative to the State of the Union," *ibid.*, Doc. 38.

[2] Robertson played an important part in the negotiations which prevented a hostile collision between federal and state troops during January. See Tyler to Robertson, January 5 [26], 1861, *Official Records . . . Armies*, Series I, Vol. I, 253; Robertson to Moore, February 3, 1861, in the *Montgomery Advertiser*, February 7, 1861; Moore to Robertson, February 3, 1861, *ibid.*

the grand committee of conference proposed by the General Assembly of Virginia.

2d. The commissioners to be appointed by the Southern States must consent to stand on the proposed "basis" of submission to Northern aggression.

3d. The commissioners to be appointed by the Northern States must agree to recommend the passage of the South under the yoke, on the terms proposed.

4th. A Black Republican Congress must agree to submit the terms of submission to be ratified or rejected by the several States.

5th. In the mean time, Virginia, Florida, Maryland and South Carolina must submit to the coercion applied by Federal garrisons stationed in their midst.

6th. The Convention of Virginia must ratify the proposed terms of Virginia's submission.

7th. Every other Southern State must, in Convention assembled, agree to submit to Northern aggression, on the same terms.

Why this is worse than the "house that Jack built." If it were possible to overcome all these obstacles *at all*—which we may venture to say, with confidence, it is not—Mr. Seward's *status quo* [3] would be more than consumed by their consummation.

What then? Shall we not only make up our minds to submit, but also wait in the cold, like poor King Harry at the Pope's out [*sic*] gate, and for three long years, until it shall graciously please our Northern masters to accept the terms of our submission? Nay! With God's help we will not wait. Or, if we shall wait, it will only be until the 4th of March, when coercion will certainly be applied, with a stringency which will altogether preclude waiting, and oblige us to take more than one step, backwards or forwards, and that in double quick time. The "double quick," backwards, must be a very difficult step, by the bye, and is altogether unknown in military tactics. Why, then, does our General Assembly urge Southern States to wait at all? Waiting only gives the enemy time—time to prepare and apply all the means of coercion—and if South Carolina and Florida, aye, and Virginia, too, intend to rid themselves of Federal garrisons at all, they had better take the step, while yet it may be accomplished without the shedding of blood.

[3] Seward, in his speech January 14, had said that he would consent to a national convention in two or three years, after the popular excitement had subsided.

146. Disunion the Necessary Antecedent of Abolition

(*Louisville Daily Journal,* January 26, 1861)

The appalling success of the vilest conspiracy ever formed against the freedom and happiness of a people in "precipitating the Cotton States into Revolution," so fills the mind with dismay as to hide from distinct view some of the worst consequences of this crime. A like disturbance of the intellectual and moral powers, by wonder, amazement, and submissiveness to unmatchable audacity, has unquestionably paralyzed the thinking people of the seceding States, and made them meekly quiescent under the destruction of their country, their fortunes, and their hopes.

We have already shown how the separation of these States, *if that separation is made on the slave line,* must inevitably lead to the rapid extinction of slavery. Mr. Boyce,[1] of South Carolina, now carried away with the prevailing insanity of his people, took the very same ground ten years ago. His reasons were unanswerable then; they are just as true and as unquestionable now.

The Constitution of the United States recognizes and protects slavery. The Southern States enjoy a large share of political power in this strong and vigorous Government, *on the basis of slavery.* The civilization which the Southern States are working out in connection with slavery is, by the growing power and strength of this great movement, placed in an attitude to command the respect and consideration of the world. The anti-slavery propagandists of Europe dare not assail us, except by insult and vituperation, which we can afford to despise. The large majority of the Northern people are, and ever have been, faithful to the Constitutional compact in regard to slavery, so far as its large and general provisions are concerned. That Northern majority, pleading the sacred obligation of the Constitution, has restrained and kept down the Abolition fanaticism. Hence, for years, the Abolitionists have hated and cursed the Constitution of the United States, because that alone stood in the way of their fiendish purposes. They were the first and the most venomous Disunionists. Under the Constitution the entire slave border is covered and protected by those Border Free States, who respect slavery, because they love and venerate and cherish the Constitution which makes us one people. The election of Abraham Lincoln would never have been brought about but by the complicity

[1] William W. Boyce, Member of Congress, 1853–1860.

of Southern Disunionists in so arranging the political chess-board as to secure that result.

Neither that election nor anything else but Disunion can get the Constitution out of the way of Abolition practices. All the power and force of these fanatics has been directed to that coveted result. Take slavery out of the Constitution of the United States, and then the whole free State border could be abolitionized—turned from friends into enemies of slavery. And no possible police or military force can watch a land line two thousand miles long, so as to prevent men and women from walking across it. Then too the entire Southern coast would be open to the piratical incursions of the Abolitionists of Europe as well as of America.

Checked by the moral power of the Constitution of the United States, the Abolitionists of America are an inconsiderable fraction of the population. However formidable in spirit and in zeal, in numbers they are contemptible. But the Abolitionists of Europe are the entire population of the Western nations of that Continent. The gross ignorance and the deep venom of European fanaticism on the subject of American slavery are almost inconceivable to our countrymen. The whole literature, the whole population, the governing and the subject classes, are equally charged with this ignorance and with this venom. Nothing has prevented the outbreak of this feeling in the most offensive and dangerous forms of interference with American slavery but the strong arm and the formidable power of the United States. Dissolve this Union on the slave line, let all the Northern States become a united anti-slavery power, aiding and abetting instead of restraining and overawing the abolitionism of Europe, and where would American slavery be?

Knowing the intense desire of the Abolitionists for Disunion, and the anxiety with which they have looked to that event as the only means of gratifying their cherished passion, every one must see that it is in keeping with the cunning and treachery of such a dire fanaticism to obtain the control of a Disunion organ in the South. The Editor of the Charleston Mercury has done more than any other man in the South to create the bitter sectional animosity and the senseless Disunion fanaticism now so prevalent there, under the pretence of advocating the cause of slavery.

The Jesuits, long since, taught the world that the most effectual way to injure any cause is to become its most violent and unscrupulous propagandist, and so lead on its votaries to destruction. Can it be that the Editor of the Charleston Mercury is the colleague and sworn brother of Garrison and Wendell Phillips? They have worked together faithfully for the same object by the same means. Disunion is the common object. Violence, insult, denunciation, and brazen falsehood, have been the common means. The Charleston Mercury has reprinted the Abolition journals for circulation in the South. If the Editor of the Charleston Mercury is not the loved and trusted brother of the Abolitionists, he has been the most effective and influential agent of that malign association. By his valuable aid they have accomplished their first cherished design—Disunion. The extinction of slavery in blood, and the ruin of the South, will be the next move, to which this first one has opened the way.

But the Abolitionists have not yet quite succeeded in their whole scheme of Disunion. *The separation has not yet been made on the slave line.* The victory therefore is partial. If the Border Slave States remain in the Union, slavery will still be a part of the Constitution of the United States, and under its protection. This barrier therefore will still be in the way of these firebrands. The conservative masses of the North, fighting under the ægis of the Constitution, will continue to resist their mad fanaticism. The amazing stupidity of some of the Southern States, in running away from the Union, may, indeed, weaken the conservative force in the North, but it will unquestionably be sufficient to maintain and vindicate the Constitutional rights of the remaining Slave States, *with the hearty and intelligent co-operation of those States.*

To infect the Border Slave States with the contagious madness of the people who are firing cannon and ringing bells and rejoicing with horrid festivity over the destruction of the only government that could successfully maintain their rights, liberties, and happiness, is now the favorite enterprise of Northern Disunionists. Unhappily their Southern allies are doing the most of the work. Lust of place and power has induced vast numbers of aspiring politicians to give themselves to the base purpose of deluding and cheating the people into Disunion. The same lust has blinded their own minds, so that they cannot see the abyss into which they are trying to plunge their country.

The people of Kentucky have looked on in amazement at the progress of this distemper. The young, the ardent, the impulsive, are first seized and practised upon. These secured, the weak are easily drawn in; and, then, the timid, conservative majority is overawed by violence and clamor into passive acquiescence. Again we say to our people that they must rouse up now to all the manliness and keen intelligence of the Kentucky character, or we, too, will be made the victim of this nefarious plot. The machinery is in full operation at Frankfort, and all over the State. PRECIPITATION is the word! All the wisdom of the past, all the safeguards of the Constitution, all the consecrated principles of our free institutions, are to be put aside and crushed beneath the car of this Juggernaut of Disunion.

We call upon every precinct in the Commonwealth to form at once its Union club, to raise the Union Banner, to carry on actively the enrollment of Union champions, and to send strong resolves, not only, but strong men to Frankfort. Your representatives now there need every assistance to enable them to resist the blandishments and the intimidation and other worse means of influence with which they are incessantly plied. Let men of stern integrity and of clear intelligence go up from every part of the State to stand by the members of the Legislature, to encourage, sustain and strengthen them in standing by the Constitution and the country. And let every man who values freedom and independence, and has sense enough to know that these can be secured only by the preservation of this Union, bestir himself and make it his chief business, as long as we are in this hazard, to teach the young the principles of statesmanship learned in the school of Washington and Madison, and Clay and Crittenden, and to strengthen and encourage young and old together to abide by those principles, and to resolve that the heritage bestowed upon us by our fathers shall be handed down to our children.

147. DISUNION THE DOOM OF SLAVERY

(*Republican Banner,* Nashville, January 26, 1861)

Those who are plotting the disruption of this Government and the establishment of a Southern Confederacy, claim to be the only true friends of the South and its institutions. Those who are for maintaining the Government are denounced as Republicans, abolitionists, &c. Any man with half a man's reasoning power can see that the friends of the existing Government are the only true friends of slavery. The prosperity of the South—its wealth and refinement—has resulted from the existence of the institution of slavery—and that institution has depended mainly for its existence upon the protection afforded it by the Constitution, which has bound the free States of the Confederacy as well as the slave to its maintenance. No other government in the world has been able to sustain slavery so successfully as this—none, indeed, to sustain it at all. The constitutional support of seventeen free States, united with fifteen slave States, and forming one of the first powers of the earth, has extended over this institution a protection which has kept the anti-slavery sentiment of the whole world at bay, as far as any practical interference jeopardizing our safety is concerned. But how will it be after the present government is dissolved, and the Northern States are absolved from their Constitutional obligations, and instead of being parties to the maintenance of slavery, as they are under the Constitution, become its open and avowed enemies, not in the abstract, but practically, and as a republic? It is clear to be seen that the South will be greatly and fatally weakened, and the doom of slavery irrevocably fixed.

In this opinion we are endorsed by one of the most sagacious leaders of the present movement in South Carolina. In 1851 the Hon. W. W. Boyce stood out successfully against secession, though in 1860 he was forced to yield, seeing that in ten years those engaged in "educating the Southern mind," and "firing the Southern heart," had made such rapid progress as to render resistance self-immolation, and very few politicians at this day are in the habit of carrying their convictions of right to such an extent. But the arguments of Mr. Boyce against secession in 1851, are unanswered either by himself or his co-secessionists in 1860, and they will not be answered. Then, after speaking of "the hostile spirit of the age to the institution of slavery," he said:

Secession, separate nationality with all its burdens, is no remedy. It is no redress for the past; it is no security for the future. It is only a magnificent sacrifice to the present, without in any wise gaining in the future. . . . For the various reasons I have stated, I object in as strong terms as I can, to the secession of South Carolina. Such is the intensity of my conviction on this subject, that if secession should take place—of which I have no idea, for I cannot believe in the existence of such a stupendous madness—*I shall consider the institution of slavery as doomed, and that the Great God, in our blindness, has made us the instruments of its destruction.*

148. THE CRITTENDEN AMENDMENT

(*Richmond Enquirer,* January 29, 1861)

This last hope of the timid has to encounter other difficulties than mere Black Republican opposition in Congress. If successful in that body it has to run the gauntlet in the States, and before the people, to become an amendment to the Constitution. How is it possible for it ever to be adopted? To become an amendment to the Constitution, it or any other proposition must be ratified by three-fourths of the States. Here, at the outset, appears a fatal difficulty. Does the "three-fourths" apply to the thirty-four States, or to those only which have not seceded. The submission of any amendment to the States must be preceded by the settlement of the question of the right of secession. If the Black Republican doctrine against secession obtains, and the seceded States are held to still belong to the Union, then it will require twenty-six States to adopt the amendment. But eight of the States will have seceded and will not submit the proposed amendment to their Legislatures, and such action necessitates the concurrence of *every* State still in the Union to the proposed amendment. If any one State refused to adopt it, the amendment fails for want of the Constitutional number. Is it probable that *every* Black Republican State will adopt an amendment that is satisfactory to Virginia? Is it probable that Virginia will be satisfied with an amendment acceptable to *every* Black Republican State? Does not this show the folly of looking to the Crittenden amendment? Before that or any other amendment can become a part of the Constitution there has to be some of the *tallest backing down* done, either by the North or the South, that has ever been witnessed in this or any other country. If the Black Republicans are willing to acknowledge the secession of the Southern States, and to submit propositions of amendment to three-fourths of the remaining States, then there may be some probability of the adoption of the amendment. But will the Black Republicans, as preliminary to yielding what they have so steadfastly refused to grant, acknowledge the right of secession and then set about the work of re-construction upon principles that rob their recent victory of all benefits and place the rights of the South in unquestioned prominence upon the letter of the Constitution. We do not wish to be understood as admitting that the Crittenden amendment places the rights of the South thus patently upon the constitution, but that any amendment to which Virginia can agree must be so plain that he who runs may read, and the wayfaring politician, though a Black Republican and Abolitionist, cannot err therein. Can any man, not rendered ridiculously credulous by his love of Unionism, for one moment believe that the Black Republicans will surrender their principles, haul down their flag and acknowledge that, victorious at the popular election, they have ignominiously surrendered all to the demands of rebels and traitors? It is absurd to expect men, besotted by fanaticism, triumphantly installed in authority, clothed with the forms of law, and armed with the army and navy, would yield to the demands of those they hold to be traitors and rebels.—What, then, is the duty of the people of Virginia to themselves and their posterity? To wait the eventuality of an amendment that must be lost, or to place the State in an attitude of defense? In our opinion the people of Virginia should, by their votes, put the "right men in the right place," and, then, voting down the reference clause of the Convention bill, stand before the world in the proud attitude of determined resistance to persistent and shameful aggression.

Upon the Convention, about to assemble in Virginia,[1] will devolve the noble work of continuing the contest for freedom and liberty—a contest once triumphantly won, but which may be lost by ignominious submission to Northern aggression, or by truckling acquiescence in inefficient amendments. The vicissitudes of war may overtake us in resistance to Northern armies, we may be overrun by Northern enemies, our industrial resources ruined, our commerce confiscated; but if we cannot live the equal of a Yankee, a privilege low enough, we can, at least, fall fighting for freedom. Men of Virginia, your love of freedom and equality eighty years ago won the admiration of the wisest, the best and the purest statesmen of the world. Your possession of slaves enabled you to estimate the privilege of freedom and the right of equality more highly than those States of the North, who now deny your equality and will soon seek to conquer your liberty. Edmund Burke, in his great speech upon "conciliation with America" said:

There is, however, a circumstance attending these Colonies, which, in my opinion, fully counterbalances this difference, and makes the spirit of liberty still more high and haughty than in those to the Northward. It is that in Virginia and the Carolinas they have a vast multitude of *slaves*. Where this is the case in any part of the world, those who are free are by far the most proud and jealous of their freedom. Freedom is to them not only an enjoyment but a kind of rank and privilege. Not seeing there that freedom, as in countries where it is a common blessing, and as broad and general as the air, may be united with much abject toil, with great misery, with all the exterior of servitude, liberty looks among them, like something that is more noble and liberal. I do not mean, sir, to commend the superior

---

[1] The convention bill, passed by the legislature on January 14, provided for an election on February 4 of delegates to a state convention which was to assemble on February 13.

morality of this sentiment, which has at least as much pride as virtue in it; but I cannot alter the nature of man. The fact is so and these people of the Southern Colonies are more strongly, and with a higher and more stubborn spirit, attached to liberty than those to the Northward. Such were all ancient commonwealths; such were our Gothic ancestors; and, in our days, were the Poles, and such *will be all masters of slaves, who are not slaves themselves.* In such a people the haughtiness of domination combined with the spirit of freedom fortifies it, *and renders it invincible.*

Such was Burke's opinion of the slaveholders of '76, those sires of the Government, who won our first battle for freedom and equality, and bequeathed their blessings to us. Shall we transmit them unimpaired to our posterity, or shall we succumb to Yankee demands, and violate the Constitution by surrendering to Northern aggressions, either through cowardly submission or by shameful agreement to inefficient amendments? We demand for the manly courage of Virginia the *privilege of fighting* before being solicited to acknowledge ourselves cowards and to seek temporary protection under the ægis of the Crittenden amendment.

The example of our forefathers forbid their descendants to abate their just demands—their noble history teaches that when we have reached the point where forbearance ceases to be a virtue, that, so far from seeking compromise, the genius of liberty demands of us not *to accept concessions.* The denial by the Northern States of our "indubitable, inalienable, and indefeasible right to reform, alter or abolish" the government, is the assertion of *their* right to hold us in subjection.

To acquiesce in this denial or assertion is to subvert the freedom of the Federal Union into a "government against which *a claim of liberty* is tantamount to high treason"—a government *submission to which is equivalent to slavery.*

A compromise which does not recognize the secession of the Southern States must be adopted by *all* the remaining States, since one-fourth of the States, holding themselves no longer members of the Union, will not consider the proposition of amendment. It is preposterous to suppose that the Republicans will yield what can satisfy Virginia, or that Virginia can accept what the Republicans will yield. Virginia may patch up a compromise which may become an amendment, and thus bound by her action, may find herself cut off by its rejection by the cotton States; and what would be her condition in that extremity—bound to the Northern Confederacy by the adoption of her amendment, and yet denied a market for her slaves by the self-protecting legislation of the cotton States? At the mercy of the dominant majority of the North, without the power of the South to aid her in future conflicts, Virginia would soon be over-run by the increase of her slaves, and forced, for the protection of the whites, to legalize the destruction of the blacks.

Virginia should demand that propositions of amendment be first adopted by the Northern States, and then submitted to the Cotton States so that the Border States may not be caught under the dead-fall of an amendment adopted by the North, but rejected by the South. This may appear harsh, but Virginia and the border States must guard against being inveigled into an amendment which being rejected by the cotton States would leave Virginia bound by its adoption to the North.

We have no faith in amendments, since we have no reason to suppose that States which have proven themselves faithless to the present Constitution would be true to it when amended. The present Constitution guarantees the rights of the Southern States, and has never been complained of by them. It is the *violation* of the Constitution, in letter and spirit, that constitutes the grievances of the South. No amendments can provide against such violation since faithless confederates will disregard the amendment, as they despise the Constitution.

149. THE BORDER SLAVE STATES AND THEIR SLAVES

(The Daily Delta, New Orleans, January 30, 1861)

The world of ideas and sentiments is never able to separate itself, in the final solution of political and social problems, from the world of facts. In the present juncture the Cotton States of the South, which have vital material interests obviously at stake in the issue—which have everything, as regards those interests, to lose by failing to meet menace and aggression with a prompt and effectual assertion of their rights, and everything to gain by a policy of timely preparation and utter repudiation of a Government whose forms were converted into instruments of assault—these States do not hesitate, but decide at once upon immediate and unqualified secession. They do not stand upon the order of their going, but go at once. They present a memorable, an unexampled, a sublime spectacle of a number of free and enlightened communities, drawing a common conclusion from the same state of facts, and acting independently, but consentaneously and sympathetically, for the achievement of a common end. Separate, they are yet co-operative; each acting for itself, they all concur to strengthen the common cause and secure a common triumph. The occasion amply justifies the policy they are pursuing; history will record it in terms of admiration.

But the state of facts has not been the same with the border slave States. Or, rather the appearance of facts has been different to them, and consequently their action has been different. The cotton States could see nothing to hope for in lingering as provincial appendages of a Union which had degenerated into a despotism. They saw plainly enough that they were doomed to death by an unrelenting sectional hate, whose destiny was to take no step backward. They knew that if they remained they would remain as condemned prisoners. And they knew that, whatever respite might be granted, mercy itself would be a cruel mockery, and that execution would follow at the convenience of a crucifying bigotry which wished to humiliate and torture, with insults, stripes, and a crown of thorns, the victim it had resolved to sacrifice. The border slave States also had rights assailed, and interests imperiled, and scoffs and indignities to look for. But they did not perceive the same remedies for present and coming evils. Transition from the old Union into independence presented to them, or appeared to present, peculiar difficulties, hardships, and hazards. Existing facts, in a word, argued for hesitation, and they hesitated. Existing facts urged the policy of inactivity, and they remained inactive. And they still, for the most part, hesitate, and still linger without decided action. In sentiment, and in conviction of right, they profess to be with us of the cotton States, but on the question of immediate interest they have seen proper, thus far, to refuse to cast their lot with ours. We believe they have taken a wrong view of the facts of the situation, which, if they do not reconsider the question and arrive at other deductions, will bring upon them the most dangerous, perhaps fatal, consequences.

The slaveholding communities of the border slave States desire domestic tranquillity. They are sensitive to every political movement that may threaten to harass their borders with Abolition disturbance, or to involve them in a war having as an object on one side to disorganize their social system and destroy the value of one large element of their wealth. But we would submit to the border slave States that, in case they choose to linger as the nethermost portion of the North, if their borders would not be still more harassed, if their society would not be still more convulsed, if their slave property would not be still more exposed, and still more certainly doomed to destruction than all these would be in case they chose to join the seceding States of the South, and help build up a Southern Confederacy, which, separate in all things essential to individual State policy, would be a firm, inseparable, impregnable solidarity in a conviction of common rights and defense of common interests.

Are the border slave States willing to make themselves a powerless appendage to Northern territory? Do they think that so incongruous and ludicrous a fringe on Abolition skirts would not inevitably be draggled in the mire, and torn into shreds? More than this, in courting the friendship or forbearance of their Northern enemies, are they willing to alienate the cotton States which are now their friends? United to the South, the Northern arm that threatens them would be paralyzed. But severed from the South, they would not make a friend of the North, while they would provoke the just hostility of the South. Between this nether and this upper millstone, what would become of their slaveholding interest? It would be ground into atoms; and they would do well to contemplate the fate of St. Domingo and Jamaica as prophetic of their own.

We do not mean that in pursuing a course that would alienate the other Southern States—in seceding from the South, and adhering to the North—they would excite an animosity in the Southern States which they deserted, that would lead of itself to war. We mean that, even should no war arise between the North and the South, or between any two or more States, the desertion of the border slave States would hardly fail to provoke a hostile peace policy on the part of the remaining Southern States, acting individually or collectively, which would be sure to wound the border slave States in their most sensitive point. For about half a century those States, in respect to slave labor, have been producers, and the other slave States have been consumers. For the same period, those States have had the benefit of a prohibitory tariff on slave labor—have enjoyed the protection of Federal legislation against the importation of foreign slave labor—have carried on a flourishing monopoly of the production and sale of slave labor. Now, is it likely that a Southern Confederacy would desire to perpetuate this tariff, this protection, this monopoly, for the special advantage of States which sought the alliance of its enemies? By no means. Whether the Southern Confederacy should or should not adopt the old Federal Constitution, it is pretty certain that it would not make haste to adopt the old Federal legislation on the subject of slavery in any one of its phases. This would leave the foreign slave trade as it was before 1808. Perhaps regulative laws would be applied to the foreign slave trade, including the Virginia, Maryland, Kentucky and Missouri slave trade, which would then be foreign. If there were discriminations, they would scarcely be in favor of States which had joined themselves to an unfriendly power, and against Cuba and Africa, with which we have no cause of quarrel and from which we have nothing to fear. Indeed, it would be the plain policy of the States composing the Southern Confederacy, if they could procure the slave labor they wanted from other sources, to take measures to prevent the border slave States from effecting the exodus of their slave population into the South and converting it into gold that would swell the general assets of the Northern enemy. Grant that the South would be disposed to approximate as much as possible to free trade; yet they might think it well in this case to make a singular exception. They might deem it a just, as well as prudent, policy to readopt the old Federal legislation prohibiting the foreign slave trade, as far as it would apply to Missouri, Kentucky, Virginia and Maryland, but no further. But suppose the South should readopt, without modification, the old Federal legislation in question—that would effectually close the door to the Southward exodus of slaves from the border slave States.[1]

It is not pleasant to contemplate the effects which any of these lines of policy would bring upon the border slave States. But what else could they expect after seceding from the South and adhering to her enemies? Could they expect the protection of Southern legislation from the evils arising from their desertion of the South? Could they expect the South to help them Abolitionize their territories, and do the work of John Brown without inflicting the loss of a dollar, or leaving a single troublesome free negro within their borders? Were they to unite with the South in a policy of common protection of Southern interests and institutions, they might reasonably expect a liberal and forbearing policy on the part of their sister Southern States. But, forsaking the South in her hour of greatest trial and peril, they could only expect the South to pursue a policy best calculated to promote her various interests, and least calculated to benefit or favor her ancient enemies, or new allies of her ancient enemies.

[1] The Constitution for the Provisional Government of the Confederate States of America prohibited the African slave trade and gave Congress power to prohibit the introduction of slaves from any State not a member of the Confederacy. Adopted by the Convention, February 8, 1861.

Some dangers, to be sure, the border slave States would incur by uniting with the South; but those dangers are almost nothing compared with the terrible evils they would invite by separating from the South.

But even if the South should exercise no legislative hostility towards the border slave States—even if the South should entertain friendly, and not inimical, feelings for slave States that had refused to join her standard and had taken position under that of the Northern aggressor, it is by no means certain that the situation of those States would be improved in the least. Perhaps it would be worse. An unfriendly disposition displayed by the South towards those States in consequence of their Northern connection might induce the Northern power to treat them with forbearance, possibly with fostering solicitude. For their benefit it might abstain from prohibiting the inter-State slave trade; it might abstain from legislation making it a capital offense to send or convey slaves into a foreign territory for sale. Lincoln is at this moment bidding for them with a policy similar to this. But if friendly feelings existed, or were suspected to exist, between the border slave States and the South, it would be sure to bring upon those States the most vindictive spirit and oppressive legislation. The owners of 500,000 slaves in Virginia alone could thus be imprisoned and gradually starved into abolishing property valued at $300,000,000; to say nothing of the unspeakable evils, social, industrial, financial, of 500,000 free negroes being turned loose on the State.

Thus, whether the South should deal kindly, or deal unfriendly, with the border slave States, their situation would be thick-set with unavoidable hardships; their present would be a dreadful suspense, and their future would present only terrific visions of danger and still more terrific certainties of disaster. The moment they cast their lot under the shadow of Northern power, they would enter the penumbra of their doom. Eclipse and darkness would come in due process of destiny.

150. REPUBLICAN POLICY

(*Louisville Daily Journal,* January 31, 1861)

"Touch it off gently," said Pat standing before the mouth of a cannon and supposing it was only primed. "Touch it off gently, and I'll catch the ball in this basket." It was touched off as gently as possible, but Pat and the basket were never seen again. Thus do many of the Republican leaders of the present day blunder along as they approach the terrible crisis of our country's destiny. They seem to think that they can manage the explosive forces of human passion and civil war, and pocket a net profit upon the whole operation. Notwithstanding the repeated declarations of Congressmen from Southern States, notwithstanding the emphatic declarations of a dozen Gubernatorial messages and the solemn acts and resolutions of a majority of Southern Legislatures, notwithstanding a thousand unmistakable indications of deep, strong, and unchangeable feeling in the Southern States, a portion of the leaders of the Republican party have gone on steadily ignoring all these portentous signs of the times in a policy which they must have known, if they had capacity to understand the plainest indications, would imperil the Union. They coolly rejected all propositions to unite upon any recognized conservative national candidate, and, while the bonds that hold our Union together were snapping under the strain, they labored with a zeal and power worthy of a better cause to break asunder all the remaining links of Union by instilling into their followers the bitterest prejudice and hatred against the slaveholding States. That infamous and vindictive libel written by the renegade Helper was circulated by the hundred thousand as a campaign document of the Republican party, endorsed by some of its leading men.

After all this—after deriding and depreciating the power, the character, and the resources of the Southern States, we should not perhaps be surprised at the votes cast by their dupes, but we have a right to expect from the leaders of the party a higher order of intelligence, which should rise above the tricks and deceptions of an electioneering campaign and realize the true condition of the country, since even their followers by hundreds of thousands have manifested their eager desire for an amicable and patriotic settlement of our national contest. We are sorry to say, that, if such intelligence exists, it is very slow in coming forth to meet the crisis, if we are to judge from leading Republican newspapers. The paltry humbugs of the late campaign are still kept up, until we are led to doubt whether the language of much of the Republican press does not arise from such a narrowness of mind and ignorance of the people of the United States as utterly disqualify the writers for the responsibilities of political journalism. We are tempted to believe that not a very large portion of the Republican journalists have sufficient knowledge of human nature or of the resources and character of the Southern States to make their opinions worth anything in the present crisis.

Just before the Presidential election we were gravely assured by Mr. Greeley of the Tribune that the election of Lincoln would have a wonderfully quieting effect upon the country, that it would be *like oil poured upon the waters,* and would promptly remove all sectional excitement. Not believing Greeley altogether a fool, we were compelled to suppose that he had reconciled his conscience to the necessity of winning an election by transparently false pretences. If he would now claim credit for sincerity in that prediction, he would prove a degree of ignorance or imbecility which would excuse his present transcendent follies. The Tribune, the Times, and other leading Republican papers are gravely urging the coercion of all the seceded States by an embargo or blockade, which, they maintain, would gently switch them back into the Union without involving the calamities of war or inflicting any injury upon the North. Nay, they are even calculating that all the commerce of the country would be driven to Northern ports; that Southern cotton would be sent North by land, and that the Northern cities would make a handsome speculation by thus playing gracefully and daintily at the great game of war. To such stuff as this we would reply emphatically—gentlemen, unless you are resolutely bent on realizing all the horrors of war, you need not deceive your readers any longer by such delusive assurances. If you know no better yourselves, if you really believe that your nice and comfortable calculations will be verified, and, that the Southern States will succumb like mischievous children to a little flagellation, we are amazed at your folly and can scarcely conceive how men of respectable intelligence on other subjects could be so utterly deluded in reference to this great question.

Can you for a moment doubt that the blockade of the Southern States would be resisted by all their warlike energies? Surely your partizan prejudices have not wrought such self-deception. Can you anticipate any other consequence than the annihilation of all American commerce by privateers, except so far as it may be protected by the presence of men-of-war?

Do you not plainly see that Northern manufacturers would lose not only for a time but perhaps forever their Southern market—that emigration to the North would be arrested by the want of employment and by burdensome taxes, and that the calamities of war would be terribly realized by every inhabitant of the Northern States?

If the policy of a deluded party should drive the South into consolidated Union in defence of its demanded rights, do you suppose that eleven millions of as warlike population as the world contains, familiar with the use of arms and occupying a country full of innumerable strongholds furnished by Nature, would shrink from a war of invasion however desolate? That such a war must produce immense suffering and devastation on both sides is self-evident; but to anticipate the conquest of such a people as the men of the South or to suppose that their proud bearing and lofty spirit could be lowered by any such attempt at military coercion is but the delusion of a fanatic or the dream of a comfortable scribbler who speculates at ease in his arm chair, but knows nothing of the stern realities of war.

You count upon the black population as an element of danger and weakness only, forgetting, that, as agricultural laborers, they count as efficiently in war as if they were in the field. Perhaps you count upon the horrid policy of insurrection—if this enters largely into your estimates you are incapable of profiting by the lesson which you might have learned from the failure of John Brown.

Do not, we pray you, trifle any longer. An armed rebellion, converted into unconquerable revolution, proves that you were mistaken in all your calculations during the late campaign. If your editorial language expresses your real convictions, we assure you most solemnly that you are still more mistaken now. You know that we have labored with a zeal and earnestness greater than your own for the preservation of our glorious Union from perils which you have been so slow and so reluctant to recognize. We speak to you now plainly —we cannot polish our language and diminish its force. We entreat you by your regard for our *whole country,* in all of which every citizen has a common interest, to trifle no longer with this crisis, and to delude your readers no longer with the vain hope that any alternative remains but prompt and manly conciliation or wide-spread ruin to our whole country.

We have done nothing to bring on this crisis, nor have we expected to make any political capital out of our country's misfortunes. We address you, Republican leaders, not as politicians, but in the name of humanity, in the name of patriotism, when we ask you to forget, as others have done, the paltry interests of party and give our country once more peace and prosperity. We need not repeat for the thousandth time our expression of the conviction, that the Southern Secessionists have acted unadvisedly, rashly, flagrantly, acted in strange and manifest disregard of the great interests of their own section and in violation of all loyalty to the Constitution and the laws, but a little calm and dispassionate reflection would convince you that the sectional and aggressive language and deeds of yourselves and your deluded followers, continued and aggravated through a long series of years, could in the nature of things have no other tendency than to inflame and provoke the fiery spirits of the South to such a course as they have taken. You well know that wrong will generally be revenged with wrong.

151. THE GRAVE MISTAKE

(*The Daily True Delta,* New Orleans, January 31, 1861)

Virginia has made a call upon her sister states of the south to meet her by delegation in the city of Washington on the 4th proximo, there and then to discuss such measures of redress as the present alarming emergency in public affairs may make advisable, to devise a plan of settlement, that will, if adopted, restore the Union to its integrity, and which will for ever prevent the question of slavery being made a subject of controversy or discussion outside of the states wherein it now exists or may at any time hereafter be established. To this appeal of our great sister state there appears at present little likelihood of any favorable response from the seceding states, and we profoundly regret it; first, because any suggestion or mode of settlement, or project of co-operation that might emanate from a source so justly entitled to respect, could not fail to combine all that is compatible with the nicest sense of honor and the most exacting sense of right; and secondly, because now, as always, we deprecate that course of action which would separate the cotton states now or hereafter, socially or politically, from our powerful and faithful brethren of the frontier states. The grave mistake, however, is made by the advocates of conciliation in Virginia and other frontier states in supposing that the political element now in the ascendency in the cotton states desires, seeks for, or would be satisfied with any plan of settlement that the united demands of the whole south, strengthened by the just, honest and patriotic democratic sentiment of the free states, could extort or voluntarily procure from the inflated enemies of the institution of slavery in the free states; consequently, the efforts Virginia, Kentucky, Maryland and Missouri may make to that end will be unsupported by the states that have already sought in revolution a redress of the grievances of which the frontier states mainly had to complain. The refusal of the immediate secessionists to leave any matter open to friendly discussion; to provide a common ground for all the above states to occupy whence to confront their free state opponents; their determined opposition even to allow the sense of the people to be taken on the extreme measures of redress they have, in a moment of great sectional excitement, managed to have passed, by conventions, the members comprising which were chosen by a popular vote far below that to which the state is entitled, and their persistent declarations that they are determined upon making the secession of the cotton states a permanent separation from the free states, all combine to expose the error, now so generally entertained in Virginia and other frontier slave states, that any mode of settlement, no matter how complete and satisfactory to the south it may be made, will induce all the cotton seceding states to return to the Union they have so precipitately abandoned. Already South Carolina has rejected the peaceful and friendly overtures of Virginia to unite her action with that of the Old Dominion, by declaring that her resolve is taken, that the severance she has long contemplated, as well as labored to bring about, is an accomplished fact, and that, out of the confederation, she is resolved to stay out; consequently, no course Virginia and other frontier slave states may commend or unite in adopting, no plan of adjustment of past disputes, no renunciation, however solemn or obligatory, of right to interfere with slavery where it now exists or may hereafter extend, by the free states, will reconcile her to return to communion with them or to be a constituent of a republic of which they are members. This is frank, outspoken and unmistakable upon the part of the Palmetto state; it is the ultimatum of a people who hate the Union, who have long loathed it, who regard it as an incubus upon their prosperity, a clog to their progression, a reproach to their pride, their spirit and their independence. Our readers will have learned from our columns long since our opinions of the course South Carolina would undoubtedly adopt in such a contingency as that which has occurred. We over and over again told our readers that the disruption of the democratic party at Charleston was the first movement in the programme of disunion; that the men of Carolina were honorable, high-minded, talented and resolute, and unlike the mercenary herd of vulgar and venal politicians with which we are brought in contact in this region and the people are cursed; they meant what they said and acted from a foregone conclusion. The result is now before the nation. South Carolina is out of the Union; has long panted after this separation; has irrevocably determined never to return to it. We know her people well; we therefore look upon all endeavors to conciliate her by concessions, no matter how great or comprehensive, as of no avail, and we have made up our mind to regard her as lost to any future reconstruction that may be obtained or resolved upon. The question then is, shall Louisiana adhere, like South Carolina, to a determination of eternal separation from the Union, or will she respond to the invitation of Virginia and make common cause, inside or out of the Union, in maintenance of their just rights, their slave property, and their security in common? Those who are in favor of the principles of South Carolina, who sincerely believe that faith with the Northern states cannot be maintained, that no compromise, no compact, no obligation, however sacred or patriotic, will bind them, will of course repudiate the appeal of old and honored Virginia; but are the people of Louisiana of these; and have they reflected fully upon the mighty and varied interests she has to provide for and secure, which the other seceded states can afford to ridicule and ignore? We regard the Union as irreparably divided—need we assure our readers with what regret and affliction we make the admission? South Carolina will, we are confident, never return to it peacefully, and otherwise the people will never allow her to be brought; therefore Virginia errs in supposing that state can be made a party to any new basis of arrangement of the slavery issue; but it is otherwise with Louisiana, and we hope she will not, through unauthorized channels, reject the overtures the great frontier slave state may commend to her acceptance.

152. The Commission to Washington—the Virginia and Kentucky Resolutions

(*Louisville Daily Journal*, February 1, 1861)

Again as in 1798–99, have Virginia and Kentucky interposed in harmonious action for the vindication of the American Constitution and for the protection of the American people. In the first case their action was to prevent the establishment of a Federal Monarchy. In the present instance it is to arrest the violent dismemberment of a common country, the horrors of civil war and of fratricidal strife, and the ultimate establishment of monarchical institutions in their most intense and aggravated form.

We have always looked upon the Kentucky character with pride and pleasure. But in our humble judgment the profound wisdom, the true statesmanship, the noble patriotism, the rare capacity to hold the even balance between the most vicious extremes of opinion, and the manly firmness to resist and beat back the contagious madness of widespreading fanaticisms, exhibited by the people of Kentucky within the last twelve months, are without a parallel in the history of nations.

Hopeful as we are of auspicious results from the commission of conference at Washington, we cannot avoid seeing that in the movement, as originated in Virginia, there is one element of disastrous omen. All the force and efficacy of what we believe to be a foul conspiracy against the country and its government is contained in the one pregnant confession of the conspirators—precipitation. All that has been done in execution of the conspiracy has been under the inspiration and by the power of that single idea. To take advantage of the furious excitement and maddening disappointment of the Presidential election, and then to drive the people onward from step to step without allowing them time for one week of calm and cool reflection, has been the pernicious, and, alas! too successful policy of the Disunion leaders. In every seceding State the wildly excited passions of the people, not their deliberate judgments, have pronounced the fatal sentence of destruction upon the noble and beneficent government which in a wonderfully short period has made us one of the foremost nations of the earth, and altogether the most prosperous. In every one of these States there has been a large proportion of reflecting men, whether a minority or a majority is uncertain, appalled at the progress of events, and overawed into silence and submission by the tumultuous and mobocratic violence of the destructive. A gentleman in Louisiana, sadly contemplating the scenes around him, writes that, whatever in other respects may be the issue of this revolution, the question of the capacity of the people for self-government by these proceedings is irreversibly decided in the negative.

Unhappily the Virginia plan of conference and conciliation is tainted with this same malignant poison—precipitation. No time is to be allowed for the passions of the people, North or South, to cool. Even now the canvass for the Convention is in progress in Virginia, and the faith of the people is imposed upon, and their excited feelings still further exasperated by lying despatches from Southern Disunionists, *and by intense provocatives from the Northern wing of the Disunion faction.* And there is no time or chance for correction. A competent knowledge of the facts of the case and dispassionate consideration of them are utterly and absolutely precluded in the trial of this, the most momentous issue ever submitted to the determination of any people.

And what is to be expected from the present Congress, or from the State Legislatures now in session? For the most part, the members of these bodies are the very froth from the top of the waves of the Slavery excitement. If the ISSUE, of the continuance or the destruction of this government, and of this Union, *is to be fairly tried, upon its merits, by a competent tribunal,* time must be given for the people, North and South, to speak, after they have recovered from the intoxicating effects of the late disastrous election:—disastrous alike to the victors and to the vanquished. To permit a final decision without an appeal to the sober second thought of the whole people, to give up in despair, to destroy this government, to dissolve this Union, to launch this country upon the untried and unimaginable horrors of revolution and intestine war, because the narrow-souled representatives of a rabid fanaticism do not, at the first summons, retrace their steps, and take back all their words, is to allow its fullest operation to the very essence and venom of the foul Disunion conspiracy.

It is with painful apprehension, therefore, that we have seen the Legislature of Virginia permitting the Disunion conspirators, Messrs. Garrison, Philips, Toombs, Yancey, & Co., to insert the small end of their riving wedge in the very plan of conciliation which that Legislature so patriotically conceived.

What wise and good purpose can be answered by haste and precipitation? What decent pretext is there for an extemporaneous revolution? Why should the enlightened people of these States assimilate themselves to the half-naked savages of Mexico and Central America, who change their governments with as much facility as they change their few and filthy garments? Cannot the question of Union or Disunion be much more effectually tried and rationally determined, one, two, or three years hence, than now, on a sudden and unreflecting impulse? Or, are we afraid that we shall be deprived of the power of thinking and acting by that time? Is it so indeed that we are frightened from our propriety as men in their great controversy? Have we been scared by the dreadful nightmare of the man Lincoln coming down upon us with his regiments of Suckers from Northern Illinois? And are we running away now from our rights in the Union, and from our duty as thinking and intelligent men, because of that horrid vision? Oh! shame, shame upon the false traitors who have persuaded the people of so many noble States so to dishonor themselves and their lineage as to throw away in one wild freak of tumultuous passion the glorious heritage transmitted to them by their fathers, and in the same terrible delirium to determine forever the destiny of their country! The same cheating game is being played now in Virginia, and, if successful there, it will of course be tried again in Kentucky; with all the advantage of that unhappy success.

If the Commission to meet in Washington on Monday next can do nothing more or better, we ask them to make a strong and unanimous appeal to all the constituencies they may represent, to adjourn the final determination of this mighty issue for at least one year. Let the same opportunity be given for wise counsel and deliberate judgment in the determination of a nation's existence, as our jurisprudence secures for the decision of any great question of personal right. In the meantime all parties can prepare, not only for the reasonable trial of the issue, but for the possible determination of that issue in a final separation. This is the only course that becomes the American people as intelligent and brave men. In counseling otherwise, the advocates of Disunion most emphatically declare their own consciousness of the badness of their cause, that they dare not submit to the calm, deliberate scrutiny of the people.

153. THEY ASK US TO WAIT

(*Daily Courier*, Louisville, February 1, 1861)

In the midst of the political convulsions now disturbing every section of the country, the end of which none can foresee, and before the momentous events of which all are powerless, we are told to be calm, asked to wait, begged to be still.

And by whom and to what end?

There was a time when the advice now thrust upon us might have been appropriately given to others.

The North should have been urged to stay their hands when they resisted the admission of Missouri as a Slave State; when they sought to assail slavery through Congress, which body they flooded with anti-slavery petitions; when they attempted to apply the Wilmot Proviso to all the Territories of the United States; when they smuggled California into the Union as a Free State; when they deprived Texas of a portion of her territory; when they prohibited the slave trade in the District of Columbia; when they were trying to abolish slavery in the Federal Capital; when they were sending armed emissaries of regularly incorporated Emigrant Aid Societies to drive Southern men with their property from Kansas; when they were distributing HELPER's infamous book broadcast over the land; when they were canonizing JOHN BROWN, the robber and murderer; when they were indorsing the doctrines of the Philadelphia platform at the polls in 1856; when they were inaugurating in the Federal Government the doctrine of the irrepressible conflict in the election of ABRAHAM LINCOLN to the Presidency; when they were tendering men and money for the subjugation of the South; and when they were proclaiming, as with one voice, that there could be no more compromises with slave-holders—at any time in the last forty years it would have been proper and timely to have urged the people of the Free States to pause, to delay, to be still.

But there has been no pause in the movements of the enemies of slavery. Their policy has ever been aggressive and progressive. They have waged an irrepressible conflict against the peculiar institution. They have assailed it by every means possible, in every form of attack conceivable, and at all times and under all circumstances.

With the increase of power their policy became more dangerous; the injuries they inflicted and the wrongs they did became more serious; and finally a disruption of the Confederacy followed inevitably aggressions which seemed to leave no other means of redress and no other hope for peace and security.

And now, the Abolitionists of the North and the Submissionists of the South beseech Kentucky and the Border Slave States to keep cool, to wait, to delay action.

The Cotton and Gulf States are gone. They have been driven out of the Union by a course of conduct which left them no alternative but separation and independence, or submission and degradation. They have gone never to return; and they will soon be followed by others. The aggressors and their sympathizers, seeing that the Border States are becoming aroused and will soon go with their sister Slave States, ask us to wait—to try LINCOLN.

And why?

Do they promise us any new guarantees? Do they even intimate a willingness to compromise by yielding nothing themselves and giving us a portion only of what the Courts have decided that we are entitled to? Do they give us any assurance that they will not carry out to the letter in its strictest spirit the policy of the Chicago platform?

No! They promise us nothing. They will concede nothing. They will not yield one iota. They ask us of the Border Slave States to cut loose from the other Slave States and remain with those who denounce slavery as a relic of barbarism, and slave owners as equally criminal with thieves and murderers, and to do this without even a promise of better treatment hereafter than we have received heretofore.

They ask us to wait, hoping to persuade the loyal people of the Border Slave States to adopt a course that will divide those whom God and nature made one—the Slave States. They will promise nothing —the Free States—but they will exhaust every expedient to stay the action of Kentucky and Virginia. They will hold out expectations they never intend shall be realized; they will promise to negotiate after the inauguration; they will alternately coax and threaten; they will do anything except abandon their sectional and unconstitutional doctrines; and these they intend shall be, in the recent language of Cassius M. Clay, *"through peace or blood,"* "eternally triumphant!"

We warn the people of Kentucky to beware of the arts of political management—to shut their ears and close their eyes to the specious seeming and plausible deceptions of the Lincoln and the Submission leaders.

Words are cheap; and they are quite as often used to conceal ideas as to express them. Actions are less liable to be misunderstood. If the people of the North intend to do us justice—if they intend that the Slave States may live with them on terms of equality and in peace— if they wish to restore the Union *they* have destroyed, let them at once—not after awhile—accept at least the Crittenden amendments, which concede far too much, but which the Border Slave States would probably agree to, and then we may begin to hope that such a reaction has taken place in Northern sentiment as to make it possible for the Free and the Slave States to live together in peace. Until they do this, or give some practical manifestation of returning reason, it is treason in any Southern man to listen to their insulting demands or become a party to the attempts to delude and ensnare the Border Slave States.

154. Civil War Will Be Abolition

(North Carolina Standard, Raleigh, February 5, 1861)*

If the difficulties between the North and South should not be settled during the next six months, war will be the result. There will be three or four Confederacies. It will be impossible for the Northwestern and Gulf States to avoid war,—the navigation of the Mississippi will lead to it. California and Oregon will set up for themselves. The isthmus route to California may be disputed and obstructed. Some of the Northern States will seek an alliance with the Canadas, and this will lead to intervention by Great Britain. England, France, and Spain will become interested and entangled in American affairs. The flags of the new Confederacies will be insulted on the high seas, and privateers will prey on their commerce. War, or impending war, or the state of alarm in which the country now is, will arrest industry, check commerce, and impair confidence between man and man. If war once breaks out it will rage in the interior, on our seacoasts, on the high seas, and on our frontiers. One section will let loose the Indians on another section. Twenty millions of Northern people will at once become our enemies.—They will war upon us along a line of three thousand miles from the Atlantic to the Pacific. One section will call in foreign troops against another section. One Confederacy will humble itself before the powers of Europe to get better commercial terms than the other Confederacies. Meanwhile war will rage. Negro property will cease to be valuable, because the products of slave labor, and of all other labor, will be in a great degree cut off from the markets of the world. The negroes will know, too, that the war is waged on their account. They will become restless and turbulent. Heavy taxes will result from these wars. These taxes must be paid mainly out of slave labor. Strong governments will be established, and will bear heavily on the masses. The masses will at length rise up and destroy every thing in their way. State bonds will be repudiated. Banks will break. Widows and orphans will be reduced to beggary. The sword will wave everywhere paramount to all law. The whole world outside the slaveholding States, with slight exceptions, is opposed to slavery; and the whole world, with slave labor thus rendered insecure and comparatively valueless, will take sides with the North against us. The end will be—*Abolition!* There are other considerations touching slavery which we shall not refer to here,—every intelligent mind will at once understand us, and will weigh those considerations for itself.

It is criminal to say there is "no hope for the Union." If five hundred of the public men of the two sections could be transported, or confined in dungeons for six months, the Union would be restored and reconstructed during that period, and it would be more glorious and prosperous than the one now threatened with destruction. The disunionist *per se* is either a *mad* man or a *bad* man. He who prefers disunion to Union, and who labors to provoke and aggravate the two sections against each other, is an enemy to his race. He who is for discord instead of concord, for war instead of peace, *for disunion for disunion's sake,* is guilty of a crime more stupendous than any which has been committed since Cain slew his brother.

155. VIRGINIA AND THE PEACE CONFERENCE

(*The Daily Herald,* Wilmington, N. C., February 6, 1861)

Persons who think that those who are called "Union" men in the telegraphic reports of the Virginia election are opposed to secession for existing causes, misapprehend the use of the word in this case. Virginia is committed to the Crittenden plan of adjustment if the Black Republicans will concede it, but if the Washington City Conference, now in session, shall fail to effect a settlement upon that, or some other basis, *guaranteeing to the South full protection* in all territory South of 36 degrees 30 minutes, with the right of transit, &c., Virginia will be as sure to secede as South Carolina was the day after Lincoln's election. Virginia loves the Union, but not with such intense affection as to give up all her rights to preserve it, and those who suppose that she will not demand all of them in the Washington City Conference, or that she will temporize, and try to patch up the Union on terms dishonorable to herself or the South is, in our judgment, vastly mistaken.

And this is what satisfied us that the Peace Conference will accomplish nothing. Nothing but a clear back down from the Chicago platform, and an amendment to the Constitution, as demanded by the South, will satisfy the Border States, or ought to satisfy them. Is it reasonable, is it not madness to suppose that the Black Republican party will do this? Does it not shock common sense, and violate all experience, and is it not contrary to human nature to believe that a party which has for twenty-five years been struggling with fanatical

zeal for the establishment of a *principle,* upon which to administer
the government, will, in the very moment of victory, and when the
sweets of power, long untasted, are within its grasp, surrender that
principle which is its life, and suffer those sweets to turn to ashes
on its lips? Is not Mr. Lincoln sacredly pledged to administer the
government upon the principles of the Chicago platform and has he
not very recently authoritatively denied any intention to compromise
those principles?—How can he and his party give the lie to the whole
of their lives, and agree to protect slavery in *any* territory North or
South, when the one idea upon which he was elected is the restriction of slavery to its present limits? And this with them is not, like
ordinary political questions, a mere matter of expediency, or economy.
It is a *religion,* a matter of education from earliest infancy with them
which they cannot surrender with honor, or the least degree of self
respect.

This, together with the evident determination of the seceding States
not to return to the Union must satisfy any reasonable man of the
utter hopelessness of preserving the Union.

156. The Border State Conferences

(*The Daily Picayune,* New Orleans, February 8, 1861)

At the same moment when the Southern seceding States are uniting
in convention at Montgomery to create a new government for a new
Union, the border States are holding another convention at Washington City for the purpose of restoring, if possible, the old order of
things.

This convention was invited by the Legislature of Virginia, in
order, as expressed in the preamble to the resolutions which contain
the proposal, "to make a final effort to restore the Union and the constitution in the spirit in which they were established by the Fathers
of the Republic."

The invitation has brought together a representation highly respectable in the character and public influence of the delegates appointed
from the border slave States, and from a considerable number of
Northern border States. Virginia, Delaware, Maryland and Kentucky
are powerfully represented. Ohio and New Jersey have sent delegations, and we believe Pennsylvania and New York, North Carolina

and Tennessee. Illinois refused, and so we think did Indiana.[1] States that are not represented directly will doubtless be consulted through their leading citizens whom the alarming state of public affairs will have brought together at Washington. There will be no want of outside and inside effort to find a basis for conciliation upon which it may be hoped that a new Union, including all the States, may be constructed.

The preservation of the Union by any of the forms of the present constitution is so plainly impossible that the first and fundamental idea of any convention which looks to a further association of these thirty-four States under one government must be that the old constitution is suspended in fact as to six of the States, and that its powers can never be renewed over them but by the result of negotiations commenced and concluded with them as independent States. They have taken positions from which it is impossible to retreat if they desired it. The dissolution of the relation of each with the Federal authorities has constituted each, by her own theory of right, an integer State, no longer competent to take part in the deliberations of the adhering States on questions of change in the government she has thrown off. If they desire to make changes to meet her views, it must be done without her, and whatever they do cannot be presented for her concurrence as one of themselves, but for her acceptance as an independent State, free to negotiate, and as free to reject as to accept. This is the position of all the seceded States, now seven in number. They have left themselves no longer the capacity to vote as States in the Union, on any proposition for amending the constitution. Whatever is done that way in the way of conciliation, must be done without them, and submitted to them afterwards, as the original constitution was submitted to the original thirteen. Each State will be competent to accede to the amended constitution as absolutely as if it were an entirely new instrument, and as absolutely free to decline it, and remain independent.

If it were otherwise, and it be conceded by the seceding States that they can vote on proffered changes, under the forms of the constitution as when they were members of the Union, the corresponding

---

[1] Twenty-one of the thirty-four States were represented. Delegates from South Carolina, Florida, Georgia, Alabama, Mississippi, and Louisiana met on the same day at Montgomery to form a Southern Confederacy. All other States were represented in the Washington Conference Convention except Texas, Arkansas, Michigan, Wisconsin, Minnesota, California, and Oregon.

obligation would follow, to submit to the adverse decision of the tribunal to which they had consented. To amend the constitution, requires three-fourths of the thirty-four States—now Kansas is admitted [2]; that is to say, twenty-six States. Nine States could defeat any amendment. It follows, that if the seceding States, which have left the Government because eighteen States have pronounced against them —which eighteen has since become nineteen—on a matter of life and death to them, should consent to refer the same questions to a tribunal in which nineteen can foreclose the chance against them, by refusing to vote for the amendment, and *nine* can defeat any proposition they please, it would be equivalent to an agreement to surrender themselves to the judgment of nine of the Abolition States, with the pledge, necessarily implied, to acquiesce in their verdict.

Acts of secession have given formal notice that seven [3] of the States will have no part whatever in proceedings which carry their case before such a tribunal, and which give, by implication, a right to expect that they will submit to such a verdict. They are out of the reach of being outvoted by the Abolition States and there is no way of dealing with them but by negotiating with them separately or conjointly as individual States, who may perhaps be willing to confer upon a fair plan for a reconstructed Union, and perhaps not.

The adhering States do not, however, agree in considering these seven States as actually out of the Union; but persist in shaping their measures—as if they were to be retained by some measure either of compulsion or concession. In the Border State Convention a difference of opinion on this head will be developed very soon. Some of the States there will hold that a State may rightfully secede; and several, including all the Southern delegations, will be resolute in asserting that there shall be no attempt to assert Federal supremacy by force. These differences may obstruct the action of the convention in *limine,* and prevent them from considering any plan for conciliation at all.

But these considerations waived or overcome, the real difficulties commence.

They are manifold. They may not agree on what shall be proposed. Congress may not consent to pass them by a two-thirds vote for the action of the State Legislatures. Three-fourths of the State Legislatures may not agree to them; and if they should, the seceding States

[2] The bill for the admission of Kansas, as finally amended by the Senate, passed the House January 28, 1861.

[3] Texas seceded on February 1, but her delegates did not reach Montgomery in time to participate in framing the Provisional Constitution.

may refuse to accept them as satisfactory and prefer to remain separated.

If the other form be tried, of calling a convention by the demands of three-fourths of the States to consider the border State plan, three-fourths of the Legislatures may not concur; a general convention, if called, may fail to agree; or, if agreeing, the plan may still be rejected by the seceding States, each of whom can act for itself.

These difficulties are made insuperable by the fact that seven of the States, which were interested, while in the Union, in amending the form of government so that they could remain, are out of it, and can take no part in the deliberations, or no action, while the theory of the adhering States, through their representatives in Congress, is that these seven States must be counted in the determining of the result. In all movements for amending the constitution, thirty-four States are still reckoned as parts of the Union, and for constitutional amendments, twenty-six are necessary in order to make three-fourths.

The secession of seven States leaves only twenty-seven to deliberate and to act, and of these nineteen are non-slaveholding and eight slaveholding. On the Federal theory that the Union is not and cannot be dissolved but by the assent of a general convention, every proposition for amendment must obtain the concurrence of twenty-six States, and the whole number of States which can act being but twenty-seven, it is obvious that the vote of any two of the twenty-seven will defeat any proposition whatever. Kansas and Vermont can overrule the other twenty-five, and thus settle all chance for restoration of harmony among the thirty-four by shutting out the possibility of even a submission of terms for adjustment of any kind by the subsisting government, even to the adhering States.

A chance for settlement which depends so entirely on the all but unanimous support, through all its stages, of the Black Republican States, is too remote a vision of credulous hope or unsubstantial figment of the imagination to be the basis of any acts by the Southern people either compromising their rights, or their powers and modes for protecting them.

Who ever has seen anywhere the signs that eighteen Black Republican States will accede to such terms as will be satisfactory to the eight adhering Southern States, or tolerated by the seven seceding States, may have faith in a propitious close of these border State propositions, within the frame of the old constitution, and he would have the further faith that the same converted majority will deal with secessionism as a conceded fact, and submit their propositions to free negotiation. That would be to concede at last what is denied at the outset—the right of independent action. Why, then, should it not be acknowledged at once, and dealt with as a basis for all attempts at conciliation, that the Union is dissolved, *pro tanto,* and that the ad-hering States should take all steps needful for their own facility in acting, to negotiate fairly upon the grounds of re-union, or the terms for separation.

If conducted in that spirit, the border conference may result in good by presenting the ultimata of concession in regard to the disputed questions on both sides, and preparing the way for either a fair presen-tation of a basis for reconstruction or the general abandonment of the effort as hopeless, with a peaceful agreement for each section to pursue its happiness in its own way.

In any other point of view, the Border Convention will prove a total failure, in its main design, for conciliation, although we cannot doubt that it will be of service in preparing the public mind for acquiescing in the necessities which it shall show to be beyond the control of the wisest and most moderate men in the nation.

157. HE MEANS COERCION

(*Daily Courier,* Louisville, February 13, 1861)

A few days ago, Mr. LINCOLN told Mr. HUTCHINSON, of Boyle county, in this State, that if Kentucky intends to stand by the resolu-tions adopted by an almost unanimous vote in the House of Represen-tatives at Frankfort, she "*should prepare for war.*" Speaking of the resolutions, he said:

If Kentucky means to say that if the Federal Government undertook to recapture the Southern forts and collect the revenue and war ensue, she will unite with the South, LET HER PREPARE FOR WAR.

On Monday he made a speech at Indianapolis,[1] in which he asserted in terms scarcely ambiguous his intention when inaugurated to retake the forts which the seceding States have taken possession of, to collect the revenue in the ports of such States, and to enforce the laws of the United States therein, notwithstanding they are to-day, according to that great American lawyer, Chancellor KENT,[2] himself a Northern

[1] For the several speeches of Lincoln during the month of February, *en route* to Wash-ington, see *Life and Works of Abraham Lincoln,* V, 86–133.

[2] James Kent, sometime Chancellor of New York State, and Professor of Law in Columbia College.

man, entitled to a position among the free and independent nations of the earth!

This according to his reasoning is neither war nor coercion; but practically it is the one and an attempt at the other, and will be met as such—it is a war proposition couched in language intended to conceal the enormity of the crime beneath pretexts too absurd to require exposure and fallacies too flimsy to deceive the most stupid. When this policy is carried into the administration of the Federal Government, it is war—war without a declaration of war, waged under false pretenses, and justifiable only to that fanaticism of which Mr. LINCOLN is at once the embodiment and representative.

In the same speech he swept away, as far as his bold and reckless assertions could sweep away, everything like State rights, State sovereignty, or State independence, and advanced the novel and dangerous doctrine that what the counties are to a State, the States are to the Federal Government—no more and no less!

The States created the Federal Government; the counties are created by the States of which they form a part; but Mr. LINCOLN, while subordinating the creature in one instance to the creator, and properly, in the other makes the creator the subject of the creature!

The inference is, that as a State is bound to enforce the laws in a refractory county, so the Federal Government, only the agent of the States, must enforce the laws in the seceding States!

An absolute, consolidated government, in which the States are powerless and dependent, follows the success of this doctrine; and this is what Mr. LINCOLN and his friends intend shall render his Administration memorable. A more vigorous head will be needed then; and a King, or a Dictator, will necessarily follow.

Enough is already known to leave no doubt as to Mr. LINCOLN's intentions; and Heaven alone can avert war, immediately after the 4th of March.

The seven States now out will then constitute a Government themselves. The independence of this Government will be recognized by the nations of the earth.—Upon it Mr. LINCOLN will wage war. He will call on Kentucky for men and arms. How many of her sons will march under the command of New England officers to shoot down their fellow-countrymen of Alabama and Georgia and Mississippi? How many Kentuckians will draw their swords against men fighting on their own soil and around their own homes for liberty and independence?

And if war follow the inauguration of this fatal and unjustifiable policy, whether Kentucky furnish men or not, she must, if she remain with the North, pay a large share of the expense of keeping a hundred thousand men in the field for the destruction of those fighting for rights common to her citizens and to themselves. Where will the money be obtained to enable Mr. LINCOLN to retake the forts in Louisiana, Georgia, Alabama, and South Carolina, and to execute the laws of the United States in the Southern Confederated States? It will require at least $100,000,000 a year, for God only knows how long! This amount must be raised by taxation direct or indirect; and the people of Kentucky will be required to pay at least one-eighteenth of it—more than five millions a year to help ABRAHAM LINCOLN and his Black Republicans to subjugate the Southern States!

Mr. LINCOLN's purposes are known. War may be expected soon after March 4th.—Kentucky will be compelled, in that event to fight for the North and to help the North pay the expenses of the war, or to take sides with her Southern sisters, and by presenting a bold and united front, compel an early recognition of independence.

If she should do the first, she will come out of the conflict bankrupt, ruined, powerless and dependent, to remain the tail end of a Northern Confederacy, in which she will be despised, insulted, and wronged to a greater extent than even our past experience enables us to conceive of: if she should prefer the last, the struggle will be less protracted, less expensive, less disastrous in its immediate effects, and in her future relations she will be respected, powerful, and secure.

We should do all we can to prevent war; but if madness rule the councils of the next President, as it now seems certain will be the case, Kentucky must take a stand with the South, or bid farewell to all her greatness and all her pride, and be an outcast among her sisters.

158. THE PEACE CONGRESS

(*The New Orleans Bee*, February 14, 1861)

Dispatches from Washington intimate pretty clearly the improbability of the adoption by the Peace Congress of any measure of adjustment at all satisfactory to the conflicting sentiments of the North and South. In the Congress there are numbers of Commissioners from various States. In fact, some of the most ultra Black Republican commonwealths in the Union are represented in that body. These men oppose a solid bulwark against all practical propositions of settlement. They affect to be sincerely desirous of witnessing a peaceful arrangement of impending difficulties, but no plan for that purpose meets their approbation. The Congress is manifestly constituted of elements too heterogeneous to coalesce. In this respect it resembles the Congress of the United States. Southern men and Black Republicans cannot view the subject of the grievances of the slaveholding States in the same light. Differing as to the question of wrong, they must necessarily differ as to the remedies suggested. Hence it is altogether likely that the Peace Congress will prove a failure. We cannot imagine now any scheme for saving the Union by conceding Southern rights which will receive the sanction of delegates from New England and the Northwest, and therefore we believe the members will separate without promoting the object for which they assembled. But if by some unexpected and almost miraculous display of harmony the Peace Congress should really elaborate some feasible project for reuniting the States, what earthly chance would it have of adoption by a constitutional majority of the Congress of the United States? None whatever, as we have repeatedly shown. The political character of the two Houses, especially since the withdrawal of the Representatives of six Southern States, forbids the slightest hope of such a consummation.

High expectations of the result of the deliberations of the Peace Congress were entertained by those sanguine citizens who yet cling to the idea that something will turn up to save the Union from disruption. For ourselves we have indulged in no such hopeful spirit. There could of course be no objection to an effort of the border States to effect an arrangement; but the certainty of failure, to our mind, was foreshadowed the very instant the non-slaveholding States began to appoint delegates. We knew that the latter would clog and hamper the deliberations, and would oppose the policy of the former, and this even in the doubtful presumption that they were sent to Washington from an honest disposition on the part of their constituents to arrive at a peaceable and equitable solution of the difficulty. It should be borne in mind that Black Republicanism has two elements. One refuses to recognize the right of the South to demand additional guarantees, declares the Constitution in its present form all-sufficient, styles secession treason, and would unhesitatingly combat it with fire and sword. The other professes an infinite amount of solicitude for the preservation of the Union, admits that the South may not be altogether in the wrong, and thinks that some compromises should be offered rather than proceed to extremities. From the first of these concession of any sort is out of the question. Politicians of the school of SUMNER, and WILSON, and WADE, and GREELEY will not consent to negotiate, and will not, therefore, take part in a Congress convoked for purposes of conciliation. The other element is the only one represented in the Congress. It is less openly mischievous and intractable, but in the end will prove equally so. It will concede nothing really valuable, even while mouthing its love of the Union and ardent desire for peace.

The experiment of a Peace Congress will prove abortive. Were its prospects less gloomy than they are, they would be overshadowed by the disastrous influence of recent elections in Virginia and Tennessee. It is true that in Virginia, although there are few unconditional Secessionists chosen, there are still fewer unconditional Submissionists, but the Black Republicans accept the term "Union" attached to the majority of the delegates in no other sense than that of unswerving hostility to the policy of the cotton States. Tennessee, if the reports are correct, has rendered a verdict which will fill them with ecstasy.[1] The defeat of the Convention in that State will serve to convince them that under no conceivable circumstances will the border States take side with the South. That this is a gross and grievous error can be demonstrated by the resolutions against coercion which by nearly a unanimous vote have passed the Tennessee Legislature[2]; but Black Republicanism like GALLIO, cares for none of these things. It rejoices at what it considers a heavy blow dealt at the South; and secure in its fancied hold upon the border States, will undoubtedly be less inclined than ever to accede to such terms as might alone re-establish the Union. The enemies of the South will discover their misapprehension of the views of the border States when they attempt to enforce the laws of the United States in the South; but in the meantime, the partial triumphs they have achieved will render them more impracticable than ever. This is another barrier to the success of the Peace Congress.

---

[1] The question of calling a state convention was defeated in Tennessee, February 9, by a popular vote of approximately 69,000 to 59,000.

[2] "Resolutions of the Legislature of the State of Tennessee relative to the Resolutions of the Legislature of the State of New York tendering men and money to the General Government to be used to coerce certain sovereign States into Obedience to the General Government." *House Mis. Doc.*, 36 Cong., 2 Sess., Doc. 22.

159. A Dangerous Mistake

(*The Daily True Delta,* New Orleans, February 15, 1861)

It is very clear that the northern presses and politicians, democratic as well as black republican, overlook the true condition of affairs in and the actual public opinion of the southern states in this conjuncture. That this is so, nothing can be more conclusive than the gross errors of the former in ascribing the secession movement entirely to a universal discontent upon the slavery issue exclusively; and on the other side, the republican, the reiterated ascription to it of a strong Union party on the basis of the *status quo* preceding Lincoln's election. Now the northern democracy deceive themselves by supposing that any settlement of federal affairs will or can reconcile the nullifiers of the last thirty years to a continuance in a Union they abhor and have incessantly labored to overthrow; because they, unlike the mercenaries of Buchanan, who have almost all co-operated with them, are animated by a principle, whether it be right or wrong, religiously entertained; while the latter would just as lief live under a despotism or the devil, if their subsistence were only guaranteed. No concession, no compromise, no sacrifice of feeling or of interest, on the part of the free states, which would fall short of securing to this party and its leaders a permanent control of the government, will then be satisfactory to them; and consequently it is a mere waste of effort to apply to them on the subject, and the extreme of folly to suppose that they will relinquish the success they have, through the treasonable complicity of the administration, already obtained. How, then, it may be asked, ought the free states in this emergency, which their eternal interference with and agitation of the slave issue has mainly produced, deport themselves; what propositions can they fairly make, and which the numerical majority of the people of the south, who are devotedly attached to the Union as it was, will accept to bring about a pacification of the country, to prevent its further disintegration and to bring back some at least of the seceding states to the confederation? The answer is easily given: forever exclude the slave question from Congress, determine it in accordance with the requirements of the constitution and according to the actual condition and growth of the Union, and not upon principles wholly inapplicable and not to be entertained. The Union party of the south is, we contend, a majority of the people, aye, a majority in the very states which have withdrawn themselves from the confederacy; but, as an humble exponent of their wishes and opinions, let us warn the north against the fatal error of supposing that they are Union supporters at any price. If a great majority of the people of the south value above all things the preservation of the government bequeathed to them as a heritage by the bravest, the wisest, the most unselfish and the most patriotic of men, it is because of the liberty, equality and impartial justice it has and would still secure under an unpartisan and honest administration of its affairs, to every citizen; because Washington and his compeers framed, organized and approved it; because it has made us, as a people, great, powerful and prosperous; because our freedom, our security and our happiness were the envy and the admiration of the world; and not because—let us with all emphasis repeat—there was not a profound sentiment of dissatisfaction entertained at the eternal meddling with a subject which only those interested in it need care to discuss; a feverish uneasiness engendered touching the sacredness of rights which every man who regards his obligations as a citizen, his duty as an American, and his liberty as a man, would, irrespective of abstract notions, faithfully protect and maintain. For reasons all understand, the policy of this government became one of territorial acquisitiveness; for this object a war was provoked with a neighboring power, and another contemplated with a European government, and northern and southern statesmen alike sanctioned and approved it. This war terminated in the extension of our national domain, and then arose the domestic question, the fruitful source of all our woes, of its future disposition, and whether northern or southern ideas should prevail in its government. In this controversy, which became wholly one of politicians, the supremacy of the people was overlooked, disregarded and contemned, just as it has been in the revolutionary proceedings we are now witnessing, and from which we are so severe sufferers; for had it been otherwise—had the people been left to occupy the territories after their spontaneous fashion, taking their slaves with them, if soil and climate invited, and leaving them at home, where they could be profitably employed, should the contrary be indicated—all would have been well; the extension of our frontiers would have, from time to time, been witnessed, most likely without bloodshed, trouble or expense, and our greatness, power, wealth, freedom and independence would have been uninterrupted and consolidated. This, however, was not to be; for on one side the enemies of slavery would insist in restricting its constitutional rights, and on the other the avowed enemies of the Union south and all those who were led to believe that no peace or security could be obtained from the free states, were united in demands which could be obtained only by a dissolution of the federal pact. We now stand a disunited and distracted people; but still, if reason, justice, common sense and genuine patriotism are allowed to rule, all may be made well again, and perhaps forever; and present causes of perturbation, ill blood and family estrangement upon the slavery issue be permanently extinguished. Let not the north, however, deceive itself; let it not delude itself into the belief that the people of these southern states, aye, of these southern states which have seceded from the Union in defiance of the well-understood wishes of the mass of their population, will consent to remain in or return to the Union unless, once for all, definitely and irrevocably, the slavery issue be determined, and their just rights in the country as it is or may hereafter be are amply secured. We yield to no living men in our love for the American Union; we love it for all that makes government valuable in the eyes and cherished in the affections of men, and for the liberty and equality it assures; and we loved it, God knows, more truly, sincerely and loyally, because under its protecting ægis we found in it in our youth a welcome, a home, comfort, kindness, troops of friends and that freedom of speech and of the pen, and sacredness of personal rights, of which men since the creation had dreamed but never before had been so fortunate as to realize. Millions like us would endure much, rather than sever their connection with such a government. Millions like us find their hearts filled with affliction, their spirits depressed, their hopes of liberty and equality surviving such a catastrophe blasted, as the certainty of the destruction of this great and free government appears more and more imminent; and while we cannot wholly exculpate the south, or its politicians rather, for what has occurred, we would earnestly and fraternally urge upon every upright, just and faithful citizen of the free states at this time the duty, above all other considerations, of presenting such a basis of settlement of the differences between us as the north can honorably offer, and the south honorably accept. Let no northern man, then, suppose that if the extreme issue be forced upon us, there will be any difference of opinion among us here as to our duty; we are for healing divisions before that fearful alternative is presented; but once presented, and as one man the south will stand or fall together. Once more, and finally, we implore our brethren north and south, particularly those men in power in both sections contrary to the well understood preferences of a majority of the people, to reflect well and duly weigh the terrible responsibility they will incur who destroy this form of government and array its children in irreconcilable antagonism to each other.

160. Mr. Lincoln's Speeches

(Daily Missouri Republican, St. Louis, February 15, 1861)

The speeches of Mr. Lincoln, since the commencement of his *progress* to Washington, have been looked for with great interest, in the hope that they might give some inkling of his Administrative policy, and present, also, some insight into the character of the man. So far as his *policy* is concerned, it may be said that he did not use too strong terms to his Kentucky visitor, when, after being told that the Kentucky Legislature had, by nearly an unanimous vote, passed resolutions against Coercion of the Seceding States, he told Kentucky to "prepare for war." His speech at Indianapolis is in perfect consonance with this idea. The forts, arsenals, mint and custom-houses, in possession of the Seceding States must be *retaken,* according to the President, and to do this the army must be called into requisition, as well as the navy, and so civil war begins—the North against the South, and the latter to be subjugated at all hazards.

Mr. Lincoln may begin this war if he likes it, but the end of his term will see him further than ever from the object in view, nor can he ever bring back the slave States into the Union by the employment of a military force; and if coercion be attempted—if war be made in the territory of the Border States, he will meet an army at the threshold quite powerful enough to destroy him.

At Columbus, Ohio, the President *improvised* a little—and certainly it is the most remarkable speech on record. The burden of it is that "nobody is hurt"—"nobody is suffering" from the present condition of affairs, pecuniary and political. Was the like of that ever heard? What could he have meant? With a perfect knowledge that the Union has been virtually dissolved—that six of the States have renounced this confederacy and formed a new government; with official information that the government was bankrupt, and that on the 4th of March not a dollar will be found in the Treasury, but pressing demands for at least eight millions, acknowledged to be due, but without the means of payment; with a knowledge that the Secretary of the Treasury had asked for means of any kind to meet the necessities of the office, and that even the indorsement of States had been solicited to give character to the national credit; with a congressional appropriation of the credit of the United States for from fifty to sixty-five millions of dollars, authorized for the ordinary wants of the Government; with communications before him, stating that not a dollar of money could be obtained by him for carrying on his government until all difficulties between the States are settled—he proceeds to tell us, that "nobody is hurt," and "nobody is suffering," from the present condition of the country.

"Nobody hurt—nobody suffering"—what does this mean? We ask the people of St. Louis to respond to this inquiry? How has it happened that commerce is checked in every department; that our merchants are forced to curtail, and even to close their business; that hundreds and thousands of worthy men are thrown out of employment, and left with their families to starve—how is this the case if, according to Mr. LINCOLN, there is "no suffering?" What say you, men of the foundries, and of the machine shops, and of the factories, and the carpenter shops, and of all the other industrial classes, is there no suffering among you, and in your families? What say the masons, and the bricklayers, and the men who aid in building houses, is there "no suffering" among you since Mr. LINCOLN's election? Have you full employment and good wages, and are you happy in your present condition of want, if not poverty? What say the draymen, the laborers, the men who strive for honest employment, and yet cannot get it, are you not "suffering," and are you not "hurt" by the present condition of affairs, growing out of the election of Mr. LINCOLN? Politically and socially, did the United States ever present such an aspect of complete wreck and abandonment, and yet Mr. LINCOLN tells us "nobody is hurt" and "nobody is suffering!"

So, too, we have no doubt that the Black Republicans of this city will tell us, that all is prosperous; that, though we have reached the starvation-point, it is incumbent on us that we should vote their ticket for the Convention; that it may become necessary, but it is *for our wholesome* [*sic*], that they should shoot down some portion of the people on Monday next; that they have organized for this purpose, and it would be wrong for us to deprive the "Black Guard" of this pastime. Mr. LINCOLN's Columbus speech and the entertainments provided for the people in the lower wards of the city bear no little similarity to each other, in the indifference which they manifest for the welfare and the peace of society.

161. The Progress of the Presidents

(Daily Nashville Patriot, February 16, 1861)

Mr. Lincoln left Springfield on Monday last for Washington, where he is to assume the Executive control of the United States on the 4th March next. He is taking in his route the capitals of States and important cities, is receiving enthusiastic welcomes, and making speeches, in all which there is evidently, an under-current of war. It appears certain that the inclinations of Mr. Lincoln's mind all tend in that direction. The revenues must be collected, and what was once the undisputed property of the Union, but is now claimed by a new power, must be retaken and held. The right of secession is properly denounced, but the President elect seems never to have dreamed of a right of revolution, or the possibility of a *de facto* government. He hopes at no time to be false to anything that the people have been taught to expect of him. He is anxious for the condition of the country, but cannot see that anybody is hurt, that anybody is suffering. He cannot comprehend how four billions of property can be forever excluded by the strong arm of power from equal rights in common territories, under an equal Constitution and equal laws, and be injured. His political reflections have never been turned to that grave problem. He seems never to have perceived how a majority in a representative republican government could, on becoming permanent, become tyrannical, and how a minority may be thereby degraded and oppressed. These ideas were not set down in his manual of statesmanship.

On the other hand, Mr. Davis left his home two or three days later, for Montgomery, where he is to assume the Executive control of the "Confederate States of America"—which means that he is to engineer an experiment to build up a new government. He makes no stops except the usual few minutes at railway stations. At most of these the people gather around the cars, shout, throw up their hats, sometimes fire a salute, and if it is night the few houses around have some extra lights stuck about the windows. Mr. Davis appears on the platform, bows politely, and in a very few sentences tells the people what he means to do. He dismisses all questions but the main one in hand, and that is to go on with the experiment, complete the machine and maintain the new government against all disputants in every form and at every hazard. He seems not to expect peace, and with a boldness and directness becoming the occasion, tells the people that he will carry the war where it is easy to advance—to the densely populated cities, where there is food for the sword and the torch. If they come down to spoil his fields and his crops, he will grow them over again; but their cities cannot rise again so easily—the grass will grow where the pavements are worn off by the tread of commerce. England will recognize the Confederate States, and a glorious future awaits them. He is for peace, he even hopes for peace, but is none the less prepared for war. And with this the locomotive whistles, he bows, replaces his hat, and speeds on his way to Montgomery—leaving nobody in doubt as to what he means.

Thus the two men progress to the respective seats of their care and responsibility. Mr. LINCOLN goes by short stages, a circuitous route, with frequent rests. He eats his meals leisurely, sleeps comfortably, and goes as to a festival of ease and pleasure. DAVIS goes the shortest route, with all the speed of steam, sprinkles his steak with pepper and with it gulps a cup of coffee, doesn't sleep at all, and goes directly forward to his post, as to a scene of labor and of danger. LINCOLN has no business in Washington before about the 4th March, and is careless about getting there—DAVIS has immediate and urgent business in Montgomery, and he goes like an earnest man to attend to it. LINCOLN is tedious—DAVIS as swift as steam.

If there is anybody in the country who thinks the "Confederate States of America" are not in earnest, he had as well review that opinion, and accept things as they are.

162. LINCOLN'S POSITION

(*The New Orleans Bee,* February 20, 1861)

The oracular utterances of the gentleman who is on his way to Washington to be inaugurated President of the United States, have proved so deficient in perspicuity as to puzzle and perplex people not much given to the labor of elucidating the obscurities of language. Mr. ABRAHAM LINCOLN has undertaken, during the circuitous route chosen for his journey to the Federal City, to make brief popular harangues at prominent places along his itinerary. He started at Indianapolis, and will probably close at Washington. His speeches vary considerably in character. When he was addressing the Black Republicans of Indiana, Mr. LINCOLN let fall significant hints respecting the probability of coercion. At Cincinnati he overlooked the Ohio River, and embraced within the scope of his vision the opposite shore of Kentucky. This reminded him of the expediency of moderation, and his words were politic and his tone subdued. After a while he reached Pittsburg, and then he thought it perfectly safe to tickle the rapacity of the Pennsylvanians by unstinted panegyrics on a protective tariff. Thus his remarks have assumed somewhat of the hue and local coloring of the people amongst whom he was sojourning when he uttered them. He seems disposed to play the part of a wily politician, and to adapt himself willingly to the predominant tastes of his audiences.

There are circumstances, however, which tend to show that Mr. LINCOLN spoke his real sentiments when he addressed the people at Indianapolis. This was the first of his speeches, and was delivered in presence of a multitude which was known to sympathize most warmly with his anti-slavery views. Besides, it is stated upon the strong authority of the New York *Tribune,* that the speech was carefully prepared in Springfield, and brought to Indianapolis in manuscript. Our readers will bear in mind the peculiar character of that discourse. It dealt with the great question of the day in a singularly hypothetical and interrogative style. Without venturing clearly and boldly to announce his purposes and policy, Mr. LINCOLN propounded queries to his audience touching the nice distinctions between coercion by invasion, the enforcement of the revenue laws, and the recovery or retention of United States property. In this speech the doctrine of the radical wing of the Black Republicans was dimly shadowed forth. Either it is vague, weak, meaningless and stupid, or its author sought to create the impression that when he should assume the reins of the Government, he would pursue the course recommended and urged by his ultra partisans. His language receives this construction from the public journals of the North which are most familiar with his principles and intentions. It matters little that the speech is loose, inelegant and destitute of the slightest grace of oratory. Its meaning is what we seek, and we think his organs interpret it correctly.

If, then, we are to accept ABRAHAM LINCOLN's Indianapolis address as foreshadowing the employment of force against the States of the Southern Confederacy, it may be asked whether civil war must henceforth be considered inevitable? We should hesitate before giving an affirmative reply. There are many serious obstacles to the fulfillment of Mr. LINCOLN's belligerent aspirations. He and his faction are extremely anxious to limit the secession movement to those States which have already withdrawn. They know that the border States—even the most submissive—have plainly intimated their determination to resist all coercive measures. They have no desire whatever to drive Virginia, North Carolina, Tennessee, Arkansas, Missouri, Maryland and Kentucky out of the Union, for they hope by the agency of these States to re-establish the Union, or to strengthen a Northern Confederacy. Considerations of expediency will therefore be apt to render Mr. LINCOLN and his myrmidons chary of overt attempts to subdue the South.

Again, there is manifestly and undeniably a growing schism in the Black Republican party. One half are in favor of violent measures; the other half are opposed to them. We have seen the evidences of these dissensions in the diametrically different remedies for the crisis proposed by various organs of the party. Concession, compromise and even peaceful separation have their advocates, while the Chicago platform and war against the South are the Shibboleth of the extremities. Mr. SEWARD leads the moderate wing; Senator CHASE, it is said, represents the ultraists. Mr. LINCOLN can hardly proceed to extremities without shattering his party to fragments. Indeed the process of dismemberment has already begun, and the organs on either side are lavish of mutual recrimination and abuse.

Finally, war is the most costly of all amusements, and we fancy Mr. LINCOLN can hardly hope to prosecute it vigorously with a collapsed treasury and an exhausted credit. It so happens, too, that the mass of those who are in a position to lend the Government money, are either friendly to the South, or invincibly hostile to coercion. Capitalists cling instinctively to peace, and draw together their purse strings the moment the horizon becomes darkened with a war cloud. It is easy to talk of marshaling armies and equipping fleets, but these pleasant pastimes require the disbursement of millions. How will the future President obtain the wherewithal? This consideration may and probably will throw cold water on his fit of heroism.

163. THE NORTHERN PRESIDENT

(*New Orleans Daily Crescent,* February 21, 1861)

If any one can read the speeches which Mr. Lincoln has made on his recent trip to Washington City without a feeling of intense disgust, we envy him not his disposition. Instead of displaying some of the qualities of a statesman and a patriot, he has, in point of fact, shown a "plentiful lack" of both. Instead of rising to the dignity of a President, he has fallen to the level of a stump orator, addressing, for temporary effect, a miscellaneous assemblage of the populace.

His speech at Indianapolis, which we believe was the first he delivered after leaving home, more especially challenges attention for its evasion of the real issue, its unnatural levity in the presence of great and serious events, and its illustrations drawn, not from anything grand or sublime in nature, but from the "passional attraction" of "free-love," and the "little pills" of the homeopathic practice of medicine! Who would have supposed that a man elevated to the Presidency of a nation would indulge in comparisons of this sort? Imagine George Washington or James Madison, on their way to the capital, making public speeches, destined to be read by the whole world, in which illustrations were drawn from such sources as these!

Mr. Lincoln betrays an utter inability to rise to the dignity of his subject. He resorts to the indirect and unsatisfactory and undignified expedient of *asking questions* of the populace before him, instead of coming out like a man, and saying flatly what he means. Too timid to express boldly his sentiments, he resorts to the roundabout way of putting interrogatories, thereby suggesting what he would not declare openly—and then, for fear of its being considered too great a committal, reminding the people that they must recollect he was only asking questions, not expressing opinions! Was there ever before such an instance of lack of directness and dignity in any one called to so high an office?

Then we discover also that the Northern President has totally misconceived the nature of the Government, and the Federative system by which the old Union was formed. He asks what the difference is between a county and a State, supposing the county to be equal to the State in population and territorial extent—deducing from this that a State has no more right of secession than a county! This absurd pretension shows how little Mr. Lincoln, like most other Northern politicians of all parties, knows of the character of the old Federal Union. He thinks that there is no sovereignty whatever in the respective States —that they are the dependencies of the Federal Government, instead of being the constituents of it, and that there is no such thing as a Federal Government without an unlimited surrender of their sovereignty on the part of the respective members. He thinks that the Union is the creature of the States, the latter losing their identity in the operation, for all purposes except that of tribute to the central authority. The doctrine of State Rights and State Sovereignty, it is plain to see, is something to which the President of the North is altogether a stranger.

It is but fair to say that Mr. Lincoln, as he traveled farther North, became more dignified in his harangues, and more cautious in his utterances. Under the manipulation of politicians more discreet than himself, he began to see that he must change his style. His later speeches are just as free from "passional attraction" comparisons as they are from the mistakes of the ill-informed politician.

Compare the Indianapolis speech of Lincoln with the inaugural address of President Davis, and how great the contrast! The reader of the latter cannot fail to be impressed with its dignified, manly, serious tone —its freedom from every kind of clap-trap—its abstinence from all insinuations or suggestions—its open, bold, honorable and fair statement of the opinions held by the distinguished orator. In nothing is the difference between Northern and Southern sentiment and morality better illustrated than in these two addresses. No wonder Seward, who, with all his anti-slavery bigotry and fanaticism, has some regard for outward appearances, should hesitate to accept a position in the Cabinet of one who has so poor an opinion of the popular intelligence, and so small an appreciation of the dignity of his office, as Mr. Lincoln displayed in his speech at Indianapolis.

164. What We Have Gained by Delay

(*Daily Courier*, Louisville, February 23, 1861)

The Black Republican party and their allies in the South—the Right and Left wings of the great Liberal party—have secured one important point—they have prevented the Border Slave States from taking any decisive action for the protection of their rights and the maintenance of their sovereign equality and independence, until it is too late to do anything before Mr. LINCOLN and his friends will have obtained possession of the Government.

This was one object they hoped to accomplish by the policy of "delay" proclaimed by SEWARD and echoed by Southern partisans.

The Border States, deceived by fair speeches and flattering but meaningless promises, have hoped for an honorable adjustment, for some satisfactory recognition of their rights, for a full acknowledgment of their equality; but these hopes are soon to pass away forever.

Congress has done nothing; Northern Legislatures have done nothing; Northern Governors have not even recommended anything; the Northern people have applauded and indorsed the "no compromise" course of their Representatives; and the Peace Conference, assembled expressly to save the Union, has done nothing and will do nothing;

none of these have done anything to restore the Union; but much has been done by the Governors of Free States, by the Legislatures of Free States, and by Congress to prevent an adjustment, and, God help us! to make war almost inevitable.

Firm action on the part of the Border States taken sixty days ago might have saved the Union or restored it, and would have certainly prevented bloodshed.

The decided action of the Cotton States convinced the North that they were in earnest, while the discontent manifest in some of the Border Slave States indicated to the alarmed men of the Free States the probability of a total and irreparable separation of all the Slave States, and the formation of a Southern Republic. Panic stricken at the idea of losing their best customers and the most liberal contributors to their own wealth and prosperity, the North began to think of concessions, and to exhibit a disposition to do justice to the weaker, aggrieved, and threatened section. Had the Border States then taken a firm and defiant stand, demanding their rights in the Union or their independence out of it, the North would have receded from their position, and the Constitution, at least for a time, would have been restored to its place in the temple and respected as the supreme law of the land.

But the genius of SEWARD, to which the Black Republican party is indebted for its organized existence, was brought to the rescue, and his carefully weighed words, of apparent conciliation, but real menace, seduced the Border States into the policy conceived in his brain to divide the South—the policy of delay.

It was successful; the golden opportunity was lost; the Northern people were made to believe that the Border Slave States were for the Union right or wrong, now and forever, while the people of those States were lured by deceptive appeals and insidious promises into action that encouraged this fatally erroneous belief; and now the end draweth nigh.

When it became apparent that Congress, nor the Free State Legislatures, nor any other authority known to the laws, would do anything to save or restore the Union, a conference of peace and Union men was convened at Washington, and the people have been consoled for the ill success of other attempts at pacification by the belief that the "Peace Conference" would do something to restore the good feeling, mutual confidence, love and respect that of old made our people one people.

That Conference has now nearly closed its third week, without the adoption of anything good or bad, weak or strong. The announcement may go out with this article that it has failed to do anything. Or if any stinted compromise should per possibility be put forth, it will be of such a nature and done in such a way as neither to secure the consent of the North nor to satisfy the South.

What the nature of the debates in that Conference have been, we have no accurate means of knowing. If they could be divulged to the country they would probably fill all candid men with disgust, and excite in the South intense indignation. We know enough to satisfy us on that point.

We know the nature of the Compromise urged by the Border States; that it is the least that could possibly be asked, virtually surrendering many rights, and in fact equality, to get a partial acknowledgment of our rights. We know also that most of the delegates from the Slave States are strong Union men, and that some of them may justly be termed submissionists, and that no effort has been wanting on the part of such to procure an agreement.

No agreement has been reached; nothing has been done to restore the Union; the Conference is a failure; but delay has been secured by the North, while the Border slave States are now, within a few days of the inauguration of Mr. LINCOLN, without a single Constitutional guarantee that the Free State majority will respect, or the hope of getting one such.

And yet with these results staring them in the face, a restoration of the Union made impossible, and war rendered almost certain, there are some fast friends of the Free State cause in the South to preach delay, further delay, delay until the dominant section is ready to bind us if we will peaceably submit to wear the badge of degradation, or to attempt to subjugate us if we resist!

165. Lo! The Conquering Hero Comes

(*The Daily Delta,* New Orleans, February 26, 1861)

It is not pleasant to see even an enemy reduced to the state of degradation and humiliation into which our Black Republican foe has fallen. It is a rude shock to even such recollections as we may still retain of the glories of the Confederacy of which we were formerly a part, to behold that once proud Republic, so shamed and debased before the world by the ridiculous, vulgar and pusillanimous antics of the coarse and cowardly demagogue whom a corrupt and crazy faction has elevated to the chair, once filled by Washington, Jefferson and Jackson. If Scipio, Cato or Augustus could have revisited the arena of their great deeds and illustrious virtues, at that melancholy era of Roman decline, when the Imperial scepter was put up to auction, or gravely proposed to be conferred on a horse, they would not have been subjected to a greater mortification and disgust than the fathers of the Republic of the United States would experience in beholding the disgusting demeanor of the elected chief of the Confederacy whose highest places they once graced and honored. His silly speeches, his illtimed jocularity, his pusillanimous evasion of responsibility, and vulgar pettyfoggery, have no parallel in history, save in the crazy capers of Caligula, or in the effeminate buffoonery of Henry of Valois. We have repeatedly averred that the secession of the South was instigated by higher motives than a mere hostility to Lincoln; that the simple fact of his election was not the moving cause of that great movement. But his recent conduct will compel us to confess that the debasement of being ruled over by such a President—the disgust of having to look up to such a Chief Magistrate as the head of the Republic—is quite as powerful a justification for secession as could be presented. It is evident that the South has been quite as much deceived in its estimate of Lincoln as the North and his own party have been. His bearing in the debate with Douglas produced a general impression that he was a man of some ability, as a politician and polemic. This estimate, though somewhat shaken by the character of his brief letter of acceptance of the nomination of the Chicago Convention, was confirmed by his silence during the campaign. But he is no sooner compelled to break that silence, and to exhibit himself in public, than this delusion vanishes, and the Hoosier lawyer dwindles into far smaller proportions than his bitterest enemies had ever assigned to him. In the expressive language of Mrs. Toodles to her blundering husband, he never opens his mouth but he puts his foot into it. In supreme silliness—in profound ignorance of the institutions of the Republic of which he has been chosen chief—in dishonest and cowardly efforts to dodge responsibility and play a double part—in disgusting levity on the most serious subjects, the speeches of Lincoln, on his way to the capital, have no equals in the history of any people, civilized or semi-civilized. The elevation of such a man enables us to form a fair estimate of the bitterness and venom of the hostility of the party, of which he is the chosen representative, against the South. They were not content to elevate one who was the proclaimed enemy to the Constitution, but they must needs add insult to injury, by choosing one whose personal unfitness and coarse demeanor would inflict the deepest chagrin and disgust upon the people of that section of the Union which has always regarded with the most sensitive pride the character of the high officials of the Government. In this they imitated the mad malice of Caligula, when he chose his imperial successor from his stable.

Passing over his ludicrous exposition of the wrong of secession in his Indianapolis speech, wherein a sovereign State is compared to a county in a State, and his hypocritical presentation of his views on coercion in the form of interrogatories—his declaration in Ohio, that "nobody was hurt" by his election, and that the present distress was all imaginary—his annnoucement of his tariff views at Pittsburg, that the iron of that city and the *corn* of Illinois ought to be equally protected by tariffs, as if anybody ever asked for any protection of corn, his speech of thanks to the young lady, who requested him to turn out whiskers, and his puerile appeals to everybody to keep cool and not get into a passion—we come to the closing scene of his dignified and triumphal procession to the capital, when he suffers himself to be smuggled through the city of Baltimore incognito, and sneaking by night into the capital, is delivered into the hands of his keeper, his Robert Le Dain, Wm. H. Seward, by whom he is to be put into rehearsal for the strange part for which he has been cast. Meantime that melancholy wreck of the once great military chief of the Republic is required to do police duty as commander of a few mercenaries composed of poor foreigners, picked up in the streets of the large cities, detached from the army of the United States, to guard the sacred person of the "People's choice for the Presidency of the *freest nation* in the world." There is not a General in Europe who would not deem it an offense to his military pride to be called on to perform such a duty as Scott delights in—the duty of an orderly sergeant, a subaltern or chief of police. There is not now a reigning monarch in Europe whose accession to the throne would require such precautions against violence and interruption, as have been deemed necessary in the inauguration of Lincoln. While such an exhibition of the decline of the Republic which our fathers founded can not but produce sad and regretful feelings in every American breast, it should be a consolation, a source of relief and pride to us of the South that we are no longer involved in the disgrace and chagrin which Black Republicans have brought upon the once proud and honored confederacy.

166. The Northern Delusion

(*New Orleans Daily Crescent,* March 2, 1861)

We have, on several occasions, noticed the strange misconception by the Northern people of the temper and spirit of the South, in respect of a reconstruction of the Union. They continue to assert that the Southern movement is but a temporary frenzy which will soon pass away and be forgotten. They declare, and perhaps believe, that the secession of the Southern States was accomplished by a *coup d'état,* a few bold leaders overriding the people, and hurrying them out of the Union before they had time to consider what they were doing. And, reasoning upon this belief, they declare that time and opportunity only are needed to develop the latent Union sentiment of the South, and restore the Gulf States to their former position in the Old Confederacy.

All this is a delusion, and a most fatal one. But we are inclined to the belief that the Northern people are not so much to be blamed for making this mistake as we at first supposed them to be. We believe, in many cases, they have reached this conclusion from wrong information *given to them from the South!* In other words, we have reason to suspect that there are people in the South—in this very city, perhaps —who are constantly writing letters to the North and to the Border Slave Sates, misrepresenting Southern sentiment, and creating wrong impressions with regard to the true state of affairs among us. These letters are handed about and circulated privately, and in some cases extracts from them are published in the papers. We refer to no particular instance, nor do we assert positively, of our own knowledge, that it is a deliberate design to misrepresent. It is merely a suspicion with us, but it is a suspicion corroborated by such circumstances as lead almost to absolute conviction.

The evil effects of this are apparent. The Washington correspondent of the Charleston Mercury states that a leading member of the Peace Conference from a slave State, and a true Southern man, told him that if Congress would adopt the Crittenden proposition, the Gulf States would be satisfied and would return to the Union. The gentleman undoubtedly believed it, and his belief was founded, no doubt, on representations of the sort we have alluded to—representations made by correspondents from Southern States who, either through ignorance or design, have so wrongly interpreted Southern sentiment. It can hardly be wondered at, under these circumstances, that the Border

Slave States should cherish the idea of reconstruction—a thing utterly impossible now, if not forever.

This State, more especially, is looked to as being the most anxious to return to the Union, needing only a decent pretext for so doing. How mistaken an idea this is, we need not say. The ordinance of secession passed the Convention by a vote nearly unanimous. It was accepted, all over the State, with feelings of eager satisfaction and relief. Thus far there has been no symptom of dissatisfaction, except here and there in individual cases. No public meetings have been held—no organized expression of hostility to the movement has been heard. The people of this State are free and brave; and it is an insult to them to say that they are living under a "reign of terror," and dare not give utterance to their honest convictions. If there were such a party here, of any consequence, it would soon make itself heard and felt. And the people here have an undoubted right to complain if popular sentiment, as we think is the case, is misrepresented by letters scattered over the North, and written by submissionists, some of whom, of course, are to be found in every Southern community.

We claim for our own opinions no more consideration than is accorded to those of other people. Our assertion, therefore, will go only for what it is worth, when we say that a large majority of the people of Louisiana would not agree that the State should now reënter the Union, under any circumstances whatever. To talk about Crittenden's proposition, or anybody else's proposition, or of anything else that looks to a reconstruction of the Union, is the sheerest nonsense and a waste of words. While the Border Slave States are anxiously looking to the Peace Conference at Washington, a large majority of the people of Louisiana feel no more interest in that Conference than they do in the proceedings of the London Board of Aldermen. They believe that it was gotten up for a patriotic purpose, but that the Northern States saw in it a chance for delay, and have merely kept it going until Lincoln could be inaugurated.

The Northern people, and the people of the Border Slave States, instead of relying upon the representations of correspondents, would gain a clearer insight into the condition of things here by watching the Southern press and by noting the proceedings of our Legislative Assemblies and Conventions. If there has been any indication, in any quarter of the seceded States, of a disposition to return to the Union on the Crittenden or any other proposition, we have yet to see it. The President of the Confederate States has declared that, in his opinion, the separation ought to be final and perpetual, and every representative man of Southern sentiment has said the same thing. Nearly the entire press of the South says the same thing. Now, then, if people at a distance choose to discard evidence of this sort, and rely upon the loose statements of correspondents, who merely give opinions without showing any basis for them, they may go ahead in their delusion. That's all.

167. THE DECLARATION OF WAR

(*Richmond Enquirer,* March 5, 1861)

Mr. Lincoln's Inaugural Address is before our readers—couched in the cool, unimpassioned, deliberate language of the fanatic, with the purpose of pursuing the promptings of fanaticism even to the dismemberment of the Government with the horrors of civil war. Virginia has the long looked for and promised peace offering before her—and she has more, she has the denial of all hope of peace. Civil war must now come. Sectional war, declared by Mr. Lincoln, awaits only the signal gun from the insulted Southern Confederacy, to light its horrid fires all along the borders of Virginia. No action of our Convention can now maintain the peace. *She must fight!* The liberty of choice is yet hers. She may march to the contest with her sister States of the South, or *she must* march to the conflict *against* them. There is left no middle course; there is left no more peace; war must settle the conflict, and the God of battle give victory to the right!

We must be invaded by Davis or by Lincoln. The former can rally fifty thousand of the best and bravest sons of Virginia, who will rush with willing hearts and ready hands to the standard that protects the rights and defends the honor of the South—for every traitor heart that offers aid to Lincoln there will be *many, many* who will glory in the opportunity to avenge the treason by a sharp and certain death. Let not Virginians be arrayed against each other, and since we cannot avoid war, let us determine that together, as people of the same State, we will defend each other, and preserve the soil of the State from the polluting foot of the Black Republican invader.

The question, "where shall Virginia go?" is answered by Mr. Lincoln. She must go *to war*—and she must decide with whom she wars—whether with those who have suffered her wrongs, or with those who have inflicted her injuries.

Our ultimate destruction pales before the present emergency. To war! to arms! is now the cry, and when peace is declared, if ever, in our day, Virginia may decide where she will finally rest. But for the present she has no choice left; war with Lincoln or with Davis is the choice left us. Read the inaugural carefully, and then let every reader demand of his delegate in the Convention the prompt measures of defense which it is now apparent we must make.

168. THE INAUGURAL

(*Richmond Dispatch,* March 5, 1861)

The Inaugural Address of ABRAHAM LINCOLN inaugurates civil war, as we have predicted it would from the beginning. The Black Republicans have played their deep, temporizing game with profound address and subtlety; but there is no longer any need of concealment, and the veil drops from the false prophet. The Demon of Coercion stands unmasked. The sword is drawn and the scabbard thrown away. If the fifteen Slave States had gone out in a body, this would have never been. But, as it is, the Border States lie almost at the mercy of an invader. Their forts are filled with Federal troops, whilst they have not raised a finger for defence. No doubt Fortress Monroe, in a month, will be powerfully reinforced, and ere long Virginia may be engaged in a life and death struggle for independence, honor, and for all that makes existence worth living.

We have no intention of arguing the points raised by his Sable Excellency upon the right of secession. That is a subject upon which there is the most radical disagreement between the North and South, a disagreement which he proposes to reconcile by the sword. This pregnant paragraph is all that concerns us:

I therefore consider, that in view of the Constitution and the laws the Union is unbroken, and to the best of my ability *I shall take care, as the Constitution itself expressly enjoins upon me, that the laws of the Union be faithfully executed in all the States.* Doing this I deem to be only a *simple duty on my part, and I shall perform it* so far as practicable, unless my rightful master, the American people, shall withhold the requisite means, or, in some authoritative manner, direct the contrary. I trust that will not be regarded as a menace, but only as the declared purpose of the Union that it will constitutionally defend and maintain itself. In doing this there needs to be no bloodshed or violence, and there shall be none unless it be forced upon the National authority. *The power confided to me will be used to hold, occupy and possess the property and places belonging to the Government, and to collect the duties on imports;* but beyond what may be necessary for these objects, there will be no invasion, no using of force against or among the people anywhere.

There is but one power under Heaven that can keep this man from executing his purpose, THE AMERICAN PEOPLE, which he recognizes as his Master, and in order to secure the interposition of that power, every Border State ought to go out of the Union within twenty-four hours. Even this movement, which would once have been effectual, may now be too late to avert the catastrophe, but it will at all events mitigate its force. It will increase the difficulties of the ferocious enterprise which these enemies of humanity propose; it is the only alternative, except the most abject humiliation. Henceforth, we venture to predict, there will be no difference of opinion in Virginia as to the course of duty, of interest and of honor. We have often protested against the application of the term Submissionists to any party in Virginia.—We accord to those who have counselled delay and negotiation the same sincerity of motive which we claim for ourselves. We believe that all parties are imbued with a common love of Virginia, and that the Legislature expressed the will of the whole State when it declared, by a unanimous voice, that Virginia would resist coercion. We believe that declaration will be sustained by the unanimous voice of the Virginia people; that henceforth the hatchet of internal discord will be buried, and that, shoulder to shoulder, and heart to heart, we shall stand in a solid phalanx in defence of the independence of Virginia sovereignty, and the sanctity of the Southern soil.

169. MR. LINCOLN'S INAUGURAL

(*North Carolina Standard,* Raleigh, March 9, 1861)

Our readers will find this document in our paper of to-day. On all sides we hear the question, *what do you think of the Inaugural?* We have read it with the utmost attention—we have formed an opinion upon it, and we intend to express that opinion.—We shall do this fearlessly and firmly.

Our opinions in relation to the Chicago platform, Abraham Lincoln, and the Black Republican party are well known. We are as hostile to Mr. Lincoln and to the sectional party that elected him as any reasonable man in the South. We will never submit to the administration of the government on the principles of that party so far as they relate to slavery in the Territories; but while we say this for the hundredth time, we also hold that justice should be done even to Mr. Lincoln and his party, and that he who would deliberately fan the flame of sectional strife, instead of doing all he can to put out the fires of discord which threaten to consume the temple of the Union, is guilty of an inexpiable crime. We want peace, not war. We want Union, not disunion. We want justice for the South, but we must do justice to the North. We long for light, not darkness. We believe that the Union can be preserved, and we are willing to bear and forbear—to watch and wait—to labor in a fraternal spirit to achieve this most desirable result. When the enemy offers us the olive branch we will not reject it. When he approaches us pointing to his oath, yet in a spirit of amity, we will not rush upon him with the sword. When he pleads for the Union we will point to the Constitution; and if both of us should then pause, we would then go with him to the fountain of all power, the people of the States, and seek there, and establish there, if possible, new foundations for equality and brotherhood.

So far as coercion is concerned, Mr. Lincoln occupies the very ground occupied by Mr. Buchanan.—We have compared the Inaugural in this respect with Mr. Buchanan's message, and the fact is so.—We cannot, as an honest man, denounce in Mr. Lincoln what we approved in Mr. Buchanan. The man had just taken an oath to support the Constitution and to enforce the laws. What was he to do? Was he to say to the seven cotton States, you are out of the Union? Who gave him that authority? Has Congress said it? No. Have the American people said it. No. The mails are still furnished to these States, and Mr. Lincoln says he will continue to furnish them unless they are repelled. But he says he must execute the laws, and in the next breath he virtually omits the cotton States as Mr. Buchanan omitted South Carolina, for the simple reason that he has no officers in those States and cannot execute them. He says that in "interior localities" where competent resident citizens will not or cannot hold the offices, "there will be no attempt to force obnoxious strangers" on the people. But he says he will collect the revenue in the cotton States. How? He must do it, if at all, at the Custom Houses, for he has no authority to do so on shipboard. The law provides only for the collection of the revenue at the Custom Houses. Congress has made no other provision. What then? Why he can do nothing in this respect. Mr. Buchanan could do nothing in this respect in South-Carolina, yet he said, as Mr. Lincoln says, that the laws must be enforced.

If Mr. Lincoln were mad enough to attempt to subjugate the Southern

States, or even if he were disposed to do so—as his Inaugural shows he is not—he has no army at his command. He might spare a thousand troops from the forts and frontiers, but what could these do against the armies of the fifteen slaveholding States? Then he has no money. The Treasury is empty. Then he has no authority for raising troops, even if he had money to pay them with. The "force bill" so-called, was defeated in the House of Representatives. What then? He is powerless. He is not only powerless at present, but the tone of his Inaugural shows that he is alarmed in view of the calamities that impend. Will he be stronger in future? We do not believe he will.—His party is already demoralized, and in addition to this, the great body of the Northern people will never consent to an aggressive war on the South.—If the seven cotton States had remained in the Union, both branches of Congress would have been against Mr. Lincoln by large majorities, and the Senate could have dictated all his important appointments. But they abandoned the Union—abandoned it selfishly and for no sufficient cause, and left us at the mercy, *as they say,* of a dominant sectional party. Shall we go out simply because they did? We trust not. Have we of the middle States no self-respect—no will of our own? We think we have *some* will of our own, for we are still in the Union.

Mr. Lincoln will have no more power to enforce the laws in the "Confederate States" than the late President had; and we all know that Mr. Buchanan enforced no law in South-Carolina after that State assumed to secede, and the only coercion he attempted was in the shape of letters and newspapers which he showered from his *mail batteries* all over that State.

Mr. Lincoln is inclined to favor a Convention of all the States. We think the condition of the country and the progress of events will compel him to assemble Congress at an early day. If he should do that, a Convention of all the States could be called, and such a body, we make no doubt, would be able to reconstruct the Union on an enduring basis. Failing to do that, however, it could at least provide for a peaceable separation of the States.

We do not propose to comment further on this document. It is before our readers, and each one of them will read and study it carefully for himself.—We approve portions of it, and we disapprove other portions. *It is not a war message.* It is not, strictly speaking, a Black Republican message; for while he recognizes slavery in the States as perpetual, and as never to be interfered with in any way by the abolitionists, he deliberately refrains from pressing the main principle in his platform, to wit, the exclusion of the South from all the Territories of the Union. It is not unfriendly to the South. It deprecates war, and bloodshed, and it pleads for the Union. That any portion of it will be approved by the Disunionists we have no idea. If it had breathed violence and war—if it had claimed the government for the North exclusively, and had threatened the South with subjugation, the Disunionists would have shouted for joy, as they did in Charleston when they learned that Lincoln was elected, for they would then have been sure of the attainment of their darling purpose, the permanent and final disruption of the Union.

170. THE TIMES AND THEIR REQUIREMENTS

(*The Daily Picayune,* New Orleans, March 10, 1861)

There is a growing conviction in the public mind that the coming days of this month are laden with events of the most solemn character. The manifest of cargo is sealed, and whether it shall prove to be a freight of blessings or of curses the portents are equally balanced. It seems to be considered certain that peace or civil war depends upon the manner in which the Government at Washington shall acquit themselves towards the Commissioners selected to arrange the matter of the forts and arsenals in possession of the Confederate States, as well as of those yet in the occupancy of the United States within the seceded States, and such other questions as are a consequence of the establishment of a separate sovereignty out of portions of the old Confederacy. It will be perceived that the programme embraces many delicate, grave and complicated issues; but the ones which press for solutions, as likely to embroil the two Governments in sudden hostilities, are those which relate to the occupancy of the captured forts and the disposition of such as yet remain in the possession of the United States.

The case presents one of those marvels in the progress of free government, where the dearest interests of humanity depend upon the behest of one man. Such contingencies are familiar to the European mind. The nations of the Old World catch up the utterances of Napoleon as presaging the destiny of Empire. A casual word dropped in the interchange of courtesies, a phrase moulded for the ceremonies of a reception, is enough to wreck a thousand fortunes on the stock exchange, and set the arsenals and navy yards a buzzing with the hum of warlike preparation. There the Court is the State; and kings and queens and emperors sacrifice the laboring millions as chessplayers do their pawns and lesser pieces, to save their castles or capture a crown. But in this "free" land the possibility of a state of facts arising which would invigorate the arm of any one who might chance to be President for the time, with these regal prerogatives, was not dreamed of by those who framed the constitution under which Mr. Lincoln holds his seat. Bad administration might indeed embarrass the nation, imbecility might complicate foreign relations, and cupidity brankrupt the treasury. But there the evil would cease; and the people, in contemplation of the constitution, would come to the rescue and redeem the country from misrule and corruption. In the present condition of the country, a civil war may be inaugurated despite the people, and the land drenched with kindred blood against the moral sense and wishes of every State in the two Confederacies. It is this anomaly in the accidental posture of a popular Government that darkens the future with gloom. If the question could be sent to the people there would be no fear of a collision, but held in the counsel of a single individual, there is much to excite distrust.

If Mr. Lincoln is equal to the occasion, if Mr. Seward is desirous of peace, if, indeed, the ambition of the Cabinet can reach the dignity of preserving the country at whatever cost to party, all will go well. There is abundant justification for the United States Government to address itself to the preservation of peace, in the fact that the late Congress took cognizance of the revolutionary condition of the South and refused utterly to pass laws which even had a color of coercion; a Congress, too, composed of majorities of the President's own party—rendered so by the withdrawal of Southern members from the Senate, and, from the beginning, such in the lower House. What better evidence could the President have that coercion was not the temper of the people, than the refusal of his own party to pass coercive laws, and that, too, when revolution was in progress? If his inaugural means peace, as his Secretary of State says it does, why not do the things which belong to peace? He cannot but know that an attempt to recapture the forts, or reinforce those in the occupancy of the Federal troops, is an act of war —of invasion, if you will. Why not, then, abandon what Congress has refused to give him power to maintain, and withdraw all provocatives to collision as well as abstain from adding new ones? This would be the course of a statesman—of a patriot. If the President was in earnest when he declared, before the assembled multitude at Washington, and in the face of the representatives of all the nations of the earth, that he would not inaugurate a policy that need require the shedding of one drop of blood, why maintain a posture which may provoke assault, and must keep alive hurtful as well as dangerous apprehensions? A peace policy requires the removal of incentives to war as well as abstinence from aggressive acts. Omission to remedy what may obviously produce war is just as criminal as the commission of overt acts of hostility. When the President says he will not do anything to make war, and yet fails to remove what may produce it, he but "keeps the promise to the ear whilst he breaks it to the hope."

Mr. Lincoln may be deceived by the multitudes which assembled at the various stations along the railroad to see and cheer him on his journey to Washington, and by the Union demonstrations with which he was from time to time greeted, into the belief that the entire North is ready to wage a war of extermination for its preservation. But Mr. Seward is not. He knows the value of these exhibitions. The Prince of Wales was just as enthusiastically received, and we are told Heenan met with an ovation equally as overwhelming. The Secretary of State has had experience of these demonstrations. If any time before the Chicago nomination he had traveled through the Northern States in company with Mr. Lincoln, the latter would have been overlooked in the greater show of his own popularity. But what would it have all signified? Nothing! He was overslaughed as ruthlessly as others have been; and those who have put their faith in such demonstrations have discovered to their cost that in these affairs at least, *vox populi* is *vox et praeterea nihil*.

The outside pressure upon the United States Government at this time must be great indeed. But when the offices are disposed of the Cabinet will be like a stranded ship from which the waters have subsided. It has been so with other Cabinets; and they will be left to the calming influences of partial desertion, or roused only by the patriotism which can afford to wait for vacancies. There are any number of self-sacrificing souls who are ready for brand and blood and would go right up to the cannon's mouth, if it were not for the irksome duty of filling profitable posts in the civil service. There are your sanguinary patriots—men who bear other people's losses with fortitude. Mr. Seward knows all about such folk. Will he address himself to the great task of composing his country's troubles? Will he be for firebrands or firesides? for tomb stones or hearth stones? for the tented field or contented homes? If the United States does not intend to wage war or retake the captured forts, the retention of those now held by her in the Confederate States are merely irritation—nothing more.

In this connection, the President of the Confederate States has a parallel duty to perform. He has achieved his reputation as a soldier, and we are sure he feels no desire to augment a fame that might content any man, by civil war. He will have much to do to restrain the eagerness of the young soldier, who is panting to flash his maiden sword upon his country's enemies. He will have something to do to restrain the rashness of the misguided enthusiast, who requires the bonds of union to be cemented in blood; and perhaps a little in the way of quelling such as find their advancement in disorder. We rejoice to believe that President Davis possesses a manhood above the temptations of whatever glory may be won in fraternal strife; and at the same time a firmness which cannot be shaken by inducements beneath the interests of his country.

The opinion is gaining ground that if upon the return of our Commissioners from Washington, Forts Sumter and Pickens are not at once surrendered, they will be taken at every hazard and at whatever cost of life. These are brave words; they are exciting words. But when we know that Mr. Lincoln is not in these forts, that Mr. Sumner is not there, that neither Garrison, nor Beecher, nor Webb, nor indeed any enemy of the South is in them, they lose something of their quickening power. The commander of Fort Sumter is a Southron in his birth, education, and in feeling. If he is kept there, it will be by the stolidity of an administration which for the time being stands like a leaden wall between the American people and peace. And in all the untold forays, battles, sieges, and massacres which may ensue, there will not be one of the Black Republican leaders in harm's way. The fighting will be done between persons who would be at peace with one another; by those who have had no part or lot in forming or fomenting sectional parties; who are united to the South by the ties of interest and advantageous commerce. Now inasmuch as the reinforcement of these forts would be an aggression such as Mr. Lincoln, taking the pacific view of his inaugural, has pledged himself against making, would a little patience be more hurtful to us than the reputation of having struck the first blow? If the U. S. Government fails to surrender the forts for fear of a jibe, the Confederate States are not called upon to relieve them of their embarrassment by doing for them what they dare not do for themselves. They must either reinforce or abandon the forts; we can prevent them from reinforcing easier than we can take them, and by forbearance obtain the prestige of the humaner and more deserving party. Certainly something will depend upon the report of the commissioners, and the reasons urged for whatever course Mr. Lincoln may think fit to pursue; but the Southern Confederacy is too respectable to be frightened by a sneer, and too strong to be damaged by prudence. Again we say that Jefferson Davis has achieved a position which will enable him to pay some respect to the traditions which are common to both sections of the country, without fear of incurring the charge of timidity, and may well aspire to the honors of a triumph of peace, as he has enjoyed and deserved those of war.

There is an idea afloat that the Confederate States would lose all respectability if they permitted the forts to remain in the occupancy of the United States an hour after our commissioners return from Washington. Up to the inauguration of Queen Victoria, if we mistake not, the sovereign of England signed himself King of Great Britain, Ireland and *France,* and yet we do not learn that France was any the less thought of on that account. It was a display of vanity, of which the present age got ashamed. And the retention of the disputed forts by the United States will be quite as silly a proceeding, if it be understood that they are not to be reinforced or used. They are indeed irritations, and must be reinforced to be retained, and that necessity will come soon enough for our purposes. But at last the great reason, the great desire we, in common with others, entertain for peace as long as it can be preserved with honor to the Confederacy, is, that when war comes the parties who will have the fighting to do, the rank and file, will be composed of people who would be friends if their rulers would let them. The young and generous soldier, who is ready to encounter the dangers and toils of war, will be willing to wait awhile when he reflects that not one of the locust horde of detractors and plotters against his country will ever come in reach of his thirsty blade; that he will have to go to Boston to find Sumner; to New Hampshire for Hale; and that those whom he will find are such as were wont to bring hither the rich products of the West for the sustenance of our people, and carry back the produce of the South for the comfort of theirs.

171. WHAT IS COERCION?

(*Republican Banner,* Nashville, March 14, 1861)

All who deny the right of secession are forced to admit that the secession ordinances of the revolutionary cotton States are void. These

States are, in contemplation of the Constitution and the laws, still members of the Union, and the Federal Constitution and laws are still binding upon their people. Whoever, therefore, understands himself, and is not a disunionist or secessionist *per se,* is bound by his own principles to approve the position taken by Lincoln in his Inaugural Address, upon the subject of the enforcement of the laws of the Federal Government, because these positions are the inevitable sequences of the non-existence of secession as a constitutional right. And mark how carefully he has defined and limited the exercise of the constitutional duty of enforcing the laws. First, the laws, he declares, shall be enforced, *"as far as practicable,"* and of course in all these States in which, by reason of hostility to the Federal Government, their enforcement has become *impracticable,* there will be no effort to enforce them, since Lincoln declares that strangers will not be appointed to fill the Federal offices in these States, and that the Federal Government will assault no one. No duties or imposts upon the importation of goods from foreign countries can in any Southern port be collected, without a Revenue Collector in such port; and as Lincoln announces that he will appoint no stranger to such offices in such localities, and as no resident of such States will accept such offices, the revenues will not be collected in those ports or any of them. There remains only two other modes in which they can be collected upon goods imported into this country. First, by vessels stationed outside of the ports in those States, and second, by their collection in the ports of other States, by refusing to recognize the validity of clearances from any foreign port to the ports of the revolutionary States, and the consequent shipment of foreign goods to the ports of those other States. The President has no power to adopt the first of these modes of collecting the duties or imposts upon the importation of foreign goods, and if he had, the mode is impracticable, as ships for the purpose could not, by reason of winds and storms, be at all times kept upon the stations near the entrance of the ports of the revolutionary Cotton States. But, if it were practicable, it would be no coercion of any State or its citizens. It would simply be a legal regulation of the trade between the United States and citizens of foreign States, who might import goods into the United States. The second mode is a practical one, of collecting the duties or imposts upon foreign goods without any interference by force on the part of the Federal Government with any State, or its authorities, or citizens. If any State excludes the Revenue Officers of the Federal Government from its territories, and thereby renders the collection of the revenue from duties or imports upon foreign goods impracticable within its borders, it is certainly legitimate for the Federal Government, for the purpose of avoiding collisions and civil war, to refuse to recognize the validity of clearances of goods from foreign ports to ports within such States, and by notifying foreign Governments and their citizens to cause these goods to be brought to the ports of other States. The Government, Lincoln says, will hold, occupy and possess its forts and public property, but it will assault no one, and if a civil war shall arise those dissatisfied with the government must be the aggressors. The collection of the revenue, the holding of the forts and public property, and the enforcement of the laws as far as practicable, need not be attended with violence and bloodshed, and as far as in his power there shall be no violence or bloodshed. Surely there never was a Government and its Chief Executive which evinced such a strong and decided determination to enforce its laws in such a manner as should, if possible, avoid all collision with dissatisfied States and citizens. And yet there is a persistent effort on the part of the allied faction of revolutionists, in and out of the Union, to induce the people of Tennessee to believe that the "Constitutional defence and maintenance of the Union," is coercion. The people have common sense, and their common sense enables them to understand that when a faction endeavors by armed force to take the forts of the Government, it resorts to coercion of the Federal Government; and the resistance by the Federal Government of such attempts is simply self-defence; that the faction which excludes all Federal officers from the Revolutionary Cotton States, and thus prevents the execution of the Federal laws and the collection of the Federal revenue, uses coercion against the Federal Government; and that the Federal Government in collecting its revenue by refusing to recognize the validity of clearances of goods from foreign ports to any ports in the revolutionary States, is only acting in self-defence. But this faction in Tennessee insults the understandings of the people, by asking them to believe that all the acts and proceedings of its allied faction in the revolutionary Cotton States, are and will be the acts of peace and gentleness, and that if the Federal Government shall resist any of these acts and proceedings of its allied faction in these States, such resistance will be an attempt to coerce those States. The position of this faction in Tennessee and of its allied faction in the revolutionary Cotton States is that the Congress of leaders assembled in the Conventions and in the Congress of the Cotton States has the right, by force of arms, *to coerce and to destroy the Federal Government,* and that if the Federal Government shall, either directly or indirectly, resist its armed and forcible attempts to coerce and to destroy that Government, *the act* of resistance and self-defence will be coercion by the Federal Government of the revolutionary Cotton States! Well, black may be white, wrong may be right, and night may be day, and the darkened understandings of we poor people, whom this faction and its allied faction in Tennessee regard as incapable of self-government may be unable to comprehend that these inconsistent and incompatible things are the same things. But until that faction, and its allied faction in Tennessee shall have convinced them that black is white, wrong is right, and day is night, they will hold their present opinions that the Federal Government has the constitutional right to maintain and defend the Union; that to enforce the laws of the Federal Government as far as practicable, is not coercion; that the faction which by armed forces and violence has seized some of the Forts, Mints, and Arsenals of the Federal Government, has coerced that Government; that the faction which shall by armed forces take or attempt to take the other Forts or Public Property of that Government, will thereby coerce that Government; or that if the Federal Government shall resist such attempts, the act of resistance will not be *coercion* but the constitutional defense and maintenance of the Union.

172. BORDER PRESS—RECONSTRUCTION

(The Daily Picayune, New Orleans, March 17, 1861)

It seems to us, that those of our contemporaries of the Border press who speak hopefully of a reconstruction of the Confederacy, shut their eyes to the first great necessary steps to be taken, before such a policy can be tolerated as possible, much less entertained as desirable. We do not allude to those atrabilious sheets, whose columns are blacked by detraction and scandal—whose mission is to misrepresent and slander. They, indeed, comfort and assure us in the position the South has taken; for we rise from their perusal vexed at the persistence of baffled malice but rejoiced that they are no longer our fellow-citizens; that they are strangers and aliens and foreigners to us. But the Border press is not made up of such. Many of them, who oppose secession, who regard the right to secede as apocryphal, and who spoke of the movement, when they thought it confined to a few disappointed ambitious schemers, as rebellious, wicked, and treasonable, now look upon it as a fact of such large and august proportions as to require other remedies than those which might suffice to put down a petty insubordination, or quell a local discontent. The idea of invasion conjures up a frightful picture of blazing homesteads and wasted sovereignties; the prospect of forcible reconstruction evokes the phantom of subjugated colonies, with an ever-turbulent and ever-resisting population. It is to this latter class we would address a few words, in sober earnestness, which we think may merit their consideration.

We quote a passage or two, or rather allusions to the Confederate States, by the Louisville Journal of the 11th inst., to bring the points we would specially commend to their reflection, distinctly in view. That Journal in one paragraph says, "the Southern Congress, *as it calls itself,* increases the postage of letters," &c., and in another speaks of the "*so-called Confederate States.*" The leaders of the Journal of that day are as strong and powerful in defense of the Union as they have always been, but they are not disfigured or weakened by the harsh epithets which have too often wounded more by their bitterness than the argument convicted by its logic. We take it for granted then that our Louisville contemporary has come to regard the Southern movement as something else than "treason," used in any other than the loose and vague sense of implying a difference of opinion as to the value of an organization which it regards as madness, or rashness or foolishness to resist. It may yet think it revolution; but of such magnitude and consistency as should palsy the arm that would draw the sword to repress it; for the Journal is as strong against coercion as it is steadfast for the Union.

If the terms "rebel" and "traitor" were ever applicable to the projectors of secession, if indeed there were any such as fomented revolution for selfish and unworthy ends, any who would bring the danger of civil war with its untold horrors upon their country from motives of personal aggrandizement, and of this God must judge, these epithets lose their meaning when peoples and States embraced the cause of secession and carried it forward to the withdrawal from the Confederacy. We are not "traitors" or "rebels;" for us these terms had no meaning beyond insulting. They struck above or below us; we care not which so they missed; neither were they "traitors" who differed with us as to the mode of resisting sectional aggression. Under the forms of the law they prevailed at the election, and we acquiesced in what seemed to be the decision of the people. As well might the members of the peace congress be denounced as in the line of treasonable precedent, if their mission meant anything more than a preliminary to unconditional submission. We all along understood that something more was intended;

that the secession of the border States hung upon the issue of their errand; that "rebellion" or "treason" in or out of the Union was to follow the conviction that the dominant party would make no concession, give no guarantees. Those who advocated a congress whose decision might prevent the "dilemma" of submission or secession, should make allowances for such as took for granted what has actually happened, and moved in a given direction a little in advance of the wagon. We do not call Kentucky a submission State, because she does not take the decision of an abolition Senator as the opinion of the people. That gallant and noble commonwealth regards the authorities at Washington as an obstruction, a hindrance, an estoppel of the popular sentiment, which must be soon swept away. Louisiana is not a rebel because being hopeless of a change for the better, she has done what Kentucky must do, if the causes which are sufficient to produce secession are not removed, unless Kentucky means to wait forever. The convocation of the peace congress was conceived in the recognition of a state of facts which would, nay, should produce disruption, if continued. The justification of the South is admitted in the facts of the hour; her condemnation can only be prompted by the hope which casts its halo on things to come. But too much of this.

To the point. Cannot the Journal make one little move in the way of peace? The *so called* Congress! The *so called* Confederate States! Why not say at once, "The Congress," "The Confederate States." Are they not such? Why parley with terms, when the facts demand recognition? Can the most ultra believer in the indestructibility of the Union imagine for a moment that the South will ever entertain a thought of reconstruction, whilst the *status* chosen by herself is unacknowledged? What elements do her Government or Congress require to make them a *de facto* power? They have all the attributes of cohesion, consistency, public sanction, a constitution, organized administration, and hands and hearts to defend them against assault from any, from all quarters. Whatever difference of opinion there may have been, or may be now, in regard to the time of secession, her people are a unit in acknowledging the supremacy of the Government. They accept the Conference as it stands, with the inherent right of fealty and support. Would the Journal have it otherwise? How would our contemporary relish the spectacle of a Southern commission sent to Mr. Lincoln to sue for pardon; to listen to the venerable Roman, as he presented a petition to his rail-splitting majesty, utter a speech like this: "Sir, we have sinned against Heaven and thee with a high hand and an outstretched arm, pray have mercy on our repentance for charity sake." To this complexion it must come, else we must be recognized or conquered. And what effect would such a programme have upon the interests of the border slave States? Would it make Black Republicanism less aggressive? Would it aid the strength of Kentucky? It is the nature of a sectional party to advance as the opposition recedes. Such a course, or any of which this might be considered a parody, would prostrate the conservative feeling of the North; it would supplant Black Republicanism with blacker abolitionism; it would install a reign of ruthless violence against the rights of the weaker members of the Confederacy; the claims of the South would be weighed in a balance, with a firebrand in one scale and a dagger in the other.

To be calm, would it be desirable to drive the South into the Union by any other compulsion than that of an adjustment so generous, so satisfactory and so stable, in its substance and form, as to be inevitable. To re-unite with all the antagonism of denied rights, with the sense of outrage glowing in the hearts of her people, with a deep conviction of insecurity abiding in every breast, would be as wise as to rebuild a magazine upon the smouldering embers of a seemingly quenched fire. It would be neither desirable nor prudent, if it were possible. The most ardent lover of the Union in the South would not dream of her retracing her steps now, unless the road was made smooth of the stumbling blocks which have made the progress of Union a career of strife, aggression and peril. And this brings us to what we shall propound in the way of suggestion, for the better judgment of our border friends.

The only process of a reconstruction, short of a subjugation which involves the extinction of the Saxon race South, must commence by a candid, bona fide recognition of the Confederate States, as an independent power—a recognition which carries with it the withdrawal of whatever may be regarded as offensive or repugnant to the ideas of complete sovereignty. This done, the two Confederacies will proceed in security upon their separate lines of progress and civilization. These lines will be parallel, or divergent, or they must meet at some point more or less distant. Short of that point it is useless to speak of reconstruction. If experience proves that separation is best, it will be best to keep separate. Or if separation developes inherent ineradicable antagonisms, they will get wider apart. If experience shall bring us together again, it will be by means so bland in their process, and so convincing in their development, that the consummation will challenge a unanimous consent. It is not for us to say when, or that these lines will ever, meet. We all have our opinions as to that. We all believe in physical, in commercial, in moral, and in social necessities. Physical necessity is an ever enduring force; commercial is more active but less constant; moral necessity is wayward, or rather like a metaphysical problem, less obvious in political application; social necessities have their ebbs and impulses, their floods and dry seasons. These are the forces which must keep us apart or bring us together. Their direction is obscured by passion, but passion is evanescent; it may be misjudged by prejudice or prepossession, but they are amenable to the laws of progress. The charts giving the direction of events differ according to the bias of the limner. It would be safe to follow the example of geographers, who, in their maps, trace the land marks as far they have data, and describe all beyond as undiscovered country. But this much we may safely predict, that with peace there is a prosperous future for both Republics; war has nothing good in store for either. Grant that each start afresh upon their way rejoicing; if they do not come together it will be because they should not; if they do, it will be because of enduring necessities. If they remain apart it will be because they will flourish apart. If they unite it will be upon a better understanding, and on a more satisfactory basis than they ever enjoyed.

173. The Effect of the Doctrine of Reconstruction

(*Montgomery Weekly Post,* March 26, 1861)

No matter how desirable it may seem to some that the old Union be reorganized, we have always regarded it as the height of folly to cling to foregone conclusions. To our mind there is no more prospect of a reconstruction of the old Government than there is of a return of Northern arrogance and fanaticism to right reason and self-sacrificing justice, a thing that they are incapable of doing, even if they had the disposition.—"Ephraim is joined to his Idol," and we may as well make up our mind to let him alone. It is manifestly our duty then, as well as our interest, to avail ourselves of the opportunities that present themselves, and make the best possible use of the circumstances that surround us. We find the country in a state of restless suspense—a general apprehensiveness is apparent; a looking forward to consequences of the most fearful character, mingled with the anxious hopes of many that these consequences may be averted. This is, to say the least of it, an unpleasant condition of things, calculated to impair confidence, paralize energy and obstruct the industrial pursuits of life; and for the

THE DOCTRINE OF RECONSTRUCTION 491

continuance of this state of things, almost as fatal in its consequences as ever the disasters of actual war would be, as is generally the case, somebody is to blame. This state of things has arisen and is fostered and perpetuated by a misunderstanding existing between some of the over credulous in both sections of the country. We would not impugn the motives of any, but he that revels in the dreams of reconstruction, follows an *ignis fatuous,* that misleads him and deceives others.—This kind of somnambulist, for such he must be if he fails to realize the actual state of things as they exist around him, in his distorted imagination can see the glimpses of returning justice, and the exhibitions of concession and conciliation from the representatives of Northern sentiment, where none really exists or were designed to be expressed; and on the other hand the North flatters itself with the delusive hope that this Southern movement is all an experiment, soon to be given up, and that soon the stray sheep of the South will return and bleat for admission into the original fold. These are fatal conclusions never to be realized, but only calculated to retard a settlement and perpetuate the present state of public suspense, and if continued, may eventually exhaust the patience of the friends of peace and quiet and make them resort to the arbitration of the sword, rather than remain the subjects of vacillating uncertainty. For the hope of a reconstruction entertained by the people of the North, misguided friends of the Union in the South are mainly to blame. The Border States have maintained their States in the Union for no other reason than to exercise their influence in behalf of reconstruction, and some of their representative men, in their infatuated zeal, have gone so far as to stigmatize this Southern movement as rebellion and treason, and even threaten the hemp pulling exercise as the penalty for the offence.

What then is the consequence of this position; in the first place, it stimulates the North, with the false idea, that the seceded States contemplate a return to the Union, and upon this ground, they are induced to protract, as long as possible, an acknowledgment of our position, and a recognition of our rights; and the same influence is wielded, with the same effect, by him that urges the propriety of reconstruction, as a citizen of the Confederate States. It fosters a delusive hope in the minds of the people of the North, and further exasperates those opposed to it, in the South. If then we would restore public confidence, facilitate a peaceful solution of our difficulties, and reinstate the industrial interests of the country, we should look upon the facts as they actually exist.—This new government is no visionary phantom, as some may seem to think—it is a living actual reality, its machinery is already in motion—it has its mission to perform and its destiny to realize; and it depends upon its own citizens to determine whether that destiny shall be one of glory, honor, and renown, or whether the experiment shall be pronounced a failure, and its friends the dupes of derision and folly. Then we must say that we are heartily tired of this cringing uncertain state of suspense, this halting between two opinions. We would be glad to see every man in the Southern States come out boldly and independently, either for or against the Southern Government; if he is for it, let him wield his influence to perpetuate it, and propel it forward in its career to success—if against it, throw off the garb of reconstruction, and enlist at once under the banner of BROWNLOW [1] and PRENTICE, [2] with ANDY JOHNSON, for your Captain General, and SEWARD, GREELEY & Co., for your patriotic confederates.

174. TENNESSEE AND THE WAR QUESTION

(*Daily Nashville Patriot,* April 12, 1861)

Tennessee gave no votes to Mr. LINCOLN. Her people repudiated with one mind the creed upon which his friends at Chicago asked their suffrages. That creed was sectional and ran counter to their views of right, equality and justice. They were overpowered by numbers, and Mr. LINCOLN was elected to the Presidency. Tennessee was warned that such an event would lead to an attempted dismemberment of the Union. That warning has been fulfilled in every particular. At the same time her people were advised that such an event would afford no justifiable cause in itself for revolution and a dismemberment of the Union, and admonished not to take sides with those who had pre-determined to break up the Government. They thus had notice of the probable course of events, and had time to make up their minds against the approaches of the Secessionists. They did so, and declared their decision and purpose on the 9th February to stand by the Union and to sustain and uphold the Federal flag, notwithstanding the election of a man to the Presidency whose opinions were distasteful to them. This determination proceeded from their calm judgment and their loyalty and devotion to the Federal Constitution, and not from any love to Mr. LINCOLN, or from any admiration of the principles upon which he

---

[1] William G. Brownlow, editor of *Brownlow's Knoxville Whig,* afterward reconstruction Governor of Tennessee, and United States Senator, 1869–1875.

[2] George D. Prentice, editor of the *Lousiville Journal.*

went into power. At the time they made this noble and patriotic declaration of attachment to the Union, Mr. LINCOLN had not been inaugurated, and nothing had occurred on the part of the Federal Administration then existing, to shake or weaken their devotion to the Union. They took it as it was and stood by it as it was.

Between that time and the present our State has spared no pains to effect an adjustment of our unfortunate difficulties. She has united in council with her sisters both in the North and the South, and agreed with them on a plan of settlement, which she approved and thought ought to be satisfactory to all the parties to the dispute. That plan was not accepted by a Congress friendly to the dominant party—dominant at least so far as this question, which required a two third vote, was concerned—a Congress that refused a reference of it to the people. This she tolerated with the confident hope and trust that the incoming President would do nothing to forfeit the respect or alienate the confidence of the American people, while yet the grave questions of reconciliation were in judgment. Though in terms equivocal she hailed with satisfaction the inaugural address of the President which enabled her to conclude that the policy of the Administration would be peaceful and conciliatory. While there was peace the hope that swelled in her brave and patriotic heart that the Union was not in reality dissolved; that whilst the reason and judgment of the American people were left free to act upon the momentous questions presented to them, there was a prospect that errors, wherever they may have occurred, might be corrected, that false steps, wherever taken, might be retraced, and the Union in all its majestic dimensions and glory might be restored on the free consent of a great people guilty of mistakes and freely acknowledging and nobly correcting them.

There is no patriotic son of hers who would not now rejoice in the realization and fruition of such a hope. But the indications from the North and the South are that the arbitrament of war is to be resorted to for a solution and decision of our troubles. This is not the choice of Tennessee. Let that be understood at the outset. It is contrary to her wishes, her instincts, her views of republican liberty. Her people flatter themselves that they are yet capable of self-government, and that in peace, without resorting to bayonets and cannon balls. But if war is inaugurated against her wishes and advice, it will cast upon her the responsibility of either taking sides with one or the other, or of acting independently of both. These alternatives will certainly present themselves the moment war is commenced; and in view of this contingency, we desire to call the attention of our readers to passing events. We wish them to consider these most pregnant alternatives. We give them facts, upon which they can rely, from day to day. Our own views and opinions we present with due deference to those of others. We cannot consent to wear even the semblance of dictators in an emergency like this; but having been long and attentive observers of the drift of political events, we give our own impressions and offer suggestions with freedom, and we now say that the alternatives presented to the people of Tennessee, in the event of actual war, will be the most important ever addressed to our reason. Shall we assist in a war of subjugation against our Southern brethren? Shall we aid in the permanent overthrow of a government to which we are so devotedly attached, by sustaining with our lives and our fortunes a sectional administration of that government which in theory denies us equality of right and of property? Or, shall we, by an act of revolution dissolve our relations with that government, and join the "Confederate States?" Or shall we act independently of both by forming a government of our own, in connection with such other States as may agree with us, under a constitution which will secure all our rights and meet our approval? These are the questions. However unpalatable, they must be considered and determined. With the first flow of blood we must consider them. All are fraught with difficulty and bristle with danger. The two first, on our espousing either, may lead to civil strife among ourselves. The last will land-lock us and make us insignificant to all the rest of the world. Let us direct our thought to these great questions, and for the present hold ourselves in the best attitude to secure our own present safety and that of our children, by avoiding hasty conclusions and standing where we are.

175. The Action of the Government and the Position of Kentucky

(Daily Courier, Louisville, April 18, 1861)

The leaders of the Submissionists, having so far resisted any action on the part of Kentucky looking to the united action of the South in defense of the common rights against the aggressions of a common enemy, and opposed every proposition to put her in a posture of defense, now, when war is declared and begun, when formidable fleets and large bodies of troops have been sent to inaugurate the work of coercion and subjugation, and when the demand of the President for the largest number of soldiers ever at one time called out in this country is being promptly responded to by the North, have issued a formal appeal to the people of the State to take an independent position!—to array themselves against the Government of the Free States by refusing to obey its requisitions for men and money, and, while thus making enemies of one entire section, to cut themselves off from the sympathy, friendship, and assistance of the other!

We know the courage of our people, their capacity of endurance, the extent of their patriotism, their willingness to make any sacrifice that may be demanded for the public good; but it is suicidal madness, without any gleam of sanity or show of reason, to ask the State to surround herself with enemies, to drive off those whose interests and safety are linked with hers, to deprive herself of any communication with the seaboard, to isolate herself from the world, while on the right and on the left, in front and rear, thirty millions of people are engaged in bloody strife!

These men and their associates prevented any appropriations by the last Legislature to arm the State and equip her militia.

While the note of preparation was heard in every State, and the distant thunder indicated the approaching storm, they were recreant to the obligations they owed the people, and through their efforts the Commonwealth is left without the means to equip a single regiment for service!

She is thus, thanks to them, in no condition to maintain an independent position, if otherwise it were proper or right!

We give the following extract from an address to the people of Kentucky issued yesterday morning by the "Union State Central Committee":

What the future duty of Kentucky may be, we of course, cannot with certainty foresee; but, if the enterprise announced in the Proclamation of the President should at any time hereafter assume the aspect of a war for the overrunning and subjugation of the seceding States through the full assertion therein of the national jurisdiction by a standing military force, we do not hesitate to say that Kentucky should promptly unsheath her sword in behalf of what will have then become the common cause. Such an event, if it should occur, of which we confess there does not appear to us to be a rational probability, could have but one meaning—a meaning which a people jealous of their liberty would be keen to detect, and which a people worthy of liberty would be prompt and fearless to resist. When Kentucky detects this meaning in the action of the Government, she ought, without counting the cost, to take up arms at once against the Government.

Until she does detect this meaning, she ought to hold herself independent of both sides, and compel both sides to respect the inviolability of her soil. The portentous meaning in question is not discernible at this time, and we believe it never will become discernible. We, however, have deemed it fit, in consideration of all the extraordinary features of the time, to anticipate this possible contingency.

According to these wise men, the sending of a powerful fleet of armed ships to the South, the transportation of thousands of regular soldiers to the shores of the Confederate States, and the preparation to send seventy-five thousand Abolition volunteers to coerce four millions of our brethren into obedience, not to the Constitution and laws enacted under it, but to a Government that has subverted the Constitution and destroyed the Union, is not "a war for the overrunning and subjugation of the seceding States!" What is it then? If it is not attempted coercion, what is it?

Is it possible that any man, any body of men, in this State, really believes that "the enterprise announced in the proclamation of the President" has not "assumed the aspect of a war for the overrunning and subjugation of the seceded States?"

And yet this is the position taken by the "Union State Central Committee of Kentucky!"

But it is a position that will be scouted by the whole people of the State—a position untenable and palpably absurd!

No! The enterprise announced in the proclamation of the President, *has* "assumed the aspect of a war for the overrunning and subjugation of the seceded States"—it is a war for the enslavement of the people of the South—it is a conflict which unites the Slave States in a "common cause"—it is an act of armed, unauthorized, and unprovoked aggression "which people worthy of liberty would be prompt and fearless to resist"—and the time has come when Kentucky "ought, without counting the cost, to take up arms" with the other slaveholding States to maintain her sovereignty, to defend the rights of her citizens, and to preserve their liberties!

And yet these men, who advised delay and inaction while the North were arming for the conflict; who objected when it was proposed to place the State in a defensive condition; who cried out against "precipitation" when it was suggested that the whole question should be submitted to the people for decision; now, while the Free States are collecting their legions, burnishing their guns, sharpening their swords, molding bullets, and organizing vast armies with which to attempt to "overrun and subjugate" the South, and after hostilities have actually commenced, still insult the intelligence and spirit of the people by crying peace, peace, and advise "a little more slumber, a little more folding of the arms to sleep!"

Great God! is there to be no end to this folly?

Is this madness still to rule where reason should reign?

Is the advice of this committee to be followed, and Kentucky so to be thrust, all unarmed, unprepared, and defenseless, into the "jaws of death," "into the gates of hell"?

People of Kentucky! every act of these men since the 6th day of November last has tended to humiliate you.

Every movement of theirs has encouraged and invited the aggressions of your enemies.

Their advice has served to divide and distract you.

Their policy, which prevailed in your Legislature, has left you without the means of resistance to usurpation and tyranny.

The hopes they have held out to you have been dissipated by the march of events.

The predictions they made have all been falsified by subsequent acts of the people and States of the North.

War, which might possibly have been prevented by decision and promptness on the part of the Border Slave States, has been precipitated by the hesitation, vacillation, and delay, which, through their counsels, has marked the course of these States.

Will you trust them longer? Dare you still listen to their appeals? Will you yet be guided by their counsels?

The Administration has given you, fellow-citizens, in the proclamation of the President—magnanimously given you—just twenty days from the Saturday of last week in which to decide!

Will you use that time in active preparation for the conflict? Will you diligently prepare in the respite given you, for resistance to tyranny for the defense of your homes and the protection of your household gods? or will you still follow those "blind leaders" whose incapacity and unfitness has been demonstrated by past events beyond the possibility of doubt?

At the expiration of the time given you for decision, *we* tell you, that you MUST take sides with the United North and aid in "overrunning and subjugating the seceded States," or make common cause with the latter: *they* tell you, that you must put yourselves in a position of resistance to the Government of the nineteen Northern States, and thus bring upon you their power, and, by refusing, to co-operate with the South, stand alone, isolated, and unaided in your contest with the Federal powers!

In either event, you array yourselves against the Federal Government: on the one hand, you will stand side by side with fourteen other Slave States; on the other hand, you will fight alone.

176. DUPLICITY OF LINCOLN AND HIS INSTRUMENTS [1]

(*The Daily Delta,* New Orleans, April 18, 1861)

The duplicity and treachery of Lincoln and Seward have served greatly to increase the hostility of our people against the United States Government. Never was seen in the chief executive or the high officer of any respectable nation such a display of low cunning and dishonorable artifice. Besides his faithlessness to our Commissioners in leading them to believe that they would in time be recognized and treated with; and that peaceful relations would in the meantime be maintained, there have been various instances of treachery and deception by Lincoln towards individuals, which will contribute to illustrate the disgusting baseness of this pitiable creature, this burlesque of a President. One of the victims of this duplicity of Lincoln was no less an individual than Judge John A. Campbell, of the Supreme Court of the United States. Judge Campbell had been induced to withhold his resignation of his seat on the bench by the earnest entreaty of the venerable Chief Justice and by the hope of using his influence to give a peaceful direction to the agitations between the two Confederacies. Accordingly, when our Commissioners reached Washington, Judge Campbell offered his services as an intermediary between them and Lincoln and Seward. In this position it was supposed he would be equally acceptable to both parties. It was to him, a Judge of the highest tribunal of the Government of the United States, that Lincoln and Seward gave the most positive assurances of peaceful purposes and of his determination not to reinforce the forts. This assurance was given as late as the 8th of April, after the orders had been sent from the War Department to fit out the naval expedition and move the troops southward to reinforce Sumter and Pickens. We have this fact from a member of Judge Campbell's family.

But this is not the only instance of vile treachery towards a prominent

---

[1] An admirable discussion of this controversial point, by an historian who inclined to the opinion that there were no dishonest men on either side, may be found in James Ford Rhodes, *History of the United States from the Compromise of 1850,* III, 329–356.

official, Senator Gwin, of California, before leaving Washington, having received from Seward repeated assurances that as soon as the Executive could be relieved of the hungry gang of office cormorants who were then besieging him, he would recognize the Southern Commissioners and take measures for a peaceful separation. At the request of Seward Mr. Gwin made a visit to Lincoln and presented to him his view of the impossibility of coercing the South into the Union. Mr. Gwin spoke as an impartial observer of the conflict, as the representative of a State not involved in it. When he had concluded his statement, Mr. Lincoln declared with great appearance of sincerity, that he fully concurred in his views, and that his policy was one of peace and conciliation. Mr. Gwin came South and communicated to all his friends in this section his belief in these purposes of Lincoln. Nelson and Etheridge, two Union members of Congress from Tennessee, received like assurances, and when they returned home communicated them to their constituents. Their communication contributed greatly to strengthen the Union feeling in Tennessee.

The closing incident in the series of acts of duplicity of Lincoln was the intrigue which was fortunately suspected and defeated by Gov. Pickens and Gen. Beauregard. It was the plan to obtain possession of Fort Sumter, which was conceived by one Fox, an officer in the United States Army, and a brother-in-law of Blair, the Postmaster General. Fox's plan was to concert with Anderson an arrangement of signals from Fort Sumter by which small boats and launches might be enabled to steer into the bay during the night, and to avoid the South Carolina batteries. To promote this scheme Talbot was appointed Assistant Adjutant General, and obtained the permission of Gov. Pickens to leave the fort and proceed to Washington. On his arrival there he and Fox were closeted with Gen. Scott and with Lincoln's Secretaries of War and Navy, and the plans for the concerted signals and communications between the fort and squadron were arranged and agreed upon. With these plans Talbot and Fox returned to Charleston and asked permission to proceed to the fort, declaring that their purpose was to make arrangements for the evacuation. But the Carolinians began to suspect these individuals, and refused them leave to go to the fort, and ordered them off, thus defeating a plot, to consummate which the lowest and the most vulgar falsehood and treachery had been employed. These are only a few of the devices of the low cunning and cowardly duplicity of the miserable pretenders who now fill the high places in the once respectable Government of the United States.

177. President's Proclamation—Despotism

(Daily Missouri Republican, St. Louis, April 19, 1861)

The Republican party at the North have found the long-sought opportunity of waging a war upon the South and its institutions. Filled with the idea that the Federal Government is a consolidated Republic, that the States are mere geographical divisions—*counties* on a large scale—this Northern geographical party is about to send down its hordes of armed men upon the seceding States of the South. South Carolina, by its attack upon Fort Sumter, has given the Republicans the war cry of treason and rebellion, and now they expect the Northern people as a unit to band against the South, and by overwhelming force to crush out the liberties of the seceding States. They must be forced by an army of seventy-five thousand to submit to the laws of the General Government, when they have, through their legally constituted Governments, thrown off its bonds, and have sought to enter into peaceable alliance with it. While the people have been seeking a peaceable settlement of the difficulties which attended their affairs, the Republican Administration, with words of peace on its tongue, but with the sword of hatred in its heart, lulling suspicions but biding its time, has made its preparations to cry havoc! and let slip the dogs of war—and behold the proclamation of the President who permits lies to be twisted from him, as it is charged by his own supporters and admitted by himself to the man he had deceived.

But this truthful President is not content with levying war upon the seceded States. He issues a proclamation, and assumes an authority to levy war without the assent of Congress. Without the authority of any law he summons 75,000 troops to repossess the forts, places and property which have been seized from the Union. And pray! do the seceded States of South Carolina, Georgia, Florida, Alabama, Mississippi, Louisiana and Texas, seven States, constitute no part of this Union? Has it come to this that the Union is an entity, distinct from the States which compose it? Is it a bundle without sticks, all binding and nothing to bind? Is the Federal Government a power as distinct from the States as was the British Government distinct from the colonies when they declared their independence? We protest against such horrid doctrines. Once admitted, and American freedom will soon stand trembling before the Presidential throne. The States are the true guardians of our freedom and our rights, and when their power is gone, the master at the Federal capital is the ruler over subject millions—an emperor, elected or self-appointed, as the times determine.

But the President's proclamation is a despotic usurpation of authority not granted in the Constitution, not authorized by the law of the land. True, the President pretends to quote authority for his act—and so any usurper can quote some law that he thinks may be twisted to his purpose, and the devil can quote scripture, also, or did so on one occasion—but the law quoted gives no authority for the acts done. The people of the United States should, through their Representatives, at once impeach ABRAHAM LINCOLN of high crimes and misdemeanors, and put him on trial before his judges. The President quotes the language of the 2d section of act of Congress of February 28, 1795, as his authority for this levying war. He is commander-in-chief, his orders must be obeyed without question! That section provides, "that whenever the laws of the United States shall be opposed, or the execution thereof obstructed in any *State,* by combinations too powerful to be suppressed by the *ordinary course of judicial proceeding, or by the powers vested by* [*sic*] *the marshals by this act,* (the proclamation cites it, *"or by the powers vested in the marshals by law,"* as if there were some special or general law upon the subject,) it shall be lawful for the President of the United States to call forth the militia of *such State,* or of any other State or States, as may be necessary to suppress such combinations and to cause the laws to be duly executed; the use of militia so to be called forth may be continued, if necessary, until the expiration of thirty days after the commencement of the next session of Congress."

The power given to the Marshals by *this act,* is found in section 9, "That the *Marshals* of the several districts, and their deputies, shall have the *same* powers in executing the laws of the United States, *as Sheriffs and their deputies in the several States* have by law in executing the laws of the *respective States."*

In those two sections is found all the authority conferred upon the President to make this war upon the Southern seceding States. The Constitution, a document little regarded now-a-days by North or South, says Congress shall have power to declare war, and to raise and support armies; but Mr. LINCOLN does it now; he needs no Congress; he is preparing his *coup d'état,* and, like the French President, he calls upon the people to support him, and the frantic North rushes forth to hail the man who has the backbone, and who is ready to prove by hard knocks "that we have a Government." The next thing is to declare martial law at Washington, although the Constitution says the privilege of the writ of *habeas corpus* shall not be suspended unless in cases of rebellion or invasion the public safety may require it. And the law can only be suspended by act of Congress, and yet suspension is spoken of, and so far is the Government suspected, that men are actually afraid of martial law.

The first section of the act gives the President authority, whenever the country is invaded, or is in imminent danger of invasion, to call forth such number of militia as he may judge necessary to repel the invasion, and to issue his order for that purpose. In the case of insurrection against a State, he can, upon application of the Legislature, or Executive of that State, call upon the militia of any other States.

Under the first section it has been decided that the danger of invasion must be determined by the President, and that the other departments of the Government must submit to that decision, as the discretion is left with him. But how different the language of the second section, under which he purports to act. When the execution of the laws of the United States are obstructed by combinations too powerful to be suppressed by the *ordinary course* of *judicial proceedings,* or by the powers *vested* in the Marshal *by this act.* What judicial proceeding has been resisted? What Marshal's writ has been taken from him? What judgment or decree fails of its due execution? What *posse comitatus* is found unable to assist the Marshal in procuring obedience to the mandate of his writ? What Judge has certified to the President that the Marshal cannot execute the laws? What Collector of a port finds himself unable to collect the duties imposed by law, and finds his authority set at naught? Not one. None of these things have been done; but the Judges have resigned; there are no Marshals; there are no Collectors, and thus the army is called upon to *execute the laws.* No writ is required, no judicial process asked, but the mailed hand is stretched forth, and, avoiding conciliation, the maxim is, all means to *crush.*

Alas! it is becoming not a question of secession and treason, but a question of our own and our children's freedom—a question whether our liberties are secured by laws or whether they are subject to the will, the mere will of despotism.

178. [THE WAR OF REVENGE]

(*The Review,* Charlottesville, Va., April 19, 1861)

When War—and Civil War—has come, it is neither politic nor in good taste to recur to the past. Political foes will soon stand side by side in the shock of battle. We accept War as a fact. From wickedness, or from some strange hallucination, the President has summoned the country to arms—to fight among themselves. Whoever is to blame about Fort Sumter, why the affair was not dropped there, or confined to Fort Pickens, we are at a loss to conjecture. What object but *revenge,* can have stimulated the immense military preparations in progress, or a purpose to "re-capture" other forts, we cannot discover. We have desired to weigh fairly both sides of this question. We know there is one sentiment at the North, and one sentiment at the South. The Northern journals rest the coercive measures which are being initiated on the necessity of maintaining the Union, and vindicating the Government. We admit very freely that in any ordinary case of resistance to the constituted authorities, force, even war, ought to be resorted to. In 1832 the Government would in our opinion have been fully justified in putting into execution the Force bill. The object of Government is to perpetuate itself, and to uphold its authority.

In the present case a section of country comprising some eight hundred thousand square miles, and eleven millions of people is about to be arrayed in hostility to the government. A sectional line has been drawn, the people on one side of which under the name of "the Government," are marshalling to compel to their ways of thinking the people on the other side. In 1861, it is proposed to carry conviction to fourteen American States by the sword. The Government so far from establishing and perpetuating its authority, is driving from itself new States, and laying the foundation of permanent separation and undying enmity. It is not a case of insubordination. It is the protest of one half of a confederation against the other half.

After ten years—or a generation—have passed—and every green field has been stained with blood—and many a gallant soldier has bit the dust—and bereavement or impoverishment has entered every home in the South, will the South be prepared to go back to the old ways? Shall the free spontaneous outgoings of the American spirit draw its impulses from the instructive promptings of improved artillery and rifled muskets? Will Virginia and Alabama be chastised into the peaceable election of members to the Federal Congress? Will blows with the edge or the flat-side of cavalry sabres teach them to cast electoral votes for a Northern president?

In case of success, the most that the "United States Government" can hope for, is the permanent military occupation of the Southern States. We through this journal have battled for the cause of the American Union, until we exposed ourselves at the hands of some of the best men in the community to the charge of being wanting in patriotism and sectional pride. We have reprobated the dismemberment of this Union in terms of the bitterest and most unmeasured condemnation. Upon an humble theatre, and with humble abilities, we have contended for the Union as a man contends for his life. We have encountered pecuniary injury, and the estrangement of valued friends, in the path of what we believed to be a duty to the welfare of the State, the interests of the American nation, and the cause of human liberty. And now while President Lincoln holds in suspense the uplifted gauge of battle, we warn him in the name of the former Union party in Virginia, that there are no divisions here now that the curtain has begun to rise. If he sends war upon the people of the South, he will meet a united and continued resistance until he will retreat as Pyrrhus did from Italy, or the legions of France retired from Moscow. Peradventure he will retrace his steps as the Persians fled from Marathon, or the English from Bannockburn. The history of Scotland may afford him an instructive lesson. After centuries of war—after the fields of Falkirk and Flodden—Scotland was still unconquered. After four hundred years that Union was effected peaceably which could never be established by force.

We find it difficult to believe that Abraham Lincoln, speaking the same language, professing the same religion, belonging to the same advanced race—born even upon Southern soil—really contemplates serious war. We can hardly realise that any man of fair ability and fair morality in the United States would in earnest inaugurate civil war between Americans. If he were to let loose the devils in hell, he could not get up such a tragedy. We still hope in conformity with his reply to the Virginia Commissioners that his design is at present limited to "the border of the country." That would be trifling in its results to a collision of large armies in the interior. It is the policy of both parties to settle this contest at sea, and at the frontier forts. Mr. Lincoln may try the experiment of coercion to this extent. It will probably only drive all the border States to secession, and succeed in establishing the permanent division of the Union by the slave line. When he should be weary, he would have the satisfaction of having added six or eight States to those already seceded.

This method of conducting the war, *may* be his policy. The danger is that, even if he has the inclination, he may not be able to restrain the storm which he has roused. The conflict will, we fear, gradually extend, and a long and bloody continental war be the result.

Judging by the temper of the people of this community, this last result will be rather invited than avoided. The public heart is stirred to its lowest depths. The War feeling is swelling and surging like the waves of the sea. Who can resist a whole people, thoroughly aroused, brave to rashness, fighting for their existence?

179. THE BORDER STATES MUST UNITE AND ACT!

(*North Carolina Standard,* Raleigh, April 20, 1861)

The proclamation of Abraham Lincoln, which we publish to-day, has completed the sectionalization of the country. The two extremes are now arrayed against each other with warlike purposes, and the only hope for peace is in the border States. *They* may interpose and stay the hand of brother uplifted against brother.

We shall not discuss the past. We have no regrets to express and nothing to retract. We glory in our course as a Constitutional Union man. The Union men are, at least, "guiltless of their country's blood." They have labored long and faithfully, under opprobrium and insults, to save the government and the Union, and at the same time their own native land. But revolution and war are now upon us. The time for "watching and waiting" has gone by—we must now UNITE and ACT. The Union cannot be maintained by force. Men cannot be whipped into freedom. Freemen cannot be compelled to send members of Congress to Washington. The proclamation of Lincoln is a gross usurpation. He has broken the Constitution. He has assumed and is now exercising undelegated power. He has deceived, and would now ruin his country. The Confederate States have grievously erred,—they fired the first gun at Charleston,—they provoked the war; admit all this, and still there is no justification for an attempt on the part of Mr. Lincoln to involve the whole country in war and bloodshed.—He looks to "devastation." That is war. He says it shall be as light as possible. Unchain the tornado and then bid it become a zephyr!—command Niagara to freeze as it falls! Civil war is the worst of all wars. It is worse than "devastation"—it is spoliation, anarchy, arson, murder, rape, annihilation!

We have read the late Northern papers carefully and sadly. The Northern people appear to be uniting by large majorities against us. The attack on Fort Sumter aroused and banded them—the proclamation of the President fired and cemented them in one common purpose, and that purpose is *war to the knife*. We cannot become parties to the subjugation of our Southern brethren. The federal government cannot be maintained by force *applied to sovereign States*. Local combinations and insurrections may be put down by force, and should be; but to attempt to drive and subdue sovereign States by armies is to exercise unjust, undelegated, arbitrary power. The people of North-Carolina would not call for this, in any event, towards Massachusetts or Maine; and they will not submit to it when attempted towards the Confederate States. We must unite and command the peace, if possible; if we fail in that, *we must fight*. This is the duty of the border States. They will prove equal to the crisis. They can muster five hundred thousand fighting men. They will take Washington City, if necessary, and hold it; and they will continue the conflict, *if it be forced upon them,* until the present federal government is demolished and a new one established on its ruins.

180. ACTION! ACTION!! TENNESSEANS TO THE RESCUE OF TENNESSEE

(Nashville Union and American, April 20, 1861)

It can not too earnestly be urged upon the people of every neighborhood in Tennessee to organize, arm and prepare for the fight, without a moment's delay. The time for argument and mere declamation has passed. The people are now called on to act, and act promptly. It is deeply to be regretted that the Legislature did not, at its last session, take the proper steps to place the commonwealth in a complete and efficient state of military preparation. But regrets are now useless, and the people must prepare themselves at once, as best they can, without waiting for the Legislature. Let military companies be formed everywhere and drilled daily, using such arms as they can find. In the meantime, we can assure them that our State authorities will not be inactive. Every means will be used to secure improved arms in the shortest possible time that is practicable. Let the military organization go on in every county and district. An hour is not to be lost. We may be called on to defend our homes and our firesides sooner than many of us expect. The attitude of the people is revolutionary, and the vengeance of the LINCOLN Government may be directed against them. We should not be surprised at an attempt to take military possession of the State, to prevent volunteers from being organized to sustain the South. The usurpations at Washington demonstrate that the constitution is a dead letter with the Government. We repeat, let our people thoroughly prepare for the fight, so as to be ready to meet the invader at the border with Tennessee's "bravest and best," and throw themselves on the very "crest of the battle," to chastise the insolent and tyrannical foe, and if need be, to march and meet him beyond our borders, Tennesseans! arouse yourselves to action, arm and organize!

The great revolution in public sentiment in Tennessee which, has been inaugurated by the hostile attitude of the Lincoln Government and its dangerous usurpations of authority, has culminated in an almost universal sentiment of resistance, and a conviction that Tennessee must separate herself from a Union, thus perverted to the purposes of tyranny, and must unite herself at once with the Conferderate States, whose Constitution and Government offer us a secure asylum against oppression.

This revolution is not the work of leaders or politicians, as all can see. It is the spontaneous uprising and upheaving of the people. It is as irresistible as the mighty tide of the ocean, and is sure to bear our beloved State into a speedy alliance with the Confederate States. This is our manifest destiny, and it will be accomplished without the intervention of leaders and despite their opposition. The attempt to place Tennessee in a position where her moral and physical energies will be broken and destroyed, by declaring that she will not take sides against the Union, will never be accepted by Tennesseans. They will never see their Southern brethren subjected to the horrors of war without the boldest and most efficient resistance; and to make this resistance effectual, they must at once join the Confederate States, and lock shields with them in this contest. The adoption of any other plan than this will prove most fatal, as we earnestly believe. It will be unworthy of a gallant and chivalrous people, it will alienate the sympathies and love of our Southern brethren and will not secure the rights, honor and interests of Tennessee. It will do more than this. It will greatly encourage the LINCOLN Government in their fiendish attempt to subjugate the Southern States. Such a measure is not a peace measure, and those who advocate it are not peace makers. Peace is only preferable to war, when it can be obtained without the sacrifice of manhood, honor and equality. And even then, it cannot be had by continually crying "peace, peace," when the enemy are already preparing the instruments of war and marshalling his [sic] armies in the field. Peace or war is no longer a question. War has been solemnly proclaimed by the President's proclamation and is being waged with all the energy and resources of the Government. The people of Tennessee have only a few days to prepare for it. Then, why harass the public mind by proclaiming what Tennessee ought to do, "should a purpose be developed by the Government of overrunning and subjugating our brethren of the Seceded States," when the President has formally proclaimed such a purpose and is hourly marshalling his forces and moving his fleets to destroy and subjugate.

Great God! Is not this enough to satisfy the most indifferent and passive mind of his designs upon the South? And must we wait, wait, wait, until his armies are marching across our fields, desolating our cities and insulting and destroying our people, contenting ourselves with declaring that we will do so and so, if they hurt anybody. Never, no never. We will throw ourselves upon the crest of battle, meet the insolent and mercenary invader, unite our strength with the gallant sons of Virginia, South Carolina, Alabama, Mississippi, and the other Confederate States, and will gallantly lead in repelling him from the land which he can never desecrate, without such a costly sacrifice as will teach him never again to set his unholy feet upon southern soil. In this war we must conquer a peace. Peace cannot now be had by words of warning and defiance. That time has long since passed. We only invite the invader by such a ruinous policy. We cannot believe there are any in our State who would wish to do this. But certainly their course would surely lead to it in the present perilous and imminent crisis.

We have thrown out these thoughts in consequence of a card which appeared in two of the city papers yesterday morning, signed by several highly respectable gentlemen, addressed to the people of Tennessee, and recommending them simply to arm themselves and stand ready for the emergency, but shaping out no positive policy for the future, except that they stand by the Union and the peace of the country and that they try another conference of the unseceded slaveholding States, and that the State resist at all hazards if LINCOLN attempt the subjugation of the Confederate States. If LINCOLN has any truth in his most solemn avowals and acts, he is now rapidly attempting to do that very thing. We apprehend that the people will give to this document the weight which it deserves and no more, discarding altogether, in so perilous a crisis, the antecedent position and influence that have been attached to the names of its signers. In predicting that LINCOLN would never attempt coercion, a large number of these gentlemen have entirely divested themselves of any claim to the name of prophets. Their advice will therefore be taken by the people for just what it is worth—which is nothing.

181. THE PROGRESS OF REVOLUTION—THE DUTY OF TENNESSEE

(*Daily Nashville Patriot,* April 24, 1861)

The well authenticated events of the past ten days are sufficient, we imagine, to convince every reasonable mind of the utter hopelessness of a peaceful solution of the intersectional troubles which have divided the country for some years. Though these events have been attended with a degree of excitement, general and all-pervading, unknown to the present generation, they sufficiently indicate that war alone can lead us to peace. The events at Fort Sumter and the quick-following proclamation of Mr. LINCOLN calling upon all the non-seceding States for troops, together with the prompt response from the non-seceding slaveholding States refusing obedience to the call, has obliterated all party distinctions in the North and united the whole people of that section in support of the war of subjugation upon the South which is now in progress. This fact is unquestionable. We know of no influential individual or journal in the whole North who or which advocates peace, or looks to anything but the umpirage of War between the two sections. We hear but one voice from that entire region. Among all the former opponents of the party which now has control of the Federal administration, there is not one of whom we know, of high or low degree, who is not willing to stand by the administration in the vigorous and desolating prosecution of that war. We cannot deceive ourselves if we would; and for our own part we would not if we could. Whilst we have resisted this dire alternative from the beginning and urged with all our power peace and union, we are forced to the conclusion that the one is altogether out of the question, and the other is gone irretrievably.

In this condition of things our own State has been placed in a peculiar position. In the first place she declared her devotion to the whole

Union so long as it could be maintained on the principles of justice and equality to every State and to each individual. This appears now to be impossible. At the same time she declared her disbelief in the idea and doctrine of "peaceable secession," but reserving to herself the inalienable right to throw off by an act of revolution the authority of the government of the Union, when by its mal-administration it became intolerable to her. She also reiterated the principle of the Declaration of Independence that all free government is based upon the consent of the people, and took decided ground against the doctrine of coercing the seceded States into an unwilling Union by force of arms. Such we understand to have been the position of Tennessee from the beginning. We understand her people to occupy the same position still. It now remains for her to determine her path of duty under these principles, and to pursue that path at all hazards. To do otherwise would be to sacrifice her honor and her liberty, and rather than do either she will suffer annihilation. This is the first question for her to decide, and in so deciding she must put herself in a condition to execute her judgment. She must therefore arm her sons. Let her make no account either of blood or treasure, but arm to the teeth, and sooner than shrink from *duty,* sooner than sacrifice her honor, her liberty, or her rights, give up everything else. It is these only for which freemen live; without these life itself is intolerable. Let but the great cardinal principle of free consent be overturned and freedom is at an end. To this we must look first, and in standing on this ground we must accept all the consequences, whatever they may be.

We have already set out in this glorious pathway. We have refused to furnish soldiers to aid a sectional Administration in its nefarious attempt to overturn the Constitution and to substitute in its place an unjust and unequal party platform. This is our first step. But it is not our only step. To refuse to furnish men, and at the same time consent to furnish money to carry on this war of subjugation would be worse than nonsense. We will not only not furnish men, but we must cut off money supplies. To do this we must declare in some form our independence of the government which seeks to rob us of the rights of freemen. Let us do this as soon as possible, and thus give ourselves wholly to the cause of justice and liberty. In view of past events and those every hour occurring this is demanded at our hands, without regard to consequences. We can provide for results as they come. Let us defend Tennessee from this war of subjugation and dishonor at every cost. Let us first ride successfully the storm of Revolution upon

which we are thrown, and then we can determine in which harbor
we shall cast anchor for future safety. In the battles which are coming
we will stand in need of aid, and that aid must of necessity come
from the slaveholding States—all of them. During the war there must
be a united South, whether afterwards or not. The identity of object
and the community of interest existing in all the slaveholding States
must and will unite them for the purpose of the war which is forced
upon us, and in such manner and to such extent as shall make that
union most effective against a common enemy. In the raising of men,
the supplying of means and in the conduct of the war there must be
either entire unity or the most perfect concert. Whoever disbelieves
these fundamental truths will be undeceived by experience.

Tennessee does not claim the right of secession, but she acts, like
freemen ought always to act, upon the inherent right of revolution. She
is already by the action of her Chief Executive and by the almost
unanimous sentiment of her people in a revolutionary attitude, and
she must and she will complete it. But to her, words are of little worth,
and banners and flags are nothing except as the emblems of great
principles. Therefore we invoke the people all over the State to permit
nothing of this sort to come between them and their first and paramount duty.—Every breeze from the North tells us to arm for our
own defense, every suggestion of reason and right appeals to us to
fight the battles of the South as against a despotic North. This is
enough for us now, and we must leave minor questions to their own
day and time.

182. THE WAR

(*The New Orleans Bee,* May 1, 1861)

The more moderate of the Northern papers still persist in the preposterous assertion that the people of that section have taken up arms
simply to preserve the Union. Now, in the first place, this is not true,
and in the next, if it were true, it would not in the slightest degree
diminish the enormity of Mr. LINCOLN's conduct. We say it is not
true that this war is waged for the maintenance of the Union. The
North knows better than that. She may be cruel, intolerant, aggressive
and fanatical, but she is shrewd enough to fathom motives, and sensible
enough to understand the impossibility of bringing together the
ruptured members of the Confederacy, and of keeping them together
if they could be momentarily forced into juxtaposition. The Union is

the pretext—the subjection of the South once for all to the supremacy of sectional foes is the real object of the war. Equally true is it that if the North really had at heart the perpetuity of the Union, Mr. LINCOLN's policy has been none the less barbarous and unjustifiable. Unless he is a born idiot, which we do not believe, he must be aware that to send armies to occupy the South, and fleets to blockade her ports; to seize on all provisions and other articles destined for the South; to maltreat all who sympathize with us, and to display envenomed hostility to us by every possible manifestation, is not exactly calculated to increase the cohesive affinities between the South and North. LINCOLN, instead of remitting them, is driving in the wedge of separation with all his force. He has acted as if his real design had been to place an eternal and impassable barrier between the two sections. This has been the effect, let his views have been what they may.

Away then with the false and hypocritical assumption that the North is engaged in a crusade against the South to preserve a Union broken beyond the power of human skill to reconstruct! Better for the TARTUFFES and MAWWORMS of the North frankly to avow their implacable enmity to us, and their intention to conquer and enthral us, if possible. There would be some honesty in such a confession. There is none whatever in the wretched pretense with which they seek to mask their odious principles.

The truth is, and it is well for us to comprehend and appreciate it—this is no holiday game between the two sections. Mr. LINCOLN's protestations and proclamations disavowing the intention to invade the South are worthless pieces of paper, because they are the production of a public functionary whose entire course since his inauguration has proved him deplorably deficient in every manly attribute. Mr. LINCOLN has signalized his brief career by a monstrous mass of perfidy and falsehood, and is therefore unworthy of the smallest credit. The North is bent on war. Facts demonstrate it. Every usage of war has been put in practice. The blockade of our ports, the stoppage of supplies to the South, the wanton and Vandal-like conflagration of Government stores and fortifications exposed to capture by the South, the efforts to control the navigation of the Mississippi, the deliberate persecution, insult and injury of all Southern sympathizers who unhappily fall into Northern hands, the fell spirit of violence and despotism openly acknowledged by Administration sheets, the threats of invasion and extermination—all indicate beyond the possibility of a doubt the disposition and purposes of the North. We are to have war, and probably on an extended scale. We have no confidence in the well meant but fruitless attempts to arrest the progress of the conflict. Mr. LINCOLN is aware that the South is arming only for defense, and asks nothing better than to be suffered unmolested to pursue the even tenor of her way. The responsibility of hostilities lies with him. He can suspend them whenever he pleases. He has no desire to call off his bloodhounds, and the war will therefore go on.

It is well, too, to guard against another common error—that of depreciating the adversary. Rank folly were it to deny the courage of the people of the North. They belong to the revolutionary stock, and have displayed their valor in many a battle field. They are as brave as the men of the South, and were their cause a just one, were they, as we are, defending their houses and firesides, their freedom and independence against ruthless invaders, they would be, as we trust we shall prove, invincible. Yet they are as numerous as the swarms of barbarians which the frozen North sent from her loins to overrun the Roman Empire, and this is their great advantage. But against this we place our devotion, our unanimity, our strong defensive attitude, our easily protected territory. Let them come in in their courage and their numbers, and the South will resist the shock as steadily and successfully as she resisted the veterans of the British army on the plains of Chalmette.

183. ACTION OF THE LEGISLATURE—ACTION OF THE PEOPLE

(Republican Banner, Nashville, May 9, 1861)

The lateness of the hour at which the action of the Legislature was divulged on Tuesday,[1] and the official documents placed in our hands, prevented us from accompanying their publication with any comment. We propose to give our views this morning in the briefest and most concise form possible.

Upon the question of arming the State, calling out volunteers and making a liberal appropriation for the expenses thereof, there will be found, we imagine, no division of sentiment among our people. All concur in the absolute necessity of this measure.

---

[1] The Tennessee legislature passed a Declaration of Independence, and approved the terms of a military alliance drawn up by Commissioners H. W. Hilliard for the Confederacy and A. W. Totten, G. A. Henry, and W. Barrow for Tennessee. The vote on the ratification was 14 to 6 in the Senate, and 42 to 15 (15 not voting) in the House. The Declaration of Independence was ratified June 8, by a popular vote of 104,913 to 47,238. For the terms of the military alliance, see "Convention between the States of Tennessee and the Confederate States of America," *Official Records . . . Armies,* Series IV, Vol. I, 297–298.

There may be some, and we have no doubt there are, who will object to the formal declaration of independence passed by the Legislature and submitted to the people—some who desire to continue, as far as any action of the Legislature or the people in their political capacity is concerned, their existing connection with the "old Union," while in reality we are in arms against that government unconditionally, and determined to resist its authority to our utmost ability, as well in behalf of the whole South, as in our own behalf. This position is too palpably absurd and untenable, in our judgment, to be long adhered to by even the few who now occupy it. No argument, it seems to us, can be made in its support, and none is necessary to show its weakness.

The next question—and the one upon which we apprehend the most likelihood of a division of the people of the State at the June election—is as to the adoption of the Constitution of the Provisional Government at Montgomery. We have heretofore thought that that question should be left open until after the conclusion of the war, when it could be considered more deliberately, and when the character of that constitution, and its adaptation to the peculiar interests and character of the people of Tennessee and of the Border Slave States, could be more calmly and fully considered. These reasons still hold good, but the exigencies of actual war which are daily pressing more closely upon us, suggest other considerations, which, in our judgment, should outweigh all the objections heretofore urged to the adoption of this constitution by the people of Tennessee. We are out of the old Union—entirely and finally. No one can anticipate the remotest chance for a reconstruction of the whole Union, and no one now contemplates, or ever did contemplate, the permanent severance of Tennessee from the South and its Union with a Northern Confederacy. The idea of a Middle Confederacy, which by the way never met with the approval of our judgment, was based mainly upon the expectation that the Southern tier of free States, and perhaps some of the middle Free States, would become parties to it. The position of those States at this moment must dissipate this expectation from the mind of every man. This alternative is therefore effectually disposed of. Then what are we to do? Where are we to go? The opponents of an immediate political connection with the Confederate States admit that that is our inevitable destiny eventually, but they urge that events should be left to take their course, and we should content ourselves at present with a close military league. If we are to go there eventually—and no one can doubt that we must inevitably become a part of that government—why delay? Why temporize? What are we to gain? To all intents and purposes we are severed from the Black Republican Government. We repudiate and scorn and spit upon the men and the spirit by whom and by which the best government the world ever saw has been perverted into an engine of oppression to one half of its people, because they held an institution, recognized in the fundamental law, obnoxious to these Union savers. Our attitude to the Federal Union is as hostile as any action of our law makers or our people can make it. By a military league with the South we give up to the Confederacy, practically and in effect, as exclusive and full control of our destiny as by a full political connection. In the former case we are without representation in the counsels of that government—in the latter our voice and our influence will be heard and felt, and our local and peculiar interests protected.

It is objected, however, that the Constitution of the Confederate States recognizes the doctrine of secession, and therefore no consistent opponent of that heresy can conscientiously vote for it. Admit that this doctrine is recognized, and the constitution in other respects unexceptionable. In the position which Tennessee now occupies—her allegiance to the old Constitution finally thrown off, and her attitude of actual hostility to the government claiming to act under it clearly and boldly assumed—her alliance with the Confederate States openly proclaimed, and her resources taxed to their utmost capacity to make good the terms of that alliance—should she hesitate upon this single objection to an abstract principle, to make the Union with the Confederacy complete in a political sense, and secure for herself all the advantages as well as encounter all the perils and exigencies, of this change of her political *status?*

But what is secession, and why should its presence in or absence from the Constitution of the Confederate States influence our action? As an abstract principle it is an absurdity. It is simply to claim a constitutional right to rebel against the Constitution. It is an assumption that the framers of the Constitution made provision in the instrument itself for its own destruction, the same as though the builder of a steamboat, upon which he is to embark his family and his all, should anticipate a contingency when he would desire to see the whole establishment blown up, and should instruct the builder of the boilers to make provision for that contingency. But, *practically,* what is secession? Merely another name for *revolution,* an inherent and inalienable right which no people can delegate to makers of Constitutions or framers of governments. Tennessee is in a state of revolution. She has revolted against the Federal Union, but bases her right so to act upon higher grounds than a Constitutional right. The recognition of the right of secession, then, amounts to nothing, practically, and it is the same whether the right is acknowledged in the fundamental law of a government or not; whenever that fundamental law is perverted, and its spirit destroyed, to the injury and oppression of any part of its people, they will assume the responsibility of secession or revolution, as has been demonstrated by the recent action of the people of the South. As long as the honor, interests, happiness and prosperity of a free people are consulted, and their constitutional rights secured in the administration of the government, so long will that government exist, harmoniously, and the minority cheerfully submit to the majority. But right or no right of secession, no government can be long maintained which utterly and flagrantly disregards these important and indispensable requisities of permanency and security.

We have protracted our remarks far beyond our original intention. It will be inferred from what we have said that in our opinion sound policy and every consideration of interest, in view of the respective attitudes of the North and South, dictate that the people of Tennessee should unite as one man and give their unanimous endorsement to the action of the Legislature, as far as made public. There may be many points upon which some of us could make out strong bills of exceptions. But we should consider the position of the State—consider the moral effect of a united support of that position—and, forgetting the past for the sake of the future, out of whose present darkness we hope to speedily see gleams of light, which shall gradually become more palpable until the breaking of a perfect day—and ignoring minor differences, come up as patriots and brothers to the support of the main issue, in which all are in heart united.

APPENDIX I

Platform of the Alabama Democracy

Adopted at Montgomery, January, 1860

1. *Resolved by the Democracy of the State of Alabama, in Convention assembled,* That holding all issues and principles upon which they have heretofore affiliated and acted with the National Democratic party to be inferior in dignity and importance to the great question of slavery, they content themselves with a general re-affirmance of the Cincinnati Platform as to such issues, and also endorse said platform as to slavery, together with the following resolutions:

2. *Resolved further,* That we re-affirm so much of the first resolution of the Platform adopted in Convention by the Democracy of this State, on the 8th of January, 1856, as relates to the subject of slavery, to wit: "The unqualified right of the people of the slaveholding States to the protection of their property in the States, in the Territories, and in the wilderness in which Territorial Governments are as yet unorganized.

3. *Resolved further,* That in order to meet and clear away all obstacles to a full enjoyment of this right in the Territories, we re-affirm the principle of the 9th resolution of the Platform adopted in Convention by the Democracy of this State on the 14th of February, 1848, to wit: "That it is the duty of the General Government, by all proper legislation, to secure an entry into those Territories to all the citizens of the United States, together with their property of every description, and that the same should remain protected by the United States while the Territories are under its authority.

4. *Resolved further,* That the Constitution of the United States is a compact between sovereign and co-equal States, united upon the basis of perfect equality of rights and privileges.

5. *Resolved further,* That the Territories of the United States are common property, in which the States have equal rights, and to which the citizens of every State may rightfully emigrate with their slaves or other property, recognised as such in any of the States of the Union, or by the Constitution of the United States.

6. *Resolved further,* That the Congress of the United States has no power to abolish slavery in the Territories, or to prohibit its introduction into any of them.

7. *Resolved further,* That the Territorial Legislatures, created by the

legislation of Congress, have no power to abolish slavery, or to prohibit the introduction of the same, or to impair, by unfriendly legislation, the security and full enjoyment of the same within the Territories; and such constitutional power certainly does not belong to the people of the Territories in any capacity, before, in the exercise of a lawful authority, they form a Constitution preparatory to admission as a State into the Union; and their action in the exercise of such lawful authority certainly cannot operate or take effect before their actual admission as a State into the Union.

8. *Resolved further,* That the principles enunciated by Chief Justice Taney, in his opinion in the Dred Scott case, deny to the Territorial Legislature the power to destroy or impair, by any legislation whatever, the right of property in slaves, and maintain it to be the duty of Federal Government, in *all* of its departments, to protect the rights of the owner of such property in the Territories; and the principles so declared are hereby asserted to be the rights of the South, and the South should maintain them.

9. *Resolved further,* That we hold all of the foregoing propositions to contain *cardinal principles*—true in themselves, and just and proper, and necessary for the safety of all that is dear to us, and we do hereby instruct our Delegates to the Charleston Convention to present them for the calm consideration and approval of that body—from whose justice and patriotism we anticipate their adoption.

10. *Resolved further,* That our Delegates to the Charleston Convention are hereby expressly instructed to insist that said Convention shall adopt a platform of principles, recognising distinctly the rights of the South as asserted in the foregoing resolutions; and if the said National Convention shall refuse to adopt, in substance, the propositions embraced in the preceding resolutions, prior to nominating candidates, our Delegaes to said Convention are hereby positively instructed to withdraw therefrom.

11. *Resolved further,* That our Delegates to the Charleston Convention shall cast the vote of Alabama as a unit, and a majority of our Delegates shall determine how the vote of this State shall be given.

12. *Resolved further,* That an Executive Committee, to consist of one from each Congressional district, be appointed, whose duty it shall be, in the event that our Delegates withdraw from the Charleston Convention, in obedience to the 10th resolution, to call a Convention of the Democracy of Alabama, to meet at an early day to consider what is best to be done.

APPENDIX II

RESOLUTIONS OF THE DEMOCRATIC ANTI-KNOW-NOTHING PARTY OF ALABAMA

Adopted at Montgomery, January, 1856

We, the delegates of the Democratic and Anti-Know-Nothing party of Alabama, in convention assembled, do adopt the following resolutions:

1. That the following principles constitute the true basis of the National Democratic organization.

First. The perfect equality of privileges—civil, religious and political—of every citizen of our country, without reference to the place of his birth. Second. The qualified right of the people of the slaveholding States to protection of their property in the States, in the Territories, and in the wilderness in which territorial governments are as yet unorganized. The Democratic platform is based on the recognition, not of one, but of both these principles; and when efforts are made to separate these two questions, the Democratic party, resting upon its platform, says: We cannot compromise either proposition, but stand united upon both.

2. That we hold the American Union secondary in importance only to the rights and principles it was designed to perpetuate; that past associations, present fruition, and future prospects will bind us to it so long as it continues to be the safeguard of these rights and privileges.

3. That the State of Alabama, in the judgment of this Convention, will and ought to resist, even (as a last resort) to a disruption of every tie which binds her to the Union, any action of Congress upon the subject of slavery in the District of Columbia, or in places subject to the jurisdiction of Congress, incompatible with the safety, the domestic tranquillity, the rights and honor of the slaveholding States; or any refusal to admit as a State any territory hereafter applying, because of the existence of slavery therein; or any act prohibiting the introduction of slavery into the Territories of Utah and New Mexico; or any act repealing or materially modifying the law now in force for the recovery of fugitive slaves.

4. That any interference by Congress for the prohibition of slavery in any of the Territories, would be an inexcusable and unconstitutional infringement of the rights of the South, which it is the deliberate sense of this Convention, it would be the duty of Alabama to resist even to a disruption of the ties that bind this State to the Union!

5. That the act of Congress, providing Territorial Governments for Nebraska and Kansas, embodies the principle of Congressional non-interference upon the subject of slavery in the Territories, and that the provisions of that act, so far as they relate to that subject, meet the hearty concurrence and approval of this Convention.

6. That the restoration of the Missouri compromise line by Congress would be a great wrong, resistance to which, even to the extent of a disruption of the Union, would be a sacred duty with all who cherish the essential principles of Constitutional right and State equality.

7. That it is the deliberate conviction of this Convention, that in view of the great practical questions which now involve and menace their dearest rights and most important interests, the people of the slaveholding States should unite for the protection of their threatened rights, and for the prevention of further aggressions upon their domestic institutions; and

that they should positively refuse longer to affiliate with any National party which will not distinctly and unequivocally recognize and maintain the full measure of their rights under the Constitution.

8. That it is expedient that we should be represented in the Democratic National Convention upon such considerations as are hereinafter expressed.

9. That the delegates to the Democratic National Convention, to nominate a President and Vice-President, are hereby expressly instructed to insist that the said Convention shall adopt a platform of principles, as the basis of a National Organization, prior to the nomination of candidates, unequivocally asserting, in substance, the following propositions: 1. The recognition and approval of the principle of non-intervention by Congress upon the subject of slavery in the Territories. 2. That no restriction or prohibition of slavery, in any Territory, shall hereafter be made by any act of Congress. 3. That no State shall be refused admission into the Union because of the existence of slavery therein. 4. The faithful execution and maintenance of the fugitive Slave law.

10. That if the said National Convention shall refuse to adopt the propositions embraced in the preceding resolution, our delegates to said Convention are hereby positively instructed to withdraw therefrom.

11. That this Convention appoint an Executive Committee, to consist of one person from each Congressional District, whose duty it shall be, in the event that the action of the said National Convention is not in conformity with the seventh resolution, to call a Convention of the Democracy of Alabama to meet at an early day, to consider what is best to be done.

12. That we hail with unaffected satisfaction the movement of Georgia to prescribe the terms upon which we will associate in party brotherhood with any National organization.

13. That we sympathise with the friends of the slavery cause in Kansas, in their manly efforts to maintain the rights and interests of the Southern people, and that we rejoice at their recent victories over the paid adventurers and jesuitical hordes of Northern abolitionists; that the deep interest felt and taken by the people of Missouri in the settlement of Kansas, and the decision of the slavery question in it, is both natural and proper, and that it is their right and duty to extend to their Southern brethren in that Territory every legitimate and honorable sympathy and support.

14. That we are uncompromisingly opposed to the political organization called the Know-Nothing order, having no sympathy with their secrecy, their oaths, their unconstitutional designs, their religious intolerance, and their political proscription; and that, under whatever name or in whatever shape its members present themselves to the public, advocating the principles of that Order, they will alike meet our stern opposition.

15. That the signal triumph in Virginia, North Carolina, Georgia, Mississippi, and other States, of the Democratic party, and of the patriotic Whigs, who co-operated in achieving these results over the Know-Nothing

organization, is conclusive evidence that, in the great practical questions involved in that contest, Southern men may honorably and successfully combine, without regard to past political distinction, to save the Constitution from desecration, and the South from being prostrated before the power of Northern fanaticism and misrule.

16. That those men in the non-slaveholding States who have nobly advocated the passage of the Kansas-Nebraska act, and the Fugitive Slave law, as measures of justice to the South, deserve our thanks, and are entitled to our confidence.

17. That the administration of President Pierce meets our cordial approval; and the bold and statesman-like enunciation of Constitutional principles, in his recent message to the Congress of the United States, entitles him especially to the gratitude of the South; and this Convention earnestly recommend him to the National Democratic Convention for nomination as a candidate for re-election to the office of President of the United States.

INDEX

Abolitionism, would invade the South under a Republican Administration, 141, 240; the main strength of Republicanism, 154; and non-slaveholders, 175

Abolitionists, reaction against, after Harper's Ferry raid, 30

Alabama, delegation to Charleston Convention, 11; resolutions of state Democratic Conventions, 39-40; instructions to Charleston delegation, 40; delegation excluded at Baltimore, 136-137; platforms of Democratic party, 517-521. See Alabama Platform

Alabama Platform, 517-518; an advanced position, 11-13; consistent with previous record, 38-40

Amendments, constitutional, as the alternative to separation, 248; nature of, demanded by South, 266-267, 352; of no value to South, 298-299; should not have been proposed by South as a matter of policy, 348; of little value without a revolution in Northern sentiment, 368-369; rendered impossible by attitude of Republican congressmen, 372-373; must be preceded by a recognition of the right of secession, 429-430; can be secured on a basis of negotiation only, 449-452

Anti-slavery sentiment, aggressive character of, 359

Atlanta Conference, and disunion, 16, 24; effect of failure upon Republican party, 52; its failure a rebuke to Southern ultraists, 56-57

Ashby de la Zouche, 6

Baltimore Convention, Democratic party, and Douglas delegations from Southern states, 90-91; address of Southern congressmen with respect to, 108-110, 121-123; and right of Southern delegations to seats, 122-126

Bell, John, strength in Southern states, 161

Benjamin, Judah P., 117

Benton, Thomas H., and the origin of squatter sovereignty, 88-89

Bigler, William, 69

Blockade of Southern ports, suggested by Republican press, 436

Bocock, Thomas S., 37

Border State Convention, proposed by Louisville *Journal,* 304; endorsed by Governors Tyler and Magoffin, 417

Border States, and secession sentiment, 264-265; and insecurity of slave property under a Republican administration, 359-360; no cause for complaint against cotton states, 357-359; and the question of coercion, 371; controlled by desire for tranquillity, 431; gain nothing by delay, 444-445, 467-468; and Lincoln's proclamation, 505-506

Boteler, Alexander B., motion to create Committee of Thirty-three, 327

Botts, John Minor, 292

Boyce, William, member of committee of thirty-three, 328; on secession and emancipation, 422, 426

Breckinridge, John C., Frankfort speech, 4-5; his election would intensify sectional strife, 149; strength in Southern states, 184; not the candidate of a disunion party, 194; his election would lead to disunion, 196; weakness in Northern states, 208

Breckinridge Democratic party, a disunion party, 160

Bright, Jesse D., 69

Briggs, George, 37

Brown, Joseph E., Governor of Georgia, message to legislature proposing retaliatory legislation, 242-246

Brownlow, William G., regarded as an abolitionist, 179, 492

Buchanan, James, 87; incapacity to deal with national crisis, 293-294; inconsistency of message to Congress, 307-308, 318-320

Burch, John C., resolution proposing a national convention, 373n

Burlingame, Anson, 299

Butler, William O., 89

California, and Southern rights, 41-42

Campbell, John A., relations with Seward and Confederate commissioners, 498

Capers, Henry D., 16 n

Cass, Lewis, 89

Charleston Convention, and Southern rights, 69-70; satisfaction of South-